Lecture Notes in Computer Science 9353

Commenced Publication in 1973
Founding and Former Series Editors:
Gerhard Goos, Juris Hartmanis, and Jan van Leeuwen

More information about this series at http://www.springer.com/series/7409

Konstantinos Chorianopoulos · Monica Divitini
Jannicke Baalsrud Hauge · Letizia Jaccheri
Rainer Malaka (Eds.)

Entertainment Computing – ICEC 2015

14th International Conference, ICEC 2015
Trondheim, Norway, September 29 – October 2, 2015
Proceedings

 Springer

Editors
Konstantinos Chorianopoulos
Ionian University
Corfu
Greece

Monica Divitini
Norwegian University of Science
   and Technology
Trondheim
Norway

Jannicke Baalsrud Hauge
Bremer Institut für Produktion und Logistik
   (BIBA)
University of Bremen
Bremen
Germany

and

KTH Royal Institute of Technolgy
Stockholm
Sweden

Letizia Jaccheri
Norwegian University of Science
   and Technology
Trondheim
Norway

Rainer Malaka
University of Bremen
Bremen
Germany

ISSN 0302-9743   ISSN 1611-3349   (electronic)
Lecture Notes in Computer Science
ISBN 978-3-319-24588-1   ISBN 978-3-319-24589-8   (eBook)
DOI 10.1007/978-3-319-24589-8

Library of Congress Control Number: 2015949473

LNCS Sublibrary: SL3 – Information Systems and Applications, incl. Internet/Web, and HCI

Springer Cham Heidelberg New York Dordrecht London

Springer International Publishing AG Switzerland is part of Springer Science+Business Media
(www.springer.com)

Preface

We are proud to present the proceedings of the 14th International Conference on Entertainment Computing (ICEC 2015). After Brazil (2013) and Australia (2014), ICEC was back in Europe, for the first time in Norway.

The conference was hosted in Trondheim, from September 30 to October 2, by NTNU, The Norwegian University of Science and Technology. As a result of a university merge, starting with January 2016, NTNU will be the biggest university in Norway with circa 38,000 students. Thanks to NTNU, the research institute Sintef and an ecosystems of knowledge intensive companies, Trondheim is one of the main Nordic centers of innovation, research, and development.

Entertainment computing is a diverse field bringing together computer science, social and cultural sciences, psychology, art, design, and many other disciplines.

Therefore, entertainment computing is one focal point of exchange between these different disciplines. ICEC 2015 aimed at celebrating the multidisciplinary nature of the area, and this is well demonstrated in this edited book by the variety and scientific quality of this year's program.

Overall, we received more than 100 unique submissions, from 31 countries, demonstrating the global interest for this research area and for ICEC 2015. Out of the total submissions, after a rigorous peer-review and meta-review process, we accepted 26 full papers and six short papers. To complement the oral presentations, the ICEC 2015 program also included six demos and 16 posters. Moreover, the main conference program was complemented by five workshops and two tutorials focusing on special topics of interest. In summary, ICEC 2015 offered an exciting program that provided an excellent overview of the state of the art in entertainment computing and an occasion for bringing research forward and creating new networks.

We are very proud of the final selection of papers, which would not have been possible without the effort and support of our excellent Program Committee, including 53 top researchers from 23 countries. We would like to thank all members of the Program Committee and all additional external reviewers for their work and commitment.

We thank our keynote speakers Florian "Floyd" Mueller, Yvonne Rogers, Alf Inge Wang, and Axel Tidemann.

Finally, this event would not have been possible without the help of all the great people who assisted us at NTNU, including our technical staff and student volunteers. We would like to specifically thank NTNU Videre for support with local organization and registration, the technical and administrative group at the Department of Computer and Information Science for the technical support before and during the conference, Tore R. Jørgensen for his support with the conference organization, and Francesco Gianni for his aid in the editing process of the proceedings. We also thank our sponsors and supporting organizations.

July 2015   Konstantinos Chorianopoulos
                                                      Monica Divitini
                                              Jannicke Baalsrud Hauge
                                                      Letizia Jaccheri
                                                      Rainer Malaka

Organization

General Chair

Letizia Jaccheri — Norwegian University of Science and Technology (NTNU), Norway

General Co-chair

Konstantinos Chorianopoulos — Ionian University, Greece

Program Co-chairs

Monica Divitini — Norwegian University of Science and Technology (NTNU), Norway

Rainer Malaka — University of Bremen, Germany

Local Chair

Sobah Abbas Petersen — Sintef, Norway

Industry and Sponsor Chair

Andrew Perkis — Norwegian University of Science and Technology (NTNU), Norway

Web and Publicity Chair

Alf Inge Wang — Norwegian University of Science and Technology (NTNU), Norway

Doctoral Consortium Chair

Helmut Hlavacs — University of Vienna, Austria

Workshop Chair

Jannicke Baalsrud Hauge   BIBA, University of Bremen, Germany;
                               Kungliga Tekniska Högskolan, Sweden

Grand Challenge Co-chairs

Aisling Kelliher   Carnegie Mellon University, USA
Andrew Perkis   Norwegian University of Science
                               and Technology (NTNU), Norway

Conference Advisory Committee

Matthias Rauterberg   Eindhoven University of Technology,
                               The Netherlands
Sydney Fels   The University of British Columbia, Canada
Hyun Seung Yang   KAIST, Republic of Korea

Program Committee

Nikos Avouris   University of Patras, Greece
Sander Bakkes   University of Amsterdam, The Netherlands
Christoph Bartneck   University of Canterbury, New Zealand
Rafael Bidarra   Delft University of Technology,
                               The Netherlands
Staffan Björk   Chalmers University of Technology
                               and University of Gothenburg, Sweden
Pedro González Calero   Complutense University of Madrid, Spain
Luis Carriço   University of Lisbon, Portugal
Marc Cavazza   University of Teesside, UK
Luca Chittaro   HCI Lab, University of Udine, Italy
Sung-Bae Cho   Yonsei University, Korea
Paolo Ciancarini   University of Bologna; Italy
Esteban Clua   Universidade Federal Fluminense, Brazil
Kendra Cooper   The University of Texas at Dallas, USA
Nuno N. Correia   Goldsmiths, University of London, UK
Frank Dignum   Utrecht University, The Netherland
Ines Di Loreto   University of Troyes, France
Jerome Dupire   CEDRIC/CNAM, France
Owen Noel Newton Fernando   NTU (Nanyang Technological University),
                               Singapore
Chris Geiger   University of Applied Sciences Düsseldorf,
                               Germany

David Geerts   KU Leuven, Belgium
Kathrin Maria Gerling   University of Lincoln, UK
Michail Giannakos   NTNU, Norway
Nicholas Graham   Queen's University, Canada
Marc Herrlich   TZI, University of Bremen, Germany
Junichi Hoshino   University of Tsukuba, Japan
Kristine Jørgensen   University of Bergen, Norway
Börje Karlsson   Microsoft Research Asia, China
Evangelos Karapanos   University of Madeira, Portugal
Haruhiro Katayose   Kwansei Gakuin University, Japan
Antonio J. Fernández Leiva   Universidad de Málaga, Spain
Joaquim Madeira   Universidade de Aveiro, Portugal
Tim Marsh   Queensland College of Art, Griffith University,
                                       Australia
Maic Masuch   University of Duisburg-Essen, Germany
Irene Mavrommati   Hellenic Open University, Greece
Simon McCullum   Gjøvik University College, Norway
Zlatogor Minchev   Bulgarian Academy of Sciences, Bulgaria
Lennart Nacke   University of Ontario, Canada
Ryohei Nakatsu   National University of Singapore, Singapore
Anton Nijholt   University of Twente, The Netherlands
Valentina Nisi   University of Madeira, Portugal
Manuel Oliveira   SINTEF, Norway
Arttu Perttula   Tampere University of Technology, Finland
Johanna Pirker,   Graz University of Technology, Austria
Yusuf Pisan   University of Technology, Sydney, Australia
Mike Preuss   TU Dortmund, Germany
Matthias Rauterberg   Eindhoven University of Technology,
                                       The Netherlands
Teresa Romão   DI/FCT/UNL, Portugal
Walt Scacchi   University of California, Irvine, USA
Hyun Seung Yang   KAIST, Korea
Nikitas Sgouros   University of Piraeus, Greece
Flavio Soares Correa da Silva   University of São Paulo, Brazil
Elpida Tzafestas   University of Athens, Greece
Guenter Wallner   University of Applied Arts, Vienna, Austria

Additional Reviewers

Aida Azadegan   Mariela Nogueira-Collazo
Augusto Baffa   Katharina Emmerich
Francesco Bellotti   Laura Giarre'
Fernando Birra   Zuzanna Hofman
David B. Carvalho   Raul Lara-Cabrera

Theodore Lim
Edirlei Soares De Lima
Stefan Liszio
Simone Mora
Malte Paskuda
Mark Rice
Johann Riedel

Andre Rodrigues
Ralf Schmidt
Alexandre Ribeiro Júnior Silva
Ioana Stanescu
Luis Valente
Gabriel Zachmann

Supporting Organizations and Sponsors

International International Federation for Information Processing (IFIP)
The Research Council of Norway (NFR)
Trondheim Municipality
NTNU - Norwegian University of Science and Technology
Brainstorm
SINTEF
Adressavisen
Kahoot
NxtMedia
Interaction Design Foundation
ERCIM
JoinGame

Contents

Full Papers

Short Papers

Posters

Demonstrations

Workshops and Tutorials

Full Papers

A Mobile Game Controller Adapted to the Gameplay and User's Behavior Using Machine Learning

Leonardo Torok, Mateus Pelegrino, Daniela G. Trevisan,
Esteban Clua, and Anselmo Montenegro

Federal Fluminense University, Computing Institute
Rua Passos da Pátria 156 – E – 3rd floor, São Domingos, Niterói, Brazil
mateuspelegrino@gmail.com,
{ltorok,daniela,esteban,anselmo}@ic.uff.br

Abstract. When playing games, the user expects an easy and intuitive interaction. While current controllers are physical hardware components with a default configuration of buttons, different games use different buttons and demand different interaction methods. Besides, the player style varies according to personal characteristics or past gaming experiences. In previous works we proposed a novel virtual controller based on a common touchscreen device, such as smartphone or tablet, that is used as a gamepad to control a game on a computer or game console. In this work we include machine-learning techniques for an intelligent adaption of the layout and control elements distribution, minimizing errors and providing an enjoyable experience for individual users. We also present different usability tests and show considerable improvements in the precision and game performance of the user. We expect to open a new way of designing console and desktop games, allowing game designers to project individual controllers for each game.

Keywords: Touch surfaces and touch interaction, input and interaction technologies, machine learning and data mining, games and play.

1 Introduction

When playing a game, one of the main features that will define the perception that the user will have about its experience is the quality and fluency of the game controls, responsible for commanding the player's in-game avatar. Therefore, in the whole area of games, one factor that is very important for gameplay experience is the controller, or the control scheme. The most memorable gaming experiences created were generally based on good controls schemes. They are usually intuitive, allowing a new player to immediately start interacting without difficulties, and provide a deep interaction, with a vast array of possible actions in the easiest way. Similarly, an inadequate controller design is one of the first characteristics of games that are frequently remembered as unpleasant experiences with very few redeeming qualities. This direct relationship between controls and the overall quality of a game is easy to

© IFIP International Federation for Information Processing 2015
K. Chorianopoulos et al. (Eds.): ICEC 2015, LNCS 9353, pp. 3–16, 2015.
DOI: 10.1007/978-3-319-24589-8_1

understand. The controls are the bridge between what the user want to do and what his avatar will actually do in the game. In the past, most games were simple and gaming controllers actually employed just a few buttons. Nowadays, controllers are presented with dozens of buttons, directional pads, analog sticks and even motion sensing and touch capabilities. While these interface devices may give a huge amount of interaction possibilities, they impose many constraints for the game designer, since he must use the same hardware for any kind of game, and increase the learning curve for players. A regular gamepad has a fixed size and shape, with the same buttons in the same position and with the same size, independently of who is using it or his ergonomic preferences. While this constraints provide a standardized interface that user may be more comfortable with and provide a simpler interface for the game designer, we would like to create an alternative for designers that are willing to explore different and fully customizable interfaces to extend their concepts from the game to the controller.

On the other hand smartphones and tablets opened a new paradigm of game interface, giving more freedom to game designers when projecting an interface. The new and simpler paradigm of control imposed by these mobile devices was responsible for bringing millions of casual players to the gaming world. The virtual controls allow mobile games to abandon older paradigms and design interfaces without regular buttons, creating a novel control scheme. Users can drag objects on the screen, perform gestures (such as pinch, rotate, etc) and still use regular virtual buttons. This flexibility allows game designer to design not only the game's visuals and gameplay element, but also the control interface, with any shape and interaction paradigm they wish and possessing only the buttons that are necessary for the game. While this already happens in most mobile games, their gameplay is usually simplified and the interfaces are created with different paradigms. The proposed approach tries to blend the vast capacity of input options and general game complexity of the more traditional console experience with the flexibility provided by touchscreen interfaces.

With our previous proposal, each game can have a custom interface, with the correct amount of buttons for its specific needs or even replacing buttons altogether with different interface elements, like regions in the screen where the user can input commands with specific multitouch gestures. The controller now becomes a part of the game design, fitting into the experience that the designer intends. The adaptive controller resulted in a patent application [17] and it is important to notice that it was created to fill a practical purpose and is intended to be released as a solution to end users.

However, this flexibility brings some challenges: touchscreens cannot replicate the same precision of a traditional controller and the control interface projected by the game designer is not necessarily the best possible interface from an ergonomic standpoint and may need some tweaking to reach the optimal configurations. To solve this problems, our solution introduces an adaptation that derives the personal preferences of the user from a series of basic events, such as button presses, or internal state changes, adapting itself to the user and his ergonomic needs based on machine-learning approaches. To perform this task, different algorithms mine information from game events, smoothly adapting the interface using machine-learning methods. The controller will try to smoothly fix the position and size of the buttons in order to eliminate or reduce errors, with the potential to improve the accuracy of a touch screen interface and correct a suboptimal default configuration, according to the users' needs and characteristics, such as hand size and mobility. In the end of this paper we show how our proposal increased the game experience for popular and commercial games, comparing a basic controller interface with and without our proposed adaptations.

2   Related Work

An adaptive user interface is an interactive software system that improves its ability to interact with a user based on its partial experience [15]. Rogers et al [19] developed models that treat uncertain input touch and use this to deal with the handover of control between both user and system. They demonstrate a finger map browser, which scrolls the map to a point of interest when the user input is uncertain. Keeping the same goal, but in a different way, Weir et al [24] used a machine learning approach for learning user-specific touch input models to increase touch accuracy on mobile devices. They proposed mapping data or touch location to the intended touch point, based on historical touch behavior of a specific user.

Bi et al [4] conceptualized finger touch input as an uncertain process, and used statistical target selection criterion. They improved the touch accuracy using a Bayesian Touch Criterion and decreased considerably the error rate. However, even improving the accuracy in a higher level, the user keeps missing the buttons and the interface needs to calculate the intended target. While personalized inputs have been commonly used, such as key-target resizing on soft keyboards [2], this type of adaptability has some disadvantages. One that immediately comes to mind is the limitation of only working in of language processing, adapting the interface according to the language's model and the user's typing behavior. Our work is not just destined to fit the interface more comfortably to the users according to their type of usage, but also aims to avoid errors. In order to achieve that, we use the data about correct and incorrect virtual button presses to change different properties of the button.

Touchscreen devices were already used as gaming controllers, with commercial solutions already available, such as GestureWorks Gameplay [9] that allows the user to play using an Android smartphone as a controller and to customize the layout of his joystick. However, none of these products present a solution to the limited precision in touchscreen input and are not capable of determining the best ergonomic configuration for the user, which has to design the controller manually, resulting in a sub-optimal configuration. In a previous work [26], we developed a framework for building customizable controller based on a mobile device and in [17] we presented a mobile controller that is created and designed by the game developer specifically to his game, but does not include any kind of adaptation to improve the designed interface. This novel interface resulted in a patent filled at INPI [18], that includes the concept of a gaming controller that can be customized for each game and includes machine learning to improve its usability.

In [26] we made a first attempt for simple adjustments, moving buttons in accordance with heat maps generated by the touches. The biggest limitation in our previous attempts is that no intelligence was being used for the movements, so that a touch in the inner side of a quadrant will have the same weight of a touch in the outer area of the quadrant, creating a biased result. In the present work we propose a much more sophisticated and novel approach, based on a K-means classifier, treating all points without any bias issues. While the usability results in [26] were based on subjective opinions provided by the users, we now developed an approach capable of automatically monitoring the user behavior, collecting all input data during user interaction and creating a log file with each user's error rate when trying to touch a button and several other statistical output. With these data, it was possible to perform several statistical analyses and determine in a formal way if the controller's adaptations are increasing the player's performance and the gameplay experience. To determine the optimal configuration for the learning algorithm, this work included pilot tests that allowed us to perform several improvements and fine-tune the controller to achieve an even better adaptation to the user's needs.

3   Proposed Adaptive Interface

The adaptive controller is composed of a physical component (a smartphone or tablet) and a software component (client and a server). The mobile device will run the client software, presenting the user interface, collecting input data, performing the machine learning routines and adaptations and sending all inputs to the computer that runs the game and the server component, receiving the inputs and converting them to events that perform in-game actions. The mobile app is created with the Android SDK [1] in the Java language, using the Weka library [25] to perform the machine learning routines, with all input data being stored in an internal SQLite database. The desktop application is also programmed in Java and receives the commands from the controller..

To achieve the desired adaptation to each user's play style it is necessary to perform several adaptations. For this work, it was decided to perform two different changes in the controller's layout: size and position of buttons. These adaptations are performed at the same time for each button. The size adaptations aims to facilitate the usage of the most important buttons for the current game, increasing the size of the most used buttons in the controller and decreasing the size of the buttons that are less used.

The second type of adaptation is the button's position. The basic concept here is to try to detect the position for a specific button that will guarantee that the majority of users' touches actually hit the button. A machine-learning algorithm will determine the position that maximizes the user's precision. In our implementation we included size and position redefinitions, but many other properties can be changed in the future, such as color, shape and force feedback.

To keep the interface consistent, several rules and boundaries were specified: The maximum size of each button is defined and conflicting areas are analyzed, verifying if the areas of any button intersects with a neighbor. The data used to evaluate the controller's correctness is a database with all the touches performed by the user. The screen is mapped in Cartesian coordinates and each touch in the screen is stored in a database. The machine-learning algorithm will use the most recent stored data (detailed in the section 4). Each touch will be classified as correct or incorrect. Correct touches are those that hit any button in the screen and are mapped to an action, while incorrect touches did not hit any button, representing a situation where the user tried to perform an action and failed. We defined that in our heuristic the size will increase for the most used buttons and decrease for the least used ones. A simple algorithm that tracks and counts the amount of times each button is used was included. A list of buttons is created, ordered by the amount of touches on each one. This list is divided in 3 parts, with the first one containing the most used buttons and the last one containing the least used ones. The controller will increase the size of the most used buttons while decreasing the least used ones to their original size. This list is update once per iteration, always following the current player's needs.

The position adaptation heuristics demands a more sophisticated process, that tries to find the points in the screen that represent the centers of the most used areas. A clustering algorithm presents a good solution for this case, classifying a set of points, or to touches, in classes that represent the buttons. Due to the characteristics of this problem, we decided by using K-means.

The input data, the most recent user touches, is passed to a K-means unsupervised learning algorithm, which is a vector quantization method for data mining [20]. This classifier receives a set of points and separates them in K classes of related entries. In our case, the algorithm is initialized with random points, a common approach for K-means. Although is a NP-hard problem [11], several heuristics allow a quicker solution that converges surprisingly fast to a local optimum. Given $x = \{x_1, ..., x_m\}$ the goal of the classifier is to partition X into k clusters with similar values [20], defining prototype vectors $\mu_1, ..., \mu_k$ and an indicator vector r_{ij} which is equal to 1 if, and only if, x_i is assigned to the cluster j. The distortion measure and the distance of each point from the prototype vector will be minimized:

$$J(r,\mu) = \frac{1}{2}\sum_{i=1}^{m}\sum_{j=1}^{k} r_{ij} \left\| x_i - \mu_j \right\|^2, \tag{1}$$

where $r = \{ r_{ij} \}$ and $\mu = \mu_j$. In order to find r and μ a two stage strategy is used. First, μ is fixed and the objective is to determine r. The solution for the i-th data point x_i can be found by setting:

$$r_{ij} = 1 \, if \, j = argmin \left\| x_i - \mu_j \right\|^2, \tag{2}$$

and 0 otherwise. In this case, r is fixed and μ will be determined. J will be a quadratic function of μ that can be minimized by setting the derivative of μ_j to 0:

$$\sum_{i=1}^{m} r_{ij}(x_i - \mu_j) = 0 \, for \, all \, j \quad , \text{rearranged as} \quad \mu_j = \frac{\sum_i r_{ij} x_i}{\sum_i r_{ij}}. \tag{3}$$

Since $\sum_i r_{ij}$ counts the number of points assigned to cluster j, the algorithm sets μ_j to be the sample mean of the points assigned to cluster j. The algorithm runs several iterations until it stops when the cluster assignments do not change significantly anymore. Originally, K would be the number of virtual buttons, but the algorithm was adjusted to use a more reliable metric, defining K as the number of buttons that were used in the current gaming section. This approach avoids the creation of redundant classes and unnecessary centroids that represent the same button.

The K-means algorithm will return several subsets of the input dataset grouping the closest points in the same class and returning the respective centroid for each class. The users' touches will be located in the area of a button or at least close to it, since the use is trying to hit the buttons. After several interactions, we will observe a pattern of touches close to each button, allowing the K-means clustering to separate inputs in classes that represent each buttons area and part of the surrounded space. After finding the centroids, each one will be paired with the closest button. In cases where there are two centroids and the closest button is the same, the correct pair will be created based on the minimal distance, leaving the other centroid without assigned buttons. The centroid paired with the button will be considered as the its optimal position, representing the mean point of all inputs directed to that button. With this data, the controller will start to move the button gradually towards the centroid of its class, until the center of the button is located precisely in the corresponding centroid. These changes on the buttons are visual and the user can observe the adaptations being performed in real time.

4   Usability Tests and Results

In order to validate how our proposed adaptation behaves with the final user and his gameplay experience, we conducted a usability test, observing the effectiveness and user satisfaction regarding our adaptations. To perform this evaluation, we divided it in two stages: the pilot tests and the final user tests. The pilot test was realized to set and define important adaptation parameters to the final test, determining an optimal configuration to the adaptation.

The evaluation used two different controllers, an adaptive and a non-adaptive, both with the same functionality and layout. It was not told to the users that our controller is adaptive and were just informed that they would test two different joystick prototypes with two game genres: platform with Super Mario Bros. (Nintendo) and the 2D shooter Sonic Wings (Hamster Corporation), totalizing four evaluation sessions per user.

Fig. 1. The setup used for testing.

Our comparison sections were focused in comparing the adaptive controller with a regular version, that represents a game controller created by a game designer with a layout that is intended to provide the best experience for these specific games. However, it is hard to determine if an interface is optimal, requiring several usability tests. This approach is costly and demands a precious time that will not be available for any game developer. With these usability tests, we expect to show how an adaptive controller can improve a customized game controller and optimize it to a more ergonomic configuration. Comparisons with current physical controllers were discarded, since the objective of this work is to provide a fully customizable interface that is also capable of adapting itself to improve its usability. As such, we are trying to provide a functionality that does not exist on traditional controllers and our tests are focused in demonstrating the benefits that these adaptations can bring to an initial unoptimized interface created by a game designer.

Our group of volunteers consisted of 16 users, 9 male and 7 female, with ages ranging from 18 to more than 60 years old. The user group was selected and separated in two different groups: 8 expert users and 8 novice users. The first group was composed basically by users that play games on consoles or PC regularly, are used to play with a joystick and play videogames for more than 10 years. The second group was made by users with less experience with games and mostly consumers of casual and simple games. An Asus Nexus 7 tablet (2012 version) running the Android OS 4.4.4 was used in all usability tests. The capacitive touchscreen has a diagonal of 7.0 inches with an aspect ratio of 16:9 and a resolution of 1280 x 800 pixels. Figure 1 shows the interaction setup for our tests.

The adaptive controller must be configured with two parameters that will interfere in the final adaptation process: the movement limit of the button per iteration, measured in pixels, and the amount of the most recent points sent to the K-means algorithm. For the first one, a higher value will make the controller change its layout faster. In the second parameter, a lower value will make the controller consider only recent points, adapting faster to the current conditions of the interaction. In the pilot tests, three different configurations were tested with several games from different genres: conservative, intermediary and aggressive, presented on this order on Table 1.

The results showed some interesting conclusions. The faster adaptation allowed the controller to answer quickly to changes in the user play style, such as situations where the user changed the position of his hands without noticing, or changes in the own game, like bonus stages with different level designs. In a subjective evaluation, the faster adaptation provides a controller that adapts better to the game and has a quick response to correct the user's mistakes. The empiric feeling that this adaptation was better was also confirmed by our success rates.

Table 1. Results of the pilot tests.

Setup	Sonic (success rate)	Lifeforce (success rate)
5 pixels, 100 points	97.56	96.62
10 pixels, 30 points	97.86	97.63
100 pixels, 10 points	98.58	97.71

Once the adaptation parameters were defined we started the usability tests with the users. Each evaluation session was limited to 5 minutes of gameplay and approximately one minute of training before starting the test. The training session consisted of a free user interaction while the evaluator read the test script describing the function of each button as well as the game goals. The evaluation comprises both a subjective survey collected by a questionnaire and an objective investigation registered by the collected log data during the user's interactions. The subjective evaluation includes perceived performance and usability issues.

All events caused by the user-control device interaction were written to a log file, registering the touches, the controller's success rate for each period of time, the success rate of each button, the final success rate, score and quantity of lives spent in the game. The success rate is a value between 0 and 100, which represents the percentage of correct touches. The success rate per buttons is calculated in a similar way, but only taking in account the touches destined to that specific button. Each correct touch is associated to the button the user pressed and each incorrect touch is associated with the closest button.

All subjects used both controller versions with both games in an alternated order to eliminate any training effect caused by the evaluation order. Thus, each user had his unique sequence of test. To select the sequence, which the user would test, we performed a permutation between both controllers' version and game genres. The adaptive version will be referred as KA (K-means adaptive) while the non-adaptive version will be referred as NA.

After determining the most suitable design for our tests, we created hypotheses to validate the proposed interface:

H1: Adaptive controller will increase the user success rate for the novice users.

H2: Adaptive controller will increase the user success rate for the expert users.

H3: Adaptive controller will increase the user success rate independently of his experience.

H4: Adaptive controller will increase the user success rate independently of game genre.

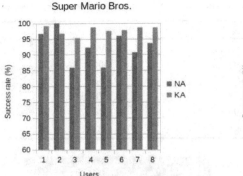
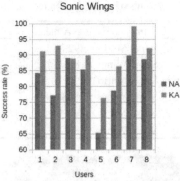

Fig. 2. Success rate for the novice users on Super Mario Bros (left) and Sonic Wings (right) using the K-means adaptive controller (KA) and the non-adaptive controller (NA).

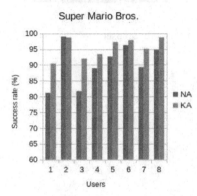
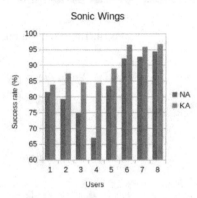

Fig. 3. Success rate for the expert users on Super Mario Bros (left) and Sonic Wings (right) using the K-means adaptive controller (KA) and the non-adaptive controller (NA).

To perform a comparison between both versions of the controller in our objective analysis, we will compare the mean final success rate of all users in one group with the same metric for the other group. After that, a Wilcoxon signed-rank test, a non-parametric statistical hypothesis test, is performed (significance level of 0.05 and the two-tailed hypothesis defined), returning the p-value, that indicates if the difference between the results achieved for both groups is significant. The decision of using a non-parametric test was motivated by the unknown distribution of the test results, since a parametric test requires a previous knowledge about the data distribution, that must be normal. For our groups' sizes, a p-value smaller than 0.05 represents a significant difference. Figure 2 and 3 presents the success rates for all users in both groups for all evaluation sessions. . Only two users do not present a better success rate with the adaptive version compared with the non-adaptive one. Figure 4 shows the initial and final configuration achieved by the adaptive controller for a user. Figures 5 presents the success rate over time for each user group, while figure 6 presents the success rate over time for both combined user groups.

Table 2. Results of the Wilcoxon test and mean success rate for both controllers for all groups.

Group	Game	NA mean (%)	KA mean (%)	p-value
Novice	Super Mario	92.89	98.11	0.03906
	Sonic Wings	84.73	90.42	0.01563
Expert	Super Mario	90.95	96.17	0.01563
	Sonic Wings	82.41	88.10	0.007813
All	Super Mario	92.43	97.57	0.0004272
	Sonic Wings	83.79	89.33	0.0001

Fig. 4. The initial and final configurations for an user.

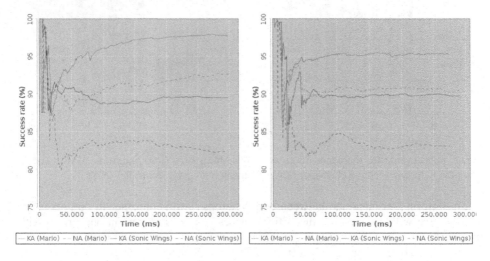

Fig. 5. Average success rate for all novice (left) and expert (right) users on Super Mario Bros and Sonic Wings for both controllers.

Table 2 shows the means for all users separated by group and for all users combined in a single group. We can see that for both games, the novice users had a higher success rate with the adaptive controller. The p-value was also less than 0.05, showing that the difference is significant and we can reject the null hypothesis. With these results, we can accept the hypothesis H1 that adaptive controller increases significantly the success rate for novice users. In a similar way, the expert users had a higher success rate in all cases. The p-value allows us to reject the null hypothesis and to consider the difference significant, validating the hypothesis H2.

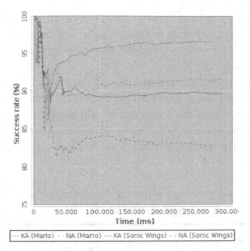

Fig. 6. Average success rate for all users on Super Mario Bros and Sonic Wings for both controllers.

However, during our evaluations of the log files, we noticed that the success rate for users of both groups were similar, leading us to believe that maybe our initial assumption that novice and expert users would use a game controller differently could be incorrect. In this case, all users would actually represent a single group and this would be an indication that the interaction with the gamepad could be more affected by other factor, such as ergonomic factors. Hence, we compared both groups to conclude if there is a significant difference between them. First we set the game Super Mario Bros. and confront the non-adaptive version for both groups. The p-value is 0.3828, so the result is not significant at $p <= 0.05$. With the same game, but confronting both adaptive results of groups the p-value is 0.1484, which is higher than the significance level, and then the difference is not significant. Setting the game to Sonic Wings and confronting the results of the non-adaptive version for both groups, we obtained a p-value of 0.8438, that shows that the difference is not significant. Lastly, with the adaptive in this game, the p-value of 1 and we concluded that this result is also not significant.

Surprisingly, the difference between both groups is not significant, showing that the level of experience probably is not an important factor in the usability of a game controller. With this result, we can combine all users in a single group. Now, it is necessary to test if, for this larger group of users, the adaptive joystick still is better than the non-adaptive version. Table 2 indicates the means and p-values for the unified group containing all users. The adaptive controller success rate was higher than the non-adaptive version, as indicated by the means. The p-values, smaller than 0.05, indicates that the difference is significant and we can reject the null hypothesis. With these last tests, we can conclude that the hypothesis H3 is valid and the adaptive controller increases significantly the success rate independently of the users' experience. Finally, we tested the hypothesis H4 comparing the adaptive version in Super Mario Bros with the adaptive version on Sonic Wings, including all sixteen users. The obtained p-value was 0.0001526. This result is significant and we can conclude that H4 is rejected and the adaptation can achieve different results in different game genres. This indicates that the controller can adapt itself better in some games and is influenced by the genre.

The second part of the analysis corresponds to the subjective results. In our survey most users believed they played Super Mario Bros. and Sonic Wings better with KA (respectively, 69% and 81% of the users) and would use the KA controller in a second play session (88% of the users in both cases). The users also rated the ease of use for both controllers, with the results in table 3 showing a clear advantage for the KA controller.

Table 3. User's opinion about the ease of use of the controllers according to a Likert scale, where 1 is "Very hard to use" and 5 is "Very easy to use".

	Super Mario Bros.		Sonic Wings	
Difficulty	NA	KA	NA	KA
Very hard	6%	0%	6%	0%
Hard	44%	19%	38%	0%
Normal	31%	25%	38%	31%
Easy	19%	38%	13%	50%
Very easy	0%	19%	6%	19%

5   Conclusions and Future Works

New forms of video game controllers are being proposed by the game industry to attract more players and enhance the immersion during gameplay. Many users avoid playing games due to the complexity observed in input devices, pushing them away from the video games community. Using a mobile device as a game controller gives the opportunity for designing specific interfaces for each game, making the interaction more accurate and adapted for individual gameplay mechanic.

Our work not only investigated whether the proposed adaptation improves the user-control interaction, but also gave insights into the general conditions under which the adaptations perform well. We can conclude that the adaptive controller brings benefits to great part of the users and from this brief evaluation we can start pointing an ideal interface.

A great surprise was to discover that the adaptation helps experts, casuals and even non-players. More than that, the interface showed similar results for both groups. In both game genres, our version of the controller showed an average improvement of more than 5%. Although in terms of percentage this is not a huge difference, when realizing that a user touches more than 2500 times when playing Sonic Wings and more than 500 when playing Super Mario Bros, we can consider that we had a great improvement in accuracy. The similar results for both groups also creates the possibility of evaluating other factors, like hand size and mobility. We would also want to evaluate the relation between how many times a button is used and its real importance for the game, determining if reducing the least used buttons really is the best approach for all game genres.

Our system is based on games with no source code, which means that we don't have access to the gameplay implementation. In future works we intend to include our system to commercial game engines, so that the control can change in accordance to the game context. The authors also pointed the study of other ways of adaptability, changing not only the button size and position, but also the shape. We also intend to investigate how this kind of user-control adaptation could improve the game interaction of different user groups, such as older users or despaired children, which usually have some motor skills limitations. The machine-learning algorithm is another topic for further studies. Other clustering algorithms can be evaluated, like K-medoids and K-medians.

References

1. Android SDK and Eclipse plugin.
   http://developer.android.com/sdk/index.html?hl=sk
2. Baldwin, T., Chai, J.: Towards online adaptation and personalization of key-target resizing for mobile devices. In: IUI 2012, pp. 11–20 (2012)
3. Bezold, M., Minker, W.: Adaptive multimodal interactive systems. Springer, 5 (2011)
4. Bi, X., Zhai, S.: Bayesian Touch – A Statistical Criterion of Target Selection with Finger Touch. ACM UIST 2013, 51–60 (2013)
5. BlueCove. https://code.google.com/p/bluecove/
6. Brandao, A., Trevisan, D., Brandao, L., Moreira, B., Nascimento, G., Vasconcelos, C., Clua, E., Mourao, P.: Semiotic inspection of a game for children with down syndrome. In: 2010 Brazilian Symposium Games and Digital Entertainment (SBGAMES), pp. 199–210 (November 2010)
7. Burke, J.W., McNeill, M., Charles, D., Morrow, P., Crosbie, J., McDonough, S.: Serious games for upper limb rehabilitation following stroke. In: Proceedings of the 2009 Conference in Games and Virtual Worlds for Serious Applications, VS-GAMES 2009, pp. 103–110. IEEE Computer Society, Washington, DC (2009)
8. Dretske.: Explaining Behavior. Reasons in a World of Causes. MIT Press, Cambridge (1988)
9. GestureWorks Gameplay on Steam.
   http://store.steampowered.com/app/296610
10. Golomb, M.R., McDonald, B.C., Warden, S.J., Yonkman, J., Saykin, A.J., Shirley, B., Huber, M., Rabin, B., AbdelBaky, M., Nwosu, M.E., Barkat-Masih, M., Burdea, G.C.: In-home virtual reality videogame telerehabilitation in adolescents with hemiplegic cerebral palsy. Archives of Physical Medicine and Rehabilitation, e1 91(1), 1–8 (2010)
11. Gonzalez, T.F.: On the computational complexity of clustering and related problems. In: Drenick, R.F., Kozin, F. (eds.) System Modeling and Optimization. Lecture Notes in Control and Information Sciences, vol. 38, pp. 174–182. Springer, Heidelberg (1982)
12. Joselli, M., Junior, J.R.S., Zamith, M., Clua, E., Soluri, E.: A content adaptation architecture for games. In: SBGames, SBC (2012)
13. Joselli, M., Silva Junior, J.R., Zamith, M., Soluri, E., Mendonca, E., Pelegrino, M., Clua, E.W.G.: An architecture for game interaction using mobile. In: 2012 IEEE International Games Innovation Conference (IGIC), pp. 73–77 (August 2012)

14. Laikari, A.: Exergaming - gaming for health: A bridge between real world and virtual communities. In: IEEE 13th International Symposium on Consumer Electronics, ISCE 2009, pp. 665–668 (May 2009)
15. Langley, P.: Machine learning for adaptive user interfaces. In: Brewka, G., Habel, C., Nebel, B. (eds.) KI 1997. LNCS, vol. 1303, pp. 53–62. Springer, Heidelberg (1997)
16. Malfatti, S.M., dos Santos, F.F., dos Santos, S.R.: Using mobile phones to control desktop multiplayer games. In: Proceedings of the 2010 VIII Brazilian Symposium on Games and Digital Entertainment, SBGAMES 2010, pp. 74–82. IEEE Computer Society, Washington, DC (2010)
17. Pelegrino, M., Torok, L., Trevisan, D., Clua, E.: Creating and Designing Customized and Dynamic Game Interfaces Using Smartphones and Touchscreen. In: 2014 Brazilian Symposium on Computer Games and Digital Entertainment (SBGAMES), pp. 133–139. IEEE (2014)
18. Pelegrino, M., Zamith, M., Mendonça, E., Joselli, M., Torok, L., Clua, E.: Controle orgânico virtual para jogos por dispositivos eletrônicos com tela sensível ao toque configurável e adaptável ao uso. Patent INPI BR 1020130300039 (filled in November 2013). http://www.inpi.gov.br/portal/artigo/busca_patentes (Accessed: February 2013)
19. Rogers, S., Williamson, J., Stewart, C., Murray-Smith, R.: Fingercloud: uncertainty and autonomy handover in capacitive sensing. In: ACM CHI 2010, pp. 577–580 (2010)
20. Smola, A., Vishwanathan, S.: Introduction to Machine Learning, pp. 32–34. Cambridge University (2008)
21. Stenger, B., Woodley, T., Cipolla, R.: A vision-based remote control. In: Computer Vision: Detection, Recognition and Reconstruction, pp. 233–262 (2010)
22. Vajk, T., Coulton, P., Bamford, W., Edwards, R.: Using a mobile phone as a wii-like controller for playing games on a large public display. Int. J. Comput. Games Technol., 4:1–4:6 (January 2008)
23. Wei, C., Marsden, G., Gain, J.: Novel interface for first person shooting games on pdas. In: OZCHI 2008: Proceedings of the 20th Australasian Conference on Computer-Human Interaction, OZCHI, pp. 113–121. ACM, New York (2008)
24. Weir, D., Rogers, S., Murray-Smith, R., Löchtefeld, M.: A user-specific machine learning approach for improving touch accuracy on mobile devices. In: ACM UIST 2012, pp. 465–476 (2012)
25. Weka: Data Mining Software in Java. http://www.cs.waikato.ac.nz/ml/weka/
26. Zamith, M., Joselli, M., Siva Junior, J., Pelegrino, M., Mendonça, E., Clua, E.: AdaptControl: An adaptive mobile touch control for games. In: SBGames, pp. 137–145 (2013)
27. Zyda, M., Thkral, D., Jakatdar, S., Engelsma, J., Ferrans, J., Hans, M., Shi, L., Kitson, F., Vasudevan, V.: Educating the next generation of mobile game developers. IEEE Computer Graphics and Applications 27(2), 96, 92–95 (2007)

A Participatory Approach for Game Design to Support the Learning and Communication of Autistic Children

Thiago Porcino, Daniela Trevisan, Esteban Clua,
Marcos Rodrigues, and Danilo Barbosa

Federal Fluminense University, Niterói, Rio de Janeiro, Brazil
thiagomp,daniela,esteban}@ic.uff.br,
{marcosrodrigues,danilo}@id.uff.br

Abstract. In this work we propose to apply a participatory design process for developing mobile games focused on learning and communication of autistic children. This study employs a game to help people with autism and describes the complete design process used in this research. As a result of the design process was possible to note the necessity to allow high customization and personalization of digital activities in order to promote the user engagement and gameplay ability. Moreover, more details are provided about the developed game. Two customized interactive activities were developed: Questions & Answers and the Emotional Thermometer that were evaluated with therapists, autistic children and HCI specialists. Finally, it is described the importance of therapists in game design process and the requirements for redesigning the application interface.

Keywords: Autism, children, learning, communication, mobile, participatory design, game.

1 Introduction

Autism is a general term for people who have one or more brain disorders that affects social interaction with different degrees: verbal and nonverbal communication, interests and behaviors. [1]

Autistic Spectrum Disorder (ASD) is a global development disorder that affects 1 in 68 children in the U.S., and may even be considered to be approaching epidemic status [2]. Although a significant portion of the population is affected, a great deal of myth and misinformation is associated with this disorder [1]. As a result, these children face a scenario that is not only complicated due to their symptoms but worsened by a lack of comprehension and support.

It has been proven that many of the negative effects of autism can be minimized when treatment is initiated early [10]; therefore, appropriate tools are essential for the cognitive development of children with ASD. However, these tools should consider certain specific characteristics of the children in order to be effective projected.

Although each case is unique, individuals with this disease share some limitations, which are not always easy to define. For example, difficulties with generalizing and

© IFIP International Federation for Information Processing 2015
K. Chorianopoulos et al. (Eds.): ICEC 2015, LNCS 9353, pp. 17–31, 2015.
DOI: 10.1007/978-3-319-24589-8_2

attention to detail make it difficult to find appropriate pedagogical activities for children with ASD, as associating designs and other representations with their real counterparts are too complicated. Many of these children are unable to communicate correctly, and some reach adulthood without the ability to communicate verbally.

Children with ASD appreciate the safe and replicable environment of computer tools [1, 7]. However, as pointed in the Related Works session, there is a lack of tools and games that are guaranteed to be flexible and scalable, with experiences that are integrated, free, and, above all, accessible.

Accordingly, the contribution of this work can be summarized in two fold: the design process applied to develop a mobile game in order to assist parents and teachers in teaching these children and moving them towards a potentially independent life, while providing tools to facilitate communication; and the application itself. This application uses the benefits of devices such as smartphones and tablet PCs in order to allow more concrete experiences. This differs from the majority of software available on the market because it allows a high degree of customization and integration. This study is the first step in a participatory design process based on an initial prototype, which in turn was guided by the studies of the characteristics of autistic children.

2   Related Works

There are various applications for mobile devices that seek to facilitate communication and stimulate learning and cognitive development in people with autism. However, few integrate these functionalities in a cohesive and personalized environment. SCAI Autismo, an augmentative and alternative communication tool (AAC) [11, 21] based on PECS, shows cards containing an image and text on the screen. The cards include "I," which contains an image that may be personalized with a photo, affirmative and negative, and desires like drinking water, sleeping, and eating dinner. They may be selected sequentially, reproducing a pre-recorded audio, so that the child can express a desire. TalkinPictures [24], also based on PECS, is a commercial application that has categorical hierarchies of cards and permits a greater degree of personalization, using a text-to-speech solution in order to include new options added by the user. meaVOX [25], which was developed by the Universidade Federal Fluminense, is similar to TalkinPictures, but instead of using text-to-speech, it permits sounds to be recorded and associated with the cards, and uses a desktop program to configure the application data. The game "What's the Word" [26] (4 pictures 1 word) not only aids in literacy but also encourages the ability to generalize. Each challenge includes four separate figures. The player must discover the common element between them and choose a group of scrambled letters that form the correct word.

In fact, none of these games permits the challenges to be customized, and players are restricted to the options offered by the developer upon installation of the program or through in-app purchases.

3   Design Process

In order to develop an appropriate tool to attend the needs of therapists, parents and children, we establish a close communication with the Center of Optimization for Rehabilitation for Autists (CORA). It is a non-profit entity that helps dozens of families. Currently, CORA has 5 therapists: one psychologist, one speech therapist, one music therapist, and two educational psychologists. At the moment of this research, approximately 45 patients were being treated, including children and adolescents from 5 to 16 years, being 14 of them females. There is a study and activity room and the main hall, where group activities are performed. In the kitchen, there is a sink and a table for lunch and breakfast. There is no equipment that would put patients at risk. The study room has 5 individual tables. This is the room where the learning activities are conducted. When the children have successfully performed tasks, they can visit the game room and participate in their favorite activities as a reward. The game room has a rubber floor and some toys such as balls and dolls. The main room is the place where the children interact as a group through games or toys, such as interviewer and interviewee, where a child is the interviewer and asks questions to the others sitting at the table.

3.1   Defining Context of Use

Analysis of the context in which the application would be used included interviews, questionnaires, and examination of footage taken previously of routine activities that were conducted at the beginning of the study. The questionnaire used has been made available in Appendix A [27].

The responses to the closed questions revealed that although the therapists were between 30 and 65 years of age, they frequently used the mobile devices with success, and considered them useful tools for therapy, because patients generally already have had contact with them and appreciate using this type of technology at home, mainly for electronic games. The majority of them are or were married, have at least one autistic child, and demonstrated great satisfaction with and commitment to their job at CORA. Only one is currently pursuing higher education; all the others have already concluded or are pursuing post-graduate education. Therefore, one may conclude that all are equally capable of providing valuable opinions on the needs of the patients, using the proposed application without much difficulty, and participating in the process of assessment while helping the child. They also indicated that the mobile devices, especially tablets, are appropriate for use both with patients and therapists, as was expected.

Using open questions, we noted that the activities most used to help patients learn are games involving the association of concepts, for example, pairing figures, as well as activities that involve music or other sound elements. The exercises are usually adjusted for each child according to his or her interests. We also observed that the children enjoy watching their favorite television programs and using computers, which was mainly seen when they always responded to particular input in the same manner. As for the association of concepts, the importance of realism was highlighted, that is, concepts must be represented by actual images and not fictitious ones because autistic children have difficulty understanding symbols. It was also suggested that the application should address issues related to speech, reading and social issues.

During the interviews, besides repeating the points raised in the questionnaire, it was noted that some therapists already use applications on their mobile devices (not always especially for autistic children) to assist in therapy. However, a single application may not be appropriate for multiple children, and various applications are needed to assist different patients.

The filmed activities were mostly group games focused on movement, encouraging fine motor development. It noted that during group sessions and more recreational and physical activities, the children were very extroverted and cooperative. However, they were less engaged in individual activities focused on learning, such as color association.

Accordingly, it was possible to confirm many of the premises obtained in prior studies as well help acquire new knowledge. Three types of people were identified from the data [4]: the therapists, who had very similar backgrounds, and the other two representing typical children who attend CORA. These are the target user profiles for the application: autistic children up to 10 years of age who mainly have communication problems. A scenario describing routine activities was also prepared, focusing on problems that might arise in these circumstances. This data guided the subsequent stages, and was more definitively prepared through the participatory design process. Factors such as the need for concrete elements, feedback sound, repeatability, appropriateness of the activity for each child in terms of both the area to be trained and individual interests, and focus on the association of concepts was strongly addressed during the application's development

3.2   Participatory Design

Participatory design is an approach that attempts to include the interested parties in the design process, i.e., all those directly or indirectly involved with the product [16]. In order to immerse the autistic children in the participatory design process, the Interface Design Experience for the Autism Spectrum (IDEAS) method was applied. The goal of this method is to include autistic children along with a team of specialists in the activities involved in designing a system, in a participatory design process [16].

The participatory design technique was used to guide development, ensuring that the proposed solutions meet the real needs of the end users in addition to encouraging a feeling of ownership of the application. The procedures were conducted together with two therapists jointly with the occasional cooperation of others, and comprised three meetings of about 1 hour divided into the following stages:

1. Review of the changes planned in the previous meeting;
2. Presentation of the changes implemented;
3. Validation and criticism of changes
4. Creation of new ideas
5. Definition of subsequent changes

Changes are defined as any modification to the current state of the application, whether an alternative of existing functions or creation of new ones. Between the meetings, the adjustments arising from the critiques and new modifications were implemented.

4   Design Solution

At the conclusion of the participatory design process, two main digital activities were performed: Questions and Answers and Card Keyboard, with the sub-game Emotional Thermometer. Below are given definitions for some terms that are referenced throughout the following sections:

Card
The activities are based on this component. It has a name and may have an image, text, and audio, all of which are optional.

Tutor
The therapist, father, or mother of the child, responsible for accompanying him or her during the usage of the application, answering questions, stimulating and personalizing the experience.

The game Questions and Answers (Fig. 1) was planned as a tool for assisting in learning, and comprises a series of questions. Each card includes a main card, represented by a large image that should be associated with one of the available options (also cards), which can be represented by a smaller image or text (if the child can read). Both the question and its answers may contain an audio instructing the user on how it should be answered, or refining the referenced concept when it is selected, respectively. If the user selects the correct option, the system provides positive feedback with a sound, and shows a dialogue box with the word "Correct!". The background is then changed for the next question. If the answer is incorrect, a different sound and the text "Incorrect" appears. The user may take as many attempts as he or she wishes, and return to the previous questions. The next question can only be reached by successfully answering the current one. In order to finish the game, the player must answer all the questions.

Fig. 1. Questions and Answers game interface.

Two alternative communication games were developed. The first one is the Emotional Thermometer (Fig. 2), based on a solution proposed by Attwood [3, p. 155] [23, p.131], is a horizontal sequence of photographs of the faces of children with different facial expressions. These are organized in a range of emotions from irritated to bored to very happy, using a slider component (Fig. 3) underneath so that the user may indicate the emotion that most closely matches his or her own. This resource is available in the game Questions and Answers, and can be accessed by pressing the screen for more than 500 milliseconds; in this way, if the user wants to stop the activity, the tutor may activate the thermometer or request that the child explain how he or she is feeling.

Fig. 2. Emotional Thermometer slider.

Fig. 3. Slider for emotional calibration.

The other communication game is the Card Keyboard (Fig. 4) based on the Picture Exchange Communication System (PECS) [23]. It comprises different cards that contain an image and a sound, divided into three categories:

Who?: Subject who performs the action. e.g., I, you.

Action: Action. e.g., want, do not want.

Which one?: Object to which the action is applied. e.g., food, bath.

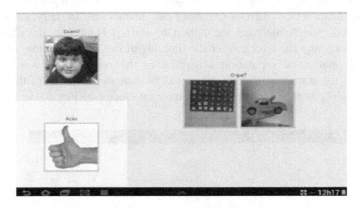

Fig. 4. Card Keyboard game interface.

The main objective is to make the children use the cards in order to communicate what they want or do not want to do. In this manner, they can avoid frustration and the potential of attacks resulting from not knowing how to verbalize their wishes. This activity has its own area, as it must be accessed when there is a clear purpose, and not as the result of actions in other parts of the application.

In order to satisfy the requirement to provide sound feedback, taking advantage of the sensory interests of children with ASD in a general manner, images, text, and sounds were combined in the game, and touch was used as a way of interacting, thereby taking advantage of the benefits for learning and the developments achieved using this type of interface [13,17]. The touch interface is more concrete than using a mouse; touching is a natural gesture with immediate feedback, which the child already knows. However, it was decided during the design meetings with the therapists that it would be more useful to add the possibility of using drag-and-drop in the game Questions and Answers in order to strengthen the association between the principal card and the option selected. This type of interaction is also more appropriate for children as pointed in [6]. This is represented visually by a colored line linking the initial touch point to the current finger position, and also adds a colored frame around the principal card as well as the option underneath the user's finger, if applicable.

As a relevant result from the participatory design sessions was possible to identity the need to have facilities for customization of game objects. In order to allow customization, all the cards may be modified by the tutor using the device's microphone, camera, and image gallery. In this way, the topics and options in Questions and Answers can be applied to the word that the child understands, incorporating subjects of interests and increasing engagement. Similarly, the Card Keyboard can represent the child's reality, for example, her or his own photo for the "I" card, and photos of favorite meals to represent for example "food." It was also decided that the order of questions should be modifiable to allow a gradual increase in the difficulty and grouping of related questions, as well as the order of the cards within each Card Keyboard category. The interface was kept as simple as possible, showing only the elements required for the current activity (which runs in full screen, without a notification bar), thereby removing any distractions. Initially, each tool had its own section, which included the option to start it (targeting the child) or to configure it (targeting the tutor). After the first day of use in the session, however, it became clear that more separation according to the user profile was necessary. Consequently, the start screen of the game has buttons to start each of the activities and button slightly farther away to enter the tutor interface (see Fig. 5).

Fig. 5. Start game screen.

The screen elements always correlate to the various interactions, visually and through sounds, indicating the ability to select active selection and thereby providing feedback to the user. Repeatability was achieved, allowing the user to return to any step of any activity.

5   Evaluation

The DECIDE framework [4], which defines the planning, execution and analysis of an Human Computer Interaction evaluation was used to establish the procedures and issues in assessing the proposed solution. The objectives, represented by questions to be answered at the end of the evaluation process, were:

- Is the child capable of understanding and independently using the game Questions and Answers until the end?
- Is the child capable of understanding the objective and successfully expressing himself using the alternative and amplified communication methods?
- When performing the proposed tasks, is the child capable of carrying out the required actions?
- Is s it possible to adjust the activities to the child's reality?
- Was the child experience with the game enjoyable?

Because the main users of the application will be autistic children, the majority of whom have little or no verbal capability, the only reliable way of obtaining the answers to these questions would be through usability and accessibility tests. Therefore, this method of evaluation was chosen, using a process filmed with the consent of both of the children's parents and respecting the appropriate ethical considerations.

The procedures to be executed were explained in a meeting with the parents and the therapists; any questions were answered, and the researchers' contact information was provided to ensure transparency. The game was also presented, so that they could approve its use by their children. The necessary equipment (a digital camera and an Android tablet) was reserved and prepared. Preparation of the tablet included extensive tests of the device's functions in order to ensure a fluid and bug-free experience; the activities were pre-configured with various questions and cards, following guidance from the therapists. Finally, the evaluation itself was performed. The methodology used for evaluation is thoroughly described below.

5.1   Methodology

For filming, 6 usage sessions addressing the explicit requirements of the TEACCH program were conducted [15]. The structure of the sessions was based on Benton et al. [8]. Each session involved a researcher filming and coordinating the procedures and answering any questions that might arise, a therapist acting as the tutor, and an autistic child age 3–10 who were experiencing her or his first contact with the game. The role of the therapist was to help the child, in the event of questions, to perform the actions necessary to complete the tasks, as well as to encourage him or her to continue. This also helped to address the need for routine once the child became accustomed to attending. For the same reason, the sessions were carried out at the CORA facilities, at the children's normally scheduled therapy time.

In order to address the difficulty of organization and sequencing, a list of tasks to be performed during the session was prepared. For all the items, this list was presented to the child at the beginning of the session and resumed after the conclusion of each task to promote concentration and the concept of the goal. The child was offered the opportunity to check off the items if they wished to create a feeling of participation and winning. The tasks performed include:

- Watch a video demonstrating the use of the game Questions and Answer.
- Play Questions and Answers.
- Watch a video demonstrating the use of Card Keyboard (nonverbal participants only).
- Use Card Keyboard (nonverbal participants only).
- Paint stars that correspond to a Likert satisfaction scale [14].
- As a reward for completing all the tasks, play any game installed on the tablet for 5 minutes (popular game options were offered).

At the end of the session, the therapist completed a questionnaire regarding the child interaction in order to facilitate more qualitative details in the evaluations.

Table 1. Evaluated Children.

Child	Ag	Sex
C1	5	Male
C2	10	Femal
C3	3	Male
C4	4	Male
C5	6	Male
C6	10	Male

5.2   Method of Interaction Analysis

To analyze the filmed content in the most objective manner possible, the DEVAN (Detailed Video Analysis) tool was used [5, 22]. Recently researchers have adapted the DEVAN tool to analyze the usability test videos for a game for children with Down syndrome entitled JECRIPE - Stimulation Game for Preschool Age Children with Down Syndrome [18]. This project used a table adapted for the children to measure elements such as fun and modified the table to contemplate the specific problems of interactions in this genetic disorder. In this method, various evaluators complete a form, and each record is composed of a code representing an interaction problem together with a timestamp for the moment of its occurrence. A second timestamp may be added if it lasts longer than a defined limit (in this case, four seconds). Because resources were limited, the same three non-specialist researchers involved in the study were used as evaluators. The table of codes was based on the one used by Macedo et al. in [18], with the inclusion of the ACX entry (exploratory action) representing autistic children's specific tendency to focus on details and lose focus on the context. The coding scheme used can be seen in Table 1.

5.3   Analysis of Results

When validating a method, it is very unlikely that different evaluators will agree exactly by giving identical results for all evaluation sessions. The any-two agreement method measures the extent of agreement on what problems the system contains for pairs of evaluators [12]. For each comparison the number of agreements, disagreements and single points were recorded, always considering the margin of 4 seconds to be counted as the same observation point. The script created to conduct this comparison is available in [20].

Due to the subjectivity of the analysis and the evaluators' lack of experience, the level of agreement reached was considered low for all of the comparisons. As can be seen in Table 2, the best any-two agreement was 21.29%, with a total of 45 unique observed points, 50 deviations and only 26 agreements. In an extreme case, there were 210 deviations in the lowest any-two agreement comparison. This demonstrates a probable difference in the understanding of the codes, as the observed points were very concordant, leaving few unique points.

Table 2. DEVAN method adapted for children with Down syndrome [18].

Code	Description	Definition
ACE	Wrong Action	An action does not belong in the correct sequence of actions. An action is omitted from the sequence. An action within a sequence is replaced by another action. Actions within the sequence are performed in reversed order. The user performs a wrong action unintentionally.
ACP	Intentional Wrong Action	The user knows that the action is wrong, but still performs this action only to have fun.
AJU	Help	The user cannot proceed without help or the researcher has to intervene in order to prevent serious problems. The user is helped to do some action.
ANT	Dislike	The user indicates disliking something.
CON	Puzzled	The user indicates not knowing how to proceed.
IMP	Impatience	The user shows impatience by clicking repeatedly on objects that respond slowly, or when it takes too much time to reach the desired goal.
PAS	Passive	The user stops playing and does not perform the expected action.
PEX	Execution Problem	The user has physical problems during interaction with the game. The user has motor skill problem.
PPR	Perception Problem	The user indicates not being able to hear or see something clearly, not understanding how to proceed.
RAN	Random Actions	The user performs random actions.
STP	Scenario Stopped	The user stops the scenario before reaching the goal.
TED	Bored	The user indicates being bored by sighing or yawning.

Table 3. Results of Any-Two Agreement.

EvaluationA x Evaluation	Any-Two	Agree	Disagree	Unique A	Unique B
Evaluation 1 x Evaluation	13,00	36	210	23	8
Evaluation 1 x Evaluation	21,49	26	50	43	2
Evaluation 2 x Evaluation	13,11	16	79	17	10

6 Discussion

Based upon the analysis of the results and observations made during the sessions, the following were the most problematic points found in the proposed solution:

- Occasional delayed response in the application.
- Buttons and images were too small; it was reported that some children do not see well.
- Child accidentally accessed the tutor (therapist) interface.

In the game Questions and Answers:
- Method for entering the Thermometer function is not intuitive and may be activated unintentionally.
- Child was not able to clearly determine when an answer was incorrect, and insisted on the error.
- Child did not feel rewarded upon completing the game.
- Child repeatedly attempted to drag-and-drop toward the option-question, an interaction not contained in the application, instead of the question-option.
- Child felt disoriented when question content changed. For example, when moving from questions about animals to questions about superheroes, or when changing from questions with just figures to questions with text.
- Child felt bored or unmotivated during the questions.
- Child attempted to select the option but touches the wrong space and chooses the wrong selection by accident.

In the sub-game Emotional Thermometer:
- Child did not understand the purpose of the screen.
- Child did not know how to return to the previous environment.

In the game Card Keyboard:
- Child did not understand the purpose of this screen.
- Child did not follow instructions to select the cards.
- There are no feedback showing the end of the sentence.
- There may be many different options for the same concept. For example, there may be several cards for food, such as pasta, beans and hamburger. This makes comprehension and selection difficult.

At the beginning of the evaluations, questions regarding the proposed solution were prepared. It was hoped that the answers to these questions would be obtained after the procedures carried out. Based on the observations, the following conclusions were made:

Is the child capable of understanding and independently using the game Questions and Answers until its conclusion? The verbal children were high-functioning autistic patients with a higher level of concentration and abstraction;

consequently, they did not have significant problems performing any of the proposed tasks. However, nonverbal children or those developing their language skills required constant assistance from therapists. The problems that were observed cannot be attributed to lack of experience with the technology, as they were all familiar with tablets. Therefore, this objective was partially achieved, requiring us to address the existing problems so that it can be used with a broader range of patients on the autism spectrum.

Is the child capable of understanding the objective and successfully expressing himself or herself using the alternate and broadened communication methods? No alternative communication method was considered successful. This may be for various reasons: lack of a clear objective, i.e., a specific message to be codified for the child though the tool, with appropriate feedback demonstrating the meaning of the sentence; inexperience on the part of the therapists, who guided the activity, with this type of tool; difficulties inherent to the severity of the child's condition; and short time of use. Teaching a new form of communication is a slow and gradual process.

Upon performing the proposed tasks, is the child capable of performing the required actions? The children had some common problems when attempting to perform the actions that were required, generally in relation to the direction of movement or to the stopping point. However, most of the time they were able to carry out their intentions.

Can the activities be adjusted to the child's reality? Because only a short amount of preparation time was available before the session, and because the therapists were not familiar with the children's personal preferences, it was not possible to adjust the application to all of them. However, several series of questions in the game Questions and Answers were prepared between the session days and managed to arouse the interest of some patients. Furthermore, some of the nonverbal children demonstrated interest in the ability to take their own photograph and place it in Card Keyboard, although they did not understand the objective.

Was the user experience agreeable for the child? The results of the Likert painted star scale are not reliable, since the children were encouraged by the therapists to paint the stars; additionally, they did not seem to understand the meaning of this activity. However, based on the videos and personal impressions, it was possible to perceive various reactions ranging from boredom and disinterest to curiosity and excitement, so much so that future studies may address the excited response to rewards.

Based on the problems raised and on the answers to the initial questions, a new design proposal was developed. This proposal will be submitted to the CORA therapists, beginning a new series of iterations in the participatory design process, the results of which may create new interesting observations.

The resulting game application will be made available at no cost and under an open source license in Google Play. Currently, its code and executable version are hosted at [20].

7   Conclusion

The experience acquired with this game design process shown that involvement of therapists was essential in the participatory design process, and the process of evaluation yielded valuable information that can only be achieved through actual use by end users, allowing a thorough analysis of the game interaction. However, due to the difficulty involved in the scope of the problem where extra care was required with the autistic users during the study in order to avoid any stress or discomfort from the proposed activities, further design iterations were not possible. Data was only collected at CORA place because of the difficulty in finding the user targeted who could participate in the study, but it would be helpful to find more users who could participate in future usability and accessibility tests.

The results obtained from the DEVAN method and subsequent analysis using the any-two agreement yielded excessively low concordance. It would be interesting to investigate the reasons for these disparities, clarifying any confusion in defining the codes. The analysis was performed by three non-specialist evaluators, which can affect the results. An essential task for removing doubt in this process is including more evaluators, including specialists, and comparing the new results with the previous ones.

Several suggestions for redesigning the application interface were mentioned during the design process and evaluation stage. These changes will be implemented in a future project, following new participatory design iterations. These new versions should be used to conduct and analyze new usability tests, permitting comparison between this new data and the results from the previous interface.

References

1. Sole-Smith, V.: Common myths about autism spectrum, Meredith Coporation (2014). http://www.parents.com/health/autism/myths-about-autism/
2. Baio, J.: Prevalence of autism spectrum disorder among children aged 8 years - autism and developmental disabilities monitoring network, 11 sites, United States, 2010. MMWR Surveill Summ. 63 Suppl. 2, 1–21 (2014)
3. Attwood, T.: The complete guide to Asperger's syndrome/Tony Attwood, 1st hardcover ed. Jessica. Kingsley Publishers, London (2006)
4. Preece, J., Rogers, Y., Sharp, H.: Interaction Design: Beyond Human-Computer Interaction. Wiley, New York (2002)
5. Barendregt, W., Bekker, M.M.: Developing a coding scheme for detecting usability and fun problems in computer games for young children. Behav. Res. Methods 38(3), 382–389 (2006)
6. Barendregt, W., Bekker, M.M.: Children may expect drag-and-drop instead of point-and-click. In: CHI 2011 Extended Abstracts on Human Factors in Computing Systems, CHI EA 2011, pp. 1297–1302. ACM, New York (2011)

7. Barry, M., Pitt, I.: Interaction design: A multidimensional approach for learners with autism. In: Proceedings of the 2006 Conference on Interaction Design and Children, IDC 2006, pp. 33–36. ACM, New York (2006)

8. Benton, L., Johnson, H., Ashwin, E., Brosnan, M., Grawemeyer, B.: Developing ideas: supporting children with autism within a participatory design team. In: CHI 2012 Proceedings of the SIGCHI Conference on Human Factors in Computing Systems, pp. 2599–2608. Association for Computing Machinery (ACM), New York (2012)

9. Bondy, A., Hortonm, C.: The picture exchange communication system: Helping individuals gain functional communication. Autism Advocate 3, 21–24 (2010)

10. Corsello, C.M.: Early intervention in autism. Infants & Young Children 18(2), 74–85 (2005)

11. Grigis, D., Lazzari, M.: Augmentative and alternative communication on tablet to help persons with severe disabilities. In: Proceedings of the Biannual Conference of the Italian Chapter of SIGCHI, CHItaly 2013, pp. 17:1–17:4. ACM, New York (2013)

12. Hertzum, M., Interaction, C.F.H., Jacobsen, N.E.: The evaluator effect: a chilling fact about usability evaluation methods. Int. Journal of Human-Computer Interaction (2001)

13. Hourcade, J.P., Bullock-Rest, N.E., Hansen, T.E.: Multitouch tablet applications and activities to enhance the social skills of children with autism spectrum disorders. Personal Ubiquitous Comput. 16(2), 157–168 (2012)

14. Jamieson, S., et al.: Likert scales: how to (ab) use them. Medical Education 38(12), 1217–1218 (2004)

15. Mesibov, G.B., Shea, V., Schopler, E.: The TEACCH Approach to Autism Spectrum Disorders. Springer, New York (2004)

16. Muller, M.J.: Participatory design: the third space in HCI. Human-computer interaction: Development process, 165–185 (2003)

17. Rasche, N., Qian, C.Z.: Work in progress: Application design on touch screen mobile computers (tsmc) to improve autism instruction. In: 2013 IEEE Frontiers in Education Conference (FIE), pp. 1–2 (2012)

18. Macedo, I., Trevisan, D.G., Clua, E., Vasconcelos, C.N.: Observed Interaction in Games for Down Syndrome Children. In: Proceedings of the 48th Annual Hawaii International Conference on System Sciences, HICSS 2015, Kauai, vol. 48, pp. 320–327 (2015)

19. Rodrigues, M.: ASD-Teaching-Tool (2014). http://github.com/mrodrigues/ASD-Teaching-Toolr

20. Rodrigues, M.: Devan-any-two (2014). https://github.com/mrodrigues/DEVAN-Any-Two

21. Romski, M.A., Sevcik, R.A.: Augmentative communication and early intervention: Myths and realities. Infants & Young Children 18(3), 174 (2005)

22. Vermeeren, A.P.O.S., den Bouwmeester, K., Aasman, J., de Ridder, H.: Devan: A tool for detailed video analysis of user test data. Behaviour and Information Technology 21(6), 403–423 (2002)

23. Williams, C., Wright, B., Young, O.: How to Live with Autism and Asperger Syndrome: Practical Strategies for Parents and Professionals. Jessica Kingsley Publishers (2004)

24. Google Play. TalkinPictures. https://play.google.com/store/apps/details?id=com.androidinlondon.autismquicktalk&hl=en_US

25. meaVOX. Alternative communication for all. http://meavox.com.br/

26. What's The Word Answer. https://www.whatsthewordanswers.com

27. Appendix A (only in Portuguese). https://github.com/thiagomalheiros/asdTools_Docs

A Real Time Lighting Technique
for Procedurally Generated 2D Isometric
Game Terrains

Érick O. Rodrigues and Esteban Clua

Department of Computer Science, Universidade Federal Fluminense,
Rua Passo da Pátria 156, Niterói - RJ, Brazil
erickr@id.uff.br, esteban@ic.uff.br

Abstract. This work proposes an automatic real time lighting technique for procedurally generated isometric maps. The scenario is generated from a string seed and the proposed lighting system estimates the geometrical shape of the 2D objects as if they were 3D for further light interaction, therefore producing a 2.5D effect. We employ opacity maps to overcome an issue generated by the geometrical shape estimation. The solution is a coupled approach between the CPU and GPU. The produced visuals, gameplay and performance were evaluated by gamers, programmers and designers. Furthermore, the performance, in terms of frames per second, was evaluated over distinct graphics cards and processors and was satisfactory.

Keywords: procedural generation, lighting, isometric, 2.5D, real time.

1 Introduction

As the processing power of computers improves over time, so does the opportunity for more complex game architectures and mechanics. Procedural Content Generation (PCG) techniques for games enable the construction of more immersive, defying, lasting and realistic games. The game Spore, for instance, employs several concepts of evolution, where creatures, textures and game spaces are procedurally generated to simulate natural selection, evolution and exploration of an infinite universe. In addition, PCG has the feasibility to reduce manual design efforts of nearly every part of the game and the time required for game development [1] while having the potential of contributing greatly to the reduction of the game data.

Shadows and lights in games are frequently computed on the basis of 3D geometries of scene objects. Although isometric terrains produce a visually pleasing result, resemble a 3D world, and conform to the effort reduction in game production due to disregarding 3D models and working with 2 dimensions instead, such as in [2] and as shown in Figure 1, their illumination is not trivial due to the lack of geometrical data. A possible solution for this is the usage of normal maps or even a simplistic volume information associated to the 2D scene that is

© IFIP International Federation for Information Processing 2015
K. Chorianopoulos et al. (Eds.): ICEC 2015, LNCS 9353, pp. 32–44, 2015.
DOI: 10.1007/978-3-319-24589-8_3

employed as a guide for light and shadow interaction [3,4]. However, these kind of solutions require dedicated design of the scene elements, which in many cases may be impracticable.

Fig. 1. Final fantasy tactics, one of the most famous games that adopts the isometric perspective.

This work proposes (1) a novel technique for estimating the geometry of 2D sprites in the isometric environment and (2) an approach for tracing lights and shadows of the scene based on the CPU and GPU. Both of these steps are automatically generated. In other words, given a certain scene having several distinct 2D sprites and no access to any kind of geometrical information nor normal maps, we propose a lighting system that interacts with the 2D environment and produces 3D-like illumination.

2   Literature Review

Currently, the literature on PCG is scattered across numerous fields. However, it is primarily related to Computer Science in areas such as Computer Graphics, Pattern Recognition, Games, Artificial Intelligence and Multimedia Computing. The earliest games that employed PCG were produced around 1980. The exploration game Elite is one of the earliest and employed a Pseudo-Random Number Generation (PRNG) to produce a very large universe [5]. When applying PRNG, the data is generated using a seeded algorithm, which allows the process to be deterministic. This is an important feature since the automatically generated data can be consistently reproduced and therefore tested [6]. Perlin Noise, for instance, is a PRNG developed to make computer generated images look more realistic [7].

PCG is constantly being applied to a large amount of commercial games. Rogue is a dungeon crawling game of the 1980s. Unlike adventure games of the time, Rogue randomly generated the dungeon layout and the location of items. Furthermore, PCG was applied to a couple of games at the time such as

Telengard, Nethack and Elite but further nearly vanished from the mainstream of commercial games. PCG was easy to implement in games of this period, which run over DOS. As soon as the frameworks became more complex, the appliance of PCG became even more complex and was consequently rarely regarded.

In 1996, Diablo resurrected PCG and roguelike games to the mainstream of commercial games. Diablo procedurally generates its levels and loot. Its sequel, Diablo II, maintained the PCG characteristic of the former. Every time a player starts the game, the maps and levels are assembled distinctly. Both Diablo and Diablo II are 2D games in the isometric perspective. The first Diablo game featured no lighting effects apart from what can be done with sprites. Diablo II, on the other hand, used a simplistic pre-built geometry of the scene to apply an incipient 2D illumination.

Randomness is one of the basis of PCG. In general, what mainly changes amongst several approaches is the chosen threshold of randomness and the way it is applied to the problem. Evolutionary algorithms, which involve random mutations, are often applied to the procedural generation of characters [8], terrains [9], tracks for racing games [10] and others. However, as previously addressed, deterministic algorithms can also be classified as procedural. Although the result of the computation is always the same for a combination of input parameters, the set of parameters itself (seed) may be randomly generated. In this work, the generated lights and shadows vary related to the position of the light and to the environment in a deterministic fashion. Therefore, the maps, as well as the positions, are the seed of the algorithm.

Ebert et al. [11] introduced several methods for procedurally generating game contents. Among these methods, algorithms for generating solids, gases, water, fire, noise, cloud, earth textures and materials, for instance, were regarded. Kelly et al. [12] surveyed techniques for procedurally generating cities, focusing on individual buildings, road networks and cityscapes. Smelik et al. [13] surveyed procedural generation of terrain and urban environments. At last, Hendrikx et al. [5] surveyed several aspects of PCG for games and categorized the existing algorithms in 6 main distinct classes: Game Bits, Game Space, Game Systems, Game Scenario, Game Design and Derived Content. The class (1) Game Bits comprises the generation of texture, sound, vegetation, buildings, behavior, fire, water, stone and clouds; (2) Game Spaces, on the other hand, aggregates indoor maps (e.g., rooms in general), outdoor maps (e.g., terrains) and bodies of water (e.g., river, lakes and seas). Furthermore, ecosystems, road networks, urban environments and entity behavior are comprised by the (3) Game Systems class. Notwithstanding, puzzles, storyboards, story and levels are fit in the (4) Game Scenario class. If the algorithm refers to the creation of mathematical patterns underlying the game and game rules then it was categorized as (5) Game Design. Finally, news and leaderboards are fit in the (6) Derived Content class.

The approach proposed in this work does not fit properly in any of the classes defined by Hendrikx et al. [5]. That is so because we are the first to introduce a methodology that procedurally estimates the geometry of 2D sprites for further light interaction. In our methodology, we draw the light rays to a texture and further pass it to the fragment shader. Thus, it could be partially comprised by the Game Bits category. However, since the entire methodology does not just generate a texture, it appears to be misclassified. Perhaps a new class called Game Effects could be added to the definition of Hendrikx et al. for a proper categorization.

3 The Approach

The map architecture followed the Entity Component System (ECS) definition. That is, every graphical component of the game is an extension of the Entity class that has a (x, y) position property. In this work we propose the usage of auxiliary layers that overlap each other. Thus, each tile or block of the map, as shown in Figure 2, is composed of the block sprite plus at most 3 layers of overlapping sprites such as shown in the third image of Figure 2.

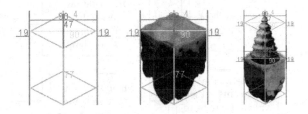

Fig. 2. Tiles or blocks of the map.

The blocks of the map are then assembled together. The assemblage is straight-forward: the nth block is placed at the right position of the $(n-1)^{th}$ block, as long as there is no line break. If a line break is present, assuming that the first block of the previous line is called p, then the n block is placed at the bottom of p in the y direction, and at the center of p and $p + 1$ in the x direction. A randomly generated map is shown in Figure 3.

Fig. 3. Randomly generated map.

The approach consists of, at first, creating an obstacle map every time a new map is loaded and storing it in memory. At every iteration of the render method, the light sources that appear within the scene are processed and drawn to a texture of slightly greater size than the screen. The light rays are traced using the Bresenham's Line Algorithm [14]. The produced texture is then bound to the fragment shader and the fragment shader alters the colors of each fragment according to the light texture. The entire process is illustrated in Figure 4.

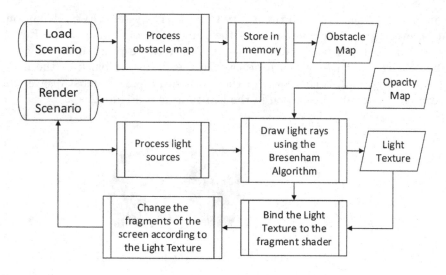

Fig. 4. Overall steps of the proposed approach.

3.1   Obstacle Map

As previously addressed, when a new map is loaded, a 2D boolean obstacle map is created to store information that is used to halt the tracing of light rays if they hit an opaque object. A heuristic was used to compute the obstacle map and is shown in Algorithm 1. Figure 5 illustrates the Δy of an arbitrary block. The height of Δy was empirically chosen to be 25 pixels in our case, where each sprite of the block is 128x128 pixels wide.

Fig. 5. The Δy in an arbitrary block.

while *not every block b has been iterated* **do**

    1. read Δy lines of b and store the largest sequence of non-transparent pixels for each line;

    2. take the sequence of occurrences s that has the least deviation to the mean;

    3. set the pixels of s as true in the obstacle map;

    4. take the central pixel of s and set their upper and lower $s.length/4$ pixels of the obstacle map as true;

end

Algorithm 1. Constructing the obstacle map.

Thereafter, a box-shaped noise reduction was applied to erase any tiny obstacle from the obstacle map. That is, we consider a $n \times n$ window and displace this window over the obstacle map verifying if there is less than n pixels set as obstacle within the window. If so, the top-left pixel of the window is unset as obstacle.

3.2   Light Rendering

Once at each l frames, the light rays are traced, interacting with the obstacle map. The Bresenham Algorithm [14] was used to trace these lines and was properly adapted to the problem as shown in Algorithm 2. At every light source within the screen a surrounding rectangular area of size $a \times b$ is regarded for tracing the light rays. A total of $4ab$ light rays are traced towards every pixel of the border of this area from the central pixel of each light source.

The Algorithm 2 receives the coordinates of the light source's origin and the coordinates of every pixel of the rectangular border. The pixels corresponding to the traced rays are drawn in a particular order: from the center of the light source to the pixels of the rectangular border. During this process, if any of these pixels corresponds to an obstacle pixel in the obstacle map, then the tracing halts at this specific pixel. If no obstacle is found, the algorithm draws the intensity and transparency of the light texture's pixel based on the function $i(\Delta j, \Delta i) = 255/(1 + max(\Delta j, \Delta i))$, where Δj and Δi represent the distance of the iterated pixel with regard to the central pixel of the light source and assuming that the texture is 8-bits depth (max value: 255).

It is interesting to note that not necessarily a light ray must be traced for every pixel of the rectangular border. Some of these pixels can be skipped to improve the overall performance and the eventual produced gaps can be further corrected in the shader at the GPU with some kind of blurring algorithm [15]. Furthermore, we previously defined that the light rays are traced at every l frames. Thus, while the light texture is not updated among these l frames, the texture should be displaced (inverse translation) according to the main central moving character, to avoid incorrect placements through the screen of a light that was generated at a certain position at a certain frame. Finally, if the generated light texture is directly drawn to the screen, then the result would look like

```
method traceLightRay(int orgX, int orgY, int dstX, int dstY);
begin
    int w = (dstX - orgX), h = (dstY - orgY);
    short dx1 = 0, dy1 = 0, dx2 = 0, dy2 = 0;
    if (w < 0) dx1 = -1; dx2 = -1; else if (w > 0)  dx1 = 1; dx2 = 1;
    if (h < 0) dy1 = -1; else if (h > 0) dy1 = 1;
    short longest = absolute(w); short shortest = absolute(h);
    if !(longest > shortest) then
        longest = absolute(h); shortest = absolute(w); dx2 = 0;
        if (h < 0) dy2 = -1; else if (h > 0) dy2 = 1;
    end
    int numerator = longest >> 1; boolean finished = false;
    for int i=0; i ≤ longest and !finished; i++ do
        if pixel(orgX, orgY) is not blocked then
            enlighten pixel(orgX, orgY);
        else
            finished = true;
        end
        numerator += shortest;
        if !(numerator < longest) then
            numerator -= longest;
            orgX += dx1; orgY += dy1;
        else
            orgX += dx2; orgY += dy2;
        end
    end
end
```

Algorithm 2. Adapted Bresenham Algorithm.

Figure 6. The white pixels on top of the trees and bushes represent the obstacle map.

The arrows in Figure 6 indicate issues generated by the current approach. That is, the bushes that are at a lower position in the vertical direction than the light's center should be completely dark, not half enlightened as it currently is. Furthermore, the part of the tree pointed by the red arrow should have been enlightened, but the current approach projects a shadow in this area.

To overcome this issue we introduce the concept of opacity maps. Each sprite of the scene (excluding the floor blocks) has its own opacity map. An opacity map is a boolean matrix that indicates if a certain pixel of the sprite is transparent or not, given a certain threshold. Thus, the opacity maps of the sprites are subtracted or added to the light texture. If the iterated sprite is at a higher position than the center of the light in the vertical direction, the opacity map of the same is added to the light texture and their illumination coefficient are properly computed. Otherwise, if the sprite is at a lower position, then its opacity map is subtracted from the light texture. The result of this correction is shown in Figure 7.

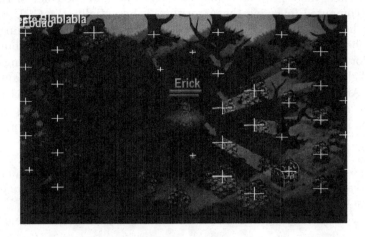

Fig. 6. Light texture being directly rendered on top of the sprites.

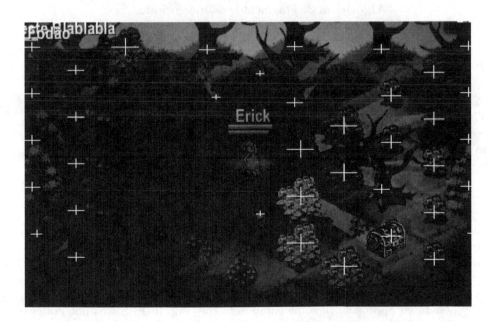

Fig. 7. Opacity maps added to the light texture.

After modifying the light texture according to the opacity maps of the surrounding sprites, the texture is bound to the shader and the color of the fragments are computed following the Algorithm 3. Essentially, the GPU will just receive the light texture and change the colors of the fragments according to the previously bound texture. Moreover, in our implementation, the framebuffer was also used for drawing all the scene sprites priorly to applying the lighting effects. Once the light texture is in the GPU, a simple box-blur algorithm is applied to the same. Although the computations in the GPU are an essential part of the process, the method is much more associated to the CPU. Therefore, processors with shared memory between the GPU and CPU will benefit from the approach.

Data: texColor being the color of the fragment, ambientClarity being a float that stores the ambient clarity and lightTexture being the texture binded to the shader

begin

$\quad$ (...);

$\quad$ float luminance = texColor.r*0.349 + texColor.g*0.114 + texColor.b*0.537;

$\quad$ vec4 lightFactor =

$\quad$ luminance*lightTexture/(ambientClarity*ambientClarity+0.1);

$\quad$ vec4 texFactor = texColor*sqrt(ambientClarity);

$\quad$ texColor = texFactor + lightFactor;

end

Algorithm 3. Fragment shader algorithm.

4   Results

Figure 8 shows the final result with two light sources on both characters [16]. The ambient clarity in this occasion was set to 0.4. The blurring gives a final nice aesthetics and allows the possibility of skipping some light rays during the tracing to speed up the overall performance. If the texFactor variable in Algorithm 3 is multiplied by lightTexture, then what is not hit by the light texture would appear completely dark.

Furthermore, we do not specifically generate shadows. That is, we assume that every pixel that does not have an associated light ray is a shadow. However, if one desires to cast shadows instead of light rays, then the light ray tracing just need to be inverted. In other words, at its current state, the light rays are traced until they reach an obstacle. To cast shadows, the shadow rays should be painted after the light rays reach the same obstacle.

The achieved Frame Rate Per Second (FPS) was satisfactory for a procedurally generated approach. In some computers the drop in FPS was not noticeable. Figure 9 illustrates some of the obtained FPS among distinct processors and graphics cards. It is interesting to notice that, in fact, the bottleneck of the approach is at the CPU and at the communication between the CPU and GPU. The processors that have an integrated GPU obtained better results due to

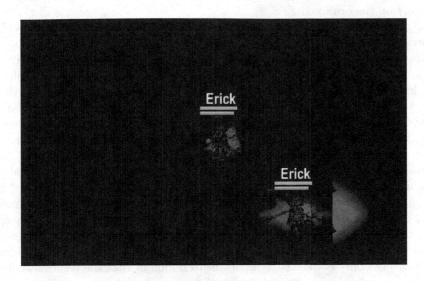

Fig. 8. Visual result.

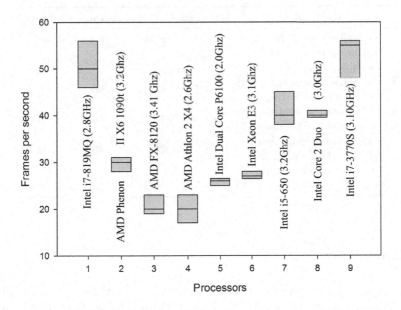

Fig. 9. A benchmark of the approach.

memory bandwidth issues. The overall power of the GPU alone did not influence positively on the obtained FPS.

The graphics cards used in each case from 1 to 9 were, respectively: (1) Nvidia GeForce GTX 850M,(2) Nvidia GeForce GTX 550ti, (3) Nvidia GeForce 630, (4) ATI Radeon HD 5550, (5) Intel HD Graphics, (6) ATI Radeon 280X Windforce, (7) Intel HD Graphics, (8) Nvidia GeForce GT 440 and (9) Intel HD Graphics. It is clear that the Intel processors performed in a more efficient fashion than AMD, specially in the chips that have an integrated graphics card. In addition, it appears that when processors and graphics cards are of the same manufacturer, the FPS is slightly benefited such as on case 4 if compared to 3. However, we cannot assure that correlation.

Beyond that analysis, we have also collected feedbacks from 61 evaluators including gamers, designers and programmers regarding the usability, benefits and visuals produced by the approach. Among them 40 were designers, 55 gamers and 42 programmers. Their analysis are summarized in Table 1. The last concept of the table is related to a comparison between the proposed approach and a non-interactive approach, such as the one in image (b) in Figure 10 (including movement, not only static). It is important to highlight that the resultant colors between (a) and (b) are a little different, though we have tried to minimize that difference as much as possible.

Table 1. General concepts analysis.

Concept	Designers	Gamers	Programmers	Mean
Overall rating (0 to 10)	8.72	8.74	8.85	8.65
Possible game production speed up rating (0 to 10)	9.50	9.27	9.28	9.18
Would active the lighting with no noticeable FPS drop (%)	97.5	85.4	90.4	85.2
Would active the lighting even with noticeable FPS drop (%)	67.5	58.1	66.6	60.6
Would reduce resolution to activate the lighting (%)	47.5	38.2	40.4	39.3
Find it better than no interaction, Figure 10-(b) (%)	86.5	80.3	80.1	79.4

5   Conclusion

The obtained results with our proposed approach are satisfactory in the visual and performance aspects. We have shown that the inclusion of automatic illumination in procedurally generated isometric scenes can be achieved without the need of proper designing or modelling. Furthermore, we have also shown that our method is independent of the sprites topology shapes.

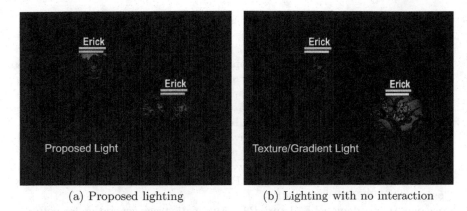

(a) Proposed lighting   (b) Lighting with no interaction

Fig. 10. Comparison of the light interaction.

Moreover, the approach may contribute as an architectural basis for a framework that can procedurally generate isometric maps of the addressed configuration. Due to the fact that the geometrical shapes of the objects on the scene and the lighting interaction are procedurally generated, there is no need to be concerned with anything other than the seed generation, which involves no 3D modelling and, therefore, greatly diminishes the workload. As a future work, we intend to develop a sandbox framework, making it possible to include in different tools.

We can conclude from the collected feedback that the approach is very interesting from the perspective of the user, especially on the PCG-related aspects. The greatest ratings were on the possibility of speeding up the production of games if the proposed lighting is regarded. However, we can also conclude that the majority would not use or activate the proposed lighting if the drop in FPS is such that it affects the gameplay experience. This argument came in a more accentuated fashion from gamers than from developers (designers and programmers). Fortunately, with regard to some computers specifications, the proposed lighting produces no apparent FPS drop. As future work we would also like to improve the CPU bottleneck.

References

1. Lee, Y.-S.: Context-aware petri net for dynamic procedural content generation in role-playing game. Computational Intelligence Magazine 6, 16–25 (2011)
2. Doytsher, Y., Hall, J.K.: Simplified algorithms for isometric and perspective projections with hidden line removal. Computers and Geoscience 27, 77–83 (2001)
3. Kilgard, M.J.: A practical and robust bump-mapping technique for today's gpus. In: Game Developers Conference: Advanced OpenGL (2000)
4. DesLauriers, M.: Normal mapping.
   https://github.com/mattdesl/lwjgl-basics/wiki/ShaderLesson6

5. Hendrikx, M., Meijer, S., Van Der Velden, J., Iosup, A.: Procedural content generation for games: A survey. ACM Transactions on Multimedia Computing, Communications, and Applications, 9 (2013)
6. Smith, A.J., Bryson, J.J.: A logical approach to building dungeons: Answer set programming for hierarchical procedural content generation in roguelike games. Proceedings of the 50th Anniversary Convention of the AISB (2014)
7. Perlin, K.: An image synthesizer. In: Proceedings of the 12th Annual Conference on Computer Graphics and Interactive Techniques, vol. 19, pp. 287–296 (1985)
8. Collazo, M.N., Cotta, C., Fernndez-Leiva, A.J.: Virtual player design using self-learning via competitive coevolutionary algorithms (2014)
9. Raffe, W.L., Zambetta, F., Li, X.: A survey of procedural terrain generation techniques using evolutionary algorithms. Proceedings of Congress of Evolutionary Computation 10, 2090–2097 (2012)
10. Loiacono, D., Cardamone, L., Lanzi, P.L.: Automatic track generation for high-end racing games using evolutionary computation. IEEE Transactions on Computational Intelligence and AI in Games 3, 245–259 (2011)
11. Ebert, D.S., Musgrave, F.K., Peachey, D., Perlin, K., Worley, S.: Texturing and Modeling: A Procedural Approach, 3rd edn. Morgan Kaufmann Publishers (2003)
12. Kelly, G., McCabe, H.: A survey of procedural techniques for city generation. ITB Journal, 14 (2006)
13. Groenewegen, S.A., Smelik, R.M., de Kraker, K.J., Bidarra, R.: Procedural city layout generation based on urban land use models. In: Proceedings of the 30th Annual Conference of the European Association for Computer Graphics, pp. 45–48.
14. Bresenham, J.E.: Algorithm for computer control of a digital plotter. IBM Systems Journal 4, 25–30 (1965)
15. Waltz, F.M., Miller, J.W.V.: Efficient algorithm for gaussian blur using finite-state machines. In: Proceedings of SPIE 3521, Machine Vision Systems for Inspection and Metrology VII (1998)
16. Rodrigues, E.O.: 2d shader light and shadow system, https://www.youtube.com/watch?v=jpmRXUH2qFU

Adaptive Automated Storytelling Based on Audience Response

Augusto Baffa, Marcus Poggi, and Bruno Feijó

Departamento de Informática, PUC-Rio, Rio de Janeiro-RJ, Brazil
{abaffa,poggi,bfeijo}@inf.puc-rio.br

Abstract. To tell a story, the storyteller uses all his/her skills to entertain an audience. This task not only relies on the act of telling a story,
but also on the ability to understand reactions of the audience during
the telling of the story. A well-trained storyteller knows whether the audience is bored or enjoying the show just by observing the spectators
and adapts the story to please the audience. In this work, we propose a
methodology to create tailored stories to an audience based on personality traits and preferences of each individual. As an audience may be
composed of individuals with similar or mixed preferences, it is necessary
to consider a middle ground solution based on the individual options. In
addition, individuals may have some kind of relationship with others
that influence their decisions. The proposed model addresses all steps
in the quest to please the audience. It infers what the preferences are,
computes the scenes reward for all individuals, estimates their choices
independently and in group, and allows Interactive Storytelling systems
to find the story that maximizes the expected audience reward.

Keywords: Social Interaction, Group decision making, Model of Emotions, Automated Storytelling, Audience model, Optimization application.

1 Introduction

Selecting the best events of a story to please the audience is a difficult task. It
requires continued observation of the spectators. It is also necessary to understand the preferences of each individual in order to ensure that the story is able
to entertain and engage as many spectators as possible.

Whereas an interactive story is non-linear, because it has several possible
branches until the end, the objective of a storyteller is to find out the best ones
considering an audience profile, the dramatic tension and the emotions aroused
on the individuals.

Empathy is the psychological ability to feel what another person would feel if
you were experiencing the same situation. It is a way to understand feelings and
emotions, looking in an objective and rational way what another person feels[2].
Based on the empathy, it is possible to learn what the audience likes. This allows
selecting similar future events along the story and, therefore, to maximize the
audience rating.

© IFIP International Federation for Information Processing 2015
K. Chorianopoulos et al. (Eds.): ICEC 2015, LNCS 9353, pp. 45–58, 2015.
DOI: 10.1007/978-3-319-24589-8_4

The proposed method aims to select the best sequence of scenes to a given audience, trying to maximize the acceptance of the story and reduce drop outs. The idea behind this approach is to identify whether the audience is really in tune with the story that is being shown. A well-trained storyteller can realize if the audience is bored or enjoying the story (or presentation) just looking at the spectators.

During story writing, an author can define dramatic curves to describe emotions of each scene. These dramatic curves define how the scene should be played, its screenshot, lighting and soundtrack. After the current scene, each new one has a new dramatic curve which adds to the context of the story[1].

The reactions of the audience are related to the dramatic curves of the scene. If the audience readings of the emotions are similar to the emotions defined by the dramatic context, then there is a connection (empathy) between audience and what is being watched[6,7].

In this work, we propose a methodology to create tailored stories to an audience based on personality traits and preferences of each individual. The global objective is to maximize the expected audience reward. This involves considering a middle ground solution based on the individual options of the audience group. In addition, individuals may have some kind of relationship with others, characterizing an interaction among the audience and ultimately influencing their decisions.

The proposed model addresses all steps in the quest to please the audience. It infers what the preferences are, computes the scenes reward for all individuals, estimates their choices independently and in group, and allows Interactive Storytelling systems to find the story that maximizes the expected audience reward.

This paper is organized as follows. Section 2 discusses on emotion modeling and on its application to audience characterization and behavior expectation. The following section presents the main aspects of automated storytelling. Section 4 is dedicated to modeling the expected audience reward maximization. The interaction of individuals in the audience is the object of section 5. Section 6 proposes a heuristic to solve the optimization model in section 5. Analysis and conclusions are drawn in the last section.

2   Emotions and Audience

During film screening, the audience gets emotionally involved with the story. Individuals in the audience reacts according to their preferences. When an individual enjoys what is staged, he/she tends to reflect the same emotions that are proposed by the story. The greater the identification between the individual and the story, the greater are the emotions experienced.

As an audience can be composed of individuals who have very different preferences, it is important that the storyteller identifies a middle ground to please as many as possible. Knowing some personality traits of each individual helps to get the story closer to the audience.

2.1 Model of Emotions

The emotional notation used to describe the scenes of a story is based on the model of "basic emotions" proposed by Robert Plutchik [9,10]. Plutchik's model is based on Psychoevolutionary theory. It assumes that emotions are biologically primitive and that they evolved in order to improve animal reproductive capacity. Each of the basic emotions demonstrates a high survival behavior, such as the fear that inspires the fight-or-flight. In Plutchik's approach, the basic emotions are represented by a three-dimensional circumplex model where emotional words were plotted based on similarity [11]. Plutchik's model is often used in computer science in different versions, for tasks such as affective human-computer interaction or sentiment analysis. It is one of the most influential approaches for classifying emotional responses in general[4].

Each sector of the circle represents an intensity level for each basic emotion: the first intensity is low, the second is normal and the third intensity is high. In each level, there are specific names according to the intensity of the emotion, for example: serenity at low intensity is similar to joy and ecstasy in a higher intensity of the instance.

Plutchik defines that basic emotions can be combined in pairs to produce complex emotions. These combinations are classified in four groups: Primary Dyads (experienced often), Secondary Dyads (sometimes perceived), Tertiary Dyads (rare) and opposite Dyads (cannot be combined).

Primary Dyads are obtained by combining adjacent emotions, e.g., Joy + Trust = Love. The Secondary Dyads are obtained by combining emotions that are two axes distant, for example, Joy + Fear = Excitement. The Tertiary Dyads are obtained by combining emotions that are three axes distant, for example, Joy + Surprise = Doom. The opposite Dyads are on the same axis but on opposite sides, for example, Joy and Sorrow cannot be combined, or cannot occur simultaneously [11]. Complex Emotions - Primaries Dyads:

- antecipation + joy = optimism
- joy + trust = love
- trust + fear = submission
- fear + surprise = awe
- surprise + sadness = disappointment
- sadness + disgust = remorse
- disgust + anger = contempt
- anger + antecipation = aggression

This model assumes that there are eight primary emotions: Joy, Anticipation, Trust, Fear, Disgust, Anger, Surprise and Sadness. It is possible to adapt the Plutchik's model within a structure of 4-axis of emotions [13,1] as shown in Figure 1.

The Plutchik's model describes a punctual emotion and it is used to represent an individual or a scene in a specific moment. In order to describe the emotions of a scene, the Plutchik's model is converted to a time series of emotions called "dramatic curve". The dramatic curve describes the sequence of emotions in a

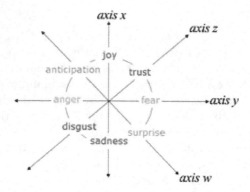

Fig. 1. Simplified 4-axis structure - families of emotions

scene in an interval of one second per point. It follows the structure of 4-axis based on Plutchik's wheel and maps the variation of events in a story.

2.2 Audience Model

In Psychology, there are many models to map and define an individual's personality traits. One of the most used is called Big Five or Five Factor Model, developed by Ernest Tupes and Raymond Christal in 1961 [15]. This model was forgotten until achieving notoriety in the early 1980s [12] and defines a personality through the five factors based on a linguistic analysis. It is also known by the acronym O.C.E.A.N. that refers to five personality traits.

The personality of an individual is analyzed and defined throughout answers to a questionnaire that must be completed and verified by factor analysis. Responses are converted to values that define one of the factors on a scale of 0 to 100. In this work only two traits are used to create the individual profile: Openness to experience $\mathcal{O} \in [0, 1]$ and Agreeableness (Sociability) $\mathcal{A} \in [0, 1]$. Each personality trait is described as follows:

Openness to Experience. The openness reflects how much an individual likes and seeks for new experiences. Individuals high in openness are motivated to seek new experiences and to engage in self-examination. In a different way, closed individuals are more comfortable with familiar and traditional experiences. They generally do not depart from the comfort zone.[5]

Agreeableness (Sociability). Agreeableness reflects how much an individual like and try to please others. Individuals high on agreeableness are perceived as kind, warm and cooperative. They tend to demonstrate higher empathy levels and believe that most people are decent, honest and reliable. On the other hand, individuals low on agreeableness are generally less concerned with others' well-being and demonstrate less empathy. They tend to be manipulative in their social relationships and more likely to compete than to cooperate.[5]

2.3 Concept of Empathy

According to Davis [2], "empathy" is defined by spontaneous attempts to adopt the perspectives of other people and to see things from their point of view. Individuals who share higher empathy levels tend to have similar preferences and do things together. In this work, he proposes a scale of "empathy" to measure the tendency of an individual to identify himself with characters in movies, novels, plays and other fictional situations. Also, the emotional influence of a movie to the viewer can be considered "empathy". It is possible to identify a personality based on the relationship between an individual and his favorite movies and books. Furthermore, it is possible to suggest new books or movies just knowing the personality of an individual [7]. Following these ideas, it is possible to relate empathy to a rating index. During an exhibition, if the viewer is enjoying what he is watching, there is an empathy between the show and the spectator. This information is used to predict what the spectator likes and dislikes.

3 Interactive Storytelling

In recent years, there have been some efforts to build storytelling systems in which authors and audience engage in a collaborative experience of creating the story. Furthermore, the convergence between video games and film-making can give freedom to the player's experience and generate tailored stories to a spectator. Interactive Storytelling are applications which simulates a digital storyteller. It transforms the narrative from a linear to a dialectical form, creating new stories based on audience by monitoring their reactions, interactions or suggestions for new events to the story.[8] The proposed approach of a storytelling system should be able to generate different stories adapted to each audience, based on previously computed sequence of events and knowledge of preferences of each individual on the audience.

3.1 Story Model

A story is a single sequence of connected events which represents a narrative. The narrative context may be organized as a decision tree to define different possibilities of endings. During the story writing, the author can define many different ends or sequences to each event (or scene). Each ending option forwards to a new scene and then to new ending options, until story ends. For example, Figure 2 demonstrates a story of three scenes modeled as a decision tree. Each scene has two ending options: A and B. If the storyteller chooses option A twice, the story ends on End1 by the sequence Scene1, Scene2 and Scene4. In this

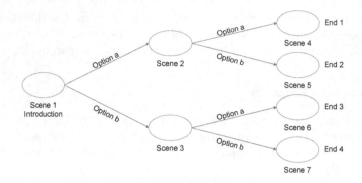

Fig. 2. Story as a Decision Tree

example, there are 4 different ends. This means that there are 4 different ways to tell the story.

To evaluate the proposed model and algorithm, the tests are performed using an event tree corresponding to a non-linear variation of the fairy tale Little Red Cap[1]. The event tree is described in Table 1 and presented in Figure 3. In some events, there are possibilities of branches such as the moment when the girl meets the wolf in the forest. The original story is represented by the sequence of events π : {EV1, EV2, EV3, EV4, EV5, EV7, EV8, EV9, EV10, EV17, EV11, EV13, EV15}.

Table 1. Little Red-Cap story events

Event	Description	Event	Description
EV1	Mother warns the girl	EV11	Girl escapes
EV2	Girl leaves her home	EV12	Wolf devours Girl
EV3	Girl is in the forest	EV13	Girl finds the Hunter
EV4	Girl finds the wolf in the forest	EV14	Wolf gets the girl
EV5	Wolf cheats the girl	EV15	Hunter kills the wolf and saves Grandma
EV6	Wolf attacks the girl	EV16	Wolf kills the Hunter
EV7	Wolf goes to Grandma's house	EV17	Wolf attacks the Girl at Grandma's house
EV8	Wolf swallows Grandma	EV18	Wolf eats the Girl after his escape
EV9	Girl arrives at Grandma's house	EV19	Wolf devours the Girl in Grandma's house
EV10	Girl speaks with Wolf	EV20	Wolf devours the Girl in the Forest

Each scene describes what occurs to the characters and the story, and also has an emotional description called "dramatic curve". The dramatic curves are based on Plutchik's wheel of emotions and describes how emotions should manifest during the scene. Soundtracks, screenshots and lighting can be chosen based on the dramatic curves.

The sequence of scenes tells the story, describes a complete emotional curve and "tags" the story as "genre".

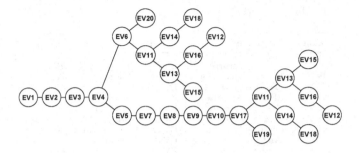

Fig. 3. Little Red-Cap story as a decision tree

3.2 Modeling Emotions to Events

During the story writing, the scenes are described as a tree of events. Each event in the tree is associated to a dramatic curve and must be modeled containing the following information:

- Name: unique name for the event (each event has a unique name);
- Text: describes what happens during the event;
- Dramatic Curves: emotional time series presented on figure 1: Joy/Sadness (axis x), Fear/Anger (axis y), Surprise/Anticipation (axis w) and Trust/Disgust (axis z).

The Tree of events has different paths, connecting to different future events, until the end of the story. When the story is told, it is selected a single branch to each event. The dramatic curves representing the original story sequence of events are demonstrated in Figure 4. Table 2 illustrates the emotions involved in each of 20 events present in the story.

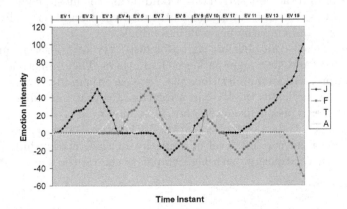

Fig. 4. Dramatic Curves of Little Red-Cap original sequence of Scenes

Table 2. Dramatic Curves for Little Red-Cap events

Event	Emotion	Event	Emotion
EV1	Joy + Surprise	EV11	Joy + Anticipation
EV2	Joy + Anticipation	EV12	Sadness + Angry
EV3	Trust + Surprise	EV13	Joy + Anticipation
EV4	Fear + Surprise	EV14	Angry + Disgust
EV5	Fear + Trust	EV15	Joy + Angry
EV6	Angry + Anticipation	EV16	Sadness + Surprise
EV7	Sadness + Anticipation	EV17	Angry + Anticipation
EV8	Angry + Surprise	EV18	Sadness + Angry
EV9	Joy + Fear	EV19	Sadness + Angry
EV10	Trust + Surprise	EV20	Sadness + Angry

3.3   Uncovering Audience Preferences

Every time an individual likes a scene or story, he/she tells what he/she likes and what does not. This information is then used to analyze and determine which are the individual preferences. The information from the dramatic curve indicates the emotion that has been liked and is used to classify genres. The favorite scenes of an individual are used to ascertain which are the emotions that stand out. The genres of the stories are set primarily by the main emotions of the scenes. Throughout readings of emotions which stand out, it is possible to know which genres the individual prefers and which scenes of a new story are emotionally similar.

Considering the personality traits, individuals who score high in "openness" like a greater variety of genres (often opposed) in comparison to others. Individuals low in "openness" generally prefer the same things and choose the same genres. In this case, there are less options to please individuals low in "openness".

The task of selecting a scene that pleases a person is to find which of the possible options approaches their preferences. The task selection becomes difficult when we try to find the best option that would please the most people in a group. In this case, it is necessary to consider other information about individuals as "agreeableness" and empathy between individuals.

Individuals who score high in "agreeableness" try to approach quickly the choices of others and have more patience than others. They sometimes prefer to accept other preferences and decisions just to please them all.

The empathy indicates the level in a relationship that individuals have. For example, when two people like each other, they may want to do things together, thus it indicates a higher level of empathy. In the other hand, people who want avoid each other have a low level of empathy in this relationship. Generally, individuals in a relationship with high empathy choose the same options or a middle ground.

4   Maximizing the Audience

Given a tree of events, each ending (a leaf of the tree) uniquely determines a sequence of scenes or the story to tell. This corresponds to the path from the root of the tree to ending leaf. Finding the most rewardable path for a given audience amounts to evaluate an utility function that captures how the audience feels rewarded by the scenes and also the choices the audience makes at each branch. The tree of event can be represented as follows:

Let S be the finite set of events (scenes) of a story. Let also $\Gamma^+(s)$ be a subset of S containing the child nodes of node s. The utility function is given by $E(s, i)$ which determines the expected value of state s for individual i and represents a measure of similarity between 0 and 1. Finally, let $Prob(s_{l-1}, s_l, i)$ be the probability with which individual i chooses state s_l to follow state s_{l-1}. Remark that the probabilities $Prob(s_{l-1}, s_l, i))$ must add one for each branch and for each individual, since one branch must be selected on each state.

Consider now a sequence of states $\pi = \{s_0, \ldots, s_k\}$ that represents a path from the root to a leaf. The proposed model evaluates path by computing its expected utility which is given by the expression:

$$f(\pi) = \sum_{l=1}^{k} \sum_{i \in I} (E(s_l, i).Prob(s_{l-1}, s_l, i)) \tag{1}$$

Let $R(s)$ be the maximum expected utility that can be obtained starting from state s. The following recursion determines $R(s)$.

$$R(s) = \begin{cases} \sum_{i \in I} (E(s, i).Prob(p(s), s, i)) + \max_{s' \in \Gamma^+(s)} R(s') \\ \sum_{i \in I} (E(s, i).Prob(p(s), s, i)), & \text{for } s \text{ a leaf} \\ \sum_{i \in I} E(s, i) + \max_{s' \in \Gamma^+(s)} R(s'), & \text{for } s \text{ the root} \end{cases} \tag{2}$$

where $p(s)$ is the predecessor of s. By computing $R(s_0)$, the root's reward, an optimal sequence π^*, with maximum expected reward, can be retrieved in a straightforward way.

We conclude the model by proposing an evaluation for the individual probabilities of choice on each story branch. This is done by assuming this probability is proportional to the expected individual reward of the branches. This leads to the expression:

$$Prob(s, s', i) = \frac{IR(s', i)}{\sum_{s'' \in \Gamma^+(s)} IR(s'', i)} \tag{3}$$

where $IR(s, i)$ is the expected reward at state s for individual i, which is given by:

$$IR(s, i) = E(s, i) + \max_{s' \in \Gamma^+(s)} IR(s', i).Prob(s, s', i) \tag{4}$$

This model allows determining the best sequence of scenes for and audience provided there is no interaction within the audience. We address this case in the following section.

5   Audience Interaction

To create tailored stories for an individual it is just necessary to check what he/she likes most, based on its own probabilities but when an individual participates of a group he/she needs to deal a middle ground. The dynamic of choosing the best story to an audience is based on the fact that the individuals will watch the same story, share a minimal intimacy and want spend sometime together. In a similar way, it is possible to say that they are trying to watch television and need to choose a television program that please the entire group. During this interaction, each individual tries to convince others about his preferences. Some individuals may agree with these suggestions based on the relationship they share, but others may introduce some limits. After some rounds, some individuals give in and accept to approach other preferences [14]. The decision of accepting others' do not eliminate personal preferences but introduce a new aspect to the options. According to the proposed model some options that originally are not attractive will be chosen because of the induced social reward imposed by the probability function of choosing it. This means that for some individuals, it is better to keep the group together than take advantage of their preference. Furthermore, as explained in section 2.2, individuals high in "openness" do not care so much about their own preferences because they like to experiment new possibilities. They may be convinced by friends or relatives and will tend to support their preferences.

In order to model the audience behavior, we propose an algorithm based on a spring-mass system. Consider that all preferences are modeled by the real coordinate space ($\Re^2$) and each individual of the audience is represented by a point positioned on his preferences. Each point (individual) is connected to n springs (where n is the number of individuals). A spring is connected to its original position and other $n-1$ springs are connected to the other points. Then, we have a total of $\frac{n \times (n+1)}{2}$ springs. The objective function aims to approach each point, considering the constraints of the springs. Each spring is modeled based on the individual personality traits and relationship levels between them.

Let $K_{ii} = (1 - \mathcal{O}_i)$, be the openness level of each individual i and $K_{ij} = \mathcal{A}_{ij}$ be the agreeableness level for each pair of individuals i and j. In this model, we are assuming that "agreeableness" may also be influenced by the relationship between i and j and it is possible to describe an individual resistance by others' preferences. After some experiments, we realize that it is possible to start an audience from $\mathcal{A}_{ij} = \mathcal{A}_i$ and fine tuning $\mathcal{A}_{ij}$ after some rounds.

Given $e_{ij} \in [-1, 1]$, the empathy level between each pair of individuals, and x_i^0, the original position in space for each individual i, let $d_{ij}^0 = \left\| x_i^0 - x_j^0 \right\|$ be the original distance between individuals and let $L_{ij} = (1 - e_{ij}).d_{ij}^0$ be a weighted empathy level. The objective of the following model is to find the final positions x_i minimizing the distances between the individuals d_{ij}, weighted by their agreeableness level K_{ij} and considering L_{ij}.

$$\min \sum_{i \in A} \sum_{j \in J : i \neq j} K_{ij}.(d_{ij} - L_{ij})^2 + \sum_{i \in I} K_{ii}.d_{ii}^2 \tag{5}$$

subject to

$$d_{ij} = \|x_i - x_j\| \quad \forall i, j \in A, i \neq j \tag{6}$$

$$d_{ii} = \|x_i - x_i^0\| \quad \forall i \in A \tag{7}$$

The constraints (6) link the distance variables d_{ij} with the coordinate variables x_i and x_j when individuals i and j are different. Constraints (7) are used to obtain the distance d_{ii} which each individual has moved from its original position. Figure 5 describes the operation of the Spring-mass system with 2 individuals.

Since this model is not linear, it is not possible to use a linear solver to obtain the optimal solution. Therefore, we use a meta-heuristic approach based on simulated annealing to obtain a good approximate solution. The simulated annealing algorithm is presented in Section 6.

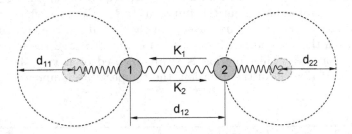

Fig. 5. Spring-mass example with 2 individuals

6 Solving the Audience Interaction Model

Simulated annealing is a meta-heuristic for optimization problems based on thermodynamics. Given a large solution space, it solves the optimization problem by finding a good solution near the global optimum[3]. At each iteration of the algorithm, it changes the current solution within a neighborhood and considers the new solution as the current one if there is any improvement on the objective function or, if there is no improvement, it may consider it based on a randomized criteria.

The neighborhood used for the audience problem is defined by all possible movements of each individual in other to minimize the distances between all individuals according to spring constraints. Let $\overrightarrow{a}$ be the current position of individual a, $\overrightarrow{b}$ be the referential position based on all relationships between the individuals and s_a be the "agreeableness" level of the personality of individual a. It is possible to calculate the step of a movement δ_x for individual a using equations (8)–(10).

$$\overrightarrow{b} = \left(\sum_{j=1}^{n} \frac{a_y^j . e_{ij}}{e_{ij}}, \sum_{j=1}^{n} \frac{a_x^j . e_{ij}}{e_{ij}} \right) \tag{8}$$

$$\alpha = (b_y - a_y)/(b_x - a_x) \tag{9}$$

$$\delta_x = \begin{cases} -\sqrt{s_a^2/\alpha^2 + 1} & a_x > b_x, \\ \sqrt{s_a^2/\alpha^2 + 1} & \text{otherwise} \end{cases} \tag{10}$$

The final position after moving the individual a is given by $\vec{a}_{final}$ as follows:

$$\vec{a}_{final} = (\delta_x + a_x, \delta_x.\alpha + a_y) \tag{11}$$

The simulated annealing method is shown in Algorithm 1. The algorithm receives as input an initial solution S_0, limits on the number of iterations M, on the number of solution movements per iteration P and on the number of solution improvements per iteration L. During its initialization, the iteration counter starts with 1, the best solution S starts equal to S_0 and the current temperature T is obtained from the function $InitialTemp()$, which returns a value based on the instance being solved. On each iteration, the best solution is changed within the neighborhood by function $Change(S)$ and the improvement is calculated on ΔF_i. This solution is then accepted or not as the new best solution and, at the end of the iteration, the temperature is updated given the factor α.

Algorithm 1. Simulated Annealing

```
procedure SA(S_0, M, P, L)
    j ← 1
    S ← S_0
    T ← InitialTemp()
    repeat
        i ← 1
        nSuccess ← 0
        repeat
            S_i = Change(S)
            ΔF_i = f(S_i) − f(S)
            if (ΔF_i = 0)||(exp(−ΔF_i/T) > Rand()) then
                S ← S_i
                nSuccess ← nSuccess + 1
            end if
            i ← i + 1
        until (nSuccess = L)||(i > P)
        T ← α.T
        j ← j + 1
    until (nSuccess = 0)||(j > M)
    Print(S)
end procedure
```

---

7   Analysis and Conclusions

The proposed methodology was initially applied on students of our graduate program in order to evaluate the emotional characteristics of the individuals. This allowed a positive view of techniques and validated the initial hypothesis.

Then, the final experiments were conducted using 20 generated audience[1] instances with 20 individuals each on instances divided in three groups: 8 entirely mixed audiences with 60% of individuals supporting an emotion, 8 audiences with similar individuals and 4 mixed audiences with one opinion leader. The opinion leader instances were generated by describing an influential individual to others[2]. This starting point permitted a qualitative evaluation of the application of the whole methodology based on discussion among the ones involved in the experience.

The resulting story endings for each audience are presented on Table 3. Stories generated to mixed audiences before interaction considered average preferences while stories generated after interaction (SA) tend to select the majority preference. The proposed Red Cap story has a natural tendency for a Sadness + Angry endings (EV12, EV18, EV19, EV20) since there are more final events of these emotional features than Joy + Angry endings (EV15 only). However, the proposed method was able to select expected story endings according to the audience preferences. Also, the preliminary evaluation of an opinion leader suggested there is a sound basis for results that may effectively converge to the choice of audience rewarding paths.

Table 3. Selected Story Endings for Audiences

Emotion	Mixed	SA	Similar	Opinion Leader
Trust	EV 12	EV 15	EV 15 short	-
Surprise	EV 12	EV 12	EV 20 short	-
Joy	EV 12	EV 15	EV 15	EV 15
Sadness	EV 12	EV 12	EV 12 short	EV 12
Disgust	EV 12	EV 12	EV 20 short	-
Anger	EV 12	EV 18	EV 18	EV 18
Fear	EV 12	EV 12	EV 12	EV 12
Anticipation	EV 12	EV 15	EV 15 short	-

Next step amounts to carrying out more thorough and relevant experiments which requires not only larger groups but also stories that truly draws the audience. In this preliminary analysis, an evaluation of the model parameters also allowed to conclude that their determination may lead to conditions which can represent a wide range of groups, thus leading to a representative model.

Our evaluation is that the proposed methodology can still incorporate more factors of emotional behavior, group interaction and storytelling aspects. The goal is to experiment thoroughly on a wide spectrum of stories and audiences.

---

[1] An audience is a set of individuals.
[2] We considered that the empathy from others to an opinion leader is near to 1 but his/her empathy to others is low.

Acknowledgements. This work was partially supported by CNPq (National Council for Scientific and Technological Development, linked to the Ministry of Science, Technology, and Innovation), CAPES (Coordination for the Improvement of Higher Education Personnel, linked to the Ministry of Education), FINEP (Brazilian Innovation Agency), and ICAD/VisionLab (PUC-Rio).

References

1. Araujo, E.T., Ciarlini, A.E.M.: Verification of temporal constraints in continuous time on nondeterministic stories. In: Proceedings of the 10th International Conference on Entertainment Computing (2011)
2. Davis, M.: A multidimensional approach to individual differences in empathy. JSAS Catalog of Selected Documents in Psychology, 10 (1980)
3. Dréo, J.: Metaheuristics for Hard Optimization: Methods and Case Studies. Springer (2006)
4. Ellsworth, P., Scherer, K.: Appraisal processes in emotion. In: Davidson, R.J., Scherer, K.R., Goldsmith, H.H. (eds.) Handbook of Affective Sciences, pp. 572–595 (2003)
5. John, P., Srivastava, S.: The big-five trait taxonomy: History, measurement, and theoretical perspectives. In: Pervin, L.A., John, O.P. (eds.) Handbook of Personality: Theory and Research, vol. 2, pp. 102–138 (1999)
6. Jones, E., Nisbett, R.: The actor and the observer: Divergent perceptions of the causes of behavior (1971)
7. Kallias, A.: Individual Differences and the Psychology of Film Preferences. PhD thesis, University of London (2012)
8. Karlsson, B., Ciarlini, A.E.M., Feijó, B., Furtado, A.L.: Applying a plan-recognition/plan-generation paradigm to interactive storytelling. In: Workshop on AI Planning for Computer Games and Synthetic Characters (2006)
9. Plutchik, R.: The emotions: Facts, theories, and a new model. Random House, New York (1962)
10. Plutchik, R.: A general psychoevolutionary theory of emotions. In: Plutchik, R., Kellerman, H. (eds.) Emotion: Theory, Research, and Experience, Theories of Emotion (1980)
11. Plutchik, R.: The nature of emotions. American Scientist (2001)
12. Rich, E.: User modeling via stereotypes. Cognitive Science 3, 329–354 (1979)
13. Rodrigues, P.: Um Sistema de Geração de Expressões Faciais Dinâmicas em Animações Faciais 3D com Processamento de Fala. PhD thesis, Pontifícia Universidade Católica do Rio de Janeiro (2007)
14. Tortosa, M., Strizhko, T., Capizzi, M., Ruz, M.: Interpersonal effects of emotion in a multi-round trust game. Psicológica 39, 179–198 (2013)
15. Tupes, C., Christal, R.: Recurrent personality factors based on trait ratings. Technical report, Air Force Systems Command (1961)

ADITHO – A Serious Game for Training and Evaluating Medical Ethics Skills

Cristian Lorenzini, Claudia Faita, Michele Barsotti, Marcello Carrozzino, Franco Tecchia, and Massimo Bergamasco

PercRo, TeCIP institute, Scuola Superiore Sant'Anna
Via Alamanni 13b, 56017 - San Giuliano Terme, Pisa
{c.lorenzini,c.faita,m.barsotti,carrozzino,
f.tecchia,bergamasco}@sssup.it

Abstract. This paper presents "A Day In The HOspital", a Digital Serious Game aiming at providing a technological tool for both evaluating and training ethical skills of medical staff personnel. During the game, the player interprets the role of a physician who has to perform a decision-making process that involves his ethical and medical skills. Usability and sense of Presence have been assessed through a specific post-game Likert-questionnaire.

In order to evaluate the potential of the game as a medical training tool, experimental sessions have been conducted with two different groups of participants ("non-medical" and "medical" groups) and game outcomes have been statistically compared. Participants belonging to both the experimental groups report a high level of game Usability and sense of Presence. Finally, the statistically higher game score obtained by the "medical" group demonstrates the usefulness of ADITHO for evaluating and training ethical skills.

Keywords: Digital Serious Game, Biomedical Ethics, Virtual Reality, Virtual Environments, Decision Making, Medical Training, Ethical Evaluation, Collaborative Training, Physician-Patient Relationship.

1   Introduction

Virtual Reality (VR) can be defined as a three-dimensional, computer generated environment which can be interactively explored by a user. Nowadays, VR is increasingly being used as a tool for education, training, teaching and dissemination purposes.

At the same time, a growing interest in the use of video games for educational scope has been observed. As a part of Information and Communications Technology, video games are considered potentially powerful learning environments [1]. In this context Digital Serious Games (DSG), definable as "video games for purpose other than entertainment" [2], have been developed. In the literature, DSGs are mostly used in the field of education [3, 4] and they are classified by several criteria based on the type of educational content, the principle of learning, the targeted users or the game technologies [5, 6]. DSGs developed in three-dimensional scenarios could be consid-

© IFIP International Federation for Information Processing 2015
K. Chorianopoulos et al. (Eds.): ICEC 2015, LNCS 9353, pp. 59–71, 2015.
DOI: 10.1007/978-3-319-24589-8_5

ered as a subset of VR. In a VR-based DSG, factors such as Immersion and Presence are topics of crucial importance. Immersion is a powerful experience that contributes to the amount of information acquired, skills developed, and subsequent transfer of knowledge to real environments [7, 8]. In the same way, the sense of Presence, definable as the subjective feeling of being in a different place from where one physically is [9, 10], can increase motivation and provide a more engaging experience [11].

Training based on video games shows several benefits ranging from the safety training to the ability in transfer the acquired knowledge and skills to the operational environment [7, 12]. DSGs can also support the development of several competencies such as analytical and spatial skills, strategic skills, recollection capabilities and psychomotor skills [2].

In the last decades, a great deal of research has pointed out the need of highly trained and educational health care professionals to avoid medical errors. The use of DSGs in health provide an efficient tool for increasing interest in training, education and evaluation of medical personnel [13, 14]. Ethics in clinical professions is a matter that involves all the health care professionals, whatever their specialization. The importance of ethics in clinical profession is underestimated within the context of the whole medical curriculum. In particular, while students learn the theoretical contents of ethical knowledge, they commonly do not acquire more than a poor ability to act based on this knowledge [15]. The goal of education in ethics and professionalism should be oriented to develop a method to track students' capacity to apply their knowledge and skills in professional clinical scenarios [16]. It has been demonstrated that following an ethical approach is of fundamental importance for creating a shared decision-making process which is the ideal treatment for difficult clinical case scenarios [17, 18]. Moreover, in order to make an ethically correct decision, it is important to create both a strong collaboration with other healthcare operators and a relationship with the patient and his family [19, 20]. As aforementioned, DSGs have been developed for training or informing regarding topics such as healthcare, social learning and ethics [21]. To the best of our knowledge no DSG regarding the Medical Ethic have been developed and evaluated yet.

Motivated by the above, we have developed a first person VR-based DSG, "A day In The Hospital" (ADITHO), aiming at training and evaluating physician's ethical skills. In the presented game, the user plays the role of a physician who has to make a clinical decision based on the information he collects during the game. By simulating realistic clinical scenarios, ADITHO allows players to deal with complex relationship and to gain new skill on medical ethics. The use of 3D environments allows the user to experience a strong immersion and sense of presence that are factors that commonly imply an enhancement of the learning process [10].

ADITHO has been developed as a part of SONNA (www.sonna.unisi.it), a larger research project aimed at investigating novel technology-enhanced learning methodologies based on the use of social media and 3D Virtual Environments [22]. The implemented game architecture allows to easily extend the game to other different clinical case. The usability of the game has been already evaluated in a preliminary study with users non expert in medical field [23]. In this paper the potentiality of the developed game as a tool for training and evaluating ethical skills is investigated through two experimental sessions conducted with two groups of users which differ in their expertise in medical matters.

The "playability" of ADITHO, in terms of Usability of the system and in the users' perceived quality of the game experience, has been also investigated through a post-game questionnaire.

2   Material and Methods

This section discusses the experiment presenting first the materials comprising the game architecture and the storyboard of the scenario. Then the methods are discussed presenting the experimental procedure, the questionnaires used for evaluating the game experience and the criteria adopted to assess the ethical profile of participants.

2.1   Game Storyboard

The game takes place in a hospital ward where a young patient suffering from Cystic Fibrosis (CFi) is in treatment. CFi is a genetic disorder frequent in young Caucasian populations and it was selected for this game storyboard because it rises up important decision-making processes to deal with in the ethical field [24].

In the proposed game, the player in the role of a physician has to decide the best strategy for treating the CFi patient using his ethical competences and collecting information by talking with the patient himself, his relatives and with other physicians and caregivers.

ADITHO starts with the choice of the avatar gender and a help guide screen that describes all main commands. At the beginning, the user is located in the hospital hall and a nurse reminds him to visit the CFi patient. Then, a series of events connected with the evolution of the clinical case are presented to the player.

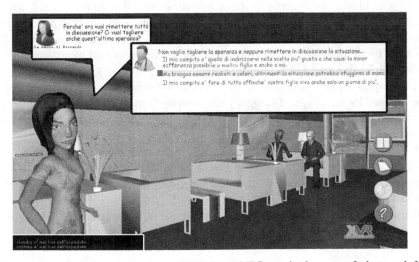

Fig. 1. Screenshot of a dialogue with an NPC. Other NPCs are in the scene. In bottom left, the notification that indicates that 2 other players are in chat room.

In order to proceed through the game story, players have to interact with other agents of the game (Non-Player Characters, or NPCs). The interactions with other NPCs are based on dialogues in which players select a sentence within a set of available ones (Fig. 1). Players can also perform several other actions that contribute to acquire information, such as reading e-mail, watching films, browsing the web, reading the patient's journal, etc. The game also provides a collaborative feature in order to simulate the real information-sharing process between the medical staff. Different players that are playing in the same moment can meet each other in the coffee room of the virtual hospital.

2.2   Game Architecture

The game architecture is realized with a separation between the Core Game Engine (CGE) and a set of Game Information (GI). CGE has been implemented using the XVR technology [25], a framework that enables the realization of web-based and/or stand-alone interactive VR applications. GI describe the game in terms of a set of resources (images, sounds, video, 3D objects, etc...) and game mechanics (actions). An action is composed by functionalities and enabling conditions and it represents the relationships between the user's interactions and the resources.

Depending on the CGE global states, a set of specific enabling condition could be verified allowing the corresponding action to be activated. Actions' functionalities consist by a set of reactions that could modify the CGE global state or the game scene. The separation between CGE and GI makes the architecture of the game versatile and thus the game could be easily expanded to other clinical cases in order to satisfy different educational needs.

With the purpose of giving users a greater sense of immersion in the environment, the game is also provided with sound feedback.

The game client can connect to a centralized server; this enables users who are simultaneously playing the game to communicate through an integrated text chat in the coffee room. Each user is visualized with an avatar of the appropriate gender (Fig. 2). When a user enters the coffee room, other players are informed by means of a non-invasive notification (see Fig. 1, bottom left).

All dialogues are described in GI, and they are automatically adapted based on the gender chosen by the player. Dialogues are composed by sentences and/or questions with related answers. Sentences develop a linear dialogue whereas questions may generate an oriented graph structure without loops depending on the user's replies. In Fig. 1 is shown a screenshot of the game in which the player has to choose a sentence among three possible once, whereas in Fig. 3 is depicted a general scheme of a dialogue. Each answer contributes to calculate the ethics score of the user (more details are discussed in Section 2.3).

All users' avatars and NPCs are animated virtual humans realized with Autodesk 3D Studio Max and Motion Builder and integrated in the XVR environment.

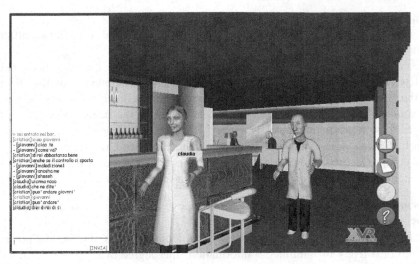

Fig. 2. Screenshot of the game chat room showing avatars of two players (a female and a male). The text chat is shown on the left whereas the player's username appears when the mouse hover over her/him.

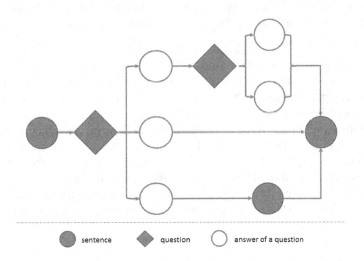

Fig. 3. The oriented graph of a general dialogue. Sentences produce one exit way only; questions produce two or more exit ways, called answers.

2.3 Evaluation Methods

This section describes the methods used for evaluating the questionnaire answers (concerning Usability and the perceived sense of Presence) and the game scores.

Usability and Sense of Presence Evaluation

The game Usability and sense of Presence have been evaluated through two different questionnaires.

In order to evaluate the Usability of the system, the System Usability Scale (SUS) [26] has been adopted. SUS is a 10 items Likert-scale questionnaire used to investigate the subjective assessment of usability by covering effectiveness, efficiency and satisfaction of the experience. Each statement indicates the degree of agreement or disagreement in a 5 points scale. The users' levels of immersion and involvement in the virtual game were evaluated by means of the Presence Questionnaire (PQ) [10]. PQ is composed by 19 items, rated on a 7-points Likert-scale. It uses 4 factors that exert their influence on presence by affecting both involvement and immersion:

- Control Factor (CF) about degree, immediacy, anticipation, mode and physical environment modifiability;
- Sensory Factor (SF) about modality, environmental richness, multimodal presentation, consistency of multimodal information, the degree of movement perception and active search;
- Distraction Factor (DF) about isolation, selective attention and interface awareness);
- Realism Factor (RF) about scene realism, information consistent with the objective world, meaningfulness of the experience, separation and anxiety/disorientation [10].

The PQ questionnaire was then customized in order to fit with the purpose of our study. We excluded 7 items of the questionnaire because we considered it not appropriate and not pertaining to the characteristics of the VR experience of ADITHO. We then selected 12 items that allow us to capture: (i) the ability to control the relation of sensors to the environment (Q1-Q5 and Q10-Q11); (ii) the consistency of the all information conveyed by the virtual world (Q4, Q6, Q8, Q12); (iii) the ability to focus on VE experience (Q9) and (iv) the realism of the stimuli perceived during game experience (Q7). All of these 12-items refer to the four factors explained before.

Finally, in order to improve the game experience in future application, participants were asked to fill an open-ended question in which they provided feedbacks and suggestions.

Ethical Profile Evaluation

In order to evaluate the participants' ethical profile, a numerical score is assigned during the game, depending on users choices, using a combination of two different criteria.

The first criterion is based on the latest Code of Medical Ethics 2014 (CME) [20], a system of moral principles establishing the ethical rules of behavior of physicians. Using CME criterion, each answer choice results in a score in the range [0, +4]. Since ethics looks at the inner attitudes and to the intentionality of the agents [27], the second criterion is founded on the four main principles of biomedical ethics postulated by Tom Beauchamp and James Childress [28]:

- the principle of respect for autonomy (A), according to which physicians recognize self-determination of patients and equip them with the means to make reasoned informed choices;
- the principle of beneficence (B1), considering the balance of benefits of treatment against the risks and costs;
- the principle of non-maleficence (B2), stating that the harm of each treatment, even if minimal should not be disproportionate to the benefits of treatment;
- the principle of justice (J), concerning the distribution of scarce health resources, and the decision of who gets what treatment.

Because of their similarities, principles B1 and B2 were combined in a single principle (B). Moreover, in order to evaluate the ethical attitude of the physician it was added another important criterion:

- communication (C), concerning the physician's capability of accompanying the patient in his diagnostic-therapeutic path sharing meaningful information and showing cooperative attitudes.

Using the four principles criterion, each answer choice results in a score in the range [-2, +2] for each principle.

Since the CME is based on ethics principles universally shared [29], a series of Spearman rank-order correlations were conducted in order to determine if there were any relationships between the scores assigned to the four principles and the ethical code (A, B, J, C, CME). A two-tailed test of significance indicated that there was a significant positive relationship between the scores assigned to each answers (Spearman's $rho(27) > .66$, $p < .01$ for all the tests).

2.4   Experimental Procedure

An experimental procedure was carried out for investigating the potentiality of the proposed game as a tool for training physicians' ethical skills.

Two experimental sessions were performed with two different groups of participants: "non-medical group" and "medical group" (see Section 2.5 for further details). The experiment was conducted in accordance with the WMA Declaration of Helsinki and subjects provided written consent to participate.

All participants had to fill-in a preliminary questionnaire concerning their personal information, their familiarity with computer games, their knowledge of VE and DSG, and their knowledge of the CME.

Before starting the experiment, a demo session was experienced by participants to get familiar with the game environment. During this phase all players were located in the hospital ward where a NPC explains the functions of the game through the assignment of specific tasks. In order to complete the demo session players had to learn how to navigate through the environment and how to talk with other NPCs.

Once all participants had finished the demo session, the experimental game session started. All users of each session have played the game at the same time, using computers connected to a network. During the game users could not verbally speak to each other. At the end of the game a summary screen with the obtained score was shown to players and all participants were required to complete the evaluation questionnaire. Finally each participant has been shown the correspondence between each multiple choice answers and CME plus A, B, J, C scores.

2.5   Participants

Twelve volunteers (3 females and 9 males) with mean age of 30.6 (range 25-43), and ten residents from "Azienda Ospedaliero-Universitaria Pisana" hospital in Pisa, Italy, (6 females and 4 males) with mean age of 27.8 (range 26-31) were recruited for the experiment. All people recruited are independent of the project.

The groups, respectively the "non-medical group" and the "medical group", did not differ either by age (t-test, p = 0.118) or by sex (Fisher Exact Test, p = 0.192). "Non-medical group" is composed by people with experience in Virtual Reality and Computer Science. This group evaluated the usability, the sense of presence and immersion in the Virtual Environment developed on the game independently form the specific topic threated. The integration between the answers of the two groups gives a more complete overview in order to evaluate the game.

As aforementioned, before starting the experiment, subjects were asked to rate both their knowledge of the Italian CME and their previous experiences with Video Games and Serious Games in a scale ranging from zero (no previous experience) to five (expert users). As expected, the groups differed by the knowledge of CME (Mann–Whitney U test, p < 0.01) but they did not differ either by previous experience with Video Games (U test, p = 0.42) or by previous experience with Serious Games (U test, p = 0.16).

3   Results and Discussion

In the following sections, results and discussion of data analysis are reported for both questionnaire answers (SUS and PQ) and for game scores.

3.1   Questionnaire Results and Discussion

In order to compare answers between the two experimental groups ("non-medical" and "medical") a series of independent-samples t-test were conducted to compare questionnaire results (in terms of SUS score and the four PQ factors scores).

Table 1 reports means and standard deviations of the SUS scores and the PQ factors scores for both the experimental groups and for the two groups merged.

Accordingly to Brooke [26], the SUS score is a percentage indicating the overall level of Usability of the game and it is obtained for each participant by the contribution of each answer score. Very high results were obtained for both groups (average scores of 74.54 ± 15.21% and 73.89 ± 21.96% for the "non-medical" and "medical" groups respectively, see Table 1). No statistical difference was found between the SUS scores of the two groups (t(20) = 0.082, p = 0.935). This means that no particular technical skills should be involved by the participants to play ADITHO. It follows that the game is "playable" for all medical personnel and it could be used for ethics training in clinical setting. This result confirms the achievement of our goal to create a tool easy to use by wide range of users.

Concerning the PQ, we analyzed separately the four different factors (CF, SF, DF, and RF, see Section 2.3 for more details) and respectively assigned a score to each subject [10]. Both groups obtained high scores for all factors (Table 1) and no significant statistical differences were found between the two groups (t(20) < 1.367, p > 0.187, for the four tests). This means that the subjective experience of participants was not affected by the topic addressed in the game, but it could be more correlated with the engagement solicited by the game story.

Results obtained in the PQ were extremely important as they support the idea that ADITHO could be a useful tool for training ethical skills. Indeed, it has been demonstrated that level of Presence positively correlates to the amount of information learnt and to performance obtained by the subjects [10, 30].

The four factors (CF, DF, RF, and SF) define the level of immersion in the environment, the impact of outside distractions and the level of the active participation through the perceived control over events in the environment; high values of these factors commonly imply an enhancement of the learning process and performance [10]. Accordingly with this interpretation, 6 out of 10 subjects belonging to the medical group self-reported that the game is "potentially very useful" in particular "to pose questions about situations that inevitably we face in our work". In addition, mostly all subjects reported that "dialogues were very involving", "the game was very interesting" and that "the game could be very useful as training tool for medical candidate".

Table 1. Final scores obtained by the two experimental groups separately and merged. First row refers to the Usability score resulted from the evaluation of SUS questionnaire. Rows 2-5 refer to PQ scores in terms of its factors. All the table data are %.

		Non-Medical Group	Medical Group	All Users
SUS [%]	SUS	74.54 ± 15.21%	73.89 ± 21,96%	74.20 ± 18.11%
PQ [%]	CF	71.15 ± 11.31%	62.57 ± 17.09%	67.25 ± 14.95%
	RF	69.82 ± 16.15%	61.85 ± 24.17%	66.20 ± 20.09%
	SF	67.84 ± 15.10%	62.28 ± 20.03%	65.31 ± 17.30%
	DF	75.00 ± 17.36%	74.29 ± 29.20%	74.68 ± 22.88%

3.2 Game Results and Discussion

As explained in Section 2.3, the users' game choices resulted each on a set of scores assigned for the CME and for the four main ethical principles: A, B, J and C. Thus, at the end of the experimental session, based on the game answers, each participant obtained an ethical profile consisting in such scores. Scores obtained by the two groups were statistically compared using the non-parametric Mann-Whitney U test for independent samples. It resulted that the "medical group" obtained a statistically higher score for each analyzed variable.

Bargraphs in Fig. 4 show the final comparison of game scores (in terms of CME and the four principles), averaged over the participants, for the "non-medical" and "medical" groups.

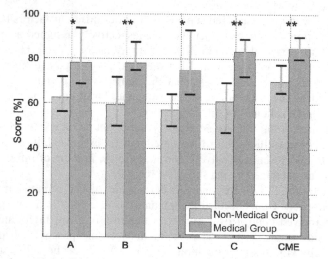

Fig. 4. Comparison of the Game Scores obtained by the two experimental group in terms of Code of Medical Ethics (CME) and the four main ethical principles: Autonomy (A), Beneficence (B), Justice (J) and Communication (C). The height of each bar represents the median value, while the upper and lower whiskers are the 25th and 75th percentiles respectively. (*p<0.05, **p<0.01).

As we expected "medical" obtained a score higher than "non-medical group" for all the scores. This is completely in line with the goal of ADITHO in which ethical competences are required in order to address the clinical case with an ethical approach. In fact, in the game professional competencies are required in order to face the clinical case with a correct ethical procedure. Moreover these results validate the efficiency of ADITHO as a useful tool for evaluating the ethical knowledge in medical personnel.

At the end of the experience each participant has been shown the correspondence between each multiple choice answers and CME plus A, B, J, C. In this way the players have become aware of the impact of their choices, improving their competence by learning from the simulated experience just lived in ADITHO.

4   Conclusion

In this paper we have presented a DSG called ADITHO together with the investigation of its potentials as a tool for training and evaluating the ethical skills of medical personnel. In a previous preliminary research, the usability of ADITHO has been assessed by performing an experiment with group of non-medical expert users [23]. In this research we have evaluated the game through an experimental test conducted on two groups of subjects: the "medical" and the "non-medical". From the analysis of the

SUS and PQ questionnaires answers, no significant differences were found between the two groups. The high overall SUS score obtained by both groups shows that the game is easily "playable" by a wide range of users. Moreover, the high sense of Presence reported by all participants suggested that users not owning particular technological skills was as highly engaged and immersed in game experience as users more experts in the use of digital technologies. It is worth noting that a high level of engagement is usually associated with an improvement in the information retention and memory. In addition, the analysis of participants' ethical profiles (i.e. the game scores) has showed that the "medical" obtained a statistically significant higher score than the "non-medical group". This fact confirms the hypothesis that ADITHO might be used as a tool for evaluating ethical skills of medical personnel. At the same time, these results suggest that ADITHO could be an efficiency-training tool to improve the ethical competencies in physicians.

We envisage carry out future work in two main directions. The first involves the exploration of new game scenarios by implementing additional storyboards dealing with other clinical cases relevantly involving ethics (e.g. living will, religion belief) and by expanding the game to other medical personnel (e.g. nurses).

The second direction focuses on the improvement of game dynamics by improving graphics and audio features and by enhancing the interaction between simultaneous players. The improved interaction will allow to evaluate more deeply the social component of the game and how it influences the sense of Presence. Finally, in order to assess the effectiveness of ADITHO as a training tool, an evaluation by using different kinds of scenario will be carried out.

The final goal of ADITHO is to be included in a larger training protocol within the context of the whole medical curriculum.

Acknowledgements. We thank Professor Francesco Giunta from University of Pisa and his residents for the time that they have dedicated in the game's experimental session.

References

1. Oblinger, D.G.: The next generation of educational engagement. Journal of Interactive Media in Education 1, Art. 10 (2004)
2. Susi, T., Johannesson, M., Backlund, P.: Serious games: An overview (2007)
3. Michael, D.R., Chen, S.L.: Serious games: Games that educate, train, and inform. In: Muska & Lipman/Premier-Trade (2005)
4. Ketelhut, D.J., Schifter, C.C.: Teachers and game-based learning: Improving understanding of how to increase efficacy of adoption. Computers & Education 56(2), 539–546 (2011)
5. Djaouti, D., Alvarez, J., Jessel, J.P., Rampnoux, O.: Origins of serious games. In: Serious Games and Edutainment Applications, pp. 25–43. Springer, London (2011)
6. Ratan, R., Ritterfeld, U.: Classifying serious games. In: Serious Games: Mechanisms and Effects, pp. 10–24 (2009)

7. Alexander, A.L., et al.: From gaming to training: A review of studies on fidelity, immersion, presence, and buy-in and their effects on transfer in pc-based simulations and games. In: DARWARS Training Impact Group, vol. 5, pp. 1–14 (2005)
8. Brown, E., Cairns, P.: A grounded investigation of game immersion. In: CHI 2004 Extended Abstracts on Human Factors in Computing Systems. ACM (2004)
9. Slater, M., Usoh, M., Steed, A.: Depth of presence in virtual environments. Presence 3(2), 130–144 (1994)
10. Witmer, B.G., Singer, M.J.: Measuring presence in virtual environments: A presence questionnaire. Presence: Teleoperators and Virtual Environments 7(3), 225–240 (1998)
11. Lombard, M., Ditton, T.: At the heart of it all: The concept of presence. Journal of Computer Mediated Communication 3(2) (1997)
12. Muchinsky, P.M.: Psychology applied to work. In: Cengage Learning (2006)
13. Wattanasoontorn, V., Hernandez, R.J.G., Sbert, M.: Serious games for e-health care. In: Simulations, Serious Games and their Applications, pp. 127–146. Springer Singapore (2014)
14. Semeraro, F., Frisoli, A., Ristagno, G., Loconsole, C., Marchetti, L., Scapigliati, A., Cerchiari, E.L.: Relive: A serious game to learn how to save lives. Resuscitation 85(7), e109–e110 (2014)
15. Campbell, A.V., Chin, J., Voo, T.C.: How can we know that ethics education produces ethical doctors? Medical Teacher 29(5), 431–436 (2007)
16. Van Zanten, M., Boulet, J.R., Norcini, J.J., McKinley, D.: Using a standardized patient assessment to measure professional attributes. Medical Education 39(1), 20–29 (2005)
17. Charles, C., Gafni, A., Whelan, T.: Shared decision-making in the medical encounter: what does it mean (or it takes at least two to tango). Social Science & Medicine 44(5), 681–692 (1997)
18. Makoul, G., Clayman, M.L.: An integrative model of shared decision making in medical encounters. Patient Education and Counseling 60(3), 301–312 (2006)
19. Wu, A.W., Cavanaugh, T.A., McPhee, S.J., Lo, B., Micco, G.P.: To tell the truth. Journal of General Internal Medicine 12(12), 770–775 (1997)
20. Federazione Nazionale degli Ordini dei Medici Chirurghi e degli Odontoiatri: Codice Di Deontologia Medica (2014). http://www.fnomceo.it
21. Pereira, G., Brisson, A., Prada, R., Paiva, A., Bellotti, F., Kravcik, M., Klamma, R.: Serious games for personal and social learning & ethics: status and trends. Procedia Computer Science 15, 53–65 (2012)
22. Carrozzino, M., Evangelista, C., Brondi, R., Lorenzini, C., Bergamasco, M.: Social networks and web-based serious games as novel educational tools. Procedia Computer Science 15, 303–306 (2012)
23. Lorenzini: C., Faita, C., Carrozzino, M., Tecchia, F., Bergamasco, M.: VR-based Serious Game Designed for Medical Ethics Training. In: Proceedings of Salento AVR (2015) (in press)
24. Walters, S.A.R.A.H., Mehta, A.N.I.L.: Epidemiology of cystic fibrosis. Cystic Fibrosis 3, 21–45 (2007)
25. Tecchia, F.: A Flexible Framework for Wide-Spectrum VR Development. Presence 19(4), 302–312 (2010)

26. Brooke, J.: SUS-A quick and dirty usability scale. Usability Evaluation in Industry 189, 194, 4–7 (1996)
27. Fineschi, V., Turillazzi, E., Cateni, C.: The new Italian code of medical ethics. Journal of Medical Ethics 23(4), 239–244 (1997)
28. Beauchamp, T.L., Childress, J.F.: Principles of biomedical ethics. Oxford University press (2001)
29. Di Pietro, M.L., Pennacchini, M.: La comparsa della bioetica nei codici di deontologia medica italiani: profilo storico e analisi dei contenuti. Medicina e Morale 52(1), 29–62 (2002)
30. Bailey, J.H., Witmer, B.G.: Learning and transfer of spatial knowledge in a virtual environment. In: Proceedings of the Human Factors and Ergonomics Society Annual Meeting, vol. 38(18). SAGE Publications (1994)

A Battle of Wit: Applying Computational Humour to Game Design

Dormann Claire

University of Ottawa / Institute of Dementia, University of Salford
Allerton Bg, Salford M6 6PU, UK
cdormann@acm.org

Abstract. There is still a dearth of humour in computer games. To spur the use of humour in games and overcome some of the difficulties in producing humour, we advance that game design can benefit from research in computational humour. The focus of this paper is thus on verbal humour and humour design. Integrating computational humour in games could facilitate humour scripting and solve one of the oldest problems in game humour related to repetition. A humour bot could enhance gamers' experiences, by stimulating social bonding or supporting comic relief. We believe that the use of computational humour for game design would enhance players' laughter and designers' creativity. Last, as game design can benefit from advances in computational humour, so virtual agents can from game research.

Keywords: humour design, computer games, players, tools, computational humour, verbal humour, one-liner.

1   Introduction

Games can challenge us, move us and affect us in many ways, including making us laugh. Humour enhances fun; it induces laughter and creates a highly pleasurable experience. The role of humour in games is manifold: humour can surprise or delight us, while it is an important component of interpersonal relations and can provide comic relief [1]. Despite a few notable exceptions such as *Portal 2* (2011) or *Borderland 2* (2012) for the more recent ones, many players and game reviewers still deplore the lack of humour in many computer games.

Indeed, crafting humour and stimulating mirth in games is not easy, and repetition and timing can be problematic. To make humour work, writers and designers need a good knowledge of humour mechanics, as well as a good dose of creativity. In an interview by Ashcraft [2], Ramis stated that writing humorous scripts for games is quite demanding, with all the many comic alternatives to produce. He added that "*it is like writing three hit movies, the scripts are impossibly long*". To spur the use of humour in games and overcome some of the difficulties in producing humour, we advance that games' design can benefit from research in computational humour.

© IFIP International Federation for Information Processing 2015
K. Chorianopoulos et al. (Eds.): ICEC 2015, LNCS 9353, pp. 72–85, 2015.
DOI: 10.1007/978-3-319-24589-8_6

This paper is centred on humour design and is situated in a long-standing investigation dedicated to stimulate the design of humorous games and comical gameplay. Furthermore, we seek to understand the players' experiences, the role of humour in game design and how it is embedded in games. Our investigation includes game players' interviews, the analysis of game scripts and walkthroughs, playtesting and the elaboration of humour patterns.

In this paper, we first review research in computational humour that can be applied to games. As computational humour relates to verbal humour, we focus on its use in games by outlining issues and game objects related to verbal humour. Then we discuss how and where games could benefit from the addition of computational humour: within the game itself as well as within the game space. We describe the foundation of a conceptual framework for the development of computational humour for games. Last, we highlight research issues related to the application of computational humour to games. We believe that as game design can benefit from advances in computational humour, so virtual agents can from game research. We hope to inspire a novel research agenda that integrates computational humour with game design and development.

2   Background in Computational Humour

Computational humour broadly includes the recognition or detection of humour and the automatic generation of humour. It spans a number of areas from the development of humour engines to the design of humour bots, humorous virtual agents and robots.

The automatic generation of humour relates to the development of verbal humour, as it is relatively easier to analyse and compute than other forms of humour. Binsted et al. [3] developed the Joke Analysis and Production Engine (JAPE), a punning riddles generator *"what do you call a murderer with fiber? A cereal killer"*. Since those early days a number of systems have been produced that generate short forms of verbal humour such as simple idiom-based witticisms with the WISCRAIC system *"the friendly gardener had thyme for the woman!"* or, generating whimsical sentences with the HAHAcronym system – *"FBI: Fantastic Bureau of Intimidation"* [4]. To improve the quality of verbal humour, specific techniques and methods have been elaborated to find the best candidate for a joke. For example, Sjobergh and Araki [5] derived a measure of funniness based on the frequencies of words that occur in jokes.

Another strand of research in computational humour connects to systems aiming to identify, index or classify humour from a large corpus such as Internet collections of jokes [6, 7]. Humour bots such as those developed by Dybala et al. [8] and Augello et al. [9] recognise and mine jokes from the Web or from a lexical database such as WorldNet.

The last important area of research connects to the design of humour bots and humorous virtual agents, or Humoroid, as Dybala called them. Augello et al. [9] created a humoristic chat bot for Yahoo Messenger, which functioned as a kind of humour partner. The system retrieved jokes after asking users what kind they wanted to hear. Their bot could also recognise different forms of humour generated by users (i.e. based on antinomy, alliteration or adult slang) and then react accordingly by providing appropriate feedback. Dybala et al. [8] developed talking agents that used humour during dialogues: their system selected a keyword from a user utterance and then outputted a short verbal humour statement. Moreover, Ptaszynski et al. [10] furthered their system to integrate an emotion analysis engine. Taking into consideration users' utterances and emotional reactions, the engine was able to detect when it was appropriate to tell a joke or not. As Stock and Strappavara [4] have pointed out, a humorous system should be able to *"recognize situations appropriate for humour, choose a suitable kind of humour for the situation, generate an appropriate humorous output, and, ... evaluate the feedback"*.

3   Verbal Humour in Game Design

To illustrate the benefit of computational humour for game design, we review briefly the use of verbal humour within games and outline issues with its production. Then we discuss humour in the game script, identifying short forms of verbal humour that are likely candidates for computational humour. More generally, we see two ways in which computational humour could be advantageous for humour design: as tools to help game writers to insert humour in games, and as tools to produce humour, or one-liners, automatically during gameplay.

3.1   Issues in Verbal Humour

Writing game scripts of games celebrated for their humour such as LucasArt games or games like *Portal 2* or *Borderland 2*, where humour plays a significant role in the game, is impressive. Bridgett [11] described different aspects of spoken (or written) game text as game story pieces (such as background "once upon a time", cut-scenes, narrators, etc.), and in-game mission dialogues (describing quests' information or instructions on how to progress in a game). The most important part of game text is conveyed through dialogues with the avatar, main Non-Player Characters (NPCs), and a host of various minor NPCs. To that, we can add various game objects ranging from in-game items, to interface elements, etc.

Of course, writing humour for games is hard. As Bridgett [11] remarked, *"depending on how many characters there are, and the AI behaviors the characters have, there could be as many as 10,000 to 15,000 individual contextual reactions that will need to be written"*. According to its creator, in Rat Race [12] humour will be integrated into dialogue-driven mini-games, adding up to hundreds of possible alternatives that will be heard in function of a player's performance. Indeed, a key aspect of game text is the sheer numbers of variations that might have to be written for a game event, character or situation; more so for games which are text-intense, such as adventure games or role-play games. Writing and designing humour in a game requires a considerable investment. Not everyone has enough knowledge or creativity to write enjoyable comedy narratives, produce jokes or one-liners at will.

Besides the sheer number of comic dialogues and humour game elements to produce, the worst problems with humour are timing and especially repetition. Timing is important in jokes, between the beginning of the joke and the punch line, to create surprise and the unexpected effect. Game timing can be disrupted by players' control and choices. More importantly, many jokes are funny once, perhaps twice, but once you have heard them ten times then they become quite annoying. In some games, like First Person Shooter (FPS) and battle sequences, some lines are repeated hundred times. Because of failure, some puns might be heard over and over. In an interview by Gonzales [13], Schafer summarised the problem quite well as, "*the hilarious boss monster who has four taunts he yells at you over and over, each of which is funny approximately one time, if you're lucky*".

3.2   Verbal Humour and Game Script

As we have seen, computational humour relates to the production of short forms of verbal humour. We subsequently refer to this as a "*Oneliner*" (for lack of a generic term) for any short forms of verbal humour including witticism, pun, putdown, teasing, banter, riddles, and so on. This is in contrast with the longer forms of verbal humour like comic narratives or dialogues.

We do not advocate nor believe that Oneliners are a panacea to insert verbal humour in games. First, humour for games should be carefully planned in function of humour mechanics, within the context of the game goal and storyline. Once a comic strategy is established, an overview of the game humour and its elements should be outlined, as a sort of humour wireframe for the game.

Second, not all verbal humours are delivered as Oneliners. Main characters and events often require a tighter control of the humour through a more complex comic script that advances the plot forward. In this situation, humour is then written as comic narratives rather than Oneliners. As many game writers have stated, writing every single character as a Oneliner firing machine is a recipe for disaster. It gets tiresome and weakens the player's ability to care about each character, and thus disrupts the effectiveness of humour within the game. However, as some stand-up comedians who have mastered the art of Oneliners to perfection show, a judicial choice and use of Oneliners can be tremendously funny.

If we take *Portal 2* (2011) as an example, as it is typical of Weatley, a comic monologue is taking place just at the beginning of the game when Weatley is trying to rouse Chell. This example illustrates the longer form of verbal humour:

"Fine! No absolutely fine. It's not like I don't have, you know, ten thousand other test subjects begging me to help them escape. You know, it's not like this place is about to EXPLODE...All right, look, okay, I'll be honest. You're the LAST test subject left. And if you DON'T help me, we're both going to die...".

Nevertheless, through the course of the game, Weatley has many Oneliners (short feedback lines), which depend on the players' actions and gameplay situations. Similarly, the cores, to put it simply, are rambling on different themes through Oneliners.

3.3   Oneliners and Games

Verbal humour permeates every aspect of computer games and we found examples for every feature, from names of objects and NPCs (e.g. Hemer Nesingway in *World of Warcraft*, 2008) to dialogues / monologues as we have seen, and to game documentation (e.g. parodies of Agony Aunt columns in *Maniac Mansion*,1987). To emphasise the usefulness that computational humour tools could have, we looked for and identified game text objects which have the Oneliner format. We searched for places in the game script which have the following characteristics: the lines are smaller and stand-alone. Moreover, these lines need more alternatives and / or occurred frequently during gameplay. We found a number of those that pertain to different script elements, from character dialogues to missions and game objects. No doubt there are many others, and their uses depend on the humour strategy, the genre of games, or players.

Barks are small parts of dialogues, a few words that characters blurt out. Barks are used to give players' feedback while making the game world alive and feel like a responsive entity. Although barks are found in many contexts, common occurrences are during battle sequences. Players can hear a hundred of them like *"I will kill you"*, *"Argh"*, *"I am dying"*, etc., over and over. Thus, barks can become quite annoying. As Hamilton stated [14], the *No One Lives Forever* series created the most memorable stealth segments. *Borderland 2* is also infamous for barks said in combat, e.g. for Nomads' *"Midget on the loose!"* and *"I miss my midget"* (on death).

Taunting and insult fights between characters are all prime candidates for computational tools. The crude gallows humour that some FPS players seem to like could be generated at various times before confronting an enemy. Taunting can also give rise to insult fights, used frequently in computer games based on boxing, wrestling, martial arts, and so on. However, the most famous comical insult fight is found in the *Monkey Island* series (1980–2000): Insult: *"Soon you'll be wearing my sword like a shish kebab!"*, Comeback: *"First you better stop waiving it like a feather-duster"*.

Comic banter or comic exchange between two characters is an excellent source of fun; it is an easy way to avoid any problems with timing, as the characters' lines follow each other. While banter between main characters could be more difficult to generate automatically, such is not the case for secondary characters. As noted by Grönroos [15] in *Dragon Age* (2009), banter in that game is triggered at random when a player explores the game world without being intrusive.

Similarly, a host of secondary characters can be used to insert humour for comic relief or comic fun. Comic relief is often provided to relieve stress and lighten the mood after a tense combat mission or grinding to level up [16]. To accommodate different players' experiences, a character in a party as the class clown is often designed as humorous, delivering a high number of Oneliners. Thus, depending on whether a game is designed as comical or uses a high number of comic characters, a huge number of Oneliners would then be needed. In *World of Warcraft* (2008) players are given the opportunity to tell predefined jokes, which vary based on the avatar's race and gender. Thus, using computational humour tool there would provide an infinite variation of these jokes so they stay fresh and still surprise the player each time, making the game more playful.

Game objects are also an important source of humour for which computational tools could be used. In comic adventure games like *Day of the Tentacle* (1983), all the objects that the players manipulate are given comic feedback. For example, the object "*Chattering teeth*" as the line "*Jumpy little sucker*". Some players delight in finding and reading all these Oneliners. A prototypical comic object used to insert humour without intruding on the main script is the radio (e.g. *Grand Theft Auto series*). Although radios can provide comic narratives, they also use a high number of Oneliners. Similarly, Oneliners can be inserted through a newspaper's headlines, a joke calendar, etc., and be varied in function of the game segments. Only the writer / designer's imagination is the limit of what might be possible.

4   Game Space and Humour Bot

As we are just beginning to explore the application of computational humour to games, we also want to highlight another example where such tools could be useful: in the game space through the addition of a humour bot in multiplayer games to enhance players' experiences.

A number of multiplayers games have an inbuilt voice and / or text chat. Most often, players can communicate privately on a one-to-one mode with a group of preselected players (e.g. member of the guild), or with everyone. Nijholt [17] proposed the use of a humour bot in the chat channel to enhance fun in computer games. Although fun should perhaps emerge primarily from the gameplay, using a humour bot has intriguing possibilities. Indeed, humour seems to be an important element of game chat and of players' experiences. A study of a game chat identified the use of humour as wordplay and amusing references to pop culture, but players also made fun of each other [18]. Similarly, Duchenault [19] found that players commonly engage in small talk and share game tips as well as humour. Players exercise their comic wit, for example, by improvising in-character dialogues. For some players, this is an essential aspect of their gameplay; the game will be fun as much as the players are fun. For those players, negative and aggressive players can ruin their experiences of the game.

Humour and laughter have a variety of possible socio-emotional functions and uses: laughing with, laughing together, and laughing at or against [20]. Humour has an important function for maintaining group relationships and to enhance players' moods to make the gameplay more enjoyable. Laughter and humour are indicative of moments of shared fun. Moreover, humour is a source of comfort and support between guild members.

Thus, a humour bot could use positive and enhancing humour to induce joking behaviour and support social bonding. This could be more important at the beginning of the game session, during idle time or, when visiting social places such as a tavern in games. The humour bot could also provide comic relief after a raid or a defeat and encourage players to level up. However, the most important and complex function of the bot might be to try to curb aggressive behaviour through humour. Players vent frustration or some aggravate others through trash-talking and swearing, as well as verbally attacking them. While some players and game communities tolerate this, such is not the case for all. Thus, a humour bot could criticise lightly this kind of behaviour, remonstrating with players in a self-mocking fashion, channelling aggression through humour and providing jokes to release tension.

Besides chatting in a group, players can also communicate through private chat. Thus, another use for a humour bot would be as a game companion or helper. It can be quite confusing and a bit daunting to learn a new gameplay and join another community of play. While some players are helpful, others are prone to taking advantage of newbies, mocking and tricking them. A number of helper agents have been developed like Sergeant Blackwell, a witty avatar that answer questions in a virtual military application [21] or, one that provides feedback on players' chess moves [22]. Thus, a humorous game companion could provide assistance to novice players through the private channel, offering in-game information, as well as enhancing players' moods through Oneliners; thus, motivating players to advance in the game by being playful rather than didactic.

5   Towards a Computational Humour Framework for Games

We have discussed ways in which computational humour could be useful and used in games. To further bring the two fields together, we present elements for a basic conceptual framework for games. We use agents or humour bots such as those developed by Dybala et al. [8] and Augello et al. [9] as a point of departure for the discussion.

5.1   Differences between Games, Bot and Agent Systems

There are important distinctions between games, agent systems and chat bots, not least that players do not usually hold a conversation directly with an NPC, as a user would converse with a virtual agent or bot. More importantly here, game worlds are far more complex than agent systems: game characters interact with each other and many objects in an ever-changing virtual world. Thus, in turn, the use of verbal humour in games is richer and more complex than the one used by agent systems.

In most cases in computational humour, the focus is on the production and output of an Oneliner. Beyond creating or retrieving the best Oneliner from a set, there is not much discussion on the type of humour produced. If virtual agents do not have much use for aggressive humour, such is not the case for computer games. Taunting and insult fights use aggressive humour like a putdown. Typically within a game, NPC allies will deliver positive and sympathetic humour, while boss monsters and enemies will use negative humour. A very simple mapping between humour polarity (i.e. from negative to positive) and types of Oneliners could consist in using putdown and insult (and comeback) for negative humour, and pun or jokes for positive humour. Beyond the structure and form of humour, the content of the Oneliner such as with ethnic jokes can also determine if a joke is perceived negatively. Thus, we might want to rate some types of jokes as negative humour.

If we devise a very simple framework for a computational humour game engine based on the work of a humour bot, the computational humour frame for games would have two important features: the polarity of humour that should be used, and as with agents or bots, what the content of the joke should relate to (see Table 1).

Table 1. Computational humour

Agent	Games	Effect
<user utterance>	<game event = trigger Oneliner>	*Player talk to Tavern Master*
	<humour event polarity >	*Positive*
<extract keywords>	<humour event charateristic>	*Drunk patron*
<query computational humour engine >	<query game humour engine>	
<retrieve Oneliner>	<retrieve Oneliner>	
<output Oneliner >	<game event Oneliner output >	*Tavern Master: jokes*
	< Oneliner counter >	

Another distinction between humoristic agents and games relates to keyword vs humour event characteristics. In the agent / humour bot, the Oneliner like a pun is produced according to the user utterance <keyword>, but such is not the case in computer games. Typically in games, Oneliners will depend on a number of factors, such as for NPCs: the types of characters (human vs dwarf), the function of characters (bartender vs soldier), setting in the game world (e.g. in a tavern or castle), or at the highest level, on the kind of game theme used (e.g. a middle age / fantasy, military, horror / zombie game, etc.). Thus, we might need to elaborate a knowledge base, a lexicon of game situations that connect humour events <tavern master> to the content of possible Oneliners to retrieve <joy of drinking>. Then the humour event characteristic would act as the keyword in agents and an appropriate Oneliner would be retrieved for the tavern master. We might also want to keep track of Oneliners that have been given to players, so as far as possible, they never hear the same Oneliner twice. Last, a review for the computational humour engine frame is given in Figure 1. As with the development of humour bots, the computational humour engine could use a very large database of Oneliners or, a mixed system that includes a humour engine that generates a Oneliner automatically when feasible and uses the database when it is not.

5.2   Using a Humour Model for Games

We might need to elaborate a humour model for game design that accounts for more variations in the use of humour than between positive and negative humour. We propose to adopt as a starting point a model based on humour styles associated with personality characteristics [23]. The four types of humour are defined as: affiliative humour (to enhance interpersonal relationships by amusing others), self-enhancing humour (related to mood and an optimistic view of life), self-defeating humour (to amuse others by saying funny things at one's expense) and aggressive humour (to put others down through sarcasm and ridicule).

Such a model could work quite well for game characters, the most frequent sources of Oneliners. However, to make the model more generic and better reflect some of the use of humour in games, we put forward some modifications. We rename the first category *Comic Humour*, for humour that makes people laugh out loud and to thus create a playful and pleasurable experience. In our experience, humour used in games can be quite exaggerated, wacky, absurd or nonsensical, more so perhaps than what we might expect as affiliative humour. The second category becomes then *Enhancing Humour*, positive humour that is utilised to support relationships or to enhance mood and diminish tension. The third and fourth categories of *Self-Defeating Humour* and *Aggressive Humour* remain the same.

While there are many examples of aggressive humour in games, self-defeating humour is not as frequent but can occur with certain class of characters such as lovable loser or comic relief characters. Affiliative humour would be the type of humour used by the tavern master, while a goofy character such as Glottis of *Grim Fandago* (1998) could be expected to use comic humour. Such a model would accommodate for different functions of humour, and we can also modulate humour according to players' choices. For example, depending on players' answers (e.g. negative), the tavern master could turn sarcastic and use aggressive humour. When transferring a humour model from one discipline to another context, it is difficult to predict entirely how the model will relate to the new domain. Thus, a humour model such as the one we have discussed should be tested with different game scripts and scenarios, and thus refined.

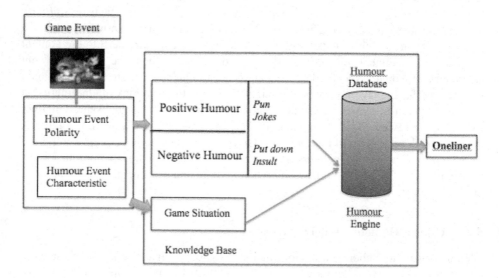

Fig. 1. Computational humour engine frame

5.3   Chat Humour Bot

As humour bots used elsewhere, based on the conversational keywords, a humour bot for a multiplayer chat should be able to retrieve Oneliners that relate to the current conversation. Using a type of humour model such as the one we have discussed would insure that the appropriate humour is delivered at the right time. As before, we might want in the first instance to establish a knowledge base of game chat situations, to decide when humour is appropriate or not (e.g. coordinating a raid) or what type of humour to initiate (e.g. self-defeating humour for swearing). Further developments could accommodate and integrate an emotion engine with the computational humour engine.

6   Discussion

To strengthen and stimulate the design and use of humour in games, we have discussed the use of computational humour tools. We have suggested two ways in which computational humour could be advantageous for humour design: as tools to help game writers and as tools to generate Oneliners during gameplay. Using a bootstrapping process more specifically attuned to games and automatic humour recognition techniques such as those described by Mihalcea and Strapparava [6], large databases of Oneliners could be developed for specific games, or game genres.

We have outlined elements for a computational humour framework for games. To develop a new research agenda in this domain there are many issues that need to be addressed. From a humour design perspective, to create a multiplayer humour chat bot we might want to study in more depth the use of humour within those games and elaborate the most appropriate knowledge base for the humour bot. Conceptual designs should be advanced and tested to evaluate the effect and players' reactions to the humour bot.

For game design, besides refining the humour model that we have discussed, we might consider developing a more formal classification for Oneliners. Inspired by humour theories and humour patterns, humour classification algorithms could then be derived to produce the best match between the game event— humour and the output— Oneliner. Such research should take into consideration and might contribute to overcoming the current limitations of computational humour recognition tools.

Game engines are becoming more efficient at tracking where players have been and what they have done. Thus, by more fully integrating data from the game engine tracking system with the computational humour engine could lead to the generation of humour that is more contextual and more reactive to the gameplay. Another element that we might introduce within a conceptual framework for computational humour in games is comic expressiveness. For NPCs, comic expressiveness would be tied up with the production of Oneliners and correspond to an NPC facial expression, body language and / or type of laughter.

We suggest that the addition of computational humour could lead to innovations in game design, within game mechanics, mini-games and ultimately perhaps the design of novel game concepts. As Root [13] stated rightly in an interview regarding some of the use of humour in games: *"Solving a puzzle, or defeating an opponent, when you are rewarded with a joke or, often as not, a bad pun, it just doesn't work. It's as if someone handed you a bag of phrases--a priest, ... a hot tub, ... and four fifths of Irish whisky--and then told you to assemble your own joke"*. But could we not just do that? Computational humour recognition tools are becoming more sophisticated; thus, a computational humour engine could also rate some types of Oneliners produced by players: the better the joke, the more points, the more goblins laugh until they die, etc. Nakatsu and Tosa [24] have developed an Artificial Intelligence (AI) comedy system based on comic dialogue generation. Could a mini-game work like a comedy stand-up performance with an NPC as a humour partner? Games that use natural language interaction such as *Façade* (2005) or *Bot Colony* [25] could benefit the most from computational humour uses.

Another emerging trend of research related to computational humour is laughter. Laughter is very expressive and is associated with the definition of humour. As with humour, the value of laughter is greatly underestimated in game design. Computational systems have been developed that are able to detect and respond to human laughs in real time [26]. Fukushima et al. [27] proposed a system composed of a set of toy dolls that laugh when the user laughs. Such laughter was shown to enhance the user's enjoyment of cartoon animations. Thus, would canned laughter enhance game enjoyment and funniness as it does in films? Would that be more desirable with some specific games, such as social types of games on the Wii? Intriguing questions also relate to the game avatar: could your avatar, breaking the fourth wall, laugh with you during gameplay and what would be the effect? Should we instead do that with the avatar sidekick? Could an avatar become funnier if the player does initiate more jokes during gameplay, etc.?

To conclude, we want to outline the benefit of game research to computational humour and agent design. Virtual agents lack the vocabulary for full comical expressiveness that game characters have. Designing a comical agent demands very different models of expressions and body postures than the more naturalistic representations generally used in virtual agent design. Thus, a virtual humour agent could also benefit from a humour model and from game character design to exploit more fully their comic potential. All research in computational humour relates to verbal humour, except for the work of Thawonmas et al. [28] on pantomime, and David and Mateas [29] on the Road Runner and Coyote jokes. The study of non-verbal forms of humour in game design through game patterns might help to bridge the gap from a high level description of humour such as slapstick / incongruity to a low level description of agent parameters. Last, the game industry has overcome the film industry in terms of revenue. Thus, games could be an ideal test bed for the development of computational humour, stimulating and driving a new research agenda forward.

7   Conclusion

Humour can surprise us, making us roll around with laughter; it creates a joyful experience and makes us more human. As Crecente [30] stated about *Dead Rising 2* (2010), there are a lot of zombie games, shooters and sandbox games but there is only one that does comedy, action and zombie. It made the game truly unique. Indeed, as LucasArt games in their time, *Portal 2* (2011) would not be the same without GLaDOS and Weatley.

Thus, to enhance and stimulate the use of humour in games and make them more enjoyable, we explore how game design could benefit from computational humour.

Computational humour would enable a greater use of humour, as it would facilitate game scripting by reducing the most monotonous humour writing tasks. It would solve one of the oldest problems in scripted verbal humour related to repetition: tired old jokes that are not funny anymore. Computational humour tools could also support the gameplay within multiplayer games, by making the player experience more engaging and enjoyable. However, the more interesting application of computational humour might be in supporting creativity and new possibilities for game design. Through our exploration of verbal humour and computational tools for game design, we hope to gain some insights to support humour design in games and with virtual agents.

Future research in computational humour and laughter for games would have to address a number of issues. These issues will range from humour design to player experiences, and the development of the computational humour engine architecture and its integration within the game engine. The field of AI and computer games, or games AI, is emerging and diversifying from research on NPC behaviour to player experience adaptation and procedural content [31]. Moreover, AI game views on NPC do not relate necessarily to making human-like NPCs but also look as we did, at other questions more typically anchored in computer game design, such as making the game more enjoyable. As far as we know, computational humour has not been applied to game design nor discussed within game AI. Thus, computational humour could become a specific strand of game AI to adapt and develop the computational humour engine for games, to make better comic NPCs, or within affective games to adapt the type and content of humour to a player's personality or mood. Let us engage in a battle of wit, and develop a new research agenda that bridges computational humour and game design, and give a new impetuous to computational humour, game AI, as well as game design.

Acknowledgment. This work was supported by the Social Sciences and Humanities Research Council of Canada.

References

1. Dormann, C., Biddle, R.: A Review of Humor for Computer Games: Play, Laugh and More. Simulation & Gaming 40(6), 802–824 (2009)

2. Ashcraft, B.: Harold Ramis On Why it's Hard to Make Funny Video games (2009). http://kotaku.com/5293133/harold-ramis-on-why-its-hard-to-make-funny-video-games
3. Binsted, K., Ritchie, G.: Computational Rules for Punning Riddles. International Journal of Humor Research 10(1), 25–76 (1997)
4. Stock, O., Strapparava, C.: The Act of Creating Humorous Acronyms. Applied Artificial Intelligence 19(2), 137–151 (2005)
5. Sjöbergh, J., Araki, K.A.: Very Modular Humor Enabled Chat-bot for Japanese. In: Pacling 2009, pp. 135–140, Sapporo, Japan (2009)
6. Mihalcea, R., Strapparava, C.: Technologies that Make you Smile: Adding Humor to Text-based Applications. IEEE Intelligent Systems 21(5), 33–39 (2006)
7. Raz, Y.: Automatic Humor Classification on Twitter. In: Proceedings of the Conference of the North American Chapter of the Association for Computational Linguistics, pp. 66–70. ACL, Stroudsburg (2012)
8. Dybala, P., Ptaszynski, M., Rzepka, R., Araki, K.: Humorized Computational Intelligence towards User-Adapted Systems with a Sense of Humor. In: Giacobini, M., et al. (eds.) EvoWorkshops 2009. LNCS, vol. 5484, pp. 452–461. Springer, Heidelberg (2009)
9. Augello, A., Saccone, G., Gaglio, S., Giovanni, P.: Humorist Bot: Bringing Computational Humour in a Chat-bot System. In: Proceeding of the International Complex, Intelligent and Software Intensive Systems, pp. 703–708. IEEE Press, New York (2008)
10. Ptaszynski, M., Araki, K., Dybala, P., Rzepka, R., Higuhi, S., Shi, W.: Towards Socialized Machines: Emotions and Sense of Humour in Conversational Agents. In: Usmani, Z.-U.-H. (ed.) Web Intelligence and Intelligent Agents (2010). http://www.intechopen.com/books/web-intelligence-and-intelligent-agents/towards-socialized-machines-emotions-and-sense-of-humour-in-conversational-agents
11. Bridgett, R.A.: Holistic Approach to Game Dialogue Production, Gamasutra (2015). http://www.gamasutra.com/view/feature/132566/a_holistic_approach_to_game_.php?print=1
12. Totilo, S.: 'Rat Race' Funnyman Hopes PlayStation 3's First Sitcom Video Game Fills Comedy Void (2007). http://www.mtv.com/news/1575219/rat-race-funnyman-hopes-playstation-3s-first-sitcom-video-game-fills-comedy-void/
13. Gonzales, L.: A Brief History of Video Game Humor (2004). http://www.gamespot.com/features/6114407/p-2.html
14. Hamilton, K.: Why Video Game Characters Say Such Ridiculous Things, Kotaku (2012). http://kotaku.com/5921878/why-video-game-characters-say-such-ridiculous-things
15. Grönroos, A.M.: Humour in Video Games: Play, Comedy, and Mischief. Master Thesis of Art, Aalto University, Finland (2013)
16. Dormann, C., Boutet, M.: Incongruous Avatars and Hilarious Sidekicks: Design Patterns for Comical Game Characters. In: Proceeding of the Digital Games Research Association (2013). http://www.digra.org/digital-library/
17. Nijholt, A.: Why and When 'Laughing out Loud' in Game Playing (2012). http://eprints.eemcs.utwente.nl/21848/
18. Wright, T., Boria, E., Breidenbach, P.: Creative Player Actions in FPS Online Video Games, Playing Counter-Strike. Game Studies. The International Journal of Computer Game Research 2(2) (2002). http://gamestudies.org/0202/

19. Ducheneaut, N., Yee, N., Nickell, E., Moore, R.: Alone Together? Exploring the Social Dynamics of Massively Multiplayer Online Games. In: Proceedings of the SIGCHI Conference on Human Factors in Computing Systems, pp. 407–416. ACM, New York (2006)
20. Zijderveld, A.: The Sociology of Humor and Laughter. Current Sociology 3, 1–64 (1983)
21. Rich, C., Sidner, C.L.: Robots and Avatars as Hosts, Advisors, Companions, and Jesters. AI Magazine 30(1), 29–41 (2009)
22. Castellano, I., Leite, A., Pereira, C., Martinho, A., Paiva, C., McOwan, P.W.: It's All in the Game: Towards an Affect Sensitive and Context Aware Game Companion. In: Proceeding of the International Conference on Affective Computing and Intelligent Interaction. IEEE Press, New York (2009)
23. Martin, R.A., Puhlik-Doris, P., Larsen, G., Gray, J., Weir, K.: Individual differences in uses of humor and their relation to psychological well-being: Development of the Humor Styles Questionnaire. Journal of Research in Personality 37(1), 48–75 (2003)
24. Tosa, N., Nakatsu, R.: Interactive Comedy: Laughter as the Next Intelligence System. In: International Symposium on Micromechatronics and Human Science, pp. 135–138. IEEE Press, New York (2002)
25. Joseph, E.: Bot Colony – a Video Game Featuring Intelligent Language-Based Interaction with the Characters (2014). https://www.botcolony.com/doc/BotColony_paper.pdf
26. Urbain, J., Bevacqua, E., Dutoit, T., Moinet, A., Niewiadomski, R., Pelachaud, C., Picart, B., Tilmanne, J., Wagner, J.: AVLaughterCycle, An Audiovisual Laughing Machine. In: Camurri, A., Mancini, M., Gualtiero, V. (eds.) Proceedings of the 5th International Summer Workshop on Multimodal Interfaces, pp. 79–87. DIST University of Genova, Genova (2009)
27. Fukushima, S., Hashimoto, Y., Nozawa, T., Kajimoto, H.: Laugh Enhancer Using Laugh Track synchronized with the user's laugh motion. In: Proceeding of CHI Conference on Human Factors in Computing Systems, Extended Abstracts, pp. 3613–3618. ACM, New York (2010)
28. Thawonmas, R., Hassaku, H., Tanaka, K.: Mimicry: Another Approach for Interactive Comedy. In: Proceedings of Conference on Simulation and AI in Computer Games, pp. 135–138. EUROSIS, Oostende (2003)
29. David, O., Mateas, M.: Beep! Beep! Boom!: Towards a Planning Model of Coyote and Road runner cartoons. In: Proceedings of the 4th International Conference on Foundations of Digital Games, pp. 145–152. ACM, New York (2009)
30. Crecente, B.: Kotaku (2010). http://kotaku.com/5524674/dead-rising-2s-dark-comedy-and-interactive-vomit
31. Yannakakis, G.N.: Game AI Revisited. In: Proceedings of ACM Computing Frontiers, Proceeding of the 9th Conference on Computing Frontiers, pp. 285–292. ACM, New York (2012)

Advanced Dynamic Scripting for Fighting Game AI

Kevin Majchrzak, Jan Quadflieg, and Günter Rudolph

Chair of Algorithm Engineering, TU Dortmund, 44221 Dortmund, Germany
{kevin.majchrzak,jan.quadflieg,guenter.rudolph}@tu-dortmund.de

Abstract. We present an advanced version of dynamic scripting, which we apply to an agent created for the Fighting Game AI Competition. In contrast to the original method, our new approach is able to successfully adapt an agent's behavior in real-time scenarios. Based on a set of rules created with expert knowledge, a script containing a subset of these rules is created online to control our agent. Our method uses reinforcement learning to learn which rules to include in the script and how to arrange them. Results show that the algorithm successfully adapts the agent's behavior in tests against three other agents, allowing our agent to win most evaluations in our tests and the CIG 2014 competition.

Keywords: Artificial Intelligence, AI, Computer Game, Fighting Game, Dynamic Scripting, Code Monkey, Real-Time, Adaptive, Reinforcement Learning.

1 Introduction

Scripting is one of the most widely used techniques for AI in commercial video games due to its many advantages [14]. One of the major downsides on scripted game AI, though, is its lack of creativity. An agent controlled by a classic script may show foolish behavior in any situation the developer has not foreseen and it is an easy prey to counter strategies because it cannot adapt.

Dynamic scripting [14] minimizes the downsides of scripting while retaining its strengths. The idea is to build a static rulebase beforehand and to select and order a subset of its rules to generate scripts on the fly. Commonly reinforcement learning is used for the selection and ordering process whereas expert knowledge is used to design rules. In many cases dynamic scripting is capable of adapting to an enemy's strategy after just a few fights [14]. These results are encouraging but the method is still too slow if enemies change their strategies frequently. Therefore, agents that are controlled by dynamic scripting in its basic form do not perform well against human players or other agents with dynamic strategies.

In the present article we introduce an improved method that meets real-time requirements and, thus, resolves dynamic scripting's shortcoming. The rest of the paper is structured as follows: We give a short introduction to the framework FightingICE used here and discuss related work in section 2. Our advanced version of dynamic scripting is presented in detail in section 3. We compare our solution with the state of the art in section 4 and close with a summary and conclusions.

K. Chorianopoulos et al. (Eds.): ICEC 2015, LNCS 9353, pp. 86–99, 2015.
DOI: 10.1007/978-3-319-24589-8_7

2 Background

We first introduce the framework used in the Fighting Game AI Competition to make the reader familiar with the most important aspects. Please refer to the official website [4] for details not covered here. We then present related work.

2.1 FightingICE Framework

The FightingICE framework, used here in version 1.01, is an open source *Beat 'Em Up* game written in Java. Developed and maintained by the Intelligent Computer Entertainment Lab. of Ritsumeikan University, Japan [4,7] it is the official software used for the Fighting Game AI Competition (FTGAIC), organized by the same group from Ritsumeikan University. The goal of the FTGAIC is to create an agent which controls one of the two characters in the game. The FTGAIC was one of the competitions held at the IEEE Conference on Computational Intelligence and Games 2014 (CIG 2014) [6].

FightingICE implements the classic concept of a Beat 'Em Up game: Two opponent characters fight each other in an arena until a winning criterion is fulfilled. Figure 1 shows a screen capture of the game taken at the beginning of a fight. As shown there, the initial state of the game has the two opponents standing at fixed positions in a neutral posture. Damage and energy values are set to zero. Both characters can move along the x- and y-axis on a two-dimensional grid by using predefined actions. In the context of the FTGAIC a round lasts 60 seconds, one second consisting of 60 frames, which equals 3600 discrete time steps per round. An agent controlling a character has to react in real-time, which means it has $1/60 \approx 0.017$ seconds to decide which action to take. The last action is reused by the framework if an agent violates this constraint.

At the end of a round, a total of 1000 points are split between the two characters based upon the damage one inflicted to the other:

$$\mathcal{P} := \begin{cases} \dfrac{\overline{\mathcal{H}}}{\mathcal{H} + \overline{\mathcal{H}}} * 1000 & \text{iff } (\mathcal{H} + \overline{\mathcal{H}}) \neq 0 \\ 500 & \text{otherwise} \end{cases} \tag{1}$$

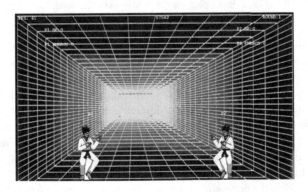

Fig. 1. Screenshot of the FightingICE framework, taken at the beginning of a fight.

where $\mathcal{H}$ and $\overline{\mathcal{H}}$ are the damage values of the two characters. A fight consists of three rounds. The winner is the agent that gained the most points during the three rounds, which means that 1501 points are sufficient to win.

What makes FightingICE interesting is an artificial lag in the data provided to an agent. At time step t, an agent receives the game state belonging to the time step 15 frames ago. This simulates a response time of 0.25 seconds, similar to a human player's. During the first 15 frames of a round, an agent receives the initial game state.

Agents can perform five different kinds of actions. *Basic actions* are the neutral posture in three variations: standing, crouching and in the air. *Movement actions* are used to move the character around. *Guard actions* can block or weaken the damage of an attack by the opponent. *Recovery actions* are automatically performed if the character has been hit by the opponent or landed after a jump. An agent cannot control the character during a recovery action. *Skill actions* are used to attack the opponent. A skill action consists of three distinct phases: startup (lasts 5 to 35 frames), active (2 to 30 frames) and recovery (8 to 58 frames). Damage is dealt to the opponent only during the active phase and only if the opponent is hit. During the other two phases, the character cannot be controlled and is particularly vulnerable to attacks of the opponent. Detailed information on the 56 different actions can be downloaded from the competition website [4].

(a) The defensive hit box of the left character (left rectangle) collides with the offensive hit box of the right character (dashed rectangle in the middle).

(b) A projectile with an offensive hit box (dashed rectangle) moves away from the attacking character with a constant velocity vector (grey arrow).

Fig. 2. Examples for hit boxes and collisions.

Whether or not a character receives damage from an attack is determined by offensive and defensive hit boxes, modeled as axis aligned bounding boxes (see figure 2(a)). The hit boxes approximate the outline of the character or of parts of the character's body. The size and position of the hit boxes depend on the current actions performed. A character is hit if the intersection of its defensive hit box and the offensive hit box of the attacker is not empty. In this case, the victim receives damage based upon the current actions of both characters. Few skill actions create moving offensive hit boxes which move through the arena, independent from the character (see figure 2(b)). They simulate magical powers, e.g. fireballs.

Some skill actions, if successful, increase the energy level of the character based upon the damage inflicted on the opponent. The maximum energy level is 1000 points.

Other skill actions consume energy, which means that they can only be performed if the character has enough energy and that the energy level is reduced by a certain amount if such an action is performed. In other words, the energy can be regarded as a reward for successful attacks and this reward can then be spent to perform other, usually very powerful, actions.

The information available to an agent is incomplete, due to the artificial lag and, to our knowledge, no universal dominating strategy exists, due to the diversity of possible attacks and counter actions. A successful agent therefore needs the ability to act under incomplete knowledge and to adapt its behavior to opponents with new strategies in real-time. Both aspects make the FTGAIC an interesting testbed for AI and learning methods.

The FightingICE framework showed nondeterministic behavior during our experiments. We believe that this noise is introduced by synchronization issues in the parallel part of the code. This adds a further obstacle an agent has to deal with. During our experiments, we did our best to minimize the influence of other processes running on the same machine, to keep the conditions as homogeneous as possible.

2.2   Related Work

In the context of this paper, the most important contribution from literature is the work by Spronck et al., *Adaptive game AI with dynamic scripting* [14], which we use as a basis for our approach. Spronck et al. use a mixture of a classic rulebase (scripting) and reinforcement learning (RL), which they call *dynamic scripting*. They apply their approach to a group of agents for a simulated and a commercial computer role-playing game. As the agents are of different types like *warrior* or *wizard*, which are capable of using very different actions, one rulebase for each type is designed manually. A learning method based on reinforcement learning selects subsets of these rulebases to create one script per agent on the fly. Spronck et al. test their group of agents in combats against other groups with similar basic abilities but static strategies. The scripts are evaluated and modified only once after each combat and it usually takes the learning method several combats to successfully adapt to an opponent. Thus, dynamic scripting in its basic form does not adapt the agents' strategies in real-time.

The primary order of rules within scripts is fixed and based on manually assigned integer values called priorities. Rules with equal priority, though, are ordered by the learning algorithm itself. Further work by Timuri, Spronck and van den Herik [18] demonstrates that the order of rules within scripts can be learned, leading to solutions of equal or better quality and a convergence rate only slightly slower compared to Spronck's original approach. Other articles on dynamic scripting suggest to generate new rules or even complete rulebases automatically [16,9,11,15]. The presented ideas and results are encouraging.

There are a number of publications that are directly related to FightingICE. The software itself is described in the article *Fighting Game Artificial Intelligence Competition Platform* by Lu et al. [7]. Up to the FTGAIC in the year 2013, all agents submitted to the competition were based on static rule bases or finite state machines. For the first time, adaptive agents like ours were submitted to the FTGAIC 2014. The source code and short descriptions of all entries can be found on the competition website [4].

The organizers of the competition themselves provide an agent called *Mizuno AI* which is based on k-nearest neighbor clustering and is able to adapt its behavior in real-time [19]. The clustering is used to predict the next action of the opponent. Mizuno AI then simulates the outcome of various counter actions and chooses the one with the best possible outcome. The agent proved to be competitive when compared to the best three entries of the 2013 competition.

Another agent that has been developed for FightingICE is described in the article of Park et al. [10]. This agent searches for similar situations in massive play data to decide on promising actions. The data has been collected and stored during training fights against the FTGAIC 2013 participants and two sample bots. The developed agent showed good results in tests against a randomly acting sample bot and Mizuno AI but it was clearly outperformed by the FTGAIC 2013 winner called T.

A different approach for Fighting Game AI commonly used is the imitation of a human player's behavior [17,13]. The article of Lueangrueangroj and Kotrajaras [8] presents an improved version of Thunputtarakul's *Ghost AI* [17], which imitates a human player's actions after an offline learning phase. The agent of Lueangrueangroj et al., however, is able to mimic its opponent's behavior in real-time. Furthermore, it evaluates the performance of learned actions and uses effective rules more frequently. As a consequence, the improved agent is able to partly adapt its actions to its opponent's strategy in real-time.

Ricciardi and Thill reduce fighting games to plain old Rock-Paper-Scissors [12]. They argue that the central aspect of such a game is to predict the action of the opponent and to react with an appropriate counter action. This problem is therefore modeled as a Markov decision problem and solved with a RL algorithm. For the simple case of only three available actions they created an agent that is able to adapt its behavior to an opponent in real-time. But as soon as they expanded the state space by adding four more actions, the RL algorithm failed to adapt the behavior sufficiently fast. This approach is therefore not applicable to a real-time game like the FightingICE framework.

A classic approach, which we found in many articles, was the use of a combination of reinforcement learning and neural networks [1,5,3]. The techniques, applied in these articles, work well for very simple games but need long training phases and are, therefore, not appropriate for real-time games. Cho, Park and Yang compare the value of genetic algorithms, neural networks and evolutionary neural networks for fighting game AI [2]. They come to the conclusion that evolutionary neural networks are the most appropriate technique among them, due to its convergence speed and ratio. But even evolutionary neural networks needed many thousand iterations to adapt to a simple opponent in their tests.

3   Adaptive Generation of Scripts in Real-Time

This section presents an improved version of Spronck's dynamic scripting method. First, we introduce an alternative and more powerful definition for rules and scripts and give some brief suggestions on rulebase design. Then we explain our learning method and apply it to an agent created for the Fighting Game AI Competition.

3.1   Rules and Scripts

An agent for FightingICE has to consider many variables, including the characters' positions, speed vectors, current actions and past actions, in real-time to decide on appropriate measures. Furthermore, it needs to take into account the simulated delay and stochastic state changes of the game. To cope with the large and high-dimensional search space we will develop a set of rules, based on expert knowledge. These rules classify and, thus, reduce the search space.

Definition 1. *A **rule** R is a mapping* $R\colon Z \mapsto \mathbb{B} \times A$. *Where* $\mathbb{B} = \{0,1\}$, *Z the set of possible game states and A the set of possible actions. We say that* $z \in Z$ ***fulfills*** *R iff* $R(z) = (1,a)$ *for some* $a \in A$.

Definition 2. $E(R) := \{z \in Z \mid z \text{ fulfills } R\}$ *is the **fulfilling set** of R. We call R an **empty rule**, iff* $E(R) = \emptyset$ *and a **default rule** iff* $E(R) = Z$.

The definition of rules in this article differs a lot from the usual understanding of the term *rule* and even Spronck's definition [14]. A rule in our context represents a sub-agent, which maps the entire state space of the game to a set of actions. As a consequence, one single rule could possibly control all of the agent's actions. This special case would be equivalent to the classic scripting approach.

The combination of rules, though, is what gives the learning method the ability to generate highly specialized scripts on the fly. In our method, if a rule is fulfilled, it thereby informs the agent that it believes to know a good solution for the current situation. In general, the fulfilling sets of rules are not disjoint and multiple rules could be fulfilled at the same time. The following definition explains how to manage these situations.

Definition 3. *Let* $S = \{R_1, \ldots, R_n\}$ $(n \in \mathbb{N})$ *be an ordered set of rules and* $Prio\colon S \mapsto \mathbb{Z}$. *S is called **script** iff*

$$Prio(R_1) \leq \ldots \leq Prio(R_n) \tag{2}$$

and

$$\bigcup_{R \in S} E(R) = Z. \tag{3}$$

We call $Prio(R)$ *the **priority** of* $R \in S$.

The execution of a script generates a candidate solution (action) based on the current game state and script. Rules that are part of the script are traversed according to their order until the first fulfilled rule is reached. This rule determines the action that is returned by the script. Equation 3 assures that every game state is part of at least one rule's fulfilling set and, therefore, the script's execution will always yield a valid result.

According to inequality 2, rules in a script are sorted by priority in ascending order. Therefore rules with low priority determine the script's result before rules with high priority. The order of rules with equal priority is not prescribed and can be decided by the learning algorithm itself. For further information on this topic, please see section 3.3.

3.2   Rulebase Design

The design of a good rulebase is a long and iterative process in many cases and it depends highly on the specific use case. For this reason, concepts that we have learned during the development of our rulebase may not hold true for other scenarios. Nevertheless, we want to give the interested reader a brief overview of our rulebase and the underlying principles.

We designed 28 rules and priorities based on expert knowledge (see appendix A). Rules with low priority are mostly counter-strategies, which are fulfilled in very few and specific situations to avoid them from dominating the script's results. Their early position in the script assures that every chance for a counterattack is taken. Many offensive rules share priority -1. Thus the learning method can independently decide which of these attacks is most effective on a specific enemy. Near the end of the script there are rules that handle situations in which their predecessors have failed. They buy time for the agent to change its strategy. To accomplish this the enemy is avoided and held at distance.

Two rules, a default rule called *PSlideDefault* and a very essential defensive rule called *MFBCtr*, are added to the script manually without taking the learning method into consideration. This kind of interference should only take place very rarely as it reduces much of the algorithms' degree of freedom. It can be an effective option in limited cases, though. The default rule receives the highest possible priority to assure that it only takes action if no other rule is fulfilled. Its job is to assure that the agent is able to decide on an action in any possible situation.

Some of the developed rules are able to perform loops of actions that, if successful, dominate and damage the opponent very effectively. We observed that in some situations these loops were canceled too soon even though they performed really well. To improve our agent's performance we decided to implement a mechanism that informs other rules on successfully running loops. The other rules will take this information into account when deciding whether they are fulfilled or not.

The quality of the agent depends highly on the script's maximum length which is set to 20 within this work. On one hand, if the limit is chosen too low the generated scripts do not reach the needed complexity to produce decent behavior. On the other hand, if scripts grow too long the agent's behavior will be dominated by rules with low priority because rules at the end of the script might never be reached. A good length depends very much on the specific game and rulebase design. 27 of the 28 developed rules are added to the rulebase exactly once. The remaining rule is an empty rule and it is added to the rulebase 17 times. This allows the learning method to vary the script's effective length between 3 and 20 rules. The rulebase contains an overall number of $27 + 17 = 44$ rules.

3.3   Learning Method

To generate scripts in real-time we need a learning method that is able to handle dynamic objective functions and to learn without examples. Furthermore, the method should be able to handle the delayed response and stochastic state changes of the game. The problem's nature allows for a very straightforward reinforcement learning algorithm that fulfills all of the mentioned constraints. The players' points and their gradients are closely connected to the agent's performance. This significantly simplifies the search for a decent evaluation function. Furthermore, reinforcement learning uses parameters that are readable and understandable for humans. Due to the presented advantages we choose reinforcement learning as the base for our learning method. Moreover, our choice allows us to benefit from the theory and results of Spronck et al. as they have also used reinforcement learning for script generation. Nevertheless, other learning methods could be considered in future research as well.

In fighting games it is advantageous to evaluate sequences of time steps rather than just single actions. This strongly reduces the impact of random noise and smooths the evaluation function. Furthermore it allows the learning method to rate the overall script's performance rather than just the value of single actions on their own.

Definition 4. *The evaluation function* $\mathcal{F}_{a,b}\colon \mathbb{N} \times \mathbb{N} \mapsto [0,1] \subset \mathbb{R}$ *is given by*

$$\mathcal{F}_{a,b} := \begin{cases} \dfrac{\overline{\mathcal{H}_{ab}}}{\mathcal{H}_{ab} + \overline{\mathcal{H}_{ab}}} & \text{iff } (\mathcal{H}_{ab} + \overline{\mathcal{H}_{ab}}) \neq 0 \\ 0.5 & \text{else} \end{cases}$$

where $\mathcal{H}_{ab}$ *(*$\overline{\mathcal{H}_{ab}}$*) is the damage that the player's (opponent's) character received during the time steps* $a, \ldots, b$.

The strategy for rule selection is controlled by weights $w \in [W_{min}, W_{max}] \subset \mathbb{N}$. Each rule in the rulebase is associated with exactly one weight. The higher a rule's weight, the likelier it will become part of the agent's script. The algorithm used for rule selection draws one rule at a time from the rulebase without replacement. The chance for a rule with weight w to be drawn is approximately w/sum, where sum is the weight of all rules that are not part of the script yet. Once a rule has been drawn, it is inserted into the script according to its priority. Rules that have an equal priority are sorted by weight. The higher a rule's weight, the earlier its position in the script. If the rules' weights are also equal, their order is random.

At the start of each fight every rule receives the same initial weight. Based on the evaluation function a reward is calculated, which the agent aims to maximize by adapting the rules' weights accordingly. In this work the weights are adjusted and a new script is generated every 4 seconds by the learning algorithm. The longer these periods of time are chosen, the longer it takes the agent to adapt to enemy behavior. But if they are chosen too short the agent's decision making will be effected by random noise. Experiments indicated that 4 seconds seem to be a good trade-off in our case.

The reward $\triangle w$ for the time period of evaluation $[a, b]$ is calculated via

$$\triangle w = \begin{cases} -\left\lfloor P_{max} \dfrac{B - \mathcal{F}_{a,b}}{B} \right\rfloor & \text{iff } \mathcal{F}_{a,b} < B \\ \left\lfloor R_{max} \dfrac{\mathcal{F}_{a,b} - B}{B} \right\rfloor & \text{otherwise} \end{cases} \tag{4}$$

where P_{max} and R_{max} are the absolute values of the maximum penalty and reinforcement. B is the value of the evaluation function $\mathcal{F}_{a,b}$ for which the agent is neither punished nor reinforced. The bigger B gets, the harder it becomes for the agent to receive reinforcement and the more frequently it will get punished. For smaller values of B the opposite is the case.

The new weight of rules with weight w that have fired (determined the result of the script) during the time period of evaluation is $w + \triangle w$. Rules that have not fired but been part of the script receive a fifth of the reward and, therefore, the new weight $w + \frac{1}{5}\triangle w$. The weights are clipped to W_{min} or W_{max} if they exit the interval $[W_{min}, W_{max}]$. The factor of $\frac{1}{5}$ is a result of trial and error and could possibly be further optimized. Our first tests were made with a factor of $\frac{1}{2}$ as suggested by Spronck et al. in their paper on dynamic scripting [14]. This value seems to be much too high for frequent weight updates, though. The weights of rules that fire rarely would reflect only the overall script's performance and neglect their individual quality. The much lower value of $\frac{1}{5}$ reduces this effect without ignoring the overall script's performance in our case.

Weights of rules, which are currently not part of the script, are adapted to assure that the the overall sum of weights in the rulebase stays constant. They all receive the same positive or negative adjustment. As a consequence their weights go down if the script generates good results and up if the script performs badly. Therefore, scripts that perform well will not be modified frequently. But as soon as the script's performance drops, even rules with previously very low weight will receive another chance to become part of the script. This is one of the major advantages of dynamic scripting.

In this work we chose $W_{min} = 0$, $W_{max} = 200$, $P_{max} = 80$, $R_{max} = 80$, $B = 0.8$ and the initial weight to be 80. In the following discussion we assume that only one of these values may be varied at the same time while the others remain constant. This assumption is necessary because the parameters influence each other mutually. Because of $W_{min} = 0$ the learning method is allowed to reduce the chances of bad performing rules of being part of the script to zero. As previously explained this does not prevent these rules from regaining weight as soon as the script performs badly. W_{max} controls the agent's variability. Spronck et al. chose the very high value of 2000 for this parameter in their article [14]. This allows the rules' weights to grow effectively unbounded. Thus, the agent's strategy will eventually become very static, once it has adapted to the opponent. In our work W_{max} is set to a much lower value because our agent will have to adapt to non-static enemies as well.

The parameter B is set to the very high value 0.8. As a result neutral and random behavior will not be reinforced and the agent will begin to adapt its behavior long before it starts to perform badly. This enables the agent to switch smoothly from one strategy to another as soon as the requirements change. If the agent does not perform well, the combination of high values for P_{max}, R_{max} and B results in rapid reorganization of the agent's script. This speed is crucial for the generation of counter-strategies in real-time and on the fly. An undesired side effect of the strict reinforcement and punishment is that the learning algorithm may discard good strategies prematurely. Then again, the nature of dynamic scripting will assure that falsely discarded strategies will eventually return if the script performs poorly without them. This process is even accelerated by the short update periods of 4 seconds. Therefore the high value of B does not only discard rules rashly, but it also assures that they get another chance very soon. In consequence, this side effect is not a major downside of our method.

If the rule's initial weights are chosen too low compared to W_{max}, it is likely that a very small number of rules will share all the available weight between them, while the other rules' weights might drop near zero. This would limit the agent's complexity and is, therefore, undesirable. On the other side, if the initial weights are chosen too high compared to W_{max}, this may lead to a lot of rules with high weights. As a consequence, the selection process will become very random. The value of 80 for the initial weights is a compromise between these contrary effects, which works well in practice for our agent.

4   Results and Discussion

In this section we will evaluate our agent's performance in fights against three other agents called *T*, *Mizuno AI* and *Airpunch AI*. To distinguish our agent from the others we name it *Code Monkey (Version 1.1)*. Code Monkey has been tested in 100 fights against each opponent with an overall number of 900 rounds and a running time of approximately 15 hours. The number of repetitions does not influence our agent's performance because it is reinitialized with no prior knowledge about its opponent before every fight. The repetitions' purpose was merely to reduce random noise in our results.

The winner of the FTGAIC 2013 called T is based on a static rulebase. The agent's source code can be accessed on the contest's homepage [4]. T prefers executing slide tackles, but they are also its own greatest weakness. Mizuno AI has already been described in section 2.2. Its ability to adapt to enemy behavior in real-time makes it a highly interesting opponent. Here, Code Monkey needs to adapt its strategy faster than Mizuno AI to succeed. The last opponent used for evaluation is AirPunch AI. This agent has been developed by our team to test Code Monkey's ability to counter air attacks. AirPunch AI jumps up in the air repeatedly to avoid being hit and then it attacks with a punch diagonally towards the ground. The illustrated combination can be repeated rapidly and a hit inflicts a high amount of damage. Because of the framework's simulated delay an enemy that uses this combination is very hard to control. It showed that AirPunch AI performs outstandingly well against most enemies what makes it even more interesting as an opponent for our agent. Airpunch AI is vulnerable to attacks that hit the enemy at a distance and in midair. The most important rule of our agent in this context is called PDiagonalFB.

Figure 3 shows the frequency of usage for Code Monkey's rules during our tests in percent. Firstly, the percentages for each fight had been calculated and then they where arithmetically averaged. For clarity, only frequently used rules are explicitly named in the figures. Percentages of the remaining rules are summed up as *Others*. More than 80% of Code Monkey's behavior against each enemy was determined by the top three to five rules. This is a major specialization since the rulebase contains 44 rules to choose from. It turns out that the rules most frequently used against T and AirPunch AI aim right at their weaknesses (please see figure 3 and the rules explained in appendix A).

Figure 4(a) shows box plots of the results (Code Monkey's points) after every round and fight. At the end of each round both agents split 1000 points between them based on the damage they received. A fight consists of three rounds and is won if the sum of the agent's points exceeds 1500. Code Monkey dominated Mizuno AI and has won

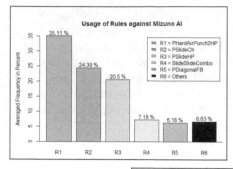
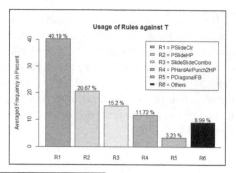

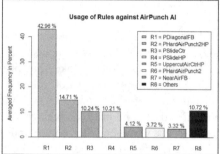

Fig. 3. The rules' averaged frequency of usage during the fights against T, Mizuno AI and Air-Punch AI.

all of the 100 fights. On average, Code Monkey gathered even more points against T and won 99 fights (one loss). It is fair to say that T, although being the winner of the 2013 competition, is no match against Code Monkey. The picture is not that clear in the comparison with AirPunch AI: Code Monkey was able to win 75% of the fights but lost the other 25% (no draws). A Wilcoxon signed-rank test with continuity correction confirms that the results are statistically significant: When testing with the null hypothesis that the true median of Code Monkey's points is 1500 and the alternative that the true median is greater, we get a p-value of 1.109×10^{-9}. Furthermore the true median is greater than 1749.5 at a confidence level of 99%. It is, therefore, save to say that Code Monkey is indeed better than AirPunch AI.

When measuring the speed of adaption, it comes down to the question: When do we know that Code Monkey successfully adapted to an enemy? We chose to compare the agent's points after every update period (4 seconds) with the points before this period. If our agent's point value has fallen, this means it received more damage than its opponent and, thus, it is likely that Code Monkey still has not adapted to the enemy well. Moreover, the use of time periods for evaluation minimizes the influence of random noise on the calculated trend.

Figure 4(b) shows the maximum number of update cycles Code Monkey needed to adapt to its enemy for each fight. We used a Wilcoxon signed-rank test with continuity correction to check if the results are statistically significant: When testing with the null hypothesis that the true median of the required update cycles per fight to adapt to

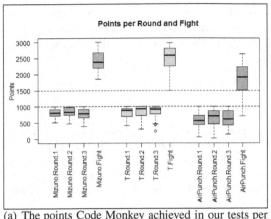

(a) The points Code Monkey achieved in our tests per round and fight.

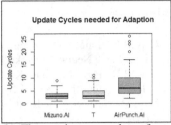

(b) The maximum number of update cycles Code Monkey needed to adapt to its enemy per fight.

Fig. 4. Achieved points and speed of adaption.

Mizuno AI, T and AirPunch AI is 3.5, 4.5 and 9 and the alternative that the true median is smaller, we get p-values of 4.935×10^{-5}, 2.745×10^{-5} and 7.165×10^{-5}. Furthermore at a confidence level of 99% the true median of the times required to adapt to Mizuno AI, T and AirPunch AI is smaller than 12, 16 and 32 seconds.

These are great results as they imply that Code Monkey is able to adapt rapidly, even to strategies that change in real-time themselves. On average it took Code Monkey twice the time to adapt to AirPunch AI and there were some outliers with even much longer times. Nevertheless, in many cases Code Monkey adapted to AirPunch AI very fast or at least fast enough to win the fight.

5 Conclusions

We presented an enhanced version of dynamic scripting and applied it to an agent for fighting games. Our agent called Code Monkey (Version 1.1) outperformed its opponents in our tests and won the CIG Fighting Game AI Competition 2014. Furthermore, our tests have shown that Code Monkey is able to adapt to static and dynamic strategies in real-time and on the fly in less than 12 to 32 seconds on average. The learning method proved to be very resistant to random noise and capable of handling stochastic state changes. In most cases the agent turned out to be reliable, even though there were a few outliers in our tests. Detailed results of the competition and Code Monkey's commented source code (including the rulebase) can be downloaded from the competition's homepage [4]. Therefore, our results can easily be replicated.

There are many promising opportunities for future work. Some examples, like the automatic ordering or generation of rules, have already been mentioned in section 2.2. Changes to the evaluation function could shift the agent's primary goal from wining to, for example, entertaining the player or behaving like a human player. In any case, there is a lot of room for creativity on this topic. In our opinion, the approach presented in this article is very relevant for practical game development. Due to the method's close relation to scripting, game developers can reuse their existing scripts and experience and still greatly increase their AI's value.

References

1. Cho, B.H., Jung, S.H., Seong, Y.R., Oh, H.R.: Exploiting Intelligence in Fighting Action Games Using Neural Networks. IEICE - Trans. Inf. Syst. E89-D(3), 1249–1256 (2006)
2. Cho, B.H., Park, C., Yang, K.: Comparison of AI Techniques for Fighting Action Games - Genetic Algorithms/Neural Networks/Evolutionary Neural Networks. In: Ma, L., Rauterberg, M., Nakatsu, R. (eds.) ICEC 2007. LNCS, vol. 4740, pp. 55–65. Springer, Heidelberg (2007)
3. Cho, B., Jung, S., Shim, K.-H., Seong, Y., Oh, H.: Reinforcement Learning of Intelligent Characters in Fighting Action Games. In: Harper, R., Rauterberg, M., Combetto, M. (eds.) ICEC 2006. LNCS, vol. 4161, pp. 310–313. Springer, Heidelberg (2006)
4. Fighting Game Artificial Intelligence Competition (2015). http://www.ice.ci.ritsumei.ac.jp/~ftgaic (accessed: February 02, 2015)
5. Graepel, T., Herbrich, R., Gold, J.: Learning to fight. In: Proceedings of the International Conference on Computer Games: Artificial Intelligence, Design and Education, pp. 193–200 (2004)
6. IEEE Conference on Computational Intelligence and Games (2014). http://www.cig2014.de (accessed: February 02, 2015)
7. Lu, F., Yamamoto, K., Nomura, L., Mizuno, S., Lee, Y., Thawonmas, R.: Fighting game artificial intelligence competition platform. In: 2013 IEEE 2nd Global Conference on Consumer Electronics (GCCE), pp. 320–323 (October 2013)
8. Lueangrueangroj, S., Kotrajaras, V.: Real-time imitation based learning for commercial fighting games. In: 2nd Annual International Conference on Computer Games, Multimedia and Allied Technology (CGAT), pp. 1–3 (2009)
9. Osaka, S., Thawonmas, R., Shibazaki, T.: Investigation of Various Online Adaptation Methods of Computer-Game AI Rulebase in Dynamic Scripting. In: Proceedings of the 1st International Conference on Digital Interactive Media Entertainment and Arts (DIME-ARTS 2006) (October 2006)
10. Park, H., Kim, K.J.: Learning to play fighting game using massive play data. In: 2014 IEEE Conference on Computational Intelligence and Games (CIG), pp. 1–2 (August 2014)
11. Ponsen, M., Spronck, P., Muñoz Avila, H., Aha, D.W.: Knowledge Acquisition for Adaptive Game AI. Sci. Comput. Program. 67(1), 59–75 (2007)
12. Ricciardi, A., Thill, P.: Adaptive AI for fighting games (December 2008). http://cs229.stanford.edu/proj2008/RicciardiThill-AdaptiveAIForFightingGames.pdf (accessed: February 02, 2015)
13. Saini, S., Dawson, C., Chung, P.: Mimicking player strategies in fighting games. In: 2011 IEEE International Games Innovation Conference (IGIC), pp. 44–47 (November 2011)
14. Spronck, P., Ponsen, M., Sprinkhuizen-Kuyper, I., Postma, E.: Adaptive game AI with dynamic scripting. Machine Learning 63(3), 217–248 (2006)
15. Szita, I., Ponsen, M., Spronck, P.: Effective and Diverse Adaptive Game AI. IEEE Transactions on Computational Intelligence and AI in Games 1(1), 16–27 (2009)
16. Thawonmas, R., Osaka, S.: A Method for Online Adaptation of Computer-game AI Rulebase. In: Proceedings of the 2006 ACM SIGCHI International Conference on Advances in Computer Entertainment Technology. ACM (2006)

17. Thunputtarakul, W., Kotrajaras, V.: Data Analysis for Ghost AI Creation in Commercial Fighting Games. In: GAMEON, pp. 37–41 (2007)
18. Timuri, T., Spronck, P., van den Herik, H.J.: Automatic Rule Ordering for Dynamic Scripting. In: 2007 AAAI Conference on Artificial Intelligence and Interactive Digital Entertainment (AIIDE), pp. 49–54 (2007)
19. Yamamoto, K., Mizuno, S., Chu, C.Y., Thawonmas, R.: Deduction of fighting-game countermeasures using the k-nearest neighbor algorithm and a game simulator. In: 2014 IEEE Conference on Computational Intelligence and Games (CIG), pp. 1–5 (August 2014)

A   Appendix

Table 1. Names, priorities and short descriptions of the rules that control our agent.

Rule	Prio	Description
MFBCtr	−10	Counters strong enemy projectiles (megafireballs).
MFBTimeExtLow	−6	Throws strong projectile (megafireball) if time is very low.
MFBEnemyDownHP	−5	Throws strong projectile if enemy is on the ground.
MFBTimeLow	−5	Throws strong projectile if energy is high and time is low.
ShortSlideCtr	−3	Counter for too short enemy slide tackle.
UppercutAirCtrHP	−3	UppercutAirCtr with higher priority.
ShortAttackCtr	−2	Counter for too short enemy attacks.
SlideCtr	−2	Jump over enemy slide tackle and counterattack from behind.
KneeAirCtrHP	−2	KneeAirCtr with higher priority.
DistanceAirFB	−1	Attack from distance using a projectile if enemy is in the air.
NearAirFB	−1	Projectile from near range if enemy is in the air.
FBCtr	−1	Counter for enemy projectiles.
PSlideHP	−1	Executes a slide tackle if possible.
SlideSlideCombo	−1	Combination of multiple slide tackles.
PSlideCtr	−1	Uses SlideCtr to attack the enemies back.
PHardAirPunch2HP	−1	PHardAirPunch2 with high priority.
PDiagonalFB	−1	Executes an uppercut and throws projectiles at the enemy if possible.
WrongDirectionCtr	0	Attack from behind if enemy is facing the wrong direction.
AirSlide	1	Attack with a punch in midair if the enemy is near.
UppercutAirCtr	1	Counters air attacks with an uppercut.
KneeAirCtr	2	Counters air attacks with a knee strike.
PHardAirPunch2	2	Jump and then a punch (type 1) in midair (if possible).
DistanceFB	3	Attacks the enemy from distance using a projectile.
FleeJump	3	Avoids the enemy by jumping away.
Uppercut	3	Executes an uppercut when the enemy is near.
PHardAirPunch	9	Jump and then a punch (type 2) in midair (if possible).
EmptyRule	20	Rule with an empty fulfilling set.
PSlideDefault	100	Executes a slide tackle if possible (default rule).

Applied Games – In Search of a New Definition

Ralf Schmidt[1], Katharina Emmerich[1], and Burkhard Schmidt[2]

[1] Entertainment Computing Group, University of Duisburg-Essen, Germany
{ralf.schmidt,katharina.emmerich}@uni-due.de
[2] Medical Faculty Mannheim, Heidelberg University, Germany
burkhard.schmidt@medma.uni-heidelberg.de

Abstract. The endeavour of transferring attributes and qualities of games and game experiences to users and contexts apart from entertainment values spanned a wide field of research over the years, along with a diversity of classifications and definitions. While respecting their uses, we argue that this diversity might also hinder cross-disciplinary research efforts on fundamental questions and cooperation with practitioners. Moreover, with the postulated development towards a ludification of culture under way, it may become more difficult and less important to distinct examples among these definitions in future.

Hence, we propose rethinking existing definitions and suggest the term of applied games as a starting point for a discussion about a more holistic and contemporary term and future common ground. This paper provides definitions of the artefact applied game and the process applied game design as well as suggestions on a classification of purposes and some research questions.

Keywords: Applied Games, Serious Games, Game Based Learning, Gamification, Game Thinking, Definition, Game Design.

1 Introduction

Games spread. Driven by technological advances and sociological acceptance, games become increasingly ubiquitous and social. The economic success and unique experiences well-designed games are able to create, is accompanied by a rising interest of utilizing these qualities for purposes other than entertainment. The term *serious games* emerged in the 70s [1] and marked the beginning of an ongoing endeavour of researchers and practitioners alike, that has led to a wide range of genres and classifications to date. As such, games and game-inspired designs, as well as the development of a game-literacy, may well play a part in understanding, engaging and solving issues of a increasingly complex future world [2]. Consequently, more people with multiple backgrounds will design game-like experiences in broader contexts, pursuing new goals, and thereby contribute to the discussion on ludification and the pervasiveness of games [3].

Being aware of similar problems in genre classifications of entertainment games [4] and in line with others [5], we argue that the range of definitions and terms we see today may be contra productive towards this development. Therefore, we suggest a

© IFIP International Federation for Information Processing 2015
K. Chorianopoulos et al. (Eds.): ICEC 2015, LNCS 9353, pp. 100–111, 2015.
DOI: 10.1007/978-3-319-24589-8_8

more holistic and contemporary. As a starting point for the discussion, this paper offers a definition of the *artefact* 'applied game' and the corresponding *process* 'applied game design', along with a high-level *classification* of purposes today's applications usually address. Applied games are defined as an *implementation of a subject, inspired by and designed along a context- and user-centric transfer of design concepts and qualities from the game world.*

After briefly reviewing the most common terms used in the field, this paper presents arguments of their usage and limitations in the academic world and practice, followed by a detailed explanation of the suggested definitions.

2   Related Definitions

The binding power and numerous forms of excitement that players experience when playing games as well as their economic success have been inspiring researchers and practitioners alike to utilize games for decades. Subsequently, many terms were coined over the years alongside a progressing ubiquity and rising acceptance of games in the research community and public.

Entertainment-Education and *Edutainment* were popular trends in the 90s and early 2000s. Educational contents and game play were only roughly interweaved. Despite a certain fun factor, these products often left players with a somewhat artificial feeling about their usefulness [6].

With a strong focus on learning and training, *serious games* is probably the most popular term nowadays. Defined in the 1970s by Abt as games which "have an explicit and carefully thought out educational purpose and are not intended primarily for amusement" (p.9) [1], serious games developed a plethora of genres over the years. Purposes common to these genres are learning and training [7]. Ritterfeld further developed the term to "any form of interactive computer-based game software for one or multiple players to be used on any platform and that has been developed with the intention to be more than entertainment" (p.6) [8]. Serious games usually fit formal game definitions, in contrast to e.g. Gamification [9]. As an annotation, another interesting part of Abt's book is seldom referenced: He proposes games as some specific way of looking at something, both in a rational/analytic and emotional/dramatic way, which may be interpreted as an early idea of game thinking, today.

Game based learning (GBL) or rather its digital equivalent DGBL is strongly connected to Prensky's broad notion of using games to design engaging and contemporary (e-)learning environments for the games generation [10]. While sharing the focus on learning with serious games, DGBLs are not necessarily full-fledged games. However, the concepts are close enough to be used interchangeably in publications. Less frequent terms sharing the strong focus on learning are *educational games, game enhanced learning* or the slightly different notion of games as *educational technology*.

Games with a purpose (GWAP) define games players use collaboratively to perform tasks computers cannot perform or not effectively perform [11]. More commonly known as 'citizen science' projects nowadays GWAP became quite popular over the years for projects with high social acceptance [e.g. 12, 13].

Gamification or rather *gameful design*, formally defined in 2011 by Deterding et al. [9], is the use of game design elements in non-game contexts. The term gamification is very popular and almost used inflationary in both academia and practice nowadays. Freyermuth and others criticise the constringent use in practice, mostly adapting 'simple' game elements to persuade or primarily target user engagement [14, 15]. However, the idea's popularity promotes a discussion about the "pervasiveness of gaming in everyday life" (p.10) [17].

Apart from the definitions above, many authors highlight the general capabilities and overall positive features of games. For example Gee explores the properties of digital games with a strong focus on learning. His numerous contributions on the topic include the description of *learning principles* [18] and the *Situated Learning Matrix* [19]. Bogost discusses the general expressive power of video games, apart from instrumental goals (i.e. serious games). He suggests that video games offer a new form of *procedural rhetoric*, describing a process of interaction by which the contents of the game are transported to the player, possibly leading to a change of attitudes and beliefs [20]. According to Schell, games are transformative, consequently suggesting the term *transformative games* for a class of 'helpful games', which primarily focus on changing the player. He stresses that "educational games are one kind of helpful games" (p.507) [21] and disagrees with the notion of seriousness as games are "meaningfully helpful" in many ways, and fun to play at the same time.

On a broader scale, all of these definitions share a common idea: the application of games (i.e. game design concepts, -elements, -attributes, -techniques) to fulfil certain goals (e.g. learning, mindset and behaviour change), whether in parts or as an actual game, within other or non-game contexts. Consequently, the term *applied game* is not new, but conceptualized differently in academia and practice. For example, the Center for Applied Games [22] proposes the use of game principles for behavioural change. The region of Utrecht (NL) launched a network site for applied game design, using it as an umbrella-term for serious games, exergames, etc. [23]. The MIT Game Lab hosted a panel on applied game research in 2012 [24] and the term defines research fields of the Zurich University of Arts [25] and the Department of Arts of Danube University of Krems [26]. Along with a Microsoft Research Group on the topic [27] and a definition by Kim [28], these developments call for a discussion about a thorough academic definition of the term.

3   Relevance and Limitations of Current Definitions

The technological developments, growing sociological acceptance of games and interest of multiple disciplines drive the development of new and innovative game concepts in everyday life. Established and well-accepted definitions allow the classification of the majority of these examples, usually along their *design specification* (e.g. serious game) and/or *target* (e.g. health game). Despite relatively broad definitions, a rising number of these examples does seem to blur between the definitions. Likewise the entertainment games business, this might drive the development of ever new terms and genre combinations to fit an example. For example, the mobile application "Zombies, Run!" [29] is often used as an example for Gamification. It applies game elements like a story, a level-like session structure and collectable items for engaging a sporting activity, that is a non-gaming context. Yet, it is also a complete game: All activities and challenges are embedded in a consistent metaphoric game world with fixed rules and variable outcome depending on interactions and resources of the users. If its purpose is understood primarily as supporting the player's healthy behaviour, it is also a serious pervasive game.

From an academic point of view, having multiple and distinct definitions is useful and important. Results and conclusions from research work are assigned to specific classifications to strengthen their value, relate to other work in the field and define limitations of transferability. Insight derived from the evaluation of a certain game is supposed to be valid for comparable applications but usually not generalizable. The same applies to comprehensive attempts to establish design methods, tools and evaluation procedures, e.g. [4, 30–32]. On the other hand, because there is room for interpretation and uncertainty which definitions suit one's work at best, inconsistent or ambiguous use of terms and classifications is increasingly common in publications, eventually leading to a fragmentation of the field [5]. With emerging cross-disciplinary research fields (e.g. game psychology) and a rising interest of disciplines in the application fields (e.g. business economics), this practice might grow into a problem. Without a discussion about a new common ground, as proposed here, it will become increasingly difficult to find and relate results to one's own work.

In addition, while the clear use of more established definitions for *specific* questions helps to advance the field, it might also hinder the work on general ones across the field. For example, a rising number of researchers of multiple disciplines (game design, psychology, social sciences,…) tried to shed some light onto the *black box* of emergent gameplay and resulting effects on players by focussing on the player's experience and the context rather than on mere design aspects [33]. The call is out for a general discussion on appropriate research methods and insights on the effects of certain game elements and the more targeted design for specific purposes of game-like applications [34]. The same applies for more varied empirical methods and results on *outcomes and purposes* of game approaches among their players and the difficulties to conduct such studies within specific contexts [4, 5, 35].

Regarding design considerations, having many definitions might additionally hinder innovative designs on a psychological level. Discussions of a currently designed prototype will take place in the light of the initially chosen classification, thereby possibly influencing the design process and limiting consideration of alternatives and innovations. The same counts for established ideas, methods and tools, although other methods (e.g. used in related, differently defined game contexts) might be more suitable, but not found due to a challenging selection of search terms among the high numbers of publications.

While relevant for academic goals, the discussion is also important for the commonly frequent cooperation with practitioners. The objectives of industrial partners and researchers often differ for natural reasons. While researchers are mostly interested in empirical fundamental work and the transfer of results, industry is mostly interested in outcome supporting the organizational goals. To our own manifold experiences, definitions relevant to researchers are of nearly no relevance for non-researching practitioners as they are complex to relate to for non-experts. Therefore, researchers often experience difficulties arguing for the main ideas and differences of definitions. The same counts for cooperation with more 'hands-on disciplines', such as the design studies and arts. Consequently, the proposed term applied games already is used within this disciplines and organizational contexts [22–27], calling for the discussion about a clear academic definition to build the basis for a common ground among researchers and research an practice alike.

When including the perspective of the user, clear differentiations get even more complicated because of individual interpretations of the experience such as the notion of the seriousness of play [20, 36, 37]. For instance, for some users "Zombies, Run!" might indeed reinforce walking and running activities. Others like the additional entertaining value to an already established habit and again others actually experience a game. Training simulations can be experienced as games in the same manner [37]. A stronger focus on the pursued and perceived outcome of a game approach could be a more natural way for a classification.

With the rising ubiquity and pervasiveness of technical platforms and hence game applications in various forms, a new discourse on games and play in society is under way [3]. The discussion about a more comprehensive term must reflect this development and take the advantages and disadvantages described here into account. With *applied games* and its corresponding terms, this paper argues for a definition that manages to bridge gaps between multiple disciplines of researchers and practitioners. It builds on what is central to most definitions, spanning a wide design space but also a stronger, user-centric focus on the purpose of an application instead on appearance and aspects of game design.

4   Applied Games

The following chapter first defines the *process* of applied game design followed by the corresponding *artefact* applied game and a suggestion on a *classification* of potential purposes in clear contrast to genres.

4.1   Applied Game Design Definition

Applied Game Design is the user-centric transfer and implementation of design concepts from the game world, in order to confer their individual, social and procedural qualities to a subject of interest, within its situated context, in order to pursue a defined goal.

Transfer. The transfer consists of two phases. A creativity process, which is characterized by an open mode thinking [38] and a gameful attitude. That is, one tries to understand a situation and users by thinking about it as if it was a game rather than what it actually is and about players rather than users or stakeholders. This gameful attitude, some may call 'game thinking', combined with a deep understanding of what games are, does help to come to creative and innovative ideas [39]. Or as game designer Eric Zimmerman put it: "(…) playful, innovative, trans-disciplinary thinking in which systems can be analysed, redesigned, and transformed into something new" [2]. The ultimate goal of this first phase is to develop *strategic design goals* and *functions*.

Consequently, the second phase is about *operationalizing the goals* on the actual context, with the user's needs and goals in mind, developing the *form*. During the closed mode [38], ideas and design goals are consolidated, prototyped, tested and rethought – constituting an actual design process. Applied game solutions usually inspire or contain affordances users interact with, the design of content, and a seamless and coherent integration to the environment and adjoining processes.

If learning or training is a primary goal of an applied game solution, its supportive character to acquire and apply the learning goals in practice constitutes a *third level of transfer* on the user's side. As a common goal to serious games, game-based learning and training simulations, applied game designs inherit all relevant research questions connected to the design and evaluation of such applications and the players transfer of knowledge the into the real world.

In contrast to the definition of serious games [1, 7, 8] and gameful design [9], applied game design does not differentiate partly or full-bodied implementations of game concepts but would incorporate both forms. They are not limited to their spatial representation but incorporate both the ubiquity of technology and space in terms of pervasiveness as well as the mixtures of digital and non-digital components. The ultimate challenge is to create an innovative applied game concept that fits both users and context and contributes to the defined strategic design goals.

Concepts. Manifold as the disciplines constituting a game in the entertainment world are the sources of innovative design of applied games. Three categories derived from games help to structure thinking during the transfer processes and formulate questions about the design approaches and goals.

Formal Concepts. Formal concepts support understanding the structure and dynamics of games. Fullerton's model describes the most important parts games consist of as well as their purposes [40]. Inspired by the model, one could ask about the rules or procedures of a business application, as an easy example and source for inspiration to redesign it. The MDA Framework helps to explore the relationships of designed mechanics (M), emergent dynamics (D) and aesthetics (A) [41]. Interaction-Feedback loops are a quite worthwhile model by Dan Cook [42]. Its core idea is an atomic view on chains of interrelated affordances, interactions and feedback that alters the player's mental model of a game mechanic and constitutes a learning process. Cook's ideas correspond with Koster's [43] theory of fun and Klimmt's considerations of multi-level I/O loops, as explanations of entertaining qualities of games [44].

Game Design Concepts. Concepts of game design form the largest category. A deep understanding of games, their mechanics and emergent qualities of game play as well as psychological backgrounds of people and subject is a precondition for a successful transfer. It is therefore one common and eligible critic to gamification that most examples only use quite shallow, behavioural implementations of most common feedback mechanics [14, 15], lacking more complex concepts that render games deep and lasting experiences. However, rethinking simple feedback mechanics of a subject alone often makes a huge difference and is a common demand in the field of usability and user experience, too. Other examples of more complex concepts likely to inspire ideas are the design of challenges and meaningful choices [20, 21] or for curiosity [45]. Some major difference of these is the focus on the experience and volitional qualities, compared to the mere goal orientation as a common focus.

Depending on the subject of applied game designs, other design disciplines are worth a look: for example, graphical styles and audio-visual representations of games, the integration of story and story elements in games, the design of game interfaces and tutorials. The major challenge is to choose the most suitable concepts and think about options to transfer the core ideas and core experiences to the subject addressed within the applied game design. One of the many research questions included in this endeavour is that about the temporal effects of the resulting design within its context. Which mechanics and elements foster a long-term motivation, which wear off quickly - and is this a bad thing at all? To continue on the example of a training simulation in business contexts, it might be all right or even desired that the applied games experience wears of when its contents are learned.

Technical Concepts. The use of technical concepts and solutions supplements the idea and greatly supports the transfer and implementation, but is not a primary focus for creativity. A solid understanding of game architecture and the ability of using game technology, game specific algorithms and technical solutions to collect game metrics and interaction technology is an important part of a comprehensive game literacy [2].

Qualities. The term qualities refers to different experiences attributed to games as well as design concepts to structure and uphold those in support of the design goals. *Individual perceived qualities* often attributed to games are feelings of self-efficacy and tension [42], curiosity [45], mastery and fun [43] and intrinsic motivation [46]. The idea here is not only rendering a subject more attractive and rewarding, but more meaningful. *Social qualities* would be those connected to team building and team playing. Equally important to real life contexts is the cause and effect of applied games to foster social intercommunication about the subject. *Procedural qualities* are ideas derived and transferred from structural and dramatic elements of games [40] and interaction-feedback loops [42, 44]. Examples are dividing a subject into levels, interweaving with a story, character design and development and the building of skill chains. These and other elements help designers to create *simulated experiences* [44] and guidance for structured, comprehensible and joyful experiences.

Subject. The subject of an applied game design defines the actual medium as well as the social, spatial and temporal design space. The simplest form of a subject would be a *single artefact*, such as a room or a display. The second category would be any form of *application*, some business software, mobile application or else, including its situated context (see below). The third category would be any form of a wider scale *process* (spatially, timely), such a strategic or operational business process, learning of a subject or pursuing a specific fitness goal. This consequently involves a much broacher design scope.

Situated Context. The more ambiguous the design goals are the more specific information and individualization in terms of person and context is advantageous. In their introduction, Moseley and Whitton correctly emphasized the purposes of games with respect to specifications of a context in contrast to "universal truths" such as games are good for motivation [47]. The interaction of a person with the environment is certainly not new to the idea of applied games. Depended on the subject, other disciplines such as Human Computer Interaction and Organizational Psychology, discovered a plethora of theories and methods to research, analyse and design for complex contexts.

Context can be structured into three spheres, typically with a declining design scope: The options and varieties of interaction with the *subject* (spatial, temporal, social) (1), its *interrelations* with other subjects and processes on a greater scale (2) as well as the social and organizational *environment* (3) (e.g organizational structure). The latter has great influence on the users within a context and therefore the design on a broader scale [16] and vice versa.

Purpose. Purposes are the strategic goals, defined for an applied game. They often consist of multiple, often diverse perspectives, such as design goals and user goals/needs that need to be respected. Purposes and their classifications are discussed in detail in section 4.3.

4.2   Applied Game

Applied games are the result of an applied game design process. They are an *implementation of a subject, inspired by and designed along a context- and user-centric transfer of design concepts and qualities from the game world.* Applied games consist of multimedia, digital and/or non-digital artefacts that constitute an individual and/or social experience for their respective users.

Quality of Applied Games. The quality of an applied game can be assessed on three distinctions. First, regarding the interpretation of the quantifiable and observable results of an interaction process, according to a defined goal, such as the interpretation of increased user activity. While it may be relatively easy to produce impressive numbers of increased overall activity, differences in quality of a specific interaction are often harder to identify. Second, the quality of support for explicit or implicit, individual user goals within the subject has to be considered. Does a health app really result in an expected behaviour change and consequently better health results? Does a social network help users to spread their network and connect emotionally to others? Third, the question is to what extend does the applied game meet its goals over time. For example, if the goal of an applied game application is to learn about some process its end point is reached when a user has internalized the process. Increased user activity on a social intranet platform on the contrary is a long-term goal that might need different design approaches and timely updates. It is crucial to include a time-perspective when setting goals and constraints of an application.

Evaluating the quality of applied games inherits the core challenges researchers and designers of serious games, game-based learning and gamification have faced for years. From a methodical viewpoint, experiences and tools about how to measure effects are rare and, because of complexity and dynamic effects of play, often difficult to measure and relate to aspects of an applied game intervention. Some criticize effect studies that may not advance the deeper knowledge about why the effects occur [34] or are not quite methodologically comparable. Consequently, Connolly and colleagues criticize the ratio of speculation about the use of games compared to actual evidence in their meta-study as well as methodological groundings [4]. Availability of resources in terms of time, money and contextual specialities, such as difficulty of sample size [35] additionally render evaluation difficult.

4.3   Classification of Purposes

Application fields [7] and genre taxonomies dominate the current practice of classifying entertainment games or applied forms of games. Both seem not suitable for the field of applied games for two reasons. First, neither the research community nor the entertainment industry did develop a commonly accepted taxonomy to date [4]. Second, according to the definition of applied games and applied game design proposed here, a *defined purpose* is more important than a classification of application fields or along its *actual design solution*. Moreover, the latter highly depends on the context, user and design group actually involved in the subject. Especially the user perspective is of high importance. It should correspond with the needs and provide usefulness to be successful and might contradict to other stakeholder's goals [32].

Conolly et al. propose a useful classification for serious games that follows a comparable approach [4]. As a subject to discussion, they introduce a refined version of their framework of learning outcomes consisting of (a) knowledge acquisition, (b) skill acquisition, (c) affective, motivational and physiological outcomes and (d) behaviour change outcomes [4]. Based on their previous work and results from expert meetings, this paper proposes a list of *strategic purposes* common to applied games to be operationalized on the context as mentioned before.

1. Attention: The design for getting, guiding and keeping attention towards a subject as well as raising awareness.
2. Motivation: The arousal or support of individual needs and motives. Designers should strive for volitional support and the design of a journey instead of a mere goal orientation wherever possible.
3. Knowledge or skill acquisition: The focus on or support for acquisition and training of knowledge, skills and behaviours by designing for meaningful experiences on the cognitive, emotional and physical level. Certainly the primary class of applied games, likewise its predecessors.
4. Process support: The aim to help users structure, restructure, facilitate or execute processes or goals. The means of this category is an actual support for planning, execution and monitoring (e.g. feedback) instead of a mere breakdown of a task into levels.
5. Joy/Playfulness: The purpose to create a subject more joyful and/or provide a playground and affordances to trigger a playful behaviour.
6. Information: The attractive and digestible presentation of information.

The list is non-exclusive and applied games will typically implement more than one purpose. Furthermore, the social context is an important complexity in design and reception of an applied game and as such part of the experience instead of a class in its own right. For example, the onboarding of social intranet users will need to get their attention and constitute options of knowledge acquisition to show users how and why the new tool is useful compared to current ones.

5   Conclusion and Outlook

This paper argues for a new academic definition in the field of game applications. With a stronger focus on what is central to related definitions and on process and purposes, the term applied game is a statement towards a common ground among academics and practitioners alike, and as such contributes to a broader discussion. In the light of a growing diversity and ubiquity of innovative examples and application fields, the current range of academic definitions and classifications does not fully support advances in the field for the several reasons discussed. Among them, an inconsistent use due to room for interpretation, relevance in practice, influence on creativity and the spreading of work on more general research questions. While respecting the uses of established definitions, e.g. for specific research questions and methods, the proposed definitions in this paper address these issues. Applied games focus on the transfer of broader qualities of games. They are classified by the definition and operationalization of strategic purposes along a user-centric applied game design process. Consequently, the goal and grand challenge of any applied game design would be to convey a meaningful best-fit combination and transfer of these qualities to the subject at hand, with respect to its users, situated context, and in pursue of the defined design goals. Along with discussions on the definitions and classification, this paper encourages cross-disciplinary researchers and practitioners alike to develop and further intensify work on a pool of research questions central to all applied game projects. Complex subjects, such as the relationships of a design to emergent gameplay and effects on the player, diverse and effective ways of evaluating the purposes in different contexts, and the design of more varied and deeper forms of experiences are long-term challenges. At last, the term applied game might constitute a common ground for an unbiased discussion of the various forms we may encounter game applications in our future everyday life. By the suggestions given in this paper, the authors hope to promote a lively and joint discussion to advance the field.

Acknowledgements. We thank C. Brosius (Die Hobrechts), S. Hoos (Useeds°), S. Scheja and P. Sykovnik (University of Duisburg-Essen) and many others for discussing and reflecting our thoughts with us. Your comments really helped to advance the subject. We also thank the German Federal Ministry of Economic Affairs and Energy (BMWi) for supporting this research.

References

1. Abt, C.C.: Serious Games. Viking, New York (1975)
2. Zimmerman, E.: Manifesto for a Ludic Century. In: Walz, S.P., Deterding, S. (eds.) The Gameful World Approaches, Issues, Applications, pp. 19–23. MIT Press, Cambridge (2014)
3. Walz, S.P., Deterding, S.: An Introduction to the Gameful World. In: Walz, S.P., Deterding, S. (eds.) The Gameful World Approaches, Issues, Applications, pp. 1–13. MIT Press, Cambridge (2014)
4. Connolly, T.M., Boyle, E.A., MacArthur, E., Hainey, T., Boyle, J.M.: A systematic literature review of empirical evidence on computer games and serious games. Computers & Education 59, 661–686 (2012)
5. Stokes, B., Walden, N., O'Shea, G., Nasso, F., Mariutto, G., Burak, A.: Impact with Games: A Fragmented Field. ETC Press under CC License. http://gameimpact.net/reports/fragmented-field/
6. Susi, T., Johannesson, M., Backlund, P.: Serious Games - An Overview. HS-IKI-TR-07-001. University of Skövde. Technical Report (2007)
7. Michael, D., Chen, S.: Serious games. Games that educate, train, and inform. Thompson Course Technology, Boston, MA (2006)
8. Ritterfeld, U.: Serious games. Mechanisms and effects. Routledge, New York (2009)
9. Deterding, S., Dixon, D.: From Game Design Elements to Gameful-ness. Defining "Gamification". In: MindTrek 2011. Proc. of the 15th Int. Academic Conference on Envisioning Future Media Environments. ACM Press, New York (2011)
10. Prensky, M.: Digital game based learning. Paragon House, St. Paul, Minn. (2007)
11. von Ahn, L., Dabbish, L.: Designing games with a purpose. Commun. ACM 51, 57 (2008)
12. Foldit Website, https://fold.it/portal/
13. UK Cancer Reserach: Play to Cure. http://www.cancerresearchuk.org
14. Ferrara, J.: Games for Persuasion: Argumentation, Procedurality, and the Lie of Gamification. Games and Culture 8, 289–304 (2013)
15. Freyermuth, G.S.: Games, game design, game studies. Eine Einführung. Transcript, Bielefeld (2015)
16. Richards, C., Thompson, C.W., Graham, N.: Beyond designing for motivation. The Importance of Context in Gamification. In: Nacke, L.E., Graham, T.N. (eds.) CHI PLAY 2014. Proceedings of the First ACM SIGCHI Annual Symposium on Computer-human Interaction in Play, pp. 217–226. ACM (2014)
17. de Freitas, S., Liarokapis, F.: Serious Games: A New Paradigm for Education? In: Ma, M., Oikonomou, A.V., Jain, L.C. (eds.) Serious Games and Edutainment Applications, pp. 9–23. Springer-Verlag London Ltd., London (2011)
18. Gee, J.P.: Good Video Games and Good Learning. Phi Kappa Phi Forum (2005)
19. Gee, J.P.: Video Games, Learning, and "Content". In: Miller, C.T. (ed.) Games: Purpose and Potential in Education, pp. 43–53. Springer, New York (2008)
20. Bogost, I.: Persuasive Games: Exploitionware
21. Schell, J.: The art of game design. A book of lenses, 2nd edn. CRC Press (2014)
22. Center for Applied Games. http://www.centerforappliedgames.com
23. Applied Game Design. http://appliedgamedesign.org/
24. MIT Game Lab Symposium (2012). http://bit.ly/1EhAt60
25. Zurich University of Arts. https://www.zhdk.ch/index.php?id=61175
26. Danube University of Krems. http://bit.ly/1PpqnX4

27. Microsoft Research APG. http://research.microsoft.com/en-us/groups/apg/
28. Kim, A.J.: What is Applied Game Design? http://amyjokim.com/blog/2015/06/10/what-is-applied-game-design/
29. Six to Start - Zombies Run! https://www.zombiesrungame.com/
30. Mayer, I., Bekebrede, G., Harteveld, C., Warmelink, H., Zhou, Q., van Ruijven, T., Lo, J., Kortmann, R., Wenzler, I.: The research and evaluation of serious games: Toward a comprehensive methodology. Br. J. Educ. Technol. 45, 502–527 (2014)
31. Lampert, C., Schwinge, C., Tolks, D.: Der Gepielte Ernst Des Lebens. Betandsaufnahme und Potenziale von Serious Games (for Health). Medienpädagogik (2009)
32. Herrmanny, K., Schmidt, R.: Ein Vorgehensmodell zur Entwicklung von Gameful Design für Unternehmen. In: van Butz, A., Koch, M., Schlichter, J. (eds.) Mensch & Computer 2014 – Workshopband. Fachübergreifende Konferenz für Interaktive und Kooperative Medien, pp. 369–378. De Gruyter, Berlin (2014)
33. Emmerich, K., Liszio, S., Masuch, M.: Defining second screen gaming. In: Chisik, Y., Geiger, C., Hasegawa, S. (eds.) Proceedings of the 11th Conference on Advances in Computer Entertainment Technology, ACE 2014, pp. 1–8 (2014)
34. Deterding, S.: Gamification Absolved? http://bit.ly/1mi9Rtv
35. Emmerich, K., Masuch, M., Schmidt, R.: Researching the Fundamentals of a Cause-Effect Relationship. In: Workshop on Designing Systems for Health and Entertainment. Advances in Computer Entertainment Technology, ACE (2014)
36. Huizinga, J.: Homo ludens. Vom Ursprung der Kultur im Spiel. Rowohlt, Reinbek bei Hamburg (1956, 2004)
37. Kerres, M., Bormann, M., Vervenne, M.: Didaktische Konzeption von Serious Games: Zur Verknüpfung von Spiel- und Lernangeboten. Medienpädagogik, 1–16 (2009)
38. Cleese, J.: John Cleese on creativity
39. Schmidt, R., Emmerich, K., Freidank, C., Masuch, M.: Serious Games. Unterhaltung, aber mit Lerneffekt. In: JuKiP, pp. 275–279. Georg Thieme Verlag, Stuttgart (2014)
40. Fullerton, T.: Game design workshop. A playcentric approach to creating innovative games. CRC Press, New York (2014)
41. Hunicke, R., LeBlanc, M., Zubek, R.: MDA: A Formal Approach to Game Design and Game Research. In: Proc. of the Challenges 2004 (2004)
42. Cook, D.: The Chemistry Of Game Design. http://www.gamasutra.com/view/feature/129948/the_chemistry_of_game_design.php
43. Koster, R.: A theory of fun for game design. Paraglyph Press, Scottsdale, Ariz (2005)
44. Klimmt, C.: Computerspielen als Handlung. Dimensionen und Determinanten des Erlebens interaktiver Unterhaltungsangebote. von Halem, Köln (2006)
45. Malone, T.W.: What makes things fun to learn? Heuristics for Designing Instructional Computer Games. In: Proceedings of the 3rd ACM SIGSMALL Symposium and the First SIGPC Symposium on Small Systems, pp. 162–169. ACM Press (1980)
46. Ryan, R.M., Rigby, C.S., Przybylski, A.: The Motivational Pull of Video Games: A Self-Determination Theory Approach. Motivation and Emotion 30, 344–360 (2006)
47. Whitton, N., Moseley, A. (eds.): Using games to enhance learning and teaching. A beginner's guide. Routledge, New York (2012)

Classification of Player Roles in the Team-Based Multi-player Game Dota 2

Christoph Eggert, Marc Herrlich, Jan Smeddinck, and Rainer Malaka

Digital Media Lab, TZI, University of Bremen, Germany

Abstract. Computer games are big business, which is also reflected in the growing interest in competitive gaming, the so-called *electronic sports*. *Multi-player online battle arena* games are among the most successful games in this regard. In order to execute complex team-based strategies, players take on very specific roles within a team. This paper investigates the applicability of *supervised machine learning* to classifying player behavior in terms of specific and commonly accepted but not formally well-defined roles within a team of players of the game *Dota 2*. We provide an in-depth discussion and novel approaches for constructing complex attributes from low-level data extracted from replay files. Using attribute evaluation techniques, we are able to reduce a larger set of candidate attributes down to a manageable number. Based on this resulting set of attributes, we compare and discuss the performance of a variety of supervised classification algorithms. Our results with a data set of 708 labeled players see *logistic regression* as the overall most stable and best performing classifier.

Keywords: multi-player games, player roles, classification.

1 Introduction

Digital games have become an important social, cultural, and economical factor. Online multi-player games attract especially large player bases and big audiences. Computer games have also matched many traditional media in terms of total revenue [14]. This is also reflected in the growing interest in competitive gaming, the so-called *electronic sports* (eSports). Stemming from it's early roots in the 1990s, it has only been in recent years that *eSports* has been showing signs of becoming a mainstream phenomenon. Parallel developments, e.g. the success of game-related online videos in the form of so-called *Let's Plays* and live broadcasting, also play an important role as an indicator and multiplier for societal impact. Game tournaments award significant prize money and there are players and teams that can make a living from playing games. *Multi-player online battle arena* (MOBA) games are among the most popular and successful games in this regard. Due to their popularity, their competitive nature, as well as their complex team-based strategies and tactics, they share many similarities with traditional physical team sports, and akin to the recent rise of data analysis in physical sports, data analysis and machine learning begin to play an important role for the development and analysis of digital games.

© IFIP International Federation for Information Processing 2015
K. Chorianopoulos et al. (Eds.): ICEC 2015, LNCS 9353, pp. 112–125, 2015.
DOI: 10.1007/978-3-319-24589-8_9

In this paper we investigate the applicability and performance of *supervised machine learning* (ML) to classify player behavior in terms of specific roles within a team of players of the game *Dota 2*, a popular contemporary MOBA game. Such information could be useful for game designers to better understand how their game design influences emergent gameplay and player behavior but also for players, both casual and professional, who want to analyze their own performance or who want to learn from others. It could also support casters and moderators in commentating and presenting matches. Furthermore, this research might hold implications for social and other research concerned with (human behavior in) games. While ML has been applied to games and traditional sports, most works are either interested in questions like spatial behavior, trying to predict the match outcome, or otherwise trying to correlate performance to certain events or behaviors. In contrast, we aim at building a classifier that is largely independent of individual player performance and that is also not tied to the overall match outcome but that is able to identify a player's role in terms of the non-formally defined roles established as common grounds within the *Dota 2* or MOBA community.

This paper contributes to the state of the art in several ways: We provide an in-depth discussion and novel approaches regarding the construction of complex attributes from low-level data extracted from *Dota 2* replay files, together with an evaluation of these attributes with respect to different classifiers. Based on the resulting reduced set of attributes, we compare and discuss the performance of a range of supervised classification algorithms, including logistic regression, random forest decision trees, support vector machines (in combination with Sequential Minimal Optimization), naive Bayes and Bayesian networks, classifying both with a newly established larger set of player roles, as well as with a reduced set inspired by related work [5].

2   Related Work

We restrict the discussion to three main areas: traditional physical sports, comparable works that focus on different games or genres, and works that also focus on *Dota 2*, yet have different classification goals.

Recognizing behaviors in traditional sports typically requires some form of image processing or other recognition techniques to extract usable data. While there is no need for image processing in our case since positional information is directly available, there are similarities that might be applicable to MOBA games. Tovinkere et al. [16] make use of the trajectory of the ball in soccer games to detect events. Combined with player positions and a rule-based-system, which was built with domain-specific knowledge, this leads to a large number of detectable events. A very similar approach is presented by Li et al. [10] for ice hockey games. A notable domain difference compared to works for soccer is that not only the position of the goal is considered, but also the moment when the blue line is crossed. In basketball games, as presented by Fu et al. [4], the actual tracking of the ball is less important for certain tactics. In order to detect offensive strategies they make use of the fact that defenders are closer to their basket than the offensive team to predict ball possession. The strategy is then recognized by comparing player positions relative to each other with expected patterns. While in MOBA games there is no ball or puck that could be tracked, using relative player positions might be applied to certain events (e.g. team fights; see section 6). In addition to positional information, Zhu et al. [21] also utilize information like score boards and game time that are typically on display during TV broadcasts to improve their predictions for soccer games. *Dota 2* replays (see section 5) contain similar information, e.g. amounts of damage, kills, healing etc. that could be combined with positional information.

An approach to ML in computer games in general was proposed by Drachen et al. [2]. They suggest using unsupervised learning algorithms, specifically k-means and *Simplex Volume Maximization*, to cluster player behavioral data. They use two very different games for a proof of concept. Knowledge of the game design is used with both titles to define the attributes used for the algorithms. This also means that the chosen attributes strongly differ. In contrast to our work, their goal is specifically to aid developers in terms of general game design, for example by finding underused mechanics. Because of that a few game specific attributes are selected and unsupervised learning is applicable. Our approach targets behavior that is not tied as directly to just one or two mechanics. Therefore we expect that we need a larger set of attributes and employ supervised learning methods. Other notable works are based on the real-time strategy game series *Starcraft*. Liu et al. [11] target the identification of a specific player from *Starcraft 2* replays by his or her personal play style. In contrast, we are looking for players behaving according to a certain common role, which can be seen as trying to remove personal play style and performance as noise. Synnaeve et al. [15] present a method for an adaptive artificial intelligence (AI) in *Starcraft: Brood War*, which uses similar features. Instead of units, their method collects data on the produced buildings to recognize build orders. The prediction is then made with a Bayesian model. Their work in turn is partly based on the works of Weber et al. [17], who use produced buildings, units and upgrades as attributes. In MOBA games we cannot rely on such attributes alone. The most similar attributes to the production in *Starcraft* would be the items players are buying for their hero. However, unlike *Starcraft*, players almost never have a fixed income, which has a big influence on the items players are buying. Items are also often more connected to specific heroes than to player roles.

A notable work on *Dota 2* is presented by Gao et al. [5]. They target the identification of both the heroes that players are playing, and the role they are taking. They define a basic model with three roles a player can fulfill that are predicted with an accuracy of about 74%. For comparison in addition to our more complex set of classes, we also applied our attributes to the reduced set of roles by Gao et al. (see section 7) with signification improvements in terms of accuracy over their results. It must be noted, though, that we had no access to their test data. Other works about *Dota 2* are mostly based on skill-related questions or social studies. For example, Pobiedina et al. [13] come to the conclusion that the national diversity of players as well as the number of friends playing together has a significant influence on team success. Nuangjumnonga et al. [12] research correlations between the leadership behavior (such as authoritarian and democratic) and the roles the players are fulfilling in the game. Notably they use the roles *Carry*, *Support* and *Ganker*, which we will also cover in section 6. Yang et al. [20] identify combat patterns to predict game outcomes with an accuracy of 80%. More recently, another contribution by Drachen et al. [3] investigated skill-based differences in the spatio-temporal team behavior of *Dota 2* matches. They find higher-skilled players to move more actively and closer to their teammates around the map. For collecting positional information they make use of a spatial division of the *Dota 2* map into zones, looking at zone changes, which shares some similarities with our method to detect early game movement (see section 6) that focuses on the number of entered zones.

3 Background: Dota 2

Based on the popular modification *DotA* (Defense of the Ancients) for the game *Warcraft 3*, *Dota 2* is is a typical example of the MOBA genre. Most popular MOBAs (including e.g. League of Legends, Heroes of Newerth, Smite, etc.) are identical in terms of the basic gameplay but differ in specific details, e.g. heroes, skills, additional mechanics, graphics, maps, etc.. *Dota 2* is played in teams of five. Each player controls a *hero* character with specific strengths and weaknesses, abilities, matching items and so on that is picked from a large pool at the beginning of each round. The choice of a specific hero is an important aspect of the game. Teams need a balance of heroes with different abilities that are able to fulfill certain roles with respect to the team tactics and strategies, resembling traditional team-based sports. Although the core setup appears simple, it can lead to a large variety of complex team-based behaviors, roles, and strategies. Heroes develop their abilities in a heterogeneous manner and become stronger throughout the game by collecting experience points and gold, which the players can invest into items that support the heros abilities or provide other advantages

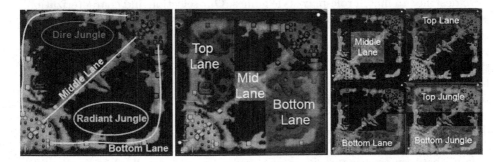

Fig. 1. Left: *Dota 2* map layout with lane annotations Mid: Areas used for determining the player lane Right: Area masks to reduce false positives for early gank detection

to the team. As shown in figure 1 (left), the map is split into three lanes. Each lane has three defensive towers (green / red squares in figure 1) (e.g. left) that constantly attack enemies within their range. The goal of the game is to destroy the enemys main building (the *Ancient*) after destroying all towers leading to it on a lane. Along each of the lanes, a wave of *non-player characters* (NPC), called *creeps*, runs from the base of each team to the base of the enemy. Creeps are important sources for gold and experience and can be utilized for attacks. Finishing blows to them are called last hits and are often used as an efficiency benchmark. Additionally, there are camps of neutral creeps (hostile towards both factions), in the map areas marked as *Dire Jungle* and *Radiant Jungle* in figure 1 (left). Another possibility to earn gold and experience is killing enemy heroes. Players lose some gold with each death and have to wait a certain amount of time until their hero is revived at their base. Surprise attacks on enemy players from behind while they are dealing with creeps are a common tactic. In *Dota 2* this behavior is called *ganking*. Each match is separated into *three phases*, called the *early game*, *mid game* and *late game*. There are no exact time thresholds for these phases and transitions (based on the behavior of the players and the strength of their heroes) can be subtle. The *early game* typically lasts for about 10-15 minutes. In this phase players mostly stay on their side of the map and collect experience points and gold by killing creeps. The *mid game* is the game phase that differs the most in every match. It depends heavily on the heroes chosen by each team. At some point in the game, heroes get so strong that even towers are no real threat to them anymore and heroes will be fully developed and equipped to their maximum abilities. This phase is called the *late game*.

4   Player Roles

There are recurring *roles* (or play styles) that players choose and try to follow for a specific game. These roles are not formally defined but have established themselves informally among players. It is important to note that these roles describe a different facet of play than classic player type classifications (e.g. after Bartle [1]) which aim to classify expressed character traits of the players and were designed to match role-play style games. Our selection and characterization of roles is based on a comparison of online guides, videos and commentary of professional players and commentators. Definitions and naming conventions of player roles will in any case differ slightly among the player base and shift over time as the game evolves, constituting another challenge for ML applications in this area. We do not view this mutability as a limiting factor but rather as a realistic constraint. We provide characterizations and in-depth explanations on the attribute calculation and selection (section 6) in order to facilitate reproducibility and comparability with other classification schemes.

In the end, we isolated nine player roles for the main ML task, which strike a balance between covering common play styles in great detail while leaving out some exotic styles which are rarely observed or are minor variations of other styles. Additionally, we employ a set containing only three rather general roles that have been used in other work for comparison. In general, we tried to avoid performance-based characterizations or attributes as much as possible as we were not interested in distinguishing bad from good players. The isolated roles were: *Carries* - who are usually weak and need protection early on, but are very strong in later stages, often deciding games. Carries typically end up with a high amount of last hits, gold per minute and overall kills, but they can get them in quite different ways. Therefore, we define two kinds of carries called *active carries* and *farming carries*. Active carries engage enemy players and participate in team fights to gain experience and gold, while farming carries focus on utilizing enemy or neutral creeps for character development. *Gankers* try to waylay enemy heroes with surprise attacks, sometimes very early in the game. *Support* players in different ways try to help other players, sometimes even sacrificing themselves. We define three kinds of support players to cover different strategies. *Babysitter support* players protect teammates (usually a carry), staying very close to them. In contrast, *roaming supports* are active around the map and even waylay other players similar to gankers. However, they still let other team members take the greater share. *Farming supports* also take their share of experience and gold. However, they spend their gold on support items and they avoid interfering with the carry. *Pushers* continuously try to clear out enemy towers, thereby pushing their lane. *Feeders* are players that somehow get taken advantage of or show very bad performance during the whole game. This is a special role we added to be able to separate such players that do not show any useful observable behavior. *Inactive* players represent another special class of players that - due to technical difficulties or other reasons - do not actively participate.

5   Data Collection

Dota 2 games are stored as replay files (*replays*). Replays contain all low-level game events that occurred during a game and allow the engine to re-simulate whole games. This approach has different advantages and disadvantages. It is very flexible because watching a replay is not limited to watching only one player's perspective or watching at the same speed as the original game. However, this comes with the cost that it is not simply playing back a recording, but the full game logic simulation has to be processed. For our goal this also means that, while low-level events and some additional data needed for attribute construction can be read directly from the replays, constructing some attributes will require significant additional processing (see section 6). We built our attribute construction processing on top of the Java-based replay parser *Clarity* by Martin Schrodt.

Adequately labeling replays requires watching the whole game, sometimes several times for different players. This is a time-consuming task. Therefore we designed and implemented a tool to crowd-source the labeling (of the play style) to the *Dota 2* player community. The tool allows anyone to quickly upload labeled match summaries, based on local replay files, to an online database. The tool was advertised by calls to the player community through established community websites and available for download from our website. Players were free to label whatever games they liked, which could be either their own games or games taken from other sources like online replay archives. For the second community call we also asked users to label a specific, seemingly problematic game (in terms of ambiguous player roles) to gain more insight into the issues as discussed in section 7. The labeled replays contain a large variety of players from different skill levels. In addition, we manually labeled a set of replays from the tournament *The International 2014*, which contains only replays of highly professional players. Overall our final data set contained 708 labeled players.

6   Attribute Construction and Evaluation

The full set of attributes we considered for evaluation is presented in table 1. While some attributes correspond directly to low-level events or summary data, attributes that capture positional information and fighting behavior require more complex processing of the replay data. We experimented with different attribute filters implemented in the Java library WEKA [7] to determine the best set of attributes using our labeled examples. These include algorithm-independent subset selections, for example the *CfsSubsetEval* class based on the works of Mark Hall [6]; algorithm-dependent subset selections, most notably the *WrapperSubsetEval* class based on works from Kohavi et al. [9]; and several classes, such as *InfoGainAttributeEval*, as presented in the works of Witten et al. [19, p. 487-492]. Our results with the *WrapperSubsetEval* class with best-first search are presented in table 1. We have chosen this algorithm for our final attribute selection because it resulted in the highest accuracy with our labeled data set. For classification we selected all attributes that were present in at least four folds, excluding *assists*, as this resulted in the overall highest accuracy. In the following sections we describe the algorithms and heuristics we developed to calculate the attributes that cannot be directly obtained from replay files. They can be grouped into five rough categories: space and movement, early ganks, team fights, support items, and damage types. Not all of the attributes we describe in this section were finally chosen to be used for classification within this work but they might prove valuable for future works.

6.1   Space and Movement

Player Lane. Many roles depend on the *lane* (see figure 1) a player is *most active* in during the *early game*. This information also provides the foundation for other attributes, e.g., the *lane partners*. Players typically have three main positions at the beginning of the game: *top lane*, *mid lane*, or *bottom lane*. Additionally, the *jungle* areas can be used, or players can have a *roaming* position, meaning that they move around the map instead of staying in a certain area. The typical areas in which players are positioned most of the time for each lane according to our observations can be seen in figure 1 (middle). During the very early game (0:30-6:00) the position of each player is checked every two seconds

Table 1. Attributes evaluated for classification. Attributes marked with + are not directly available from replays. Attributes marked with * were finally selected for classification. Number of Folds shows in how many folds an attribute was selected by WEKA's WrapperSubsetEval class using 10-fold cross-validation for logistic regression.

Attribute	Number of Folds
KDA Ratio* = (Kills + Assists) / (Deaths + 1)	10
Last Hits*	10
Early Ganks*+	10
Number of Support Items*+	10
Damage to Neutral Creeps*+	10
Damage to Regular Creeps*+	10
Lane Partners*+	10
Kills*	9
Experience*	5
Deaths*	5
Assists	5
Team Fight Participation*+	4
Early Movement (Visited Cells)*+	4
Damage to Heroes*+	4
Solo Lane+	2
Damage to Towers+	1
Chosen Hero	0
Gold	0

and for each player a region counter is increased if the player is present. Players that are positioned in one of the three lanes at least half of the time are assigned to the *corresponding lane*. If this is not the case, they are flagged as *roaming*. Unfortunately, trying to detect the *jungle* position with the same approach does not work as these areas would necessarily overlap with the areas of the lanes. Instead, the damage that players do to *neutral creeps* is tracked (see *damage types* below). If an empirically determined damage threshold of 6000 is surpassed, the position is set to *jungle* regardless of any other positional information.

Lane Partners and Solo Lane. The number of lane partners is determined by comparing the *lane* attribute calculated as described above between players. Players in the *roaming* or *jungle* position are always assigned *zero* lane partners, while players sharing the top, mid or bottom lane are assigned the corresponding *number of* their *teammates* in the same lane. We also included a *solo lane* attribute as an alternative to the lane partners. This attribute is always true if a player is assigned to one of the three main lanes without any teammate and otherwise false.

Early Movement. Some roles are characterized by how active players are on the map during the early game. Although this attribute might depend on skill as is indicated by Drachen et al. [3], this could also be caused by active play styles being more prevalent in higher-skilled matches. Unfortunately, the movement activity cannot simply be determined by tracking the total movement of players, as all characters are usually running back and forth even when they do not change their general position. For this reason, we make use of the structure of positional information in *Dota 2* replays. Positions in replays are specified by a 128x128 grid and additional offsets. As we do not need the accurate coordinates, which might also introduce a lot of noise into the classification, we divide grid positions by ten, effectively resulting in a grid consisting of 13x13 cells. During the early game, we count the *total number of cells* that each player visits and assign it to the respective attribute.

6.2   Early Ganks

Early ganks are a key indicator for aggressive player roles, such as *roaming supports* and *gankers*. We collect every fight that is not considered a *team fight* (see below) first. Players are considered to be within the fighting area if they are within 10% of the map size. We use a time threshold of 5 seconds to find the end of a fight and an empirically determined damage threshold of 100 to avoid false positives. Within the collection of fights we detect *early gankers* based on the *lane* attribute described in section 6.1. Based on the assigned lane, we define extended areas in which players are expected to fight, which can be seen in figure 1 (right). If a player is participating in a fight that is not taking place in the expected area for their lane, we increase the corresponding *early gank* attribute by one. For players in the *roaming* position, every fight participation therefore increases the attribute. Due to expected false positives this attribute does not necessarily reflect the exact number of early ganks but a large value should reliably provide a strong indication for them.

6.3   Team Fights

Team fights are typically considered to involve most players of both teams and often decide the outcome of a match. In a standard match there is usually at least one player of each team assigned to each of the three main lanes. If both teams decide to assign both of the remaining two players to the same lane, this leads to a situation where fights involving six players might happen early on. However, these types of fights should not be considered team fights according to the description above. Therefore, we define a minimum of seven players to participate in a fight to label it as a team fight. In addition, we use empirically determined *spatial*, *damage* and *time thresholds* to extract team fights from the attack events contained in the replays files. For each such event a fight entry is instantiated that at first contains only the two players directly involved in the event. Additional players are added to the fight if they either take or receive damage within a radius of 20% of the map size (the team fight zone). Fights are ended if no corresponding attack events occur for 5 seconds. The total damage dealt or received within the team fight must surpass a threshold of 2000 to further reduce false positives. After all team fights have been counted, each player is assigned the percentage of team fights they were involved in as the corresponding attribute.

6.4 Support Items

The right items are key to *support roles*. However, many items that are useful for support players also have their uses for other roles. Therefore, based on available game guides we manually compiled a list of items that are exclusively used by support players: *Courier*, *Flying Courier*, *Observer Ward*, and *Sentry Ward*. Item purchases are not directly reflected in the available data from the replay files. Therefore, we periodically check the inventory of each player and increment a counter for support items if a new item from our list is found. The resulting count is finally assigned to a corresponding attribute for each player.

6.5 Damage Types

We determined the following damage categories based on player roles and requirements of other attributes: damage to heroes, damage to towers, damage to neutral creeps, and damage to regular creeps. We extract this information from the replay files by utilizing a categorized database of all units in the game and comparing identifiers of attacker and victim for each damage event.

7 Classification Results and Discussion

Based on the attribute selection described in section 6, several different classifiers were trained and evaluated using 10-fold cross-validation on our data set. The choice of candidate classifiers was based on existing works and complemented by commonly used classification approaches. It included: *Logistic regression* (LR), *random forest decision trees* (RF), *support vector machines* with *sequential minimal optimization* (SMO), *naive Bayes* classifiers (NB), and *Bayesian networks*. The WEKA library and tools provided the technical platform. The classifiers were evaluated according to several established performance metrics (accuracy, mean absolute error (MAE) [18], and area under ROC (AUC) [8]) and we also analyzed the confusion matrix. All performance metrics were calculated by using the WEKA default implementations, which are described in the reference documents [19], with optimized parameters.

Table 2 lists the accuracies and MAEs of all classification approaches, as well as the weighted AUC averages. Table 3 presents the confusion matrix of the LR classifier. With accuracies of around 75%, MAEs around 0.08 and AUC values around 0.95 the results are not perfect but quite promising with respect to the complex classification task and the limited data set. Our analysis revealed neuralgic points that might be good starting points to improve the results in future work. For further analysis we limit ourselves to the LR case as the overall most stable and best performing classifier of our selection. Taking a closer look

Table 2. Summary of 10-fold cross-validation accuracies, mean absolute errors and weighted averages of the AUC for the full set and for a reduced set of classes

Classifier	Accuracy	Mean Absolute Error	Wgt. Avg. AUC
Full set of classes			
Random Forest	76.27%	0.0905	0.943
Logistic Regression	75.85%	0.0826	0.947
SMO	75.28%	0.1753	0.926
Bayesian Networks	72.03%	0.0801	0.933
NaiveBayes	70.76%	0.0769	0.933
Reduced set of classes			
Bayesian Networks	96.58%	0.0322	0.995
SMO	96.15%	0.2308	0.975
Logistic Regression	96.15%	0.0381	0.993
Naive Bayes	95.58%	0.0383	0.994
Random Forest	91.17%	0.1162	0.985

Table 3. Confusion Matrix for logistic regression using 10-fold cross-validation.

a	b	c	d	e	f	g	h	i	classified as
163	6	13	11	1	0	2	3	0	a = Carry - Active
12	**101**	0	0	0	1	9	0	0	b = Carry - Farming
27	3	**28**	0	3	0	0	0	0	c = Ganker
10	0	0	**113**	5	0	0	5	0	d = Support - Babysitter
1	0	2	8	**57**	0	0	3	0	e = Support - Roaming
5	0	0	0	2	**8**	1	0	0	f = Support - Farming
7	14	0	1	0	0	**30**	0	0	g = Pusher
6	0	3	7	0	0	0	**31**	0	h = Feeder
0	0	0	0	0	0	0	0	**6**	i = Inactive

at the confusion matrix (table 3) reveals that there are two frequent cases of misclassification: *Active carry* versus *ganker* and farming carry versus *pusher*. In order to gain better insight we manually analyzed a number of problematic games and players and we could observe that in these games the *early gank* detection could be problematic because of the unclear transition between game phases (esp. early to mid game). As mentioned in section 6 we empirically determined a fixed time threshold for early game detection that – on average – worked well but not for exceptional cases that were present in some games; e.g. players leaving their lanes either extremely early or extremely late. A second factor that we noticed originated from roles looking very similar even to the human eye, although for apparently different reasons. For example, the *farming carry* wants as much gold and experience as possible and the *pusher* on the other hand wants to destroy towers as fast as possible but these goals in many cases can be achieved by the same actions. The *active carry* and the *ganker* are both involved in many player versus player fights. As we based our initial role definitions on established information sources for the game, our results highlight that some of the accepted roles do in fact bear overlaps because even though they define a certain player behavior, the distinction in some cases seems to be made solely by the players' intentions, which cannot be directly observed. A third factor that might play an important role is what we call performance noise in cases where players are not able to demonstrate a certain role clear enough. Although the special roles *feeder* and *inactive* were added to reduce performance effects, borderline cases may not be detected. A fourth factor we identified are dynamic role changes that are demanded by the situation or enforced by the competing team. This is problematic because our attributes and classification are currently based on large time spans or even the whole game. A solution might be detecting roles for smaller time spans within the game, however, this would also necessarily reduce the amount of game data available due to the shorter time span and dividing the game into meaningful phases is in itself a very challenging task.

We conducted a small study on the issue of ambiguous roles, asking three *Dota 2* experts to manually classify ten players in one of the problematic games. The responses were highly divergent with up to four different labels being provided for some players. This illustrates that the classification task is difficult, even for human experts, which is an interesting insight for the MOBA community and game designers. We classified the professional tournament data set (203 players) to look deeper into the possible influence of performance noise and achieved an accuracy of 81% percent. Although based on a limited data set, this indicates that performance might indeed be an issue. Yet, limiting the original data set to only the players of the winning teams did not result in any notable differences in classification performance (accuracy 75.62%, MAE 0.0842, weighted AUC 0.936). This suggests that individual performance noise might be an issue but not the team performance as a whole. We also classified our data set with the same attributes but with a reduced set of classes (*carry*, *support*, and *solo lane*) inspired by Gao et al. [5] to compare the power of our attributes and to assess the influence of the number of classes. Before classification with the same attributes as before we relabeled our data according to the following rules: all types of *carries*, *gankers*, and *pusher* were relabeled as *carry* and all types of *supports* were relabeled as just support. Entries labeled as *inactive* were completely removed before training and classification (cf. [5]). Players labeled as *feeders* were manually looked up and relabeled by a human expert to the best fitting class. The results of a ten-fold cross-validation are also presented in table 2. Again, LR proved to be among the best performing and most stable classifiers. However, for the reduced set of classes, Bayesian networks also performed well. While the results overall improved compared to the full set of classes, there are still some residual errors. Compared to the results of Gao et al. [5], classification with our attributes achieved a higher accuracy for our data set. A direct comparison is not possible since the data sets differ. Still, the results indicate that classification with a reduced set of classes works well and could already be employed for many applications.

Summarizing, we can state that the full set of classes shows promising results but also highlights that, although these classes are accepted by game experts, some are ambiguous even to humans manually labeling the data. Furthermore, we identified the reliable distinction of game phases as a major challenge. Additionally, looking at global game roles per match has proven to have limits, due to dynamic roles switching within shorter time spans. Lastly, performance noise exists, although of the mentioned factors, this one is comparatively well controlled by our attributes (in accordance with the design goals, as differences between winners and losers or even compared to professionals were not significantly large).

8   Conclusion and Future Work

We presented and discussed an approach to apply machine learning techniques for the classification of player roles in the MOBA game *Dota 2*. Since most MOBA games share many key game mechanics, our approach should be applicable to other games of the same genre or even to similar team-based games of other genres with slight modifications. Investigating a larger set of attributes, we isolated a manageable set and employed that reduced set to estimate the applicability of a range of classifiers according to established performance metrics. While the classification accuracy for the whole set of classes is limited, with approx. 75%, it is still promising and for our data set logistic regression was clearly the overall most stable and best performing classifier. Classification for a reduced set of classes was very successful with an accuracy of 96%, which is already suitable for many applications. Again, LR – although not the best performing classifier – proved to be very stable and well suited to this domain.

Looking at the limitations of our results highlights several important challenges. First, the definition of classes seems to be primarily intention-defined rather than behavior-defined for some classes, which makes them very difficult to detect. Still, our approach could be useful as a pre-processing step for a tool that allows game designers, players, or casters to look at games and player roles, e.g, by highlighting problematic games. Second, the distinction of specific games phases is an important issue that is not trivial to solve. It affects the classification of certain roles that are characterized by behavior related to certain phases in the game and further complications arise from the fact that roles may change during a game. Third, performance noise is a factor, e.g., if players are not able to act out their intended role. However, we presented indications that our attributes are insensitive to performance up to a certain degree by comparing the results of limiting classification just to the winning team or just professional players. In the future we plan to look more closely at the mentioned problem of identifying the game phase and transitions more reliably. It might also be beneficial to detect roles not for a whole match but rather for phases or sections to account for role changes during the game.

References

1. Bartle, R.: Hearts, clubs, diamonds, spades: Players who suit muds. Journal of MUD Research 1(1), 19 (1996)
2. Drachen, A., Sifa, R., Bauckhage, C., Thurau, C.: Guns, swords and data: Clustering of player behavior in computer games in the wild. In: CIG, pp. 163–170. IEEE (2012)
3. Drachen, A., Yancey, M., Maguire, J., et al.: Skill-Based Differences in Spatio-Temporal Team Behaviour in Defence of the Ancients 2. In: Proc. of IEEE Games, Entertainment, and Media (GEM), IEEE (2014)
4. Fu, T.S., Chen, H.T., Chou, C.L., Tsai, W.J., Lee, S.Y.: Screen-strategy analysis in broadcast basketball video using player tracking. In: Yang, J.F., Hang, H.M., Tanimoto, M., Chen, T. (eds.) VCIP, pp. 1–4. IEEE (2011)
5. Gao, L., Judd, J., Wong, D., Lowder, J.: Classifying dota 2 hero characters based on play style and performance. In: Univ. of Utah Course on ML (2013)
6. Hall, M.A.: Correlation-based Feature Subset Selection for Machine Learning. Ph.D. thesis, University of Waikato, Hamilton, New Zealand (1998)
7. Hall, M., Frank, E., Holmes, G., Pfahringer, B., Reutemann, P., Witten, I.H.: The weka data mining software: An update. SIGKDD Explor. Newsl. 11(1), 10–18 (2009)
8. Huang, J., Ling, C.X.: Using auc and accuracy in evaluating learning algorithms. IEEE Transactions on Knowledge and Data Engineering 17, 299–310 (2005)
9. Kohavi, R., John, G.H.: Wrappers for feature subset selection. Artificial Intelligence 97(1-2), 273–324 (1997); special issue on relevance
10. Li, F., Woodham, R.J.: Analysis of player actions in selected hockey game situations. In: CRV, pp. 152–159. IEEE (2005)
11. Liu, S., Ballinger, C., Louis, S.: Player identification from rts game replays. In: 28th Int. Conf. on Computers and their Applications, CATA (2013)
12. Nuangjumnonga, T., Mitomo, H.: Leadership development through online gaming. In: 19th ITS Biennial Conference, ITS, Bangkok (2012)
13. Pobiedina, N., Neidhardt, J., del Moreno, M.C.C., Werthner, H.: Ranking factors of team success. In: WWW (Companion Volume), pp. 1185–1194. WWW Conf. Steering Committee, ACM (2013)
14. Statista: Video games revenue worldwide from 2012 to 2015. http://statista.com/statistics/278181/ (access: August 05, 2015)
15. Synnaeve, G., Bessre, P.: A Bayesian Model for Plan Recognition in RTS Games Applied to StarCraft. In: AIIDE. AAAI Press (2011)
16. Tovinkere, V., Qian, R.J.: Detecting Semantic Events in Soccer Games: Towards A Complete Solution. In: Proc. of IEEE Int. Conf. on Multim. & Expo (2001)
17. Weber, B.G., Mateas, M.: A data mining approach to strategy prediction. In: CIG, pp. 140–147. IEEE, Piscataway (2009)
18. Willmott, C.J., Matsuura, K.: Advantages of the mean absolute error (MAE) over the root mean square error (RMSE) in assessing average model performance. Climate Research 30, 79–82 (2005)
19. Witten, I.H., Frank, E., Hall, M.A.: Data Mining: Practical Machine Learning Tools and Techniques, 3rd edn. Morgan Kaufmann Publ. Inc., SF (2011)
20. Yang, P., Harrison, B., Roberts, D.L.: Identifying patterns in combat that are predictive of success in moba games. In: Proc. of Foundations of Digital Games (2014)
21. Zhu, G., Huang, Q., Xu, C., Rui, Y., Jiang, S., Gao, W., Yao, H.: Trajectory Based Event Tactics Analysis in Broadcast Sports Video. In: Proc. of the 15th Int. Conf. on Multimedia, pp. 58–67. ACM, New York (2007)

Design-Based Learning in Classrooms
Using Playful Digital Toolkits

K.J. Scheltenaar, J.E.C. van der Poel, and M.M. Bekker

Department of Industrial Design, Eindhoven University of Technology, The Netherlands
{k.j.scheltenaar,j.e.c.v.d.poel}@student.tue.nl,
m.m.bekker@tue.nl

Abstract. The goal of this paper is to explore how to implement Design Based Learning (DBL) with digital toolkits to teach 21st century skills in (Dutch) schools. It describes the outcomes of a literature study and two design case studies in which such a DBL approach with digital toolkits was iteratively developed. The outcome is described in the form of a framework that explains how to consider different perspectives, such as the DBL process, the role of the teacher, the use of a digital toolkit and the framing of the design brief in relation to setting learning goals that are suitable for a school context. The design cases indicate that DBL with digital toolkits can play a valuable role in teaching 21st Century skills, such as problem solving, creativity, and digital literacy to children in schools, if the other components of the framework, such as school's learning goals, are taken into account.

Keywords: playful learning, design-based learning, creative learning, digital toolkits, construction toolkits, children, 21st century skills.

1 Introduction

Changes in society and economy have led people to reflect on what education should look like. With the Lisbon strategy created in 2000 and the Europe 2020 strategy, Europe set the goal for becoming "the most dynamic and competitive knowledge-based economy in the world" [1]. One of the methods to achieve this is a focus on skills and "lifelong learning" by reinforcing the role of education. Countries in Europe have started to translate these ideas into consequences for the curricula provided in schools. A promising approach is using design-based learning (DBL) to address the stimulation of 21st century skills [2] [3]. Twenty-first century skills are a set of skills consisting of: creativity, critical thinking, problem-solving capabilities, communication, collaboration, researching, innovation (entrepreneurship), digital literacy and reflection [4] [5] [2]. The Netherlands has already started to integrate 21st century skills and DBL into their curriculum [5] [2], England has also translated (part of) the European strategy into a new curriculum for education that encompasses DBL with design thinking learning goals [6].

DBL is a playful approach to learning: it allows children to seamlessly combine play and learning in a very fluid process. This is similar to how children use their

© IFIP International Federation for Information Processing 2015
K. Chorianopoulos et al. (Eds.): ICEC 2015, LNCS 9353, pp. 126–139, 2015.
DOI: 10.1007/978-3-319-24589-8_10

imagination, try out ideas, and think about what they see [4]. While DBL is already being used at technical higher educations and even at a limited amount of special technology focussed high schools in the Netherlands called "Technasia", there seems to be little experience with designing DBL approached for a younger target group (primary and secondary school) with 21st century skills as a learning goal [7] [8].

The goal of this paper is to explore and define all different elements needed for implementing DBL *in a playful way*, using *digital toolkits*, to teach 21st century skills in current (Dutch) primary and secondary schools. We present our insights in the form of a descriptive framework. Furthermore, in our process we explore how DBL toolkits might be used in schools, this will be presented in the form of two case studies which we used for qualitative research.

2   Related Work

The SLO (Dutch foundation of education development) states that the development of 21st century skills should be offered in primary and secondary schools to prepare students for the future [9]. The Netherlands has included this advice in the format of learning goals for the Dutch educational system. The Dutch learning goals have shifted over the past years from developing mostly theoretical knowledge to the development of skills and knowledge.

Other countries also acknowledge the need for a change in education stimulating 21st century skills. The United States responds with their STEM programme (Science, Technology, Engineering, Mathematics) while the UK encompass design activities in their curriculum [10]. Although the details of the approaches may be different, the underlying motives of all countries are similar: preparing the new generation for the 21st century by transforming education.

2.1   Learning Goals and Styles

Previous learning goals for Dutch education (1993) as defined by the SLO had a heavy focus on theoretical skills and knowledge in the form of 103 core learning goals for primary education and 300 core goals for secondary education [11]. In 2006 the SLO decided to leave more room for a school's own interpretation of the learning goals. They created 58 main learning goals for primary education and 58 main learning goals for secondary education that focus more on the learning process and less on pure theoretical knowledge [12].The learning goals now also encompass 21st century skills like "the ability to research" and "reflecting on own and others work". However, the focus is still mostly on theoretical learning processes and less on domain crossing competencies like 21st century skills.

The target group of this project consists of secondary school students from first and second class and primary school students in their final years. These students are between 10-15 years of age. Children of this age are in the formal operational stage according to Piaget's theory of cognitive development [13]. In this stage a person becomes capable of hypothetical and deductive reasoning and able to think about thinking and abstract concepts. Piaget's theory is a theory on which a lot of aspects of current education are based.

As described in the introduction, new skills and knowledge are required to be able contribute in a 21st century workplace. This has also created new views on learning such as the constructivist perspective on learning [14]. This perspective describes that learning and knowledge are an active construction of creating meaning by the learner. Kolb describes learning as the process whereby knowledge is created while experiences are transformed [15]. This perspective can also be described as learning by reflecting and doing.

The constructivist perspective has an influence on the role of the student, on the design of the curriculum and assessment, and on the role of the teacher [16]. A 21st century curriculum should allow for active student participation and control, offer ample opportunity for interaction, and provide an authentic context for students' learning. DBL gives the opportunity to integrate these aspects.

2.2   Design-Based Learning

At secondary school, children are often used to executing assignments and meeting the goals set by the teacher. Because of this, children often tend to do their work in a way they think that satisfies their teacher [5]. In kindergarten however, children often learn by going through a specific kind of design-like exploration process: "Imagine, create, play, share, reflect" in which they set their own goals and targets [4]. This iterative process can be compared to DBL.

DBL can provide an entirely different way of teaching in which students become co-owner or creator of a research/design assignment. Students learn to think critically and are better connected to what they are doing [5]. DBL furthermore allows teachers to combine the development of theoretical knowledge and 21st century skills and allows the students to immediately apply what they learn in a social context [2] [3].

Although the effectiveness of a teaching method is often difficult to prove, initial research done on DBL is promising. Kolodner describes a large project in the United States concerning a newly developed DBL method called "Learning by Design" [3]. In this study 240 students participated in a study over multiple years. Kolodner found that students learn to become better critical thinkers and are stimulated to put more effort into their work at school. General (21st century) competencies like collaboration and negotiation skills will be faster to develop compared to by using traditional learning methods. A big challenge is the fact that the classroom culture has to change and that the teacher has to be very flexible. In addition to this the way a teacher applies DBL heavily influences the achieved learning results, arguably even more than with traditional education styles [3].

2.3   Toolkits

DBL is often accompanied by 'tangible' learning. The choice for combining DBL and tangible learning is often made because children learn better while playing and exploring in the physical world [17]. Another benefit is a great amount of engagement;

children are less likely to consider a tangible appliance as a traditional learning tool [18]. This is confirmed by Giannakos and Jaccheri with their OurToys program. With OurToys, children build their own digital game/story with physical objects [19]. The program raised awareness for technology, intensified the experience, invited children to explore boundaries and increased collaboration while learning and playing.

The traditional Kindergarten approach provides materials for children to play with. Children with different interests and learning styles can use the same materials, each in their personal way. The Kindergarten tools enables children to go through a design-like process and make innovative creations [4]. Resnick states that it is important to transform the traditional tangible Kindergarten tools into different types of tools, media and materials with a regard to age appropriateness and current era [4]. Since the late 1960's researchers argue that the particular properties of the constructive building blocks offered to children limit or enhance what they can build, create and learn [20]. Due to this, the development of electronic, physical toolkits for learning to support creating and teaching the added value of technology has been growing since 1980. Besides toolkits, learning events to teach children about technology and design exist, such a Lego League Junior and STEAM maker festival.

Most of the currently existing toolkits and events are however focused on a very specific set of skills and knowledge and are not embedded in a school context. This can for example clearly be seen with Littlebits [21] and the Arduino/Raspberry Pi platform [22] (figure 1). Both mostly focus on physical digital electronics and/or programming and offer no clear directions for teachers on how to implement learning activities with the toolkits. Just making is not enough to guarantee learning [23]. Lassiter et al. state that it is needed to empower students to control their learning in authentic projects with real-world problems [24].

Fig. 1. Arduino on the left and LittleBits on the right.

3   Method

The approach for this project has two layers, the development of a framework and embedded in this process two design cases that have been conducted. The framework is developed by combining insights from a literature study and our two design case studies. The concepts of the two design cases were iteratively developed by applying a user centred design approach, incorporating input from diverse stakeholders. The design cases contributed to the development of the framework but are in addiction to this a result on its own, showing how DBL with digital toolkits could look in practice [25]. Finally, in the conclusion we will discuss and reflect upon the uncovered requirements and the two final DBL concepts we created.

3.1   Framework

To examine what factors influences embedding DBL to teach digital literacy and design thinking in schools, a holistic exploratory research approach is applied. A literature study is done to uncover factors mentioned in previous work, combined with various design cases with stakeholder input (e.g. four teachers, two educational experts, one publisher and two curriculum developers) to develop concrete solutions in real world contexts of primary and secondary education. Four stakeholder workshops were organized to gather the experience of multiple experts in an efficient way: Two workshops with experts from primary education and two with experts from secondary education. In these stakeholder workshops early design concepts (four concepts for PE and four concepts for SE were discussed and used to uncover requirements for implementing DBL in (Dutch) education. Consulted experts are experts from the field of primary and secondary education, having a background as teacher, curriculum developer, curriculum publisher, teacher educator or designer of educational tools. All gathered insights are combined and integrated in multiple different iterations for the framework. The final version of the framework describes a collection of requirements for implementing a toolkit for learning in (Dutch) education. In the following section the framework will be explained in more detail.

3.2   Design Cases

We will describe two design cases done in the context of Dutch education. Two toolkits for learning were iteratively developed using a user centered design process for two age groups (primary and secondary school, respectively 10-12 year and 12-14 year old children). The end users and stakeholders from the field of education were heavily involved in the design process with observations, user tests, expert meetings, and the stakeholder workshops.

The toolkits were developed to support the development of a subset of the 21st century skills: creativity, critical thinking, problem solving, collaboration, and reflection. This set of skills can be seen as a 'design' sub-group. To describe the final list of criteria surrounding DBL based toolkits for learning, the main insights of user testing the two design cases in context were integrated into the framework.

4   Framework

4.1   Framework Structure

The insights gained from literature research and the two research by design cases are combined in the framework to describe the different elements needed to implement DBL for developing 21st century skills in (Dutch) education.

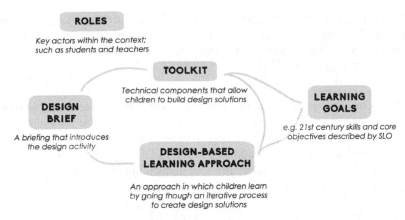

Fig. 2. Framework structure.

Figure 2 shows the components of the framework. Literature research showed that a playful learning *toolkit* must be combined with a *DBL* process. It is important to have a clear *design brief* that provides a direction and frames the design *(DBL)* process and uses the *toolkit* as an instrument for that. Together the *toolkit* and *DBL* process should offer the possibility to meet learning goals: set by the curriculum of the (Dutch) government such, 21st century skills and the development of an awareness for the value of technology in society [11]. The *toolkit* must be designed to be open ended as to be applicable with different *design briefs* and different end results [25]. Next to that it must allow children who may have different learning styles and approaches to work with it [4]. In addition, the teacher *(role)* must be able to guide the process and progress that children are going through and must (be helped to) understand the principles of a *DBL* process and the *toolkit* [24].

4.2   Framework Components

Roles. It is important that teachers must get used to a certain mind-set of children being more self-directed instead of blindly following a method. Therefore it is necessary that a design brief does not blur the creativity of teachers but gives them support without forcing in one direction. In project-based education, the teacher should be able to assess progress, diagnose problems, provide feedback and evaluate overall results [26]. This means on the one hand that the teacher must have a certain knowledge about DBL and the principles of the toolkit in order to explain and guide the progress [24]. On the other hand, teachers should also get familiar or confident that they cannot always predict the outcome of design activities.

Design Brief. It should provide the opportunity to apply a design process and should create a clear role for how the whole toolkit will be used. It should be composed in such a way that is possible to connect the design activity to other courses: this way the added value of technology (in other disciplines) can be highlighted. Meaningful contexts and scientific concepts, close to children's own imagination, enhance opportunities for discussion. Reasoning, interpretation and reflection are important for knowledge building [27] [28]. This often implies examples from everyday life and current socio-scientific issues. These themes or topics are by their nature interdisciplinary, and require teacher cooperation [28].

DBL. DBL is a teaching method that incorporates a design process to stimulate learning. The design process is introduced by the design brief. There are multiple design processes that can be used, the chosen design process should allow a connection between activity and learning goals. In addition to this, a DBL approach must offer two levels: the level of applying the process as a tool and learning through the process by for example reflections, and gaining course based knowledge.

Toolkit. The framework shows the importance of the usability of the toolkit, the toolkit should be general enough that children with different learning styles can work with it but it should also offer the possibility to dig deeper in the materials and functions of the toolkit [4]. These layers must make it is possible to create multiple iterations in their design process. The iterations will enforce the design process due to observing, reflecting, discussing and improving. The toolkit should be designed in such a way that it can fit multiple design briefs, allowing for reuse of the teaching method.

Learning Goals. A last important insight is that the approach had to support the ability to measure if learning goals are achieved. This has to be facilitated by both briefing and design process. This becomes a clear challenge when you compare developing skills and a certain mind-set with examining answers on a test that have only one possible solution.

5   Design Cases

5.1   Design Case 1: Spark! Toolkit for Learning

With the Spark! design case, secondary school students (first and second class, 12- 14 years) are targeted.

Fig. 3. Spark! Toolkit for learning with end result of one lessons.

Concept – Spark! Toolkit for Learning

With the Spark! concept, students create solutions for societal problems. Throughout the Spark! process, both teacher and students are supported with a briefing that stimulates to achieve depth. Everything needed for a Spark! lesson for two students is provided in one wooden case, which can be used for different (societal) problems. The full process needs at least three hours but should ideally be spread over multiple lessons, depending on teaching style, the skill level of students and required results. The following design process is used in the Spark! concept:

1. Identifying and describing the problem: E.g. the introduction of for example street litter as a societal problem.
2. Generating ideas: Brainstorming to generate multiple solutions.
3. Sketching concepts: Stimulating students to converge and think ahead through sketching.
4. Prototyping concept(s): Tangible prototyping phase in which concepts come alive.
5. Test & improve: User testing and an iteration for improvement.
6. Present & reflect: Reflection, answering of critical questions and giving a short presentation.

Spark! supports tangible learning by having students physically prototype and experiment with technology by combining general arts and crafts materials, LED's, conductive glue, a specially modified Arduino and visual programming. The form and contents of the whole Spark! toolkit is intended to make students feel like designers. Technology used in the toolkit is selectively exposed.

Scenario. During a Spark! lesson, the teacher functions as a facilitator of learning to stimulate all duos in his classroom to reach enough depth to safeguard development. Duo's form a team and function like a design agency. The selectively exposed technology allows students to experience the power of technology by prototyping their design solutions and making them work while at the same time not scaring them with too difficult technological aspects. Results of a design duo (e.g. with the design case "decreasing the amount of street litter") can range from talking trashcans that should convince people to throw their garbage in the bin to playful litter collection baskets that require people to playfully throw away their trash and sort the garbage at the same time.

Evaluation. *Participants:* Spark! has been tested during three user tests. Two students (12-13 years old, VWO) participated in the first test. Four students (12-13 years old, VWO) participated in a session that lasted 100 minutes. Fourteen students (aged 12-13 years old, HAVO) participated in 5 lessons of 50 minutes. During the first two user tests the first author of this paper took on the role of teacher. For the third user test all lessons were independently given by a teacher.
Design: The Spark! concept as shown in figure 3.
Procedure: The first user test had the goal to test the overall usability of the learning toolkit. The second user test examined the amount of influence students had on each

other and tested to what extend students could complete the process independently by using improvements done after the first user test. The third user test tested the final design, in which a teacher independently gave the class to 14 students, using the briefing for teachers to help him give the lessons.

Analysis: reflection on outcomes based on observations during the user test by both designer and teacher. A short survey for both students and teacher held after the third user test.

DBL process: Students were able to complete the whole design process using the provided briefing by going through all provided steps. Students seemed to have fun during the whole design process and were proud of their end results. Students collaborated intensively during the whole process and were able to come up with various design solutions for the proposed societal problem

Learning goals: Students were challenged in the area of creativity, critical thinking, problem-solving capabilities and reflection skills (21st century skills) and were also challenged concerning Spark4Arduino (the visual programming environment) and making electronic circuits (knowledge). It was however difficult to establish how much they exactly learned during the user test. During reflection students mentioned they learned about Snap4Arduino, making an electronic circuit and thinking about and defining problems and general societal problems like street litter. The user tests showed reflection is difficult for students. The second and third user test showed that after reading ''prompt questions'' students were able to formulate more grounded answers to the main question. Prompt are questions like: *''Why do we think this solution works?''*. Reflection remained to be difficult for the students however, often needing help from the teacher to reach enough depth. In addition to this, all involved teachers during the process saw opportunities to connect physics and sociology objectives to Spark!.

Design brief and DBL support: Guidance and examples in the briefing helped students independently complete the design process. However, observations showed that students are easily influenced in one direction and that they do sometimes need help from the teacher to achieve enough depth with difficult tasks like reflection. The second user test showed that the introduction course for the technological parts of the toolkit enabled students to use the toolkit for prototyping independently. Using the briefing for teachers, the teacher of user test #3 could give a clear introduction of the lesson for children. The teacher also made his own planning for using Spark! Taking 5 lessons of 50 minutes for the whole process. 5 lessons were however a little bit too short for fully completing the process. The prototyping phase took more time than the teacher expected.

Toolkit property reflections: The students creatively use all contents of the toolkit to make their prototypes. Students also combined the materials and tools from the toolkit with other materials and tools that they sometimes even brought in from outside the classroom. Different materials also allowed students to come up with different design solutions.

5.2   Design Case 2: Dolly X4.2

The focus was on Dutch children (11-12) within their final years of primary school.

Fig. 4. DollyX4.2, the method and the user test setting.

Concept. Dolly X4.2, is a method developed to introduce DBL and give children the opportunity to make the design process their own in order to develop 21st century skills. The method creates the awareness that technology is everywhere, it shows the added value of technology and it provides depth by exploring technical principles in detail. Furthermore, the method can be connected to other courses. The method is based on growth: groups of children create their own fantasy animal that relates to other created animals in the classroom. The phases of growth: "Pre-birth"; understand what is needed to be born. "Birth"; understand what is needed to survive as individual. "Growing up"; understand what is needed to be part of a population and what is the relation to other animals. The name "DOLLY X4.2" is inspired by the cloned sheep 'Dolly', children are triggered to think like inventors and create their own animal. The intended use, covers at least 15 sessions of 1 hours. The methods elements:

— A teacher guide describing the different process phases of the method and the reason behind each phase. It contains design activity cards for each phase that explain the activity, show connected learning goals and what kind of materials you need.
— A toolkit containing transparent objects with different electronic circuits that demonstrate an action – reaction principles (from the categories: colour, vibration, sound and temperature). For example, a sensor that captures a colour and a RGB LED that displays the same measured colour.
— Worksheets for students that guide children in decision-making steps. Children have to write down why they made a certain when they create a fantasy animal. For the teacher it is possible to review answers in their own time and see what the children based their choices on.
— An evaluation instrument that helps to measure progress of gained knowledge and skills over time. With this form, the level of reflection can be scored. Level 1 describes that children have put no extra thought in why they wanted a certain characteristic (it's just cool) while level 3 describes a higher level because children have thought about how animals survive.

Scenario Concept. The method consists of three process phases. The purpose of phase one is to, by exploratory learning, try out different technical modules.

Small activities after each module will be an introduction to the DBL approach. Phase two and three provide an iterative design process and include different activities. The teacher is able to follow a script described in the method or to select provided design activities that fit the curriculum. In total, the three phases can be integrated within one school year.

Evaluation. *Participants:* Two tests have been executed to examine elements of the developed concept. In each test two groups of four children participated (16 children). *Design:* The DOLLYX4.2 concept as shown in figure 4.
Procedure: The main question of the first test was: do children understand that they can use the modules of the toolkit to build their fantasy animal and can they use the technical principles as functions of their animal? The main question of the second test was: do children understand the principles of the modules and can they explore them? Both user tests were conducted at a Dutch primary school. The teacher took a role as supervisor, while in both tests the second author took the role as teacher.
Analysis: reflection on outcomes based on observations during the user test by both designer and teacher.

DBLA: All children were able to create a fantasy animal on paper and formulate different characteristics, such as 'I want my animal to be pink because it is my favourite colour' or 'I want my animal to be invisible because it will be able to hide from predators'. The different reasons showed an already different levels of reflection. The evaluation tool provided the possibility to score these levels. In an interview afterwards the present teacher expressed the added value about the way these skills could be measured because of the rating and time management possibilities. During the process of making design decisions together, children improved their designs constantly. For example, children first had to draw their super animal. Secondly they had to select 5 characteristics and mention why they selected them.

Learning goals: Some children had difficulties with describing the working principles of the modules during the second test and needed some explanation before they realized what they could do with it. After they explored a few modules, the children were given a short design brief in which they had to solve a problem. It revealed that children integrated knowledge gained during previous design activities in their solution. This was observed without mentioning they had to implement this knowledge. For example, children had just explored modules about temperature, vibrations and sound and did implement this knowledge immediately.

Design brief properties: In both tests children were enthusiastic and eager to think of a 'super animal' together. The children were able to read the explanation on paper because the text was lively and written from their perspective (image that YOU were a super smart inventor...). The children were already well informed by their teacher who had made sure the children knew what they could expect. This resulted in much curiosity from the children. This curiosity will probably stay over time because different (design) activities can be introduced.

Toolkit properties: Most children were curious about the inner workings of the modules and liked the fact that they could see the electronics. They were surprised that they could influence what happened (by action, reaction principles) and how they could suddenly come close to technology. For some children it was hard to make the connection between the technical modules and the animal that they created on paper, therefore the actual building of an animal was hard. For example one kid asked: "But does the animal have to hold the battery all the time?" This confusion is possibly due to the fact that the children did not have an introduction about the working principles of the modules during test one (in an ideal situation this would be a phase before the animal creation phase). A little explanation helped them to imagine new ways of using the modules, for example by using a colour sensor and an RGB LED as eyes.

6   Conclusion and Discussion

In this paper we present a framework for teaching (a sub-set of) 21st Century skills with digital toolkits in a (Dutch) school context. Two design cases and a literature study have been conducted to examine how DBL could offer children a different and playful approach to learn 21st century skills with digital toolkits. The framework and the two case studies create a basis for others on how to develop an integrated approach that suits a school context.

- A toolkit in combination with a DBL approach offers creative, playful learning. The user tests confirmed that children are indeed less likely to see lessons with a tangible toolkit as a traditional learning tool. The added value of technology can be exposed when combining a technology toolkit with design cases and activities that are related to real-world problems. This makes a connection between society and technology. Real world problems furthermore keep the activity close to the own imagination of children. The cases showed that children engaged with the topics in the design briefs, were eager to find design solutions and had fun while doing so.

- It is possible to stimulate 21st century skills with DBL and digital toolkits. We also found it is possible to combine teaching 21st century skills and course-based learning goals through DBL. It is important to connect existing course based learning goals to future learning goals (21st century skills). Without addressing both current and future learning goals, a digital toolkit is not applicable in practice. Connectedness makes sure that the toolkit covers more areas then just technology, this makes it more appealing for schools to implement it. Therefore, when other similar design based learning solutions are created, a designer should carefully focus on what children can learn on a current course-based level and on a future learning goal level (21st century skills).

- Children can relatively independently complete design processes when provided with a well thought out design process, toolkit and briefing. There are multiple criteria surrounding these aspects to DBL with toolkits. These criteria are defined in the framework mentioned in section 4. A teacher has relatively little time per student. Because of this a good briefing is a very important aspect in the framework. A briefing can however not replace a teacher. A teacher will remain to be the facilitator of learning, actively stimulating and helping children where necessary.

Although our design explorations delivered promising first results, further research is needed to get a better understanding on how an integrated DBL approach can be embedded in a real school context. The challenge in applying the framework is in developing an integrated solution tailored to a **specific context**: e.g. embedded in a school context, linking to appropriate course learning goal, using a digital toolkit that can be applied by the teacher in a set of learning activities. The framework provides a good starting point for further work. For example on how the properties of digital toolkits can best be linked to different types of course-based learning goals. In addition to this, our user tests showed that although our design solutions are specifically designed for usage in classrooms, the teacher still has to put a lot of effort in getting to know design based learning and applying it in class. This was also described by Kolodner [3]. Twenty-first century skills seem to form the future of education, actual development of these skills is however difficult to measure. Implementing and measuring 21st century skills in a non-isolated way will ask for a big change in the current form of education. In our opinion and in the opinion of most consulted experts, this will however improve the connection between education and (future) society.

Acknowledgements. We would like to thank all stakeholders and the children who joined our user tests. From the stakeholders we would like to thank the Jan van Brabant College, Theresialyceum, Heerbeeck College Best and De Sonnewijzer for participating in our user tests. The 'Design based learning of 21st century skills with technology toolkits at schools' project received funding from the Municipality of Eindhoven as part of the project 'Eindhoven Education 2030'.

References

[1]   European Parliament: The Lisbon Strategy 2000 – 2010 An analysis and evaluation of the methods used and results, European Parliament, Brussels (2010)

[2]   Klapwijk, R., Holla, E.: Leidraad onderzoekend en ontwerpend leren. Wetenschapsknooppunt Zuid-Holland, Delft (2014)

[3]   Kolodner, J.L., Camp, P., Crismond, D., Holbrook, J., Puntembaker, S., Ryan, M.: Problem-Based Learning Meets Case-Based Reasoning in the Middle-School Science Classroom: Putting Learning by Design(tm) Into Practice. Journal of the Learning Sciences, 495–547 (2003)

[4]   Resnick, M.: All I really need to know (about creative thinking) I learned (by studying how children learn) in kindergarten. In: C&C 2007

[5]   Thijs, A., Fisser, P., van der Hoeven, M.: 21e eeuwse vaardigheden in het curriculum van het funderend onderwijs: een conceptueel kader. SLO, nationaal expertisecentrum leerplanontwikkeling, Enschede (2014)

[6]   Department for Education United Kingdom, National curriculum - GOV.UK, September 11, 2013. https://www.gov.uk/government/collections/national-curriculum

[7]   Hummels, C., Frens, J.: The reflective transformative design process. In: CHI 2009 Extended Abstracts on Human Factors in Computing Systems, pp. 2655–2658 (2009)

[8]   den Brok, P.J., van Diggelen, M.: Implementatie van Technasia. Eindhoven School of Education, Eindhoven (2013)

[9]   van der Graft, M., Kemmers, P.: Onderzoekend en Ontwerpend Leren bij Natuur en Techniek: Basisdocument over de didactiek voor onderzoekendkend en ontwerpend leren in het primair onderwijs. Stichting Platform Bèta Techniek, Den Haag (2007)

[10] White House Office of Science and Technology Policy, Preparing Americans with 21st Century Skills, White House Office of Science and Technology Policy, Washington, D.C. (2014)

[11] SLO, Kerndoelen Primair Onderwijs, SLO, nationaal expertisecentrum leerplanontwikkeling, Enschede (2006)

[12] Onderbouw-VO, Karakteristieken en kerndoelen voor de onderbouw. Onderbouw-VO, Zwolle (2006)

[13] Piaget, J.: Piaget's theory. Springer, Heidelberg (1976)

[14] Dochy, F., Segers, M., De Rijdt, C.: Assessment in onderwijs: nieuwe toetsvormen en examincring in studentgericht onderwijs en competentiegericht onderwijs. Uitgeverij LEMMA BV, Utrecht (2002)

[15] Kolb, D.A.: Experiential Learning: Experience as the Source of Learning and Development. Prentice Hall, Englewood Cliffs (1984)

[16] Birenbaum, M.: New insights into learning and teaching and their implications for assessment. In: Optimising New Modes of Assessment: in Search of Qualities and Standards, pp. 13–36 (2003)

[17] Piaget, J.: How children form mathematical concepts. Scientific American 189, 74–79 (1953)

[18] Terrenghi, L., et al.: A cube to learn: a tangible user interface for the design of a learning appliance. Personal and Ubiquitous Computing, 153–158 (2006)

[19] Giannakos, M.N., Jaccheri, L.: An enriched artifacts activity for supporting creative learning: Perspectives for children with impairments. In: Anacleto, J.C., Clua, E.W.G., da Silva, F.S.C., Fels, S., Yang, H.S. (eds.) ICEC 2013. LNCS, vol. 8215, pp. 160–163. Springer, Heidelberg (2013)

[20] Blikstein, P.: Gears of our childhood: constructionist toolkits, robotics and physical computing, past and future. In: Interaction Design and Children IDC, New York (2013)

[21] littleBits Electronics Inc., littleBits: DIY Electronics For Prototyping And Learning, May 12, 2015. http://littlebits.cc/

[22] Arduino, Arduino - Home, May 12, 2015. http://www.arduino.cc/

[23] Resnick, M., Rosenbaum, E.: Designing for tinkerability. In: Designing for Tinkerability, New York, Routledge, p. 164 (2013)

[24] Lassiter et al.: Training and Inspiring Educators in Digital Fabrication: A Professional Development Framework, February 9 Research

[25] Resnick, M., Martin, F., Sargent, R., Silverman, B.: Programmable Bricks: toys to think with. IBM Systems 35, 443–452 (1996)

[26] Blumenfeld, P.C., et al.: Motivating Project-based Learning Sustaining the Doing Supporting the Learning. Educational Psychologist 26(3-4), 369–398 (1991)

[27] Hennessya, S., Wishartb, J., Whitelockc, D., Deaneya, R., Brawnb, R., Velleb, L.I., McFarlaneb, A., Ruthvena, K., Winterbottom, M.: Pedagogical approaches for technology-integrated science teaching. Computers & Education 48(1), 137–152 (2007)

[28] Sjøberg, S.: Science and Technology in Education - Current Challenges and Possible Solutions. Meeting of European Ministers of Education and Research, Uppsala (2001)

Embedding and Implementation of Quantum Computational Concepts in Digital Narratives

Nikitas M. Sgouros

Department of Digital Systems, University of Piraeus
18534, Piraeus, Greece
sgouros@unipi.gr

Abstract. Quantum computational concepts introduce a host of new ideas for describing and implementing computational processes based on notions of superposition, entanglement, interference and measurement. This paper explores how such quantum mechanical ideas can be used in the development and implementation of computational narrative environments. In particular we focus on the use of quantum computing concepts for the representation of character state and beliefs, the development of point-of-view and context-sensitive processes for decision making along with the representation of the notion of conflict. We describe the implementation of these ideas in QuNL, our novel, special-purpose declarative language for narrative construction along with QuNE its associated interpreter. Both systems are available on the Web for testing and experimentation.

Keywords: Quantum Computing, Computational Methodologies for Entertainment, Narratives.

1 Introduction

Narrative forms an important backbone on which major entertainment forms ranging from movies or theater to games are based. One of the most significant forms of narrative centers on Aristotle's view of tragedy [1]. In the Aristotelian conception of narrative an original conflict between antagonistic forces develops out of an initial situation. The conflict moves from this initial situation towards its antagonistic climax through a sequence of escalating conflicts consisting of actions and counter-actions and then towards an unambiguous solution at the end. The evolving performance conforms to the demands of *unity* and *totality* [1]. Unity means that the performance consists of a single dramatic sequence, or if there are more than one, that one ("the primary plot") predominates clearly over the others. Totality means "that everything is there that somehow belongs to it" and, in negative terms, "that all elements that are not indispensable are omitted".

Central to this narrative conception is the notion of the 'hero' i.e., the protagonist whose beliefs, goals, behavior and final fate is the subject of the story. Another important notion is that of the 'anti-hero ' i.e. a protagonist that opposes the hero and possesses incompatible qualities to those of the hero. The existence of the hero and

© IFIP International Federation for Information Processing 2015
K. Chorianopoulos et al. (Eds.): ICEC 2015, LNCS 9353, pp. 140–154, 2015.
DOI: 10.1007/978-3-319-24589-8_11

anti-hero forms a dipole around which a clash erupts, escalates and finally resolves transforming our experience at the end of the event. This is a basic description that we believe fits a lot of stories, game plots, theater plays, operas etc. that can be conceptualized as the conflict between a hero and anti-hero enacting the battle between good and evil, wealth and poverty, love and hate etc. While the aristotelian principles of narrative have been successfully applied over the ages to events with a predetermined fixed plot structure such as stories, movies or theater plays, their application in interactive events, such as games, where the participants have significant degrees of freedom in their behavior and, therefore, a fixed plot structure is not guaranteed to be followed, is more problematic. The problem stems from the fact that the outcome of the conflicts taking place in a game is inherently indeterminate. Consequently, computational abstractions for interactive narrative should take into account the indeterminate nature of these events and describe them as such.

This paper explores how narrative elements can be framed in quantum computational terms. We describe how quantum mechanical notions such as superposition, entanglement, interference and measurement can handle important narrative aspects such as the representation of character state and beliefs, the development of point-of-view and context-sensitive processes for decision making along with the representation of the notion of conflict. Furthermore, since quantum models are inherently indeterminate they can provide ways to capture the effects that context has on the observation and evolution of an interactive narrative.

We explore the use of quantum computational concepts in narrative generation through the construction of QuNL, a declarative language for describing subjective elements in narrative construction and QuNE a special-purpose interpreter for executing QuNL programs on a classical computer. QuNL programs are fed to QuNE (Quantum Narrative Engine), a special-purpose interpreter that constantly evaluates the applicability of protagonist actions and establishes the effects of each applied action. QuNE is implemented in C++ and an on-line version is available at (http://www.epinoetic.org/Assets/QuNL.html) along with a description of the QuNL language (http://epinoetic.org/?page_id=37). A QuNL code example that can be fed to QuNE can be found at (http://www.epinoetic.org/Assets/QuNLexample.txt) .

The rest of this paper is structured as follows. Section 2 provides a brief overview of the basic notions in quantum theory and computing that are relevant to our research. Section 3 describes our quantum concepts for character state and beliefs in narrative. Section 4 describes our quantum theoretic notion of conflict in narrative, while section 5 shows how narrative evolves using quantum computational notions. Finally, section 6 presents related work and discusses our research results.

2   Quantum Computing Overview

Although at first sight it might seem idiosyncratic to suggest that a theory that deals with the behavior of subatomic particles can serve as the basis for thinking about computational forms of narrative, we believe that there are very interesting insights to be gained from drawing parallels between these two areas of research. In this section we seek to describe in a simplified manner the major features of quantum theory that are relevant to this endeavor (see [2] for a thorough introduction).

Quantum theory is concerned with modeling the behavior of subatomic particles. The behavior of such a particle p is characterized by its *state*. The state of a particle can be expressed in terms of a basis consisting of a set of n vectors. We refer to these basis vectors as *pure* states $|x_i\rangle$ using the Dirac *ket* notation that is popular in quantum theory. Each $|x_i\rangle$ is a n-dimensional vector, for example $x_0=[1,0,...,0]^T$, $x_1=[0,1,...,0]^T$, ..., $x_{n-1}=[0,0,...,1]^T$, such that the set of x_i's forms an orthonormal basis of the complex vector space C^n. The state $|\psi_p\rangle$ of particle p is a linear combination of the x_i's, therefore

$$|\psi_p\rangle = c_0{}^* \ |x_0\rangle + c_1{}^* \ |x_1\rangle + ... + c_{n-1}{}^* \ |x_{n-1}\rangle$$

where the c_i 's are complex numbers referred to as *complex amplitudes*. Unlike classical physics a particle can be in a *superposition* of states, therefore our particle p can be in all of the $|x_i\rangle$ states simultaneously. Consequently the current state of the system corresponds to a vector in Hilbert space. The particular blending of states it is in is described by the vector of complex amplitudes $[c_0, c_1, ..., c_{n-1}]^T$ in its state description. Although p is in a superposition of states, when we *observe* (*measure*) it, it ends up (collapses) in only one of its $|x_i\rangle$ pure states. Therefore while a quantum system can exist in a multitude of states simultaneously it is the measurement process that interacts with the current superposition of the system and actively creates a single state for the system to be in. The probability $Pr(\psi_p = x_i)$ that p will be observed in state $|x_i\rangle$ is given by the normalized squared length of the state's amplitude:

$$\Pr(\psi_p = x_i) \ = \frac{|c_i|^2}{\sum_{i=0}^{n-1}|c_i|^2}$$

In the following we always assume that $\sum_{i=0}^{n-1}|c_i|^2 = 1$, therefore:

$$\Pr(\psi_p = x_i) \ = |c_i|^2$$

The computation of these probabilities proceeds by first projecting the state vector onto the relevant pure state vector and then squaring the length of the resulting projection.

Another important feature of quantum theory is the way quantum particles are combined to form more complex systems. In classical physics the combination of two independent systems each with n and m degrees of freedom respectively, results in a system with n+m degrees of freedom. This is not the case in the quantum context where the combination of the two systems results in a system with n*m pure states. This happens because the state of the new system is computed using the *tensor product* $\otimes$ of the two initial states and it contains all the combinations of its initial states. However, not all states of multi-particle systems can be decomposed into a tensor product of a set of more simple states. We refer to the ones that cannot be decomposed in such a way as *entangled* states. Entanglement seems to be a fundamental phenomenon in quantum mechanics for which there might be no equivalent in classical physics. The states of entangled particles are correlated, therefore if we observe the state of one of them then the states of the rest are instantaneously affected even though they may be quite far away from each other. It is not clear yet how particles become entangled in nature although in quantum computing there exists sequences of operators that act on *qubits* (a qubit is a unit of information on a two dimensional state space) and set them in an entangled state.

Another basic notion in quantum mechanics is that of the *observables*, i.e., the parameters that can be observed in each state of the state space. Observables can be thought of as the set of questions that we can pose at a specific state of the system. As we noted before, each time we pose a question to a system (i.e. we perform a measurement on it) the system exits its superposition and settles in one of its pure (definite) states. What is interesting is that, in general, when we pose a sequence of questions to the quantum system, its final state depends on the order in which these questions are posed, therefore measurements do not commute in general. We refer to this ordering effect as *interference* between the various measurements. In essence, interference is one way of capturing the effect of the context in which a measurement is performed. Another effect of ordering in the measurement process is that while a system can reach a definite state after a measurement, it can then enter a new superposition after a subsequent measurement corresponding to a different question is performed. Therefore, it is not always the case that a sequence of measurements removes uncertainty by setting the system into a definite state since this depends on the choice of basis in which the measurement is performed. Heisenberg's well-known uncertainty principle which states informally that there is an inverse relationship between the accuracy of measuring the position and momentum of a quantum particle illustrates this phenomenon in the case of observables that do not commute.

In terms of dynamics, a quantum system evolves either through the application of a *unitary operator* on its current state which transforms it into a new state or through the execution of a measurement. A unitary operator is a linear operator that modifies the direction of a vector in a Hilbert space without changing its length. In quantum computing each operator is represented by a unitary matrix and referred to as a quantum gate. The application of a sequence of unitary operators on a state is deterministic. In contrast, as we indicated before, the execution of a measurement is probabilistic. In general then a quantum computation can evolve using both methods under the following sequence of steps:

1. the system is placed into an initial state, e.g. $|\psi\rangle$
2. a sequence of unitary operators   (quantum gates) is applied to $|\psi\rangle$
3. the output of step 2 is measured giving us the final state of the system.

3   Representation of Character State and Beliefs

The quantum-theoretic notion of superposition forms the basis for representing the state of our narrative protagonists. At each point in time each protagonist has a unique state that can be expressed as a superposition of alternative pairs of qualities. These pairs of qualities correspond to different points of view (moral, economic, health, social etc.) for referring to the protagonist state.

In particular, we represent the various qualities of the hero and anti-hero as unit vectors in two dimensional complex space C^2. These vectors are organized in pairs each of which defines a basis for describing the state space of a protagonist. For example, if the narrative is about poor versus rich then we can define two such qualities forming a 60^0 and a -30^0 angle with the x axis respectively (see Fig. 1) as:

$$|poor> = [\cos(60^0), \sin(60^0)]^T \text{ and } |rich|> = [\cos(-30^0), \sin(-30^0)]^T$$

These qualities form an orthonormal basis $W = \{|poor>, |rich>\}$ for describing the state space of a protagonist in terms of wealth. In this case the states of our hero and anti-hero can be represented as two superpositions with respect to W. For example, if at time t_1 our hero is more likely to regard himself as poor while the anti-hero more probably regards himself as rich then these protagonists can be in the following superpositions:

$$|hero(t_1)> = 0.8*|poor> + 0.6*|rich>$$
$$|anti-hero(t_1)> = 0.6*|poor> + 0.8*|rich>$$

where $|hero(t_1)>$ and $|anti-hero(t_1)>$ represent the states of the hero and anti-hero, respectively, at time t_1.

What these relations indicate is that both protagonists in terms of wealth are simultaneously 'poor' and 'rich', i.e. they are in a superposition of these two possible inconsistent states. If the hero at time t_1 seeks to make up his mind on whether he is rich or poor this is equivalent to measuring his state and in this case there is a 64% $(=0.8^2)$ chance that he will be measured 'poor' and a 36% $(=0.6^2)$ that he will come out as 'rich', while the reverse holds for our anti-hero.

A protagonist then can be conceptualized as a quantum system generating various qualities. At each point in time each protagonist has a state represented as a unit vector in C^2. The squared length of the projection of his state vector on a quality vector corresponds to the probability with which the state can generate the particular quality when measured.

Such a protagonist state can be simultaneously described in terms of various qualities. Each protagonist can use his own set of bases for describing his state. The orientation between the various bases that describe a protagonist state provide a geometric representation of the correlations between the qualities forming these bases. In essence, this set defines the system by which each protagonist internally encodes the correlations between his qualities along with his conception of the qualities of the other protagonists, thus providing a method for differentiating each protagonist as a character and furnishing him with a distinctive world view.

For example, there can be two different bases for morality M_{hero} and $M_{anti-hero}$ for our hero and anti-hero respectively. We define the M_{hero} basis as $M_{hero} = \{ |good_{hero}>, |evil_{hero}> \}$ while the $M_{anti-hero}$ basis can be $M_{anti-hero} = \{ |good_{anti-hero}>, |evil_{anti-hero}> \}$ with the orientation of their unit vectors shown in Fig. 1. The hero can internally describe his state using the W and M_{hero} bases while the anti-hero can internally describe his state using the W and $M_{anti-hero}$ bases. As a result, each of the protagonists has a different conception of morality because each one views the world using a different morality basis. Furthermore, M_{hero} and $M_{anti-hero}$ can form different angles with the W basis. Consequently, each protagonist has a different conception of the correlation between morality and wealth because of the particular orientation between the morality and wealth basis in his basis set that controls how each basis can be expressed in terms of the other. Thus each protagonist possesses his personalized belief system.

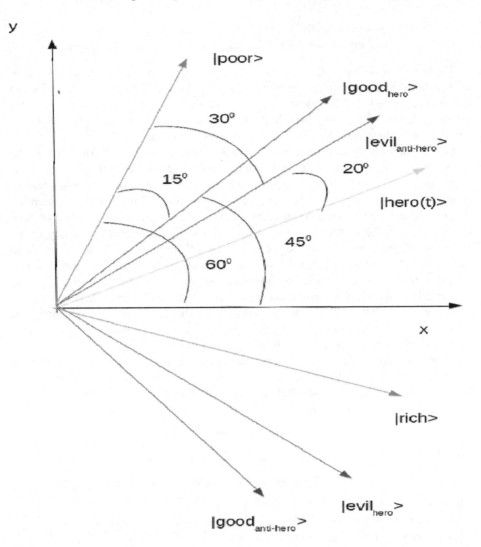

Fig. 1. Orientation between the bases M_{hero}, $M_{anti-hero}$ and W on the xy plane. The unit vectors of the M_{hero} basis are in blue, the ones of the $M_{anti-hero}$ are in black while the unit vectors of W are in red. Each one of these bases consists of orthonormal vectors.

Furthermore, such a quantum geometrical abstraction allows us to represent how each protagonist observes the state of the other protagonists in his own belief system. This is performed through the expression of the state of the other protagonists using the various bases that express the observer state.   For example, if we assume that the vector |hero(t)> in Fig. 1 represents the current state of the hero forming a 20^0 angle with the |evil$_{anti-hero}$> vector and consequently a 70^0 angle with the |good$_{anti-hero}$> vector then the state of our hero as seen by the $M_{anti-hero}$ basis of the anti-hero is written as:

$$|hero(t)\rangle = \cos(20^0)*|evil_{anti-hero}\rangle + \sin(20^0)*|good_{anti-hero}\rangle \Rightarrow$$
$$\Rightarrow |hero(t)\rangle = 0.93969*|evil_{anti-hero}\rangle + 0.34202*|good_{anti-hero}\rangle$$

Therefore, according to the anti-hero's morality our hero is probably an 'evil' man as there is a 88.3% chance to be observed as 'evil' compared with a 11.7% chance to be observed as 'good'. This view is inconsistent with the conception of the hero for himself in terms of morality since his state is closer to the $|good_{hero}\rangle$ vector than the $|evil_{hero}\rangle$ one. Therefore, the hero possibly regards himself as 'good'.

In general, each protagonist is not expected to have access to the *'true'* state of the other protagonists neither to the details of the *'true'* bases in which they express their state. As a 'true' state or basis of a protagonist we refer to the state and bases that he actually uses in his behavior. Therefore, each protagonist can use his own conception of the state and the bases that are used by others. For example, from the point of view of the anti-hero the $|hero(t)\rangle$ state that he used to view the hero's morality in the previous computation may not be the 'true' state of the hero but what the anti-hero thinks it is. As a result, there is not necessarily some global 'true' knowledge shared by all protagonists and each one of them behaves according to his subjective conception of the environment. This greatly increases the expressive power of our narrative model allowing us to represent misconceptions or misunderstandings between the protagonists. These situations of discrepant awareness can have significant dramatic potential according to theories of drama [3].

If we conceptualize the whole narrative as a quantum system composed of protagonist subsystems then the state of the whole system can be computed as the tensor product of the protagonist states. In general, if $|i\rangle = [x, y]^T$ and $|j\rangle = [z, e]^T$ then their tensor product is computed as:

$$|i\rangle \otimes |j\rangle = [x*z, x*e, y*z, y*e]^T$$

and if $|A\rangle = (a*|i\rangle + b*|j\rangle)$ and $B = (c*|k\rangle + d*|p\rangle)$ then

$$|A\rangle \otimes |B\rangle = a*c*|ik\rangle + a*d*|ip\rangle + b*c*|jk\rangle + b*d*|jp\rangle$$

where $|ij\rangle$ is used as a shorthand for $|i\rangle \otimes |j\rangle$

For example, if we want to describe the state $|\psi(t)\rangle$ of the narrative at time t in terms of morality bases M_{hero} and $M_{anti-hero}$ where:

$$|hero(t)\rangle = 0.8*|good_{hero}\rangle + 0.6*|evil_{hero}\rangle$$
$$|anti-hero(t)\rangle = 0.6*|good_{anti-hero}\rangle + 0.8*|evil_{anti-hero}\rangle$$

then:

$$|\psi(t)\rangle\rangle = |hero(t)\rangle \otimes |anti-hero(t)\rangle \Rightarrow$$
$$\Rightarrow |\psi(t)\rangle = 0.48*|good_{hero}good_{anti-hero}\rangle + 0.64*|good_{hero}evil_{anti-hero}\rangle +$$
$$+0.36*|evil_{hero}good_{anti-hero}\rangle + 0.48*|evil_{hero}evil_{anti-hero}\rangle$$

This representation now means that, at time t there is a 23,04% (= 0.48^2) chance that both our protagonists are observed as being good with respect to their individual bases, a 40,96% (=0.64^2) chance of our hero being observed as good and the anti-hero as evil etc.

QuNL allows us to define the various bases and basis unit vectors that represent alternative points of view in the unfolding narrative using the *Basis* statement. Each Basis provides a reference frame for representing the protagonist states with regards to two opposing qualities. For example *wealth@hero* can be defined as a basis that corresponds to a 2D coordinate system with an x-vector called 'rich' with value [cos(30.0), sin(30.0)] and a y-vector called 'poor' with value [cos(120.0), sin(120.0)] where the angle values are in degrees. The following QuNL statement describes all this information:

Basis wealth@hero <- rich [cos(30.0), sin(30.0)] poor [cos(120.0), sin(120.0)];

In addition, a Basis can be defined with respect to an already defined basis as in:

Basis health@hero <- healthy sick #Angle 10.0 #WithRespectTo wealth@hero;

In this statement a new basis 'health@hero' is defined consisting of an x-vector named 'healthy' and a y-vector called 'sick' each of which forms a 10 degree angle with the corresponding x- and y- vectors of the 'wealth@hero' basis. The #Angle and #WithRespectTo keywords are used to indicate the relative angle and the reference basis respectively.

QuNL also provides the *Protagonist* statement for describing the initial state of a story character. For example, the statement:

Protagonist hero <- #Amplitude [cos(45.0), sin(45.0)] #WithRespectTo health@hero;

describes the initial state of a protagonist named 'hero' as a unit vector with value [cos(45.0), sin(45.0)] in the coordinate system defined by Basis 'health@hero'.

In conclusion, our quantum-inspired conception of a protagonist state can capture ambiguity and internal conflicts in his character through the notion of a superposition. In this conception the observed (measured) qualities of the protagonist emerge in real time at the point of measurement reflecting the interaction between the protagonist state and its environment. This is because the measurement process changes the state of the protagonist by projecting it into one of its basis vectors. Furthermore, this quantum conception offers a geometric interpretation that can capture the correlations between the qualities of a protagonist through the construction and orientation of several bases that form a personalized belief system. This geometric interpretation can also be used to capture the correlations between the states of different protagonists.

4   Quantum Theoretic Conceptualization of Conflict

Conflict is an essential concept in aristotelian narrative as it provides a way of resolving the questions posed by an event and of propelling the story forward. As a result, conflict is a transformational event. In order to operationalize conflict we turn to the notion of entanglement and explore its potential use in our narrative model.

In quantum theory it is not always the case that the current state of a composite system can be expressed as the tensor product of its subsystems. For example, let us consider the state $|\psi(t_3)>$ such that:

$$|\psi(t_3)> = \frac{1}{\sqrt{2}} * |good_{hero}evil_{anti-hero}> + \frac{1}{\sqrt{2}} * |evil_{hero}good_{anti-hero}>$$

State $|\psi(t_3)\rangle$ corresponds to a scenario in which the $|good_{hero}\rangle$ and $|evil_{anti\text{-}hero}\rangle$ vectors are perfectly correlated and the same holds for the $|evil_{hero}\rangle$ and $|good_{anti\text{-}hero}\rangle$ vector pair. Consequently whenever the state of the hero coincides with the $|good_{hero}\rangle$ vector the state of the anti-hero will automatically coincide with the $|evil_{anti\text{-}hero}\rangle$ vector and vice versa. An analogous situation holds between the $|evil_{hero}\rangle$ and $|good_{anti\text{-}hero}\rangle$ vector pair. In addition, the entanglement relation specifies that there is a 50% chance for the event '$|good_{hero}\rangle$ and $|evil_{anti\text{-}hero}\rangle$' to happen and the same holds for the '$|evil_{hero}\rangle$ and $|good_{anti\text{-}hero}\rangle$' combination. As a result, each of our protagonists has a 50% chance to be observed as 'good' and if this happens then the other one becomes 'evil'. More specifically, state $|\psi(t_3)\rangle$ has three distinctive features:

(1) It can be proven that it cannot be decomposed into a tensor product of its two protagonist components, therefore it is not a product of the usual rules of state synthesis. This is because $|\psi(t_3)\rangle$ is analogous to what is called a Bell state in quantum mechanics [2]. In particular, two other state combinations that a tensor product would generate ($|good_{hero}good_{anti\text{-}hero}\rangle$ and $|evil_{hero}evil_{anti\text{-}hero}\rangle$) are absent from $|\psi(t_3)\rangle$. As it does not emerge out of the 'normal' rules of system synthesis, $|\psi(t_3)\rangle$ essentially corresponds to a disruption in system evolution.
(2) There is perfect correlation between the states of the system involved in it. More specifically, the hero and anti-hero states in $|\psi(t_3)\rangle$ exhibit perfect correlation because if the state of the hero is measured as $|good_{hero}\rangle$ then we automatically know that our anti-hero is in the $|evil_{anti\text{-}hero}\rangle$ state and vice versa.
(3) It is indeterminate because although the states involved are perfectly correlated we do not know in advance in which one of these correlations the system will collapse after measurement.

We refer to state $|\psi(t_3)\rangle$ as an *entangled* state.

In the case of conflict although it is quite hard to come up with an exact definition, we can nevertheless adopt a consensus view that associates conflict with a disruption of the status quo of a system. This disruption arises out of a maximal level of contradictions in the evolution of the system. In this respect conflict and entanglement are both disruptive events in the life of a system. Similar to entanglement, conflict in narrative:

(1) results in establishing correlations between the states of the parties involved usually in the form of a winner and a loser.
(2) its final result is indeterminate. There is always an element of surprise in conflict and even the most powerful can end up on the losing side. This fact provides the dramatic suspense that is necessary to engage the audience in the event. Furthermore, both parties have something to gain or lose, i.e., there is always risk in conflict.

Therefore, entanglement can be used to establish 'zero-sum' types of correlations between the protagonists where one man's win is another man's loss such as the state represented by $|\psi(t_3)\rangle$. Such 'zero-sum' correlations correspond to the archetypical notion of conflict in aristotelian narrative. This is the case because each story needs to have a clear, unambiguous resolution and placing our protagonists in orthogonal states (e.g. life/death, love/hate, freedom/jail) in the end provides the clearest conceptual separation of their final fate.

In QuNL entanglements are established using the *Entangle* statement. This statement takes three arguments each one enclosed in brackets ([]) that describe how the states (e.g. ?subj and ?obj) in its first argument will be correlated (variables in QuNL are denoted as identifiers beginning with '?'). The second argument of this statement defines the probability P with which the correlation described in its third argument can be established through measurement. Finally, the third argument describes the pair of unit vectors of two bases (e.g. A and B) in which the values of the entangled states will collapse after measurement with probability P. Then the probability of the ?subject and ?object states collapsing on the other pair of unit vectors of bases A and B is 1-P and is computed automatically by the system. For example in the following Entangle statement:

(Entangle [?subj ?obj] [?p*?h] [rich(wealth@?subj) poor(wealth@?obj)])

we have that P = ?p*?h, A = wealth@?subj, B = wealth@?obj and the statement establishes the following entanglement relation between the ?subj and ?obj states:

$$(?p*?h)*|rich(wealth@?subj)poor(wealth@?obj)>+$$
$$(1-?p*?h)*|poor(wealth@?subj) rich(wealth@?obj)>$$

5   Narrative Dynamics

In our quantum conception of narrative the state of each protagonist is represented as a unit-length vector in Hilbert space. The story uses a number of bases in which each such state can be expressed thereby representing the belief system and the qualities of each protagonist and allowing each state to have multiple interpretations depending on the basis in which it is expressed. Based on this conception we can identify three ways to affect narative evolution (its dynamics): (1) Protagonist decisions (2) Protagonist actions (3) Belief Revision

Protagonist decisions are equivalent with the process of measuring his state in some basis. Consequently we can represent each decision as a collapse of the protagonist state in one of the basis vectors, thereby modifying the state vector.

Protagonist actions are more general than decisions in that they modify the superposition corresponding to the protagonist state without necessarily causing it to collapse to any basis vector. This is achieved by modifying the amplitudes of the pure states involved in a superposition. In essence protagonist actions correspond to unitary operators in quantum theory. In addition protagonist actions can change the state of other protagonists. For example, if the hero finds a well-paid job then his state in Fig. 1 should rotate closer to the |rich> vector since the possibilities of improving his wealth are now brighter.

Furthermore, protagonist actions can result in the entanglement of protagonist states. For example, our hero may try to become rich by stealing the anti-hero's treasure chest. If the stealing action succeeds it will result in the hero becoming rich and the anti-hero poor while if it fails the hero will remain poor and the anti-hero rich. Therefore the stealing action can be thought of as establishing the following entanglement between the hero and anti-hero:

$$|\psi(t_5)> = \alpha * |rich_{hero}poor_{anti-hero}> + \beta * |poor_{hero}rich_{anti-hero}>$$

where a and b squared will reflect the probability of the stealing action either succeeding or failing respectively.

Whenever conflict entanglements are established they create clear correlations between states, therefore they impose a set of constraints on how different state vectors change. The amplitudes of the entangled states may not remain fixed but they can change during the event reflecting the effects of the protagonists behavior. For example, if the hero consumes a magic filter that makes him invisible then his chances of succeeding in stealing the anti-hero's treasure should improve and that should be reflected in the amplitudes of the entanglement he participates related to his stealing action. Therefore, modification of the state of a protagonist can either cause an entanglement to be resolved if it collapses to a state participating in such an entanglement or it can change the probabilities of the events described in the entanglement.

Each protagonist action can be triggered in a particular context. Such a context can consist of actions that have already taken place or of probabilities for the appearance of certain states and the relations between them. For example, a stealing action such as the one we described above can be materialized under a context in which the subject of the action is primarily 'evil' and he thinks that the person he wants to steal from is probably 'rich'. If the thief is the hero and the victim is the anti-hero this means that in order for the stealing action to occur the probability of the hero's state collapsing to the $|evil_{hero}>$ vector in Fig. 1 should be above a certain threshold while the probability of the anti-hero's state collapsing to the $|rich>$ vector should be greater than another threshold.

Finally, belief revision corresponds to a change in the protagonist's conceptualization of his state. This happens when the protagonist modifies one or more of the bases he uses to express his state. For example, our hero may convince himself that being rich is not such a bad thing. This will be materialized by transforming (rotating) the M_{hero} basis in Fig. 1 so that the $|good_{hero}>$ vector comes closer to the $|rich>$ vector.

Each protagonist uses a set of alternative bases in which he can express his state. However, each protagonist can have a clear preference over which of the vectors of each basis his state should be closer to or, optimally, coincide with. We call a set of such vectors the protagonist's *preferred* states. For example, our hero may regard the vectors $|good_{hero}>$, $|rich>$ described in Fig. 1 as belonging to the set of his preferred states. This set then represents the set of goals that he wants to satisfy in the narrative. Depending on the geometry of the vectors involved it is not always possible to maximally satisfy all these goals. The optimal scenario for the protagonist would be if all the vectors in its preferred states were identical, therefore collapsing its state to any one of them would maximally satisfy his goals. If this is not the case then the protagonist should seek to transform his state vector through a sequence of decisions and/or actions to a position that represents an optimal compromise between achieving all these goals. Alternatively, he could revise his beliefs by transforming their respective bases so as to achieve either a maximal or an optimal positioning of the basis vectors included in his preferred states set with his state vector. Finally, he could decide to drop some of the goals in his preferred states set reflecting the fact it is hard or worthless to achieve them.

The distance between the current protagonist state and its optimal position in the preferred set of each protagonist can provide us with a measure of the *dramatic tension* that exists in his behavior. This distance is equal to the sum of the inner products between the state vector and each of the vectors in his preferred state set. The sum of the dramatic tensions for all protagonists can be used to estimate the overall dramatic tension in the event.

In QuNL the *Ethos* statement defines a set of qualities that a protagonist seeks to achieve as closely as possible ('ethos' is hellenic for the guiding beliefs of a person) therefore it corresponds to his preferred states. For example, the statement:

Ethos hero <- rich(wealth@hero) healthy(health@hero);

denotes that the protagonist 'hero' seeks to move his state as close as possible to the positions of the vectors 'rich' of basis 'wealth@hero' and 'healthy' of basis 'health@hero'.

Aristotelian narrative typically proceeds through the involvement of the protagonists in a sequence of developments that causes a rise in the overall level of dramatic tension. At some point tension reaches a maximum value corresponding to a climactic point in the event. This point triggers the resolution of all outstanding events leading to the story end. According to Aristotle, this resolution should be total and unambiguous affecting all unresolved events in the story and delivering a clear message in terms of ethics to the spectator. We model resolution as the measurement of some protagonist state in the event that makes it collapse to one of its basis vectors. This can be the result of a decision or an action taken by a protagonist or of a measurement executed on an entangled state (e.g. the outcome of a conflict). The performance of such a measurement can trigger a cascade of resolutions affecting all entangled states in which a protagonist is involved with his new pure state along with the establishment of new states for the rest of the protagonists that participate in these entanglements. Ideally the resolution of the psychagogical event should take place at its *climactic point* that is the point in which overall dramatic tension in the event reaches its maximum value.

In QuNL a *Praxis* statement represents the subjective imprint of an action ('praxis' is hellenic for 'action') that a protagonist may use in order to achieve the qualities in his Ethos. The following statement defines a Praxis named 'Steal'.

Praxis Steal <-

  #Bindings (?subj != ?obj)

  #Context (?p <- Prob ?subj = evil(morality@?subj)

                ?p > 0.7

                ?h <- Prob ?obj = rich(wealth@?subj)

                ?h > 0.9

)

   #Effects (

      (Entangle [?subj ?obj] [?p?h] [rich(wealth@?subj) poor(wealth@?obj)]));*

Each Praxis statement contains three fields, *#Bindings, #Context* and *#Effects*. The #Bindings field contains statements constraining the values of the Praxis variables independent of the context in which the Praxis can be executed. For example in the case of the Steal action above the #Bindings statements denote that the subject of the action should be different from the person to which the action is directed.

The #Context field contains a set of statements that describe the context under which the action can take place. For example, in the Steal Praxis statement above the statement:

$$?p <- Prob\ ?subj = evil(morality@?subj)$$

computes the probability with which the superposition of the protagonist state bound to the value of the variable ?subj can be found through measurement to be equal to the vector 'evil' of the basis 'morality@?subj' where again the variable ?subj is appropriately bound. The value of this probability is then assigned to the variable ?p. The following statements in the context of the particular Steal action then indicate that in order for this action to be considered for execution the prospective thief has to think of himself as being primarily evil (with a probability > 0.7) and he also has to think of the victim as being rich (with a probability > 0.9).

In addition the Praxis context can contain a *Metro* statement ('metro' is hellenic for measure). A Metro statement causes a measurement of a state in a given basis. For example, the statement

$$?d <- Metro\ \#State\ hero\ \#WithRespectTo\ romance$$

will cause a measurement of the state 'hero' in the basis 'romance'. The result of the measurement will be the name of the unit vector of the basis 'romance' in which the superposition 'hero' will collapse. This result will be stored in the variable '?d'. Finally, the #Effects field describes the effect of this action according to the persons involved in it. In our example execution of a Steal Praxis statement entangles the wealth states of the protagonists involved. In general in its current version a *Praxis* statement can have three effects:

1. Create entanglements between various protagonist states.
2. Transform one or more superpositions.
3. Stop narrative generation because a final resolution for the story has been found.

A QuNL program is fed to the QuNE interpreter which loops continuously seeking to identify all Praxis statements that can be executed during each cycle. For each protagonist the interpreter selects randomly and executes one of the Praxis statements that can run and the loop continues until there are no Praxis statements available for execution or narrative generation is stopped as a result of a Praxis execution.

6   Related Work and Discussion

Our research seeks to actively explore the use of quantum computational concepts in computational narratives. In this respect we described how quantum theory provides us with innovative means of expressing and formal methods for computing subjective elements of stories such as character construction, contextual and point-of-view decision-making, discrepant awareness and goal-directed behavior. Our research is inspired from and complements similar research efforts in social sciences and education [4-7] that seek to leverage the power of quantum theory and geometry in their respective fields.

A large part of the research in creating computational forms of narrative focuses on the use of AI planning techniques that are enriched in order to capture character intentionality and event causality in stories e.g. [8-10]. These methods assume that there is a definite event and character state at each point in the narrative along with explicit plan or rule-based structures for computing narrative developments. We differ from these approaches since we use indeterminate and vector-based rather than set-theoretic and determinate representations for narrative concepts such as protagonist state and beliefs and express the effects of protagonist actions in terms of either potentialities (unitary operations) or correlations (entanglements) rather than definite causal effects. Furthermore, each protagonist does not form a multi-step action plan but he reacts to narrative developments in context-sensitive ways. In essence our narrative model describes a computational mechanism by which each protagonist forms subjective views of the unfolding narrative and incorporates these views into decision-making and action selection processes. Such a quantum-based abstraction can work alongside classical AI narrative systems where the quantum model will be responsible for taking context-sensitive decisions and/or selecting appropriate actions. Since actions are executed in a non-quantum reality their results can be fed to a classical AI system for further refinement and execution. The outcomes of action execution can then be fed back to our quantum model so that a new decision/action selection process can begin.

Although our narrative approach is based on quantum theory, it is not faithful to quantum mechanics. For example and to the best of our knowledge there is no model of entanglement in quantum physics that allows the amplitudes of an established entanglement relation to become modified. Future work will seek to represent narrative elements in multi-dimensional vector spaces, investigate how our ideas can be applied to other entertainment forms such as music or visual arts and develop user-friendly authoring tools for creating quantum-based narratives.

Acknowledgements. Presentation of this research was partially supported by the University of Piraeus Research Center.

References

1. Aristotle, Poetics
2. Nielsen, M.A., Chuang, I.L.: Quantum Computation and Quantum Information. Cambridge University Press (2010)
3. Pfister, M.: The Theory and Analysis of Drama. Cambridge University Press (1991)
4. Busemeyer, J.R., Bruza, P.D.: Quantum Models of Cognition. Cambridge University Press (2012)
5. Haven, E., Khrennikov, A.: Quantum Social Science. Cambridge University Press (2013)

6. Goff, A.: Quantum tic-tac-toe: A teaching metaphor for superposition in quantum mechanics. American Journal of Physics 74(11) (2006)
7. Kitto, K., Boschetti, F.: Attitudes, ideologies and self-organization: information load minimization in multi-agent decision making. In: Advances in Complex Systems, vol. 16(2 & 3). World Scientific Publishing Company (2013)
8. Riedl, M.O., Young, M.R.: Narrative Planning: Balancing Plot and Character. Journal of Artificial Intelligence Research 39, 217–268 (2010)
9. Porteous, J., Cavazza, M.: Controlling narrative generation with planning trajectories: The role of constraints. In: Iurgel, I.A., Zagalo, N., Petta, P. (eds.) ICIDS 2009. LNCS, vol. 5915, pp. 234–245. Springer, Heidelberg (2009)
10. Sgouros, N.M.: Dynamic Generation, Management and Resolution of Interactive Plots. Artificial Intelligence 107(1), 29–62 (1999)

EmotionBike: A Study of Provoking Emotions in Cycling Exergames

Larissa Müller[1,3], Sebastian Zagaria[1], Arne Bernin[1,3], Abbes Amira[3],
Naeem Ramzan[3], Christos Grecos[4], and Florian Vogt[1,2]

[1] Department Informatik, University of Applied Sciences (HAW) Hamburg, Germany
[2] Innovations Kontakt Stelle (IKS) Hamburg, Germany
[3] School of Engineering and Computing, University of the West of Scotland, UK
[4] Independent Imaging Consultant

Abstract. In this work, we investigate the effect of how exercise game
design elements generate deliberate real-time sensed emotional responses
in gamers. Our experimental setup consists of a cycling game controller,
a designed 3D first-person cycling game to provoke emotions, a data
recording system, and an emotion analysis system. The physical cycling
game controller is an enhanced computer controlled bike-exercise-trainer
that enables handle bar steering and sets pedal resistance. Our developed
3D first person cycling game provokes emotions with game elements in
different game settings: timed race, parcours traversal, and virtual world
exploration. Our recording system synchronously captures video, game
controller activity, and game events for emotion analysis. In this case
study, we show evidence that crafted computer exergame elements are
able to provoke subject emotions displayed in their facial expressions,
which can be quantified with our developed analysis method. The game
elements selected in the specific gameplay situations follow patterns that
give inside and judge of individual players involvement and emotional
tension. Our emotion analysis of game events provides insights into player
reactions during specific game situations. Our results show that strong
differing responses by individuals may be taken into account in the design
of game mechanics. For example, the falling event of level 3 showed that
two opposing strong reactions could be triggered in players. The emotion
analysis methods may be used in other types of games. Hereby we believe
that a combination of questionnaires and our in situ emotion analysis
provide valuable feedback to aid decision in for game design and game
mechanics.

Keywords: Exergame, Affective Gaming, Physical Activity, Cycling
Game, Big Five Personality Test, Facial Expression, Emotion Provocation, Emotion Recognition

1 Introduction

Games, as one form of entertainment, enable the telling of stories by immersion
into imaginary worlds. Game content is designed during development to provide

© IFIP International Federation for Information Processing 2015
K. Chorianopoulos et al. (Eds.): ICEC 2015, LNCS 9353, pp. 155–168, 2015.
DOI: 10.1007/978-3-319-24589-8_12

rich and unique experiences and engage players. Provoked emotions play a significant role in the design of game scene moods and game character persona. These provoked emotions are either fixed in design or evolve through choices in the game flow. The individual emotional reactions of players during gameplay are a great source to individualize storytelling and provide another level of interaction.

In our work, we introduce the concept of emotion provocation in a physical cycling game. The physicality is hereby important since it requires physical effort in order to progress the game. To showcase the provocation concept we successfully provide our case study to show how game elements are able to provoke emotions. The experiments were conducted with a custom cycling controller, cycling game and emotion analysis. In addition, we investigate the influence of the emotional reaction by consideration of the big five personality traits.

2   Related Work

Relevant research can be found in the domain of affective computing and affective gaming. Different sensor types have been utilized as sources of affect information. Applied sensors include vision-based sensors that recognize facial expressions, body actions and physiological sensors including ECG, PPG, GSR, Respiration, and HR. A good overview of affective sensors provided in the survey by Kotsia et al. [1]. In this work we focus at this point on facial expression recognition to minimize invasiveness of the subjects. An interesting direction was demonstrated by Bailenson et al. [2], who combines facial feature recognition and physiological responses including electrocardiogram and skin conductance.

One research field using emotional dialogue systems aims to create human or animal like behavior in robots. Human Robot Interaction (HRI) enables bidirectional interaction between robots and humans, where social interacting elements such as Kismet [3] and Flobi [4], virtual avatars [5] and abstract surfaces [6] have been created. Social interaction requires modeling of intrinsic emotions [5] to create believable persona. Dialogue systems are often based on multimodal interaction [7] and offer users a more natural and transparent interaction [8]. Based on existing research we followed the paradigm of natural user interfaces and developed a physical cycling game controller to enhance the accessibility of the system. Tan et al. [9] discovered that physiological data relates to the game experience.

Provoking user emotions is a concept that has been explored previously in different contexts. The most commonly provoked user state is stress, because it is relatively easy to provoke and reliable to measure. It can be sensed with a combination of EEG, Blood Pressure, ECG and GSR [10][11].

In emotion recognition analysis systems chose predominately continues emotion dimensions (e.g. pleasure, arousal, dominance) or discreet emotion categories (e.g. basic emotions) as the output representation [12] [13]. In our work we chose a discreet emotion category, including joy, disgust, anger, fear, neutral, sad, surprise, and contempt, based on the availability of a recognition system. To obtain emotion measures from facial expressions our work utilizes the automatic FACS [14] coding tool CERT [15].

For the CERT assessment of emotion for computer-mediated tutorial dialogues Grafsgaard et al. [16] reported the importance to perform a bias adjustment, due to inter-person variation. For this study we do not adjust this bias, since we intend to show the ability of our physical exergame to provoke emotions and show differences. In our work, we relate facial expression reactions to game events.

A subset of the research field affective computing, which uses previously discussed techniques to create more entertaining and immersive experiences in games, is called affective gaming. Gilleade et al. [17] defined affective gaming as a form of gameplay where the current emotional state of the player is used to alter the game mechanics. For example, altering the behavior of user input, changing the game environment, artificial intelligence behavior or displaying visual feedback depending on the current emotional state. Currently there are many works which triggers game events in relation to the player's emotional state but there are fewer works that directly link recognized emotions to events that occurred during gameplay such as [18] [19].To take full advantage of interactive entertainment applications it is crucial for game design to analyse the effectiveness of emotions triggered by game events. Parnandi et al. [20] proposed an affective game, analyzing EDA and SCR data to control the game difficulty. They also defined a number of requirements enhancing affective game design and controls. Those requirements are incorporated in the presented cycling controller: be intuitive, engaging, easy to learn, highly dynamic and enabling multiple forms of manipulation, such as steering and speed. Many works in affective gaming focus on horror scenarios, because of the strong influence on stress levels [18] [19]. Another way to enable an emotional dialogue is to apply biofeedback. For example, games including biofeedback [21] and an integrated emotion recognition [22][23].

For general exercise, Biddle [24] linked physical activity to mood and emotion. Looking at exercise and video games, Warburton et al. [25] showed that interactive games are able to enhance exercise experiences. Specifically for cycling exergames, Hoda et al. [26] demonstrated that combining games with a physical bike increases the speed and the average rpm of participants by motivation, resulting in an improved exercise. These results provide evidence that exergames add entertaining value and motivation for people with basic activity levels to exercise. To our knowledge, our study is the first emotion assessment in a cycling exergame.

3   Experimental Setup

To conduct our case study we designed an experimental setup for physical cycling game scenarios, capture game and interface controller events as well as emotional responses in facial expression. Our experimental setup, shown in Fig. 1 consisted of four main components: data acquisition, emotion sensors, controller, and visualization. The emotion sensors component generalized input data from cameras and physiological sensors. The emotion provoking game provided scenes on a

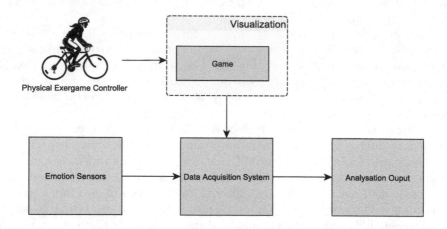

Fig. 1. Overview of Experimental Setup

42-inch flat panel display to participants and sent relevant events to the data recording system.

The data acquisition system records synchronized emotion sensor data, game and controller events in a database. In our case study, the emotion sensors investigated consisted of a Kinect camera that provided HD video at 30 fps and which recorded frontal facial images for offline emotion analysis.

3.1 Cycling Game Controller

In our cycling game controller, user inputs are generated by an ergometer, including speed calculated from pedal rpm and pedal resistance that can be software controlled. The exergame controller needs to be intuitive, easy to learn, highly dynamic and enable multiple forms of adaptation. Thus a custom constructed handle bar allowed rotation up to 180°. The cycling game controller is based on a semiprofessional exercise machine[1], which provides a maximum pedal resistance of 1000W. The ergometer operates on an embedded system and connects with a network interface to read and control parameters such as resistance and speed. Fig. 2 shows the hardware setup consisting of display screen, cycling game controller, face illumination lamp and Kinect 2 camera.

4   Cycling Game to Provoke Emotions

With our cycling game we aim to provide a unique and engaging natural user interface to participants. The cycling game is realized with the Unity3d game engine[2]. The resulting in house game is tailored to the needs of the experiment to

---

[1] Daum premium 8i ergometer
[2] http://unity3d.com

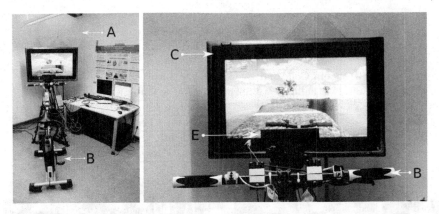

Fig. 2. Hardware Setup of the EmotionBike: Face Illumination Lamp (A), Cycling Game Controller (B), Screen (C) and Camera (D)

provide different game styles resulting in five different levels, which provide users with different objectives. The different levels allowed us to explore the effects of different game types in controlled environments for our case study. In particular the investigated provoking game events were separated for easy recognition of emotions in facial expressions.

The overall cycling game can be categorized as a fun racer; it has no ambition to be physically accurate as a real world bicycle. This game concept allows a broad range of gameplay mechanics and game events that would not be appropriate in a realistic physical simulation. The player may physically accelerate and steer. The generated controller input is directly transferred into the game, simulating a virtual bicycle in near real time, as shown in Fig. 4. This is essential for a cycling game since insufficient controls may influence the overall user perception and evoke frustration.

4.1   Game Scenarios

The five levels are designed with game elements as stimuli for specific emotions. If the designated game event occurs a message is sent including event type and timestamp. Table 1 lists all levels and events with the intended emotion provocations in players. A training level, not listed in Table 1, allows the user to get familiar with the cycling game controls. This training level presents to the player neither challenge nor obstacle and has the goal to ride from the start to the finish line.

Level 1: The goal is to race a street track from start to finish. The streets are populated with roaming teddy bears, shown in Fig. 3a. If the player bumps into a bear then the bike stops immediately and the bear explodes, in which case a *teddy hit* event is created.

Table 1. Game Levels, in Game Events and Intended Emotions

Level	Event	Emotions
1	Teddy Hit	Joy
2	Coin Collected	Joy / Surprise
3	Falling	Surprise / Anger / Joy / Fear
3	Boost	Surprise / Joy
4	Spider Attack	Surprise / Fear
4	Resistance	Effort
5	Jump Scare	Disgust / Fear / Joy / Surprise

(a) Street Race with Teddy Bears   (b) Race Track Collecting Coins

Fig. 3. Game Display of Level 1 and 2

Level 2: The main goal of the level, shown in Fig. 3b, is to collect all 20 coins. If the player crosses the finish line and has not collected all coins, then the player is teleported back to the start line. The level ends when all coins are collected and the finish line is crossed.

Level 3: The level starts on a mountain road. In order to finish this level it is necessary to jump over a giant gap. To succeed, the player is required to cross a booster gate, shown in Fig. 4, in proper alignment with a ramp to catapult the bicycle over the gap. Since the alignment and steady steering is very challenging, player often need multiple attempts to succeed.

Level 4: At the beginning the player climbs up a hill, which drastically increases the physical resistance of the paddles, shown in Fig. 5a. On reaching a plateau filled with dense and tall grass, the player is attacked by spiders that push the virtual bicycle around. Due to the occluded environment these spiders are hard to spot in order to detour. In addition, the player may trigger walls traps that rise unexpected and block the way for a short amount of time.

Level 5: In this *Night Ride* level the player cycles through a dark and thick forest. The only light source providing vision is a bicycle headlight, shown in Fig. 5b. Eventually self-illuminated coins guide the player on a path through the

Fig. 4. Game Display of Level 3: Hill Jump with Booster

(a) Mountain terrain (b) Night Ride

Fig. 5. Game Display of Level 4 and 5

forest. Just before reaching the finish the player triggers a *Jump Scare* event, were all player controls are disabled and monsters spawn in front of the bicycle and produce a horrible shout. The monsters are shrouded in red lights and a grainy film effect distorts the players vision.

5 Experimental Design for the Case Study

5.1 Participants Profile

In this case study eleven participants are evaluated, three females and eight males aged between 19 and 41 with an average age of 27. At the start of the experiment participants were given a questionnaire including questions concerning personal information, fitness level, and game experience. The personal information part included questions designed by Satow [27], which allows the categorization of the participants according to the big five personality model (openness to experience, conscientiousness, extroversion, agreeableness, and neuroticism). Dividing the participants into small groups with similar personality did decrease the individual differences in the analysis. Preliminary results indicated that people with high extroversion displayed higher emotional reaction.

Seven participants stated that they played video games approximately 2-3 hours per week and described themselves as casual gamers. The other four participants declared that they did not play games regularly. In addition, participants were asked about their game controller experience with modern control mechanisms including Wii remote and Kinect. Seven participants confirmed that they had experience. Further all participants stated that they performed sports, but only seven on a regular basis. Nine out of the eleven participants stated that they cycled on a weekly basis, ranging from one to four hours.

5.2   Experiment Procedure

All participants started by filling out the questionnaire mentioned earlier. They were informed about their right to abort the experiment at any time. To start the physical experiment they had to mount the exercise trainer and the game was started, beginning with a training level to get familiar with the interface mechanics and the game world. During the gameplay an experimenter guided the player with pre-defined phrases through the game to explain critical parts of a level. For example, in level four the participants had the opportunity to skip to the next level after exceeding a number of trials because of the high difficulty. At the end of the experiment participants were asked to provide a statement about their physical strain perception in the range from 1 to 7, as defined by Borg [28]. The reported mean strain for our participants was 3.9.

6   Analyses of Emotion Provocation

6.1   Analysis Method

During our experiments, all participants facial expressions were assessed by observers and after completion of each level participants were asked to self assess their emotions. The recorded facial videos are analyzed with the Computer Expression Recognition Toolbox (CERT) [15] providing a probability for all eight

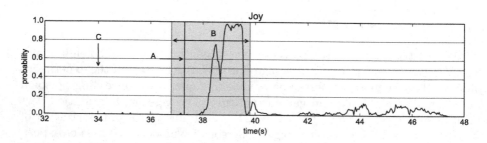

Fig. 6. Example Emotion Analysis for Data of Level 5: Black vertical line marks a game event (A), interval (B) shows the analysis window, red line (C) marks the detection threshold, black line shows an emotion response curve.

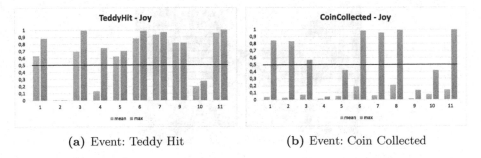

(a) Event: Teddy Hit   (b) Event: Coin Collected

Fig. 7. Analysis Results of Emotion Probabilities for 11 Subjects for the Emotion Joy

basic emotions (joy, disgust, anger, fear, neutral, sad, surprise, and contempt) per video frame. CERT recognition is based on a support vector learning approach of frontal face images and includes pose correction. Grafsgaard et al. [16] suggests that facial expression probabilities may vary significantly between individuals. In order to access this variation phenomenon we compared the machine facial expression analysis with the observer- and self-assessment. The probability values near the provoking events are compared with our target emotions. For each event a time windows of 3 seconds (0.5 seconds before and 2.5 seconds after an event) was evaluated for occurring emotion probability peaks. An example event analysis is shown in Fig. 6. For all subjects each target event maximum and mean basic emotion probability were extracted. Provoked emotion responses are taken into account for the summary results if they exceed a threshold of 0.5.

6.2   Experimental Results

Level 1: Fig. 7a indicates that nine out of eleven participants felt joy during *Teddy Hit* events. Participant eight did not hit any teddy bears due to successful avoidance and participant two did not recognize the *Teddy Hit* because the teddy bumped from behind. Participant four had a low mean value but a relatively high max value indicating that he felt joy at least once. In this evaluation ten self and observer assessments supported our analysis results.

Level 2: Seven participants had each a high joy response connected to the *Coin Collected* event, at least one time. The low mean value, shown in Fig. 7b indicates that provocation was not maintained for the duration of collection of the 20 coins. Rather than the coin collection itself, circumstantial situations such as near misses in collection and anticipation of finishing the level, provoked a stronger response. An interesting effect was that six participants had high max surprise values. The mean values were low indicating that they displayed surprise by the *Smiley Particle Effect*, shown in Fig. 8.

Level 3: In this level two events were triggered. The first event occurred while driving through a booster. Eight participants displayed joy at least once. Five participants displayed surprise reactions. Fig. 9a and Fig. 9b present the max

Fig. 8. Game Display of Level 2 with Particle Effect

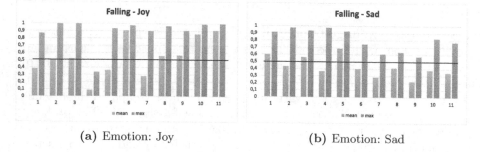

(a) Emotion: Joy   (b) Emotion: Sad

Fig. 9. Analysis Results of Emotion Probabilities for 11 Subjects for the Falling Event

and mean probabilities for joy and sadness. Ten participants displayed joy at this event and eleven participants expressed sadness, making this finding interesting. This effect can be explained since falling down the cliff occurs repeatedly. The ambition of most of the participants was very high and both joy and sadness were detected. Our observation, that joy is often detected in frustrating situations as many people smile in natural frustration has been reported by Hoque [29]. Respectively nine self and nine observer assessments labeled frustration.

Level 4: Only four participants had a high value for surprise by a *Spider Attack*. But the high resistance throughout the level led to an often mentioned physical strain by the participants.

Level 5: The surprise effect of the *Jump Scare* event displayed the most varying emotion responses. Emotional facial expression displayed included one for disgust, two for fear, two for surprise and four for joy, shown in Fig. 10. This result neither correlates with the self-assessment nor with the observer-assessment, because they unanimously stated that they felt scared.

The resulting data show that participants who describe themselves as gamers showed less than maximal surprise or fear. They stated that they expected the events due to their game experience. Some emotions such as surprise and joy decreased in maximum value the more frequently they occurred. Other emotions including anger increased when it occurred more often e.g. during *Falling*

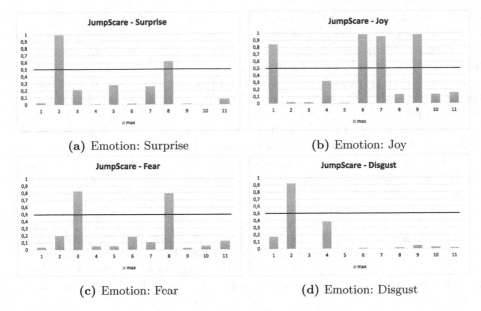

(a) Emotion: Surprise   **(b)** Emotion: Joy

(c) Emotion: Fear   **(d)** Emotion: Disgust

Fig. 10. Analysis Results for Emotion Probabilities for 11 Subjects for the Jump Scare Event

Table 2. Summery of Provoked Emotion with Game Events for 11 Participants

Level	Event	Target Emotion	Part. prov. in %
1	Teddy Hit	Joy	82
2	Coin Collected	Joy	63
3	Falling	Joy	91
3	Falling	Sad	100
4	Spider Attack	Surprise	36
5	Jump Scare	Surprise	18
5	Jump Scare	Joy	36
5	Jump Scare	Fear	18
5	Jump Scare	Disgust	9

events. The emotion of joy occurred 0.5 seconds earlier than average in level 2, where the main objective was to collect all coins. Thus all participants became more focused and our aim of emotional engagement was reached. The Big Five personality traits showed that people with a high value in extroversion had a higher maximum value in expressing joy. They had a maximum probability of 0.89 against 0.76 for introverted participants.

7 Conclusion

This work presents a new physical cycling game interface that records and analyses emotions. Our case study demonstrates that tailored game events can provoke specific emotions, as shown in Table 2. In summery, the *Teddy Hit* and *Falling* game elements are able to provoke specific emotions for most subjects, while the game elements *Coin Collected* and *Jump Scare* provoke a more varied response in the type and probability of emotion.

In this work we present an analysis method to measure emotional reactions to specific game events. The analysis for game events will aid game development and its design process by comparing alternative designs or studying resonance and engagement of players. In addition, this method provides a quantified measure of emotion reactions for a user experience analysis. Emotion response analysis can vary between groups of users and therefore may be correlated with factors including personality traits, gender or age. These factors will enable better specific reaction predictions..

Acknowledgment. We thank Kai von Luck for his support and feedback to this work. Further we express our gratitude to Kai Rosseburg for providing the photos in Fig. 2 and to Wojtek Gozdzielewski, Sobin Ghose, Jonas Hornschuh, Ralf Jettke and Erik Matthiessen for supporting our project. We also thank Enno Putzar for video recording.

References

1. Kotsia, I., Zafeiriou, S., Fotopoulos, S.: Affective gaming: A comprehensive survey. In: Comp. Vis. and Pat. Recog. Works (CVPRW), pp. 663–670. IEEE (2013)
2. Bailenson, J.N., Pontikakis, E.D., Mauss, I.B., Gross, J.J., Jabon, M.E., Hutcherson, C.A., Nass, C., John, O.: Real-time classification of evoked emotions using facial feature tracking and physiological responses. International Journal of Human-Computer Studies 66(5), 303–317 (2008)
3. Breazeal, C.L.: Sociable machines: expressive social exchange between humans and robots. PhD thesis, Massachusetts Institute of Technology (2000)
4. Kipp, A., Kummert, F.: Dynamic dialog system for human robot collaboration: playing a game of pairs. In: Int. Conf. on Human-Agent Interact., pp. 225–228. ACM (2014)
5. Becker-Asano, C.: WASABI: Affect simulation for agents with believable interactivity, vol. 319. IOS Press (2008)
6. Müller, L., Keune, S., Bernin, A., Vogt, F.: Emotional interaction with surfaces - works of design and computing. In: Herrlich, M., Malaka, R., Masuch, M. (eds.) ICEC 2012. LNCS, vol. 7522, pp. 457–460. Springer, Heidelberg (2012)
7. Wahlster, W.: Dialogue systems go multimodal: The smartkom experience. In: SmartKom: Foundations of Multimodal Dialogue Systems, pp. 3–27. Springer (2006)
8. Dumas, B., Lalanne, D., Oviatt, S.: Multimodal interfaces: A survey of principles, models and frameworks. In: Lalanne, D., Kohlas, J. (eds.) Human Machine Interaction. LNCS, vol. 5440, pp. 3–26. Springer, Heidelberg (2009)
9. Tan, C.T., Leong, T.W., Shen, S.: Combining think-aloud and physiological data to understand video game experiences. In: ACM Conference on Human Factors in Computing Systems, pp. 381–390. ACM (2014)

10. Munia, T.T.K., Islam, A., Islam, M.M., Mostafa, S.S., Ahmad, M.: Mental states estimation with the variation of physiological signals. In: Informatics, Electronics & Vision (ICIEV), pp. 800–805. IEEE (2012)
11. Sharma, N., Gedeon, T.: Modeling stress recognition in typical virtual environments. In: International Conference on Pervasive Computing Technologies for Healthcare, ICST (Institute for Computer Sciences, Social-Informatics and Telecommunications Engineering), pp. 17–24 (2013)
12. Gunes, H., Pantic, M.: Automatic, dimensional and continuous emotion recognition. International Journal of Synthetic Emotions (IJSE) 1(1), 68–99 (2010)
13. Calvo, R.A., D'Mello, S.: Affect detection: An interdisciplinary review of models, methods, and their applications. IEEE Transactions on Affective Computing 1(1), 18–37 (2010)
14. Ekman, P., Friesen, W.V.: Measuring facial movement. Environmental Psychology and Nonverbal Behavior 1(1), 56–75 (1976)
15. Littlewort, G., Whitehill, J., Wu, T., Fasel, I., Frank, M., Movellan, J., Bartlett, M.: The computer expression recognition toolbox (cert). In: Automatic Face & Gesture Recognition and Workshops, pp. 298–305. IEEE (2011)
16. Grafsgaard, J.F., Wiggins, J.B., Boyer, K.E., Wiebe, E.N., Lester, J.C.: Automatically recognizing facial indicators of frustration: a learning-centricanalysis. In: Affective Computing and Intelligent Interaction (ACII), pp. 159–165. IEEE (2013)
17. Gilleade, K., Dix, A., Allanson, J.: Affective videogames and modes of affective gaming: assist me, challenge me, emote me. In: Proc. of DIGRA (2005)
18. Vachiratamporn, V., Moriyama, K., Fukui, K.I., Numao, M.: An implementation of affective adaptation in survival horror games. In: Computational Intelligence and Games (CIG), pp. 1–8. IEEE (2014)
19. Nogueira, P.A., Aguiar, R., Rodrigues, R., Oliveira, E.: Computational models of players' physiological-based emotional reactions: A digital games case study. In: 2014 IEEE/WIC/ACM International Joint Conferences on Web Intelligence (WI) and Intelligent Agent Technologies (IAT), vol. 3, pp. 278–285. IEEE (2014)
20. Parnandi, A., Son, Y., Gutierrez-Osuna, R.: A control-theoretic approach to adaptive physiological games. In: Affective Computing and Intelligent Interaction (ACII), pp. 7–12. IEEE (2013)
21. Nacke, L.E., Kalyn, M., Lough, C., Mandryk, R.L.: Biofeedback game design: using direct and indirect physiological control to enhance game interaction. In: Proceedings of the SIGCHI Conference on Human Factors in Computing Systems, pp. 103–112. ACM (2011)
22. Negini, F., Mandryk, R., Stanley, K.: Using affective state to adapt characters, npcs, and the environment in a first-person shooter game. In: IEEE Games, Entertainment, and Media, Toronto, Canada, pp. 109–116 (2014)
23. Raaijmakers, S., Steel, F., de Goede, M., van Wouwe, N.C., Van Erp, J.B., Brouwer, A.M.: Heart rate variability and skin conductance biofeedback: A triple-blind randomized controlled study. In: Affective Computing and Intelligent Interaction (ACII), pp. 289–293. IEEE (2013)
24. Biddle, S.J.: Chapter 4: Emotion, mood and physical activity. In: Physical Activity and Psychological Well-Being, p. 63, Psychology Press (2000)
25. Warburton, D.E., Bredin, S.S., Horita, L.T., Zbogar, D., Scott, J.M., Esch, B.T., Rhodes, R.E.: The health benefits of interactive video game exercise. Applied Physiology, Nutrition, and Metabolism 32(4), 655–663 (2007)
26. Hoda, M., Alattas, R., Saddik, A.E.: Evaluating player experience in cycling exergames. In: Multimedia (ISM), pp. 415–420. IEEE (2013)

27. Satow, L.: Big-five-persoenlichkeitstest(b5t): Test-und skalendokumentation (2012). http://www.drsatow.de
28. Borg, G.: Anstrengungsempfinden und körperliche aktivität. Deutsches Ärzteblatt 101(15), 1016–1021 (2004)
29. Hoque, M.E., Picard, R.W.: Acted vs. natural frustration and delight: Many people smile in natural frustration. In: Automatic Face & Gesture Recognition and Workshops, pp. 354–359. IEEE (2011)

Evaluating the Impact of Highly Immersive Technologies and Natural Interaction on Player Engagement and Flow Experience in Games

Raffaello Brondi[1], Leila Alem[2], Giovanni Avveduto[1], Claudia Faita[1],
Marcello Carrozzino[1], Franco Tecchia[1], and Massimo Bergamasco[1]

[1] PERCRO Lab., Scuola Superiore Sant'Anna,
Via Alamanni, 13b, 56010, Pisa, Italy
r.brondi@sssup.it
[2] Games Studio, University of Technology, Sydney, Australia

Abstract. Social interaction in videogames has a big impact on players experience and is often used to increase enjoyment and retention. In the current study a highly immersive setup based on the Oculus Rift and depth cameras and exploiting natural user interaction is compared with a classical Keyboard & Mouse configuration in the context of a videogame experience taking place in a shared Virtual Environment. The research aims at assessing the impact of new technologies and interaction metaphors on users engagement when playing social games. Initial findings from our study suggest that while players perform better using the classic Keyboard & Mouse setup, the new technological setup and the Natural User Interface offer higher level of engagement and facilitate user flow state.

Keywords: Flow, Collaborative, Social Game, Natural User Interfaces, Player Engagement, Social Presence, Game Design, Mixed Reality, Virtual Reality.

1 Introduction

The importance of the social component as motivation for playing has been pointed out by many researches [18, 3], both in digital and non-digital games. When playing with other people involvement as well as enjoyment of the game increase. Lazarro describes in her work [10] the main reasons that brings people to play games identifying four keys, or pathways, leading players to emotion in games. Social interaction is one of these four aspects. Yee [19, 18] offers a clear slice of the characteristics and behaviours of Massively Multiplayer Online Role-Playing Games (MMORPGs) players. He analysed the motivation of over 30000 MMORPG users, identifying three main components that define the motivation to play online games: achievement, immersion and, again, the social component.

Social interaction in videogames is mostly defined by the ability of players to communicate with the others. The less is the effort required in order to learn how to interact with the others, the better is the experience gamers will have.

© IFIP International Federation for Information Processing 2015
K. Chorianopoulos et al. (Eds.): ICEC 2015, LNCS 9353, pp. 169–181, 2015.
DOI: 10.1007/978-3-319-24589-8_13

By providing additional ways to interact in games, players can customize their experience, choosing the most familiar and effective forms of communication for them. The social component is therefore heavily influenced by the available technologies. Nowadays the hardware evolution has lead to powerful solutions able to substantially improve the interaction of players with the Virtual Environment(VE). The spreading of depth cameras and sensorized controllers is shaping the way we play. Natural User Interfaces[1] (NUIs) are becoming more and more popular. New richer interaction metaphors can be designed in order to improve the game engagement in a social scenario. With the availability of cheap highly immersive visualization systems (e.g. the Oculus Rift), a completely new experience can be provided to the players.

The presented work aims at assessing the impact on player engagement and social presence of new highly immersive technologies combined with NUIs. During the experiment subjects have played a collaborative jigsaw puzzle game in a shared VE using two different interaction metaphors mapped on two different technological setups. The first interface exploits Keyboard & Mouse, one of the most traditional gaming interface, as a medium between the player and the VE, while the other uses a Head Mounted Display(HMD) and a depth camera implementing a NUI.

The paper is structured as follows: first a review of previous works addressing player engagement and social presence is presented. Then the study methodology is explained: the technological setup and NUI used to conduct the experiment, the participants sample, the procedure and metrics are introduced. Finally the salient results are discussed and guidelines for the development of future games are provided.

2   Literature Review

If players do not enjoy the game, they will not play the game [16], therefore player enjoyment is the most important goal for computer games. There are multiple factors contributing to the overall game engagement [15, 7, 1]; flow and social interaction are two of them. Flow has been defined by Csikszentmihalyi as a state of mind in which a person is completely involved and immersed in an activity [4, 2]. The concept of flow is central to game evaluation [12, 16, 7, 1].

Social interaction represents another key aspect when designing videogames. People often play games to interact with others, regardless of the task [16]. Players use games as mechanisms for social experiences: "It's the people that are addictive not the game" [10]. Several researches investigated how the social component in videogames affects user engagement and satisfaction [5, 18].

Given the relevance of these two factors on gaming experience, it is extremely important to maximize their effects when designing a game.

---

[1] Natural User Interface is a term used to identify human-computer interactions based on typical inter-human communication. These interfaces allow computers to understand the innate human means of interaction (e.g. voice and gestures).

Social interaction in videogames is mostly defined by the ability of players to communicate with the others and, more than other aspects in videogames, it is heavily affected by the technological facilities used. This difference is even more important when players are not physically co-located and the communication among them relies only on the technological layer. Using different hardware solutions new interaction metaphors can be enabled: motor activity-centered games exploit new console controllers (e.g. Wii Remote); depth sensors allow full body interaction. Game designers can take advantage of them to create new *communication channels* or improve the existing ones.

Gajadhar et al. [6] evaluated the effects of co-player presence on player enjoyment according to three common two-player settings (virtual, mediated, and co-located). They used a basic technological setup in which subjects play *PONG* varying the closeness of the players. They found that players enjoy more the co-located setting due to the increased affordance for communication. Nowadays the increasing availability of novel hardware devices (e.g. Depth cameras, HMDs, inertial sensors) provides new and interesting alternatives to game designers. It is possible to develop novel, powerful and extremely immersive social experiences overcoming the existing communication gap between co-located and remote players. It is today possible to de-materialize the players and teleport them in a shared virtual world where the game takes place.

Sajjadi et al. [14] investigated whether the choice of interaction mode\controller has an impact on the game experience. They tested a collaborative game using the Oculus Rift and Sifteo Cube[2]. They didn't found any significant difference between the two interfaces on the game experience. They instead observed that almost all participants using the Oculus Rift looked for alternative way of communication trying to use gestures to interact with the partner even if not enabled by the technological setup.

Lindley et al. [11] focus on the impact of the new interfaces involving body movements on player engagement and social behaviour. They found that the amount of social interaction is higher when using input devices which allow body movements, resulting in an higher engagement in the game.

Kauko and Häkkilä [8] compared the effect of two different technological setups on social interaction. Subjects played the same multi-player game first on their mobile phones facing each other and then on a typical game-console setting side-by-side. They found an increase in the social interaction in the first setup which enables a socially richer game experience.

Even if both flow and social factors contribute to an increment of game engagement, it is still not so clear which kind of interactions occur between them. Sweetser and Wyeth [16] assert that social interaction, being not an element of flow, can interrupt immersion in games, as real people provide a link to the real world that can knock players out of their fantasy game worlds. Similarly Lindley et al. [11] suppose that by encouraging social interaction, players will in some sense have been drawn out of the game environment and into the real world breaking the flow.

---

[2] An interactive game system built on building blocks and domino tiles.

Fig. 1. Snapshot of the system highlighting the players pointers during a KM game session.

Fig. 2. Each column shows a user playing in the physical environment and one of the binocular view of the Oculus.

All the previous works highlight the importance of communication between gamers in multiplayer videogames. Being able to effectively interact with your partner is extremely important. At the same time the social communication works as a link with the real world because often happens outside of the game. This can affect the flow experience which represents another fundamental aspect for game enjoyment. New technologies offer powerful alternatives to enable new ways of communication. In this study we evaluated a new NUI designed in order to fuse all the required *communication channels* inside the game world. The present experiment aims at assessing if the adoption of new technologies can satisfy the needs for communication richness in social games.

3   Method

The current work aims at assessing the impact of new highly immersive technologies combined with natural interaction on player engagement and social presence. Particular attention has been directed to the relation between flow experience and social interaction. The subjects participating in the study play a collaborative jigsaw puzzle game in a shared VE using two different interaction metaphors tied to different visualization systems.

In the following, first the technological setup and interaction metaphors under evaluation are presented. Then the game used to perform the study is described. Finally participants, procedure and metrics are presented.

3.1   Technological Setup and Interaction Metaphors

Two identical networked hardware setups have been used to play the collaborative game. Each system is composed by: (1) a gaming-grade workstation; (2) an Oculus Rift DK2 HMD; (3) a Primesense Carmine 1.09 RGB-depth (RGBD) camera; (4) a wireless headset with microphone; (5) two coloured thimbles.

The first interface proposed exploits Keyboard & Mouse, one of the most classic gaming interface, as a medium between the player and the VE. Players can navigate the environment by using the mouse to change the view direction and the keyboard to move their point of view. They can grab and position the puzzle tiles and zoom in and out by using the mouse. Verbal communication is enabled by using headphones and microphones. Each player can see both his and the partner's pointers (see Fig. 1). We refer to this setup as "KM" from here on.

The second interface provides a natural interaction between the player and the VE using an implementation of [17]. The user wearing the HMD is free to move naturally in a physical\virtual environment of about 3 by 3 meters. User head's tracking is performed by using the inertial measurement unit built-in the Oculus and the tracking camera shipped with it. The perception of the self and the partner as well as the natural interaction with the VE are enabled by depth cameras and inertial\visual tracking techniques. Two coloured thimbles placed on the index and thumb of the dominant hand are tracked using the acquired RGBD data. Through a simple collision detection algorithm applied to the positions of the thimbles, the user is able to naturally interact with the virtual objects by grabbing and moving them in his\her peripersonal space (see Fig. 2). The participants are able to communicate both verbally and using their bodies (e.g. using gestures). No haptic feedback is provided. We refer to this setup as "OU" from here on.

3.2   The Game

A collaborative jigsaw puzzle game has been developed for the experiment. This popular game genre combines a low complexity with an high level of attention and interaction. Even if videogames of this type are usually two-dimensional, we designed the game to be played in a three-dimensional environment in order to exploit the immersive capabilities of the HMD. The collaborative component of the game, based on the Complementarity and Shared Goals design patterns [13], allows to evaluate the effect of social interaction between participants on the game engagement and flow.

The game scene is composed by a virtual room with a table on a side. A countdown timer, the scoring board and a poster showing the solution are hung on a wall. The puzzle is made up of 48 tiles randomly disposed on the two sides of the table. Each tile is represented by a gray parallelepiped with the top face textured with a part of the puzzle image. In the middle of the table a board divided in two sections defines the placeholders where the puzzle has to be arranged on (see Fig. 1 and Fig. 2).

The game is played at the same time by two players physically located in two different rooms but sharing the same VE. The actions performed by a player to the environment are visible to the partner (e.g. scoring, tiles movements and positioning). During KM sessions the players can see his/her own and partner's mouse pointers. During OU sessions the RGBD captures of the bodies are streamed between the two setups. A proxy for each player, made by a textured mesh reconstructed from the RGBD data and a virtual head replicating the user movements, is shown in the VE (see Fig. 2).

Both participants can interact with each tile at any time. When a tile is currently grabbed by a user, the other player can not interact with it until it is released. A tile dropped close to a free board placeholder is attracted and automatically positioned on top of it. If correctly positioned, the tile collapse on the placeholder and cannot be moved anymore. Sound feedbacks notify correct or wrong tile positioning. Each player is able to place tiles only on the half board belonging to him/her. Trying to position a tile on the half board belonging to the partner, causes the tile to jump away in a random position. Each player can see only the half solution owned by the partner so that players need to help each other. The two players are characterized by different colors, red and blue. Each element belonging to a user (score, grabbed tile, etc) is modulated with the correspondent color.

The aim of the collaborative game consists in working together with the partner in order to solve the puzzle before the time is over. Players have seven minutes to correctly place all the tiles on the board.

The shared team score is calculated according to the following rules:

- +2 points for each correctly positioned tile
- +1 point for each 5 seconds left when the puzzle is completed
- −1 point for each tile not correctly positioned when the time is over

3.3 Participants

The participants have been recruited among colleagues and students. A total of 24 subjects, 15 males and 9 females healthy subjects, aged between 23 and 50 $(32, 04 \pm 6, 84)$ took part at the experiment. Only 2 of them were not native Italian speakers. During the recruitment they have been asked to read and sign the informed consent. Thus they filled an entry questionnaire (EnQ) used to collect demographic information like gender, age and level of education. In the EnQ users had also to rate, on a 5 points Likert Scale from 0 to 4, their experience with the use of computers (average $2, 88 \pm 0, 85$), videogames (average $2, 12 \pm 1, 33$), use of immersive virtual displays(average $1, 54 \pm 1, 21$), puzzle games (average $2, 04 \pm 1, 2$) and online puzzle games (average $0, 83 \pm 1, 05$).

3.4 Procedure

During the recruitment, participants have been asked to play a single player version of the puzzle game using keyboard and mouse as input devices. In a social game the challenge is heavily influenced by the different abilities of the participants [2]. Owning similar skills is extremely important in order to make the game challenging for both players and prevent boredom or frustration. For this reason a pre-experiment aimed at assessing the puzzle-solving abilities has been conducted in order to couple participants according to their dexterity. The subjects were unaware of the real objective of this session. Hence twelve couples have been formed.

Before the experiment, each couple has been informed about the outline of the experimental session. The players have been then divided on the two identical setups (see Sec. 3.1) prepared for the experiment, located in two different rooms and network connected. The subjects, spatially not co-located, have been able to communicate by using only the communication channels provided by KM or OU session. In addition, each user performed a 5 minutes trial session to get familiar with the NUI provided playing a simplified (12 tiles) single player version of the puzzle game. Two different puzzle images have been used.

The experiment adopted a within-subjects design. Each couple played two sessions, one for each interaction metaphor, KM and OU. Players were allowed to read again the instructions before each game. The order in which the two game sessions as well as the puzzle images were presented to different couples has been randomized.

3.5   Metrics

In order to analyse the player engagement, we have reviewed available questionnaires focusing on user engagement and social experience. Qin et al. [12] focus too much on the game narrative aspects while Seif El-Nasr et al. [15] in their metric do not consider player flow experience. GameFlow [16] represents the baseline from which both Immersion Experience Questionnaire(IEQ) [7] and Game Engagement Questionnaire (GEQ) [1] have been developed and it is outdated by these two research works. Analysing the questions composing IEQ and GEQ, we found that even if the two questionnaires namely address different factors, immersion and engagement, they are very similar. We therefore decided to adopt GEQ which is completed by the social questionnaire named Social Presence in Gaming Questionnaire (SPGQ) [9], addressing another fundamental aspect of our research.

At the end of each game session, players have answered a post condition questionnaire (PCQ) composed by a subset of the GEQ items (competence, flow, tension\annoyance, challenge, negative affect and positive affect), a subset of the SPGQ items (empathy and behavioural involvement), awareness and satisfaction questions. When the two conditions have been played, an exit questionnaire (ExQ) has been presented to both players in order to collect their preferences and motivations, friend relationship, general impressions and suggestions. Finally an informal debriefing session between the experimenters and both players has been conducted to further register impressions and anecdotes.

Besides data collected through questionnaires and interviews, objective measurements have been recorded through the game in both the preliminary and the experimental sessions. Usage and performance data collected comprehend: (1) completion time and score, (2) frame-rate and network latency, (3) outcome and tiles positions, (4) positions and headings of player head. Each session was video and audio recorded for further investigations. Experimenters assisted all the sessions taking notes of noteworthy events.

4   Results

The questionnaires results have been analysed in order to assess the impact
of the different technological setups and interaction metaphors on user engagement, social presence, awareness and performances. Following the instructions
provided by the authors in [1], the answers to GEQ and SPGQ questionnaires
have been aggregated in order to obtain a value for each one of the eight items
taken from the two questionnaires. A Wilcoxon signed-rank test has been used
to statistically compare questionnaires results for the two conditions as the distribution of the data was not Gaussian. A paired t-test has been used to compare
performances.

4.1   Awareness, Satisfaction and Performances

As reported in Fig. 3, players had a good awareness of the other's actions, locations and intentions in both setups.

All the participants rated both experiences as very satisfying as shown by the
question *"Please rate your overall satisfaction"* reporting an high score in both
sessions. Answers to the ExQ showed a clear preference of the participants for
the OU session. To the question *"Which kind of user interface do you prefer?"*,
16 players ($\sim 66.7\%$) answered the natural one.

Figure 3 shows the performances registered during the game sessions. Data reports a significant difference between the two setups in terms of frequency of tiles
correctly ($W = 8.00, p = 0.015$) and wrongly ($W = 11.00, p = 0.028$) positioned.

4.2   Game Engagement and Social Presence

The results of GEQ questionnaire indicate an overall positive evaluation of both
game setups (see Fig. 3). Participants felt competent in both sessions without

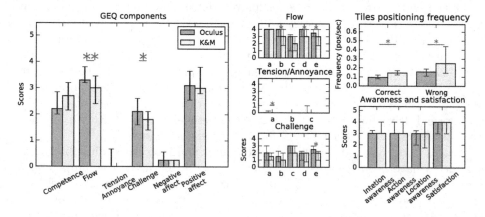

Fig. 3. Game Engagement Questionnaire, performances and awareness results (*$p \leq$
0.05; **$p \leq 0.01$). Bars reports 25th and 75th percentiles.

any particular difference. Even if in both setups players have reported a high level of flow, the psychological absorption has been significantly greater in the OU session (see Fig. 3). The single questions of the GEQ flow item (see Fig. 3), (b) *"I forgot everything around me"* ($W = 4.00, p = 0.048$), (d) *"I was deeply concentrated in the game"* ($W = 5.00, p = 0.013$) and (e) *"I lost connection with the outside world"* ($W = 6.00, p = 0.046$), highlight the main differences characterizing the OU experience.

Challenge has been medium-rated by participants. Players found the OU session significantly more challenging with respect to KM ($W = 22.5, p = 0.011$). Low values for tension/annoyance and negative affects have been highlighted for both the sessions. A slightly higher value of annoyance, (a) *"I felt annoyed"* ($W = 0.0, p = 0.023$), have been registered when playing with the Oculus. Players reported a high positive affects in both sessions.

Participants high-rated both social components, Empathy and Behavioural Involvement. No relevant differences has been found in the results.

5   Discussion and Future Work

In the present work we have explored the effect of two different interaction metaphors and technological setups on game experience taking place in a shared Virtual Environment. A number of design implications and trade-off can be deduced starting from the findings of this study.

Almost all the players enjoyed the OU metaphor and most of them (66.7%) found it preferable to the classic Keyboard & Mouse interface even if it resulted to be more challenging. The playing experience with the Oculus has been perceived as more engaging and entertaining. Almost all the participants who preferred the KM metaphor appreciated the lower complexity of the interface, which results more familiar and comfortable for people who daily use computers. They were able to become proficient in a shorter period, while the OU configuration required more time to get comfortable with. Most participants (71%) during the final debriefing asserted to have appreciated the natural interaction with the environment and the partner because it makes the experience more similar to the reality (*"I felt like I was really playing with him a real puzzle!"*).

In the Keyboard & Mouse setup users mostly use the mouse to point tiles to be grabbed and locations where to put them on. While the mouse indication is the preferred method, verbal communication was nonetheless extremely important to support it. Players used to describe the graphic features of the tiles to grab (e.g. *"Take the big red bird!"*) and sometimes to number the destination placeholder (e.g. *"Put it on the third column, four cells up."*). In the Oculus setup, participants extensively used all the available communication channels provided in order to complete the task. Experimenters observed that most of the players preferred using hands gesture to interact with the other (see Fig. 2): *"Wow, I can point out them!"*. Verbal communication was nonetheless extremely important to support gestures. Also in this case many participants described the tiles to grab or the action to undertake verbally in addition to using their hands.

All the subjects reported that the NUI was more challenging with respect to the KM metaphor, however only one player found the OU metaphor not enjoyable and too complex to be used. The majority of players (75%) have considered the Keyboard & Mouse more immediate and faster. Nonetheless, during the KM session, experimenters observed that many players tried to use body language and gestures to interact with the other, even if these communication channels were not available. The same attempt to communicate with the partner using gestures has been reported also in [14]. Hence providing a natural interaction seems to be important during social activities. If the NUI would be completely transparent, removing any artificial medium between the user and the social sphere, probably it would be perceived easier and more enjoyable than the mediated communication (e.g. Keyboard & Mouse).

The game environment has been designed in order to maximize the space needed by a player during a game session and stimulate participant's movement to evaluate the spatial awareness in a social shared environment. In the OU setup, due to the nature of the technology and the choices made, players were able to see just a part of the scene at once and therefore were forced to walk and rotate the head in order to play. On the contrary, when playing using the KM setup, players had a global view of the entire scene, without being required to move. Even if it was possible to change the point of view using Keyboard and Mouse, nobody did it. This aspect may have affected the interfaces comparison in terms of usability. Adopting a different game design forcing the players to move and rotate the view in the KM as in the Oculus setups, would probably generate different results. It would be interesting to evaluate this different conditions.

Thanks to the high immersion and sense of presence induced by the technology, participants during OU session perceived the proxy of the other more as a physical presence rather than a virtual representation. This makes the experience more engaging. At the same time, the absence of any physical feedback and the possibility to pass through the representation of the partner has been perceived by some players odd and sometimes a bit annoying for the purpose of the game, while cheerful by others. The essential KM interface resulted to be more functional to the task but, as observed by the experimenter and highlighted in the open questions, less funny and more impersonal. We plan to explore possible solutions addressing "virtual proxy compenetration" in dedicated experiments where different stimuli and virtual warnings will be provided to avoid proxy collisions (e.g. using a "virtual aura" to signal proximity) or to reduce the related visual impact (e.g making the representation of the other player transparent as it comes closer).

Differently from what presumed, there was no significant differences between the two configurations concerning the awareness of the partner. Even if the OU metaphor provides more detailed and richer information on what the other user is doing, players were able to equally distinguish other's intentions and actions in the two setups. This is mainly justified by the heavy usage of verbal communication to coordinate the team actions. Partner location awareness obtained similar results. Players focusing on the puzzle completion do not require rich and accurate information about partner location and consider equally satisfying the two modalities.

Almost all the participants were Italian native speakers with two exceptions. Experimenters noticed that players speaking different languages benefited more from the NUI. Language misunderstandings were compensated by gestures. Due to the small number of non Italian native speaker it has not been possible to evaluate the real impact on the user engagement. It would be interesting to further investigate the impact of linguistic differences on player engagement.

The sample used in the experiment was composed by people who daily use computers. All the participants were at ease with the use of Keyboard & Mouse. It would be interesting to evaluate the impact of the two metaphors on a more variegated sample to highlight possible differences related to previous personal skills.

In this work a wider communication interface has been presented in comparison with a traditional Keyboard & Mouse setup. Both the interaction metaphors have been tested in a social collaborative shared environment. Flow experience is one of the key factor to make a game engaging as like as the social component. Players completely engrossed in a game reach the flow state. As a consequence of the deep absorption, as described by Jennett et al. [7] in their work, being increasingly immersed in a game decreases one's ability to re-engage with the "real world". During the debriefing session, a player talking about the OU experience said: *"The interruption has a much stronger impact; the break is much clearer"*. The study results show a significant increment in the participants flow experience in the OU configuration. The deep immersion provided by the technological solution together with the natural interaction have led to a greater absorption in the game. Sweetser and Wyeth [16] speculate on the effect of the social and flow components in games. They assert that reaching the flow mental state is impeded by the social activity which establish a link between the player and the real world. In the OU setup using the NUI, being the social interaction fused into the virtual environment, players do not need anymore to "leave" the game in order to interact. The link with the real world requested by the social communication is therefore broken. In order to investigate this effect, it would be interesting to develop a single-player version of the game using the same immersive setup and the NUI. If the provided communication channels would be expressive and transparent enough to make the virtual experience seeming real, the comparison with the multi-player game should not highlight any relevant difference in terms of flow experience. On the contrary, it would be possible to observe a significant increment in the flow due to the greater engagement reachable with the social component.

6   Conclusion

Based on the results, we can conclude that the players had an overall good game experience with the developed interface providing natural interaction, which proved to be an interesting alternative to the classic Keyboard & Mouse interface. The technological setup composed by the Oculus Rift combined with the NUI can be used to increase game engagement. No significant differences have been observed on the social presence between the two setups and both of them were perceived equally positive.

When designing social games a broad communication bandwidth enriches players gaming experience and increases enjoyment. A natural interaction with the environment, like the one provided in the study, allows the users to experience ways of communication similar to what they use in real-life. This turns out to be extremely important to support the richer interaction happening during collaborative tasks.

Thanks to the new technologies, nowadays it is possible to de-materialize the players and teleport them in a shared virtual world where the game takes place. Games can be played without the medium of any interface but using the own body as a way to interact with the VE.

Even if the new natural interaction has been described as more intriguing and enjoying, the classic setup based on Keyboard & Mouse resulted to be a better choice when performances matter. The study highlights that the implemented natural interaction results more challenging and requires more time to become productive. Nonetheless it will be interesting to evaluate if the performance gap can be reduced, or even nullified, by continuous training.

The OU settings have reportedly generated a significantly higher level of flow over the KM. This is mainly related to the natural interaction which enables new communication channels making the experience more real (a player said: "It was like playing a real puzzle"). Previous works [16, 11] suppose a negative influence of social interaction on the flow experience. Encouraging sociability, players are in some sense drawn out of the game environment, back into the real world, breaking the flow. We suppose that the negative influence could be overcome providing natural communication channels embedded in the game world.

Looking at the current and upcoming available technologies, immersive social environments exploiting Natural User Interfaces have the potential to improve players game engagement and enjoyment defining the next gaming experience.

Acknowledgement. Authors wants to acknowledge Games Studio, University of Technology of Sydney (UTS), for the support provided during this research. We would also like to show our gratitude to Professor Yusuf Pisan who provided insight and expertise that greatly assisted the research.

References

[1] Brockmyer, J.H., Fox, C.M., Curtiss, K.A., McBroom, E., Burkhart, K.M., Pidruzny, J.N.: The development of the game engagement questionnaire: A measure of engagement in video game-playing. Journal of Experimental Social Psychology 45(4), 624–634 (2009)

[2] Chen, J.: Flow in games (and everything else). Communications of the ACM 50(4), 31–34 (2007)

[3] Cole, H., Griffiths, M.D.: Social interactions in massively multiplayer online role-playing gamers. CyberPsychology & Behavior 10(4), 575–583 (2007)

[4] Csikszentmihalyi, M.: Flow. Springer (2014)
[5] Ducheneaut, N., Moore, R.J.: The social side of gaming: a study of interaction patterns in a massively multiplayer online game. In: Proceedings of the 2004 ACM Conference on Computer Supported Cooperative Work, pp. 360–369. ACM (2004)
[6] Gajadhar, B.J., de Kort, Y.A.W., IJsselsteijn, W.A.: Shared fun is doubled fun: Player enjoyment as a function of social setting. In: Markopoulos, P., de Ruyter, B., IJsselsteijn, W.A., Rowland, D. (eds.) Fun and Games 2008. LNCS, vol. 5294, pp. 106–117. Springer, Heidelberg (2008)
[7] Jennett, C., Cox, A.L., Cairns, P., Dhoparee, S., Epps, A., Tijs, T., Walton, A.: Measuring and defining the experience of immersion in games. International Journal of Human-Computer Studies 66(9), 641–661 (2008)
[8] Kauko, J., Häkkilä, J.: Shared-screen social gaming with portable devices. In: Proceedings of the 12th International Conference on Human Computer Interaction with Mobile Devices and Services, pp. 317–326. ACM (2010)
[9] de Kort, Y.A., IJsselsteijn, W.A., Poels, K.: Digital games as social presence technology: Development of the social presence in gaming questionnaire (spgq). In: Proceedings of PRESENCE, pp. 195–203 (2007)
[10] Lazzaro, N.: Why we play games: Four keys to more emotion without story (2004)
[11] Lindley, S.E., Le Couteur, J., Berthouze, N.L.: Stirring up experience through movement in game play: effects on engagement and social behaviour. In: Proceedings of the SIGCHI Conference on Human Factors in Computing Systems, pp. 511–514. ACM (2008)
[12] Qin, H., Patrick Rau, P.L., Salvendy, G.: Measuring player immersion in the computer game narrative. Intl. Journal of Human–Computer Interaction 25(2), 107–133 (2009)
[13] Rocha, J.B., Mascarenhas, S., Prada, R.: Game mechanics for cooperative games. ZDN Digital Game, 73–80 (2008)
[14] Sajjadi, P., Cebolledo Gutierrez, E.O., Trullemans, S., De Troyer, O.: Maze commander: a collaborative asynchronous game using the oculus rift & the sifteo cubes. In: Proceedings of the First ACM SIGCHI Annual Symposium on Computer-Human Interaction in Play, pp. 227–236. ACM (2014)
[15] Seif El-Nasr, M., Aghabeigi, B., Milam, D., Erfani, M., Lameman, B., Maygoli, H., Mah, S.: Understanding and evaluating cooperative games. In: Proceedings of the SIGCHI Conference on Human Factors in Computing Systems, pp. 253–262. ACM (2010)
[16] Sweetser, P., Wyeth, P.: Gameflow: a model for evaluating player enjoyment in games. Computers in Entertainment (CIE) 3(3), 3–3 (2005)
[17] Tecchia, F., Avveduto, G., Brondi, R., Carrozzino, M., Bergamasco, M., Alem, L.: I'm in vr!: using your own hands in a fully immersive mr system. In: Proceedings of the 20th ACM Symposium on Virtual Reality Software and Technology, pp. 73–76 (2014)
[18] Yee, N.: Motivations for play in online games. CyberPsychology & Behavior 9(6), 772–775 (2006a)
[19] Yee, N.: The psychology of mmorpgs: Emotional investment, motivations, relationship formation, and problematic usage. Avatars at work and play: Collaboration and Interaction in Shared Virtual Environments 34, 187–207 (2006b)

Evolutionary Changes of Pokemon Game: A Case Study with Focus On Catching Pokemon

Chetprayoon Panumate[1], Shuo Xiong[2], Hiroyuki Iida[1], and Toshiaki Kondo[2]

[1] Japan Advanced Institute of Science and Technology, Japan
{panumate.c,xiongshuo,iida}@jaist.ac.jp
[2] Sirindhorn International Institute of Technology, Thailand
tkondo@siit.tu.ac.th

Abstract. Game refinement is a unique theory that has been used as a reliable tool for measuring the attractiveness and sophistication of the games considered. A game refinement measure is derived from a game information progress model and has been applied in various games. In this paper, we aim to investigate the attractiveness of Pokemon, one of the most popular turn-based RPG games. We focus on catching Pokemons which are important components in the game. Then, we propose a new game refinement model with consideration on a prize cost and apply it to catching Pokemons. We analyze in every generation of the game. Experimental results show that a game refinement value of catching Pokemons which has been changed many times tries to reach to an appropriate range of game refinement value: $0.07 - 0.08$ for which previous works have confirmed.

Keywords: Game refinement theory, engagement, Pokemon.

1 Introduction

Game theory [13] originated with the idea of the existence of mixed-strategy equilibrium in two-person zero sum games. It has been widely applied as a powerful tool in many fields such as economics, political science and computer science. Game refinement theory is another game theory focusing on attractiveness and sophistication of games based on the concept of information of game outcome uncertainty [7] [11]. The early works (e.g., [4] [8] [17] [20] [21]) focused on various types of games such as sports, board games and video games. The game refinement values of those popular games support the previous assumptions of a balanced range of game refinement value which is around $0.07 - 0.08$ [22]. Classical game theory concerns the optimal strategy from the player's point of view, whereas game refinement theory concerns the optimization from the game designer's point of view.

In this study, we aim to investigate the attractiveness of Pokemon, one of the most popular turn-based RPG games [6]. While many efforts have been devoted to the study of Pokemon with focus on different points such as education [9], media science [15] and social science [6], the present study focuses on another

© IFIP International Federation for Information Processing 2015
K. Chorianopoulos et al. (Eds.): ICEC 2015, LNCS 9353, pp. 182–194, 2015.
DOI: 10.1007/978-3-319-24589-8_14

important aspect of Pokemon: engagement or entertainment. Catching Pokemon is an important part that makes Pokemon game very attractive and widely popular.

For this study, we raise a research question: why has catching Pokemon mechanism been changed so many times in its history? To answer this question, we try to quantify the attractiveness of catching Pokemon in every episodes based on the game refinement theory. We propose a reasonable model of game information progress to derive a game refinement measure for catching Pokemon, while we consider prize cost to catch Pokemons.

In this paper we first give a short sketch of Pokemon game, especially for catching Pokemon. Then we present the fundamental idea of game refinement theory, and our new approach to the application of catching Pokemon with consideration on prize cost. Moreover, analyzed results obtained from various episodes are discussed and concluding remarks are given.

2   Catching Pokemon

In this section, we present a short history of Pokemon. Then, we focus on catching Pokemon which is our main target to apply game refinement model with consideration on prize cost. Moreover, some essential Pokemon capturing mechanism and equations are described.

2.1   Pokemon

Pokemon [2] [16] is a series of games developed by Game Freak and Creatures Inc. and published by Nintendo as part of the Pokemon media franchise. First released in 1996 in Japan for the Game Boy, the main series of role-playing video games (RPG) has continued on each generation of Nintendo's handhelds. Games are commonly released in pairs each with slight variations and then an enhanced remake of the games is released in a few years from the original release. While the main series consists of role-playing games, spinoffs encompass other genres such as action role-playing, puzzle and digital pet games. It is the second bestselling video game franchise worldwide, next to Nintendo's own Mario franchise. We show, in Table 1, a brief history of Pokemon.

The basic goal of Pokemon game [10] is to win the badges of gyms and become the champion of the league. For this purpose, one has to make his/her own team strong enough to win every battle in the game. Hence, in this study, we chiefly focus on the detail in catching Pokemon which is the main means to collect Pokemons and build one's own team.

2.2   Catching Pokemon

At the very initial stage to start a game, a Pokemon is given as a starter Pokemon for the coming adventure. The player may be able to catch other Pokemons by his/her effort, except some Pokemons given automatically due to the story of the game.

Table 1. History of Pokemon

Generation	Number of Pokemons	Year	Version
1st	151	1996	Pokemon Red & Green
		1997	Pokemon Blue
		1998	Pokemon Yellow
2nd	251	1999	Pokemon Gold & Silver
		2000	Pokemon Crystal
3rd	386	2002	Pokemon Ruby & Sapphire
		2004	Pokemon Fire Red & Leaf Green
			Pokemon Emerald
4th	493	2006	Pokemon Diamond & Pearl
		2008	Pokemon Platinum
		2009	Pokemon Heart Gold & Soul Silver
5th	649	2010	Pokemon Black & White
		2012	Pokemon Black2 & White2
6th	719	2013	Pokemon X & Y
		2014	Pokemon Omega Ruby & Alpha Sapphire

Importantly, the final goal of Pokemon game is to catch every Pokemon and make one's Pokedex, a portable device which provides information regarding the diversified species of Pokemon, be completed. Moreover, Table 1 shows that the number of Pokemons incessantly increases. We therefore understand that catching Pokemon is one of the most important parts in Pokemon game.

Catching Pokemon can be simply described that a player has to reduce the current HP of a target Pokemon as much as possible. HP [12] is an attribute assigned to each entity in game that indicates its state in combat. When HP of a player character reaches zero, the player may lose a life or their character might become incapacitated or die. So, to catch Pokemon, it is reasonable that the more Pokemon's HP is reduced, the weaker the target Pokemon is. Then, the player has to throw a ball, working as a catching device, to the Pokemon. Importantly, if the Pokemon is fainted, the catching attempt is unquestioningly failed. Additionally, using high quality ball or giving bad status to target Pokemon makes it easier to be caught.

According to Table 1, Pokemon has six generations to date. Each generation has own different catch rate mechanism except third generation and fourth generation, where these two generations follow the same mechanism. Below we show the detail for each catching mechanism [5].

$$P_1 = \frac{S}{B} + \frac{\min(C+1, B-S)}{B} \times \frac{\min(255, F)+1}{256} \tag{1}$$

Where, $F = \left\lfloor \frac{\left\lfloor \frac{M \cdot 255}{G} \right\rfloor}{\max(1, \lfloor \frac{H}{4} \rfloor)} \right\rfloor$

$$P_2 = \frac{\max(\frac{(3M-2H) \cdot C}{3M}, 1) + S + 1}{256} \tag{2}$$

$$P_{34} = \frac{\frac{(3M-2H)\cdot CB}{3M} \cdot S}{255} \tag{3}$$

$$P_5 = \frac{\frac{(3M-2H)\cdot GCB}{3M} \cdot S \cdot \frac{E}{100}}{255} \tag{4}$$

$$P_6 = \frac{\frac{(3M-2H)\cdot GCB}{3M} \cdot S \cdot O}{255} \tag{5}$$

P_i stands for probability of catching Pokemon at ith generation. S is a variable for additional status. Normally, it is easiest to catch a Pokemon when its status is either asleep or frozen. The difficulty increases if the status is poisoned, burned, or paralyzed. The status none is the hardest case because it means that Pokemon is now very strong and ready to break any balls. C is a capture rate. Every Pokemon has its own capture rate status between 3 and 255. The value 3 means that it is very hard to catch that Pokemon, it is for super rare or legendary Pokemon. The value 255 means that it is very easy to catch, it is for common Pokemon which can be found regularly. B is a variable for ball used. There are many kinds of ball in this game. Some balls have special property which fit for some Pokemons whereas it also does not fit for other Pokemons. In this experiment, we focus on three kinds of common balls: Poke Ball, Great Ball and Ultra Ball, which can be bought in mart.

G (for P_1) represents a variable for Great Ball modifier. Due to some bugs in the first generation, this variable makes Great Ball has a higher average catch rate than Ultra ball even though Ultra Ball is more expensive. G (for P_5 and P_6) is a variable for grass modifier. It depends on the place where the player meets Pokemon. For example, if the action catching Pokemon takes place in thick grass, it is harder than normal grass. E denotes Entralink power. During normal gameplay this value is not effective. However, by playing Entralink missions with their friends over local wireless, they can receive capturing power from another player, which enables them to increase the chance of catch rate. O stands for O-Power bonus. This value replaces the Entralink modifier of the fifth-generation games to factor in Entralink powers sixth generation analogue, O-Powers.

M means maximum HP. It can be exactly calculated by Equation (6) for first and second generation, and by Equation (7) for third generation onward. H stands for current HP. It is reasonable that the more Pokemon's HP is reduced, the easier target Pokemon is caught. Importantly, if one makes the target Pokemon fainted, the catching attempt is unquestioningly failed.

$$HP_{12} = \frac{(IV + BaseHP + \frac{EV}{8} + 50) \times Level}{50} + 10 \tag{6}$$

$$HP_{3456} = \frac{(IV + 2 \cdot BaseHP + \frac{EV}{4} + 100) \times Level}{100} + 10 \tag{7}$$

IV is an individual value which is randomly generated by the game at the time when one meets that Pokemon first. There are six IV due to each Pokemon has six battle status. To calculate HP, *IV* of HP is used. *BaseHP* means initial HP status of Pokemon considered. It depends on what kind of one's Pokemon is. Some Pokemons have outstanding BaseHP while other Pokemons have poor *BaseHP*. Rationally, Pokemon with poor *BaseHP* should have another great initial status. However, legendary Pokemon may have excellent value in every initial status. *EV* stands for special value which Pokemon will receive when finishing a battle. It depends on what kind of Pokemon has been defeated. Some Pokemons give *EV* of HP while other Pokemons give *EV* of another status. *Level* denotes a level of Pokemon considered. It simply starts from 1 to 100. The more Pokemon's level increase, the stronger Pokemon becomes.

Moreover, there are various works which have been carried out with Pokemon, for example, in the domains of mathematics [1] and computer science [3]. In this paper, we focus on catching Pokemon which is an essential component in Pokemon game. Pokemon Catch Rate Calculator [5] is an application that enables us to calculate Pokemon catch rate in many situations and every generations. We use this tool for calculating the chance of catching Pokemon. In the next section, we show our new model, game refinement model with consideration on prize cost, which is applied to catching Pokemon.

3   Assessment of Catching Pokemon

In order to quantify the attractiveness of catching Pokemon, we first give a brief sketch of the basic idea of game refinement theory. Then we show our proposed model and its application to various episodes of Pokemon.

3.1   Game Refinement Theory

A general model of game refinement was proposed based on the concept of game progress and game information progress [17]. It bridges a gap between board games [8] and sports games [19]. We first show a general model of game progress in order to derive a game refinement measure. Then, we apply this idea to various games while identifying reasonable game progress models of given games, and compare them using game refinement measures.

The game progress is twofold [19]. One is game speed or scoring rate, while another one is game information progress with focus on the game outcome. Game information progress presents the degree of certainty of a game's result in time or in steps. Having full information of the game progress, i.e. after its conclusion, game progress $x(t)$ will be given as a linear function of time t with $0 \leq t \leq t_k$ and $0 \leq x(t) \leq x(t_k)$, as shown in Equation (8).

$$x(t) = \frac{x(t_k)}{t_k} \, t \tag{8}$$

However, the game information progress given by Equation (8) is unknown during the in-game period. The presence of uncertainty during the game, often until the final moments of a game, reasonably renders game progress as exponential. Hence, a realistic model of game information progress is given by Equation (9).

$$x(t) = x(t_k)(\frac{t}{t_k})^n \qquad (9)$$

Here n stands for a constant parameter which is given based on the perspective of an observer of the game considered. Only a very boring game would progress in a linear function however, and most of course do not. Therefore, it is reasonable to assume a parameter n, based on the perception of game progress prior to completion. If the information of the game is completely known (i.e., after the end of the game) and the value of n is 1, the game progress curve appears as a straight line. In most games, especially in competitive ones, much of the information is incomplete, the value of n cannot be assumed, and therefore game progress is a steep curve until its completion, along with $x(t_k)$, t_k, $x(t)$ and t, just prior to game's end.

Then acceleration of game information progress is obtained by deriving Equation (9) twice. Solving it at $t = t_k$, we have Equation (10).

$$x''(t_k) = \frac{x(t_k)}{(t_k)^n}(t_k)^{n-2} \, n(n-1) = \frac{x(t_k)}{(t_k)^2} \, n(n-1) \qquad (10)$$

It is assumed in the current model that game information progress in any type of game is encoded and transported in our brains. We do not yet know about the physics of information in the brain, but it is likely that the acceleration of information progress is subject to the forces and laws of physics. Too little game information acceleration may be easy for human observers and players to compute, and becomes boring. In contrast, too much game information acceleration surpasses the entertaining range and enters frustration, and at some point beyond that could become overwhelming and incomprehensible. Therefore we expect that the larger the value $\frac{x(t_k)}{(t_k)^2}$ is, the more the game becomes exciting, due in part to the uncertainty of game outcome. Thus, we use its root square, $\frac{\sqrt{x(t_k)}}{t_k}$, as a game refinement measure for the game under consideration. We call it R value for short shown in Equation (11).

$$R = \frac{\sqrt{x(t_k)}}{t_k} \qquad (11)$$

There are many works done before [14], the brief result is shown in Table 2. From Table 2, we can propose suitable approach for various game types by using the described model. We see that sophisticated games have a R value in the appropriate range, $0.07 - 0.08$. It has been proposed that information acceleration is one of the direct factors of engagement or excitement for all game types.

Table 2. Measures of game refinement for major board games and sports games

Game	R
Chess	0.074
Go	0.076
Basketball	0.073
Soccer	0.073

3.2   Game Refinement Model with Consideration on Prizing Cost

While early work [18] focuses on playing cost, this work focuses on prizing cost. We propose V as a value of each prize captured and P as a probability of successful capturing the prize. Therefore, the game information $x(t_k)$ can be described as an average of P and V, as given in Equation (12).

$$x(t_k) = \frac{1}{n} \sum_{0<i<n} P_i V_i \tag{12}$$

Next, we apply our $x(t_k)$ in game refinement measure R in Equation (11). For this case, we have to calculate by percentage as shown in Equation (13).

$$R = \frac{1}{10} \sqrt{\frac{1}{n} \sum_{0<i<n} P_i V_i} \tag{13}$$

In order to apply this model to catching Pokemon, V, a value of each prize captured, can be calculated by the degree of rareness of target Pokemon. Normally, each Pokemon has its own capture rate which shows how hard to capture the target Pokemon, which means like a rareness of Pokemon. Therefore, we propose an equation for calculating the rareness of each Pokemon, V, as shown in Equation (14)

$$V = \frac{Max - Cap + Min}{Max - Avg} \tag{14}$$

Max means the maximum of capture rate and Min means the minimum of capture rate. Likewise, Avg means the average of capture rate and Cap means that target Pokemon's capture rate. Generally, the minimum of capture rate in Pokemon game is 3, which means that it is very hard to catch. The maximum of capture rate in Pokemon game is 255 which means that it is very easy to catch this Pokemon. For the average of capture rate, it can be directly calculated which equals 100.25. Therefore, Equation (14) can be reduced in Equation (15).

$$V = \frac{256 - Cap + 3}{256 - Avg} \tag{15}$$

For probability of successful prize capturing, P, it can be calculated by Pokemon Catch Rate Calculator [5]. To use this calculator, we reasonably assume some parameters as explained below.

- Used Pokemon: We use 110 Pokemon samples which come from the first episode of Pokemon because we cannot use Pokemon from new episode to the first episode Pokemon Catch Rate Calculator. Moreover, the first episode of Pokemon contains 151 Pokemons but some Pokemon can be found from evolution. So we considerably cut some Pokemons which cannot be found as natural one.
- Current HP: We use 50 percent of full HP. It is the middle from 0 to 100.
- Pokemon level: It should be the average level of natural Pokemon in every episode which is approximately calculated by the lowest level and the maximum level of natural Pokemon in every episode. Finally, we already calculated average Pokemon level equals 25.69, approximately 26.
- Ball: There are many kinds of ball in Pokemon game. In this experiment, we focus on three main balls: Poke Ball, Great Ball and Ultra Ball.
- Status: Generally, if a Pokemon is asleep or frozen, it will be easiest to catch. If it is poisoned, burned or paralyzed, it is easier to catch but harder than asleep or frozen status. The hardest status for catching is none status. Hence, we use paralyzed status as an average status.

By this assumption, we obtain average of P for each generation and ball used as shown in Table 3

Table 3. Average catch rate

Generation	$R_{PokeBall}$	$R_{GreatBall}$	$R_{UltraBall}$
1st	39.14	63.98	52.55
2nd	33.36	42.60	47.86
3rd & 4th	53.33	67.12	74.85
5th	57.03	69.54	76.50
6th	57.07	69.51	76.50

Finally, we apply our new game refinement model with consideration on prize cost to Catching Pokemon. According to Equation (13), the result is shown in Table 4.

Table 4. Measures of game refinement for catching Pokemon with three main balls

Generation	$R_{PokeBall}$	$R_{GreatBall}$	$R_{UltraBall}$
1st	0.047	0.062	0.059
2nd	0.042	0.050	0.056
3rd & 4th	0.054	0.064	0.071
5th	0.058	0.067	0.072
6th	0.058	0.067	0.072

4   Discussion

For our new game refinement model with consideration on prize cost as shown in Equation (13), we can consider it as a new approach to quantify attractiveness of games. With this model, it enables us to explore new domains of game which cannot be investigated by previous models. The core of this model consists of two parameters, P that stands for the probability of successful capturing and V that stands for a value of each prize captured. For P, if we know the equation it can be calculated with the answer as the probability. If not, it can be calculated by simulating and collecting the data. For V, we have to carefully consider on what the related parameters of the prize's value are. Then, we establish the reasonable equation in order to measure the value of each prize.

Moreover, it has to be calculated in percentage system. We can apply this model to another game by creating reasonable equation. For the application to catching Pokemon, we collected data of catching Pokemon from Pokemon Catch Rate Calculator [5]. Then, we applied game refinement theory in the manner prescribed in Section 3.2. The results in Table 4 are compared in Figure (1).

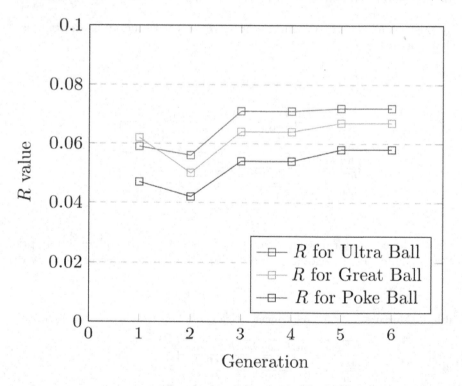

Fig. 1. Changes of game refinement values with three main balls compared

For Poke Ball, we can see that in first generation the R value is quite low. Furthermore, in second generation, the R value is lower than first generation.

Nevertheless, R value is extremely increased in third generation and continuously go this way in fifth and sixth generation. Finally, it reaches 0.058 which is the maximum of R value using Poke Ball in sixth generation.

For Great Ball, we can see that in first generation the R value is not too low. However, in second generation, the R value is awfully decreased from 0.062 in first generation to 0.50. In third generation, R comes back to 0.064 which is slightly higher than first generation. Then, it continuously increases and finally reach 0.067 in sixth generation.

For Ultra Ball, we can see that in first generation R value is rather low. It then decreased from 0.059 in first generation to 0.056 in second generation. However, in third generation, R significantly increased to 0.071 which is more than another R value from another ball in another generation mentioned before. Then, it continuously increased to 0.072 in sixth generation which falls between the appropriate ranges of game refinement value: $0.07 - 0.08$.

Next, we consider each generation applied. According to Figure (1), in first generation, due to some errors, although Ultra ball is the best ball in these three kinds of balls but it has lower average catch rate and R value than Great ball. That means in first generation some mechanism need to be fixed. In second generation, we can see that R value for Ultra Ball is larger than Great Ball. That means the problem in previous generation was fixed. However, in second generation, every ball has trivially lower R value than other generations. That means the second generation's mechanism which is fixed from first generation does not work well and it should be fixed again. Suddenly, in third generation, R value is remarkably developed and every ball in this generation has quite good R value. Moreover, third generation catching mechanism is used in fourth generation which confirm the efficiency of this mechanism. For fifth and sixth generation, even though it uses the different catching mechanism but the calculated R value is closely same. The calculated R value of these mechanisms is very fine.

Moreover, we can consider the equation, both catching Pokemon equation and HP equation, directly. We see that the catching Pokemon mechanism which has been changed so many times try to add new parameters. For example, in fifth generation, Equation (4), proposing E which is Entralink power. This enables players to receive a capture power from another player. This variable is changed to O which is an O-Power bonus in sixth generation, Equation (5). We will see that both E and O increase a chance of capturing which may increase R value.

To compare HP equation, we consider the modification from HP_{12} to HP_{3456} by reducing Equation (7) to Equation (16).

$$HP_{3456} = \frac{(\frac{IV}{2} + BaseHP + \frac{EV}{8} + 50) \times \frac{Level}{2}}{50} + 10 \tag{16}$$

By comparing Equation (6) with Equation (16), we will see that $BaseHP$ and EV has the same coefficient while IV and $Level$ is changed. With this modification each Pokemon has lower HP value which trivially makes catching Pokemon easier.

Nevertheless, to get the more exact R value, we should apply the idea of focusing on playing cost from early work [18]. In catching Pokemon, we can apply this idea by considering the cost of ball. We know that Poke Ball's cost is 200, Great Ball cost is 600 and Ultra Ball cost is 1200. These costs have not been changed since the first generation of Pokemon until now. However, we cannot directly use the pure playing cost value because it will lead the R value to be unreliable. We need to propose a reasonable function such as prize cost factor which was shown in Equation (13). To propose a reasonable function of playing cost, we need more data from other balls. Therefore, this work ignores this point and further works should carefully consider this issue.

Moreover, the experiments conducted in this study have many assumptions mentioned before. Further investigation may be made from difference aspects. Below we show a few examples.

- Used Pokemon: Normally, each episode will have its local Pokemon, a Pokemon that can be found in nature in that episode. We may consider each episode by those local Pokemons. So, each episode will use different Pokemon.
- Current HP: Current HP may be given randomly.
- Pokemon level: By following the used Pokemon assumption, we will consider each episode so that we can use each episode's average level of natural Pokemon as a Pokemon level in the experiment. So, each episode will use different Pokemon level.
- Ball: We may focus on another ball.
- Status: We may assign a status for each Pokemon at random.

In conclusion, We can see that in first generation the result shows slightly lower values but it gradually increases in third generation and also in fifth and sixth generations. Finally, for Ultra Ball in third to sixth generation, the calculated R value of catching Pokemon falls between $0.07 - 0.08$ which has been supposed to be a reliable game refinement value for many games that have undergone sophistication. The slightly lower value for the first and second generations implies that at that time the balance of catching mechanism, the relation between rareness of Pokemon and chance of catching was not optimized yet. Therefore, the catching mechanism was developed successively and it eventually reaches the appropriate range of R value. However, the experiments in this study was performed with a simple model under many assumptions. Further works may try to focus on playing cost or use new assumptions.

5   Conclusion

We believe that catching Pokemons is an essential component of Pokemon game's engagement. This work is an attempt to find a reason why the mechanism for catching Pokemons has been changed so many times. To tackle this problem, we have applied a game refinement theory with a new model which considers a prize cost as shown in Equation (13). We have introduced a value of prize captured, V, because each prize has its own unique value. For the Pokemon case, we can calculate the value of captured prize by considering the rareness. We have proposed an equation for calculating the value V from the rareness described in Equation (15). We used Pokemon Catch Rate Calculator, a reliable Pokemon catch rate simulator, as an essential tool in this research. The result is shown in Table 4 and is compared in Figure (1).

Our result confirms that the mechanism for catching Pokemons has been changed in a proper way by editing some details in the catch mechanism which directly increases R value since the first generation to sixth generation. With the changing to an appropriate R value, we conclude that this is the reason why the mechanism for catching Pokemon has been changed so many times. Moreover, we can predict that in the next generation, the catching mechanism will have R value in an appropriate range.

It is obvious that game refinement theory can effectively be used in many domains of games such as classical board games, video games and sports, including Pokemon, by establishing a reasonable game information progress model. It can be used as a helpful tool to measure the attractiveness of a game and it also enables game designers to make a target game more sophisticated. As a conclusion, we have observed that a suitable game refinement value is around $0.07 - 0.08$, with many studies done before confirmation.

Additionally, the proposed model of game refinement which considers a prize cost can be applied in other domains where the value of each prize is unequal. We will be able to establish a reasonable equation to calculate a value of each prize. However, it is understood that the work presented in this study is a simple model with no complicated factors, and more studies are required. Further works may include to collect data in other types of ball or in other games which may have a catching component.

Acknowledgement. The authors wish to thank the anonymous referees for their constructive comments that helped to improve the article considerably. This research is funded by a grant from the Japan Society for the Promotion of Science, in the framework of the Grant-in-Aid for Challenging Exploratory Research (grant number 26540189).

References

1. Aloupis, G., Demaine, E.D., Guo, A., Viglietta, G.: Classic nintendo games are (computationally) hard. In: Ferro, A., Luccio, F., Widmayer, P. (eds.) FUN 2014. LNCS, vol. 8496, pp. 40–51. Springer, Heidelberg (2014)
2. Bainbridge, J.: It is a Pokemon world: The Pokemon franchise and the environment. International Journal of Cultural Studies 17(4), 399–414 (2014)
3. Chen, S.D.: A Crude Analysis of Twitch Plays Pokemon arXiv preprint arXiv:1408.4925 (2014)
4. Diah, N.M., Nossal, N., Zin, N.A.M., Higuchi, T., Iida, H.: A Game Informatical Comparison of Chess and Association Football ("Soccer"). Advances in Computer Science 3(4), 10, 89–94 (2014)

5. Dragonflycave   pages,   Pokemon   Catch   Rate   Calculator. http://www.dragonflycave.com (accessed, 2015)
6. Horton, J.: Got my shoes, got my Pokemon: Everyday geographies of children popular culture. Geoforum 43(1), 4–13 (2012)
7. Iida, H., Takeshita, N., Yoshimura, J.: A metric for entertainment of boardgames: Its implication for evolution of chess variants. In: Nakatsu, R., Hoshino, J. (eds.) Entertainment Computing. IFIP, vol. 112, pp. 65–72. Springer, Heidelberg (2003)
8. Iida, H., Takahara, K., Nagashima, J., Kajihara, Y., Hashimoto, T.: An application of game-refinement theory to Mah Jong. In: Rauterberg, M. (ed.) ICEC 2004. LNCS, vol. 3166, pp. 333–338. Springer, Heidelberg (2004)
9. Lin, Y.H.: Integrating scenarios of video games into classroom instruction. In: First IEEE International Symposium on Information Technologies and Applications in Education, ISITAE 2007, pp. 593–596. IEEE (2007)
10. Lin, Y.H.: Pokemon: game play as multi-subject learning experience. In: The First IEEE International Workshop on Digital Game and Intelligent Toy Enhanced Learning (DIGITEL 2007), pp. 182–184 (2007)
11. Majek, P., Iida, H.: Uncertainty of game outcome, proceedings of inter academia. In: 3rd Int. Conf. on Global Research and Education in Intelligent Systems, Budapest, Hungary, pp. 71–180 (2004)
12. Moore, M.: Basics of Game Design, pp. 151–194. CRC Press (2011). ISBN 1439867763
13. Neumann, J.: Zur theorie der gesellschaftsspiele. Mathematische Annalen 100(1), 295–320 (1928)
14. Nossal, N., Iida, H.: Game refinement theory and its application to score limit games. In: Proceedings of IEEE GEM (2014)
15. Ogletree, S.M., Martinez, C.N., Turner, T.R., Mason, B.: Pokemon: Exploring the Role of Gender. Sex Roles 50(11-12), 851–859 (2004)
16. Pokemon pages on wikipedia. http://www.wikipedia.com (accessed, 2015)
17. Sutiono, A.P., Purwarianti, A., Iida, H.: A mathematical model of game refinement. In: Reidsma, D., Choi, I., Bargar, R. (eds.) INTETAIN 2014. LNICST, vol. 136, pp. 148–151. Springer, Heidelberg (2014)
18. Rachaya, C., Nossal, N., Iida, H.: Game refinement model with consideration on playing cost: A case study using crane games. In: 2015 7th International Conference on Knowledge and Smart Technology (KST), pp. 87–92 (2015)
19. Takeuchi, J., Ramadan, R., Iida, H.: Game refinement theory and its application to Volleyball, Research Report 2014-GI-31(3), Information Processing Society of Japan, pp. 1–6 (2014)
20. Xiong, S., Zuo, L., Iida, H.: Quantifying Engagement of Electronic Sports Game. Advances in Social and Behavioral Sciences 5, 37–42 (2014)
21. Xiong, S., Iida, H.: Attractiveness of real time strategy games. In: International Conference on Systems and Informatics (ICSAI 2014), pp. 264–269 (2014)
22. Xiong, S., Zuo, L., Chiewvanichakorn, R., Iida, H.: Quantifying engagement of various games. In: The 19th Game Programming Workshop 2014, pp. 101–106 (2014)

Game-Based Interactive Campaign
Using Motion-Sensing Technology

Alf Inge Wang, Mari Hansen Asplem, Mia Aasbakken, and Letizia Jaccheri

Dept. of Computer and Information Science,
Norwegian University of Science and Technology, Trondheim, Norway
{alfw,letizia}@idi.ntnu.no,
{mariashasa,mia.aasbakken}@gmail.com

Abstract. The article describes an evaluation of a prototype for doing game-based interactive advertisement campaigns in crowded public spaces using motion-sensing technology. The prototype was developed using OpenNi, XNA and Kinect, in which people who pass by a large display would be reflected on a large screen in the form of a silhouette and automatically become a part of a game. The goal of the game is for the players to gather falling objects into a container using the body to direct the objects. The objects move around when the objects collide with the silhouette of the player. The graphical representation of the falling objects and the container can be changed to fit various advertisement purposes.

The game-based interactive campaign was tested at four different public locations, and was evaluated through observations and questionnaires. Our findings suggest that there is a potential for using motion control in game-based interactive campaigns in public settings. The game attracted a good amount of attention, and seemed to tempt the curiosity of passers-by. An observed trend was that participants were comfortable playing in public and got easily engaged. Children and adolescents in groups were by far the most active participants.

Keywords: Interactive advertisement campaigns, motion-sensing control, games, evaluation.

1 Introduction

As the world around us has become filled with more and more advertisements in the form of posters or public displays, people have learned to ignore such campaigns, and grabbing the attention of passers-by has become more challenging. LCD and plasma screens make it easy and cheap to create digital campaigns that can be replaced on the fly and opens an opportunity to incorporate interaction with the user, for example in the form of touch interfaces and body recognition. After over 20 years where graphical user interfaces have consisting of windows, icons, menus and pointing devices, there has been an increased interest in new interfaces based on multi-touch technology and gestures [1]. To control devices with body gestures have now become common for gaming systems like Nintendo Wii, PlayStation Move and Microsoft's Kinect, as well as smart-TVs and other smart devices. The casual game revolution

© IFIP International Federation for Information Processing 2015
K. Chorianopoulos et al. (Eds.): ICEC 2015, LNCS 9353, pp. 195–208, 2015.
DOI: 10.1007/978-3-319-24589-8_15

introduced through smart phones, tables and game consoles like Nintendo Wii has made gaming common among both genders and among young and old [2]. By combining motion sensor technology and gaming, new types of interactive campaigns can be created that are far more engaging and enjoyable for the target audience. There has not been much research on using this type of technology for interactive campaigns, and it is an exciting area to explore. We are especially interested in how people perceive participating in interactive campaigns in public areas and the opportunities and limitations using such technology.

This paper presents an evaluation of a motion-controlled game that was developed to explore the opportunity of doing interactive advertisement campaigns using motion-sensing technology such as Microsoft Kinect. The testing of the game took place in a waterpark, a university campus, a movie theater, and a shopping mall. The goal of the evaluation was to investigate how people react to interactive campaigns using motion-control game technology in regards to joining the game, using body gestures for control, engagement, social aspects, and how the game affects the people's attitude towards a product.

2   Material and Method

This section presents the related work, the prototype of the motion-controlled interactive campaign game, and the research goal, questions and method.

2.1   Related Work

Gestural interaction is often referred to as "natural user interfaces", but they are not necessarily easy to learn or remember, and the same gesture can mean different things depending where you are [3]. However, despite some usability issues, gesture controls such as the Kinect in social games work very well as users quickly become immersed in the game [4]. Examples of using gesture and movement for various purposes are the Nautilus game where users can play in an interactive virtual space [5], and interactive art installations [6-8]. The immersion that motion-sensing technology can create along with the opportunity of public interactivity, makes this technology promising for running advertisement campaigns.

Public digital displays can be found all around us in public and semi-public spaces, and their main purpose is often advertising or displaying information [9]. A problem in the past has been the lack of interactivity they provide, but this is changing as (multi-) touch and motion-sensing technology becomes cheaper and more common. Many studies on interactive public displays have revealed an important problem: It is hard to get people to interact with them and a commonly cited reason is social embarrassment [10]. The main problem is transitioning from peripheral awareness (doing some activity away from the screen, but being peripherally aware of it) to focal awareness (focusing on the screen, watching it being used and talk about). One effect that help users move from peripheral to focal awareness occur when some people are standing around an installation and showing an interest in it, which leads to a progressive increase in the number of people in the immediate vicinity of the installation (the honey pot effect [10]).

The Audience Funnel is a framework for investigating public displays by describing the different phases that make up the interaction process [11]. Between these phases there are thresholds that the user must either cross or that cause them to abort the interaction. The phases are 1) Passing by, 2) Viewing and Reacting, 3) Subtle Interaction, 4) Direct Interaction, 5) Multiple Interaction, and 6) Follow up Actions. The first four phases are attention-based while the last two focus on motivation.

Muller et al. describe some general models for attracting attention and these are Behavioral urgency, Bayesian surprise and Honey pot effect [12]. Behavioral urgency refers to the fact that certain things, such as the abrupt appearance of a new object, moving or looming stimuli, and some luminary contrast changes capture attention. Bayesian surprise refers to the difference between what someone expect and what she or he experienced in a situation, and adding elements of surprise that will be unexpected to the user can grab their attention. The honey pot effect is described above.

There is not a lot of research on understanding the motivating factors behind a user's activity, but the Magical Mirrors study identified a set of motivating factors [12] based on work by Malone [13]: Challenge and control (motivation based on user mastering something that has appropriate challenge level), Curiosity and exploration (solve or complete something that might be uncertain or incomplete), Choice (let users have control), Fantasy and metaphor (enrich the experience), and Collaboration (easier or more entertaining).

There have been some projects that have experimented with interactive displays or installations. One example is the Magical Mirrors where the installation consisted of four displays placed next to each other in a store front window in downtown Berlin [14]. The display showed a mirror image of the scene in front of it, and by using motion detection from a simple video, added optical effects to the image, such as ribbon following a moving hand or flowers growing from your hand. Another example was the CityWall installation in Helsinki [15], where a multi-touch screen in a store front window provided users with a timeline full of photos of the city downloaded from Flickr. Users could zoom in on the timeline and organize photos by moving, rotating and resizing them. A less public, but still collaborative interactive display is the BlueBoard device, intended for both personal and collaborative use in a work setting [16]. The BlueBoard is a plasma display with touch technology and an RFID reader some users can be identified by sweeping their card. It allows users to pull up personal information quickly and to collaborate on sketching ideas, sharing content and so on. Another example was Volvo's interactive commercial prior to screening the movie Ratatouille at twelve movie theaters across the UK where the audience controlled a Volvo through an obstacle course by holding their arm up into the air and moved their arms in the direction they wanted the car to go [17]. Another example of a commercial use of motion sensor technology is the virtual fitting room where an interactive display shows the user wearing various virtual clothes that move according to body movements detected by a Kinect motion detection device [18]. Our approach is different from the described projects in being a game. Our motivation for choosing the game approach was to increase the immersion and engagement.

2.2   The Prototype

The game is a simple motion gesture game where the goal is to gather similar falling objects into a container of some sort. Once a certain number of objects have been collected, an advertisement campaign such as an image of an offer or a coupon code will be shown. The falling objects are controlled by moving the player's body so that the silhouette collides with them. Because the silhouette of a person appears on the screen as soon as they pass the sensor, she or he will immediately be a part of the game. The objects that fall down, the background, the container and the winning image can be easily replaced, thus changing the appearance of the game. The falling objects behave as physical objects and bounce of the silhouette, making it a challenge to get them into the container. Figure 1 shows a screenshot from a two-player game with two people in the background.

Fig. 1. Screenshot from a two-player game

The game prototype was made using XNA and utilizing the OpenNI (communication and management of motion sensor) and Farseer (physics engine) libraries. The OpenNi framework defines APIs developers can use for accessing Natural Interaction devices. It gives access to vision and audio sensors, and middleware that analyzes data from sensors. Examples of application areas for OpenNI are speech recognition, body motion tracking, and capturing body/hand gestures. The Farseer physics engine is an open source 2D physics engine made for the Microsoft .Net platform based on the BOX2D physics engine used for instance in the Angry Birds game from Rovio. Farseer uses four central concepts in order to simulate a moving body that can collide and interact with another body: World (a location of bodies, fixtures and constraints), Body (keeps track of a position in the world and is the backbone for fixtures), Shape (2D geometrical object in space), and Fixture (acts as glue and attaches the shape to the body and adds material properties like density, friction and restitution).

2.3 Research Goal, Questions and Method

To provide a framework for conducting the research described in this article, the Goal Question Metric framework was used [19]. In the goal question metric approach we first define a research goal (conceptual level), then define a set of research questions (operational level), and finally describe a set of metrics to answer the defined research questions (quantitative level). The metrics used in our evaluation was a mixture of qualitative and quantitative data [20]. The research goal was defined as:

The purpose of this study was to understand and evaluate how users relate to motion-controlled applications in a public space.

The research goal was decomposed into the following research questions:

- RQ1: Are people comfortable becoming a part of and playing a motion-controlled game in a public space without explicitly giving permission?
- Metrics: Observation on site and questionnaire.
- RQ2: Which users are easiest to engage?
- Metrics: Observations.
- RQ3: Do people get engaged playing an interactive motion-controlled campaign?
- Metrics: Observations and questionnaire.
- RQ4: What roles do the social aspects play for participating in an interactive motion-controlled campaign?
- Metrics: Observations and questionnaire.
- RQ5: Does interactive motion-controlled campaign change the attitude of the people involved?
- Metrics: Observations and questionnaire.

Based on the research questions above, a questionnaire was designed. The observations were conducted by the two developers of the game. More details about the research design and questionnaire can be found in [21].

3 Results

This section presents the results from the evaluation of the prototype.

3.1 Observations

The interactive campaign was tested out in four different locations: The entrance area of a waterpark, at the a large corridor at the university campus with access to multiple lecture halls, cafeteria, offices and shops, the entrance of a candy store in a movie theater, and in an open space at a downtown shopping mall as shown in Figure 2.

Fig. 2. Testing out the game-based interactive campaign

In the waterpark there was a relatively constant stream of people but not typically crowded in the entrance area, as people tend to spend a short time passing through the reception to enter the waterpark. Especially adults did not pay much attention to the stand and mostly focused on getting into the waterpark. The most eager groups were definitely elementary and middle school children. These children were drawn to the screen to try out the game. In some cases, the children encouraged their parents to try the game. Most of the children who played were very active, and they would run around, jump and yell, without seeming to be affected by the fact that the game was placed in a public space.

The testing of the interactive campaign at the university campus attracted a lot more participants. Most people who passed it did notice, and went from being passers-by in the audience funnel to viewing and reacting [12]. A fairly large portion of those who looked at the screen did not try to participate in the game. Some would walk by while doing a superfluous movement, such as waving an arm, without stopping, while others would exclaim: "Look, we're on TV" or "Is that us? No? Yes it's us!" Although the goal of the game is presented in the center of the screen, several people chose to have fun in the outer area of the screen. A small group of students danced and watched their silhouettes, while two other tried playing volleyball with the balls in the game. Some tried to grab a single ball with their hands, while others played around with capturing as many balls as possible between their arms. A large majority of those who stopped and started playing were in groups of two or more people, and most of them male. Mixed groups also stopped, but then most the female students played. Another way some experimented with the game was to use physical objects they were holding to control the game or even a backpack to hurl the balls around. When students won the game, the price was an advertisement for a lunch offering in the local store. The students were generally reluctant to the advertisement at the end of the game, but were positive to an alternative approach to advertisement.

The third location to test the interactive campaign was in front of the candy store in a movie theater. A problem in the movie theater common area was to be able to stand out, as there were many other screens and advertisement in the room. The graphics in the game for this location was falling popcorns and a popcorn container. At first very few noticed the interactive campaign, until a person standing in front of the screen accidentally started to move around popcorns. He got his friends over to the screen and then more people were drawn to the game (the honey pot effect). One surprise was that some thought the game was touch screen based and tried to control the game touching the screen.

The forth location was an open area in a shopping mall. The game was here tested both without and with a prize for winning the game. Offering a gift certificate as a prize greatly increased the amount of time people spent on playing and the amount of people who wanted to play. One observation at the mall was that the most frequent players were groups of teenage girls. Some boys that played did not try to win the game but rather used various body parts to move the balls around. Some men in their early twenties kicked balls to each other and had fun in this way. Another pattern in the mall was that those who stopped played for a very short period of time (about one minute). Another problem in the mall was that people standing behind the player would make it hard for the players to complete the task. The announcement of the prize made people more eager to figure out how to win the game and play longer and more. The prizewinners were drawn among the winners of the game.

3.2   Empirical Results

In the evaluation of the interactive campaign we had a total of 105 respondents, where 28 did not play the game and 77 played the game. 69% of the respondents were female vs. 31% male (similar gender distribution for those who played and those who did not play). The age distribution of the group is shown inn Figure 3.

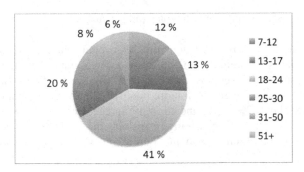

Fig. 3. Age distribution of respondents

The largest group was the 18-24 years old (41%), as a large portion of the respondents were students playing the game at the university campus. The age distributions of those who played the game and those who did not play the game is shown in Figure 4.

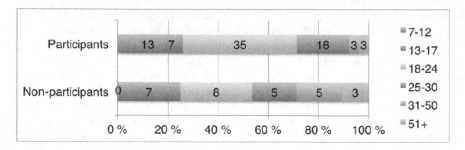

Fig. 4. Age distribution of those who played and those who did not

The first statement in the questionnaire focused on how comfortable the respondents were with being "thrown into" a game while passing by, without explicitly giving their consent to their silhouette being projected on the screen and suddenly being part of the game. Figure 5 shows the results where 84% of those who had played the game agreed or strongly agree that it was ok to be part of the game without consent on beforehand. The respondents not playing the game were more skeptic as only 52% agreed or strongly agreed to be comfortable becoming a part of the game without giving explicit consent.

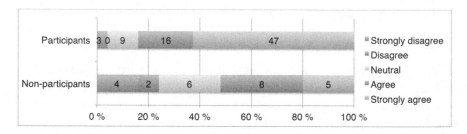

Fig. 5. Descriptive statistics on joining game without consent

The second statement in the questionnaire was about whether or not being comfortable with playing such a game in a public space (with many people around). The results from this statement are shown in Figure 6. Similar to statement one, respondents that played the game were much more positive to playing in public compared to those who did not play (79% agree and strongly agreed for those who played vs. 46% for those who did not play). One striking result was that as little as 5% of those who played found it to be a problem to play in a public area with people around.

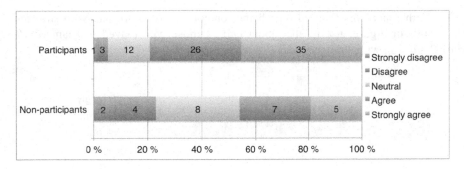

Fig. 6. Descriptive statistics on playing the game in public space

The third statement of the questionnaire focused on the immersion of the players by asking if they became unaware of their surroundings while playing the game. The results are shown in Figure 7, and give a clear indication that the game was immersive as much as 65% of those playing the game agreed or strongly agreed that they became unaware of their surroundings while playing. Also notice that as little as 13% of the players disagreed to this statement.

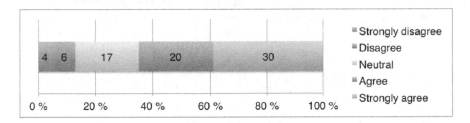

Fig. 7. Descriptive statistics on immersion

The fourth statement of the questionnaire consisted of two parts. First we asked whether they had played the game with other people or not. 56 out of 77 respondents (73%) had played the multi-player mode. Part two of this statement asked if they thought it was more fun to play with someone, and the results are shown in Figure 8. The results clearly state that it was more fun to play with another person (88% agreed or strongly agreed).

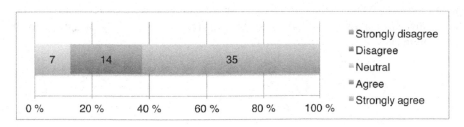

Fig. 8. Descriptive statistics on social enjoyment

The fifth statements focused on whether or not it was ok to play with strangers. The results in Figure 9 show that about half of those who played the game (51%) were ok playing with strangers, and 17% were negative.

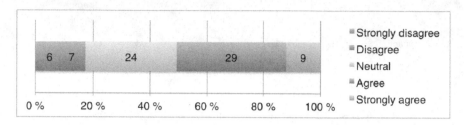

Fig. 9. Descriptive statistics on playing with strangers

The sixth statement of the questionnaire focused on whether the game caught the respondents' attention to a greater degree than a poster would have done. The results are shown in Figure 10. It is interesting to see the large difference between those who played the game and those who did not. 91% of those who played the game claimed that the game was more efficient in catching the audience attention compared to a poster. For those who did not play the game, 56% agreed. However, only 16% of the same group disagreed to this statement.

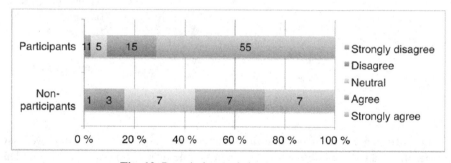

Fig. 10. Descriptive statistics on attention

The seventh statement of the questionnaire consisted of two parts where the first part asked whether the players had won the game or not. The winners of the game where then asked whether they were more likely to buy the advertised product after playing the game. The results in Figure 11 show that 33% were more positive to buy the product after playing the game vs. 44% disagreed or strongly disagreed to the same statement.

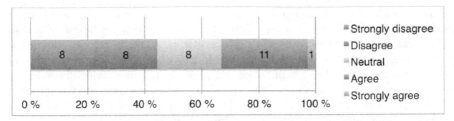

Fig. 11. Descriptive statistics on commercial effect

In the eight and final statement of the questionnaire, the respondents who played a version of game without advertisement for a specific product were asked if they would be comfortable participating in an corresponding advertising campaign. The results in Figure 12 show that 76% agreed or strongly agreed to participate in an interactive advertise campaign.

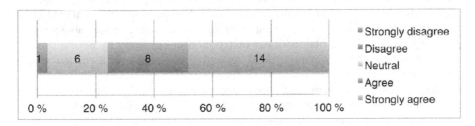

Fig. 12. Descriptive statistics on willingness to be part of campaign (29)

4   Discussion

One focus in our evaluation was to investigate how people felt about playing a motion-controlled game in a public space without giving explicit permission to participate. In our study the great majority (over 80%) felt comfortable being part of a game without giving permission, and many expressed excitement about seeing themselves being represented on the screen. Some participants commented on feeling silly and being a bit embarrassed by playing in the public. However, the majority of the participants reported that they became unaware of their surroundings while playing, which contributed to making it less embarrassing. We also observed several teenage girls who felt it was embarrassing, but still wanted to play in order to win the gift certificate. There were also many who just passed by the installation without noticing the installation, which means that they did not move out of the *passing-by phase* as defined in the Audience Funnel by Müller [11]. However, once someone actually saw the game and reacted to it, they would often perform some subtle interaction like a wave or slowing down to look at their silhouette.

Another focus in the evaluation was to investigate what user groups were most active and engaged interacting with the installation. This can be affected by several factors, such as the type of application, the design of it, rewards, location/context of the installation, and comfort level of playing in public. As we expected, male users were more willing to stop and play at three of our test locations. However, at the shopping mall, the majority of players were girls and the same group of girls came back several times to play to try to win a gift certificate. At the university campus, we did not see any groups of only girls that would play, but girls in groups with boys would stop and interact. The age of the people playing the game varied depending on where the installation was placed. At the shopping mall and the waterpark where there was a wider variety of age among the people there, those who played the most and seemed to become most engaged where children and young teenagers.

For most of the tests, people did not play for a long time and the average playing time varied between 76 and 104 seconds. We suspect that the short playing times have to do with the fact that people in a public space are generally heading some-where and have other plans than playing with an interactive campaign. These findings correspond to findings for the Magical Mirrors installation [12]. However, the playing time and the engagement increased when we announced the chance of winning a gift certificate. Results from the evaluation of the Magical Mirrors installation showed that 70% of those who had direct interaction with the installation did multiple interactions. We did not see similar results in our study, but we suspect that the Magical Mirrors' four displays in a row could can explain the difference. It was also possible to get people to revisit and play with our installation in our study by have a prize to win. Some groups of participants played several times in a row to increase their chances of winning a price.

Another focus in our study was group dynamics. As expected, passers-by who were in groups were much more likely to stop and play, and play for a longer time when stopping. People who were walking alone were much likely to pass over from the view and reacting and subtle interaction phases of the Audience Funnel to the direct interaction phase, while those who were in groups and discovered themselves on the screen very often interacted directly. Over 70% of the respondents to our questionnaire played together with others, and an overwhelming majority of them said that they thought the game was more fun because they played with someone else. Half of those who played alone said they would have played for a longer time if they had been playing with someone else. We also observed that those who played in groups seemed to be significantly less self-conscious while playing. Sometimes we observed that if one person in a group wanted to play, he or she would convince others to join because it would become less embarrassing.

5   Conclusion

In this article we have presented an evaluation of an interactive campaign using motion-controlled game technology along with a simple game concept of collecting falling balls into a container using body gestures. The first research question asked whether people are comfortable becoming a part of and playing a motion-controlled game in a public space without explicitly giving permission (RQ1). Our observations and results from the questionnaire shows that the large majority (84%) of those who played the game think it was ok to join an interactive advertisement game without consent, while those who did not play were more skeptic (52% thought it was ok). We also observed the same pattern regarding playing a game controlled by the user's body in public where 79% of those who played the game thought it was ok vs. 49% of those who did not. Further, few respondents stated that they were negative to join the game without consent and playing in public.

The second research question asked about which users were easiest to engage (RQ2), and the general answer is children and adolescents. However, for teenager and older, the engagement is very dependent on the number of people around, where the interactive campaign is located, and if the user is a part of a group or not.

The third research question asked whether people got engaged playing an interaction motion-controlled campaign or not (RQ3). As many as 65% of those who played the game agreed to become unaware of their surroundings while playing, and only 13% disagreed. This shows that if interactive motion-controlled campaigns are designed well immersion is not a problem.

The fourth research question asked about how the social aspects play a role when participating in an interactive motion-controlled campaign (RQ4). 88% of those who played the game agreed that it was more fun to play the game as multi-player. From the observations we also noticed that it was easier for many to play together than alone, making it important to provide multi-player support for such interactive campaigns. Further, 51% of those who played agreed to that it was ok to play with strangers vs. 17% disagreeing.

The fifth and final research question asked about the effect of using motion-controlled campaigns (RQ5). The statistics showed that 91% of they who played the game said that the interactive motion-controlled campaign had a better effect than a poster vs. 56% for those who did not play. Further that 33% of those who won the game were more positive to buying the product vs. 44% that disagreed to the same statement. For those who played a game without advertisement, 76% were positive to participate in an interactive advertisement similar to the game.

From the observations, we noticed that a major success factor getting high attendance and motivation for playing through the game is to provide prizes for the winners of the game. This is especially true for teenagers, youths and adults. Also we found that many playing the game did not play the game as designed, but just having fun with it without trying to win.

References

1. Petersen, N., Stricker, D.: Continuous natural user interface: Reducing the gap between real and digital world. In: ISMAR, pp. 23–26 (2009)
2. Juul, J.: A casual revolution: Reinventing video games and their players. The MIT Press (2012)
3. Norman, D.A.: Natural user interfaces are not natural. Interactions 17, 6–10 (2010)
4. Nielsen, J.: Kinect Gestural UI: First Impressions. Jakob Nielsen's Alertbox (2010)
5. Strömberg, H., Väätänen, A., Räty, V.-P.: A group game played in interactive virtual space: design and evaluation. In: Proceedings of the 4th Conference on Designing Interactive Systems: Processes, Practices, Methods, and Techniques, pp. 56–63. ACM (2002)
6. Trifonova, A., Jaccheri, L., Bergaust, K.: Software engineering issues in interactive installation art. International Journal of Arts and Technology 1, 43–65 (2008)

7. Satomi, M., Sommerer, C.: game_of_life: interactive art installation using eye-tracking interface. In: Proceedings of the International Conference on Advances in Computer Entertainment Technology, pp. 246–247. ACM (2007)

8. Costello, B., Muller, L., Amitani, S., Edmonds, E.: Understanding the experience of interactive art: Iamascope in Beta_space. In: Proceedings of the Second Australasian Conference on Interactive Entertainment, pp. 49–56. Creativity & Cognition Studios Press (2005)

9. José, R., Cardoso, J.C.: Opportunities and challenges of interactive public displays as an advertising medium. In: Pervasive Advertising, pp. 139–157. Springer (2011)

10. Brignull, H., Rogers, Y.: Enticing people to interact with large public displays in public spaces. In: Proceedings of INTERACT, pp. 17–24 (2003)

11. Michelis, D., Müller, J.: The audience funnel: Observations of gesture based interaction with multiple large displays in a city center. Intl. Journal of Human–Computer Interaction 27, 562–579 (2011)

12. Müller, J., Alt, F., Michelis, D., Schmidt, A.: Requirements and design space for interactive public displays. In: Proceedings of the International Conference on Multimedia, pp. 1285–1294. ACM (2010)

13. Malone, T.W.: Toward a theory of intrinsically motivating instruction*. Cognitive Science 5, 333–369 (1981)

14. Michelis, D.: Interaktive Großbildschirme im öffentlichen Raum. Springer (2009)

15. Peltonen, P., Kurvinen, E., Salovaara, A., Jacucci, G., Ilmonen, T., Evans, J., Oulasvirta, A., Saarikko, P.: It's mine, don't touch!: interactions at a large multi-touch display in a city centre. In: Proceedings of the SIGCHI Conference on Human Factors in Computing Systems, pp. 1285–1294. ACM (2008)

16. Russell, D.M., Trimble, J.P., Dieberger, A.: The use patterns of large, interactive display surfaces: Case studies of media design and use for BlueBoard and MERBoard. In: Proceedings of the 37th Annual Hawaii International Conference on System Sciences, p. 10. IEEE (2004)

17. Wang, A.I., Føllesdal, E.A.: Evaluation of a social multiplayer game featuring multimodal interaction. In: Proceedings of the IASTED International Conference on Software Engineering and Applications (SEA 2010) (2010)

18. Magazine, W.: Augmented Reality: Kinect Fitting-Room for Topshop, Moscow. Web: http://www.wired.com/2011/05/augmented-reality-kinect-fitting-room-for-topshop-moscow/ (2011)

19. Basili, V.R.: Software modeling and measurement: the Goal/Question/Metric paradigm. University of Maryland for Advanced Computer Studies (1992)

20. Wohlin, C., Runeson, P., Höst, M., Ohlsson, M.C., Regnell, B., Wesslén, A.: Experimentation in software engineering. Springer (2012)

21. Asplem, M.H., Aasbakken, M.: Evaluation of an Interactive Campaign, Exploring the use of a motion-controlled game in a public space. Master Thesis, Norwegian University of Science and Technology (2012)

Gamification and Family Housework Applications

Anne Berit Kigen Bjering[1], Marikken Høiseth[1], and Ole Andreas Alsos[2]

[1] Department of Product Design, Norwegian University of Science
and Technology (NTNU), Kolbjørn Hejes vei 2B,
[2] Department of Computer and Information Science, Norwegian University of Science
and Technology (NTNU), Sem Sælands vei 9, 7491 Trondheim, Norway
ab.bjering@gmail.com

Abstract. This conceptual work represents an initial exploration into a little researched area, namely app design for families. We explore how gamification is incorporated in applications that target family housework, also known as *chores*. During the last five years an increasing number of apps aim to transform routine based housework into entertaining activities. Many parents think it is important that children, at an early age, learn about family values and responsibilities that comes with the role as a family member. However, a gamified approach towards housework can influence family interaction in both positive and negative ways. We analyze a selection of so-called chore apps by building on an existing classification framework for educational apps and applying concepts of game design elements. Our findings show (1) that existing apps tend to be mostly instructive and partly manipulable, (2) that they tend to focus on external rather than intrinsic motivation, (3) that they target family members individually, rather than the family as a whole. We discuss the results from a motivation perspective by drawing attention to three concepts that relate to intrinsic motivation: Competence, autonomy and relatedness.

Keywords: Gamification, housework, family, motivation, children, parents.

1   Introduction

This paper is connected to an ongoing project that aims at developing a system to motivate children between 6 and 12 years to contribute with housework. The idea is based on own experience and observations of parents wanting children to participate at home, but struggling to engage and motivate them. Housework refers to tasks such as cleaning the house, doing laundry, preparing meals and doing the dishes. The system is intended to address children, but it should be relevant for the whole family.

The purpose of this paper is to shed light on the topic of gamification in apps targeting family housework by drawing on concepts from motivation theories. Deterding et al. [1, p.9] define gamification as "the use of game design elements and game thinking in a non-gaming context". Doing housework can typically be considered a non-game context. Building on the idea of gamification, a recent trend in apps is to target housework aiming to transform boring chores into entertaining activities. This gamified approach towards housework seems especially relevant for

© IFIP International Federation for Information Processing 2015
K. Chorianopoulos et al. (Eds.): ICEC 2015, LNCS 9353, pp. 209–223, 2015.
DOI: 10.1007/978-3-319-24589-8_16

families with children in elementary school age, but also for preschool-aged children. One reason for this is that many parents want their children to learn about responsibilities that come with the role as a family member. Another reason is that many children, along with parents, use applications on a daily basis for playing, learning and sustaining social interaction. Thus, the recognition that both housework and games are strongly present in many modern families has led to development of apps that seek to combine the two.

Our point of reference is a Scandinavian context. Here, gender equality policies are based on the idea that "women and men should have the same opportunities, rights and responsibilities in all significant areas of life...This includes shared responsibility for work in the home and with children" [2]. However, research about younger couples in the Nordic countries shows that "daily life practice often differed from their ideals" and that families in these countries "report more disagreement about the division of housework" compared to "countries with more traditional gender regimes" [3].

Taking this as a starting point, the paper is structured as follows: Section 2 introduces different approaches that families use to organize their housework. Section 3 presents some key concepts from motivation theory and gamification. Section 4 describes the research method. Section 5 presents the results, in 3 position axes. In section 6 we discuss the results. Finally, section 7 offers concluding remarks and suggestions for future research. Through this conceptual work, we aim to inspire and challenge game developers to create better apps for families.

2   Approaches to Organize Family Housework

There is a large amount of literature in sociology and related disciplines that provide interesting perspectives on how families organize and negotiate housework. For instance, Solberg [4] views childhood as a social construction, understanding conceptions about childhood to be part of culture that transforms in time and space, end explores children's roles in Norwegian family housework contexts. Informed by gender and welfare state theories, a lot of research investigates relations between national practices and policies and how women and men spend their time on housework [2], [5]. Research shows that men have a greater share of housework in Scandinavian countries, where women's economical and political power is greater, and in nations where divorce culture is strong [2]. Taking a social learning perspective, researchers demonstrate how attitudes about gender and housework are shaped in early childhood and that parental practices strongly influence children's own future expectations and attitudes about housework distribution [2], [6].

Families use different strategies to encourage children's contributions to housework. Bjering [7] used a combination of questionnaires, observations and home interviews with the whole family to investigate how Norwegian families organized their family life and chores. As explained in the following, a wide variation was found:

Verbal Instructions and Demonstrations: Parents include children in housework by show and tell; they use verbal instructions and demonstrations to motivate the children and to make clear what their tasks are and how to perform them.

Books: Some parents use books which thematize housework [8, 9]. These books attempt in a pedagogical way, often through a character, to bring attention to the benefits of helping at home and how to do it. Our literature search showed that most of these books are for children aged 2-5 years.

Calendars, Boards and Checklists: Several of the parents used homemade solutions to motivate children to help with chores. Many of these took form as boards with checklists, task lists or calendars where the children get a sticker or a magnet for every finished chore. Some of these are also available as products on the market.

Digital tools: Parents had three main attitudes towards digital tools to help with chores. A few parents already used digital tools (usually checklists) to help get an overview of the chores. Another group of parents did not use digital tools for this, but wanted to try it. The last group of parents was negative towards digital tools for tracking chores.

Rewards: Most of the parents stated that they praised their children after they have finished a chore. In addition, parents usually follow one of the following reward strategies: 1) to see chores as everyone's responsibility and therefore non-paid work, or 2) to pay the children for each chore they do, or 3) to pay a weekly or monthly allowance when the child completes the agreed set of chores (some parents deducted an amount from the allowance if the child failed to complete the agreed chores).

3   Theoretical Background

3.1   Motivation and Reward

Many theories exist on motivation, and different perspectives have led to a great variety. Motivation is the direction of behavior and its energy, originally meaning *"to be moved"* to something" [10]. Taking it further, one can say that there must be an interaction between a person and a task, for the person to be motivated. The orientation of the motivation answers why we want to move or act; namely the reasons or goals. Throughout the years two major fields have gained more interest than others: behaviorism and social cognitive theory [11].

Behaviorism is based on the theory that people are motivated only because of external responses to stimuli. The best known psychologists in this field are Ivan Pavlov and B. F. Skinner, both of them doing motivation research on animals such as rats [12]. They saw that the animals reacted in predictable ways to rewards and punishment, and extrapolated the results onto the human being. In short, they saw extrinsic motivation as the best way to encourage people to do activities.

Social cognitive theorists were skeptical to parts of Skinner´s work, mostly because his approach assumes that people are "industrial machines", and not social human beings with the capability of thinking [13]. Edward Deci and Richard Ryan are two influential psychologists in this field, with their theory of *Self-determination* (SDT). SDT says that people have inherently a strong internal desire for growth, but that the surroundings must support this; if they do not, the internal desire might die [14].

Social cognitive theory focuses on people´s desire to flourish and to do what makes them happy. Whereas intrinsic motivation is about our willingness to do a task for the enjoyment or interest of the task itself, extrinsic motivation refers to a separable outcome or consequence [15]. Intrinsic motivation as explained by Deci and Ryan, correlates well with Csikszentmihalyis concept of flow: whatever produces flow becomes its own reward [16]. To be in flow one must have equally high skills and challenges.

Deci and Ryan also point out that rewards might have negative effects if they are poorly implemented. The reward might actually decrease the interest for an activity, and cause people to choose the least challenging task, because it is the safest way to a reward. By doing so, people do not get in flow, and the intrinsic motivation is lost. According to SDT, intrinsic motivation and human needs consist of three major elements: *competence, autonomy and relatedness* [14].

Some motivational theories are especially adapted to the work setting [17]. In some ways one can say that doing household chores is a part-time job. It is therefore interesting to look at some work motivation theories as well. Hackman and Oldham´s job characteristic model [18] is based on the principle that employees derive motivation from completing a task, and it builds upon SDT. The following three psychological states relate to motivation: 1) The task must be meaningful, 2) The task must give you responsibility, so that you can plan and do the task the way you think is best and 3) You need feedback - how effective have you been, when doing the task?

Especially when doing chores, we should acknowledge that some jobs are actually quite boring - e.g. to clean the toilet. According to this model, we should find ways to provide meaning. This means that one has to show importance of the work, and how the effort affects other people in the organization, or the family in our case. Herzberg´s motivation and hygiene theory distinguishes between two factors: those that genuinely motivate staff, and those that can provide small amounts of dissatisfaction if they fall below acceptable levels [19]. Examples on the latter, called hygiene factors, are pay, working conditions and relationship with supervisors. Examples of motivating factors are achievement, responsibility, recognition and the nature of the work (how exciting it is by itself). The recommendation is to set realistic, but challenging tasks and recognize and celebrate achievements publicly. Moreover, autonomy is important in this theory as well.

Should we think differently when trying to motivate children? Focusing on children's motivation, Bandura´s theory about self-efficacy and Covington's self-worth theory are considered central [20]. Self-efficacy refers to how people judge their own operative capabilities, thus what they think they are able to do with their skills under certain circumstances [21]. Self-worth refers to the value that people places on their own perceived abilities, qualities, and attributes [22].

Why should children have chores while growing up? As members of a family, children's responsibility for selected and meaningful tasks can benefit their sense of self-efficacy and self-worth on the home arena. Under the right conditions, taking part in the house chores can foster competence, autonomy and relatedness in both children and parents. Toddlers see success as a result of effort; high effort enhances the chance of mastering a task. When the children get older, their expectation about success is more attached to skills or capabilities, and less to effort [20]. This means that they start comparing themselves to others. Covington underlines that children's perception of their own skills is a major part of their self-perception, and has therefore an impact on the self-esteem and motivation [22].

In different situations people can respond differently to activities, and either be demotivated (do not care), intrinsically motivated (want to do it for the genuine pleasure) or extrinsically motivated (want to do the activity to get something in addition to the task). Regarding children's motivation to contribute with housework - how can we pull the right triggers so that the environment will facilitate intrinsic motivation? This is where gamification can play a role. Children, like adults, use applications on a daily basis to play, learn and sustain social interaction. Research about children's internet use in European countries shows that children access the internet at younger and younger ages; many preschoolers are already experienced game players [23].

3.2   Gamification

The field of "Gamification" has the past years gained significant interest and the actual term can be explained as the application of game design elements and game mechanics, in none-game contexts [1]. Gamification can be used to create engagement, solve problems, change behavior or create better experiences [24]. It has been used mainly in the software industry, but now fields such as marketing, tourism, health and education see a potential for including game elements in their services and businesses [25].

Gamification builds upon the elements and design of games, but it does not constitute a game in itself. To better understand how gamification works, we take a look at games. What are games, and what makes games fun? What motivates us to play? The Danish videogame researcher Jesper Juul defines games with six elements [26]: 1) There is a set of rules, 2) A variable and quantifiable outcome, 3) Different outcomes are assigned different values (e.g. positive and negative), 4) Interactive: The players can influence the outcome by doing some effort, 5) The players are emotionally attached to the outcome, 6) Negotiable consequences: The game can be played with or without real-life consequences. Only when all of these criteria are present, we have a game.

Other ways to define a game include elements as players, conflict, competition and collaboration, rules, feedback systems, quantifiable outcomes and voluntary participation [27, 28] and self-representation with avatars, narrative context, time pressure, reputations/ranks/levels and teams [29].

The core of gamification is to apply a set of external motivation elements, which should facilitate intrinsic motivation - the desire to play along. Drawing on Deci and Ryan´s SDT, Schell (2011) and Deterding (2011) point out the importance of the three aforementioned principles for gamification to achieve intrinsic motivation: 1) Competence: The feeling of mastering a system, by achieving clear and visual goals, 2) Autonomy: The freedom of choosing to participate or not, and not being controlled and 3) Relatedness: Interaction with other people, such as family and friends.

Gamification has also received quite some criticism. Schell outlines a gloomy scenario in which every activity in life becomes a game play - 10 points for brushing your teeth, 20 points for looking at advertisement, 30 points for eating the right cereal etc., and questions whether this is the kind of society that we really long for [30]. There has been lots of arguing about how we should apply game mechanics, and whether it serves its purpose or not.

Recognizing that current debates on gamification are contested and not yet moving beyond superficial scoring systems, Cody Reimer draws attention to Johan Huizinga's work on play and his concept of the magic circle [31]. The magic circle is understood as the boundary of game play - as a "temporary world within the ordinary world" wherein the player experiences immersion and engagement [32]. As such, experiencing the magic circle aligns with experiencing intrinsic motivation and flow. Focusing on gamification in education, Reimer argues that because we can already understand education and life as a game, gamification should be understood as "a means to reveal the ways in which education or school is already a game" rather than considering gamification as a means to motivate students [31]. Applying these ideas thus means that we are challenged to shift the way we look at the non-game context. In our case, it encourages us to ask: How to reveal the ways in which housework is a game?

Game designer Margaret Robertson has a similar way of looking at the problem with gamification, or what she calls pointsification, and how it is being applied: "What we're currently terming gamification is in fact the process of taking the thing that is least essential to games and representing it as the core of the experience. Points and badges have no closer a relationship to games than they do to websites and fitness apps and loyalty cards. (...) They are the least important bit of a game, the bit that has the least to do with all of the rich cognitive, emotional and social drivers which gamifiers are intending to connect with" [33].

We agree with the criticism of the excessive use of points and reward systems. However, we adopt the claims holding that gamification, by moving beyond the superficial application of mere points, has the potential to foster immersion and engagement by considering the wide range of game design elements. This can be understood as a move from a behaviorist perspective to ideas upon which SDT builds (Constructivist paradigm).

4   Method

In this study we analyzed apps as the main method. The analysis was initially performed as a market/competition analysis. Therefore it lacks some of the scientific rigor that normally would have been applied. This part describes the way we performed the app search, app selection, and how we analyzed them.

To explore how gamification is incorporated in applications that target family housework, we searched for suitable apps from the main app providers, *App Store*, *Google Play*, and *Windows Phone Store*. We also searched through 12 forums (such as *allparenting.com, bestappsforkids.com,* and others), news sites, web magazines, as well as social media to get an overview of the most used and best rated apps. In this semi-structured Internet search we used the search terms *chores, apps, motivate, house, family, game.* The search was carried out in February and March 2015 and resulted in around 60 apps that aimed to motivate children to do specific tasks at home or to change their habits and behavior, or to help parents raise their children. We focused primarily on English-speaking apps.

Based on the number of positive and negative reviews, and whether they targeted children or children *and* parents, we selected 15 apps for further analysis. In this stage we did not consider standard to-do list apps, such as *Wunderlist* or *Todoist*, as they are targeting an adult audience. To limit the number of apps, we also discarded apps that were specifically targeting merely one kind of task such as cooking. We also limited the app selection to iOS apps.

All the apps were downloaded, installed and tested to get an overview of functionality, intended user groups, usability, etc. Based on this initial app testing we selected all 15 apps for further analysis (figure 1).

Fig. 1. Selected apps

Table 1. Parameters the apps were evaluated on

Product	Description	User	Functionality	Motivation/Reward	Game elements
Name, screenshots, developer	The description from the producer or, when missing, the app home page	Description of the target users and their age	Description of the main functionality	Is the app based on external (points, badges or high score list) or intrinsic motivation?	What kinds of game elements or game mechanics were used in the app?

Pedagogical Design	User Interface	Universal Design	Technical Solution	Overall Impression
Instructive, manipulable or constructive approach?	How is the user interface created? Is it different for children and parents?	How is the app using sound, text, text size, images? Is it relying on text or images in communication?	Which technical platform and technology is used? Does the app require internet connection?	An overall subjective description of the authors' impression of the app.

We made a detailed description of each selected app. Table 1 shows the parameters that were described. The analysis was presented in one overall table for easy comparison. A one-row excerpt of this table is provided in figure 2.

For classifying the pedagogical design, we applied the framework of Goodwin and Highfield which they used to categorize educational applications [34, 35]. In line with their proposed categories, we considered whether the apps were instructive, manipulable, constructive, or a combination of these, i.e. instructive/manipulable or manipulable/constructive. Instructive apps are characterized as "game apps", using a combination of overt extrinsic rewards, providing clear goals and missions, and basing interaction on drill and practice. Manipulable apps provide opportunities for guided discovery, allowing for multiple responses and offering users various choices, whereas constructive apps are more like tools that are open-ended, incorporate limited extrinsic rewards and facilitate creativity. The framework is useful for distinguishing apps at a general level.

PRODUCT	DESCRIPTION	USER	FUNCTIONALITY	MOTIVATION/ REWARD	GAME ELEMENTS	PEDAGOGICAL DESIGN	USER INTERFACE	UNIVERSAL DESIGN	TECHNICAL	OVERALL IMPRESSION
YOU RULE CHORES Opposite Inc.	"You Rule is a powerful chore management app that gives parents ultimate control over family productivity while transforming kids into happy chore-doing maniacs."	Children are the main users, age 5-11. Up to 6 siblings can use the app.	Includes a guide on how to use the app. The children choose a character, which level up when they do tasks. Parents are a referee and approve the tasks, give out rewards.	Extrinsic: Gold coins for each task, varies in amount. The child makes a wishlist on things or adventures they want to have or do. Competition in who will reach the weekly goal first.	• Leaderboard with visual progression • Reward • Levels • Gold coins • Competition	Hybrid instructive/ manipulable: Game app, overt extrinsic rewards, goal and mission: a weekly finish line, compete with other siblings. Some capacity to make choices, e.g. level of difficulty and type of chore.	Two interfaces; one for children and one for parents. Both interfaces have a good screen resolution.	Handdrawn pictures in all slides. Visual progression. The tasks are only written in text. Music and sounds from different characters.	App for ios. Cost: 39 NOK Only available at one phone or ipad (does not syncronize through internet) English language.	Nice app, well designed with a great use of game elements. A bit strange concept of having a parent referee.

Fig. 2. Excerpt from overall table

5   Results

In this section we present results from the app analysis. We have explored how gamification, i.e. introducing game design elements into non-game contexts, is incorporated in the 15 selected apps. We present the results by positioning the apps in 3 axes, and describe what features influenced the choice of position.

5.1   Instructive, Manipulable or Constructive

We found that most apps are characterized as instructive or hybrid instructive/ manipulable, as shown in figure 3. The instructive apps contain overt extrinsic rewards and clear goals. The focus is on earning points and the task itself is reduced to a mere means to get to the important part – namely the rewards. The hybrids instructive/manipulable contain additional possibilities for guided discovery, some capacity to make choices and also multiple responses are possible.

Chore Monster is an example of an instructive app, where children tap "thumbs up" after having completed a task. This releases a certain amount of points (determined by parents). Moreover children get to spin a fortune wheel where it is possible to win different kinds of monsters; in addition children get access to short videos about monsters. *Lickety Split* is another app identified as an instructive app. This app incorporates time constraint as a game element, a so-called beat-the-clock game. As the hourglass gets filled, classical music is played and children can use it to endure a time period of 2 minutes for brushing teeth or to actually beat it when cleaning the room or putting on pajamas. Even though this app does not rely on the use of overt extrinsic reward, this app is characterized as instructive because of the clear mission and goal in addition to the focus on drill and practice.

You Rule is positioned as a hybrid between an instructive and manipulable app. The instructive element lies in that the game revolves around completing chores to earn coins, which unlocks avatar powers and can later be redeemed for rewards that children have wishlisted. The player who first finishes the weekly chores wins the game. The way of playing is through a competition intended to be among the children. As such, there is a clear focus on goals and missions. The manipulable aspect has to do with opportunities to choose levels of difficulties and kind of chores. The ways in which the characters will evolve through the new skills and powers can be understood as a kind of guided discovery. In *Dreamhouse Tasks* the tasks are related to different rooms and each room contains a number of stars, which symbolize different tasks. The tasks can be linked to a timer and when all the tasks have been carried out, the child can receive a reward (unspecified, to decide together with parents) and feed a pet character. This app is instructive in that the goals are clear and there is some use of extrinsic rewards, and manipulable in terms of guided discovery as well as some capacity to make choices.

Two apps are positioned as pure manipulable: *Tejas and Lollipop`s great cleanup* and *Little Critter: Just helping my dad*. These are interactive book apps, informing children about how to tackle messy rooms and the joy of helping out. Both apps include guided discovery by tapping things, looking for animations, learning words, finding mice and spiders, and more. One can choose to read out loud or listen to a narrative voice, as well as spend as much time as wanted on each page. This can be seen as a capacity to make choices.

None of the apps were characterized as constructive, thus apps that are open-ended, focus on creative input/interaction and facilitate intrinsic motivation rather than using overt extrinsic rewards. These findings correspond to the findings of Goodwin and Highfield in their study on educational apps [34, 35].

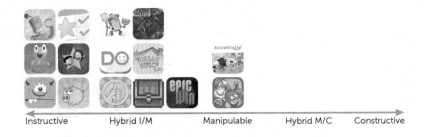

| Instructive | Hybrid I/M | Manipulable | Hybrid M/C | Constructive |

Fig. 3. Apps positioned along axis of instructive, manipulable and constructive design

5.2 Overt vs. Limited Use of Extrinsic Rewards

We found that many of the apps tend to focus on external (points, badges, highscore, etc.) rather than intrinsic motivation, as shown in figure 4. *Funify Do* is an app that uses extrinsic rewards. The children learn to earn ice cream, TV-time or other rewards, by performing tasks with assigned values. Parents need to check if the task has been done properly, before the children can get their reward. There is a clear goal, and feedback that mainly revolves around obtaining a specific reward. This is one way of showing children how parents get their income.

In the app *Allowance & Chores Bot*, a robot character gives information and encouragement about the tasks. Here, the main focus is on extrinsic rewards in the form of allowance. *iRewardChart* is similar to a traditional chart and completed chores are rewarded with stars that can be subsequently redeemed for another reward. Both these apps emphasize the overt focus on extrinsic reward through the option called "punishment"; Parents can remove money and stars if a task is not carried out according to their expectations.

Dreamhouse Tasks is placed in the middle of the axis because it uses some extrinsic motivation by incorporating stars that eventually add up to fill a progress bar. Collected stars can be used to feed a pet animal and beyond this other rewards can not be specified in the app, leaving it more open for parents and children to decide about how they choose to make use of rewards.

Only a few apps limit the use of extrinsic rewards. Two of these apps are interactive stories, as mentioned in 5.1, and aimed for the youngest children. In *Little Critter: Just Helping my Dad*, the children meet the character *Critter* who spends the day helping his father with different chores. The story presents housework in the context of social values and family life, such as the importance of helping, togetherness, self-esteem and confidence. The game elements are connected to fantasy and curiosity as the player can find and collect hidden treasures. The way of playing is for children to explore the story alone or together with a parent. Most of the graphic elements are interactive in the sense that its verbal description is expressed when pressing it. Children can thus increase their vocabulary by learning words and their pronunciation when exploring the story. In *Lickety Split,* the player is rewarded with positive verbal feedback and children's rejoicing. The way of playing is to compete with time.

Limited extrinsic rewards   Overt extrinsic rewards

Fig. 4. Apps positioned along axis of extrinsic rewards

5.3   Individual vs. Family

We found that most of the apps target family members individually, rather than focusing on the family as a whole.

Many of the apps have a twofold system, wherein children and parents have separate accounts. In this way, many of the apps give children and parents specific roles as respectively players and administrators. Even though it is quite possible for parents to participate as players on an equal footing as the children, many of the apps nevertheless provide a kind of frame that does not really encourage this. Parents are rather expected to take on a role as commander and controller, whereas children are offered the role as individual chore performers.

The idea of targeting the whole family is more present in the apps that offer story-based interaction. In *Tejas and Lollipop`s great cleanup* for example, the underlying thought is to encourage understanding about how tidying up can be a meaningful activity and make you feel at ease in your surroundings.

The focus on individual performance as opposed to a family performance can be seen in relation to the use of specific game elements, namely competition and collaboration. The apps that target individual players also tend to use competition as approach, as shown in figure 5. The two apps placed in the middle take a more team-based approach wherein competition is somehow based on social encouragement.

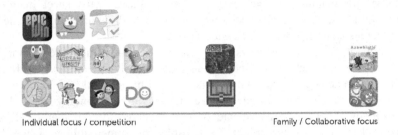

Individual focus / competition   Family / Collaborative focus

Fig. 5. Apps positioned along axis of individual focus/competition and family/collaborative focus

To sum up the results from analyzing a selection of apps that gamify chores we draw attention to the following points:

- Most apps are characterized as instructive or hybrid instructive/manipulable and there is a lack of constructive apps
- Most apps use overt extrinsic rewards
- Most apps target family members individually, rather than the whole family

6   Discussion

In this section we discuss the results from a motivation perspective by asking: How can the chore apps facilitate intrinsic motivation? We focus on the three principles from SDT: *Competence*, *autonomy* and *relatedness*.

Referring to the pedagogical design of the selected apps, the most commonly used approach is characterized as instructive or as hybrid instructive/manipulable. There is a lack of constructive apps. In a way, this can be compared with only offering ready-made worksheets for coloring (instructive) as opposed to blank paper sheets. The different kinds of sheets can serve different purposes. The same can be true for apps and in our case for chore apps. The instructive apps, thus the apps combining overt extrinsic rewards, clear goals and missions as well as a so-called drill and practice method, can have different benefits for achieving intrinsic motivation in terms of competence. Facilitation of competence has to do with the feeling of mastering a system. Apps that provide clear instructions, offering a frame with explicit goals and tangible outcomes, can contribute to experiencing a task as fun and meaningful. However, this is not necessarily related to actually conducting the chore itself, rather conducting the chore may become a means to obtain something that is perceived as fun and meaningful.

By working towards an overt extrinsic reward, one can acquire specific skills and confidence in own capabilities (self-efficacy). For example, through regular repetition of making the bed or taking out the garbage one gets gradually better at it and also aware that it does not happen by itself. There is also a chance that extrinsic rewards contribute to reduce a task to something standing in the way and therefore will be halfheartedly performed. In this case, competence and intrinsic motivation will not be facilitated. A constructive approach, one offering a less rigid system, can provide opportunities for making own games. Referring to the drawing sheet metaphor - provided with blank paper sheets and some pencils, new drawings can be made each time and there is always something new to discover.

Most apps target family members individually. As shown in figure 5, individual participation is often related to competition as a game design element. An individual-competitive approach can make a game engaging and meaningful. On the other hand, this approach might also weaken one's sense of autonomy. Autonomy has to do with the freedom of choosing to participate or not. A chore system that is all about competition between siblings might be suitable for some siblings while being perceived as unfair by other siblings. Moreover, predefining a marked distinction between the roles that parents and children are expected to have, such as assigning parents the roles as the referee (distributing, defining and approving tasks) while children are represented by cartoon-like avatars (conducting tasks as efficient as possible in competition with siblings), can either reflect or indeed contravene the actual roles and how they are experienced within families. Such representations can influence the game play in different ways and affect autonomy. Gamification of chores can, however, also lead to a strengthening of autonomy. If the game is adapted to all the players in such a way that there is a balance between their skills and the offered challenges, they can experience flow and as such find participation meaningful. A pedagogical design that allows for some manipulation or construction should support autonomy.

Relatedness has to do with meaningful interaction with other people. Depending on game design elements, apps can facilitate for relatedness to varying degrees. A certain view on players as well as task is conveyed through use of game design elements and specific language. For instance, the idea to combine competition with the concepts of reward and punishment is different from the idea to combine collaboration with the concepts of inspiration and happiness. Encouraging direct collaboration within the family, as a way of playing, is an approach that can foster positive social interaction, self-worth and intrinsic motivation.

To end our discussion, we present some suggestions that can serve as inspiration for app or digital designers seeking to motivate the whole family to enjoy household chores through gamification:

- Explore how hybrid manipulable/constructive or constructive pedagogical designs can foster positive and fun ways of doing chores. Let the family be a team of "explorers" and inspire them to come up with new and better ways to solve tasks, or simply to come up with new tasks that can be done. As mentioned, blank sheets can foster creativity.
- Limit the extrinsic rewards, and focus on tasks that can provide autonomy, relatedness and competence. One way of doing this is to make the actual housework more of a game, than a checklist, like in Huizinga's magical circle [32]. Let the children pick the tasks that they want to do – this can

increase their autonomy and competence. Support the right conditions: create a positive/fun/engaging/meaningful frame to foster play.

- Focus on collaboration and the whole family, rather than on the individual. Add mechanisms that encourage parents and children to do things together. Inspire families to talk about and decide upon a set of family values. Competition can be used, but a suggestion is to have a common goal rather than an individual one.

7 Conclusion and Further Research

In this paper we explored how gamification is incorporated in 15 apps that aim to motivate people, and notably children, to contribute with family housework. First of all, we found that most of the apps are characterized as instructive or hybrid instructive/manipulable and there is a lack of constructive apps. This means that the apps do not facilitate open-ended exploration and user's own creative input. Second, we found that the apps use overt extrinsic rewards, rather than appeal to intrinsic rewards. This means that there is limited focus on the actual housework and less opportunity to gamify the activities as such. Third, we found that the apps target family members individually, rather than the family as a whole. This means that values concerning collaboration are not fully employed as drivers for intrinsic motivation.

We have come up with a list of suggestions for future chore app development. This includes focusing on autonomy, competence and relatedness, to use limited extrinsic rewards, to focus on collaboration rather than the individual, and to explore the constructive and more open field of play. The next step for future research and development is to move away from a theoretical analysis of the apps. Instead we want to study the apps in real use and involve families in a user-centered design process in order to further develop the potential that gamification might have as approach to facilitate intrinsic motivation among all family members.

References

1. Deterding, S., et al.: From game design elements to gamefulness: defining gamification. In: Pro. MindTrek 2011, pp. 9–15. ACM Press (2011)
2. Hook, J.L.: Gender Inequality in the Welfare State: Sex Segregation in Housework, 1965–2003. American Journal of Sociology 115(5), 1480–1523 (2010)
3. Bernhardt, E., Noack, T., Lyngstad, T.H.: Shared housework in Norway and Sweden: advancing the gender revolution. Journal of European Social Policy 18(3), 275–288 (2008)
4. Solberg, A.: Negotiating childhood: Changing constructions of age for Norwegian children. In: James, A., Prout, A. (eds.) Constructing and Reconstructing Childhood: Contemporary Issues in the Sociological Study of Childhood, pp. 126–144. Falmer Press, London (1997)
5. Miller, P., Bowd, J.: Family time economies and democratic division of work. Journal of Family Studies 20(2), 128–147 (2014)
6. Cunningham, M.: Parental Influences on the Gendered Division of Housework. American Sociological Review 66(2), 184–203 (2001)

7. Bjering, A.B.: Design of a digital application to motivate families to do domestic chores together (Master thesis), Department of Product Design. Norwegian University of Science and Technology (2015)
8. Bringsværd, T.Å., Soli, T.: Når to skal rydde. Gyldendal, Oslo (2006)
9. Wolde, G., Birke, E.: Emma støvsuger. Aschehoug, Oslo (2002)
10. Deci, E.L., Ryan, R.M.: Intrinsic motivation and self-determination in human Behavior. Springer Science & Business Media (1985)
11. Werbach, K., Hunter, D.: For the win: how game thinking can revolutionize your business. Wharton Digital Press, Philadelphia (2012)
12. Skinner, B.F.: The behavior of organisms: an experimental analysis. Appleton-Century, Oxford (1938)
13. Bandura, A.: Social cognitive theory of self-regulation. Organizational Behavior and Human Decision Processes 50(2), 248–287 (1991)
14. Ryan, R.M., Deci, E.L.: Self-determination theory and the facilitation of intrinsic motivation, social development, and well-being. American Psychologist 55(1), 68–78 (2000)
15. Ryan, R.M., Deci, E.L.: Intrinsic and Extrinsic Motivations: Classic Definitions and New Directions. Contemporary Educational Psychology 25(1), 54–67 (2000)
16. Csikszentmihalyi, M.: Flow: The psychology of optimal experience. Harper & Row, New York (1990)
17. McGrath, J., Bates, B.: The little book of big management theories... and how to use them. Pearson, Harlow (2013)
18. Hackman, J.R., Oldham, G.R.: Motivation through the design of work: test of a theory. Organizational Behavior and Human Performance 16(2), 250–279 (1976)
19. Herzberg, F.I.: Work and the nature of man. World Pub. Co., Cleveland (1966)
20. Skaalvik, E.M., Skaalvik, S.: Skolens læringsmiljø: selvopfattelse, motivasjon og læringsstrategier. Akademisk Forlag, København (2007)
21. Bandura, A.: Self-efficacy: Toward a unifying theory of behavioral change. Psychological Review 84(2), 191–215 (1977)
22. Covington, M.V.: The Self-Worth Theory of Achievement Motivation: Findings and Implications. The Elementary School Journal 85(1), 5–20 (1984)
23. Holloway, D., Green, L., Livingstone, S.: Zero to eight. Young children and their internet use. EU Kids Online, London (2013)
24. Zichermann, G., Cunningham, C.: Gamification by Design: implementing game mechanics in web and mobile apps. O'Reilly Media, Sabastobol (2011)
25. Xu, F., Weber, J., Buhalis, D.: Gamification in tourism. In: Xiang, Z., Tussyadiah, I. (eds.) Information and Communication Technologies in Tourism 2014, pp. 525–537. Springer (2013)
26. Juul, J.: The game, the player, the world: Looking for a heart of gameness. PLURAIS-Revista Multidisciplinar da UNEB 1(2) (2010)
27. Salen, K., Zimmerman, E.: Rules of play: game design fundamentals. MIT Press, Cambridge (2004)
28. McGonigal, J.: Reality is broken: why games make us better and how they can change the world. Vintage books, London (2012)
29. Reeves, B., Read, J.L.: Total engagement: using games and virtual worlds to change the way people work and businesses compete. Harvard Business Press, Boston (2009)
30. Schell, J.: The Pleasure Revolution: Why games Will Lead the Way. [Video]. November 2011.
    http://www.youtube.com/watch?v=4PkUgCiHuH8&feature=youtu.be

31. Reimer, C., Play to order: what huizinga has to say about gamification. In: Pro. Games + Learning + Society Conference, pp. 272–274. ETC Press (2011)
32. Huizinga, J.: Homo ludens: a study of the play-element in culture. Beacon Press, Boston (1955)
33. Robertson, M. Can't play, won't play, October 2010 [cited 2015 05.05.].
    http://hideandseek.net/2010/10/06/cant-play-wont-play/
34. Goodwin, K., Highfield, K.: iTouch and iLearn: an examination of "educational" apps. In: Early Education and Technology for Children Conference (2012)
35. Goodwin, K., Highfield, K.: A framework for examining technologies and early mathematics learning. In: Reconceptualizing Early Mathematics Learning, pp. 205–226. Springer (2013)

IdleWars: An Evaluation of a Pervasive Game to Promote Sustainable Behaviour in the Workplace

Evangelos Tolias[1], Enrico Costanza[1], Alex Rogers[1], Benjamin Bedwell[2],
and Nick Banks[3]

[1] Electronics and Computer Science, University of Southampton, Southampton SO171BJ
{et2e10,ec,acr}@ecs.soton.ac.uk
[2] Horizon Digital Economy Research, University of Nottingham, Nottingham, NG72TU
Benjamin.Bedwell@nottingham.ac.uk
[3] Centre for Sustainable Energy, Bristol BS34AQ
Nick.Banks@cse.org.uk

Abstract Energy reduction is one of the main challenges that countries around the world currently face, and there is potential to contribute to this by raising awareness towards sustainability in the workplace. We introduce *IdleWars*, a pervasive game played using smartphones and computers. In the game, workers' proenvironmental or wasteful behaviour is reflected in their game score, and displayed through eco-feedback visualisations to try and call attention to energy wastage and potentially reduce it. A field deployment, over two weeks in a medium sized organisation, revealed that the physical and competitive elements of the game work well in engaging participants and stimulating discussion around energy wasted and conservation. However, the game turned out to encourage also some anti-conservation behaviours, as participants appropriated the game and extended its rules, sometimes in a way that favoured engagement and fun rather than proenvironmental behaviour. More in general, our study uncovered how both the game and idle time reduction in itself can rub against the daily practices of the workplace where the study was run.

1 Introduction

Energy reduction is one of the main challenges that countries around the world are currently facing, and it has been pointed out that there is an important energy saving potential in the work environment [11,4]. A large part of this potential is related to energy wastage [9,19], i.e. equipment being left on when not in use. As an example, according to the Personal Computer (PC) energy report [14], in the UK 27% of the workers who regularly use a PC reported that they do not always shut down their computers, 14% reported that they shut them down only occasionally, while 9% reported to never shut them down. This energy wastage results not only in additional cost for the industry, but, more importantly, in unnecessary carbon emissions.

We refer to the time that a computer is left on while not in use as "idle time", and we argue that idle time reduction offers a rich opportunity to study interventions to promote behaviour change in the work place. It is worth emphasising that the aim of this work is researching behaviour change interventions, rather than directly addressing reduction

© IFIP International Federation for Information Processing 2015
K. Chorianopoulos et al. (Eds.): ICEC 2015, LNCS 9353, pp. 224–237, 2015.
DOI: 10.1007/978-3-319-24589-8_17

of computer energy consumption. Indeed, there are already commercial solutions available on the market to reduce computer idle time by automatically switching computers off at predefined times (e.g. 1E NightWatchman[1], Cisco EnergyWise Suite[2]). Adopting computer idle time[3] reduction as a research vehicle is useful because it provides a convenient scenario (as detailed below) to design and evaluate behaviour change intervention, which could then be applied to other forms of resources wastage.

In this paper we present an approach that combines a *game* with *eco-feedback* [5] in the work environment. We introduce *IdleWars*, a pervasive game played using smartphones and desktop computers. In our game, workers' proenvironmental or wasteful behaviour is reflected in their game score, and displayed through eco-feedback visualisations. Our aim is to use a game as an engagement mechanism to activate intrinsic motivations [17], and to try and bring the workers' attention to their computer based energy wastage and reduce it.

The rest of this paper is structured as follows. The next section presents a brief discussion of related work around eco-feedback and games related to sustainability. Subsequently, we introduce the design of IdleWars and its rationale, followed by its technical implementation. We conclude by reporting an initial two-week deployment of the game in a real workplace, which demonstrates that workers immediately grasped the game design and engaged with it.

2   Related Work

Froehlich et al. [5] provide a review of eco-feedback technology and interventions, discussing the potential benefits of cooperation between the academic fields of HCI and environmental psychology. More specifically, they argue that HCI design for proenvironmental behaviour change can be informed by models (e.g. rational choice models, norm activation models) and strategies already popular in environmental psychology (e.g. information, goal setting, comparison). To date, research related to eco-feedback is mostly focused on the domestic environment [5]. For example, Jain et al. [10] investigated visualisations based on consequence interventions like comparative feedback, historical feedback (current day, last week), rewards and penalties. Their results show that there is a link between interface engagement and energy conservation.

Few papers have investigated eco-feedback in the work environment. Siero et al. [19] investigated behaviour change related to energy conservation in two units of a metallurgical company. The first unit received feedback and goal setting interventions, whilst the second unit additionally received comparative feedback (its performance was compared to that of the first unit). Their analysis suggest that employing comparative feedback results in higher energy conservation. Pousman et al. [15] proposed *Imprint*, a system that tracks the documents people print in the work environment, and provides a visualisation of the resources consumed in this way on a semi-public display. The authors suggest that their design employs a "ludic engagement strategy" [6] to stress environmental issues related with energy and paper consumption. Schwartz et al. [18] installed plug-level

---

[1] http://www.1e.com/nightwatchman-pc-power-management/

[2] http://www.cisco.com/en/US/products/ps10195/

[3] A typical desktop PC and LCD display consume 55W and 15W of power respectively.

energy meters in a few offices of a research organisation and observed the reactions of employees through business ethnography. They claim that the sensors enabled workers to be aware of their own energy related behaviour in the workplace. Jentsch et al. [11] presented an energy-saving support system for work environments that leverages a variety of sensors (temperature, electricity, light, contact) to provide workers suggestions about how to act in an environmentally friendly way, however, no real-world evaluation is reported. Yun et al. [21] run a twenty-seven week field study with eighty employees investigating feedback interventions combined with manual and automatic control. The manual control enables participants to activate and deactivate a device remotely via a web interface whereas automatic control is a web-based scheduler were participants are able to define the activation and deactivation time of a device. Results showed reduced energy consumption to groups with online controls compared to just feedback. Lights and phone devices showed higher savings compared to computer and monitors. Automation control was less effective to users with an ingrained energy efficient behaviour.

Games have also been used with the aim of promoting proenvironmental behaviour, mostly in the domestic context. For example, Reeves et al. [16] presented a serious game, *Power House*, that simulates a virtual household and evaluated its consequence both in a lab study and in a field trial, reporting its success in the reduction of energy consumption. Few energy related games were specifically targeted to children and adolescents. Gustafsson et al. [7] argue that serious games make it difficult to transfer lessons from the game to the real world, therefore they propose instead a casual game approach. They report the design of a pervasive game for teenagers, played by activating and deactivating real appliances in the home (monitored through plug-level sensors). A similar approach is proposed by Bang et al. [1], who report a combination of a casual game, that follows a classic videogame gameplay, with a pervasive game in which players have to complete missions in the real world and verify their action by taking pictures with smart phones. The game aims to educate teenagers on ways to conserve energy at home, but no user evaluation is reported. In contrast to this prior work, IdleWars, the game we present here, is a pervasive game designed for adults in the work environment.

The only game designed to encourage proenvironmental behaviour in the work environment is *Climate Race* [20], which is based on a combination of implicit and explicit energy-related actions. The game tracks players' activity in the real world at the room level, through environmental sensors (e.g., switching off lights when not in the office); based on this activity players gain positive or negative points. Extra game points can be collected through specific collective actions, such as all players switching off lights when leaving the office. Our approach is different from *Climate Race* in two ways: first, it does not require sensors, as activity detection takes place in software on existing office IT infrastructure. Second, IdleWars, introduces an element of competition its the game dynamics, with the aim to increase engagement.

The idea of using computer idle time as a proxy for energy wasteful behaviour was originally proposed by Kim et al. [13], who used this measure to investigate two persuasive ambient displays: *Timelog* and *Coralog*. Both visualisations aim to eliminate computer idle time; Timelog uses a bar graph to represent the active and idle time of the computer, while Coralog uses a visual metaphor, where the proenvironmental behaviour is mapped to the health of coral reefs. Through a study, Kim et al. showed that the

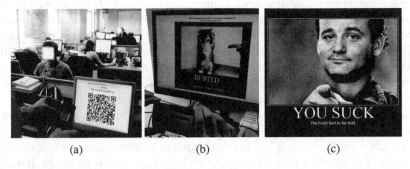

(a)   (b)   (c)

Fig. 1. (a) A participant *busting* the *idle* computer of another player by scanning the QRCode on the IdleWars screen saver. (b) A *busted* computer showing the profile picture of the player. (c) The profile image used by a participant to convey a message to players they bust.

Coralog visualisation created emotional attachment and the desire to change behaviour whereas the one based on bar charts did not. While the work by Kim et al. focusses on individual users, IdleWars uses computer idle time in the context of a game and the online nature of it provides not only personal feedback, but also comparative feedback, as detailed next.

3   Game Design and Its Rationale

We started the design process by taking into account the main contrasts between the workplace and domestic environments, to try and best apply lessons from prior work. The first important difference is the lack of incentives: employees generally do not share financial benefits coming from lower energy bills [8,4,9]. Another key difference is that workplaces often have a richer social dimension than in a domestic context, not only because generally there are more people in an office than a home, but also because these multiple social groups and layers (e.g. friends, teams, divisions, departments, cross-cutting projects, etc.) may co-exist among workers.

Against this background, we decided to design a game. We believe that through a balance of competition and collaboration games have potential to leverage and influence social dynamics, in a way that can be steered towards proenvironmental behaviour. Moreover, it was recently reported that games in the workplace have potential to provide motivation for employees to reduce their energy consumption [20]. We decided to focus on wastage around personal computer usage for several reasons: first, in the work environment the computer is mostly a *personal* tool and only its owner has the responsibility of switching it on and off, so it is possible and easy to track *individual behaviour*, in contrast to shared equipment (e.g. from shared printers to coffee machines to corridor lights), for which apportionment would be more difficult or even impossible. Second, monitoring the PC can be achieved *purely in software*, without any additional hardware, therefore keeping deployment costs and installation complexity low and making the system easily scalable.

IdleWars, the game we designed, tracks the computer status for each player. When no mouse movements or key strokes are detected for more than 5 minutes, the computer is considered inactive, or "idle". In such case, a screensaver appears on the computer screen, showing a QR code, a short url, and an additional alphanumeric code, as illustrated in Figure 1a. Any player (other than the computer owner), can then "bust" the idle computer by scanning the QR code with a smartphone, or by manually typing the short url or the alphanumeric code in any web browser (in case a smart phone is not available). Following the busting action, the screensaver of the idle computer changes to show the *profile picture* of the person who busted the computer, as illustrated in Figure 1b. At any point the "owner" of an idle computer, whether busted or not, can close the screensaver and resume the normal operation by typing in their password. If the idle computer is busted, the owner will see a full-screen profile picture of the player who busted them when they return to their desk. Once a computer has been busted by one player, it cannot be busted by anyone else.

Busting an idle computer can be considered as a metaphor for turning it off. Therefore, busting is a proenvironmental, energy-saving behaviour that we want to encourage through the game. Conversely, leaving a computer idle represents a wasteful behaviour, which in our game makes the player vulnerable to being busted by other players. The system tracks the time (in minutes) that a computer stays busted – this time is roughly related to the amount of energy that would have been saved by switching the computer off. This information is considered eco-feedback on the premise of reducing environmental impact [5]. The total time busted (which can be considered "time rescued") by each participant, the total number of busting actions, and the percentage of individual idle time are used to calculate 3 separate player rankings displayed on the IdleWars leader board, as shown in Figure 2. All metrics and ranking orientations are designed to give emphasis to positive behaviour (rather than highlighting negative behaviour).

The leader board provides players with comparative and continuous feedback about their behaviour. It is displayed on a public screen in the workplace where the game takes place, and it is also accessible as a Web page. Users can only access the Web page version by logging-in, which allows us to highlight the individual player position in each of the rankings, making it easier to read. The public display was deliberately designed not to be interactive, so it does not support scrolling, and it shows only the top performers from each ranking. The number of top participants shown depends on the size of the screen available for deployment. The choice of a public display, to be placed in a trafficked location in the workplace, aims at encouraging casual conversations and triggering gossip related to the game, with the hope to further motivate workers towards the desired behaviour.

As *privacy* was reported to be an issue of concern in the work environment [8,20], in IdleWars the idle time is presented in terms of percentage of the total time the computer is on. In this way the information about the total time each computer is active or idle is kept private. Another major concern in a work environment is *productivity*: the game must not obstruct employees. For this reason IdleWars does not implement any notification mechanism, which may be considered distracting and disruptive. Feedback is provided only through the leader board, and through the game screensaver indicating that the computer was left idle wasting energy, which acts as an ambient display.

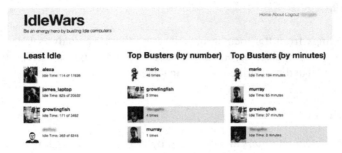

Fig. 2. The IdleWars leader board.

4 Deployment

We conducted an initial deployment to assess whether the game dynamics would engage people, and to observe whether any changes would occur in terms of computer IdleTime. The trial lasted for two weeks, and it took place at the Centre for Sustainable Energy (CSE), a non-profit organisation working on sustainable energy & policy. The organisation has 50 employees, most of them located in one workspace: an office including two communicating large open spaces, see Figure 1a for a partial view. This setup allows each player to easily see and scan the computer screen of other workers. Computer usage is an important part of the office work, main activities are e-mail, writing reports and searching the Web for information. At one end of the working space there is an open plan kitchen, used to warm up and consume meals and to make hot drinks. The leader board semi-public display was installed in front of the kitchen, to make it visible and encourage people to talk about the game and the ranking over lunch and coffee breaks.

The trial was approved by the organisation's management, and recruitment took place through an email sent to all employees, and through an announcement at a staff meeting. Participants were asked to register on a website, and at the same time provide consent to participate in the research. The game software client could also be downloaded from the site, at the end of the registration process. An experimenter assisted participants in the installation process.

Automatic interaction logs were collected throughout the duration of the trial. After the end of the trial we conducted a focus group. The format of a focus group was chosen, rather than individual interviews, due to the very limited time availability of participants. The session took place over a lunch break and it lasted approximately one hour.

A total of 26 participants (15 females) registered but only 20 (11 females) installed and used the system. All participants are staff members of the organisation. They all hold a degree level and some have post-graduate qualifications. Ages range from late 20s to early 40s, with most in their 30s. 7 of the players took part in the focus group, together with one employee who did not play but expressed interest.

5 Findings

We report findings from the focus group (through thematic analysis [3]) and present information on system usage based on the automatic interaction logs. The focus group was audiorecorded and transcribed for the analysis.

5.1 Interaction Logs

Interaction logs were automatically collected by the system, including: idle and active time, bust attempts, and web page views. During the 10 working days period, computers were left idle for 3719 minutes overall, corresponding to 8.1% of the total time they were on. If busting a computer represented shutting it down, participants would have saved 268 minutes of computer idle time, corresponding to 6.7% of the total idle time.

In total, 14 participants out of 20 busted a computer at least once. Most activity happened during the first week with 23 busting actions, whereas in the second week only 14 took place. We found that the total 37 busting actions took place on just 9 computers, which got busted from 2 to 11 times, while the remaining computers were never busted. All 7 participants who joined the focus group were involved in the actual game play, in the sense that they either busted or got busted 3 or more times.

5.2 Engagement

The focus group revealed enthusiastic engagement with the game. Participants reported running and having fun, for example: *"Yes. There was a lot of noise when P4 was sprinting across the office, shouting 'no!' [because his computer was about get busted by another participant]" [P6].* 'Fun' was also mentioned explicitly: *"...you know, it's quite fun to have someone's profile picture coming up as Bill Murray saying 'you suck'."* *[P4]* This comment refers to the profile image used by another participant, shown in Figure 1c. Indeed, another sign of engagement was the *appropriation* around the use of profile images. While we suggested participants to use an image to represent them (an avatar), three of them chose instead an image with humorous text (a so called "image macro" in Internet slang). This is because these participants realised that the profile picture would be displayed on the screen of a busted computer, so they used it to deliver a message to the people they bust. This practice was widely accepted and characterised as fun by the participants, as the previous quote illustrates.

Apparently, our participants became so engaged that game-related tension mounted around the risk of having one's computer busted: *"...it became quite a tense office, because if anybody did leave their desk and left it [the computer] on, there'd be quite a few people around it just... waiting." [P5]* This quote also indicates the development of tactics, such as players paying attention to who gets up from the desk. Another participant also described a similar tactic, to see who is in the kitchen (which is part of the office open plan) and then check whether their computers are idle: *"If you keep an eye on the kitchen... see who was in the kitchen, and then go and look at their desk." [P1]*

In contrast to the above report of the game generating 'tension' someone else told us that the game also had a stress relieving effect: *"I think particularly because we have got lots of work on at the moment, it's always nice to have something.. ..stop you [from] stressing." [P7]* The game, then, acted as a welcomed distraction from everyday issues.

To sum up, many of the comments from the focus group provide an indication of how engaging the game was and how the work environment became a more active place relieving workers from stress. The focus group also reveals how participants devised new ways of using the system to interact with each other and tactics on how to score more.

5.3   Gameplay

From the focus group it became apparent that during the game participants viewed the number of times they busted other players as a score for the game. They placed less value in the minutes they "rescued" by busting others, or in limiting the minutes their computer was idle (as described in the Game Design section). One participant explained that the number of times they busted others was perceived as a metric for one's own more "active" gameplay, while the number of minutes busted depended more on others' behaviour:

"I think there's inherently a bit more glory within sort of the number of times that you've busted, [...] because it's quite arbitrary, how long it takes somebody to come back to their computer. It's not like that's your victory as a buster.." [P5]

Another participant reinforced the idea: *"I looked at that [the idle time] briefly, but I suppose... not such an interesting bit, for me. It was more the action [of busting] that was the interesting bit." [P6]* Participants also reported a strategy to increase the number of times they busted others: after busting the computer of someone who was away from their desk, they would then unlock the computer and wait for it to become idle again after five minutes, so it could be busted one more time.

Someone else related the busting action to direct competition: *"Well, there's the point of the busting, yes [...] You can sort of say, oh, 2-0 or whatever. It's easy to compare." [P2]* This quote, as well as several other comments made throughout the focus group, suggest that our participants were very sensitive to the competitive aspect of the game.

At the same time, another participant highlighted a conflict between competitive, individualistic behaviour and sustainability:

"I think I have a bit of a thing about this ... if you encourage people to take a competitive, individualistic approach, you're kind of encouraging them to behave in a particular way which actually, in a holistic sense, isn't that good for being sustainable. So kind of bringing out certain characteristics of them ..." [P1]

We also learned that another co-worker, who did not take part in the focus group, declined to take part in the game because they disliked this mismatch between sustainability and competition: *"There was somebody who didn't play out of principle, because they thought it shouldn't become a competitive [activity]" [P1]*

In summary, the gameplay was dominated by the number of times participants busted others, which aligned with the competitive attitude most participants had during the game. However, some participants called attention to the contrast between individualistic attitude typical of competition and sustainable behaviour.

5.4   Awareness and Behaviour Change

The game triggered a discussion in the workplace about computer power management, as that was perceived to be directly related to energy waste. Participants realised that they could save energy by deactivating their computers in different ways: *"We had a discussion about what the difference between hibernation and sleep was, didn't we? And somebody broke down which one was better. Mark did some sums"* [P7]

The influence of the game extended even to those in the office who did not participate in the game. We received indirect reports that even those not playing the game felt more aware of their behaviour around energy waste, because of having people participating around them.

The discussion also highlighted technical issues related to computer power management:

"..it took so long to come back up if you hibernated your computer. So I think maybe it's a bit unrealistic to tell people they need to hibernate, because if you're away for five minutes, that's a bit of a pain.." [P1]

Other participants mentioned that different computers (running different versions of the operating system) had different power management options and different problems. For example, some applications would not reconnect to their servers after computers were resumed from sleep or hibernation.

Moreover, the focus group revealed that the game had also undesirable effects on power management. It turned out that setting computers to automatically sleep or hibernate after 5 minutes was considered as "cheating" in the context of the game. One of the participants told us: *"I did [configure my computer to automatically hibernate], and then I got pressured that I was cheating, and then reverted back."* [P4] another one confirmed: *"It's no fun [to configure your computer to automatically hibernate]. That's the thing ? it was no fun if anyone was able to do that."* [P6] Configuring the computer to automatically hibernate was deemed not acceptable by the rest of the participants, because it would take the fun of busting away. As P6 explains, if everyone activates this automation none of the computers will become idle and therefore it would become impossible to play the game.

The negative effects of the game on power management went even further. Some of the participants had the habit of switching their monitor off (albeit not the computer) when leaving their desk. However, this would make it impossible for other players to bust the computer, so they were pressured into foregoing this habit:

"P6: I think we're all in the habit of just turning off our monitors. So you had to undo that, because really we are used to turn off the monitors..
P4: ..To enjoy the game."

The discussion stimulated by IdleWars extended beyond energy consumed by computers, to a more general level. In part this generalisation was prompted by the understanding that computer consumption could be quite minimal:

"Is the expectation that the benefit will come on saving energy for the monitors, or is it from the kind of discussion that might happen around it? [...] Because actually, the amount, you know, we would have saved is vanishingly small, presumably, isn't it?" [P2]

So participants also considered energy waste, automation and behaviour change related to other office appliances, such as shared printers, or lights, as demonstrated by the following exchange:

"P4: We don't switch the lights off [...]. I used to always do it... the ones in the kitchen. I gave it up. They never get done.
P7: Are they not motion-sensitive?
P4: No. No, you can switch them [the lights] off. So you' re right... you know, we don't do things we could do."

As such, while the IdleWars game stimulated participants to forego proenvironmental behaviours such as setting computers to automatically hibernate or sleep or turning off monitors when not in use, it also raised awareness around energy waste more generally in the workplace, and encouraged the players to reflect on a broader array of energy consuming behaviours.

6 Discussion

The game design was successful in engaging participants, as demonstrated by the interaction logs, by the focus group and by the appropriation of the profile images. IdleWars sparked discussion around energy waste and conservation: participants explored different options for computer power management (sleep and hibernation) they had not considered before, and confronted their shortcomings. The sleep and hibernation shortcomings can potentially be diminished by the adoption of new hardware and software technologies (e.g. faster hard-disk drives). At the same time, the game turned out also to encourage *some* anti-conservation behaviours: discouraging users from automatically setting their computers to sleep and from turning monitors off. It is worth emphasising, then, that the game was effective in terms of *generating discussion* and even *behaviour change*, yet not necessarily for the better.

Despite the engagement, though, we could not find statistically significant differences in idle time and indeed a reduction in idle time of 5.6% is quite low in absolute terms. This could be explained by the combination of proenvironmental and wasteful behaviours that were encouraged by the game, as well as by a strong proenvironmental culture in the organisation where the game was deployed. Indeed, a computer idle time of only 8.2% is quite low, and it is clear from the logs that none of the participants left their computer on overnight.

More specifically, the game design was successful in catalysing existing social dynamics in the work environment where it was deployed: our participants collectively interpreted how the game was supposed to be played, to the point of making up additional rules (e.g. it is *forbidden* to automatically put one's computer to sleep). The main **implication** of these findings, we argue, is that they demonstrate the potential of games in the workplace to engage workers around sustainability issues, to stimulate discussion, and even encourage behaviour change.

6.1 Physicality and Visibility

Based on the focus group, the main factors behind the success of the game in engaging participants seem to be its physical elements and its competitive nature. The *physicality* contributed to make the gameplay *visible*. Participants *saw* others "sprint" across the office to save their computer from being busted. Scanning a QR-code to bust a computer is a *gesture* that everyone in the office can *see*. The idle and busted screen-savers as well as the leader board are visible in the workplace, making everyone aware of the status and activity of everyone else. The IdleWars leader board also made players' behaviour visible, revealing the proenvironmental or wasteful behaviour of the individual, and potentially even the proportion of time one spends at their desk.

These results, then, bear an **implication for future research**, opening up a question about how similar visibility could be achieved at a larger scale. Would it be possible to make this type of games work at all, for example, in larger companies, where teams are not co-located? Further research could explore the application of remote collaboration paradigms, such as ambient displays that show when a remotely located computer becomes idle and then gets busted.

6.2   Action-Reaction in the Gameplay

Being "active" seems to be a key for our participants. They found the idea of gaining points for busting someone else rewarding because they relate it directly to the prowess of the buster. In contrast, gaining more or less points because the person busted left their computer inactive for a particular length of time was perceived as depending (somewhat arbitrarily) on the fault of the another person, and therefore not of interest. Similarly, setting computers to automatically sleep after few minutes of inactivity was considered *cheating* – it is an individual responsibility, one needs to remember to turn off the computer, so they can be caught if they forget. As such, automation was found not to be *fun*. This effect is perhaps encouraged or amplified by the feedback provided by IdleWars. The action of busting a player is instantly rewarded by the feedback of having one's profile picture displayed on the screen of the "victim". The appropriation we observed around the use of the profile pictures further indicates that our participants valued this action-reaction sequence.

The lack of interest in the number of minutes "rescued" by busting can also be explained due to the fact that IdleWars does not provide instant feedback about the minutes busted: players need to go and find the leader board to reveal how many minutes the busted player had been idle for. Simply adding a minutes counter on the busted screen would make this information instantly available, and thus more salient to the players. On the other hand, a busted computer could be unlocked by anyone and busted again after five minutes. This made it possible, and even encouraged, to score repeatedly. This issue could be limited by making the unlocking of a busted computer password-protected, so that only the computer owner could perform it. This shortcoming negatively influenced the game dynamics. One strategy to limit this type of issue could be, for example, to include in the game explicit suggestions about proenvironmental behaviour, and perhaps even to make the action of busting a computer *metaphor* for switching it off.

At one level, it could be argued that the undesired effects were simply caused by a design limitation, which resulted in a misalignment between the (perceived) game goals and the desired behaviour. However, more in general, it is worth calling attention to the potential conflict between individualist competition and sustainability goals, often framed in terms of altruistic and cooperative behaviour. Indeed, at least one worker from the organisation where we deployed the game refused to take part because she felt the two attitudes should not be combined. This question highlights an opportunity for further research.

6.3 Productivity Trade-Offs?

Similar to other studies about energy conservation in the workplace [12], a tension between saving energy and productivity on the job emerged in our focus group. Idle-Wars encouraged our participants to put their computer to sleep or into hibernation, but they perceived that such practice has the potential to reduce their productivity, because it takes time to reactivate the computer and resume work when one is back at the desk, or because of software glitches. Some of these issues are strictly technological (rather than behavioural), and probably related to dated software and hardware. While hardware upgrade is likely to have a considerable environmental cost, a purely software solution (e.g. having applications that reconnect to servers in seamless fashion after computer sleep) could be attractive, if at all possible [2].

The IdleWars gameplay in itself was also pointed out to be a source of distraction: a few *keen* players admitted they would sometimes linger away from their desk to try and bust others, or they would run and shout in the office distracting bystanders. These are probably extreme cases, and indeed the reports from other participants suggest the gameplay was often integrated in the natural work breaks that take place in any workplace. However, we believe these occurrences point at another inherent tension: between job productivity and an engaging, entertaining game.

We draw two **implications** here. First, to contain the distraction caused by games like IdleWars, more efforts could be made to refine their design, using timed activation to fit within prescribed pauses, or limiting the daily amount of playing. Second, given that the aim is to help players *learn* a proenvironmental behaviour, an alternative strategy could be to frame such games as episodic, short term activities lasting just one or two weeks. The game could then become one of a number of activities (e.g. workshops) designed to draw employees attention to sustainability issues in the workplace, all to take place over a specific period. Creating anticipation for the event, by advertising it in advance, could help the engagement, as it happened in our deployment. This duration-limited approach would also be inline with the engagement naturally tapering off over time.

7   Conclusion and Future Work

In this paper we introduced IdleWars, a pervasive game designed to raise awareness and promote behaviour change in relation to energy waste in the workplace. An initial deployment, over two weeks in a medium sized organisation, revealed that the physical and competitive elements of the game work well in engaging participants. More specifically, the design was successful in catalysing existing social dynamics in the workplace where it was deployed.

Participants appropriated the game and extended its rules, sometimes in a way that favoured engagement and fun rather than conservation behaviour. IdleWars triggered discussion around computer power management options and their adoption, and more in general on energy waste in the office. In contrast, setting computers to automatically sleep after few minutes of inactivity (which is desirable in terms of sustainability) was considered "cheating" because it takes away from the game challenge. While these results point out that our specific game design needs to be revised to better align the game rules with the underlying sustainability goals, they also indicate that pervasive games like IdleWars *can* be effective tools to raise the attention to sustainability issues in the workplace, paving the way for further HCI research in this domain.

In addition to the pointers included in the discussion, in future work we also plan to leverage the *IdleWars* infrastructure, especially in terms of idle time sensing, with alternative game or eco-feedback approaches. We believe that computer idle time as a measure of proenvironmental behaviour has potential for larger scale, remote deployments, and engagement through online social networks.

Acknowledgments. This work was partially supported by the "Creating the Energy for Change" project (energyforchange.ac.uk) reference No. (EP/K002589/1) and by the Greek State Scholarships Foundation (www.iky.gr), contract No. (2012--564). We would like to thank the Centre for Sustainable Energy (www.cse.org.uk) for allowing us to trial our prototype at their premises. The dataset is available at (http://dx.doi.org/10.5258/SOTON/377465).

References

1. Bang, M., Gustafsson, A., Katzeff, C.: Promoting new patterns in household energy consumption with pervasive learning games. In: de Kort, Y.A.W., IJsselsteijn, W.A., Midden, C., Eggen, B., Fogg, B.J. (eds.) PERSUASIVE 2007. LNCS, vol. 4744, pp. 55–63. Springer, Heidelberg (2007)
2. Blevis, E.: Sustainable interaction design: invention & disposal, renewal & reuse. In: Proc. CHI 2007 (2007)
3. Braun, V., Clarke, V.: Using thematic analysis in psychology. Qual. Res. Qual. Res. in Psych. 3(3), 77–102 (2006)
4. Foster, D., Lawson, S., Wardman, J., Blythe, M., Linehan, C.: Watts in it for me: Design implications for implementing effective energy interventions in organisations. In: Proceedings of the SIGCHI Conference on Human Factors in Computing Systems, CHI 2012, pp. 2357–2366. ACM, New York (2012)
5. Froehlich, J., Findlater, L., Landay, J.: The design of eco-feedback technology. In: Proceedings of the SIGCHI Conference on Human Factors in Computing Systems, CHI 2010, pp. 1999–2008. ACM, New York (2010)
6. Gaver, W.W., Bowers, J., Boucher, A., Gellerson, H., Pennington, S., Schmidt, A., Steed, A., Villars, N., Walker, B.: The drift table: designing for ludic engagement. In: CHI 2004 Extended Abstracts on Human Factors in Computing Systems, pp. 885–900. ACM, New York (2004)
7. Gustafsson, A., Bång, M., Svahn, M.: Power explorer: A casual game style for encouraging long term behavior change among teenagers. In: Proceedings of the International Conference on Advances in Computer Enterntainment Technology, ACE 2009, pp. 182–189. ACM, New York (2009)

8. Jahn, M., Schwartz, T., Simon, J., Jentsch, M.: EnergyPULSE: Tracking sustainable behavior in office environments. In: Proceedings of the 2nd International Conference on Energy-Efficient Computing and Networking, pp. 87–96. ACM Press, New York (2011)

9. Jain, M., Agrawal, A., Ghai, S.K., Truong, K.N., Seetharam, D.P.: We are not in the loop: resource wastage and conservation attitude of employees in indian workplace. In: Proceedings of the 2013 ACM International Joint Conference on Pervasive and Ubiquitous Computing, UbiComp 2013, pp. 687–696. ACM, New York (2013)

10. Jain, R.K., Taylor, J.E., Peschiera, G.: Assessing eco-feedback interface usage and design to drive energy efficiency in buildings. Energy and Buildings 48, 8–17 (2012)

11. Jentsch, M., Jahn, M., Pramudianto, F., Simon, J., Al-Akkad, A.: An energy-saving support system for office environments. In: Salah, A.A., Lepri, B. (eds.) HBU 2011. LNCS, vol. 7065, pp. 83–92. Springer, Heidelberg (2011)

12. Katzeff, C., Broms, L., Jönsson, L., Westholm, U., Räsänen, M.: Exploring Sustainable Practices in Workplace Settings Through Visualizing Electricity Consumption. TOCHI 20(5), November 2013

13. Kim, T., Hong, H., Magerko, B.: Design requirements for ambient display that supports sustainable lifestyle. In: Proceedings of the 8th ACM Conference on Designing Interactive Systems, DIS 2010, pp. 103–112. ACM, New York (2010)

14. PC Energy Report: PC Energy Report (2009). http://www.1e.com/energycampaign/downloads/PC_EnergyReport2009-US.pdf (accessed: December 09, 2013)

15. Pousman, Z., Rouzati, H., Stasko, J.: Imprint, a community visualization of printer data. In: Proceedings of the ACM 2008 Conference on Computer Supported Cooperative Work, CSCW 2008, pp. 13–16. ACM, New York (2008)

16. Reeves, B., Cummings, J.J., Scarborough, J.K., Yeykelis, L.: Increasing Energy Efficiency With Entertainment Media: An Experimental and Field Test of the Influence of a Social Game on Performance of Energy Behaviors. Environment and Behavior (2013)

17. Ryan, R.M., Deci, E.L.: Intrinsic and Extrinsic Motivations: Classic Definitions and New Directions. Contemporary Educational Psychology 25(1), 54–67 (2000)

18. Schwartz, T., Betz, M., Ramirez, L., Stevens, G.: Sustainable energy practices at work: understanding the role of workers in energy conservation. In: Proceedings of the 6th Nordic Conference on Human-Computer Interaction: Extending Boundaries, NordiCHI 2010, pp. 452–462. ACM, New York (2010)

19. Siero, F.W., Bakker, A.B., Dekker, G.B., Van den Burg, M.T.: Changing Organizational Energy Consumption Behaviour through Comparative Feedback. Journal of Environmental Psychology, 235–246 (1996)

20. Simon, J., Jahn, M., Al-Akkad, A.: Saving energy at work: The design of a pervasive game for office spaces. In: Proceedings of the 11th International Conference on Mobile and Ubiquitous Multimedia, MUM 2012, pp. 9:1–9:4. ACM, New York (2012)

21. Yun, R., Aziz, A., Scupelli, P., Lasternas, B., Zhang, C., Loftness, V.: Beyond eco-feedback: adding online manual and automated controls to promote workplace sustainability. In: Proceedings of the 33rd Annual ACM Conference on Human Factors in Computing Systems, CHI 2015, pp. 1989–1992. ACM, New York (2015)

Interactive Digital Gameplay Can Lower Stress Hormone Levels in Home Alone Dogs — A Case for Animal Welfare Informatics

Annika Geurtsen[1], Maarten H. Lamers[1], and Marcel J.M. Schaaf[2]

[1] Media Technology Research Group, Leiden University, The Netherlands
annika.geurtsen@gmail.com
[2] Leiden Institute of Biology, Leiden University, The Netherlands

Abstract. Social isolation, when owners are not home, is a major stressor for dogs leading to separation anxiety and related behavioral and physiological issues. We investigate whether a digital interactive game requiring no human interference reduces stress response in dogs when isolated. An interactive game was developed specifically for canines. Dogs were domestically tested, totaling 15 days with and 15 days without the game. Twice-daily saliva samples were analyzed for cortisol stress hormone concentrations; ethograms were constructed. Combined data confirm that digital interactive games can lessen physiological and behavioral stress responses in dogs, and that the effect is modulated by a dog's personality.

Keywords: animal welfare, interactive games, stress, games for health and well-being.

1 Introduction

Canines are social animals, wired for a life in a pack. However, throughout time, dogs have been domesticated [15] and humans have created artificial living environments for canines (amongst other animals that we domesticated) in which they are required to adapt. The result from living in this artificial environment is that dogs are left alone at home during the day, when their human companions are at work. Social isolation [49] is considered a major stressor for a social species such as canines. Staying home alone, and thus being isolated from the pack, might have an impact on the well-being of the canine [37].

Apart from dogs possibly being bored [29], a considerable number of dogs have developed behavioral issues related to separation anxiety. A recent study conducted for the BBC [11], shows that from a randomized group of 40 dogs, at least 10 subjects showed signs of separation anxiety. Moreover, another 25 subjects that did not show anxiety signs, but slept or were lying down while the owners were absent, had cortisol levels that matched those of the dogs showing separation anxiety. Levels of cortisol have been shown to correlate positively with stress experienced by dogs [3,4,8,18]. In other words, even though these

© IFIP International Federation for Information Processing 2015
K. Chorianopoulos et al. (Eds.): ICEC 2015, LNCS 9353, pp. 238–251, 2015.
DOI: 10.1007/978-3-319-24589-8_18

dogs did not show behavioral signs, they were undergoing stress when they were isolated.

Studies investigating whether human contact reduces stress for shelter dogs show that dogs interacting with humans had lower cortisol levels than dogs that did not interact with humans [6,44]. The absence of human presence could allow for a dog to become stressed, and in order to ease the stress, the presence of a human seems required.

Studies into improving the psychological conditions for canines that live in isolation (for several hours every day) using technology is scarce. Products such as SmartDog (Four Legged Trends Ltd., 2014) and PetChatz (Anser Innovation, 2014) focus on strengthening or maintaining the bond between the owner and the dog, by providing direct, live interactions between humans and canines. Providing the canine and owner with the option to initiate contact during separation is a worthwhile aim. However, such solutions circumvent the problem by ensuring the canine is not alone.

Our research embraces the idea that if a digital interactive game is able to entertain the canine sufficiently, the canine may be enabled to become more (emotionally) independent from the human (owner) and as a result might experience less stress when separated from the human. We hypothesize that *the presence of a digital interactive game, with which a dog can play without the need of human presence or interference, can reduce the stress response in dogs when left home alone by their owners.* This is tested through an experimental study in which we measure cortisol levels in home alone dogs and combine these with video-based ethogram data. We then compare the outcomes across two conditions, namely being at home with and without a digital interactive game specifically designed for canines.

The aims of our research are threefold. Firstly, using intelligent technologies, we aim to improve the quality of life for animals. As such, our work falls within the scope of Animal Computer Interaction (ACI) and Animal Welfare Informatics (AWI) [27]. Secondly, we aim to combine data derived from physiological indicators, i.c. hormonal indicators of stress, and behavioral indicators, i.c. ethograms, to increase the data's reliability in determining a dog's psychological state. This seemingly obvious approach is nonetheless novel within AWI. Thirdly, we aim to widen the application and study of interactive entertainment beyond the human species — a goal that remains compliant with the domain of intelligent technologies for interactive entertainment.

2   Related Work

Artifacts used for and by animals have been developed in previous decades, but usually not with the intention to specifically improve their welfare. [41]. Since then, the aspirations to serve the aims of animals other than humans in studies have advanced [27,28].

Not all work exploring the relation between technical artefact and animals can be considered AWI. One end of the spectrum focuses on new ways of computing using animals, while the other end aims towards using technology to improve the living conditions of the animal. Studies have examined the possibility of animals controlling digital systems (e.g. [19,22,25,26,42,45,46]), or the use by animals of a technological medium to communicate with humans (e.g. [20,39]).

An early exploration into AWI is work by Resner [38] which enables owners to clicker train their dog over the Internet. While it is a step towards the positive end of the AWI spectrum, the quality of the interaction is asymmetrical in the sense that the dog merely follows orders, incapable of controlling the application. Training a dog over the Internet supports human needs, but not necessarily those of the canine.

To stimulate both human and animal to participate in interaction one can envision technologically mediated gameplay during which the animal is considered user of the game. The Canine Amusement and Training project [48] allows a dog to join a human in electronic gaming, while simultaneously aiming to motivate the human to spend more time with their canine. As such, it serves the needs of both the canine and human, but the dog remains dependent on the human to initiate gameplay.

A similar approach was undertaken in Cat Cat Revolution [34], a game that allows cats to chase virtual objects on a tablet, a natural behavior of cats. At least partial success of this approach can be deduced from the popularity of Free Games for Cats from Friskies (Nestlé Purina Petcare Company, 2013), tablet games designed for cats and their owners.

The game Pig Chase [14] is an example of an interface that allows the animal to participate as fully recognized user through means of embodied play. The game operates around a large touch-sensitive projection screen set up in a pig stable. On it, pigs can follow small lights with their snout, which are in turn controlled by humans playing on a tablet. Once a pig "catches" a light with its snout, it explodes into a burst of light which according to the makers (among whom animal welfare scientists) pigs enjoy and thus serves as a reward and stimulation. As such it can cognitively stimulate pigs held in captivity and combat its negative effects such as stereotypic behavior development.

Metazoa Ludens [43] is one of few studies where an inter-species game was built, used, and thoroughly evaluated. It allows pet owners to interact and play with their hamster remotely via the Internet in a mixed-reality game. The hamster is placed on an actuated flexible floor and presented moving food that it physically chases and catches. In virtual game space, the human avatar is coupled to the physical food, while being chased by the hamster's avatar. After being allowed over a period of 6 weeks to voluntarily play for one hour per weekday, standardized body condition scoring showed that hamsters' health and fitness had improved. A separate study, aimed at assessing the motivation of the hamsters to play Metazoa Ludens showed that over time the hamster's preference to play increased, allowing a conclusion that the hamsters enjoyed playing the game.

More closely related to our work is Pawtracker [36], an interface that posts sensor-based dog-created content on social media, enabling owners to track their dog's activities and share the information with friends. As such, human users know what their pet is up to when home alone. Although the study concerns itself with the issue of dogs being alone at home, it does not directly provide support or a solution for a home alone dog if anxious.

Another study [29] addresses the issue of dogs being left home alone by their owners by providing Internet mediated interactions. For example, the owner is notified when a dog is bored (lying down) and can initiate play remotely by activating a device that throws a ball. Whether this has the desired effect during canine isolation is not investigated. However the study did result in interesting findings on how canines perceive and what their (cognitive and physical) capabilities are in relation to technology.

Although quite a number of related studies exist, the field of ACI is still in its infancy. Co-designing with animals is somewhat of a struggle, and ACI studies cannot make use of certain evaluation methods commonly used in HCI studies, such as surveys. Thus new ways of evaluation must be designed, applied and tested. Although the first exploratory steps were taken, the fields of ACI/AWI will continue to grow, offering valuable insights into the cognitive abilities of animals and resulting design strategies.

3   Design Considerations

As mentioned above regarding games intended for cats, hamsters and pigs, we suggest that for dogs too, the immersive quality of play could provide a solution to social isolation. In an informal preliminary study we explored design issues for games that potentially prevent canines from getting stressed during isolation. Design choices were assessed informally according to (hypothesized) reactions of canines, feasibility of the game within the constraints of this study, practicality of the game within a domestic setting, and suitability towards the aims of our study.

To successfully design a game for canines, it must adhere to a couple of requirements. Firstly, it must provide suitable stimuli for canine sensory perception [16,24,33]. Secondly, the game must comply with canine cognitive capabilities [7,12,30,31,32], providing a satisfactory challenge to keep dogs immersed. We acknowledge that not all dogs have identical cognitive skills or play style preferences [10,23]. The resulting game may not have a similar effect on all dogs, even when capable of performing the same actions. Thirdly, because we aim to provide a game not reliant on human interference, it must work autonomously. Fourthly, [2] dogs do not seem to initiate play when (home) alone or when accompanied by another dog [47]. Therefore, the game must initiate play in order for the dog to immerse in gameplay.

To aid the design process, various commercial dog games were researched and evaluated. Tether Tug (Tether Tug Dog Toys Company, 2013) aims to stimulate individual dog play by appealing to the play action of tugging. A popular product is the Kong (KONG Company), a hollow, rubber object in which food can be placed in the form of treats or foods that can be smeared. Various other commercial parties produce artefacts designed to mentally stimulate dogs. However, all these games require human presence.

Automation and digitalization of existing games may have the potential of immersing a dog in gameplay that is intuitive and experienced as fun, while also being autonomous, such as GoDogGo Fetch Machine (GoDogGo Inc., 2009) and iFetch (iFetch Company, 2013). Keeping practicalities of our domestically situated experiment in mind, we chose to create a digital interactive game that exploits elements of the electronic game *Simon* (Milton Bradley Company, 1978), and hide and seek, using sound.

Fig. 1. Button designed specifically to be pressed by canine paws.

4   The Digital Interactive Game

The digital interactive game designed for our experiment consists of two game positions, spaced roughly 120 cm apart, and an electrically controlled dog treats dispenser positioned midway between them. Each game position consists of an audio speaker and button designed specifically to be pressed by canine paws (Fig. 1). The buttons are positioned in front of each speaker, and are basically a microswitch covered by a flexible plastic sheet (20 x 20 cm). Placing a paw on the plastic cover depresses the switch, even with minimal force applied - informal tests showed that a weight of 70 grams is sufficient to depress the switch.

The interaction rules are simple and provide direct feedback to aid the dog in understanding gameplay. The game reacts according to the steps-diagram shown in Table 1.

5   Experimental Methods

5.1   General Setup

Canine subjects were tested over a total period of 10 days: divided over 5 consecutive weekdays of stimulated condition and 5 consecutive weekdays of

Table 1. Game steps diagram

Step Action
1. Wait 20 minutes.
2. From both positions, a position P is randomly selected.
3. Position P emits a short audio sample every 10 seconds, until 2 minutes have passed *or* the button at position P was pressed.
4. If button P was *not* pressed, repeat from step 1.
5. Dispense a treat, and then wait 30 seconds.
6. Alternate position Q emits a short audio sample every 10 seconds, until 2 minutes have passed *or* the button at position Q was pressed.
7. If button Q was pressed, dispense a treat.
8. Repeat from step 1.

unstimulated condition, separated by two days without testing. All testing occurred inside the dogs natural domestic setting. On testing days, the subject was isolated for a set duration, either accompanied by the digital interactive game (stimulated condition) or without it (unstimulated condition). The duration of daily isolation varies per subject (as discussed in more detail later), as does the order in which both conditions were applied. Other animals cohabitating with the subject were excluded from the space wherein the subject was isolated.

5.2   Salivary Cortisol Measurements

Cortisol tests are commonly applied to assess the level of stress experienced by an animal [3,4,8,18]. Cortisol can be measured through different sources, such as excretion, blood and hair. We use saliva [10] to provide samples containing cortisol, because differences in cortisol concentration can be measured in saliva within a period of a few hours, whereas cortisol conserved in hair is only detectable over longer periods of time. Furthermore, saliva can be collected at any moment in time, whereas excretion would have to appear during every test within the set timeframe, which is unlikely to happen within a domestic setting. Taking blood samples is intrusive and might itself have an effect on the psychological state of the dog.

Sample Collection. Saliva samples were obtained twice daily from each subject, at the moments of departure and return of the owner, defining the subject's period of isolation. Twice-daily sampling was done due to the circadian nature of cortisol concentrations inside the body, causing concentrations to fluctuate throughout each day.

Saliva samples were obtained by the experimenter by placing an absorbing dental roll (Nobadent) between the cheek and the jawline of the dog's mouth, preventing the dog from chewing on the dental roll or swallowing it. The dental roll remained in position for one minute before being removed and placed inside a 10 ml syringe. The sample was then diluted with 2 ml of phosphate buffered saline (PBS) and pressed into a labeled test tube, which was then sealed and stored for a maximum of 4 weeks at -18 °C degrees before being analyzed in a laboratory.

Cortisol Concentration Determination. Cortisol concentrations in the samples were assessed using an enzyme-linked immunosorbent assay (ELISA) cortisol test. After a standardized sequence of steps, reactions produce a color signal in the sample substrates. Light absorbance at 450 nm is then read by a microplate reader for each sample. Higher cortisol concentrations result in less color intensity in the sample reaction product, and lower optical absorbance values (expressed as optical units).

Although the ELISA cortisol test is used to assess cortisol levels in canines frequently, a preliminary test was performed to determine whether the cortisol concentrations of the samples taken from dogs would fall within the detectable range of the ELISA cortisol test [8]. This confirmed that the cortisol concentrations in the preliminary test samples were detectable within the calibration range of 0.4 - 1.7 nm/mg.

Ethograms and Qualitative Notes. Continuous video and audio observations were recorded during the period wherein the subjects were isolated. Cortisol concentrations give an objective indication of the amount of stress experienced by a canine during the test. However, the observed cortisol concentration does not discriminate between positive arousal (excitedness) and negative arousal (anxiety). In order to add context to the cortisol concentrations, video/audio observations of the subjects behavior are analyzed [1].

Behavioral observations were quantified through a focal animal sampling ethogram also used by Scaglia *et al.* to analyze home alone dogs [40], modified to incorporate interactions with the digital interactive game. An ethogram was created for the first 30 minutes of every hour of video/audio recording, to gain a representative sample of subject behavior. Supporting qualitative notes and observations were made in addition to the quantified ethogram data. This was done to ensure that the proper context was attributed to the subjects' observed behaviors for interpretation.

6   Results

6.1   Subjects

For the study 3 canine subjects were tested in their natural domestic situation in the Groningen province of The Netherlands during Summer 2014. Table 2 shows key characteristics of the subjects, the isolation duration, and the daily times at which saliva samples were collected.

Table 2. Overview of subjects, experimental conditions and sample collection characteristics

Subjects			
ˏName	Isa	Tommie	Rosie
Breed	White Swiss Shepherd	English Springer Spaniel	Australian Shepherd
Gender	F	M (neutered)	F
Age (in years)	6	5	5
Cohabiting animals	2 cats	none	1 dog
Stimulation and sampling conditions per subject			
Stimulated condition	$21/7 - 25/7/2015$	$28/7 - 1/8/2015$	$11/8 - 15/8/2015$
Unstimulated condition	$28/7 - 1/8/2015$	$21/7 - 25/7/2015$	$4/8 - 8/8/2015$
Daily isolation hours	3 (10:30 – 13:30h)	2 (11:10 – 13:10h)	1 (20:00 – 21:00h)

6.2   Salivary Cortisol Analysis

The ELISA cortisol test was performed on a duo set of calibration samples and 60 saliva samples obtained from the subjects during the experiment. Sample optical absorbance measurements (in optical units) are usually converted to cortisol concentrations (ng/ml) by creating a standard curve from the double sets of calibration samples, for which the cortisol concentrations are known. However, rather than converting to the cortisol concentrations we use optical absorbance measures in our data analysis. Converting the absorbance measures to cortisol concentrations introduces noise. Moreover, we are interested in daily within-subject differences in cortisol levels across experimental conditions, for which absorbance measures suffice as a proxy. The range of absorbance measures encountered in samples is 2.182–2.424 optical units. Between-subject comparisons of cortisol concentrations were not made, because levels are known to differ between individuals and breeds and fluctuate throughout the day, whereas subjects were tested at different times of day. All statistical analyses assume possible effects in either direction (two-tailed) and accept significance if $p < 0.05$. To keep the text legible, the unstimulated condition is referred to as control and the stimulated condition as experimental. All results are summarized in Table 3.

Table 3. P-Values of T-tests comparing mean absorbance measurements, across various conditions for pooled and individual subjects. Significant P-values in boldface

Data	T-test compares		Pooled	Isa	Tommie	Rosie
Control	P	Pre	Post	**0.035** $(-)$	0.607 $(-)$	0.077 $(-)$	0.371 $(-)$
Exp.	P	Pre	Post	0.376 $(-)$	0.610 $(-)$	0.303 $(-)$	0.828 $(+)$
Pre	U	Control	Exp.	0.169 $(+)$	0.646 $(-)$	**0.032** $(+)$	0.305 $(+)$
Post	U	Control	Exp.	**0.034** $(+)$	0.251 $(-)$	**0.018** $(+)$	**0.024** $(+)$

(Control): Unstimulated isolation;   (Exp.): Stimulated isolation;
(Pre): Pre-isolation;   (Post): Post-isolation;   (P): Paired;
(U): Unpaired; $(-)$: Decrease; $(+)$: Increase

Under the control condition, and pooled over all subjects, individual absorption values show a small (-0.031) but statistically significant mean daily decrease (paired t-test, $p = 0.035$, $df = 14$), i.e. increase of cortisol concentrations. However, under the experimental condition, a smaller mean daily decrease (-0.011) in individual absorption values is found, which is not significant (paired t-test, $p = 0.376$, $df = 14$). These findings correspond to our hypothesis that stimulation lessens the mean individual daily increase in cortisol hormone, when compared to the control condition, in fact mitigating its statistical significance. A comparison of pre-isolation measurements between the control and experimental conditions shows a non-significant small different between means of 0.019 (unpaired two-sample t-test, $p = 0.169$, $df = 26$), where the experimental condition yields the highest absorbance value. However, when comparing post-isolation samples, the control and experimental conditions shows a small but statistically significant difference between means (unpaired two-sample t-test, $p = 0.034$, $df = 26$). This corresponds to our hypothesis that stimulation decreases the post-isolation cortisol hormone levels compared to the control condition. This effect is not found when comparing pre-isolation samples, as would be expected, because they are independent of experimental conditions.

When comparing means of daily change in absorbance values between control (-0.031) and experimental (-0.011) conditions, pooled over all subjects, the difference is non-significant (unpaired two-sample t-test, $p = 0.267$, $df = 28$). Although stimulation appears to lessen the daily increase of cortisol concentrations over all subjects, we cannot reject the null-hypothesis that the true means daily differences in cortisol concentrations are in fact equal when comparing the control and experimental conditions.

Since in theory the latter lack of significance could be caused by pooling of data over subjects, we performed analyses per subject. In short, for two subjects (Tommie, Rosie) post-isolation absorbance values are significantly higher in the experimental condition. Although this corresponds to our hypothesis, it does not hold for subject Isa. Moreover, subject Tommie also shows significantly higher experimental pre-isolation absorbance values, something that cannot be explained through our hypothesis.

6.3 Ethograms and Qualitative Notes

Quantified ethogram scores describing exhibited behaviors were converted to fractions over sample periods, representing the relative occurrences of said behavior. The amount of time subjects were visible in the video was noted. Behaviors exhibited in video view were noted, as were audio cues when subject was outside video view. Detailed ethogram data is reported in [13].

Subject Isa was barely observed on video during stimulated isolation. She was not in proximity of the digital interactive game (to which the camera was aimed). Based on the observations made during her unstimulated trials, Isa was most likely performing passive behavior at a location outside the scope of the camera. Based on collective observations made we assess that Isa exhibits little or no stress-associated behavior during isolation.

Subject Tommie exhibited more barking, whining and howling during unstimulated isolation compared to stimulated isolation, whereas more locomotion and passive behavior was observed during stimulated isolation. Barking, whining and howling are often perceived as stress related behaviors whereas passive behavior (as exhibited here) is perceived as a calm state of mind. Tommie exhibited slightly more exploratory behavior during stimulated isolation, which is often associated with a perceived sense of safety in the canine. Overall, ethogram data suggest that Tommie shows more stress-associated behavior during unstimulated isolation and more calm behavior during the stimulated isolation.

Subject Rosie performed more barking, whining, locomotion and alert behavior during unstimulated isolation compared to stimulated isolation. When stimulated, Rosie did not howl, exhibited more explorative behavior and appeared more in video, indicating she was in proximity of the game about 90% of the time. Overall, ethogram data suggest that Rosie performed more stress-associated behaviors during unstimulated isolation, whereas little or no stress-associated behavior was shown in stimulated isolation.

6.4   Game Oriented Behaviour

Subject Isa showed explorative behavior towards the game about 13% of the time analyzed. She did not play the game, however, possibly because she was not taught to play the game before stimulated isolation. Furthermore, she did not follow any training courses (agility, flyball or obedience training). She did know basic commands, but had never worked with buttons prior to stimulated isolation. Not knowing how to play the game might have resulted in a loss of interest.

Subject Tommie showed slightly more interest in the game and explorative behavior towards the dispenser by sniffing it. He did not play the game, probably because of similar reasons as described for subject Isa. Tommie does know basic commands, but at the time of testing was not involved in any training. He had not been taught to press a button. Both Isa and Tommie showed much interest in the game in the presence of humans.

The fraction of time subject Rosie was in camera view, and thus in proximity of the game, is 91% percent. She showed interest in the dispenser and even managed to displace it so as to reach the treats inside. Commonly, Rosie performed this behavior after an attempt to play the game while it was not active (no sound was made). This behavior led us to adjust the game settings on the last day of stimulated isolation. Rosie showed more interest in the game than Isa and Tommie and is the only subject who managed to successfully play the game. Rosie knows basic commands, and was engaged in agility, obedience and doggy dance training. Next to that she had worked with a button before.

7   Conclusions and Discussion

Our experiment explores the hypothesis that the presence of a digital interactive game, with which a dog can play without the need of human interference, can reduce the stress response in dogs when left home alone by their owners. Combining behavioral (ethogram) observations with physiological measurement of cortisol hormone concentrations in canine saliva we observed the following.

(1) Dogs that showed behavioral patterns associated with anxiety in unstimulated isolation showed less behavioral anxiety patterns while stimulated, and these anxiety decreases are confirmed by statistically significant differences in post-isolation cortisol ELISA measurements of these dogs ($n = 10$ per dog, 2 dogs). Such decrease in behavioral and physiological anxiety indicators is not observed for a dog that showed no anxiety indicators in unstimulated isolation. However, even when the post-isolation physiological measures ($n = 30$) are pooled over all subjects, including those of the "non-affected" dog, the decrease in physiological anxiety measures remains statistically significant. From these results we are satisfied to accept our main hypothesis to hold for dogs that show behavioral signs of anxiety during normal (i.e. without digital interactive game) isolation. For dogs that show no behavioral signs of anxiety during isolation, the hypothesis is rejected.

(2) Paired within-subject comparison ($n = 15$ pairs) of pre- and post-isolation physiological measures showed a significant increase in physiological anxiety during normal isolation. This increase is much smaller and no longer significant ($n = 15$ pairs) for isolation with the interactive game. This indicates a relevant decrease in physiological anxiety measures when introducing the interactive game. However, comparing daily isolation-induced changes of cortisol ELISA measures between normal isolation ($n = 15$) and isolation with the interactive game ($n = 15$) shows that the decrease exists, but is not significant. Therefore, we cannot with 95% confidence reject the alternative hypothesis (null-hypothesis) that the daily change in canine physiological stress indicator induced by isolation is similar in the presence of our interactive game. The observed lowered daily increase in physiological anxiety measure could be caused by chance.

(3) Behavioral analysis (and to some degree physiological measures) show that the game is not suitable for every type of dog. A dog that is not stressed or bored when isolated, without the urge to be active or cognitively challenged, will not be attracted to engaging in digital interactive gameplay. A dog in need of cognitive stimulation and known to be active might experience benefits from being able to play the game during isolation. Dogs with such personality traits often descended from breeds such as Border Collies, Australian Shepherds, Malinois and Dutch Shepherds. From our experience, it appears that dogs with these traits develop separation anxiety in particular. A digital interactive game may not only be used to treat separation anxiety, but possibly also as a method to train such dogs for preventing the development of separation anxiety.

That said, we find substantial support from combined quantified behavioral data and physiological stress indicators to conclude that positive effects of the digital interactive game during canine isolation exist and were found. Aspects that may have affected our results should be identified also. Firstly, the small number of subjects (3 dogs) limits the expressive power of our physiological data, even though substantial data per subject was gathered (20 physiological measures per dog). Cost-efficiency and practical constraints have played part in this limitation. Secondly, the variances in subject characteristics (e.g. breed, training experience, and exhibited isolation anxiety) complicate generalization of our results. Thirdly, the unfortunate coincidence of our testing with common summer holidays in The Netherlands led to shortened durations of isolation periods. We speculate that longer isolation might strengthen the found effects of digital interactive gameplay on physiological measures of anxiety.

Concerning design of interactive digital games for canines, we conclude the following from our results. Firstly, our game was designed not towards commercial viability, but to test our hypothesis. For general application its robustness could be improved and setting of specific gameplay parameters should be further explored. Secondly, one could argue that dispensing of treats can alter the psychological state of dogs, whereby it did not occur in control conditions. Treats were regarded as part of the complete interactive game experience. Thus their effect on the psychological state of our subjects is considered an effect of interacting with the game as a whole. Thirdly, this reasoning about treats must be generalized; further deconstructing game elements while testing them individually would provide valuable insights as to which game components have what effect.

From the effects observed we conclude that interactive digital gaming without human interference has the potential to improve the quality of life for home alone dogs. Hopefully our work contributes to further study and deployment of interactive digital games for improvement of animal welfare. Moreover, we have shown that physiological indicators combined with behavioral observations provide a strong basis for evaluating effects of digital interactive entertainment on animals. We look forward to interactive entertainment researchers embracing this method. Finally, we are confident to have shown that animals are users worthy of designing intelligent technologies for interactive entertainment for.

Acknowledgement. We gratefully relied on laboratory support by Petra Bakker (Leiden University), discussion with animal health and welfare specialist Marc Bracke (Wageningen University), and the dog owners voluntarily sharing their time, dogs and homes for this study.

References

1. Abrantes, R.: Dog language. Wakan Tanka Publishers (1997)
2. Aslaksen, S., Aukrust, K.: Hundens adferd når den er hjemme alene. Master Thesis, Institutt for Husdyr- og Akvakulturvitenskap, Norway (2003)
3. Beerda, B., et al.: The use of saliva cortisol, urinary cortisol, and catecholamine measurements for a noninvasive assessment of stress responses in dogs. Hormones and Behavior 30(3), 272–279 (1996)
4. Beerda, B., et al.: Behavioural and hormonal indicators of enduring environmental stress in dogs. Animal Welfare 9(1), 49–62 (2000)
5. Campbell, S.A., et al.: Some effects of limited exercise on purpose-bred beagles. American Journal of Veterinary Research 49(8), 1298–1301 (1988)
6. Coppola, C.L., Grandin, T., Enns, R.M.: Human interaction and cortisol: can human contact reduce stress for shelter dogs? Physiology & Behavior 87, 537–541 (2006)

7. Coren, S.: How dogs think: understanding the canine mind. Simon and Schuster, New York (2005)
8. de Weerth, C., et al.: Measurement of cortisol in small quantities of saliva. Clinical Chemistry 49(4), 658–660 (2003)
9. Dognition: see the world through your best friends eyes. http://www.dognition.com
10. Dreschel, N.A., Granger, D.A.: Methods of collection for salivary cortisol measurement in dogs. Hormones and Behavior 55(1), 163–168 (2009)
11. Evans, M.: Dogs: Their secret lives. Channel 4 Television (2013)
12. Gácsi, M., et al.: Explaining dog wolf differences in utilizing human pointing gestures: selection for synergistic shifts in the development of some social skills. PLoS One 4(8) (2009)
13. Geurtsen, A.: An experiment in animal welfare informatics: effects of digital interactive gameplay on the psychological welfare of home alone dogs. Master of Science Thesis, Media Technology program, Leiden University (2014)
14. Grooten, E.: Playing with pigs: researching the complex relationship between pigs and humans through game design. http://www.playingwithpigs.nl
15. Hare, B., et al.: The domestication hypothesis for dogs' skills with human communication: a response to Udell et al (2008) and Wynne et al (2008). Animal Behaviour 79, e1–e6 (2010)
16. Hare, B., Woods, V.: The genius of dogs: discovering the unique intelligence of man's best friend. Oneworld Publications, London (2013)
17. Hawkley, L.C., Cacioppo, J.T.: Loneliness matters: a theoretical and empirical review of consequences and mechanisms. Annals of Behavioral Medicine 40, 218–227 (2010)
18. Hekman, J.P., Karas, A.Z., Dreschel, N.A.: Salivary cortisol concentrations and behavior in a population of healthy dogs hospitalized for elective procedures. Applied Animal Behaviour Science 141(3), 149–157 (2012)
19. Hertz, G.: Cockroach controlled mobile robot. http://www.conceptlab.com/roachbot
20. Herzing, D.: Could we speak the langauge of dolphins? video. In: TED 2013 (2013)
21. Hirskyj-Douglas, I., Read, J.C.: Animal computer interaction design. In: ACM-W 2014, Manchester, UK (2014)
22. Holze, R., Shimoyama, I.: Locomotion control of a bio-robotic system via electric stimulation. In: Proc. IEEE/RSJ Int. Conf. on Intelligent Robots and Systems, vol. 3, pp. 1514–1519 (1997)
23. Animal hospital of North Asheville: What's your dog's style? Breeds, toys and play styles. http://www.ahna.net/what-your-puppys-style-breeds-toys-and-play-styles
24. Jensen, P.: The behavioural biology of dogs. Cabi Publishing, UK (2007)
25. Lamers, M.H., van Eck, W.: Why simulate? hybrid biological-digital games. In: Di Chio, C., et al. (eds.) EvoApplications 2012. LNCS, vol. 7248, pp. 214–223. Springer, Heidelberg (2012)
26. Maharbiz, M.M., Hirotaka, S.: Cyborg beetles. Scientific American 303(6), 94–99 (2010)
27. Mancini, C.: Animal-computer interaction: a manifesto. Interactions 18, 69–73 (2011)
28. Mancini, C., Zamansky, A.: Charting unconquered territories: intelligent systems for animal welfare. In: 40th Annual Convention of the Society for the Study of Artificial Intelligence and the Simulation of Behaviour, pp. 181–182 (2014)

29. Mankoff, D., et al.: Supporting interspecies social awareness: using peripheral displays for distributed pack awareness. In: Proc UIST, 2005, pp. 253–258 (2005)
30. Miklósi, A., et al.: A simple reason for a big difference: wolves do not look back at humans, but dogs do. Current Biology 13(9), 763–766 (2003)
31. Miklósi, A., et al.: A comparative study of the use of visual communicative signals in interactions between dogs (canis familiaris) and humans and cats (felis catus) and humans. Journal of Comparative Psychology 119(2), 179 (2005)
32. Miklósi, A., Soproni, K.: A comparative analysis of animals' understanding of the human pointing gesture. Animal Cognition 9(2), 81–93 (2006)
33. Miller, P.E., Murphy, C.J.: Vision in dogs. Journal of the American Veterinary Medical Association 207(12), 1623–1634 (1995)
34. Noz, F., An, J.: Cat cat revolution: an interspecies gaming experience. In: Proc. SIGCHI Conf. on Human Factors in Computing Systems, pp. 2661–2664 (2011)
35. Overall, K.L., Dyer, D.: Enrichment strategies for laboratory animals from the viewpoint of clinical veterinary behavioral medicine: emphasis on cats and dogs. ILAR Journal 46(2), 202–216 (2005)
36. Paarsovaara, S., et al.: The secret life of my dog: design and evaluation of paw-tracker concept. In: Proc. 13th Int. Conf. on Human Computer Interaction with Mobile Devices and Services, pp. 231–240 (2011)
37. Rehn, T., Keeling, L.J.: The effect of time left alone at home on dog welfare. Applied Animal Behaviour Science 129, 129–135 (2011)
38. Resner, B. I.: Rover@home: computer mediated remote interaction between humans and dogs. MSc Thesis, Media Arts and Sciences program, Massachusetts Institute of Technology (2001)
39. Savage-Rumbaugh, S., Fields, W.M., Taglialatela, J.P.: Ape consciousness—human consciousness: a perspective informed by language and culture. American Zoologist 40(6), 910–921 (2000)
40. Scaglia, E., et al.: Video analysis of adult dogs when left home alone. Journal of Veterinary Behavior: Clinical Applications and Research 8(6), 412–417 (2013)
41. Skinner, B.F.: Pigeons in a pelican. American Psychologist 15, 28 (1960)
42. Talwar, S.K., et al.: Behavioural neuroscience: rat navigation guided by remote control. Nature 417(6884), 37–38 (2002)
43. Tan, R.T.K.C., Cheok, A.D., Teh, J.K.S.: Metazoa ludens: mixed reality environment for playing computer games with pets. International Journal of Virtual Reality 5(3), 53–58 (2006)
44. Tuber, D.S., et al.: Behavioral and glucocorticoid responses of adult domestic dogs (canis familiaris) to companionship and social separation. Journal of Comparative Psychology 110, 103–108 (1996)
45. van Eck, W., Lamers, M.H.: Animal controlled computer games: Playing pac-man against real crickets. In: Harper, R., Rauterberg, M., Combetto, M. (eds.) ICEC 2006. LNCS, vol. 4161, pp. 31–36. Springer, Heidelberg (2006)
46. van Eck, W., Lamers, M.H.: Hybrid biological-digital systems in artistic and entertainment computing. Leonardo Journal of Arts, Sciences and Technology 46, 151–158 (2013)
47. Vestrum, I. G.: Aleneatferd hos hunder som lever i en gruppe. Master Thesis, Husdyrvitenskap program, Institutt for Husdyr- og Akvakulturvitenskap (2009)
48. Wingrave, C.A., et al.: Early explorations of CAT: canine amusement and training. In: Proc. CHI EA, pp. 2661–2670 (2010)
49. Wolfe, T.L.: Policy, program and people: the three p's to well-being. In: Mench, J.A., Krulisch, L. (eds.) Canine Research Environment, pp. 41–47. Scientists Center for Animal Welfare, Bethseda (1990)

KINJIRO: Animatronics for Children's Reading Aloud Training

Hisanao Nakadai[1], Lee Seung Hee[2,3,4], Muneo Kitajima[2,3,4], and Junichi Hoshino[2,3,4]

[1] University of Tsukuba, Graduate School of Systems and Information Engineering,
1-1-1 Tennodai, Tsukuba, Ibaraki 305-8573 Japan
[2] University of Tsukuba, Art and Design, 1-1-1 Tennodai, Tsukuba, Ibaraki 305-8577 Japan
[3] Nagaoka University of Technology, Management and Information Systems Engineering,
1603-1 Tomiokacho, Nagaoka, Niigata, 940-2188, Japan
[4] University of Tsukuba, Systems and Information Engineering, 1-1-1 Tennodai, Tsukuba,
Ibaraki 305-8573 Japan

Abstract. Reading aloud during childhood is fundamental to develop the necessary power of expression and imagination needed in our society, and is adopted by many elementary schools in language classes. Teaching reading aloud focuses on the ability to adjust the way one reads to improve the understanding of the listener. However, it is difficult for children not in class to correctly read aloud while being aware of the listeners. In this paper we propose a support robot that will allow children to enjoy reading aloud by themselves or with their family, and encourage them to do so while paying attention to their listeners.

Keywords: Animatronics robots, Aloud Training, Robot therapy.

1 Introduction

Reading books does not only enrich our lives but it is also said to be the foundation for acquiring the expressiveness and imagination needed to cope with the ever-changing environment and communication in our society [1]. To support such reading activities it is fundamental to start reading sentences aloud since early childhood, and for this reason elementary schools actively incorporate it in reading comprehension classes [2][3][4][5][6][7][8].

The elementary school read-aloud guidance focuses on the ability to adjust the voice volume, intonation and accent, to think about the listener while reading, and to read in an easy to understand way [5][6][7]. However, when children are not in class and without a listener it is difficult for them to read aloud as if reading for someone. In addition it has been pointed out that the embarrassment due to reading aloud in front of other people and the fear of being corrected when doing a mistake leads to developing the awareness of not being good at reading. R.E.A.D. (Reading Education Assistance Dogs) is a program conducted in the United States where children with reading difficulties read aloud with a dog as a companion, so that they can feel at ease while training regularly and improving their reading comprehension.

© IFIP International Federation for Information Processing 2015
K. Chorianopoulos et al. (Eds.): ICEC 2015, LNCS 9353, pp. 252–260, 2015.
DOI: 10.1007/978-3-319-24589-8_19

In this paper we propose KINJIRO, an autonomous animatronics robot for children which allows them to enjoy reading aloud with their families or by themselves, and encourages listener-aware reading. Animatronics refers to the use of robotics to imitate the appearance, motion and emotion expression of humans, animals and other characters that appear in movies and theme parks. In our system, in addition to a familiar external appearance and life-like motion generation, we added perceptive

Fig. 1. KINJIRO.

behaviors to give the feeling that the robot is listening, such as turning in the direction of the reader's voice, nodding and blinking. Thanks to an evaluation experiment with a group of elementary school children we were able to confirm the improvement of both reading span when reading by memory and listener-aware behavior.

2   Animatronics for Supporting Reading Aloud

With our reading aloud support animatronics robot (KINJIRO), not only the child can read while aware of it as a listener, but it also adopts psychological elements present in animals that relieves the child from shyness and stress (Fig.1) [11][12][13]. Parents and teachers can check how often and how long the child has been reading aloud using an application for smartphones.

2.1   Animatronics Control

When a child reads aloud, having someone willing to listen increases the motivation and the chances of continuing this activity [12]. For this reason KINJIRO reacts to the child by turning its head in the direction of the voice, nodding and showing happiness. Sound sensors in each ear of KINJIRO sample the nearby sounds at every millisecond. The neck has two degrees of freedom so that it can move up, down, left and right; ears and eyelids have one degree of freedom. When the child starts reading, if during a given interval the sensors value keeps exceeding a threshold the nodding phase begins. During this phase, if the value goes under a predicted limit it is interpreted as a pause in the sentence and triggers the execution of a nod. If the difference between left and right sensor values is sufficiently big, the head turns to face the voice. Nodding is accompanied by ear movements and blinking(Fig.2).

Fig. 2. Motion control of KINJIRO

2.2   Robot's Exterior

KINJIRO's exterior is made to let the child feel at ease and naturally induce helping behaviors in him. According to Lorenz, the characteristics of children cuteness (baby schema) activates in others the motivation to care for them [13]. Moreover, touching something fluffy like a dog's fur is considered to have a relaxing effect. For these reasons, KINJIRO is shaped to be seen as a baby animal, characterized by a big head, big mouth and small arms and legs. It is also covered in an elastic skin made of the same silicon used for special effects makeup. This makes it soft and comfortable to the touch, and allows for greater expressivity. The skin is covered with fur to resemble the touch and fluffiness of a real dog.

3   Evaluation Experiment

3.1   Goals

The goal of the experiment is to evaluate, by analyzing video recordings of children reading aloud with KINJIRO, their listener-awareness and enjoyment while reading.

Fig. 3. Internal mechanism and Production of skin.

3.2   Procedure

A child (elementary school, 2nd to 4th grade, male and female, 5 people) is made to sit in a room in front of KINJIRO and asked to read aloud. The text used for the experiment is taken from the textbook used in their respective language classes. By using a text which the child is used to, it is possible to reduce the difference among the children's reading skills. The reading experiment was repeated in three different conditions (in arbitrary order).:

- KINJIRO is present and moving (MK)
- KINJIRO is present and not moving (NMK)
- KINJIRO is not present (A)

After the experiment, children are asked to answer a questionnaire about their impressions on KINJIRO.

3.3   Video Analysis

After performing the experiment the recorded video data is analyzed. The text being read, the children's speech transcript and behavior (gaze, posture) and the behavior of KINJIRO are annotated using a timeline to examine their correspondences (Tab. 1, 2). Speech analysis is performed through ELAN, a dialog analysis tool [17].

Table 1. Description symbol of reading aloud behavior.

Transcript	content
Behavior	
B	Subjects move the eyes to book
BP	tracing books with a finger
LB	Subjects to lift the book
VR	Subjects move the eyes to the robot
Angle of	
head Fa	Front
Dla	down a little
Da	down

Table 2. Description symbol of the behavior of the robot.

Transcript	content
Nod	Nod
Ear	moving the ear
Blink	Blink
TF	Turn around

3.4   Questionnaire

To evaluate the impressions of the children about reading aloud and KINJIRO, a questionnaire in interview format has been carried out using a question panel. Q1, Q2, Q3 and Q5 use a five grade scale (5: Strongly agree, 4: Agree, 3: Neutral, 2: Disagree,

1: Strongly disagree), Q4 is an open question, Q6 and Q7 use a different five grade scale (5: Strongly like, 4: Like, 3: Neither, 2: Dislike, 1: Strongly dislike), Q8 has two options (with or without the presence of the robot).

—Questionnaire for a single subject—

Q1: Do you think that the robot listened to you when reading?

Q2: Do you think that the robot behavior changed in response to different ways of reading?

Q3: Do you want to read a book to the robot again?

Q4: How was reading a book to the robot?

Q5: Did you enjoy reading a book to the robot?

Q6: Do you like reading aloud?

Q7: After reading to the robot, did you start liking reading aloud more?

Q8: Which one was more interesting?

4   Evaluation Results

The results of the questionnaire are shown in Fig. 4. The overall impressions of KINJIRO are positive. Before the experiment, many participants gave neutral or negative answers to Q6; after the experiment, there was an increase in positive answers. Regarding Q8, most children reported a more enjoyable reading experience with KINJIRO than when reading by themselves.

Figure 5 shows a sample of the video analysis for test subject A, revealing the subject's behavior while reading aloud. The video analysis results for each subject are presented in Figs.4 and 5, and the results of the behavioral and speech features are presented in Figs. 6 and 7, respectively. The purple regions in Fig. 6 indicate when children are studying the book. During the periods indicated in blue, the children are shaking their bodies, touching their bodies with their hands, or performing other redundant movements. The red regions denote moments of looking at KINJIRO. When alone or in the presence of a stationary KINJIRO, all subjects showed many unnecessary movements and focused little on reading aloud. A moving KINJIRO attracted much more attention. However, even when KINJIRO was stationary, the children tended to look into its eyes. This behavior indicates that the children were aware of KINJIRO's presence, and thus better focused on reading aloud.

The green regions in Fig. 7 represent times of normal verbal reading. In the gray regions, the voice was small and difficult to hear, and white regions denote times of unnatural interruption or silence. Orange, red, and yellow represent various voice intensities. Subjects 1, 4, and 5 lowered their voices and lapsed into long silences when KINJIRO was stationary. Overall, KINJIRO's presence enriched the expressiveness of the subjects' speech The exception was subject 3, whose reading was fluent but expressionless regardless of whether KINJIRO was present or not, or (if present) whether moving or stationary. This subject was unaffected by KINJIRO even after a longer trial. From this result, we understand that perceptions of KINJIRO are subjective and can vary.

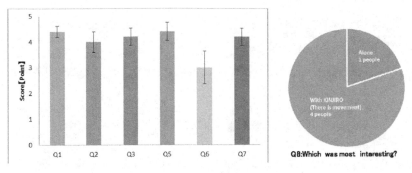

Fig. 4. Questionnaire results.

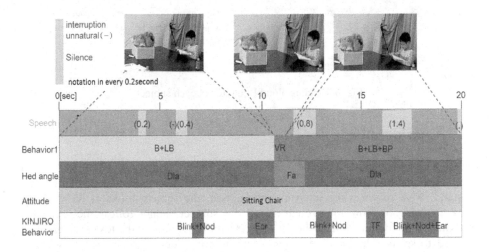

Fig. 5. Appearance of the experimental and Description of reading aloud behavior example

Overall, children who experienced difficulties in reading aloud by themselves or in the presence of a stationary KINJIRO developed clearer speech patterns when KINJIRO was present and active. The children also injected emphasis into their reading, spoke longer, and increased their expressiveness. Consequently, their reading was more easily understood. When KINJIRO was present and moving, the unnecessary movements almost disappeared, and children focused on their reading task. Moreover, the children frequently raised the book when reading and looked at the robot. According to the questionnaire results, the children felt that KINJIRO was listening to them and reacting to their reading.

These results affirm that a lifelike robot that reacts to reading aloud can improve children's verbal reading, because the children become aware of the robot's presence. Therefore, the robot can stimulate training even in children who lack the natural talent for reading aloud.

H. Nakadai et al.

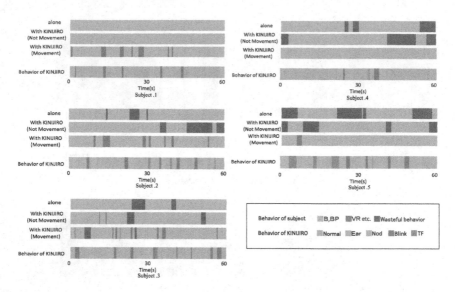

Fig. 6. Reading aloud Behavior of each subject.

5 Considerations

In Fig. 5 about subject 1, it can be observed how when reading with KINJIRO present there are numerous silences and interruptions, and the voice becomes difficult to understand. Near to when the interruptions happen, the subject looks at KINJIRO or takes up the book from the ground. Since the subject cannot follow the text when speaking while looking at the robot, it is necessary to memorize the text once and then proceed to speak. The increase in interruptions and silences when reading with the robot are probably due to this reason.

The amount of text one is able to correctly recall is called reading span, and is strongly related to one's reading comprehension capability [1][23][24]. From the data obtained from our experiment we are lead to believe that KINJIRO has a good influence on the reading span. Regarding the questionnaire, subject A's results were positive about enjoying reading aloud with KINJIRO and in Q4 answered that felt interested in the book when reading it to the robot. These results show how the subject pays attention to KINJIRO as a listener and enjoys reading aloud while looking forward to its reactions.

About subject 4, when KINJIRO is present parts of the text difficult to understand decreased and irrelevant behaviors too disappeared. In Q1 subject B answered that he thinks that KINJIRO is listening when reading aloud, thus confirming the fact that he is conscious of the robot as a listener. However, in Q8 he answered that he enjoyed reading by himself more than when with the robot. This suggests that reading with KINJIRO indeed improves reading aloud, but for the subject it may have been a source of nervousness.

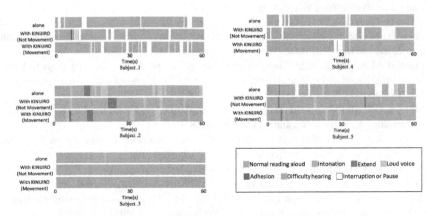

Fig. 7. Reading aloud state of each subject.

6 Conclusions

In this paper, we constructed an animatronics robot that acts as a listener, borrowing psychological elements from pets named KINJIRO. The aim was to instill enjoyment in reading aloud to a perceived listener whether alone or with family. To evaluate the efficacy of the robot as a learning tool, we recruited children to read aloud to the robot and analyzed the results using videos and questionnaires. All subjects increased their voice volume in the presence of an active KINJIRO, and their focus on the reading task and awareness of the listener was improved. Eighty percent of the subjects reported an enhanced reading experience. Since children widely differ in their personalities and capabilities, we will recruit more test subjects and extend the length of our experiments in future work. From the results, we will elucidate how a robot listener influences the verbal reading skills of children.

References

1. Saito, T.: Reading ability. Iwanami Shoten (2002)
2. Maiko, T.: Role of Oral Reading in the Development of Reading Ability: A Review. The Japan Association of Educational Psychology 61(1), 95–111 (2013)
3. Maiko, T.: Cognitive Processes in Sentence Comprehension During Silent and Oral Reading: Role of Attentional Resources and Phonological Encoding. The Japanese Journal of Educational Psychology 55(4), 538–549 (2007)
4. Takahashi, M., Tanaka, A.: Cognitive Processing during Silent and Oral Reading: Cognitive Load and Phonological Representation. Cognitive Studies: Bulletin of the Japanese Cognitive Science Society 18(4), 595–603 (2011).
   MEXT, http://www.mext.go.jp/a_menu/shotou/clarinet5./002/003/002/007.htm
5. Ingenuity of guidance that put the ability to read with an emphasis on reading aloud
6. http://www.ginowanokn.ed.jp/UserFiles/File/kyouikukenkyujyo/keikyuhoukoku/elementary/3_4.pdf

7. Language arts learning activities proposed.
   `http://www.shiribeshi-etc.jp/kyouiku/sidouan/`
8. Shaw, D.M.: Man's Best Friend as a Reading Facilitator. The Reading Teacher (publication of the International Reading Association) 66(5), 365–371 (2013)
9. Jalongo, M.R.: What are all These Dogs Doing at School? Using Therapy Dogs to Promote Children's Reading Practice. Using Therapy Dogs To Promote Children's Reading Practice. Childhood Education 81(3) (2005)
10. Melson, G.F.: Why the wild things are. Harvard University Press, Cambridge (2001)
11. Yokoyama, A.: What is the animal therapy. NHK Books (1996)
12. Lorenz, K.: Die angeborenen Formen möglicher Erfahrung [Innate forms of potential expe-rience]. Zeitschrift für Tierpsychologie 5, 235–409 (1943)
13. Nishizaka, A.: Perspective of mutual behavior analysis. Kanekoshobo (1997)
14. Masanao, M., et al.: The predictive power of working memory task for reading comprehension: An investigation using reading span test:An investigation using reading span test. The Japanese Journal of Educational Psychology 77(6), 495–503 (2007)
15. Nakamura, M.: Reading Ability of Hearing-Impaired Children (3)- Relative to Reading Span. Research Bulletin 7, 91–98 (2000)
16. Procedure of video analysis by ELAN.
    `http://shower.human.waseda.ac.jp/~m-kouki/pukiwiki_public/16.html`

Rogue-Like Games as a Playground for Artificial Intelligence – Evolutionary Approach

Vojtech Cerny and Filip Dechterenko

Charles University in Prague, Czech Republic
{woitee,filip.dechterenko}@gmail.com

Abstract. Rogue-likes are difficult computer RPG games set in a procedurally generated environment. Attempts have been made at playing these algorithmically, but few of them succeeded. In this paper, we present a platform for developing artificial intelligence (AI) and creating procedural content generators (PCGs) for a rogue-like game Desktop Dungeons. As an example, we employ evolutionary algorithms to recombine greedy strategies for the game. The resulting AI plays the game better than a hand-designed greedy strategy and similarly well to a mediocre player – winning the game 72% of the time. The platform may be used for additional research leading to improving rogue-like games and general PCGs.

Keywords: artificial intelligence, computer games, evolutionary algorithms, rogue-like

1 Introduction

Rogue-like games, as a branch of the RPG genre, have existed for a long time. They descend from the 1980 game "Rogue" and some old examples, such as NetHack (1987), are played even to this day. Many more of these games are made every year, and their popularity is apparent.

A rogue-like is a single-player, turn-based, highly difficult RPG game, featuring a randomized environment and permanent death[1]. The player takes the role of a hero, who enters the game's environment (often a dungeon) with a very difficult goal. Achieving the goal requires a lot of skill, game experience and perhaps a little bit of luck.

Such a game, bordering between RPG and puzzle genres, is challenging for artificial intelligence (AI) to play. One often needs to balance between being reactive (dealing with current problems) and proactive (planning towards the main goal). Attempts at solving rogue-likes by AI have been previously made [9,2,7], usually using a set of hand-coded rules as basic reasoning, and being to some extent successful.

---

[1] The game offers no save/load features, it is always replayed from beginning to end.

© IFIP International Federation for Information Processing 2015
K. Chorianopoulos et al. (Eds.): ICEC 2015, LNCS 9353, pp. 261–271, 2015.
DOI: 10.1007/978-3-319-24589-8_20

On the other hand, the quality of a rogue-like can heavily depend on its procedural content generator (PCG), which usually creates the whole environment. Procedural generation [14] has been used in many kinds of games [17,5], and thus, the call for high-quality PCG is clear [8]. However, evaluating the PCG brings issues [4,16], such as how to balance between the criteria of high quality and high variability.

But a connection can be made to the former – we could conveniently use the PCG to evaluate the artificial player and similarly, use the AI to evaluate the content generator. The latter may also lead to personalized PCGs (creating content for a specific kind of players) [15].

In this paper, we present a platform for developing AI and PCG for a rogue-like game Desktop Dungeons [11]. It is intended as an alternative to other used AI or PCG platforms, such as the Super Mario AI Benchmark [6] or SpelunkBots [13]. AI platforms have even been created for a few rogue-like games, most notably NetHack [2,7]. However, Desktop Dungeons has some characteristics making it easier to use than the other. Deterministic actions and short play times help the AI, while small dungeon size simplifies the work of a PCG.

And as such, more experimental and resource demanding approaches may be tried. The platform could also aid other kinds of research or teaching AI, as some people create their own example games for this purpose [12, Chapter 21.2], where Desktop Dungeons could be used instead.

The outline of this paper is as follows. First, we introduce the game to the reader, then we proceed to describe our platform, and finally, we will show how to use it to create a good artificial rogue-like player using evolutionary algorithms.

2   Desktop Dungeons Description

Desktop Dungeons by QCF Design [11] is a single-player computer RPG game that exhibits typical rogue-like features. The player is tasked with entering a dungeon full of monsters and, through careful manipulation and experience gain, slaying the boss (the biggest monster).

Disclaimer: The following explanation is slightly simplified. More thorough and complete rules can be found at the Desktop Dungeons wiki page [1].

2.1   Dungeon

The dungeon is a 20×20 grid viewed from the top. The grid cells may contain monsters, items, glyphs, or the hero (player). Every such object, except for the hero, is static - does not move[2]. Only a 3×3 square around the hero is revealed in the beginning, and the rest must be explored by moving the hero next to it. Screenshot of the dungeon early in the game can be seen in Fig. 1.

---

[2] Some spells and effects move monsters, but that is quite uncommon and can be ignored for our purpose.

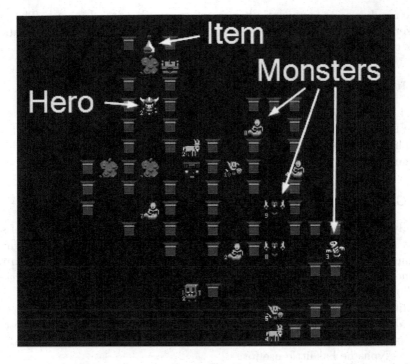

Fig. 1. Screenshot of the dungeon, showing the hero, monsters, and an item (a health potion). The dark areas are the unexplored parts of the dungeon.

2.2 Hero

The hero is the player-controlled character in the dungeon and holds a set of values. Namely: health, mana, attack power, the number of health/mana potions, and his spell glyphs. The hero can also perform a variety of actions. He can attack a monster, explore unrevealed parts of the dungeon, pick up items and glyphs, cast spells or convert glyphs into bonuses.

2.3 Exploring

Unrevealed grid cells can be explored by moving the hero next to them (at least diagonally). Not only does exploration reveal what lies underneath for the rest of the game, but it also serves one additional purpose – restoring health and mana. Every square explored will restore health equal to the hero's level and 1 mana. This means that the dungeon itself is a scarce resource that has to be managed wisely. It shall be noted, though, that monsters heal also when hero explores, so this cannot be used to gain an edge over damaged monsters.

2.4 Combat

Whenever the hero bumps into a monster, a combat exchange happens. The higher level combatant strikes first (monster strikes first when tied). The first attacker reduces his opponent's health by *exactly* his attack power. The other attacker, if alive, then does the same. No other action causes any monster to attack the hero.

2.5   Items

Several kinds of items can be found lying on the ground. These comprise of a Health Powerup, Mana Powerup, Attack Powerup, Health Potion and a Mana Potion. These increase the hero's health, mana, attack power, and amount of health and mana potions respectively.

2.6   Glyphs

Spell glyphs are special items that each allow the hero to cast one kind of spell for it's mana cost. The hero starts with no glyphs, and can find them lying in the dungeon. Common spells include a Fireball spell, that directly deals damage to a monster (without it retaliating), and a Kill Protect spell, that saves the hero from the next killing blow.

Additionally, a spell glyph can be converted to a racial bonus - a specific bonus depending on the hero's race. These are generally small stat increases or an extra potion. The spell cannot be cast anymore, so the hero should only convert glyphs he has little use for.

2.7   Hero Races and Classes

Before entering the dungeon, the player chooses a race (Human, Elf, etc.) and a class (Warrior, Wizard, etc.) of his hero. The race determines only the reward for converting a glyph, but classes can modify the game in a completely unique way.

2.8   Other

The game has a few other unmentioned mechanics. The player can enter special "challenge" dungeons, he can find altars and shops in the dungeon, but all that is far beyond the basics we'll need for our demonstration. As mentioned, more can be found at the Desktop Dungeons wiki [1].

3   AI Platform

Desktop Dungeons has two parameters rarely seen in other similar games. Every action in the game is deterministic[3] (the only unknown is the unrevealed part of the dungeon) and the game is limited to 20×20 grid cells and never extends

---

[3] Some rare effects have probabilistic outcomes, but with a proper game setting, this may be completely ignored.

beyond. These may allow for better and more efficient AI solutions, and may be advantageously utilized when using search techniques, planning, evaluating fitness functions, etc.

On the other hand, Desktop Dungeons is a very interesting environment for AI. It is complex, difficult, and as such can show usefulness of various approaches. Achieving short-term and long-term goals must be balanced, and thus, simple approaches tend to not do well, and must be specifically adjusted for the task. Not much research has been done on solving rogue-like games altogether, only recently was a famous, classic title of this genre — NetHack — beaten by AI [7].

From the perspective of a PCG, Desktop Dungeons is similarly interesting. The size of the dungeon is very limited, so attention to detail should be paid. If one has an artificial player, the PCG could use him as a measure of quality, even at runtime, to produce only the levels the artificial player found enjoyable or challenging.

This is why we created a programming interface (API) to Desktop Dungeons, together with a Java framework for easy AI and PCG prototyping and implementation. We used the alpha version of Desktop Dungeons, because it is more direct, contains less story content and player progress features, runs in a browser, and the main gameplay is essentially the same as in the full version.

The API is a modified part of the game code that can connect to another application, such as our framework, via a WebSocket (TCP) protocol and provide access to the game by sending and receiving messages. A diagram of the API usage is portrayed in Fig. 2.

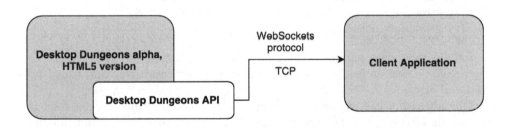

Fig. 2. The API, as a part of the game, connects to an application using a WebSockets protocol and provides access to the game by receiving and sending messages.

The framework allows the user to focus on high-level programming, and have the technical details hidden from him. It efficiently keeps track of the dungeon elements, and provides full game simulation, assisting any search techniques and heuristics that might be desired. The developed artificial players can be tested against the default PCG of the game, which has the advantage of being designed to provide challenging levels for human players, or one can generate the dungeon on his own and submit it to the game. Intermediate ways can also be employed, such as editing the dungeons generated by the game's PCG to e.g. adjust the difficulty or reduce the complexity of the game.

The framework is completely open-source and its repository can be found at `https://bitbucket.org/woitee/desktopdungeons-java-framework`.

4 Evolutionary Approach

To demonstrate the possibilities of the Desktop Dungeons API, we have implemented an evolutionary algorithm (EA) [10] to fine-tune greedy AI. A general explanation of EAs is, however, out of the scope of this paper.

4.1 Simple Greedy Algorithm

The original greedy algorithm was a simple strategy for each moment of the game. It is best described by a list of actions, ordered by priority.

1. Try picking up an item.
2. Try killing a monster (prefer strongest).
3. Explore.

The hero tries to perform the highest rated applicable action, and when none exists, the run ends. Killing the monster was attempted by just simulating attacks, fireballs and drinking potions until one of the participants died. If successful, the sequence of actions was acted out. This can be modeled as a similar list of priority actions:

1. Try casting the Fireball spell.
2. Try attacking.
3. Try drinking a potion.

Some actions have parameters, e.g. how many potions is the hero allowed to use against a certain level of monster. These were set intuitively and tuned by trial and error.

This algorithm has yielded good results. Given enough time (weeks, tens of thousands of runs), this simple AI actually managed to luck out and kill the boss. This was very surprising, we thought the game would be much harder to beat, even with chance on our side. It was probably caused by the AI always calculating how to kill every monster it sees, which is tedious and error-prone for human players to do.

4.2 Design of the Evolution

We used two ordered lists of elementary strategies in the greedy approach, but we hand-designed them and probably have not done that optimally. This would become increasingly more difficult, had we added more strategies to the list. We'll solve this by using evolutionary algorithms.

We'll call the strategies used to select actions in the game **maingame strategies** and the strategies used when trying to kill monsters **attack strategies**.

Each strategy has preconditions (e.g. places to explore exists) and may have parameters. We used as many strategies as we could think of, which resulted in a total of 7 maingame strategies and 13 attack strategies.

The evolutionary algorithm was tasked with ordering both lists of strategies, and setting their parameters. It should be emphasized, that this is far from an easy task. Small imperfections in the strategy settings accumulate over the run, and thus only the very refined individuals have some chance of slaying the final boss.

However, the design makes the AI ignore some features of the game. It doesn't buy items in shops nor does it worship any gods. These mechanics are nevertheless quite advanced, and should not be needed to win the basic setting of the game. Using them can have back-biting effects if done improperly, so we just decided to ignore them to keep the complexity low.

On a side note, this design is to a certain extent similar to *linear genetic programming* [3].

4.3 Fitness Function

Several criteria could be considered when designing the fitness function. An easy solution would be to use the game's score, which is awarded after every run. However, the score takes into account some attributes that do not directly contribute towards winning the game, e.g. awarding bonuses for low completion time, or never dropping below 20% of health.

We inspired ourselves by the game's scoring, but simplified it. Our basic fitness function evaluates the game's state at the end of the run and looks like this:

$$fitness = 10 \cdot xp + 150 \cdot healthpotions$$
$$+ 75 \cdot manapotions$$
$$+ health$$

The main contributor is the total gained XP (experience points, good runs get awarded over a hundred), and additionally, we slightly reward leftover health and potions. We take these values from three runs and add them together. Three runs are too few to have low variance on subsequent evaluations, but it yields far better results than evaluating only one run, and more runs than three would just take too much time to complete.

If the AI manages to kill the boss in any of the runs, we triple the fitness value of that run. This may look a little over the top, but slaying the final monster is very difficult, and if one of the individuals is capable of doing so, we want to spread it's gene in the population. Note, that we don't expect our AI to kill the boss reliably, 5-10% chance is more what we are aiming for.

We have tried a variety of fitness functions, taking into account other properties of the game state and with different weights. For a very long time, the performance of the bots was similiar to the hand-designed greedy strategy. But, by analyzing more of the game, we have constructed roughly the fitness function above and the performance has hugely improved.

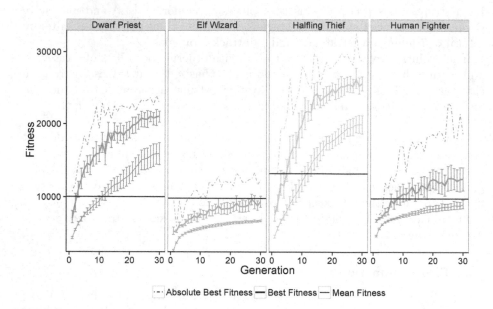

Fig. 3. Graphs describing the fitnesses of the evolution for each of our class-race settings. The three curves describe the total best fitness ever encountered, the best fitnesses averaged over all runs and the mean fitnesses averaged over all runs. The vertical line indicates the point, where the AI has killed the boss and won the game at least once in three attempts. This fitness value is different for each setting, since some race-class combinations can gain more hitpoints or health potions than other, both of which directly increase their fitness (see Section 4.3).

The improvement lies in the observation of how can the bots improve during the course of evolution. Strong bots in the early state will probably just use objectively good strategies, and not make complete blunders in strategy priorities, such as exploring the whole level before trying to kill anything. This should already make them capable of killing quite a few monsters. Then, the bots can improve and fine-tune their settings, to use less and less resources (mainly potions) to kill as many monsters as possible. And towards the late state of evolution, the bots can play the game so effectively, they may still have enough potions and other resources to kill the final boss and beat the game. The current fitness function supports this improvement, because the fitness values of the hypothetical bots in subsequent stages of evolution continuously rises.

After implementation, this was exactly the course the bots have evolved through. Note, that saving at least a few potions for the final boss fight is basically a necessary condition for success.

4.4 Genetic Operators

Priorities of the strategies are represented by floating point numbers in the $[0, 1]$ interval. Together with the strategy's parameter values, we can encode it as just a few floating point numbers, integers and booleans.

This representation allows us to use classical operators like one-/two-point crossovers and small change mutations. And they make good sense and work, but they are not necessarily optimal, and after some trial and error, we have started using a weighted average operator to crossover the priorities for better performance.

The AI evolved with these settings were just a little too greedy, often using all their potions in the early game, and even though they advanced far, they basically had no chance of beating the final boss. These strategies found quite a strong local optimum of the fitness, and we wanted to slightly punish them for it. We did so in two ways. Firstly, we rewarded leftover potions in our fitness value calculation, and secondly, a smart mutation was added, that modifies a few individuals from the population to not use potions to kill monsters of lower level than 5. After some balancing, this has shown itself to be effective.

Mating and natural selection was done by simple roulette, i.e. individuals were chosen with probability proportional to their fitness. This creates a rather low selection pressure, and together with a large enough number of individuals in a generation, the evolution should explore a large portion of the candidate space and tune the strategies finely.

4.5 Results

After experimentation, we settled to do final runs with a population of 100 individuals, evolving through 30 generations. The population seemed large enough to be exploring the field well, and the generations sufficient for the population to converge. We ran the EA on 4 computers for a week, with a different combination of hero class and race on each computer. The result was a total of 62 runs, every hero class and race setting completed a minimum of 12 full runs. A single evaluation of an individual takes about 2 seconds, and a single whole run finishes in about 14 hours (intel i5-3470 at 3.2GHz, 4GB RAM, two instances in parallel).

The data of the results contain a lot of good strategies, their qualities can be seen in Fig. 3. Every combination of hero race and class managed to beat the boss at least once, and the strongest evolved individual kills the boss 72% of time (averaged over 10000 runs). This is definitely more than we expected. Note that no AI can slay the boss 100% of the time, since the game's default PCG sometimes creates an obviously unbeatable level (e.g. all exits from the starting room surrounded by high level monsters).

The evolved strategies also vary from each other. Different race and class combinations employ different strategies, but variance occurs even among runs of the same configuration. This shows that Desktop Dungeons can be played in several ways, and that different initial settings require different approaches to be used, which makes the game more interesting for a human. The different success rates of the configurations can also be used as a hint which race–class combinations are more difficult to play than others, either to balance them in the game design, or to recommend the easier ones to a beginner.

5   Conclusion

We present a platform for creating AI and PCG for the rogue-like game Desktop Dungeons. As a demonstration, we created an artificial player by an EA adjusting greedy algorithms. This AI functioned better than the hand-made greedy algorithm, winning the game roughly three quarters of the time, compared to a winrate of much less than 1%, and being as successful as an average human player.

This shows that the game's original PCG worked quite well, not generating a great abundance of impossible levels, yet still providing a good challenge.

A lot of research is possible with this platform. AI could be improved by using more complex EAs, or created from scratch using any techniques, such as search, planning and others. The PCG may be improved to e.g. create more various challenges for the player, adjust difficulty for stronger/weaker players or reduce the number of levels that are impossible to win. For evaluating the PCG, we could advantageously utilize the AI, and note some statistics, such as winrate, how often are different strategies employed or number of steps to solve a level. A combination of these would then create a rating function.

Also, it would be very interesting to keep improving both the artificial player and the PCG iteratively by each other.

References

1. Desktop Dungeons - DDwiki, http://www.qcfdesign.com/wiki/DesktopDungeons (accessed: 12 May 2015)
2. Tactical Amulet Extraction Bot (TAEB) - Other Bots, http://taeb.github.io/bots.html (accessed: 12 May 2015)
3. Brameier, M.F., Banzhaf, W.: Linear Genetic Programming. Springer Science & Business Media (2007)
4. Dahlskog, S., Smith, G., Togelius, J.: A Comparative Evaluation of Procedural Level Generators in the Mario AI Framework. In: Proceedings of Foundations of Digital Games (2014)
5. Hendrikx, M., Meijer, S., Van Der Velden, J., Iosup, A.: Procedural content generation for games: A survey. ACM Transactions on Multimedia Computing, Communications, and Applications 9(1), 1–22 (2013)
6. Karakovskiy, S., Togelius, J.: The Mario AI Benchmark and Competitions. IEEE Transactions on Computational Intelligence and AI in Games 4(1), 55–67 (2012)
7. Krajíček, J.: NetHack Bot Framework. Master's thesis, Charles University in Prague. Czech Republic (2015) (in Czech)
8. Liapis, A., Yannakakis, G.N., Togelius, J.: Towards a Generic Method of Evaluating Game Levels. In: AIIDE (2013)

9. Mauldin, M.L., Jacobson, G., Appel, A.W., Hamey, L.G.C.: ROG-O-MATIC: a belligerent expert system (1983)
10. Mitchell, M.: An Introduction to Genetic Algorithms. MIT Press (1996)
11. QCF Design: Desktop Dungeons, http://www.desktopdungeons.net/ (accessed: 12 May 2015)
12. Russell, S., Norvig, P.: Artificial Intelligence: A Modern Approach, 3rd edn. Prentice Hall Press, Upper Saddle River (2009)
13. Scales, D., Thompson, T.: SpelunkBots API - An AI Toolset for Spelunky. In: IEEE Conference on Computational Intelligence and Games, pp. 1–8 (2014)
14. Shaker, N., Togelius, J., Nelson, M.J.: Procedural Content Generation in Games: A Textbook and an Overview of Current Research. Springer (2015)
15. Shaker, N., Yannakakis, G.N., Togelius, J.: Towards Automatic Personalized Content Generation for Platform Games. In: AIIDE (2010)
16. Smith, G.: The Seven Deadly Sins of PCG Research, http://sokath.com/main/blog/2013/05/23/ (accessed: 12 May 2015)
17. Togelius, J., Yannakakis, G.N., Stanley, K.O., Browne, C.: Search-based procedural content generation: A taxonomy and survey. IEEE Transactions on Computational Intelligence and AI in Games 3(3), 172–186 (2011)

Software Architectures and the Creative Processes in Game Development

Alf Inge Wang[1] and Njål Nordmark[2]

Norwegian University of Science and Technology,
N7491 Trondheim, Norway
alfw@idi.ntnu.no, njaal.nordmark@gmail.com

Abstract. Game development is different from traditional software engineering in that there are no real functional requirements and the customers buy and use the software only because it is engaging and fun. This article investigates how game developers think about and use software architecture in the development of games. Further, it looks at how creative development processes are managed and supported. The results presented in this article come from responses to a questionnaire and a survey among thirteen game developers. The research questions answered in this study are: what role does the software architecture play in game development, how do game developers manage changes to the software architecture, how are creative development processes managed and supported, and how has game development evolved the last couple of years. Some of our findings are that software architectures play a central role in game development where the focus is mainly on achieving software with good performance and high modifiability, creative processes are supported through flexible game engines and tools, use of scripting and dynamic loading of assets, and feature-based teams with both creative and technical professions represented, and game developers are incrementally using more game-specific engines, tools and middleware in their development now compared to earlier.

Keywords: Game development, Creative software development, Software architecture.

1   Introduction

Game development can be incredibly challenging as game technology such as game engines and game platforms changes rapidly, and code modules crafted for specific games offer less than 30 percent reuse [1]. In the early days of the video games era, game development was carried out by small teams, where the software architectures were made out of a few modules such as 2d graphics, simulation, sound, streaming of i/o and main. At this time, there was not much focus on software architecture and software engineering, but rather on how to how to create an interesting game with the limited hardware resources available. The success of the video game industry, the development of game technology and the increasing demands from the players have resulted in large and complex games developed by large teams of multiple

© IFIP International Federation for Information Processing 2015
K. Chorianopoulos et al. (Eds.): ICEC 2015, LNCS 9353, pp. 272–285, 2015.
DOI: 10.1007/978-3-319-24589-8_21

professions. The evolution of games has also resulted in an evolution of game architectures that have grown in size and complexity [2]. Today, some game projects are very large, and the game software itself has a complex software architecture with many interconnected modules. One aspect that makes software architectures for games challenging is the absolute real-time requirements and the need to support the creative processes in game development [1]. Further, the development of AAA games (major game titles) requires a multitude of computer science skills [3] as well as other disciplines as art, game design, and audio/music [4]. The direct involvement of professions with very different background (e.g. the technical team vs. the creative team) poses challenges for how a game is developed.

So far, research related to game development and software engineering has focused on requirement engineering, and there is a lack of empirical work [5]. This article presents a study on how game developers think about and manage software architecture and the creative processes that characterize game development. The study investigates the relationship between creative design and software development, and how the technical and creative teams collaborate.

2   Material and Method

In this section, we present other research relevant to this article as well as the research goal, the research questions and the research method used.

2.1   Related Work

As far as we know, there are no similar studies that focus on software architecture and creative processes in game development. In this section, we will present work in the field of software engineering and game development.

As games over the years have grown into large complex systems, the video game industry is facing several software engineering challenges. Kanode and Haddad have identified the software engineering challenges in game development to be [6]: *Diverse Assets* – game development is not simply a process of producing source code, but involves assets such as 3D modes, textures, animations, sound, music, dialog, video, *Project Scope* – the scale of a video game can be massive and the game industry is known for poorly describing and defining project scope, *Game Publishing* - brining a video game to market involves convincing a game publisher to back up financially that will affect the deliveries and development process, *Project Management* – project management in game development can be extra hard due to very tight schedules and involvement of many professions, *Team Organization* - involves building teams that enhances communication across disciplines, *Development Process* – the development process includes more than just software development, and *Third-Party Technology* – for many game developers third-party software represents the core of the project due to rising development costs and increasing complexity. In this article we will mainly focus on project management, team organization, development process, and third-party technology.

Only one systematic literature review concerning game development was found [5]. This literature review assessed the state of the art on research concerning software engineering for video games. The result of this literature review showed that the main emphasis in this research domain is on requirement engineering, as well as coding tools and techniques. Articles related to requirement engineering focuses on the problem of going from a game concept that should be fun and engaging to functional requirements, and software architectures and software designs that can produce game software realizing the game concept [7]. The initial requirements for a game can be labeled emotional requirements that contain the game designer's intent and the means which the game designer expects the production team to induce that emotional state in the player [4]. Research on coding tools and techniques include articles on development of game engines [8-10], component-based game development [11], the use of game engines [12], development of serious games [1], and challenges and solutions for networked multiplayer games [13-17]. There are also several articles that focus on software architectures for games [18-20], and design patterns for games [21-23]. These articles propose various software architectures and/or design patterns to solve problems in game development. However, unlike our article, they say very little about the processes in which the architectures and patterns are used, and how the various roles in game development affect them.

There are also articles that focus on the game development process and the involved roles. In [24], Scacchi presents how the free and open source development practices in the game community differs from traditional software engineering practices. In [25], a survey of problems in game development is presented based on an analysis of postmortems written by various game developers. According to Flood, all game development postmortems say the same things: the project was delivered behind schedule; it contained many defects; the functionalities were not the ones that had originally been projected; and it took a lot of pressure and an immense number of development hours to complete the project [26]. Petrillo et al. further details the specific problems found in game development postmortems to be unrealistic scope, feature creep, cutting features during development, problems in the design, delayed schedules, technological problems, crunch time of the developers, lack of documentation, communication problems between teams, lack of effective tools, insufficient testing, difficulties in team building, great number of defects found in the development phase, loss of key personnel during development, and over budget [25]. The problems clearly differentiate game development from conventional software development are unrealistic scope, feature creep, lack of documentation, and crunch time. You can also find these problems in traditional software development, but not to such a great extent.

Another study by Petrillo and Pimenta investigates if (and how) principles and practices from Agile Methods have been adopted in game development by analyzing postmortems of game development projects [27]. The conclusion of this study was that game developers are adopting a set of agile practices, although informally. One aspect of agile methods that is very relevant to our research is the emphasis on frequently gathering relevant stakeholders to bridge the gap between of all involved in the project [28]. This is related to our study where we investigated how the creative team, the technical team and the management collaborate and coordinate.

2.2   Research Goal, Questions and Method

The research method used in case study is based on the Goal, Question, Metrics (GQM) approach where we first define a research goal (conceptual level), then define a set of research questions (operational level), and finally describe a set of metrics to answer the defined research questions (quantitative level) [29]. The metrics used in our study is a mixture of qualitative and quantitative data [30].

The research goal of this study was defined as the following using the GQL template:

The purpose of this study was to *examine how software architecture is used and how creative processed are managed* from the point of view *of a game developer* in the context *of video game development.*

The following research questions were defined by decomposing the research goal:

- **RQ1:** What role does software architecture play in game development?
- **RQ2:** How do game developers manage changes to the software architecture?
- **RQ3:** How are creative processes managed and supported in game development?
- **RQ4:** How has game development evolved the last couple of years?

To find answers to the research questions, we used a combined approach that included a questionnaire and a literature study to back up the findings. The questionnaire consisted of 20 statements where the respondents should state how they agree using the Likert's scale [31]. In addition, we added an opportunity for the respondents to give a free text comment on every statement. The statements in the questionnaire were constructed on the basis of the research goal and the research questions presented above, and was a result from a preliminary study of the role of software architecture and creative processes in game development. The subjects of the study were recruited from the Nordic booth at Game Developer Conference (GDC 2012) as well as direct emails sent to game developers. The questionnaire and results are described in detail in [32].

3   Results

This section presents the quantitative results from the questionnaire, comments from the respondents, as well reflections from a research literature.

3.1   Design of Software Architecture (RQ1)

Table 1 shows the response to statements related to design of software architecture in game development.

The majority of the companies in our survey agreed that software architecture is an important part of the game development process (Q1), backed up with the following comment: "Oversight in the game software architecture may lead to serious dead ends, leading to a need to rewrite the entire system". One reason the software architecture is so important, is to properly manage changing requirements as well as the complexity of game engines, libraries and APIs during the project [11]. Another reason is the importance of quality attributes such as performance (frame rates), portability, testability, and modifiability, which are very hard to change after release [18]. Further, the increasing focus on network games demand more focus on security (to avoid cheating) and availability for game servers [33]. Careful design and evaluation of a software architecture is the main approach to achieve predictable and acceptable quality attributes in software development [34].

Table 1. Statements related to the design of software architecture in game development

ID	Statement	Agree	Neutral	Disagree	N/A
Q1	Design of software architecture is an important part of our game development process	69%	15%	8%	8%
Q2	The main goal of our software architecture is performance	54%	15%	23%	8%
Q3	Our game concept heavily influences the software architecture	69%	8%	15%	8%
Q4	The creative team is included in the design of the software architecture	69%	15%	8%	8%
Q5	Our existing software suite provides features aimed at helping the creative team do their job	92%	8%	0%	0%
Q6	Our existing software architecture dictates the future game concepts we can develop	15%	47%	38%	0%

To the statement whether the main goal of their software architecture was performance (Q2), over half of companies agreed. However, the comments to this statement diversify the picture somewhat: "Performance plus functionality"; "Also future change, ability to be data-driven, optimized deployment processes, ease of automation, and testability"; and "Main goals are: Performance and Memory consumption."

Almost 3 out of 4 of the game developers agreed that the game concept heavily influences the software architecture (Q3). This result was a bit surprising, as game engines should ideally make the software architecture less dependent on game concept. One respondent provided the following comment: "Entirely depends on the game concept requirements, but in general: more generic – within boundaries – the better." This highlights that the importance of separating generic modules (core) with specific game play modules. Such an approach will allow reuse of core components, and at the same time provide sufficient freedom in development of game concept. "

How much the game concept will influence the game software architecture is really a question about where the boundary between the game and the game engine. Currently, game engines are targeting one or few game genres, such as real-time strategy games (RTS) or first-person shooters (FPSs). As there is yet no taxonomy that can be used to specify all types of games, there exist few game engines that are independent of genres [18]. Plummer tries to overcome this problem by proposing a flexible and expandable architecture for video games not specific to a genre [20]. However, too general game engines will most likely provide overhead in code and thus result in poor performance and memory usage. Thus, games stretching game genres will result in software architectures that deviate from the architecture of the game engine [18].

The large majority of the respondents agreed that the creative team was included in the design of the software architecture (Q4). One way this can happen is when the same person both work with code and game design as illustrated by this comment: "Only because I am a programmer and also the lead designer. Other creative people don't know enough to be productively included." There are several ways the creative team can contribute to the software architecture, such as making decisions of what game to make, request for new in-game functionality, and request for new development features in tools. Another comment related to this statement was: "This is mostly true when working on the tools the creative team will be using. It rarely applies to in-game specific features." Experiences from postmortems of game development projects show the importance of making the technical and creative team overlap going from game concept into developing the actual game software [25]. An overlap in roles in technical and creative teams is recommended to bridge the code/art divide that many game development projects suffer from [45].

To the statement Q5, the response concludes that the game engine and the supporting tools provide features that help the creative team. This is illustrated through the following comments: "Our third-party tools do not do this, but we've developed in-house extensions that do"; and "Use two software tiers that aims at very different levels of artist integration: Visual Studio and Unity3D". The latter comment describes the situation that the creative teams not always can work with high-level GUI editors and high-level scripting, but sometimes must dive into the source code to get the game where the creative team wants it to go.

Game development is all about creativity and coming up with new game concepts. The response from statement Q6 shows that the software architecture does not to a large degree dictate future game concepts (15%). One comment that illustrates this point was: "We have engines that gives us a great benefit when building new games and we would prefer to continue on the same engines. However, it doesn't fully dictate the games we will make in the future. This is primarily market-driven." Other comments that clarify this point were: "It may influence, but not dictate whenever possible"; and "It makes it a bit more expensive to go to certain genres, but that's it." These comments indicate that the influence exerted by the existing software architecture is a direct result of a cost-benefit trade-off. The higher cost of change, the more influence the existing software architecture exert on the game concepts.

3.2   Changes to the Software Architecture during Development (RQ2)

Table 2 shows the responses to the statements Q7 to Q11 that focus on how game developers cope with changes to the software architecture.

We could not draw any conclusion regarding whether the creative team must restrict their ideas because of an existing game engine or not (Q7). The comments explain the diversity of the responses: "Technical realities are always something the creative side has to work around"; "Depending on structure. For assets handling, yes, but creatively, not so much. In latter case, the challenge is put to programmers to extend usage"; "Most of the time, the creative team is not fully aware of the game engine limitations so it is not their job to make it work by locking the creativity to things known to have been done with the engine before, the people who implements just need to make the ideas work one way or another"; and "That is not the way we do it here. The game design comes first, then we build what is necessary to make it happen." These comments indicate a trade-off between creative freedom and the technical limitations. Either the ideas must be adapted to the technology, or the technology to the ideas.

Table 2. Responses on how game developers cope with change to the software architecture

ID	Statement	Agree	Neutral	Disagree	N/A
Q7	The creative team has to adopt their ideas to the existing game engine	31%	46%	23%	0%
Q8	During development, the creative team can demand changes to the software architecture	69%	31%	0%	0%
Q9	The technical team implements all features requested by the creative team	69%	15%	8%	8%
Q10	It is easy to add new gameplay elements after the core of our game engine has been completed	70%	15%	0%	15%
Q11	During development, the creative team has to use the tools and features already available	47%	15%	38%	0%

The majority of the respondents agreed and none disagreed that the creative team can demand changes to the software architecture (Q8). There were two comments to this statement: "Depends how far in development and the size of a change, the odds of re-factoring an entire system late in production are close to nil, but the development team keeps an open mind at all times"; and "But again, only because the head of the creative team is president of the company and also wrote the original version of the game engine. If someone who doesn't know how to program came demanded changes to the software architecture, I would probably not listen very seriously." Game developers are inclined to prioritize the wants and needs of the creative team, given that the cost-benefit trade-off is favorable. Another important issue is what phase the project is in. The later in the project (production), the less changes are possible from the creative team. Boehm and Basili estimate that requirements error can cost up to 100 times more after delivery if caught at the start of the project [35]. A possible solution to this problem is to spend more time in the preproduction phases before moving to production, as it would leave relatively few surprises in the production phase [36].

The majority of the game companies agreed that the technical team implements all features requested by the creative team (Q9). There were several comments to this statement that provided more details: "It can happen that the creative team contributes on technical aspects during prototyping phase. Production quality code is left to the technical people"; "Things just aren't segmented this way in our situation"; "Of course, if the requests are decided to be implemented in the first place"; "It's very much a dialogue, we try not to have too formal split between tech and creative team when thinking about this, but prioritize what the user experience should be and when we can ship at target quality"; and "Some requested features are not tech. feasible."

Also the majority of the respondents agreed that was easy to add new gameplay elements after the core game engine has been completed (Q10). However, the comments suggest that adding new gameplay elements after completing the core game engine is often not possible, recommended or wanted: "It is simple during prototyping phase, technology-wise. However from a game concept point of view, it is highly disrecommended and the fact it is simple does not motivate the team to stack up features because the existing one are just not convincing enough :)"; "This really depends a lot, and can only be answered on a case to case effect"; and "Depends on the type of element – some may require significant underlying engine changes". One of the most common motivations for designing a software architecture is to provide a system that is easier to modify and maintain. In game development, modifiability must be balanced with performance. There are mainly two contrasting approaches to design modifiable game environments [38]: *Scripting* that requires developers to anticipate, hand-craft and script specific game events; and *Emergence* that involves defining game objects that interact according to rules to give rise to emergent gameplay. The most common approach is to create or acquire a game engine that provides a scripting language to create a game with predefines behavior. The emergence approach involves creation of a simulation of a virtual world with objects that reacts to their surroundings. The use of scripting makes it complex to add new gameplay elements, as everything is hardwired. The emergence approach makes it much easier to add new gameplay elements later in the project, with the price of being harder to test.

It was not possible to draw a conclusion on whether the creative team has to use the tools and features already available during development or not (Q11). The comments elaborated this issue: "The ones already available and the ones they request along the way"; "New tools can be made. However, it is certainly best to keep within the suite offered"; and "Our current engine (Unity) is easily extensible". This statement is really about cost. Adding new tools and features during development is costly and might also add risk to the project. However, in some cases new tools and features must be added to get the wanted results.

The response to the question about who decides if change-requests from the creative team are implemented is shown in the table below (Q12):

Technical team	Management	Creative team
10%	40%	50%

The responses to this question were mainly divided between management and the creative team, detailed through these comments: "Ultimately, the management can overrule everybody, but I would like to check the 3 options here, the creative team judges how important the change is, the technical team decides if it is realistic and the management makes sure it can be afforded. So mostly, it is a team decision"; "Actually it is all of the above, but the question would not let me put that as an answer"; "Sort of. The technical team advices what is possible, and as such has the final word. If it is

possible, the decision falls on management, as it is usually related to economic costs";
and "Depends very much on the scale of change, we try as much as possible to keep
this within and as a dialogue between the tech/creative teams, but if it means a major
change it goes to management. We also aim to be as much product/feature driven as
possible, as the primary owner is in the creative team." The responses from the developers indicate that all three branches (administration, technical and creative) are involved in the decisions about change. More game developers have also started to
adopt agile development practices, where it is more common to have frequent planning and decision meetings involving all relevant stakeholders [37].

3.3   Supporting the Creative Processes

The results that relates to how creative processes are supported through technology
and processes are shown in Table 3.

Table 3. Responses to how creative processes are supported

ID	Statement	Agree	Neutral	Disagree	N/A
Q13	Our game engine supports dynamic loading of new content	92%	8%	0%	0%
Q14	Our game engine has a scripting system the creative team can use to try out and implement new ideas	70%	15%	15%	0%
Q15	The creative team is included in our development feed-back loop (e.g., scrum meetings)	86%	8%	0%	8%
Q16	Our game engine allows rapid prototyping of new levels, scenarios, and NPC's/behavior	86%	8%	0%	8%

The response from the game developers shows that the game engines they use allow
dynamic loading of new content (Q13). However, the comments show that there are
some restrictions in when and how it can be done: "At some extent, in editor mode
yes, at run-time only a subset of it"; and "With some constraints, but the content must
be properly prepped of course." Different game engines provide different flexibility
regarding changes that can be carried out in run-time. Most game engines support
changes to the graphic as long as the affected graphical structures are the similar.
Similarly, many game engines allow run-time changes using a scripting language that
can change the behavior of the game. However, substantial changes to game play and
changes of the game engine itself usually cannot be changed in run-time.

Most of the respondents say they have a scripting system that can be used by the
creative team (Q14). However, there are also game developers in the survey that uses
with their own game engines without scripting capabilities. Especially for small game
developers, it can be too expensive, too much work or lack the competence to create
support for scripting in their own game engine. The comments related to this statement were: "Yes, but could be better and more flexible (as always...)"; and "Our
"scripting system" is typing in C++ code and recompiling the game." A recognized
problem of letting the creative team script the game engine is that they usually do not

understand the underlying low-level mechanisms related to performance [39]. Until the game engines can optimize the scripts automatically, the technical team often must assist the creative team with scripting.

The majority of the game developers in this survey include the creative team in the development feedback loop (Q15). This was not only true for smaller game developers, as a large one (500+ employees) also said that the creative team was included in development feedback loops. This is in alignment with what has been found in other studies [24, 27, 37]. The only comment related to this statement was: "Depends on the phase of the project".

The majority of respondents agreed that their game engine allows rapid prototyping of new levels, scenarios, and NPC's/behavior (Q16). Game engines supporting scripting normally provide rapid prototyping. There was only one comment related to this statement: "While most of the systems are designed with simplicity and fast iteration time in mind, certain things still requires time consuming tweaking tasks".

3.4   Changes Over Time

Table 4 shows the results on how game development has changed the recent years.

Table 4. Responses to how game developer has changed the last couple of years

ID	Statement	Agree	Neutral	Disagree	N/A
Q17	Today our company uses more 3rd-party modules than 3 years ago	46%	15%	8%	31%
Q18	It is easier to develop games today than it was 5 years ago	77%	8%	15%	0%
Q19	Middleware is more important to our company today than 3 years ago	55%	15%	15%	15%
Q20	Game development is more like ordinary software development today than 5 years ago	38%	24%	38%	0%

Close to half of the respondents agree that they use more third-party modules than 3 years ago (Q17). This confirms the predictions that buying a good middleware will provide a better result than what an organization can produce at the same prize [40]. The only comment to this statement was "It is about time ...". On the importance of middleware to game companies today, the majority of respondents agreed that the importance has increased over the last 3 years (Q19).

Further that the vast majority in the survey agrees that it is easier to develop games today than it was 5 years ago (Q18). The complexity of games and the players' expectations have increased over the years [2], but the tools and the engines have also made it easier to manage complexity as well as achieving higher fidelity. The comments from the respondents highlight that the technical part has probably become easier, but the overall challenge of game development probably not: "The challenges have changed and the quality bar has risen, it is more accessible to people less interested in nerdy things nowadays (engines like Unity reduced the low-level aspect of the development), but developing a great game is still as challenging as before, the problems to solve just have evolved"; and "Technically and graphically, yes. Conceptually, no."

The feedback on the statement regarding whether game development now is more like ordinary software development than 5 years ago was mainly divided into two camps (Q20). The only comments to this statement came from those disagreeing: "Game development requires a more eccentric creative problem solving than development in most of other industries and this will probably remain true forever ;)"; "Nope. It was software development then, and still is now"; and "I think the tools available today moves game development further away from 'ordinary software development'.)". Several differences between game development and conventional software development have been identified in the literature. One example is that games usually have more limited lifecycle than conventional software products and that the maintenance of games mainly only focuses on bug fixing without charging the end-user [41]. Another example is that game development does not include functional requirements from the end-users. Typical end-user requirements to a game is that the game must be fun and engaging [7]. The latter poses a challenge of going from preproduction phase that produces a game design document (and maybe a prototype), to the production phase where all the software, game design, art, audio and music will be produced [7]. From a software engineering point of view, a challenge in game development is to create functional requirements from a game design document that describes the game concept. Another difference between conventional software systems and games is the importance of usability. A software system might be used if it provides much needed functionality even if the usability is not the best. However, a game with low usability is very unlikely to survive [42]. Usability tests and frameworks are also used within game development, but they are tailored specifically for the game domain [43, 44].

4   Conclusion

This article presents the results from a survey and research literature on how game developers use and manage software architecture and creative development processes.

The *first* research question (RQ1) asked about the role software architecture plays in game development. The response was that software architecture is important in game development, and it is important for managing the complexity of game software as well as achieving the quality in performance, availability, security and modifiability. We also found that the game concept heavily influences the software architecture mainly because it dictates the choice of game engine. Further, that the creative team can affect the software architecture through the creation of a game concept, by adding in-game functionality, and by adding new development tools. Finally, existing software architecture may or may not dictate future game concepts depending on a cost/benefit analysis (reuse of the software architecture if possible).

The *second* research question (RQ2) asked how game developers manage changes to the software architecture. The survey response was that the creative team has to some degree adjust their game play ideas to existing software architecture based on a cost/benefit analysis. The creative team can demand changes to the software architecture during development, but this decision depends on how far the project has progressed and the cost and benefit of making the change. Decisions on change-requests are usually made by involving personnel from technical team, creative team and management, but the management has the final word. Further, we found that the technical teams to a large extent implement all features and tools requested by the creative team (within reasonable limits), and that most developers said it was easy to add new game play elements after the core game engine was complete (although not recommended late in the project). The literature highlighted two approaches to deal with adding game play elements to a game: Scripting – where the behavior of the game is pre-deterministic and acting according to a script, and Emergence - where the behavior is non-deterministic and a virtual world is created by game objects that reacts the environment around them. The former has the advantage of being easier to test, and the latter has the advantage of being easier to extend game play.

The *third* research question asked about how the creative processes are managed and supported in game development. Almost all of the game developers in this study said they used game engines that support dynamic loading of new game elements (although not everything in run-time). The majority of the respondents use game engines that support scripting. Only game developers with own developed game engines did not support scripting. Finally, the majority of the developers said they used game engines that enabled rapid prototyping of new ideas. The conclusion of this research question is that current game engines enable creative processes through support of GUI tools, scripting, dynamic and loading of element.

The *fourth* research question asked how game development has evolved the last couple of years. This question can be summarized with the following: There has been an increased use of third-party software, middleware has become more important, and it has become technically easier to develop games. Although the majority of respondents said the technical aspects of game development have become easier, game development in itself has not become easier due to higher player expectations and higher game complexity. Similarly, there was no clear conclusion whether game development has become more like conventional software development. The main differences were identified to be that in game development there are no real functional requirements, the quality attributes performance and usability are more important, and game development has its own set of tools and engines.

References

1. Zyda, M.: From visual simulation to virtual reality to games. Computer 38(9), 25–32 (2005)
2. Blow, J.: Game Development: Harder Than You Think. Queue 1(10), 28–37 (2004)
3. Crooks, C.E.: Awesome 3D Game Development: No Programming Required, Cengage Learning (2004)
4. Callele, D., et al.: Emotional Requirements. IEEE Softw. 25(1), 43–45 (2008)

5. Ampatzoglou, A., Stamelos, I.: Software engineering research for computer games: A systematic review. Info. and Software Technology 52(9), 888–901 (2010)
6. Kanode, C.M., Haddad, H.M.: Software engineering challenges in game development. In: Sixth International Conference on Proc. Information Technology: New Generations, ITNG 2009, pp. 260–265. IEEE (2009)
7. Callele, D., et al.: Requirements engineering and the creative process in the video game industry. In: Proceedings of the 13th IEEE International Conference on Requirements Engineering, pp. 240-250. IEEE (2005)
8. Bishop, L., et al.: Designing a PC Game Engine. IEEE Comput. Graph. Appl. 18(1), 46–53 (1998)
9. Cheah, T.C., Ng, K.-W.: A practical implementation of a 3D game engine. In: Proc. Of the International Conference on Computer Graphics, Imaging and Vision: New Trends, pp. 351–358. IEEE (2005)
10. Darken, R., et al.: The Delta3D Open Source Game Engine. IEEE Comput. Graph. Appl. 25(3), 10–12 (2005)
11. Folmer, E.: Component Based Game Development–A Solution to Escalating Costs and Expanding Deadlines? Component-Based Software Engineering, pp. 66–73 (2007)
12. Antonio, C.A.M., et al.: Using a Game Engine for VR Simulations in Evacuation Planning. IEEE Comput. Graph. Appl. 28(3), 6–12 (2008)
13. Bouras, C., et al.: Networking Aspects for Gaming Systems (2008)
14. Smed, J., et al.: A review on networking and multiplayer computer games. Citeseer (2002)
15. Hampel, T., et al.: A peer-to-peer architecture for massive multiplayer online games. ACM (2006)
16. Triebel, T., et al.: Peer-to-peer infrastructures for games. ACM (2008)
17. Cai, W., et al.: A scalable architecture for supporting interactive games on the internet. In: Proceedings of the Sixteenth Workshop on Parallel and Distributed Simulation, pp. 60–67. IEEE Computer Society (2002)
18. Anderson, E.F., et al.: The case for research in game engine architecture. ACM (2008)
19. Caltagirone, S., et al.: Architecture for a massively multiplayer online role playing game engine. J. Comput. Small Coll. 18(2), 105–116 (2002)
20. Plummer, J.: A flexible and expandable architecture for computer games. Arizona State University (2004)
21. Gestwicki, P.V.: Computer games as motivation for design patterns. SIGCSE Bull. 39(1), 233–237 (2007)
22. Ampatzoglou, A., Chatzigeorgiou, A.: Evaluation of object-oriented design patterns in game development. Info. and Software Technology 49(5), 445–454 (2007)
23. Nguyen, D., Wong, S.B.: Design patterns for games. ACM (2002)
24. Scacchi, W.: Free and Open Source Development Practices in the Game Community. IEEE Softw. 21(1), 59–66 (2004)
25. Petrillo, F., et al.: What went wrong? A survey of problems in game development. Computer Entertainment (CIE) 7(1), 1–22 (2009)
26. Flood, K.: Game unified process. GameDev. net (2003)
27. Petrillo, F., Pimenta, M.: Is agility out there?: agile practices in game development. In: Proceedings of the 28th ACM International Conference on Design of Communication, pp. 9–15. ACM (2010)
28. Schwaber, K., Beedle, M.: Agilè Software Development with Scrum (2002)
29. Basili, V.R.: Software modeling and measurement: the Goal/Question/Metric paradigm. University of Maryland for Advanced Computer Studies (1992)
30. Wohlin, C., et al.: Experimentation in software engineering. Springer (2012)

31. Likert, R.: A technique for the measurement of attitudes. Archives of psychology (1932)
32. Nordmark, N.: Software Architecture and the Creative Process in Game Development, Master Thesis, Norwegian University of Science and Technology (2012)
33. Hsiao, T.-Y., Yuan, S.-M.: Practical Middleware for Massively Multiplayer Online Games. IEEE Internet Computing 9(5), 47–54 (2005)
34. Bass, L., et al.: Software Architecture in Practice, p. 624. Addision-Wesley (2012)
35. Boehm, B., Basili, V.R.: Software defect reduction top 10 list. Foundations of Empirical Software Engineering: The Legacy of Victor R. Basili, vol. 426 (2005)
36. Bethke, E.: Game Developer's Guide to Design and Production. Wordware Publ. Inc. (2002)
37. Stacey, P., Nandhakumar, J.: Opening up to agile games development. Communications of the ACM 51(12), 143–146 (2008)
38. Sweetser, P., Wiles, J.: Scripting versus emergence: issues for game developers and players in game environment design. International Journal of Intelligent Games and Simulations 4(1), 1–9 (2005)
39. White, W., et al.: Better scripts, better games. Communications of the ACM 52(3), 42–47 (2009)
40. Rollings, A., Morris, D.: Game Architecture and Design - A New Edition. New Riders Publishing (2004)
41. McShaffry, M.: Game coding complete. Cengage Learning (2013)
42. González Sánchez, J.L., Padilla Zea, N., Gutiérrez, F.L.: From usability to playability: Introduction to player-centred video game development process. In: Kurosu, M. (ed.) HCD 2009. LNCS, vol. 5619, pp. 65–74. Springer, Heidelberg (2009)
43. Desurvire, H., Wiberg, C.: Game usability heuristics (PLAY) for evaluating and designing better games: The next iteration. In: Ozok, A.A., Zaphiris, P. (eds.) OCSC 2009. LNCS, vol. 5621, pp. 557–566. Springer, Heidelberg (2009)
44. Laitinen, S.: Better games through usability evaluation and testing. Gamasutra (2005), http://www.gamasutra.com/features/20050623/laitinen_01.shtml
45. Hayes, J.: The code/art divide: How technical artists bridge the gap. Game Developer Magazine 14(7), 17 (2007)

Storytelling Variants: The Case
of *Little Red Riding Hood*

Edirlei Soares de Lima, Antonio L. Furtado, and Bruno Feijó

Department of Informatics – Pontifical Catholic University of Rio de Janeiro (PUC-RIO)
Rua Marquês de São Vicente, 225 – Rio de Janeiro – Brazil
{elima,furtado,bfeijo}@inf.puc-rio.br

Abstract. A small number of variants of a widely disseminated folktale is surveyed, and then analyzed in an attempt to determine how such variants can emerge while staying within the conventions of the genre. The study follows the classification of types and motifs contained in the *Index* of Antti Aarne and Stith Thompson. The paper's main contribution is the characterization of four kinds of type interactions in terms of semiotic relations. Our objective is to provide the conceptual basis for the development of semi-automatic methods to help users compose their own narrative plots.

Keywords: Folktales, Variants, Types and Motifs, Semiotic Relations, Digital Storytelling, Plan Recognition.

1   Introduction

When trying to learn about storytelling, in order to formulate and implement methods usable in a computer environment, two highly influential approaches come immediately to mind, both dealing specifically with folktales: Propp's *functions* [34] and the comprehensive classification of *types* and *motifs* proposed by Antti Aarne and Stith Thompson, known as the *Aarne-Thompson Index* (heretofore simply *Index*) [1,39,40].

In previous work, as part of our **Logtell** project [13, 14], we developed prototypes to compose narrative plots interactively, employing a *plan-generation* algorithm based on Propp's functions. Starting from different initial states, and giving to users the power to intervene in the generation process, within the limits of the conventions of the genre on hand, we were able to obtain in most cases a fair number of different plots, thereby achieving an encouraging level of *variety* in plot composition.

We now propose to invest on a strategy that is based instead on the analysis of already existing stories. Though we shall focus on folktales, an analogous conceptual formulation applies to any genre strictly regulated by conventions and definable in terms of fixed sets of personages and characteristic events. In all such genres one should be able to pinpoint the equivalent of Proppian functions, as well as of ubiquitous types and motifs, thus opening the way to the *reuse* of previously identified narrative patterns as an authoring resource. Indeed it is a well-established fact that new

© IFIP International Federation for Information Processing 2015
K. Chorianopoulos et al. (Eds.): ICEC 2015, LNCS 9353, pp. 286–300, 2015.
DOI: 10.1007/978-3-319-24589-8_22

stories often emerge as creative adaptations and combinations of old stories: this is a most common practice among even the best professional authors, though surely not easy to trace in its complex ramifications, as eloquently expressed by the late post-structuralist theoretician Roland Barthes [3, p. 39]:

> Any text is a new tissue of past citations. Bits of code, formulae, rhythmic models, fragments of social languages, etc., pass into the text and are redistributed within it, for there is always language before and around the text. Intertextuality, the condition of any text whatsoever, cannot, of course, be reduced to a problem of sources or influences; the intertext is a general field of anonymous formulae whose origin can scarcely ever be located; of unconscious or automatic quotations, given without quotation marks.

The present study utilizes types and motifs of the Aarne-Thompson's *Index*, under whose guidance we explore what the ingenuity of supposedly unschooled narrators has legated. We chose to concentrate on folktale type **AT 333**, centered on *The Little Red Riding Hood* and spanning some 58 variants (according to [38]) from which we took a small sample. The main thrust of the paper is to investigate how such rich diversities of variants of traditional folktales came to be produced, as they were told and retold by successive generations of oral storytellers, hoping that some of their tactics are amenable to semi-automatic processing. An added incentive to work with folktale variants is the movie industry's current interest in adaptations of folktales for adult audiences, in contrast to early Disney classic productions.

Related work is found in the literature of *computational narratology* [9,32] – a new field that examines narratology from the viewpoint of computation and information processing – which offers models and systems based on tale types/motifs that can be used in story generation and/or story comparison. Karsdorp et al. [26] believe that oral transmission of folktales happens through the replication of sequences of motifs. Darányi et al. [16] handle motif strings like chromosome mutations in genetics. Kawakami et al. [27] cover 23 Japanese texts of Cinderella tales, whilst Swartjes et al use Little Red Riding Hood as one of their examples [37].

Our text is organized as follows. Section 2 presents the two classic variants of **AT 333**. Section 3 summarizes additional variants. Section 4 has our analysis of the variant-formation phenomenon, with special attention to the interaction among types, explained in terms of semiotic relations. Section 5 describes a simple plan-recognition prototype working over variant libraries. Section 6 contains concluding remarks. The full texts of the variants cited in the text are available in a separate document.[1]

2   The Two Classic Variants

In the *Index*, the type of interest, **AT 333**, characteristically named **The Glutton**, is basically described as follows, noting that two major episodes are listed [1, p. 125]:

> The wolf or other monster devours human beings until all of them are rescued alive from his belly.

---

[1] http://www-di.inf.puc-rio.br/~furtado/LRRH_texts.pdf

I. **Wolf's Feast**. By masking as mother or grandmother the wolf deceives and devours a little girl whom he meets on his way to her grandmother's.

II. **Rescue**. The wolf is cut open and his victims rescued alive; his belly is sewed full of stones and he drowns, or he jumps to his death.

The first classic variant, *Le Petit Chaperon Rouge* (Little Red Riding Hood), was composed in France in 1697, by Charles Perrault [33], during the reign of Louis XIVth. It consists of the first episode alone, so that there is no happy ending, contrary to what children normally expect from nursery fairy tales. The little girl, going through the woods to see her grandmother, is accosted by the wolf who reaches the grandmother's house ahead of her. The wolf kills the grandmother and takes her place in bed. When the girl arrives, she is astonished at the "grandmother"'s large, ears, large eyes, etc., until she asks about her huge teeth, whereat the wolf gobbles her up. Following a convention of the genre of admonitory fables, a "moralité" is appended, to the effect that well-bred girls should not listen to strangers, particularly when they pose as "gentle wolves"

The second and more influential classic variant is that of the brothers Grimm (Jacob and Wilhelm), written in German, entitled *Rotkäppchen* (Little Red Cap) [22], first published in 1812. The girl's question about the wolf's teeth is replaced by: "But, grandmother, what a dreadful big mouth you have!" This is a vital change – not being bitten, the victims are gobbled up alive – and so the Grimm variant can encompass the two episodes prescribed for the **AT 333** type. Rescue is effected by a hunter, who finds the wolf sleeping and cuts his belly, allowing girl and grandmother to escape. The wolf, his belly filled with heavy stones fetched by the girl, wakes up, tries to run away and falls dead, unable to carry the weight. As a moral addendum to the happy ending, the girl promises to never again deviate from the path when so ordered by her mother. Having collected the story from two distinct sources, the brothers wrote a single text with a second finale, wherein both female characters show that they had learned from their experience with the villain. A second wolf comes in with similar proposals. The girl warns her grandmother who manages to keep the animal outside, and eventually they cause him to fall from the roof into a trough and be drowned.

3   Some Other Variants

In [38] no less than 58 folktales were examined as belonging to type **AT 333** (and **AT 123**). Here we shall merely add seven tales to the classic ones of the previous section.

Since several variants do not mention a red hood or a similar piece of clothing as attribute of the protagonist, the conjecture was raised that this was Perrault's invention, later imitated by the Grimms. However a tale written in Latin by Egbert de Liège in the 11th century, *De puella a lupellis seruata* (About a Girl Saved from Wolf Cubs) [43], arguably prefiguring some characteristics of **AT 333**, features a red tunic which is not merely ornamental but plays a role in the events. The girl had received it as a baptismal gift from her godfather. When she was once captured by a wolf and delivered to its cubs to be eaten, she suffered no harm. The virtue of baptism, visually represented by the red tunic, gave her protection. The cubs, their natural ferocity subdued, gently caressed her head covered by the tunic. The moral lesson, in this case, is consonant with the teaching of the *Bible* (Daniel VI, 27).

Whilst in the variants considered so far the girl is presented as naive, in contrast to the clever villain, the situation is reversed in the *Conte de la Mère-grand* (The Story of Grandmother), collected by folklorist Achille Millien in the French province of Nivernais, circa 1870, and later published by Paul Delarue [18]. In this variant, which some scholars believe to be closer to the primitive oral tradition, the villain is a "bzou", a werewolf. After killing and partly devouring the grandmother's body, he stores some of her flesh and fills a bottle with her blood. When the girl comes in, he directs her to eat and drink from these ghastly remains. Then he tells her to undress and lie down on the bed. Whenever the girl asks where to put each piece of clothing, the answer is always: "Throw it in the fire, my child; you don't need it anymore." In the ensuing dialogue about the peculiar physical attributes of the fake grandmother, when the question about her "big mouth" is asked the bzou gives the conventional reply: "All the better to eat you with, my child!" – but this time the action does not follow the words. What happens instead is that the girl asks permission to go out to relieve herself, which is a ruse whereby she ends up outsmarting the villain and safely going back to home (cf. http://expositions.bnf.fr/contes/gros/chapcron/nivers.htm).

An Italian variant published by Italo Calvino, entitled *Il Lupo e le Tre Ragazze* (The Wolf and the Three Girls) [7], adopts the trebling device [34] so common in folktales, making three sisters, one by one, repeat the action of taking victuals to their sick mother. The wolf intercepts each girl but merely demands the food and drink that they carry. The youngest girl, who is the protagonist, throws at the wolf a portion that she had filled with nails. This infuriates the wolf, who hurries to the mother's house to devour her and lay in wait for the girl. After the customary dialogue with the wolf posing as the mother, the animal also swallows the girl. The townspeople observe the wolf coming out, kill him and extract mother and girl alive from his belly. But that is not all, as Calvino admits in an endnote. Having found the text as initially collected by Giambattista Basile, he had deliberately omitted what he thought to be a too gruesome detail ("una progressione troppo truculenta"): after killing the mother, the wolf had made "a doorlatch cord out of her tendons, a meat pie out of her flesh, and wine out of her blood". Repeating the strange above-described episode of the *Conte de la Mère-grand*, the girl is induced to eat and drink from these remains, with the aggravating circumstance that they belonged to her mother, rather than to a more remotely related grandparent.

Turning to China, one encounters the tale *Lon Po Po* (Grammie Wolf), translated by Ed Young [42], which again features three sisters but, unlike the Western folktale cliché, shows the eldest as protagonist, more experienced and also more resourceful than the others. The mother, here explicitly declared to be a young widow, goes to visit the grandmother on her birthday, and warns Shang, the eldest, not to let anyone inside during her absence. A wolf overhears her words, disguises as an old woman and knocks at the door claiming to be the grandmother. After some hesitation, the girls allow him to enter and, in the dark, since the wolf claims that light hurts his eyes, they go to bed together. Shang, however, lighting a candle for a moment catches a glimpse of the wolf's hairy face. She convinces him to permit her two sisters to go outside under the pretext that one of them is thirsty. And herself is also allowed to go out, promising to fetch some special nuts for "Grammie". Tired of waiting for their return, the wolf leaves the house and finds the three sisters up in a tree. They persuade him to fetch a basket mounted on which they propose to bring him up, in order to pluck with his own hands the delicious nuts. They pull on the rope attached to the basket, but let it go so that the wolf is seriously bruised. And he finally dies when the false attempt is repeated for the third time.

Another Chinese variant features a bear as the villain: *Hsiung chia P`o* (Goldflower and the Bear) [11], translated by Chiang Mi. The crafty protagonist, Goldflower, is once again an elder sister, living with her mother and a brother. The mother leaves them for one day to visit their sick aunt, asking the girl to take care of her brother and call their grandmother to keep them company during the night. The bear knocks at the door, posing as the grandmother. Shortly after he comes in, the girl – in spite of the darkness – ends up disclosing his identity. She manages to lock the boy in another room, and then obeys the bear's request to go to bed at his side. The villain's plan is to eat her at midnight, but she asks to go out to relieve her tummy. As distrustful as the werewolf in the before-mentioned French variant, the bear ties one end of a belt to her hand – an equally useless precaution. Safely outside on top of a tree, Goldflower asks if he would wish to eat some pears, to be plucked with a spear, which the famished beast obligingly goes to fetch in the house. The girl begins with one fruit, but the next thing to be thrown into his widely open gullet is the spear itself. Coming back in the morning, the mother praises the brave little Goldflower.

One variant, published in Portugal by Guerra Junqueiro, entitled *O Chapelinho Encarnado* [23], basically follows the Grimm brothers pattern. A curious twist is introduced: instead of luring the girl to pick up wild flowers, the wolf points to her a number of medicinal herbs, all poisonous plants in reality, and she mistakes him for a doctor. At the end, the initiative of filling the belly of the wolf with stones is attributed not to the girl, but to the hunter, who, after skinning the animal, merrily shares the food and drink brought by the girl with her and her grandmother.

The highly reputed Brazilian folklorist Camara Cascudo included in his collection [8] a variant, *O Chapelinho Vermelho*, which also follows the Grimm brothers pattern. The mother is introduced as a widow and the name of the girl is spelled out: Laura. Although she is known, as the conventional title goes, by a nickname translatable as "Little Red Hat", what she wears every day is a red parasol, given by her mother. One more particularity is that, upon entering her grandmother's house, the girl forgets to close the door, so that finding the door open is what strikes the hunter as suspicious when he approaches the house. The hunter bleeds the wolf with a knife and, noticing his distended belly, proceeds to open it thus saving the two victims. Nothing is said about filling the wolf's belly with stones, the wounds inflicted by the hunter's knife having been enough to kill him. Two prudent lessons are learned: (1) Laura would not forget her mother's recommendation to never deviate from the path, the specific reason being given here that there existed evil beasts in the wood; (2) living alone should no longer be an option for the old woman, who from then on would dwell with her daughter and granddaughter.

4   Comments on the Formation of Variants

It is a truism that people tend to introduce personal contributions when retelling a story. There are also cultural time and place circumstances that require adaptations; for example, in the Arab world the prince would in no way be allowed to meet Cinderella in a ballroom – he falls in love without having ever seen her (cf. "Le Bracelet de Cheville" in the Mardrus translation of *One Thousand and One Nights* [31]). Other differences among variants may result from the level of education of the oral storytellers affecting how spontaneous they are, and the attitude of the collectors who may either prefer to reproduce exactly what they hear or introduce corrections and rational explanations while omitting indecorous or gruesome scenes. On the storyteller's part, however, this tendency is often attenuated by an instinctive pact with the audience – with children, in special – in favour of faithful repetition, preferably employing the very same words. Indeed the genre of folktales is strongly marked by *conventions* which, to a remarkable extent, remain the same in different times and places. The folklorist Albert Lord called *tension of essences* the compulsion that drives all singers (i.e. traditional oral storytellers) to strictly enforce such conventions [29, p. 98]:

> In our investigation of composition by theme this hidden tension of essences must be taken into consideration. We are apparently dealing here with a strong force that keeps certain themes together. It is deeply imbedded in the tradition; the singer probably imbibes it intuitively at a very early stage of his career. It pervades his material and the tradition. He avoids violating the group of themes by omitting any of its members. [We shall see] that he will even go so far as to substitute something similar if he finds that for one reason or another he cannot use one of the elements in its usual form.

The notion of tension of essences may perhaps help explaining not only the total permanence of some variants within the frontiers of a type, but also the emergence of transgressive variants, which absorb features pertaining to other types, sometimes even provoking a sensation of strangeness. When an oral storyteller feels the urge "to substitute something similar" in a story, the chosen "something" should, as an effect of the tension-of-essences forceful compulsion, still belong to the folktale genre – but what if the storyteller's repertoire comprises more than one folktale type? As happens with many classifications, the frontiers between the types in the *Index* are often blurred, to the point that one or more motifs can be shared and some stories may well be classified in more than one type. So a viable hypothesis can be advanced that some variants did originate through, so to speak, a *type-contamination* phenomenon.

Accordingly we propose to study type interactions as a possible factor in the genesis of variants. We shall characterize the interactions that may occur among types, also involving motifs, by way of *semiotic relations*, taking an approach we applied before to the conceptual modelling of both literary genres and business information systems [12, 25, 20]. We distinguish four kinds of semiotic relations, associated with the so-called *four master tropes* [6, 10], whose significance has been cogently stressed by a literary theory scholar, Jonathan Culler, who regards them "as a system, indeed *the* system, by which the mind comes to grasp the world conceptually in language" [15, p. 72]. For the ideas and for the nomenclature in the table below, we are mainly indebted to the pioneering semiotic studies of Ferdinand de Saussure [35]:

relation	meaning	operator	trope
syntagmatic	connection	and	metonymy
paradigmatic	similarity	or	metaphor
meronymic	unfolding	part-whole	synecdoche
antithetic	opposition	not	irony

The itemized discussion below explores the meaning of each of the four semiotic relations, as applied to the derivation of folktale type variants stemming from **AT 333**.

(1) <u>Syntagmatic relation with type **AT 123**</u>. As mentioned at the beginning of section 2, the *Index* describes type **AT 333** as comprising two episodes, namely **Wolf's Feast** and **Rescue**, but the classic Perrault variant does not proceed beyond the end of the first episode. As a consequence, one is led to assume that the **Rescue** episode is not essential to characterize **AT 333**. On the other hand the situation created by **Wolf's Feast** is a long distance away from the happy-ending that is commonly expected in nursery fairy tales. A continuation in consonance with the **Rescue** episode, exactly as described in the *Index*, is suggested by **AT 123: The Wolf and the Kids**, a type pertaining to the group of **Animal Tales**, which contains the key motif **F913: Victims rescued from swallower's belly**.

The connection (syntagmatic relation) whereby **AT 123** *complements* **AT 333** is explicitly declared in the *Index* by "cf." cross-references [1, p. 50, p. 125]. Moreover the Grimm brothers variant, which has the two episodes, is often put side by side with another story equally collected by them, *The Wolf and the Seven Little Kids* [22], clearly of type **AT 123**.

Still it must be noted that several of the variants reported here do not follow the Grimm pattern in the **Rescue** episode. They diverge with respect to the outcome, which, as seen, may involve the death of the girl, or her rescue after being devoured, or even her being totally preserved from the villain's attempts either by miraculous protection or by her successful ruses.

(2) <u>Paradigmatic relation with type **AT 311B***</u>. For the Grimm variant, as also for those that follow its pattern (e.g. the Italian and the two Portuguese variants in section 3), certain correspondences or analogies can be traced with variants of type **AT 311B***: **The Singing Bag**, a striking example being another story collected in Brazil by Camara Cascudo [8], *A Menina dos Brincos de Ouro* (The Girl with Golden Earrings). Here the villain is neither an animal nor a werewolf; he is a very ugly old man, still with a fearsome aspect but no more than human. The golden earrings, a gift from her mother, serve as the girl's characteristic attribute and have a function in the plot. As will be noted in the summary below, the villain's bag becomes the wolf's belly of the Grimm variant, and what is done to the bag mirrors the act of cutting the belly and filling it with stones. In this sense, the **AT 311B*** variant *replaces* the Grimm variant.

One day the girl went out to bring water from a fountain. Having removed her earrings to wash herself, she forgot to pick them up before returning. Afraid to be reprimanded by her mother, she walked again to the fountain, where she was caught by the villain and sewed inside a bag. The man intended to use her to make a living. At each

house that he visited, he advertised the magic bag, which would sing when he me-
naced to strike it with his staff. Everywhere people gave him money, until he came
inadvertently to the girl's house, where her voice was recognized. He was invited to
eat and drink, which he did in excess and fell asleep, whereat the bag was opened to
free the girl and then filled with excrement. At the next house visited, the singing bag
failed to work; beaten with the staff, it ruptured spilling its contents.

(3) Meronymic relation with type **AT 437**. In *The Story of Grandmother* the paths
taken by the girl and the werewolf to reach the old lady's house are called, respectively, the Needles Road and the Pins Road. And, strangely enough, while walking along
her chosen path, the little girl "enjoyed herself picking up needles" [18]. Except for
this brief and puzzling mention, these objects remain as meaningless details, having
no participation in the story.

And yet, browsing through the *Index*, we see that needles and pins are often treated
as wondrous objects (motifs **D1181: Magic Needle** and **D1182: Magic Pin**). And
traversing the *Index* hierarchy upwards, from motifs to types, we find them playing a
fundamental role in type **AT 437: The Needle Prince** (also named **The Supplanted
Bride**), described as follows [1, p. 140]: "The maiden finds a seemingly dead prince
whose body is covered with pins and needles and begins to remove them ... ". Those
motifs are thus *expanded* into a full narrative in **AT 437**.

Especially relevant to the present discussion is a variant from Afghanistan, entitled
The Seventy-Year-Old Corpse reported by Dorson [17], which has several elements in
common with the **AT 333** variants. An important difference, though, also deserves
mention: the girl lives alone with her old father, who takes her to visit her aunt. We
are told that, instead of meeting the aunt, the girl finds a seventy year old corpse covered with needles, destined to revive if someone would pick the needles from his
body. At the end the girl marries the "corpse", whereas no further news are heard
about her old father, whom she had left waiting for a drink of water. One is tempted
to say that Bruno Bettelheim would regard this participation of two old males, the
father and the daunting corpse, as an uncannily explicit confirmation of the presence –
in two different forms – of the paternal figure, in an "externalization of overwhelming
oedipal feelings, and ... in his protective and rescuing function" [4, p. 178].

(4) Antithetic relation with type **AT 449**. Again in *The Story of Grandmother* we
watch the strange scene of the girl eating and drinking from her grandmother's remains, punctuated by the acid comment of a little cat: "A slut is she who eats the flesh
and drinks the blood of her grandmother!" The scene has no consequence in the plot,
and in fact it is clearly inconsistent with the role of the girl in type **AT 333**. It would
sound natural, however, in a type *in opposition to* **AT 333**, such as **AT 449: The
Tsar's Dog**, wherein the roles of victim and villain are totally *reversed*. The canniba-
listic scene in *The Story of Grandmother* has the effect of assimilating the girl to a
ghoul (motif **G20** in the *Index*), and the female villain of the most often cited variant
of type **AT 449**, namely *The Story of Sidi Nouman* (cf. Andrew Lang's translation in
Arabian Nights Entertainment) happens to be a ghoul.

No less intriguing in *The Story of Grandmother* are the repartees in the ensuing un-
dressing scene, with the villain (a werewolf, as we may recall) telling the girl to destroy

each piece of clothing: "Throw it in the fire, my child; you don't need it anymore." This, too, turns out to be inconsequential in the plot, but was a major concern in the werewolf historical chronicles and fictions of the Middle Ages [2, 36]. In 1521, the Inquisitor-General for the diocese of Besançon heard a case involving a certain Pierre Bourget [2]. He confessed under duress that, by smearing his body with a salve given by a demon, he became a wolf, but "the metamorphosis could not take place with him unless he were stark naked". And to recover his form he would "beat a retreat to his clothes, and smear himself again". Did the werewolf in *The Story of Grandmother* intend to transform the girl into a being of his species? Surely the anonymous author did not mean that, but leaving aside the norms of **AT 333** the idea would not appear to be so farfetched.

In this regard, also illustrating type **AT 449**, there are two medieval lays (short narrative poems) that deserve our attention. They are both about noble knights with the ability to transform themselves into wolves. In the two narratives, they are betrayed by their villainous wives, intent on permanently preventing their resuming the human form. In Marie de France's lay of *Bisclavret* [30] – an old Breton word signifying "werewolf" – the woman accomplishes this effect by stealing from a secret hiding place the man's clothes, which he needed to put on again to undo the transformation. In the other example, the anonymous lay of *Melion* [5], after a magic ring is applied to break the enchantment, the man feels tempted to punish the woman by inflicting upon her the same metamorphosis.

In the preceding discussion we purported to show how types can be semiotically related, and argued that such relations constitute a factor to be accounted for in the emergence of variants. We should add that types may be combined in various ways to yield more complex types, whose attractiveness is heightened by the occurrence of unexpected changes. Indeed Aristotle's *Poetics*[2] distinguishes simple and complex plots, characterizing the latter by *recognition* (αναγνορισισ) and *reversal* (περιπετεια). Differently from reversal, recognition does not imply that the world changed, but that the *beliefs* of the characters about themselves and the current facts were altered.

In particular, could a legitimate folktale promote the union of monster and girl? Could we conciliate type **AT 333** (where the werewolf is a villain) with the antithetically related medieval lays of type **AT 449** (where the werewolf is the victim)? Such conciliations of opposites are treated under the topic of *blending* [19], often requiring creative adaptations. A solution is given by type **AT 425C: Beauty and the Beast**. At first the Beast is shown as the villain, claiming the life of the merchant or else of one of his daughters: "Go and see if there's one among them who has enough courage and love for you to sacrifice herself to save your life" [41, p. 159] – but then proves to be the victim of an enchantment. Later, coming to sense his true inner nature (an event of recognition, as in Aristotle), Belle makes him human again by manifesting her love (motif **D735-1: Disenchanting of animal by being kissed by woman**). So, it is as human beings that they join.

Alternatively, we might combine **AT 333** and **AT 449** by pursuing until some sort of outcome the anomalous passages of *The Story of Grandmother*, allowing the protagonists to join in a non-human form. The werewolf feeds human flesh of his victim to

---

[2] http://www.gutenberg.org/files/1974/1974-h/1974-h.htm

the girl, expecting that she would transform herself like he did (as Melion for a moment thought to cast the curse upon his wife), thereby assuming a shape that she would keep forever once her clothes were destroyed (recall the concern of Pierre Bourget to "beat a retreat to his clothes", and the knight's need to get back his clothes in *Bisclavret*). At the end the two werewolves would marry and live happily forever after, as a variant of an admittedly misbegotten new type (of, perhaps, a modern appeal, since it would also include among its variants the story of the happy vampires Edward and Bella in the *Twilight Saga*: http://twilightthemovie.com/).

5   First Steps Towards Variants in Computer-generated Stories

To explore in a computer environment the variants of folktale types, kept in a *library of typical plans*, we developed a system in *C#* that does plan-recognition over the variants of the type indicated (*e.g.* **AT 333**), with links to pages of semiotically related types (e.g. **AT 123**, **AT 311B***, **AT 437**, **AT 449**). Plan-recognition involves matching a number of actions against a pre-assembled repertoire of plot patterns (cf. [20, 25]).

Let P be a set of m variants of a specific tale type that are represented by complete plans, $P = \{P_1, P_2, \cdots, P_m\}$, where each plan is a sequence of *events*, i.e.: $P_i = \langle e_1^i, e_2^i, \cdots, e_{n_i}^i \rangle$. These events are actions with ground arguments that are story elements (specific names, places, and objects). For instance, $P_k = \langle go(Abel, Beach), meet(Abel, Cain), kill(Cain, Abel) \rangle$. The library of typical plans is defined by associating each plan P_i with the following elements: (1) the story title; (2) a set of parameterized terms – akin to those we use in **Logtell** [14] to formalize Proppian functions – describing the story events; (3) the specification of the characters' roles (e.g. *villain, victim, hero*) and objects' functions (*e.g. wolf's feast place, basket contents*); (4) the semiotic relations of the story with other variants of same or different types (Section 4); (5) a text template used to display the story as text, wherein certain phrases are treated as variables (written in the format #VAR$_1$#); and (6) the comics resources used for dramatization, indicating the path to the folder that contains the images representing the characters and objects of the narrative and a set of event templates to describe the events textually. The library is specified in an XML file.

Let T be a partial plan expressed as a sequence of events given by the user. The system finds plans in P that are consistent with T. During the searching process, the arguments of the events in P are instantiated. For example, with the input $T = \{give(Anne, ring, Little Ring Girl), ask\_to\_take(Marie, Little Ring Girl, tea, Anne), eat(Joe, Little Ring Girl)\}$, the following stories are generated:

Story 1: give(Anne, ring, Little Ring Girl), ask_to_take(Marie, Little Ring Girl, tea, Anne), go(Little Ring Girl, the woods), meet(Little Ring Girl, Joe), go(Joe, Grandmother's house), eat(Joe, Anne), disguise(Joe, Anne), lay_down(Joe, Grandmother's bed), go(Little Ring Girl, Grandmother's house), delivery(Little Ring Girl, tea), question(Little Ring Girl, Joe), eat(Joe, Little Ring Girl), sleep(Joe), go(Hunter, Grandmother's house), cut(Hunter, Joe, axe), jump_out_of(Little Ring Girl, Joe), jump_out_of(Anne, Joe), die(Joe).

Story 2: give(Anne, ring, Little Ring Girl), ask_to_take(Marie, Little Ring Girl,
tea, Anne), go(Little Ring Girl, the woods), meet(Little Ring Girl, Joe), go(Joe,
Grandmother's house), eat(Joe, Anne), disguise(Joe, Anne), lay_down(Joe, Grand-
mother's bed), go(Little Ring Girl, Grandmother's house), lay_down(Little Ring
Girl, Grandmother's bed), delivery(Little Ring Girl, tea), question(Little Ring
Girl, Joe), eat(Joe, Little Ring Girl).

which correspond, respectively, to the Grimm and Perrault **AT 333** variants, reph-
rased to display the names of characters and objects given by the user.

Our plan recognition algorithm employs a tree structure, which we call *generalized
plan suffix tree*. Based on the *suffix tree* commonly used for string pattern matching
[24], this *trie*-like data structure contains all suffixes p_k of each plan in P. If a plan P_i
has a sequence of events $p = e_1 e_2 \cdots e_k \cdots e_N$, then $p_k = e_k e_{k+1} \cdots e_N$ is the suffix of
p that starts at position k (we have dropped the index i of the expressions p and p_k for
the sake of simplicity). In a generalized plan suffix tree S, edges are labeled with the
parameterized plan events that belong to each suffix p_k, and the leaves point to the
complete plans ending in p_k. Each suffix is padded with a terminal symbol $\$i$ that
uniquely signals the complete plan in the leaf node. Figure 1 shows an example of
generalized plan suffix tree generated for the plan sequences $P_1 = \{go(A, B), meet(A,
C), kill(C, A)\}$ and $P_2 = \{tell(A, B, C), meet(A, C), go(A, D)\}$.

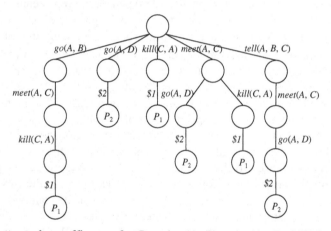

Fig. 1. Generalized plan suffix tree for $P_1 = \{go(A, B), meet(A, C), kill(C, A)\}$ and $P_2 =
\{tell(A, B, C), meet(A, C), go(A, D)\}$.

The process of searching for plans that match a given partial plan T expressed as a
sequence of input terms, is straightforward: starting from the root node, the algorithm
sequentially matches T against the parameterized plan events on the edges of the tree,
in chronological but not necessarily consecutive order, instantiating the event variables and proceeding until all input terms are matched and a leaf node is reached. If
more solutions are requested, a *backtracking* procedure tries to find alternative paths
matching T. The search process produces a set of complete plans G, with the event
variables instantiated with the values appearing in the input partial plan or, for events
not present in the partial plan, with the default values defined in the library.

After generating G through plan-recognition, the system allows users to apply the
semiotic relations (involving *connection*, *similarity*, *unfolding*, and *opposition*) and

explore other variants of same or different types. The process of searching for variants uses the semiotic relations specified in the library of typical plans to create a link between a g_i in G and its semiotically related variants. When instantiating one such variant v_i, the event variables of v_i are instantiated according to the characters and objects that play important roles in the baseline story g_i. Characters playing roles in g_i that also exist in v_i, assume the same role in the variant. For roles that only exist in v_i, the user is asked to name the characters who would fulfil such roles.

Following the $g_i \rightarrow v_i$ links taken from the examples of section 4, the user gains a chance to reinterpret the g_i **AT 333** variant, in view of aspects highlighted in the semiotically related v_i: 1. the wolf's villainy *complemented* by a rescue act (**AT 123**); 2. the wolf and his belly *replaced* by ugly man and his bag (**AT 311B***); 3. the girl's gesture of picking needles *expanded* to the wider scope of a disenchantment ritual (**AT 437**); 4. girl and werewolf with *reversed* roles of villain and victim (**AT 449**).

As illustrated in Figure 2, our system supports two dramatization modalities: *text* and *comics*. The former uses the original literary rendition of the matched typical plan as a template and represents the generated stories in text format. The latter offers a storyboard-like comic strip representation, where each story event gains a graphical illustration and a short sentence description. In the illustrations, the scene compositing automatic process takes into account the specific object carried by each character and the correct movement directions. More details on the generation of comic strips can be found in our previous work on interactive comics [28].

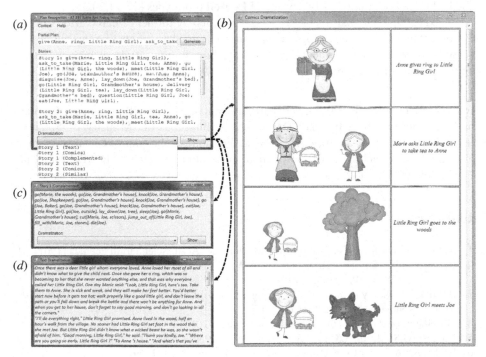

Fig. 2. Plan recognition system: (*a*) main user interface; (*b*) comics dramatization; (*c*) a variant for story 1; and (*d*) text dramatization.

6   Concluding Remarks

The imagination of storytellers far surpasses what automatic tools can produce at the current state of the art, but there is always a hope that technology can advance by the observation and analysis of human creative processes. Folktales offer a suitable model to begin with, given their amazing fertility in the proliferation of variants, favouring different – sometimes *very* different – perspectives to view what is basically the same story. Having access to a collection of variants, either of folktales or of some other similarly predefined genre, readers have a fair chance to find a given story in a treatment as congenial as possible to their tastes and personality profile.

Moreover, prospective amateur authors may feel inspired to put together new variants of their own after seeing how variants can derive from the type and motif interactions that we associate with semiotic relations. They would learn how new stories can arise from episodes of existing stories, through a process, respectively, of concatenation, analogous substitution, expansion into finer grained actions, or radical reversal.

Computer-based libraries, such as we described, should then constitute a vital first step in this direction. In special, by also representing the stories as plans, in the form of sequences of terms denoting the story events (cf. the second paragraph of section 5), we effectively started to combine the two approaches mentioned in the Introduction, namely Aarne-Thompson's types and motifs and Proppian functions, and provided a bridge to our previously developed **Logtell** prototypes [13,14,20,25].

We expect that our analysis of variants, stimulated by further research efforts in the line of computational narratology, may contribute to the design of semi-automatic methods for supporting interactive plot composition, to be usefully incorporated into digital storytelling systems.

Acknowledgements. This work was partially supported by CNPq (National Council for Scientific and Technological Development, linked to the Ministry of Science, Technology, and Innovation), CAPES (Coordination for the Improvement of Higher Education Personnel), FINEP (Brazilian Innovation Agency), ICAD/VisionLab (PUC-Rio), and Oi Futuro Institute.

References

1. Aarne, A., Thompson, S.: The Types of the Folktale. Acad. Scientiarum Fennica (1961)
2. Baring-Gould, S.: The Book of Were-Wolves, http://www.gutenberg.org/dirs/etext04/bofww10h.htm
3. Barthes, R.: Theory of the Text. In: Young, J.C. (ed.) Untying the Text: a Post-Structuralist Reader. Routledge & Kegan Paul (1981)
4. Bettelheim, B.: The Uses of Enchantment. Vintage (2010)
5. Burgess, G.S., Brook, L.C.: Eleven Old French Narrative Lays. D.S. Brewer (2007)
6. Burke, K.: A Grammar of Motives. Univ. of California Press (1969)
7. Calvino, I.: Italian Folktales. Mariner Books (1992)

8. Camara Cascudo, L.: Contos Tradicionais do Brasil. Global (2014)
9. Cavazza, M., Pizzi, D.: Narratology for interactive storytelling: A critical introduction. In: Göbel, S., Malkewitz, R., Iurgel, I. (eds.) TIDSE 2006. LNCS, vol. 4326, pp. 72–83. Springer, Heidelberg (2006)
10. Chandler, D.: Semiotics: The Basics. Routledge, London (2002)
11. Mi, C.: Goldflower and the Bear. In: Tatar, M. (ed.) The Classic Fairy Tales. Norton (1999)
12. Ciarlini, A., Barbosa, S.D.J., Casanova, M.A., Furtado, A.L.: Event relations in plot-based plot composition. In: Proc. of the Brazilian Symposium on Computer Games and Digital Entertainment (2008)
13. Ciarlini, A., Casanova, M.A., Furtado, A.L., Veloso, P.: Modeling interactive storytelling genres as application domains. Journal of Intelligent Information Systems 35(3) (2010)
14. Ciarlini, A., Pozzer, C.T., Furtado, A.L., Feijo, B.: A logic-based tool for interactive generation and dramatization of stories. In: Proc. of the ACM-SIGCHI International Conference on Advances in Computer Entertainment Technology (2005)
15. Culler, J.: The Pursuit of Signs: Semiotics, Literature, Deconstruction. Routledge (1981)
16. Darányi, S., Wittek, P., Forró, L.: Toward Sequencing 'Narrative DNA': Tale Types, Motif Strings and Memetic Pathways. In: Proc. of the Third Workshop on Computational Models of Narrative (2012)
17. Dorson, R.M.: Folktales Told Around the World. Univ. of Chicago Press (1978)
18. Delarue, P.: The Story of Grandmother. In: Dundes, A. (ed.) Little Red Riding Hood: A Casebook. Univ. of Wisconsin Press (1989)
19. Fauconnier, G., Turner, M.: Conceptual projection and middle spaces. Tech. Rep. 9401, Univ. California, San Diego (1994)
20. Furtado, A.L., Ciarlini, A.E.M.: Constructing libraries of typical plans. In: Dittrich, K.R., Geppert, A., Norrie, M. (eds.) CAiSE 2001. LNCS, vol. 2068, pp. 124–139. Springer, Heidelberg (2001)
21. Furtado, A.L., Casanova, M.A., Barbosa, S.D.J.: A semiotic approach to conceptual modelling. In: Yu, E., Dobbie, G., Jarke, M., Purao, S. (eds.) ER 2014. LNCS, vol. 8824, pp. 1–12. Springer, Heidelberg (2014)
22. Grimm, J., Grimm, W.: The Complete Grimm's FairyTales. Hunt, M., Stern, J. (trans.) Pantheon (1972)
23. Guerra Junqueiro, A.B.: Contos para a Infância, http://www.gutenberg.org/files/16429/16429-h/16429.htm
24. Gusfield, D.: Algorithms on Strings, Trees, and Sequences. Cambridge Univ. Press (1997)
25. Karlsson, B.F., Furtado, A.L.: Conceptual model and system for genre-focused interactive storytelling. In: Pisan, Y., Sgouros, N.M., Marsh, T. (eds.) ICEC 2014. LNCS, vol. 8770, pp. 27–35. Springer, Heidelberg (2014)
26. Karsdorp, F., et al.: In Search of an Appropriate Abstraction Level for Motif Annotations. In: Proc. of the Third Workshop on Computational Models of Narrative (2012)
27. Kawakami, S., et al.: On Modeling Conceptual and Narrative Structure of Fairytales. In: Proc. of 13th European-Japanese Conf. on Information Modelling & Knowledge Bases (2003)
28. Lima, E.S., Feijó, B., Furtado, A.L., Barbosa, S.D.J., Pozzer, C.T., Ciarlini, A.: Non-Branching Interactive Comics. In: Proc. of the 10th International Conference on Advances in Computer Entertainment Technology, pp. 230–245 (2013)
29. Lord, A.: The Singer of Tales. Harvard Univ. Press (2000)
30. de France, M.: The Lais of Marie de France. Burgess, G.S., et al. (tr.) Penguin (1999)
31. Mardrus, J.C.: (trans.). Les Mille et une Nuits. Bouquins Robert Laffont 2 (1985)

32. Mani, I.: Computational Narratology. In: Hühn, P., et al. (eds.) Handbook of Narratology. De Gruyter (2014), http://www.lhn.uni-hamburg.de/article/computational-narratology
33. Perrault, C.: Little Red Riding Hood. In: Beauties, Beasts and Enchantment - Classic French Fairy Tales. Planché, J.R., Zipes, J. (trans.) Meridian (1991)
34. Propp, V.: Morphology of the Folktale. Laurence, S. (trans.) Univ. of Texas Press (1968)
35. Saussure, F.: Cours de Linguistique Générale. In: Bally, C., et al. (eds.) Payot (1995)
36. Sconduto, L.A.: Metamorphoses of the Werewolf: A Literary Study from Antiquity Through the Renaissance. McFarland (2008)
37. Swartjes, I., Theune, M.: Iterative authoring using story generation feedback: Debugging or co-creation? In: Iurgel, I.A., Zagalo, N., Petta, P. (eds.) ICIDS 2009. LNCS, vol. 5915, pp. 62–73. Springer, Heidelberg (2009)
38. Tehrani, J.J.: The Philogeny of Little Red Riding Hood. PLOS ONE 8, 11 (2013)
39. Thompson, S.: The Folktale. Univ. of California Press (1977)
40. Uther, H.J.: The Types of International Folktales. Finish Acad. Science & Letters (2011)
41. Villeneuve, G. The Story of Beauty and the Beast. In: Beauties, Beasts and Enchantment - Classic French Fairy Tales. Planché, J.R., Zipes, J. (trans.) Meridian (1991)
42. Young, E.: Lon Po Po: A Red-Riding Hood Story from China. Puffin (1996)
43. Ziolkowski, J.M.: A Fairy Tale from before Fairy Tales: Egbert of Liège's 'De puella a lupellis seruata' and the Medieval Background of 'Little Red Riding Hood'. Speculum 67(3) (1992)

Tags You Don't Forget:
Gamified Tagging of Personal Images

Nina Runge, Dirk Wenig, Danny Zitzmann, and Rainer Malaka

Digital Media Lab, TZI, University of Bremen, Germany
{nr,dwenig,malaka}@tzi.de, zitzmann.danny@gmail.com

Abstract. Mobile multi-purpose devices such as smartphones are progressively replacing digital cameras; people use their smartphones as everyday companions and increasingly take pictures in their daily life. Tagging is a way to organize huge collections of photos but raises two challenges. First, tagging (especially on mobile devices) is a boring task. Second, remembering the assigned tags is important to find images with tags. We propose gamification for more entertaining tagging. Most gamification approaches use crowd-based assessments of good or bad tags, which is a good way to prevent cheating and to not assign improper tags. However, it is not appropriate for personal images because users don't want to share every image with the crowd. We developed and evaluated two mobile apps with gamification elements to tag images, a single-player and a multiplayer app. While both variants were more entertaining than a simple tagging app, the single-player app helps users to remember significant more tags.

Keywords: gamification, image tagging, mobile devices

1   Introduction

Consumer photography has fundamentally changed twice in the last 15 years. First, moving from analog to digital photography allowed users not only to easily edit photographs but also to take as many pictures as they want without considerable additional costs for photographic films. Second, multi-purpose devices (first and foremost smartphones) are more and more replacing digital cameras specialized in taking pictures. This allows users to extensively take spontaneous pictures in their daily life.

Furthermore, smartphones are often the only device for saving, sharing and presenting images. Even though there are many programs for sorting or tagging images on a PC, the possibilities for tagging images directly on the mobile device are very limited. Most mobile image applications do only tag images based on simple computer vision algorithms, e.g. Google and Apple detect people in images. Some of them tag images when they are uploaded into the cloud with computational expensive computer vision solutions. For some users this is a serious privacy issue. To prevent massive amounts of unorganized data, it would be beneficial to have apps for tagging images directly on the mobile device.

© IFIP International Federation for Information Processing 2015
K. Chorianopoulos et al. (Eds.): ICEC 2015, LNCS 9353, pp. 301–314, 2015.
DOI: 10.1007/978-3-319-24589-8_23

Tags are well suited for organizing large collections of data. Especially for images, manual tagging is better than using simple computer vision algorithms [11]. Good tags for personal images should describe the image content well, but most important, tags should help the users to organize images and to easily find them after a while. Therefore, it is not possible to judge the suitability of tags through an expert or other people. Because the quality of produced tags cannot be determined by majority vote, crowd-based tagging is inappropriate for private photos. The users need to tag their images on their own or with friends and family.

The focus of this work is on the playful interaction that helps to encourage users to contribute user-generated personal semantic data for mobile image tagging. New object recognition algorithms [19] work quite well for detecting objects in images. This is a good starting point for an automatic tagging system, but tags are not only about the image content, but also about the context. An image from a wedding cake for example could be automatically tagged with object tags like "cake" or "knife", but to find it later again it may be more important whose wedding the user attended or how she/he liked it. Such more personal tags cannot be solved by computer vision only or by verifying precompiled tags. While there are other approaches to learn [16] tags from the users, it is always necessary that the users add new tags from which the system could learn. Tagging images by crowd workers is also not a solution for private images.

Gamification is a good method to enforce people to solve boring tasks and has been used to tag images but, in most cases, only for public and not for private image collections [21]. Imagine you return from a wonderful holiday with your family, where you took hundreds of images. Even if an app helps you to tag your images, you probably won't be motivated to tag all the images. Wouldn't it be great to have a game you could play with fun alone or together with your children that tags the images alongside? Such a gamified app has to be entertaining and necessarily needs to produce tags of good quality. The user has to remember them to be able to find the images again later.

We developed two apps with gamification elements for mobile devices: a single-player and a multiplayer app. In a user study we evaluated both against each other and a simple non-gamified tagging app. The goal was to find out whether the gamified approaches are more entertaining than the simple tagging app and how game elements affect the quality of the image tags. Therefore, we conducted a post questionnaire after one week to determine whether the users can remember the tags they assigned to the images.

The rest of the paper is structured as follows. First, we introduce the related work. Afterwards, we present the gamified apps we developed. We conducted an evaluation with these two apps and tested them also against a non-gamified approach, as a baseline. Finally, we conclude with a discussion and present our plans for future work.

2   Related Work

Tags are a good way to organize large data collections, and are used of many large companies to visualize their data or in social media to enhance the visibility. Especially for multimedia data, tags are a good way to find them or to organize them. Users are more motivated to tag images for sharing/visibility purposes, but not for organizing their own data [1]. Therefore, many approaches try to tag data automatically. Image tagging is a large research field in the area of computer vision techniques. Images can be tagged automatically using a computer vision algorithm [3]. Many approaches try to detect objects in images; a good overview is given by Zhang [25]. New results [19] are very promising for detecting and tagging objects in images. All these approaches only use the image data to tag images.

In a collection of images, the co-occurrence of image features could be used to tag images [18]. Some approaches also use context information from the mobile device, like the location or the date, to recommend new tags [15]. But context is more than date and location [17]. Qin et al. [24] tried to recommend tags based on the information from all friends and the status of their mobile devices but this does not seem to be a very practical solution: it would require that all nearby users share their mobile device's sensor data.

Automatically computed tags are not perfect and lack contextual information. Humans are very good in detecting and identifying objects or text in images (a crucial ability to tag images), but in addition they also might know information about the context of the image. This is a reason why we should bring humans into the loop [14]. A way might be to recommend new tags to the users and let them add additional ones. Recent approaches try to learn new tags from user input [16]. They require extensive training and in particular personalization needs to adapt the mapping of features to tags for each and every single user. For tagging of private images, a combination of different approaches might be a solution. Apart from that, it is also possible to improve computer vision algorithms with user tags [9].

Human computation tries to motivate people to solve tasks that could not be solved by computers. Gamification is often used to better motivate people to solve these tasks in a gamified environment or in a game. Games with a purpose (GWAPs) are often used to tag images because tagging is a task which could not be fully solved computer-based and is very boring and repetitive [6, 23]. The ESP game for example is used to tag images for the Google search engine. Von Ahn showed that people do not play these games because they want to help solving tasks but want to play entertaining games; e.g. Peekaboom [22], KissKissBan [8].

Krause et al. [12] argued for GWAPs that encapsulate the task as much as possible in the game because it motivates users to play the game. However, hiding a task like inserting text is not easy to be included e.g. in a first-person shooter. Takhtamysheva and Smeddinck [20] showed that it is often sufficient enough to add only some playful elements like sound and graphics to motivate the users. Mekler et al. [13] found out that even simple game elements increase the amount of tags users assign to paintings. Especially points, levels and leaderboards should be used to boost user performance. They also showed that the intrinsic motivation is not effected by the game elements they used.

For personal images there are only a few games or gamified approaches. One example is a kind of memory game [2]. A problem of this approach is that only one expert rated the quality. Until now, it has also not been evaluated how good users can remember their own tags. Some approaches also use new interaction techniques to motivate the user [7]. But such games are only designed for selecting tags and not for adding tags, which is crucial for a good tagging system.

3   Gamified Tagging for Personal Images

Our goal was to develop apps with simple gamification elements that allow users to tag images in an entertaining way and help them to remember the tags they have created. The system should run on mobile devices because many people only use these devices to organize, present and share images. Because we believe that users can remember tags best when they create their own individual tags (not limited to a predefined list), the apps should allow free entries. Moreover, the time required for creating tags should be similar to simple tagging apps. This requires efficient (soft-) keyboard input for new text and excludes gamification of text-entry (e.g. hitting appearing characters in the manner of a Whac-A-Mole game).

Fig. 1. Simple tagging app without gamification

We aimed for an intuitively usable gamified application. A shooter game or very complex role-play would be problematic for users who are not familiar with these genres. Furthermore, it is complicated to integrate them with an un-gamified input like the keyboard. Therefore, we decided to develop a casual game that is easy to understand and to easy to play for everybody. The decision for the game genre was also influenced by the requirements that we did not want to use the crowd to verify or recommend tags. To develop something like a guessing game, wrong tags need to be created. When a user plays a game just after creating an image, nothing is known about these images and no wrong tags can be established.

Furthermore, we were interested whether a competitive task leads to more cheating or different tags and developed a single- and a multiplayer application. Both apps were realized for the Android platform using the libGDX framework. For the multiplayer system we used a server to establish the communication between the players. We tested these two apps against one simple app as a baseline. It allows adding tags to an image but without any gamification elements. Figure 1 shows the app: the user looks at an image, can add tags and edit or remove them afterwards. We call this app the simple app. The simple tagging app and the single-player app are self-explanatory for the users, for the multiplayer app we developed a small tutorial directly embedded in the app.

Fig. 2. Gamified single-player tagging app: (a) text entry and (b) tagged image

3.1 Single-Player App

The requirements for the gamified app are similar to the simple tagging app. A user should see an image, add tags and edit tags. This prototype is based on the assumption that even very simple game elements can motivate people to solve tasks [13]. Gamification of tagging with text input is not a trivial task, especially if nothing is known about the images. Only the numbers or the lengths of the tags are candidate measures for points and highscores. As users realize such mechanisms, they might be enforced to just add tags based on these measures. Therefore, we carefully balanced the gamification elements and the main task. In particular, we only used small and minimalistic but very typical game elements: background graphics that give the impression of a casual game, background music and sound for every input, graphics and points for every tag users add to an image.

The gamified variant is shown in Figure 2. In this prototype, an image is presented to the user in gamified graphics. The user has to add tags for which she/he receives points. Adding the same tag multiple times is excluded, but there are no semantic evaluations of the tags. People may add tags, which are semantically not correct (e.g. "petersparty" instead of "peter" and "party"), but they might be able to remember these tags very well.

Every point a player gets is accentuated with sound. These are the only game elements. We decided that the length of the tags do not score, because 'the longer, the better' is not true for tags and we do not want to bias the users or set them on a wrong track how to tag images. The only differences to the simple tagging app are:

- Background graphics
- Background sound and sound for adding tags
- Five points for every added tag

In the evaluation we investigated how these simple elements entertain the user and influence the recall of tags compared to the multiplayer app.

3.2   Multiplayer App

The second prototype uses the game elements of the single-player app and additional elements that enhance the game-character of the app. Competitive image tagging in a game or gamified app might be fun but leads to some problems: people might be more interested in the game and winning aspects and thus neglect the serious tagging task. This is the reason why many multiplayer apps for image tagging use a tag matching procedure for distinct users who tagged an image. Those mechanisms, like used in the ESP Game, can prevent the users from cheating. However, in our approach we use personal images which excludes crowd-based mechanisms. We also used no experts or a gold standard to evaluate the tags.

Von Ahn and Dabbish [23] distinguish three types of Human computation games:

- Input-agreement: One player gets an input and has to assign an output to it. The second player also receives an input and the output from the first player. Output is added if the user decides input and output fit.
- Output-agreement: Both players have to produce an output for a given, equal input. If the output is equal, it is added.
- Inversion-problem: One player creates the output and the second one has to decide if this output is correct.

We decided to implement a game which uses an inversion-problem because only using this technique we get new and verified tags from every round played by the users. Furthermore, not both players have to add tags with the keyboard, which is probably the most boring part. In our app, a user starts the competition by tagging an image. Then a second player joins the session and has to guess which tags are added by the first one. Alternately, the players are either tagger or guesser. Tags are shown for a few seconds on the screen and the guesser has to click on the tags that seemed to be correct for her/him. To realize the multiplayer app, we used a client-server implementation.

Each round contains six images. The tagger assigns three tags and one category (from the categories home, animals and people, landmark, event, or on the road) to an image. An overview of this approach is shown in Figure 3. The inversion-problem approach requires wrong tags: the guesser achieves points for correct tags while s/he loses points for incorrect ones. Wrong tags should not be fully improper (e.g. person for a landmark). Therefore, we decided to learn wrong tags directly from the user and introduced the *evil tag*. One evil tag is chosen by the tagger and can be used to set the guesser on a wrong track (e.g. a wrong spelled name, or a wrong event name). If a family returns from holidays and wants to tag the taken images together, this is a good way to challenge each other. Furthermore, we also used the non-selected categories as wrong tags. Users get points for a correct category and even more for a correct tag, but also discount for wrong selected tags (categories and the evil tag). For the correct category a user receives five points and for a tag, which was typed in by the other user, 25 points. We used the same discount if a user selects the evil tag or a wrong category.

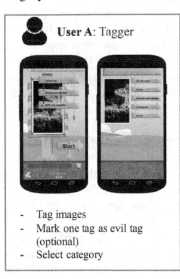

- Tag images
- Mark one tag as evil tag (optional)
- Select category

- Receive tags to click on
- Points for correct tags, discount for wrong tags
- Receive an overview

Fig. 3. Multiplayer app: Tagger on the left, guesser on the right

4   Study Design

We recruited 27 participants (20 male and 7 female) aged between 18 and 32 years (M=26). Most participants (26) own a smartphone and use its camera to take pictures. Nine of them use the camera at least once a month, 13 once a week and four of them even daily. None of our participants has ever tagged images. Twenty-two participants have games installed on their mobile device. The majority favor strategy games, followed by quiz games. But most of the participants do not play games very often.

For the user study we decided to use our own images because not every participant may comply with sharing her/his private images. Even though this has some disadvantages such as users do not know the whole story behind the images, most important is the advantage that the results are comparable. We selected 18 pictures which are good to tag, representative for mobile photos (like events, people, objects) and not displeasing. In the start questionnaire we asked the participants for the tags they would add to most of their images on theirs mobile devices. Most prominent tags are: family (added by 18 participants), holiday (16), friends (14), party (6), me (5), which corresponds to our image collection.

We evaluated the apps in a controlled lab setting using a within-subject study design. Every participant had to tag 18 images; six with every prototype. We shuffled the order of the prototypes based on Latin square. Additionally, we varied the order of the images so that every image was equally often tagged with every prototype on every position. We tested the prototypes with a Nexus 7 tablet, so the participants could see every detail of the image and all game elements.

The participants had to answer one general questionnaire at the beginning and different questionnaires after each prototype. After using the simple tagging app, they filled out the System Usability Scale (SUS [4]), which allows us to exclude that usability issues influence the tagging procedure. After the two gamified approaches, the users had to answer the Post Game Experience Questionnaire [10] to verify the motivation and emotions during the gameplay. We also used the Intrinsic Motivation Inventory [5], which is very good for gamified tasks, because we want to know if the users play the game only to solve the task or if they are intrinsically motivated to play the game.

All test runs were recorded on video. We did not enforce the participants to think aloud because this could influence the game play. After the participants have tested every prototype, they were interviewed and asked how they liked the prototypes in general, what they think about their own performances and about the quality of the tags they have created with them. We also conducted an interview at the end, asking what they liked about the apps and what might be improvements.

Because we wanted to know if the game elements help the participants to remember the tags they have created, we contacted them one week later. We asked them directly or via video chat to tag all the images again. Using this information we evaluated how good the tags, assigned with the different prototypes, are. Image tags are used to find images again later, so the recall of the tags is the crucial for the tag quality.

5   Results and Analysis

The simple tagging app had no fundamental usability problems and achieved a SUS score of $M=89.8$ ($SD=10.85$). So the differences in the following results are not caused by usability problems in the simple app, which we used as a baseline.

5.1   Gamification

For the two gamified apps, the game experience questionnaire gives quite good results but no major differences for single- and multiplayer approach. The participants rated the use of the app as a positive experience (single-player: M=3.59, SD=.71; multiplayer: M=3.87, SD=.56; 1=strong reject, 5=strong accept). They also rated the app as not exhausting (single-player: M=1.09, SD=.28; multiplayer: M=1.17, SD=.34). Furthermore, the evaluation showed that it is easy to return to reality in both apps (single-player: M=1.47, SD=.51; multiplayer: M=1.58, SD=.56) probably because of the game genre. But this is typical for mobile and also for casual games. Because there are no statistical differences between the single- and multiplayer app, we can conclude that no further results are based on different game experiences.

Using the IMI-Questionnaire we tested how motivated the people are to play with the apps and not only to solve the tagging task. These results are good and very similar for the single- and multiplayer app. The IMI results are summarized in four dimensions (scale: 1=total disagree, 5=total agree; single-player=sp; multiplayer=mp):

- *Interest* (sp: M=4.72, SD=.31; mp: M=4.89, SD=.17)
- *Competence* (sp: M=4.58, SD=.27; mp: M=4.42, SD=.12)
- *Perceived Choice* (sp: M=3.87, SD=.24; mp: M=3.74, SD=.17)
- *Perceived Pressure* (sp: M=2.61, SD=.20; mp: M=2.85, SD=.16)

Because statistical tests showed that the dimensions are not normally distributed we used a Wilcoxon test. The dimension *interest* is significantly higher for the multiplayer app (T=23.5; p<0.001; r=-0.74), *perceived choice* (T=35.5; p<0.001; r=-0.71) and *perceived pressure* (T=14.5; p<0.01; r=-0.81) are also highly significant, but not the dimension *competence*. We can conclude that the multiplayer app leads to more intrinsic motivation, which is interesting because they also have to use the keyboard and repetitive add tags.

5.2   Fun and Perceived Quality of Tags

After the participants tested all three prototypes we asked them to score every prototype with respect to the fun they had (see Figure 4) and the tag quality they think they have achieved. Every prototype was scored on a 5-point scale (1=worst, 5=best).

The simple tagging application was not rated as entertaining by most of the participants (M=3.07, SD=1.37), the single-player app was more fun (M=3.81, SD=1.00) and the multiplayer approach was rated best (M=4.52, SD=.80).

The multiplayer app was significantly better rated than the simple tagging app (t(26)=1.99, p<.001). All other relations showed no significant differences.

The participants also rated the perceived quality of the tags they added while using the different applications. All results are very good without major differences for the prototypes (simple app: M=3.93, SD=.96; single-player: M=3.89, SD=1.05; multiplayer: M=4.04, SD=.90). This corresponds with the results from the IMI questionnaire stating that there where no major differences in the perceived competence. As the participants did not have the feeling that the game part distracted the quality of the tagging task, this is quite astonishing.

In the last question we asked the participants to rate the three prototypes. The results are very clear: 88% of our participants favored the multiplayer and 83% would start tagging images with this prototype.

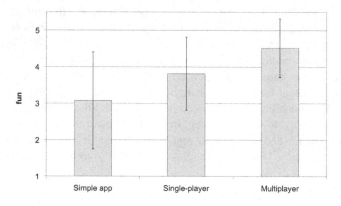

Fig. 4. Mean fun during tagging, error bars indicate standard deviation

We conclude that especially a multiplayer tagging app for playing with family and friends (and not strange people in the cloud) would be beneficial, because it motivates the users to tag their own images with fun.

5.3   Tag Recall

While one expert evaluated all tags to be sure that they all fit the images, for private images it is more important whether the users can remember their own assigned tags. All participants tagged the images one week after the initial trial again. We computed a score for each participant how good they produce the same tags again. Therefore we computed the f1-score, based on the precision

$$P=TruePositiv/(TruePositiv+FalsePositiv)$$

and the recall:

$$R = TruePositiv/(TruePositiv+FalseNegativ)$$

The f1-score is a measurement for classification tasks. We used it to measure whether tags assigned with the prototypes are equal to those in the post questionnaire.

The score describes how good people can remember the tags with each prototype (0=worst, 1=best).

$$f1 = 2 \cdot \frac{P \cdot R}{P + R}$$

Figure 5 shows the mean f1 scores and standard deviation for each prototype. The single-player (M=.72, SD=.11) application produced significant better results than the simple tagging application (M=.60, SD=.15), t(26)=1.99, p<.001. Because we did not implement any differences in these two apps despite the graphics, music and the points for a tag, we can conclude, that just these gamification elements lead to better image tags the users can remember.

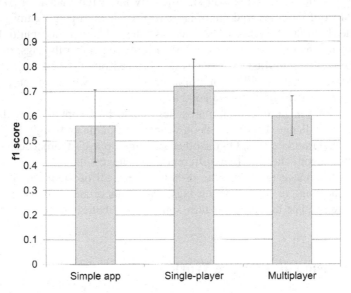

Fig. 5. Mean f1-scores for all participants, error bars indicate standard deviation

The f1-Score for the single-player application is also significantly higher than the score for the multiplayer gamified approach (M=.56, SD=.08), t(26)=1.99, p<.001 which means that our multiplayer app produced less valid tags. This might have different reasons. For instance, some elements distracted the users and they forgot some tags during the game play. Another reason might be the tag comparison between the users. Tags were only counted as correct tags, if and only if the first player has assigned the tag to the image and the second player guessed it correctly.

6   Discussion

Tagging images requires time and is a tedious repetitive task. Especially on mobile devices it is not very motivating to tag all images. Gamifying the task is a promising approach to improve the motivation. A problem is that many users are more motivated to win the game than to create good tags. Most approaches use many different people (such as *crowd workers*) to prevent the users from cheating and use the majority vote to evaluate tags. But using the crowd is not appropriate for personal images. Therefore we created a gamified approach which does not need any other users or experts: one for a single-player and one for multiple players. Both are evaluated against each other and against a non-gamified application.

In the evaluation, we provided evidence that gamification does not only turn the task into an entertaining activity but also helps remembering the assigned tags which in turn facilitates human recall. In the single-player condition, the participants remembered significantly more tags than in the non-gamified one: a few game elements helped to improve the recall significantly. The multiplayer variant was most entertaining and the participants had significantly more fun than in the simple app condition. Most of them favored multiplayer and would start tagging images because of it. This leads to the conclusion that there is a need for gamified multiplayer apps that are not only entertaining but also help the user to remember the tags. In this paper we have shown that gamified approaches do not need other experts or the crowd to create good tags. Even with a multiplayer approach we were able to create mechanisms to force the users to add good tags.

While multiplayer gamification approaches should be competitive, realizing such mechanics is a challenge. People focus on winning the game and might begin to cheat and to enter inappropriate tags. On the other side, multiplayer approaches can be used to prevent users from cheating (e.g. different users suggest the same tag). One expert evaluated all the image tags from the prototypes and all of them could be rated as correct (no cheatings or totally wrong tags). Most important, it is astonishing, that users could remember the assigned tags significantly better if they use a gamified approach.

7   Conclusion and Future Work

The approach of gamification is promising for tagging personal images. It does not only provide an entertaining alternative but also helps users to remember the assigned tags better. Furthermore, it seems that the users are not interested in cheating when tagging personal images. This allows creating apps with gamification elements that not necessarily include verification through an expert or the crowd.

In the study, the users were not interested in cheating the system at all. This might have very different reasons:

- They are focused on the tagging aspect.
- The results are influenced by the innovativeness.
- The lab setting influenced the results.

A long-term study is required to find out more about the reasons. Future work should investigate, if cheating in the long run is not a problem for personal images.

Currently we are planning to develop a gamified app for multiple players that ideally does not only make more fun but also helps to remember tags. This is interesting whenever a family or a circle of friends tag images together. A multiplayer approach with more than two players might be a solution to evaluate the tags based on the majority vote of the other players. Integrating a recommender system might allow new variegated game mechanics. We are planning to integrate computer vision algorithms and machine learning mechanisms to recommend tags or to integrate them into the system.

Furthermore, this work does only investigate the part of creating tags. Although the presented approach helps the users to remember the tags, systems and user interfaces that allow her/him to easily find the images s/he is looking for are still needed. Based on our insights we want to develop more gamified apps, not only for creating new tags, but also for the verification of tags, and combine these with a recommender system.

References

1. Ames, M., Naaman, M.: Why We Tag: Motivations for Annotation in Mobile and Online Media. In: Proceedings of the SIGCHI Conference on Human Factors in Computing Systems, CHI 2007, pp. 971–980. ACM (2007)
2. Bieliková, M.: Personal Image Tagging: a Game-based Approach. In: Proceedings of the 8th International Conference on Semantic Systems, I-SEMANTICS 2012, pp. 88–93. ACM (2012)
3. Binti Zakariaa, L.Q., Lewisb, P., Hallc, W.: Automatic Image Tagging by Using Image Content Analysis. In: Proceedings of the International Conference on Informatics and Applications, pp. 91–101. The Society of Digital Information and Wireless Communication (2012)
4. Brooke, J.: SUS - A Quick and Dirty Usability Scale. In: Usability Evaluation in Industry, Taylor & Francis (1996)
5. Deci, E.L., Ryan, R.M.: Self-Determination. John Wiley & Sons (2010)
6. Goh, D.H., Lee, C.S.: Perceptions, quality and motivational needs in image tagging human computation games. Journal of Information Science 34(5), 515–531 (2011)
7. Gonçalves, D., Jesus, R., Correia, N.: A Gesture Based Game for Image Tagging. In: Extended Abstracts of the SIGCHI Conference on Human Factors in Computing Systems, CHI EA 2008, pp. 2685–2690. ACM (2008)
8. Ho, C.J., Chang, T.H., Lee, J.C., Hsu, J.Y.J., Chen, K.T.: KissKissBan: A Competitive Human Computation Game for Image Annotation. In: Proceedings of the ACM SIGKDD Workshop on Human Computation, pp. 11–14. ACM (2009)
9. Hwang, S.J., Grauman, K.: Reading between the lines: Object Localization Using Implicit Cues from Image Tags. IEEE Transactions on Pattern Analysis and Machine Intelligence 34(6), 1145–1158 (2012)
10. IJsselsteijn, W., De Kort, Y., Poels, K., Jurgelionis, A., Bellotti, F.: Characterising and Measuring User Experiences in Digital Games. In: Proceedings of the International Conference on Advances in Computer Entertainment Technology, ACE Conference 2007, pp. 27–31. ACM (2007)
11. Kennedy, L.S., Chang, S.F., Kozintsev, I.V.: To Search or To Label? Predicting the Performance of Search-Based Automatic Image Classifiers. In: Proceedings of the 8th ACM International Workshop on Multimedia Information Retrieval, pp. 249–258. ACM (2006)

12. Krause, M., Takhtamysheva, A., Wittstock, M., Malaka, R.: Frontiers of a Paradigm: Exploring Human Computation with Digital Games. In: Proceedings of the ACM SIGKDD Workshop on Human Computation, pp. 22–25. ACM (2010)

13. Mekler, E.D., Brühlmann, F., Opwis, K., Tuch, A.N.: Do Points, Levels and Leaderboards Harm Intrinsic Motivation? An Empirical Analysis of Common Gamification Elements. In: Proceedings of the First International Conference on Gameful Design, Research, and Applications, pp. 66–73. ACM (2013)

14. Motoyama, M., Levchenko, K., Kanich, C., McCoy, D., Voelker, G., Savage, S.: Re: CAPTCHAs – Understanding CAPTCHA-Solving Services in an Economic Context. In: USENIX Security Symposium, vol. 10, pp. 3–21 (2010)

15. Proß, B., Schöning, J., Krüger, A.: iPiccer: Automatically retrieving and inferring tagged location information from web repositories. In: Proceedings of the 11th International Conference on Human-Computer Interaction with Mobile Devices & Services, MobileHCI 2009, pp. 69–71. ACM (2009)

16. Runge, N., Wenig, D., Malaka, R.: Keep an Eye on Your Photos: Automatic Image Tagging on Mobile Devices. In: Proceedings of the 16th international Conference on Human-Computer Interaction with Mobile Devices & Services, pp. 513–518. ACM (2014)

17. Schmidt, A., Beigl, M., Gellersen, H.W.: There is more to context than location. Computers & Graphics 23(6), 893–901 (1999)

18. Sigurbjörnsson, B., Van Zwol, R.: Flickr Tag Recommendation based on Collective Knowledge. In: Proceedings of the 17th International Conference on World Wide Web, WWW 2008, pp. 327–336. ACM (2008)

19. Simonyan, K., Zisserman, A.: Very Deep Convolutional Networks for Large-Scale Image Recognition. In: Proceedings of the International Conference on Learning Representations, ICLR 2015 (2015)

20. Takhtamysheva, A., Smeddinck, J.: Serious questions in playful questionnaires. In: Herrlich, M., Malaka, R., Masuch, M. (eds.) ICEC 2012. LNCS, vol. 7522, pp. 449–452. Springer, Heidelberg (2012)

21. Von Ahn, L.: Games with a Purpose. Computer 39(6), 92–94 (2006)

22. Von Ahn, L., Liu, R., Blum, M.: Peekaboom: A Game for Locating Objects in Images. In: Proceedings of the SIGCHI Conference on Human Factors in Computing Systems, CHI 2006, pp. 55–64. ACM (2006)

23. Von Ahn, L., Dabbish, L.: Designing Games With A Purpose. Communications of the ACM 51(8), 58–67 (2008)

24. Qin, C., Bao, X., Roy Choudhury, R., Nelakuditi, S.: TagSense: A Smartphone-based Approach to Automatic Image Tagging. In: Proceedings of the 9th International Conference on Mobile Systems, Applications, and Services, MobiSys 2011, pp. 1–14. ACM (2011)

25. Zhang, D., Islam, M.M., Lu, G.: A review on automatic image annotation techniques. Pattern Recognition 45(1), 346–362 (2012)

The Design Process Continues

Attending Experiential Values up to Version 1.0

Rikard Lindell

Mälardalen University, Box 883, SE-721 23 Västerås Sweden
rikard.lindell@mdh.se

Abstract. How to attend experiential values of a design throughout the implementation is still an open issue. The interplay between experience design and software engineering is problematic because of the different epistemologies of design and engineering. Interaction design is a design practice, whereas software engineering describes itself as engineering and science. There is a long tradition in design of discussing materials and the craft of making artefacts. Thus, if we have a material, it is reasonable to say that we have a craft. If programming language code is a design material, then, making a finished artefact is the shaping of material. The development process can thus continue as a design process up to version 1.0. This paper presents a design case up to version 1.0 of a music creativity app, utilising design through programming. The app design validity was evaluated in a field study at an electronica music festival. Material consciousness of code, and an open-ended, and quality-driven design process allow attention to the experiential qualities of the design.

Keywords: Experience Design, Interaction Design, Music, Creativity, Craft, Artisanship, Material, Materiality.

1   Introduction

In the experience design field we devote ourselves to create methods, practices, and knowledge to design valuable, aesthetically pleasing, and usable digital artefacts. However when our designs become finished products, their experiential qualities often get lost in the process. Buxton [1] argues that version 1.0 is critical in the software life cycle for the user experience of a digital artefact. Thus, bridging the gap between designing digital artefacts and implementing them is important. Still, how to bridge this gap remains an open issue [2-4].

This paper delineates the design process from a research prototype up to version 1.0 of an iOS music creativity app. The case portrays the relationship between design decisions, code snippets, and the resulting appearance and behaviour.

2   Background

Boehm [4] shows that software engineering has started to acknowledge usability, and that requirements of interactive artefacts cannot be defined a priori. Stakeholders

© IFIP International Federation for Information Processing 2015
K. Chorianopoulos et al. (Eds.): ICEC 2015, LNCS 9353, pp. 315–328, 2015.
DOI: 10.1007/978-3-319-24589-8_24

cannot articulate their needs to be transformed into a well-defined requirements specification. Nonetheless, models and methods in software engineering focus on solving problems and thus entail commitments to well-defined requirements [5, 6]. Engineers are trained to solve well-defined specific problems [7, 8]. Engineering focuses on convergent processes to determine one solution to one problem in a sequential refining order in an objective manner [8].

Schön [9] introduces the concept of *technical rationality* to offer an explanation of the engineer's epistemology. "Technical rationality depends on agreement about ends". Schön discusses how faith in rational, scientific, and technological solutions became dominant. These approaches were successfully applied during World War II, where the solution to a problem was to supply more resources [9]. This epistemology is part of the historical heritage in software engineering, where the metaphor of engineering is used to describe programming. Bennington [10] introduces a "top-down" engineering development model for software in 1956. This top-down instrumental approach was named "The Waterfall Model" in the 70's [5]. The Waterfall Model is still important in the development of large projects [5]. Over the last decades so called agile techniques have developed to attend use cases and features, such as the Spiral Model, Rational Unified Process, Extreme Programming and Scrum [5]. Although Scrum is designed to handle chaos and change [11], it stipulates agreements to end in so called *sprints*. In each sprint a development team commits to implement as set of usable features. These must not change during the sprint that may last up to a month. Despite the emphasis on features, Lárusdóttir et al. [3] have shown that scrum teams often fail to attend user experience values of a design.

Schön points out that technical rationality cannot solve confused and conflicting situations: "When ends are fixed and clear, the decisions to act can present themselves as an instrumental problem. But when ends are confused and conflicting, there is as yet no problem to solve. A conflict of ends cannot be resolved by the use of techniques derived from applied research; it is rather through the non-technical process of framing the problematic situation that we may organise and clarify both the ends to be achieved and the possible means of achieving them" [9]. This quote suggests that problem-setting is crucial to understand a situation to design for. Framing the problem space of the context, and cut a search tree of plentiful design proposition to reach the right user experience design of a future artefact [7, 12]. Design is the exploratory use of malleable tangible materials and provides suggestions for possible future solutions [7, 13]. The design process is tightly connected to the material and the materiality of the design [14-16]. Information technology can be regarded as a material with no recognisable features [16, 17]. However Bertelsen et al. [18] introduced materiality as a concept describing, among other digital artefacts, electronic music artefacts developed with the MaxMSP programming environment. Thus, experience designers can learn from more traditional design disciplines to be attentive to the designs' materiality [19]. Furthermore, a previous study has shown that the metaphor of material is applicable to program language code [15]. In this study the informants, users of programming languages, were concerned with the material's internal malleability. In that the language can be processed and transformed according to desire and needs.

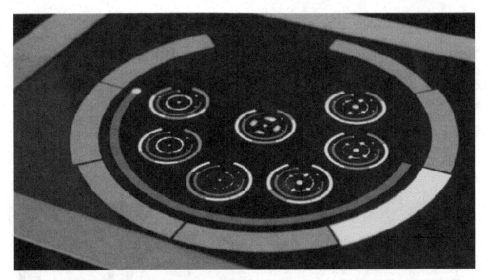

Fig. 1. The c3n play app version 1.0 running on an iPad 3 device. The photograph shows a zoomed in view of an arrangement of audio loops called a performance. Each performance consists of seven scenes indicated by the green circle segments around the performance. Each loop can be attached to any of the seven scenes. The current playing scene indicated by a fully saturated green colour.

There is a tradition of discussing material and craft and how they relate to each other [20], for instance, in the nineteenth century the discussion on handicraft and material in public education [21]. According to Adamson, "craft entail and encounter the properties of a specific material [22]." Artisans are, according to Sennett, conscious of the material and quality-driven, bordering onto the manic. They are busy perfecting their work with commitment to perform good artisanship for its own sake [23].

"Every good craftsman conducts a dialogue between hand and head. Every good craftsman conducts a dialogue between concrete practices and thinking; this dialogue evolves into sustaining habits, and these habits establish a rhythm between problem-solving and problem-finding. The relationship between hand and head appears in domains seemingly as different as bricklaying, cooking, designing a playground, or playing the cello..." [23]. The artisans are thus characterised by an ability to see and solve problems simultaneously in a dialogue between the hand and the mind. In this dialog talkbacks from the material tells the artisans what it wants to become [9]. Designers get talkbacks for their initial design ideas from design material such as sketches, storyboards, and mock-up prototypes. The goal of the design process is to frame, as much as possible, the problem for an engineering process to solve. In the ideal case, every problem is well defined and known. However, there are still design problems left unattended because the material of the design process is different from the material of the implementation process. Material consciousness of code and simultaneous problem-setting and problem-solving allow software artisans to be attentive to designs' experiential qualities in the making of the artefact [15].

3   Design Case

This design case presents the design process from a research prototype to version 1.0 of an iOS app for music creativity called *c3n play*. The development of the app was, eventually, conduced as a design project, carefully crafting the artefact in C programming language code. The design allows artists to play and collect loops, and create and edit performance arrangements. The content is presented on an infinitely large zoomable surface. The number of elements on the surface is however limited by the physical storage size of the device. The first version contains 285 loops. The user navigates with zoom and pan. Fig. 1 presents a photograph of an iPad running the app zoomed to a performance playing an arrangement of seven loops.

Fig. 2. Sketches and paper-prototypes exploring the user experience design for the research prototype.

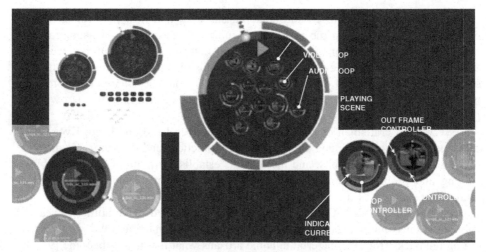

Fig. 3. This figure presents the research prototype's interface. The top left image shows an overview. The top middle image shows a performance containing audio and video loops. Each loop has scene tags connecting it to any of the six scenes. Bottom left image shows audio loops. The bottom right image shows video loops and their controls for selecting a sub-loop, beginning at IN FRAME and ending at OUT FRAME. The artist moves the sub-loop selection with the LOOP CONTROLLER to dynamically play different parts of the underlying video stream.

The starting point for the implementation of the interactive research prototype was the result of design process working with sketches, moodboards, paper prototypes

[24], see fig. 2. Fig. 3 shows the appearance of a few aspects of the research prototype's user interface. I did exploratory coding in the dynamic programming language for the design work. The coding was a conversation with the material; thus, many design problems emerged and were solved in this process. The goal was to make a sufficiently reliable artefact for field studies. Two music artists and a video artist evaluated the prototype in a multimedia performance at a festival playing electronic dance music. The collaborative design allowed the video artist to be more involved in the live performance. All artists reported this as a major advantage. Furthermore, they reported that the design in combination with touch screens gave the prototype the experiential quality of a music instrument. A video of the prototype field study can be found here: http://youtu.be/xslEtVnBnEo

4   The Making of Version 1.0

Encouraged by the results from the field study and with the advent of the iPad, I decided to make an app with this design. However, the design process had not answered all design questions. For instance, the text labels used in the prototype felt inconsistent with the design idiom. Instead of labels, we based the design on icon symbols. Inspiration for symbols came from Maya signs, electric symbols, and signs in astronomy, fig. 4 and 5. Eventually, crop circles showed to have interesting characteristics, fig. 6 (left). One can recognise a crop circle and distinguish them from each other. Fig. 6 (right) shows examples of symbols. The underlying design idea is that users will learn the meaning of the symbols from the feedback they get in interaction with the app, evoking hedonic attributes [24] of being in control.

Fig. 4. Three proposed designs for a symbolic language.

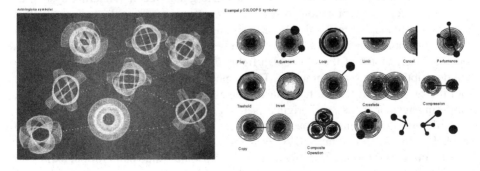

Fig. 5. Suggestion for a symbolic language based on symbols from astronomy.

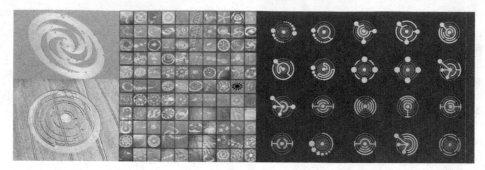

Fig. 6. Crop circles as inspiration for a symbol language (left), Corn sign inspired symbols. Each symbol can be described from a string of data (right).

The normal procedure to include graphics in an iOS app is to put PNG image files in the app's resource bundle. We implemented the in an initial attempt to create a product. This project relied on hired software engineers, and we relied on the model view controller design pattern for iOS app development. The project failed for a couple of reasons. First, the carefully selected consultants focused more on state diagrams, sequence diagrams, and design patterns than on experiential qualities. Focus on technology turned out to be disastrous because of the remaining unanswered design questions. Second, the high level technologies in iOS prescribe a specific behaviour. For example, the implementation used CoreAnimation to display content. CoreAnimation is a technology designed to provide hardware-accelerated support for animated graphics and data visualisation. The documentation does not describe the CoreAnimation constraints. Thus, it is up to the developer to empirically evaluate its usefulness. We could maybe have avoided the failure with better management and better research of the technologies in iOS; thus, better engineering. However, design problems arise as talkback from the implementation. Then, focus needs to be on experiential qualities value, instead of on technical details. Finally, the project started over, this time with no outside programmers. Our focus was the experience design, and to implement a close coupling between storage, representation, presentation, and interaction with the content.

One of the first measures was to make a scene graph vector rendering system as replacement for CoreAnimation to present content on a zoomable surface. In this environment bitmap images did not feel consistent with the appearance of the design and the zoomable interface. It felt natural to rely on the scene graph code for the symbols too. The features of the symbols in figure 7 were analysed and transformed into data descriptions for vector graphics. The symbols consist of arcs, circles, and lines from the origin. Each feature has four attributes, shell (1, 2, 3, or 4), starting angle, length (in angle, or shells), and origin offset.

A software engineering approach would have been to define a file format or use an established format, for instance SVG (scalable vector graphics) or JSON (JavaScript Object Notation). The later is a data descriptive attribute–value pairs format expressed in human-readable text that can be parsed by the JavaScript interpreter in a web browser. The Lua scripting language, used for the research prototype, also has data descriptive attribute–value pairs features. However, we carved the app in C, which is tedious and cumbersome, nonetheless we transferred the acquired skills and practice of Lua scripting to C programming. Instead of engineering a so-called *content pipeline* relying on file formats and shared libraries, the features of the symbols were described directly in C. Thus, using C as a data descriptive language.

```
void C3Symbol_createSymbols(){
    const unsigned short performanceComponents[][5] = {
    // type                 shell     angle     length offset
        {kC3SymbolShapeArc,  4,        0,        360,       0},
        {kC3SymbolShapeArc,  3,        2,        41,        0},
        {kC3SymbolShapeArc,  3,        47,       41,        0},
        {kC3SymbolShapeArc,  3,        137,      41,        0},
        {kC3SymbolShapeArc,  3,        182,      41,        0},
        {kC3SymbolShapeArc,  3,        227,      41,        0},
        {kC3SymbolShapeArc,  3,        272,      41,        0},
        {kC3SymbolShapeArc,  3,        317,      41,        0},

        {kC3SymbolShapeNil,  0, 0, 0, 0} // terminator
    };
    const unsigned short addMediaToSceneComponents[][5] =
{
    // type                 shell     angle     length offset
        {kC3SymbolShapeArc,  4,        0,        360,       0},
        {kC3SymbolShapeArc,  3,        2,        41,        0},

        {kC3SymbolShapeNil,  0, 0, 0, 0} // terminator
    };


    ...
C3ZNodeRef symbol;
    symbol = C3Symbol_createSymbol(performanceComponents);
    _symbols[kC3SymbolPerformace] = symbol;

    symbol =
C3Symbol_createSymbol(addMediaToSceneComponents);
    _symbols[kC3SymbolAddMediaToScene] = symbol;


    ...
}
```

The dataset for each symbol is parsed by the function C3Symbol_createSymbol, and the resulting scene graph node is kept in a static array. This approach has a couple of advantages: the code is cleaner because there are no dependencies to file formats, and shared libraries, and the launch time of the app is shorter because the app binary contains the compiled data. The top right of fig. 9 displays the resulting symbols for *performance* and *addMediaToScene*.

Fig. 7. In zoomable interfaces, position and scale may be arbitrary. To compensate for this, we sought a design for sliders with fixed interaction position regardless of the slider's value. Vintage telephone dials in combination with lids from McDonald's coffee cups provided inspiration for the slider design.

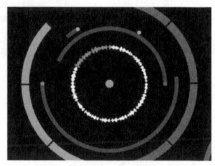

Fig. 8. A loop in a performance. The seven green tags indicate which scenes the loop is attached to. The artist tap the scene tags to attached or detach the loop to the corresponding scene. The green dot adds or removes the loop to or from the current playing scene. The blue, orange, and pink dots are slider heads at a fixed. The length of the slider's tail conveys its value.

Another example of an unanswered design problem from the research prototype was the design of sliders. In fig. 3 the sliders were arcs with various positions for the head. In a zoomable interface position and scale varies. Thus, we sought for a design with fixed positions of slider heads to make the design more consistent. In fig. 7 old dials and the layout of a plastic coffee cup lid provided inspiration for the design of sliders portrayed in fig. 8.

Fig. 9 shows an overview of c3n play. We used a spiral design language for the organisation of content. The prototype organised content in a grid, this was, however, inconsistent with the design idiom. Sub-spirals organise collections of loops in a spiral. The spiral expands with new performances and new content. The symbol for creating a new performance from the current playing loops or the symbol for appending these loops to the current playing scene creates a flow between navigating, creating arrangements and performing.

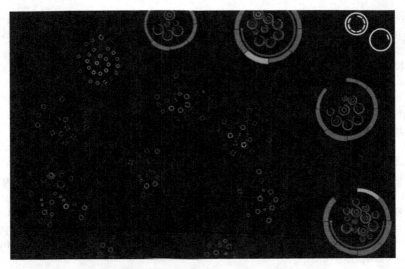

Fig. 9. An overview of the c3n play app version 1.0. A spiral of audio loops collected in sub-spirals is shown in the middle. Arrangements of loops collected in of performances are shown in the continuation of the spiral. Bright green indicates a playing scene of a performance. A tap in the left top right symbol collects the playing loops and creates a new performance. A tap on the right top right symbol adds the current playing loops to the last playing scene.

In the development of version 1.0 we used the Kanban development model. It has attracted attention by providing freedom for adaptation [24]. "Kanban leaves almost everything open. The only constraints are Visualize Your Workflow and Limit Your WIP [work in progress]. Just inches from Do Whatever, but still surprisingly powerful." [24]. The goal of a work in progress can change during the process; thus, it allows open-endedness and simultaneous problem-setting and problem-solving. The model allows the concrete material from the design process – mood boards, sketches, storyboards, videomatics etc – to be used to describe functionality. Hence, Kanban is a radically different approach than the earlier development models and allows an artisan approach in direct engagement with the features of the materials [21].

This is a link to a tutorial video for the app: http://youtu.be/gOdJwlvMOFA

5   Evaluating the Validity of the Design

We carried out the design process with professional music and video artists to perform music and video live on stage. Evaluations of prototypes have shown that the design is useful for this purpose and context. We wanted to make a design that was challenging at the first glance, but that attracts and evoke interaction, and that shows its semantics and functionality through interaction without instructions and descriptions. Our aim was to create conditions for a sense of skill among users, creating enjoyment of the design [25]. However, a new electronic musical instrument must have a low learning threshold while providing room for virtuosity [26]. The design needed to be balanced between these qualities.

Krippendorf [12] discusses the validity of a design, specifically relevant here is pragmatic validity and experimental validity. "Pragmatic validity. If the stakeholders of a design are committed to support, promote, realise, or use it, this surely is a kind of evidence that no one could ignore. Pragmatic validity lies in the hands of its stakeholders, as it should. In some sense, pragmatic validity is the ideal of a self-evident proposal that requires no further explanations." In this quote Krippendorf [27] means that users' statements about a design in various forums, reviews in online stores, and the count of followers or *likes* in social media constitute evidence to the validity of the design. In comparison with the research prototype, c3n play is a crippled app with only a few of the features necessary for professional performance use. Yet, the version 1.0 conveys the design idiom of the user experience from the research prototype. Here follows some positive user reviews of the app:

"Awsome I found it very Easy and amusing. It doesn't lag and you have a large play area, I made good beat in 6 min Max Its Worth it! Try out its an awesome app!"

"Newthinking!! Great idea and interesting interface, easy to get a groove going but still takes a while to grasp."

"great interface ,simple yet genius layout"

"Greate stuff I have tried dozens of music programs but no one is better than this app. Easy and cool to use!"

"Awesome app! I love how easy it is to play around with different sounds and compositions. The UI is interesting and solves a complex problem in a fun way!"

In an update of the iOS operating system, we missed a bug that resulted in a lower rating. "Nice app (3 of 5) I really like the app, but its not working well at the moment.pls fix "

The reviews indicated the pragmatic validity of the design. However, the 19 reviews in AppStore are a fraction of all the 4,070 downloads. The reviews are encouraging, but they do not provide a rich picture of the design's validity.

In the following quote Krippendorf [28] delineates experimental validity: "Experiments with prototypes ... [a]nswers to such questions as to whether people can recognise the prototype for what it affords, how many disruptions they experience while interfacing with it, the characters traits they would attribute to it, and which user identities the are believed to support define statistical distributions. Experimental validity ... allowing subjects to interact with a prototype, which can yield unexpected evidence in support of or against the claims advanced by its designer."

A rigorous design process still needs to be evaluated to show what meaning users attribute to the design. Evaluations show if the design fulfils the intended experience qualities.

To receive a complementary view of the design's validity, we conducted an evaluation at the Volt Festival 2014, an annual electronica music festival. We set up two iPads tablets connected to a mixer. Each tablet also had a pair of headphones. Festival visitors were invited to play. There was always music in the speakers, but if users felt unsafe, they could listen to the music they played only in their headphones. A video camera by each tablet collected data. The evening generated in total four hours of video data for 38 users. I analysed the material on users' engagement and learning. How long users played, if they made positive comments, or made suggestions for improvements to the design indicated engagement. If users seem to understand what they do, and if they asked for help, shows learning.

The average time was over eight minutes and median time was five minutes. Seven users played for 18 minutes or longer. Three of these users learned the design without introduction and one of them played entertainingly (my subjective assessment). Four of the seven needed an introduction to the design. One of these suggested improvements of the design (a button that stops all playing loops). Another user spontaneously comments: "its quite fun", "its a good one", "ah, its really cool." Two drunken users played in the late night for almost half an hour, afterwards one of them said: "this was the evening's best dance floor." This comment is somewhat narcissistic in the sense that you played better than all the artists at the festival; however, the comment indicates engagement.

Two users played for 12 or 13 minutes. These two men were intoxicated. They did not ask for help. They seemed not to learn the design.

One user played for ten minutes, she received an introduction to the system and then explored the design on her own. After six minutes, she began to dance to the music she created, an indication of engagement.

The remaining 28 users played in seven minutes or less. Ten of them had no introduction to the app, the two of these tried to use the app for a minute and did not learn how the design works. There were three of the 18 who receive an introduction to the design that did not learn the design either.

A total of seven users (including the two intoxicated) did not learn how the design works. They navigated primarily through panning, and played loops, the rest of the design's functionality remained hidden for these users.

5.1   Discussion of the Results

The evaluation was not a controlled experiment, but rather a field study without a prior stipulated hypothesis. The basis for the analysis of the data was the design's intended experiential values and to find indications if these were valid or not. Thus, one cannot say that the evaluation experiment was quantitative despite counting the number of minutes played, and how the subjects asked for help or were offered help. Since I counted and measured, I cannot say that the evaluation was qualitatively. However, the interpretation of the data was qualitative.

The app is designed for a niche. For that reason, I have prioritized interpretations from data of the users who played longer than 18 minutes. The time they devoted to play the app implies experimental design validity. However, four of the seven users needed or received an introduction to the design. This indicates that the design should be more accessible. Without a tutorial that describes the design, the first step seamed to big. It was also clear that it was difficult for users to understand the sliders. The vertical gesture manipulation that allows multiple sliders to be altered simultaneously, did not map to the sliders circular presentation.

The design of the sliders needs to be modified so that there is an affordance for vertical movement. We will also search for a design that makes it easier to get started with the app, without breaking its aesthetics, a design that leads users into the design so that they gradually learn how it works. Pohlmeyer [25] shows that a challenging design leads to satisfaction that lasts longer. The learning approach to the design corresponds to excitement in Csíkszentmihályis [29] flow model, excitement of being able to cope with something above your ability.

6   Discussion

The design case in this paper shows that the design process does not stop when the implementation start. Design through programming and treating programming language code as a design material for digital artefacts helped the making of a version 1.0 that entailed the intended experiential values. Dourish and Mazmanian suggest that there is a materiality of digital representations, and digital technologies need to be studied on their own materiality and on their particular forms of practice [30]. Previous results have shown that program language code can be considered a material [15]. Thus, masons chopping letters from stone with a chisel and a hammer can be metaphor for the description of symbols in C code. For a more sophisticated approach, a deeper analysis of the symbols could provide several glyphs that combined from a string of characters present the symbols. Yet, the stone mason's craft affected the appearance of the Roman alphabet characters. Similarly, the descriptive C code affected the look of the symbols; compare fig. 6 (right) and 8. Using C is sound for responsive, highly interactive, and performance demanding digital artefacts, especially on computationally weak devices. However, designers have increasingly developed the capacity of programming themselves, instead of relying on software engineers, through more pliable tools and dynamic languages such as ActionScript, JavaScript, and Processing.

Lárusdóttir et al. have showed that the agile software engineering method scum fails to attend experiential qualities in development projects [3]. Buxton criticised the engineering approach in his open letter on Engineering and Design [7]. The engineering community itself struggle with the issue [5]. In the design case above a year of work was lost because of engineering. Instead of engineering, as suggested in the design case, the gap between interactive prototype and version 1.0 can be bridged through a quality-driven and open-ended artisan approach characterised by material consciousness of code and careful attention to the experiential qualities of the design.

References

1. Buxton, B.: Sketching User Experiences - getting the design right and the right design. Morgan Kaufmann (2007)
2. Lai-Chong Law, E., Abrahão, S.: Interplay between User Experience (UX) evaluation and system development. International Journal of Human-Computer Studies 72(6), 523–525 (2014)
3. Lárusdóttir, M.K., Cajander, Å., Gulliksen, J.: The Big Picture of UX is Missing in Scrum Projects. In: Proceedings of the 2nd International Workshop on the Interplay between User

Experience Evaluation and Software Development. In Conjunction with the 7th Nordic Conference on Human-Computer Interaction (2012)

4. Memmel, T., Gundelsweiler, F., Reiterer, H.: Agile human-centered software engineering. In: Proceedings of the 21st British HCI Group Annual Conference on People and Computers: HCI...but not as we know it, (BCS-HCI 2007), vol. 1, pp. 167–175. British Computer Society, Swinton (2007)

5. Boehm, B.: A view of 20th and 21st century software engineering. In: Proceedings of the 28th International Conference on Software Engineering (ICSE 2006), pp. 12–29. ACM, New York (2006)

6. Kroll, P., von Krüchten, P. The Rational Unified Process Made Easy: A Practitioner's Guide to the RUP. Addison-Wesley Professiona (2003)

7. Buxton, B.: On Engineering and Design: An Open Letter. Businessweek, April 29 (2009), http://www.businessweek.com/innovate/content/apr2009/id20090 429_083139.htm (accessed April 27, 2015)

8. Löwgren, J.: Applying design methodology to software development. In: Proceedings of Designing Interactive Systems, pp. 87–95 (1995)

9. Schön, D.A.: The Reflective Practitioner - how professionals think in action. Basic Books (1983). ISBN: 0-465-06878-2

10. Bennington, H.D.: Production of Large Computer Programs. Annals of the History of Computing, vol. 5(4) (October 1983)

11. Schwaber, K.: SCRUM Development Process. In: Workshop Report: Sutherland, Jeff. Business Object Design and Implementation of 10th Annual Conference on Object-Oriented Programming Systems, Languages, and Applications Addendum to the Proceedings, vol. 6(4), pp. 170–175 (1995)

12. Krippendorf, K.: The Semantic Turn. CRC Press, Taylor & Francis Group (2006)

13. Wiberg, M.: Methodology for materiality: interaction design research through a material lens. Personal and Ubiquitous Computing 18(3), 625–663 (2014)

14. Vallgårda, A.: Giving form to computational things: developing a practice of interaction design. Personal and Ubiquitous Computing 18(3), 577–592 (2014)

15. Lindell, R.: Crafting interaction: The epistemology of modern programming. Personal and Ubiquitous Computing 18(3), 613–624 (2014)

16. Löwgren, J., Stolterman, E.: Design av informationsteknik - materialet utan egenskaper. (Design of Information Technology - the material without properties) Studentlitteratur (2004)

17. Robles, E., Wiberg, M.: From materials to materiality: thinking of computation from within an Icehotel. Interactions 18, 32–37 (2011)

18. Bertelsen, O.W., Breinbjerg, M., Pold, S.: Instrumentness for creativity mediation, materiality & metonymy. In: The Proceedings of the 6th Conference on Creativity & Cognition, pp. 233–242 (2007)

19. Redström, J.: On Technology as Material in Design. Design Philosophy Papers: Collection Two: 31-42. Team D/E/S Publications (2005)

20. Salomon, O.: Introductory Remarks, from The Teachers' Handbook of Slöjd. In: Adamson, G. (ed.) The Craft Reader, Berg, Oxford. Silver, Burett & Co excerpted, Boston (1891) (2010)

21. Adamson, G.: Thinking Through Craft, Chapter 2 Material, Berg (2007)

22. Sennett, R.: The Craftsman. Penguin Books (2008)

23. Wallace, J., Press, M.: All This Useless Beauty: The Case for Craft Practice in Design For a Digital Age. The Design Journal 7(2), 42–53 (2004)

24. Kniberg, H., Skarin, H.: Kanban and Scrum - making the most of both. C4Media Inc. (2010)
25. Pohlmeyer, A.E.: Enjoying joy: a process-based approach to design for prolonged pleasure. In: Proceedings of the 8th Nordic Conference on Human-Computer Interaction: Fun, Fast, Foundational (NordiCHI 2014), pp. 871–876. ACM, New York (2014)
26. Wessel, D., Wright, M.: Problems and Prospects for Intimate Musical Control of Computers. In: Proceedings of New Interfaces for Musical Expression (NIME 2004), Shizuoka University of Art and Culture, Hamamatsu, Japan, 3-5 June (2004)
27. Krippendorf, K.: The Semantic Turn, p. 267. CRC Press, Taylor & Francis Group (2006)
28. Krippendorf, K.: The Semantic Turn, p. 264. CRC Press, Taylor & Francis Group (2006)
29. Csíkszentmihályi, M.: Flow: The psychology of optimal experience. Harper & Row, New York (1990)
30. Dourish, P., Mazmanian, M.: Media as Material: Information Representations as Material Foundations for Organizational Practice. In: Proceedings of the Third International Symposium on Process Organization Studies (2011)

Three Apps for Shooting Sports: The Design, Development, and Deployment

Agnieszka Besz[1], Maciej Górnicki[1], Toni Heinonen[1], Tapani Kiikeri[2],
Ilkka Ratamo[2], Mika Luimula[3], Taisto Suominen[3], Aki Koponen[4],
Jouni Saarni[4], Tomi "bgt" Suovuo[5], and Jouni Smed[5]

[1] Turku Game Lab, Turku University of Applied Sciences and University of Turku
{maciej.gornicki,agnieszka.besz}@utu.fi, toni.heinonen@turkuamk.fi
[2] Rightspot Ltd., Salo, Finland
{tapani.kiikeri,ilkka.ratamo}@rightspot.fi
[3] Business, ICT and Life Sciences, Turku University of Applied Sciences
{mika.luimula,taisto.suominen}@turkuamk.fi
[4] Turku School of Economics, University of Turku
{aki.koponen,jouni.saarni}@utu.fi
[5] Department of Information Technology, University of Turku
bgt@sci.fi jouni.smed@utu.fi

Abstract. Video games rarely simulate shooting sports accurately. In this paper, we introduce three mobile applications that try to convey the essence of target shooting and biathlon to the players. We look at the applications from the perspectives of game design, implementation, and marketing. Our analysis provides a basis for developing games that take a real-world sport and help the player to appreciate the nuances of the sport, and maybe even to try it out in reality.

Keywords: mobile games, shooting sports, sport games, biathlon, game development, game design, mobile marketplaces.

1 Introduction

Sport games (together with shooters) can be called one of the original video game genres, starting from *Tennis for Two* created by William Higinbotham in 1958 [6, pp. 37–40]. Although shooting has been an integral part of video games, games focusing on shooting sports have been less common. The earliest commercial example is the rifle-shaped light gun of Magnavox Odyssey from 1972, which could be used with cartridge #10, "Shooting Gallery". Early sport games such as *Summer Games* [2], *Hyper Sports* [9] and *International Sports Challenge* [4] included skeet shooting in the events. Another typical shooting sport is biathlon, which is part of *Winter Games* [3], *Winter Olympiad 88* [17], and *Winter Olympics: Lillehammer '94* [19].

A typical feature of both the examples listed above and the modern-day video game shooting sports is that they are very simplified. They approach shooting from the point of view of a game and try make the sport as play-like as possible. This differs from the design philosophy we have engaged in our work. Our

© IFIP International Federation for Information Processing 2015
K. Chorianopoulos et al. (Eds.): ICEC 2015, LNCS 9353, pp. 329–342, 2015.
DOI: 10.1007/978-3-319-24589-8_25

approach towards these applications is more from a simulation than game. We wish to engage the user in the experience of how it really is to compete in target shooting or in a biathlon competition. Hence our applications are more like the *Microsoft Flight Simulator* [16] or the *Microsoft Train Simulator* [10] than the games mentioned earlier.

In this paper, we will present three applications for shooting sports—*Kurt Thune Training*, *Pete Patruuna*, and *Biathlon X5*—designed and developed by Turku Game Lab in co-operation with Rightspot Ltd. The plan of the paper is as follows: In Sect. 2, we describe our three applications and their intended use and underlying motivation. Section 3 continues this discussion by delving deeper into the game design, followed by a view into the implementational issues in Sect. 4. In Sect. 5, we present topics related to marketing the applications. We give a broader discussion in Sect. 6, and the concluding remarks appear in Sect. 7.

2   Three Applications

The games we have developed are not shoot-em-ups but focus on shooting as an activity with its nuances and specialities. The point of view throughout the entire development work has been sport, in an environment that is as realistic as possible. Naturally, such apps cannot be created without a thorough knowledge of the sport in question.

Kurt Thune Training was the first step to the world of shooting sport game apps. The game idea behind *Pete Patruuna* was similar, but it was intended for the young members of the Finnish Shooting Sport Federation. *Biathlon X5* combines both shooting and skiing bringing more factors such as pulse and breathing rate into focus.

2.1   Kurt Thune Training

Kurt Thune Training is a smartphone application for Android, iOS and Windows Phone aimed directly at those who have target shooting as a hobby (see Fig. 1). The application simulates realistic rifle shooting event and enables the players to practice many areas of sport shooting outside of the real-world shooting range to improve their shooting scores. The game models the sight movements of a rifle shooter as realistically as possible, which allows the players to practice coordination between the eye and finger, right timing, right aiming picture, triggering, follow through, concentration, ability to "take" top results, and make sight adjustments.

2.2   Pete Patruuna

Pete Patruuna (see Fig. 2) is a smartphone application for Android, iOS and Windows Phone platforms intended for under 14 year-old members of the Finnish Shooting Sport Federation. The application allows the player to practice air rifle shooting by practicing right timing and aiming as well as adjusting the sights in

Fig. 1. Screenshots from *Kurt Thune Training*.

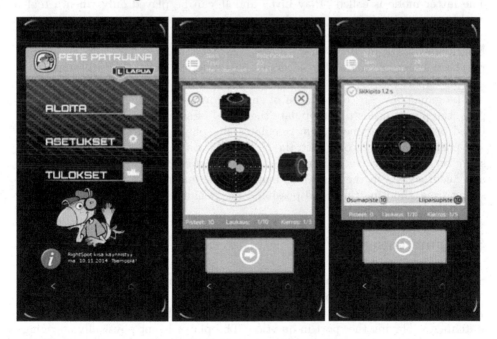

Fig. 2. Screenshots from *Pete Patruuna*.

a realistic manner. The players can also take part in a competition and compare their scores with other players' scores.

The aim of the application is to acquaint young players with shooting sports to attract new enthusiasts to the sport. The original vision behind the game was that a young person, who is an avid gamer, might get excited about the sport through the mobile game so much that they will start practicing the sport for real.

2.3   Biathlon X5

Biathlon X5 is an application made for three platforms: Android, iOS and Windows Phone (see Fig. 3). The goal of the application is to add value to the experience of watching a biathlon competition on TV and to encourage typical smartphone users to try the application and show them the phenomenon of biathlon. In *Biathlon X5*, the focus is on an entertainment, supplementary mobile service that is offered in addition to the TV screen. The interactive content of this service aims at producing additional information for the user and enhances the viewing experience with the use of a game.

The application allows the player to participate in a real-world competition in Kontiolahti, which hosted the IBU (International Biathlon Union) World Championships in March 2015, and compete with other players from around the world. The latter mode is called "Play Live" and it can be played only when a real-world competition is in progress. After each competition, the player can see the current position in the world ranking. There is also possibility to practice in the Kontiolahti track in "Play Now" mode. We have also implemented an in-app purchase system to allow the players to buy different items that will make the gaming experience better.

The gameplay is a combination of simulation and management. In the first part, the player needs to manipulate the speed of skiing by moving sliders, and based on that the game system calculates the player's heartbeat, energy level and position. In the second part, the player enters a 3D simulation of a shooting stage on a biathlon track. Here, the most important things are reflexes, wind, and accuracy. As in the real-world biathlon, the end-result is a combination of skiing time, shooting time, and possible time penalties from missed targets.

3   Game Design

Sport games create a special challenge for game designers, because many people have high expectations about what the game will be like [1, pp. 74–75]. Sport games—unlike many other games—simulate a world the player knows about by watching or playing the sport in question. The player is not physically engaging in the sport but rather playing a game embodying the spirit, atmosphere and attitude of the activity.

In this section, we focus mainly on the design of *Biathlon X5* as it is the most complicated of the three applications. Moreover, it includes and is built upon the work done in *Kurt Thune Training* and *Pete Patruuna*. Throughout the process the design of *Biathlon X5* has been discovered by following the directions of these vectors:

Fig. 3. Screenshots from *Biathlon X5*.

1. *Fidelity and realism of the simulation*: All the facts should be as correct as possible and the player should receive an experience of a real biathlon competition.
2. *Agency and usability*: The player should be immersed in the sport event.
3. *Social media and second screen functionality*: The player should be linked to the same experience with the other players as well as to the actual sports event.
4. *Monetization*: The game should produce revenue without hindering the overall playability.

These vectors are related to Murray's concept of the proper application of the affordances of the digital medium: spatiality, participation, procedurality, and encyclopedia [11, pp. 87–96]. Murray points out that for a designer it is not important to maximise the application of the affordances, and similarly here

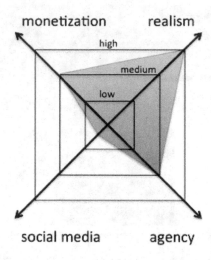

Fig. 4. The forces of the four vectors in *Biathlon X5*.

it has not been important for us to maximise the forces of these vectors (see Fig. 4). Instead, for example, in *Biathlon X5*, monetization has been important, but not in the excess. We did not want purchases being present everywhere in the application, unlike the feeling of realism, which was seen as the main goal of the project. We achieved medium level agency in the game and the social media/second screen vector played a relatively small part in the final outcome.

Whereas in *Biathlon X5* we were tackling all these vectors, the first two applications focused mainly on vector 1 and, to a lesser extent, vector 4. All these vectors have been used in the ideology of agile methods: We did not initially fix which features will be implemented in the final product, but the vectors served as ideals to aim at. At each point, when one path along any of the vectors appeared accessible, it was followed. This way we managed to come up, in time, with a product that is a complete and enjoyable game for the players, within a short development time.

Obviously, vector 1 dominated the overall design process, but it turned out to be problematic, because having the facts of the simulation and receiving a real biathlon experience contradict one another within the realm of a digital game. To give a player an experience of attending a biathlon competition means that we have to tell the player a story, where excitement is provoked by game mechanics and phenomena, such as exhaustion, are presented by game elements that serve better the production of game experience than simulation of realism.

From this perspective, biathlon, as a sport, posed an old game design conundrum: how to make a real-world endurance sport into a playable game. Most of the time in a real-world biathlon event is spent on the skiing track, which, game-wise, is not as interesting to play as shooting. For the audience, especially at home, this is a good time for social interaction. The television commentators make use of this

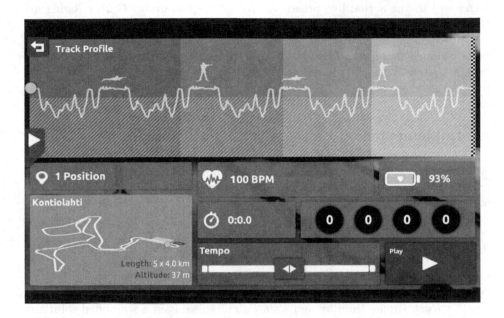

Fig. 5. Controlling the skiing.

time by analysing the athletes and relating other kinds of background information. We saw this kind of time valuable and did not want the skiing part of the game to require intensive attention—especially because vector 3 was pulling the design to another direction. Therefore, we decided to have the players to input a few parameters for the skiing (see Fig. 5). The players have only one input, tempo, that they can control during skiing. The tempo can be set for different sections of the track or it can be changed whenever the player chooses to pay attention to the game. The critical outputs that the player should observe are heartbeat rate (BPM) and the energy level (in percents).

We considered social media and involvement in the actual event an important factor, and vector 3 counted much in the initial design efforts. The original concept aimed at that the game does not disturb watching the actual live competition. Following the competition is typically a social event that the game should not hinder that significantly. Moreover, the game should improve the experience of following the live event. It can increase the social aspects, for example, by allowing the spectators to compete against one another. The game aims also at increasing the interest in biathlon and biathlon events.

Despite the initial interest, vector 3 was not followed so much later on, partly because of a tight schedule and partly because of the bad ratio of risks versus benefits. Social media is still very fresh realm and it has been discovered with serious risks of abuse. Also, it turned to be difficult to incorporate the idea of a second screen into the design, because it means that the game would be secondary to the actual live broadcast from the sport event. Games, being an interactive media by nature, are not ideal content for the second screen.

Our experiences confirm that game monetization design, vector 4, should have been included more already early on. Now, it dominated the final stages of the design process, which made it hard to include, for example, in-app purchases into the game events.

4   Implementation

All the three applications were implemented using Unity game engine [18]. During the development we encountered four implementational issues that we will address in detail here.

4.1   Database

One of the functionalities implemented in the *Biathlon X5* was the ability to compete against other users. For this reason, we created a special highscore system. In *Kurt Thune Training* and *Pete Patruuna* we used a simplified solution, but now we had to extend the multiplayer functionalities. The system is responsible for storing data on the server, retrieving it and creating new competitions. Although the idea was simple, resolving the real-time skiing of other players' overview turn out to be challenging. Therefore, the saved information is used in two ways: (1) just to display the best result of a player and, based on the score, place the players in the ranking list, and (2) to store the checkpoint times, to re-create and simulate back the skiing on the diagram. Based on that, the player can follow the other contestants like during a real-world competition. We also took security matters into account, when designing and implementing the system.

The database consists of three tables: users, race events, and high scores for all competition events. When a player starts the application, a new user is created in the database. When the player launches the competition, the application retrieves the 50 best players relevant to the selected event. After the player has finished the competition, the data is uploaded to the server. The data consists of four entries in the form of

- the checkpoint times,
- the number of misses on each shooting,
- the final time, and
- the total number of misses.

The entries are stored in JSON format. On the server side, the score is checked, and only the better score gets updated in the database table. Before accessing the server, the request needs to pass a security control, which uses a public key encryption system.

4.2   User Interface

Implementing a multiplatform user interface (UI) is always a challenging task. Especially in mobile platforms different aspect ratios, resolutions and support to old devices that have a low amount of memory available makes the UI development a slow process. In some cases, we might need two sets of UI graphics, one for low and one for high resolution devices to lower the memory footprint. For different resolutions and aspect ratios, there are different ways to achieve clear and functioning UI. One way is to focus on creating UI that can scale up or down based on different screen sizes; the other way is to make pixel-perfect UIs for each specific device or size.

The performance of the application also poses challenges. It is best to decide at the very beginning the lowest supported device for each platform that project will be released on. Moreover, the development team should always have at least one device for each platform for testing purposes during the development cycle, but, preferably, the set of test devices should cover different makers and models. Sometimes even that is not enough, but there might be variance in the same device and model from within.

4.3   Advertisements and In-app Purchases

All the three applications contain advertisements. Our system allows to create an own set of ads and place them in any place in the application, for example, on UI elements or blend into 3D objects. *Kurt Thune Training* and *Pete Patruuna* use a custom made advertising system for displaying banner ads inside menus. The system uses a web server where data and pictures is fetched to be displayed on predefined locations inside the app. Administrator can also define website addresses for specific ads.

For *Biathlon X5*, this system was extended to create and place ads also to 3D objects. In addition, *Biathlon X5* can also show Google AdMob banner and interstitial ads in menus and scene changes. AdMob was selected because it works on all mobile platforms with one plugin. To increase income we implemented an in-app system using OpenIAB plugin to help cross-platform developing. This plugin allowed a faster implementation of desired in-app purchases but required still quite much platform specific work. The implemented system allows a player to purchase new skins for the rifle or to purchase a head start that will open upcoming live competition before it becomes available to all.

4.4   Deployment

Deployment to multiple platforms even on Unity requires much work. Most problematic areas are the Unity plugins and requirements for different mobile stores. The biggest difficulties we encountered were when using plugins, which often work differently on different platforms—or they can even be totally unsupported. With *Biathlon X5*, we had particular problems with the JSON plugin on Windows Phone. Because some libraries are not supported by that platform, we had to modify the plugin to meet our requirements.

Last thing to remember are the requirements for different mobile application stores. The fastest release is possible on Android and Windows Phone, since it takes only few hours from the moment the application is uploaded. Recently, Google Play announced that it is introducing a human review process that might slow down the review time [8]. In comparison, the review of an iOS app can take about seven days after which the app will be ready to release—provided that it has passed the review. Therefore, it is best not to leave the release process for the last moment. Certain requirements can slow down the release process (especially on iOS platform). It is also good to do test release on smaller markets similar to the main target. For example, in our case we have used Finland for test releases before releasing the applications worldwide.

5   Marketing

This section presents the path leading to the current business model. The story captures the main elements of Lean Canvas tool, an adaption of traditional business model canvas of Osterwalder et al. [13] created by Ash Maurya (see Fig. 6).

Following that approach the starting point for business model design is the identification of problems that the business idea tries to solve. This problem

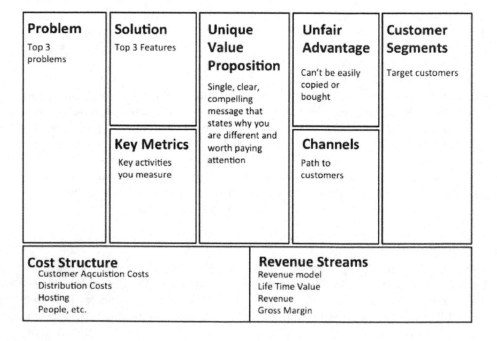

Fig. 6. Lean canvas [15].

identification is naturally strongly linked with the right customer segments. As mentioned earlier, the second screen feature was left out of this application. Still, market is two-sided, since the players of the game are not only customers but also audience to advertisers. Also, for the future development International Biathlon Union (IBU) as well as single event organizers may be customers. Therefore, the problems are here presented, not only from the end user perspective, but also from the perspective of the biathlon as a sport.

Starting from the end user, the very nature of biathlon—shooting—makes it rather difficult hobby for ordinary people. Legal regulation of shooting generates remarkable barriers to start that hobby. Therefore, most of the biathlon race followers lack own experience of the sport, which makes it harder to understand race situation, strategies, etc. That is, TV experience of the race could be deeper and more exciting. The lack of own experience makes commitment to the sport easily thinner than, for instance, in soccer, ice hockey or any other sport where the followers also have their own experience in playing those games.

Another problem for biathlon is the demographics of the followers. The viability of a sport is based on popularity and attractiveness to advertisers. Basically, the current situation is rather good, since biathlon is very popular sport in Central-Europe and in Russia. For instance, during the world cup season 2012–2013, there were 140 million TV-spectators for the most popular race. There is, however, one problem: the demographics. Most of the spectators are over 60 years old and more than half are retired. In the case of biathlon the fundamental problem, generally speaking, is to generate new followers to the sport.

In order to produce a viable service, it is critical to identify special needs for each of the segments. Within the consumer segment we can identify three rough sub segments: fans of biathlon, generic winter sports spectators and random spectators. Since there are advertisers, it is obvious that we have a two-sided market at hand. Following the logic of a two-sided market, the customers in the latter group are both biathlon race organizers (IBU, local teams) and broadcasters. Based on the previous, the value proposition for the end users is an experience very close to the real biathlon one. For the biathlon race organizers and other right holders, the value proposition is better content for the end-user and new, more committed fan-base.

The second screen case—or service for biathlon race organizers—present a typical egg–chicken problem of network markets is present. To make the firm side interested, a solid customer base is needed. In the current competitive environment it is not easy to gather critical user mass for a novel application. These factors make it difficult to sell new services to content producers. Even if there is need and will to develop more participatory services to improve user experience, the B2B-customers often choose safer solution. In this case general solution, as good biathlon simulation game as possible, is a good starting point. With a superior solution, it is possible to build up big enough end-user base also to be lucrative for business side of the two-side market.

A key factor driving the business growth is the channels delivering the product to the customers. The game is available for the customers in chosen application stores (App Store, Google Play, Windows Phone Store). In addition to delivery, the stores provide product information for the customers. The main challenge for new applications is the number of applications: in each store there are vast number of different applications competing not only for the customer attention but also for their most limited resource: time. This problem has been tried to cope with media presence: the developers of the idea has presented the game in TV and other media to make the game known to the users.

The last part of the model is the analysis of the sustainability of the competitive advantage. In this case, the original developers of the idea have a great biathlon sport know-how to reach all the relevant stakeholders and to deliver a full-scale authenticity to the players. Also, there is a dedicated multitalented team to carry out the development as well as networking capabilities to reach important interest groups and media visibility

6   Discussion

Recently, one of the objectives has been to serve new interesting content for biathlon fans and tourists visiting in biathlon events. For example, Hawking et al. [5] report that tourism service has special needs (e.g., do-it-yourself travelling) that requires tailor-made applications. These applications should offer for the users services which are relaxing and enjoyable. In addition, services should be narrative to enrich travelling experiences. Mobile devices users have currently a need for ambient intelligence, for user friendly UIs, and for services just in time (location-aware and/or context-aware).

Regarding the future, researchers have investigated intensively for years how mobile devices could be utilized in tourism. For example, Nielsen et al. [12] have categorized user experiences in four areas, namely activating, learning, entertaining, and experiencing. Especially *Biathlon X5* can provide new possibilities for sport event organizations to fulfill the users' needs in these four areas. As Pine and Gilmore [14] have stated, user experience requires a lot of financial resources. In order to increase the customer's interest we have to refine the raw materials (in this case all the content visible in the television plus all the marketing material) to new products (such as applications presented in this paper), and to new services (which are offering new user experiences in all four categories listed above).

The *Biathlon X5* project has been tested in real-life conditions in Kontiolahti IBU World Championships in March 2015. All in all, one of the advantages in this project has been to focus not only in piloting or demonstrating something new and innovative but also on commercialization. Collected feedback from the field in the world championships has been mainly promising. This first version contained content just dedicated to the Kontiolahti venue. In the future, we need more content including tracks, avatars, and shops. We believe that this kind of a hybrid game application (containing management and real-time playing) has business potential but needs a lot of more research. It will be interesting to study how players will use these type of games in a long-term period (e.g., covering a whole biathlon season). One of the future directions can be to focus also on new marketing innovations. In fact, *Biathlon X5* can be seen as an ecosystem which consists of various applications or screens which can be used simultaneously. For example, real-time playing sport fans might like to play in public environments. This could include testing players' physical and shooting conditions. Motion detection, wearable computing, and intelligent environments could give us a lot of new possibilities providing new added-value services as a part of this ecosystem. Naturally, these features of the game requires extensive usability evaluations.

One approach to develop that kind of an innovative product is to do it in collaboration with university partners like the Turku Game Lab, whose research philosophy is in applied research. This project is a typical example in which we will try to apply the latest game technologies in industrial cases. Research and development is implemented in various test generate cycles which has similarities to the IS research framework presented by Hevner et al. [7]. That is to say, we are designing artifacts, analysing problem relevancy, late evaluating research contributions typically based on usability evaluations based rigorous research methods. These test generate cycles in our case can be seen in two different stages. In the case of Rightspot, we are doing research and development which is based on agile methods. Based on improvements and alternative solutions we will get a progress which is in line with the customer's directions. Test generate cycles can be seen also in a more general perspective. We are namely testing game technologies in various cases parallel. This will open us a better understanding how these up-to-date technologies can be applied in various fields such as tourism and sport but also, for example, edutainment, healthcare and technology industry. Interacting in the same time with various clients and testing pilots, prototypes, demonstrations, and even products in various domains will improve our understanding of the potential of game technologies in new service innovation development.

7 Conclusion

Shooting sports provide an interesting area for mobile applications. Although one can label it as a niche market, it does have potential to be interesting even for an average player. In this paper, we presented three applications that aim at fulfilling this potential. We analysed the development process from various perspectives—design, implementation, and marketing—and proposed new ways for utilizing them.

Acknowledgments. Our warmest thanks go to Max Lindblad and Hanna Ahtosalo who acted as a lead programmer and a lead artist, respectively, in *Kurt Thune Training* and *Pete Patruuna*, and to Jonathan Sarry who worked on the database for *Biathlon X5*. We would also like to thank Tapani Liukkonen for his input on the historical game review.

References

1. Adams, E.: Fundamentals of Game Design, 3rd edn. New Riders, San Francisco (2014)
2. Epyx: Summer Games. Software (1984)
3. Epyx: Winter Games. Software (1984)
4. Harlequin: International Sports Challenge. Software (1992)
5. Hawking, P., Stein, A., Sharma, P., Nugent, D.: Emerging issues in location based tourism systems. In: Proceedings of the International Conference on Mobile Business, pp. 75–81 (2005)
6. Herman, L.: Phoenix: The Fall & Rise of Videogames. Rolenta Press, Springfield (2001)
7. Hevner, A.R., March, S.T., Park, J., Ram, S.: Design science in information systems research. MIS Quarterly 28(1), 75–105 (2004)
8. Kim, E.: Creating better user experiences on Google Play. Android Developer Blog, March 17 (2015), http://android-developers.blogspot.com/2015/03/creating-better-user-experiences-on.html
9. Konami: Hyper Sports. Software (1984)
10. Kuju Entertainment: Microsoft Train Simulator. Software (2001)
11. Murray, J.H.: Inventing the Medium: Principles of Interaction Design as a Cultural Practice. MIT Press, Cambridge (2012)
12. Nielsen, L.B.: Post Disney experience paradigm?: Some implications for the development of content to mobile tourist services. In: Proceedings of the 6th International Conference on Electronic Commerce, pp. 657–666 (2004)
13. Osterwalder, A., Pigneur, Y.: Business Model Generation: A Handbook for Visionaries, Game Changers, and Challengers. John Wiley & Sons, Hoboken (2010)
14. Pine, J., Gilmore, J.: The Experience Economy. Harvard Business School Press, Boston (1999)
15. Spark59, Inc.: How to create your lean canvas, https://leanstack.com/LeanCanvas.pdf (accessed April 22, 2015)
16. subLOGIC: Microsoft Flight Simulator. Software (1982)
17. Tynesoft Computer Software: Winter Olympiad 88. Software (1988)
18. Unity Technologies: Unity. Webpage (2015), http://unity3d.com/
19. U.S. Gold: Winter Olympics: Lillehammer '94. Software (1993)

Yasmine's Adventures: An Interactive Urban Experience Exploring the Sociocultural Potential of Digital Entertainment

Valentina Nisi, Mara Dionisio, Julian Hanna, Luis Ferreira, and Nuno Nunes

Madeira-ITI, University of Madeira. Campus da Penteada 9020-105, Funchal, Portugal
{mara.dionisio,julian.hanna,luis.ferreira}@m-iti.org,
{njn,valentina}@uma.pt

Abstract. Urban computing systems impact quality of life in densely populated areas. With the widespread availability of wireless networks and portable devices, urban areas are fast becoming a hybrid of the physical environment and the digital datasphere. This paper describes Yasmine's Adventures, a location aware storytelling platform that leverages on urban computing strategies to create an interactive walk through the Mehringplatz area, surrounding the Jewish Museum in Berlin. Yasmine's Adventures (YA) is a mobile application that delivers a sequence of animations clips tailored specifically to the Mehringplatz neighbourhood. The story follows an adventurous local girl as she walks home alone, visiting local landmarks. Yasmine's perceptions of the landmarks, identified by community members in an earlier workshop, reflect the real concerns of the community. This interactive experience was created to engage visitors of the Jewish Museum to explore the relatively neglected streets of the area in which the museum is situated.

Keywords: Mobile socially driven entertainment, Interactive narrative, Digital storytelling, Location aware virtual reality, Urban computing.

1   Introduction

Urban computing systems [1] can have a powerful impact on improving quality of life in densely populated areas. With the widespread availability of wireless networks and portable computing devices urban areas are fast becoming a hybrid of the physical environment and the digital datasphere. Our work falls into an area known as 'locative media' [26], which frames mobility not as a problem to be overcome but as both an everyday fact and a new opportunity to create interactive experiences that rely upon or exploit movement and space. The motivation for this work is that the conscious layering of space and narrative provides a deeply compelling experience and a high level of immersion [25]. Moreover, understanding mobility in its cultural settings requires that we pay attention to the symbolic and aesthetic aspects of technological urbanism as well as the purely instrumental [19].

This paper describes Yasmine's Adventures, a location aware storytelling platform that leverages on urban computing strategies to create an interactive trail across the

© IFIP International Federation for Information Processing 2015
K. Chorianopoulos et al. (Eds.): ICEC 2015, LNCS 9353, pp. 343–356, 2015.
DOI: 10.1007/978-3-319-24589-8_26

landscape surrounding Mehringplatz in the Friedrichshain-Kreuzberg borough of Berlin. This interactive walk was created with the goal of challenging and engaging visitors of the world famous Jewish Museum Berlin to explore the adjacent and relatively neglected streets of the area in which it is situated.

Historically (until the 18th century) one of the three major squares of the city, Mehringplatz today is quite a different place. Located in central Berlin, today the area is considered by many to be unremarkable at best, ugly and unfriendly at worst. Marked as a socially disadvantaged neighbourhood, it has acquired a negative reputation in recent decades. In contrast, the Jewish Museum Berlin, built by architect Daniel Libeskind in 2001, is an award-winning, internationally recognized building. Local residents of Mehringplatz have been actively trying for years to change the area's reputation, for example by emphasizing its multicultural identity, its tolerance and diversity, and its welcoming attitude. Such qualities are often overlooked by visitors to the area, however, who are usually focused on visiting the museum. Leveraging on the colocation of the Jewish Museum, which attracts more than 700,000 visitors per year [2], we took the opportunity to shine a spotlight on the Mehringplatz community by revealing the everyday lives, local landmarks, and important issues of the community to visitors of the museum. Through our interactive walk we created an opportunity for people to wander the local streets and establish a link between the museum and the neighbourhood in which it is embedded.

Through the interactive walk the audience follows the adventures of a free-spirited local girl named Yasmine, as she sneaks away from her class field trip to the museum and attempts to walk home alone. The story is delivered through the Yasmine's Adventures (YA), a mobile application that delivers a sequence of short animations tailored specifically to the Mehringplatz neighbourhood: revealing, through the adventures of Yasmine, the community's feelings about itself. The 2D animated stories are embedded in 3D virtual environments that reproduce the real features of the Mehringplatz streets. These 3D panoramas are revealed to users when they capture specific markers (See Fig. 3 below) strategically positioned in order to lead the audience from the Jewish Museum into the heart of Mehringplatz.

The locations where each segment of Yasmine's Adventures takes place were determined by community members as part of the RDL/UdK-led 'Pinpointing Mehringplatz' workshop [3]. Each pinpointed place holds specific positive or negative values for the local residents. By seeing the neighbourhood through Yasmine's eyes, the audience also sees it through the eyes of the community: the most beloved spaces, the areas that require change, and the spaces that are disliked or seen as problematic by the community all feature in Yasmine's story.

The Yasmine's Adventures project was developed to be showcased at the international symposium Community Now? The Politics of Participatory Design, which took place from 19-21 February at the Jewish Museum Berlin.

2   Related Work

Urban computing is generally defined as the process of acquiring, integrating, and analyzing big and heterogeneous data generated by diverse sources in urban spaces, such as sensors, devices, vehicles, buildings, and humans [20]. Urban computing investigates the ways in which computing technologies shape, are shaped by, and mediate our experience of urban space, reflecting the contemporary reality of the city as a nexus of computational infrastructures [19]. The areas of research in mobility and mobile computing applications are driven by two primary considerations: i) mobilizing static applications allowing people to carry on traditional desktop tasks while on the move; and ii) providing people with access to resources in unfamiliar spaces, helping people navigate space in terms of resources such as devices, services, or people [19]. In this context patterns of movement go beyond moving from point A to B and may enact social and cultural meanings; therefore navigation through urban space enacts aspects of cultural identity. Such work falls under location-based social networks in which individuals are connected by interdependency derived from their locations in the physical world as well as their location-tagged media content [20].

Creative interventions in this domain fall under locative media in which location and time are considered essential to the work [24], alluding to the fact that a user's context and their movement through space need to be taken into consideration during the design process for a mobile media system. Locative systems encompass a number of different fields and applications, from art to academic research, including many different authoring tools, games and narrative experiences [8]. Location Aware Multimedia Stories (LAMS) is one area of locative media. LAMS refers to cinematically rendered narrative content related to specific locations and embedded in those real spaces through the use of location aware mobile technologies [8]. LAMS combine the mobility of the audience with spatial distribution of the story content in interactive, multi-threaded narrative experiences to create a synergy that encourages the development of a sense of place from otherwise unknown spaces.

Urban spaces are rich and multilayered in symbolic and material meanings [4]. Complex layers of history alter their physical and social aspect. Today, mobile devices and the consumption of mobile multimedia are ubiquitous. By designing and producing virtual layers of information that combine with the existing material layers we can have a direct impact on how a location is perceived and experienced by visitors and residents. Nowadays cities are often augmented with different layers of multimedia content in order to tailor specific experiences for their users. Several projects in the past two decades have explored the association of digital media to urban locations with the intention of providing rich entertaining and educating experiences [5,6]. These projects have in effect laid the foundations and established guidelines for how to design mobile location aware experiences. In our case, we learned from these projects how to carefully orchestrate a complete mobile experience, pacing content to avoid overloading the audience with overlapping tasks and media. In particular a number of these projects focused specifically on empowering communities, highlighting local histories [7,8,9], counteracting media reports that damaged the reputations of disadvantaged neighbourhoods [10], and connecting communities with visitors [11].

Building on this work, we envisaged leveraging on past findings while tackling some of the challenges that still remain unresolved. For example, how to address GPS inaccuracy in pinpointing exact locations, or how to best combine and take advantage of different location aware sensors and technologies such as iButtons, RFID tags, or QR-Codes to refine the location specificity of the application [12,13,14]. Moreover, even when the technical layer of the design seems resolved, practical issues still crop up: for example, how to ensure that tags or other equipment left outdoors are not vandalized, how obtain permissions for working in public spaces, or how to reflect the specific (e.g. socio-economic) realities of a location while guaranteeing user safety.

To address some of the above issues many projects resort to virtual reality (VR) and augmented reality (AR) as means to associate content to locations. Such technologies can serve as a highly efficient means of anchoring the viewer to the real space around them [15]. However the low accuracy and frequency of AR can create jerky augmentation, which may negatively impact the user experience [16, 17]. For this reason many projects opt instead for virtual reality, which means reconstructing the environment virtually and overlaying it with content inside the 3D reconstruction. For example, in the project 'Matera: Tales of a City', the authors used virtual reality environments to share memories and stories that took place in that ancient physical location. This approach, in addition to site-specific viewing, supports location independent viewing, where the content can be uploaded to the Internet for later reflection and recollection [18]. In this way the project expands its potential audience and the timeframe in which the experience can be enjoyed by the public.

In summary, several projects over the last two decades have explored the association of digital media to urban locations with the intent of providing rich experiences that take advantage of urban technologies. The related work analyzed above has informed some of our design decisions, described in detail in the section below.

3   Designing Yasmine's Adventures Interactive Experience

3.1   The Concept

Yasmine's Adventures was conceived with the goal of exposing non-residents (in this case the symposium audience) to the issues and attractions of the Mehringplatz neighbourhood by encouraging them to see the area from the point of view of the community. The process originated with the 'Pinpointing Mehringplatz' workshops, in which local community members expressed opinions about features of the neighbourhood as pleasing, displeasing, or potentially transformational. Locations were chosen and photographed by community members themselves, led by UDK.

By analyzing the locations and content provided to us by UDK workshop organizers, we identified a convenient route leading participants from the museum into the heart of the neighbourhood. This route took into consideration the constraints of a frigid Berlin winter, hence not exposing people to harsh weather conditions for more than 20 minutes, after which any experience would become unpleasant. Based on the issues raised by the community members themselves we selected five anchor points for our interactive walk. Some had positive connotations, like the local hip hop youth space or murals that had been painted by famous artists. Other locations had negative connotations for the community, like the construction site at the center of the neighbourhood and the dirty alleys behind some of the apartments. Yasmine's Adventures echoes the positive or negative feelings about neighbourhood locations. For example, Yasmine is scared and unhappy near the construction site, because of its ugly intrusion into the landscape. Conversely she has fun at the youth club dancing to hip hop. Yasmine's Adventures highlights the community's concerns, making them visible outside the community.

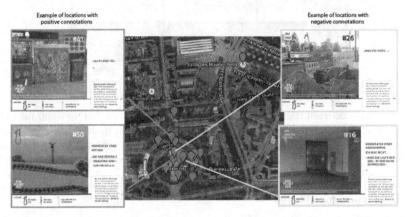

Fig. 1. Map of the neighbourhood with all 'Pinpointing Mehringplatz' locations. On the left and right are samples of content produced by the community in the original format.

3.2   The Story

In order to engage our audience in following someone through the neighbourhood, we wanted a character who would elicit empathy. For this reason we opted for a child protagonist and created Yasmine, a 7-year-old girl from the neighbourhood. Her appearance reflects the ethnic diversity of Mehringplatz. She is a curious and adventurous girl. The story starts with her school trip to the Jewish Museum, where our interactive walk was made available to the public. Yasmine is bored by the strict rules of the school trip and decides to escape, running away from the museum and walking home on her own. Along the journey she stops in various places such as the children's playground and the KMA where hip hop classes are offered (both very positive). Continuing her journey, she follows a painter to the popular street murals. She talks to the painter and learns about the murals. Then the story moves into a fantastic event, as one of the murals comes to life and a big bird depicted in it flaps its wings and flies into the air. Yasmine decides to follow the bird as it flies away, finally landing on the angel statue at the center of the square. Near the angel is where much of the unpopular construction is taking place: a location that the community would like to change. Here Yasmine starts to become worried: it is getting dark and the construction site is scary. She runs off and then, tired and scared, declares that she wants to go home. But one last obstacle must be overcome: she finds herself in an alley near the apartment block where she lives, a site that the community labelled as dirty and often full of rats. As the night turns stormy, a flash of lightning illuminates the alley, and she sees the menacing shadow of a rat. She remembers something given to her by the angel, a magic feather, and that helps her to find the way home.

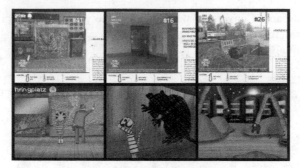

Fig. 2. Connection between community content and Yasmine's story. Left to right: the first top and bottom pictures show the mural and Yasmine learning about murals in Mehringplatz by talking to the painter. Second top and bottom: the dirty alley as reported by the community, where Yasmine meets the rat. Last top and bottom: the construction site in Mehringplatz.

3.3   The Experience Design

Ideally our audience would become aware of the interactive walk at the Jewish Museum through the ticket desk or posters. If interested they would be given a phone or instructed how to download the application to their own device and how to use the app. The user then has to go outside the museum and look for visual cues or markers. These markers, located in strategic spots, are easy to see and access. The markers are A5 postcards depicting scenes from Yasmine's Adventures. By pointing the phone's camera at the marker and capturing it, a 3D reconstruction of the surrounding environment loads and is displayed on the screen. Once the 3D environment appears the user is prompted to scan the real environment looking for story content. Thanks to the phone's accelerometer and compass, the 3D reconstruction of the environment follows the user's movements, updating the screen with a 3D version of the real environment outside. Within the 3D environment story elements are highlighted by an orange circle. The orange circle is a loading cue: it means that story content related to that precise spot in that location is loading. The user stops and waits until the video animation is fully loaded and then watches it. The animation depicts adventures in that specific location.

When the video is over, the user returns to the 3D environment screen by clicking a back button, and scans the real environment for more stories. If no more stories are available, the user can go back to the 2D map and follow the indications of where to go next to see more adventures of Yasmine. The application covers content in six different locations, all reconstructed in 3D. One or more 2D animations of Yasmine's Adventures are found in each location. The story is sequential so the locations have to be visited in the correct order. Yasmine's story ends after all six locations highlighted on the map have been visited. The user then returns the device. The walk lasts approximately 20 minutes: the duration was a design consideration due to the cold Berlin winter, which could lead to an unpleasant or unfinished experience.

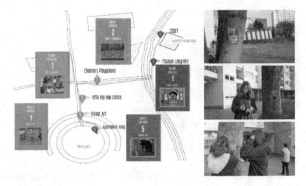

Fig. 3. Left: The experience points with content associated to the visual marker. Right: The visual markers placed in the real environment and participants interacting with them.

3.4   Technical Description

The implementation of the mobile application that delivers the Yasmine's Adventures Experience was programmed in C# using the Unity[1] game engine. The main interface is composed of a scrollable map, a 'close' button, and a 'capture the marker' button (see Fig. 4). In order to recognize and capture the visual markers we used Vuforia, third party software developed by Qualcomm[2] and available as a plugin for Unity. Vuforia is a mobile vision platform offering many features to generate vision-based computing experiences. Vuforia allowed us to associate a 'visual marker' with specific content, in our case a 360-degree 3D panorama. The use of this plugin allows us total freedom in the design of the 'visual marker' since it detects and tracks features that are naturally found in the image itself and compares them with a known target resource database[3].

Each marker is associated with a 360-degree 3D virtual environment. To achieve the 360-degree interaction we used the Durovis Dive plugin developed by Durovis[4] expressly for Unity. Durovis Dive transforms a mobile device into a virtual reality headset using a nylon viewer that features two adjustable lenses. These lenses project an image of the virtual scene into each eye. This feature is combined with head-tracking software that makes use of the mobile device's inbuilt gyroscope. For our purposes we tweaked the software so that we did not have to use the viewer for the 3D effect, and only required the virtual scene to display on the mobile device. For this we were able to implement an interactive 360-degree virtual environment playing from a Samsung Galaxy S4 mobile device.

---

[1]   http://unity3d.com/
[2]   https://www.qualcomm.com/products/vuforia
[3]   https://developer.vuforia.com/library/articles/Training/Image-Target-Guide
[4]   http://www.durovis.com

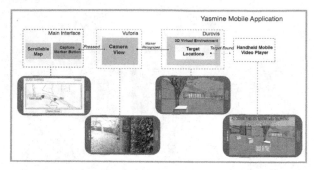

Fig. 4. Yasmine mobile application flow. Top: The flow of the technical implementation can be seen. Bottom: Corresponding screenshots.

For YA we recreated five three dimensional virtual locations of the neighbourhood in which to disseminate the animations. The 3D models had to be low poly to reduce the processing power needed to render them. The real locations chosen were modeled and textured according to the visual style of the animation (see Fig. 5). The entire surrounding environment in the locations is rendered in shades of grey except for the exact location where the story happens. This way the colored features of the environment attract the attention of the user to the content. Once the target location in the virtual environment is found and users lock their scanning movement on it, the animation video loads and plays. When the video playback finishes Unity resumes, showing if there is more content to explore or not. All the multimedia content is stored on the mobile device and no data connection is needed.

Fig. 5. Screenshoot of sections of the 3D panoramas at the KMA location. The green circle indicates content presence and loading(central picture)

3.5   Mixing Realities

While designing the Yasmine's Adventures Experience we had to make several design and technology choices. In the following section we will describe our design rationale in detail. In order to be able to highlight the precise connection of the content to specific points on the location, we opted for reconstructing the environment surrounding the users as a 3D environment. In fact replicating the real environment surrounding the user on the device and placing content in the 3D environment itself allowed us unprecedented precision in communicating to the player the relationship of the content to that exact space. GPS alone would not have given us precise support for the connection between the stories of Yasmine and the places pinpointed by the community. At the same time, the real space around the user still acts as reference, as the 3D world depicts the same environment.

We decided to adopt physical visual markers to indicate the presence of content around the neighbourhood streets. Adopting markers in order to trigger the related 3D reconstruction of the surrounding environment allowed us to place the markers in the vicinity but still in a safe and accessible place for the player to stop, capture and view the content. Once the marker is captured, the user can move from the place where the marker was positioned and still carry the reference to the content in the 3D environment of the device. Through the act of scanning the 360-degree environment the user becomes familiar with the surrounding peripheral space. S/he can then lock the motion in the direction of the related content, which is the same precise spot in the 3D environment. After viewing the content the user can resume looking around and checking the real surrounding place to reflect on what s/he just saw. The replication of real space in 3D also evokes a sense of wonder and contrast between real and virtual. Through this design we wanted to open up space for imagination, assisting the viewer in thinking about the space in different ways (e.g. from the point of view of a neighbourhood child), or deepening immersion in the story itself.

As the project has a strong community focus, while designing the application we envisaged the eventual possibility of community members and visitors adding more stories or comments to the highlighted locations, as well as adding new ones. We foresaw the experience in later iterations fostering dialogue and eliciting ideas and comments from residents and non-residents alike. Such changes would add a layer of feedback and participation of the user and eventually of the community itself. The details of such an extension of the system have not yet been designed or discussed in detail, belonging to the possible future work and directions of the project.

Furthermore, we envisaged the experience as contained in the 3D panoramas and animations available for sharing with non collocated audience via the Internet. In this way it would be available to appeal to a larger audience without losing the site specificity of the story, which would remain captured in the 3D reconstructions of the environment. A sort of virtual representation of Mehringplatz and the issues highlighted by its own community would be created, sharable and updatable through the Web.

3.6   Pilot and Findings

We piloted the YA application during the Community Now? symposium, which took place at the Jewish Museum Berlin in February 2015. The aim of the pilot was to collect feedback for further refinements of the application and guidance for the design of a wider user study. The walk was available to symposium guests during the lunch break. A special desk was set up just outside the symposium lecture room with three researchers and ten mobile phones available for guests to borrow. Participants borrowed the mobile phones with the interactive application already installed. The researchers at the desk explained how to use and interact with the application, how to find and capture the markers along the way, and where to return the devices at the end of the experience. After the explanation two of the researchers followed the users as they interacted with the story, shadowing them and observing their actions. The users were told that the researchers would be around and available to help and answer questions if they encountered any problems. At the end of the experience there was a one-page questionnaire for users to complete with details of their experience. Because we were testing an experience we decided to focus on flow [21]. Flow is a subjective state in which the person is intensely involved in a task, ignoring other stimuli and being fully invested in a precise challenging but achievable activity [21]. Flow theory has been applied in many different domains of experience, including sport, art, work, games, and HCI [22]. The questionnaire includes some demographics and a section intended to evaluate the flow of the experience through several Likert scale questions. Flow is a fairly stable concept, but the techniques used to measure flow vary significantly. For the purpose of our pilot evaluation we used a simplified version of the flow questionnaire described in [23]. The questionnaire also included space to write down free comments for qualitative assessment of the experience.

Several participants took the walk and communicated reactions to the researchers in person, while four completed the flow questionnaire. The pilot was a limited qualitative probe into the experience, in order to gain insights and lay groundwork for the design of a wider study. Pilot findings are described in detail in the following section. The results involve the analysis of the feedback gathered through observations, questionnaires, written comments, and loose feedback during the experience and the rest of the symposium day.

Flow of the Experience: Flow experience is achieved in conjunction with activities that are simultaneously and equally providing fluency (e.g. 'I knew what I had to do each step of the way', 'I felt that I had everything under control') and a high level of absorption (e.g. 'I didn't notice time passing'). From the four completed questionnaires the results are promising. All users indicated high levels for losing the notion of time and medium-high levels for being absorbed in what they were doing. The degree of challenge was appropriate despite the fact that most users had low familiarity with this kind of interactive experience. In terms of fluency, users reported that they did not have difficulty concentrating and felt like they had everything under control, which indicates some fluency. Although the sample is not significant these initial results are encouraging in indicating the presence of a flow state while participating in the experience.

Orienting the User in Finding and Viewing the Content: From the voiced and written comments of the users and the observations of researchers on the ground it was clear that people were having difficulty identifying the first marker. One user in particular mentioned that the term 'visual marker' invited him to expect a marker similar to a QR code. In order to mitigate the problem, suggestions ranged from using a different name for the marker, to making an introductory video. The video would clarify details of the experience and explain how the system worked so users would not have to rely on a human guide to explain to them how to take the tour.

Moreover, the indicator of presence and loading of video content in the 3D panorama (the orange circle) was flagged as difficult to spot. Researchers on the ground had to help users find the indicator on the screen and ask them to wait until it indicated full loading before moving away from that spot. As a result, some people did not always find the video content inside the 3D panorama and would move to the next location, missing out on a sequential fragment of the story. Some users who did spot the orange indicator did not realize that the content was loading (slowly) and would move to the next location too quickly, losing partially loaded content and missing out on the story.

Closure for the Experience: Some users reported that the experience somehow lacked closure: 'I felt like I needed a conclusion at the end of the experience explaining more details' (U4). In addition, the practical task of returning the devices was not streamlined properly. Many users went for lunch and kept the device with them, intending to return it later. This problem was partly caused by the fact that participants had lunch near the location of the last story, and we did not enforce bringing back the device since the weather was cold and people were hungry. But the outcome of the pilot made us reflect on how devices could be returned without the users having to going back to the museum.

Comments from the Questionnaire: Three users explicitly reported enjoying the experience, in particular the graphics, layout, and interface: 'It was fun! I liked the interface and the layout' (U2); 'very inspiring' (U3). Some users suggested the experience would be inspiring as a community tool for sharing opinions about their neighbourhood, as well as to entice visitors to engage with an area, although it needed refinements. One user praised the connection of geocaching with social content from the community: 'I liked the idea of combining geocaching and socio-cultural information.' The same user highlighted how such a method fostered deeper engagement and exploration of the locations. Users reported that they saw things in the neighbourhood they would have not otherwise, such as the murals: 'It's a great way to look in detail at certain points' (U3).

4   Discussion and Future Work

Our preliminary evaluation of the YA provided useful insights for improving the interactive experience. In this section we describe the changes introduced after the pilot.

We created an introductory video with information on how to use the mobile application, its purpose, and the overall experience. In this video we replaced the problematic 'marker' term with the more descriptive 'postcard'. The orange circle indicating content and loading of the animation file was changed to a bright green which was much more visible than the previous. Some additional explanatory text was added beside the green circle in order to alert users to wait until the loading of the animation was finished. We added text to 3D environments containing more than one animated story to tell users to continue searching for stories after the first had been viewed. Refinements to the story clips were made to add context and make some stories more complete: for example, an extra scene at the beginning of the first story showing the children getting off the school bus in front of the Jewish Museum.

Details were added to the landscape to improve aesthetics and user engagement: for example, more leaves on the trees and hedges, a harder rain during one of the dramatic scenes, and more detail in the characters' expressions. Extra dialogue between Yasmine and the locals was added so that more information about the neighbourhood could be conveyed to the audience. A final epilogue clip was also made in order to wrap up the experience in a more satisfying way. In the last clip the links between Yasmine's Adventures and the issues highlighted by the community during the workshop were explained in detail. Details about returning the device were also added to the epilogue.

Pilot testing of the YA guided the design and deployment of a wider evaluation of the mobile urban experience. On the basis of the pilot experience and feedback received we designed a more detailed questionnaire probing the audience on immersion and flow aspects of the experience as well as their level of engagement with the neighbourhood. The evaluation was carried out in the same location one month after the symposium. We managed to recruit 20 users and engaged them in a 20-minute walk with the YA system, a 15-minute exit interview, and a 10-minute questionnaire. Preliminary findings support the assumption that the application promotes relatedness and exploration of the local neighborhood. Final results from the wider study are currently being consolidated and analyzed.

5   Conclusions

Location and time are essential elements for designing compelling urban computing experiences that rely upon or exploit movement and space. The overlapping of space and narrative provides opportunities to design compelling experiences with a high level of immersion. However, designing such experiences generates many challenges: most of them not related to the technicalities of the application but rather to considerations of user context, behaviour, and perception.

In this paper we presented the design process, pilot and refinements of the interactive, location based Yasmine's Adventures Experience. The experience was designed in collaboration with the UDK design research group aiming to better integrate the Jewish Museum Berlin with the surrounding neighbourhood of Mehringplatz. We described our design process and the pilot evaluation of the first final prototype using the concept of flow. In flow state we lose track of time and anxiety and our level of focus maximizes our performance and pleasurable feelings coming from the activity.

Despite the cold weather and brevity of the pilot, insightful feedback was collected and important refinements were made to the application. The application was well received and further work is in progress to refine and disseminate more detailed knowledge in the area of location aware narratives and mobile storytelling applications for social benefit and community integration. Our users found Yasmine's Adventures aesthetically pleasing and engaging. The mobile application was successful in inspiring people to learn more about the neighbourhood and the community's concerns. Location aware storytelling is one of the most compelling areas in the development of urban computing, but it also involves complex experiences that require further research in terms of methodology and evaluation criteria required for effective deployment.

Acknowledgements. This initiative was inspired by the Community Now? research project. We acknowledge the help of Bianca Herlo, who invited us to the symposium, and Iohanna Nicenboim from the UDK Design Research Group for giving us access to the content output of their community workshop 'Pinpointing Mehringplatz'. We wish to acknowledge the help of our fellow interns Rui Trindade and Paulo Bala and the support of the Associate Robotic Laboratories LARSyS (PEst-OE/EEI/LA0009/2013). The project has been developed as part of the Future Fabulators project (2013-1659/001-001 CU7 COOP7), funded by the EU Culture and Media program.

References

1. Paulos, E., Goodman, E.: The familiar stranger: anxiety, comfort, and play in public places. In: Proceedings of the SIGCHI Conference on Human Factors in Computing Systems (CHI 2004), pp. 223–230. ACM, New York (2004)
2. Berlin Jewish Museum Annual Report, 2011-2012, Museum Berlin (2013)
3. http://community-infrastructuring.org/pinpointing-mehringplatz/ (April 27, 2015)
4. Stevens, Q.: The Ludic City: Exploring the Potential of Public Spaces. Taylor & Francis (2007)
5. Reid, J., Hull, R., Cater, K., Fleuriot, C.: Magic Moments in situated mediascapes. In: Proceedings of the 2005 ACM SIGCHI International Conference in Advances in Computer Entertainment Technology, Valencia, Spain, June 15-17, pp. 290–293 (2005)
6. Benford, S., Giannachi, G., Koleva, B., Rodden, T.: From Interactions to Trajectories: Designing Coherent Journeys through Users Experiences. In: Proc. CHI 2009, Boston Massachusetts, USA, April 4-9 (2009)
7. Nisi, V., Haahr, M.: Weirdview: Interactive Multilinear Narratives and Real-Life Community Stories. Crossings: eJournal of Art and Technology 4(1) (2004)
8. Nisi, V., Oakley, I., Haahr, M.: Location-Aware Multimedia Stories: Bringing Together Real and Virtual Spaces. In: Proceedings of ArTech 2008, Porto, Portugal (2008)
9. Christopoulou, E., Ringas, D., Stefanidakis, M.: Experiences from the Urban Computing Impact on Urban Culture. In: 2012 16th Panhellenic Conference on Informatics (PCI), October 5-7, pp. 56–61 (2012), doi:10.1109/PCi.2012.53.
10. Nisi, V., Oakley, I., Posthuma de Boer, M.: Locative narratives as Experiences: a new perspective on location aware multimedia stories. Touchpoint Journal 1(3) (2009, 2010)
11. Dionisio, M., Nisi, V., van Leeuwen, J.P.: The iLand of madeira location aware multimedia stories. In: Aylett, R., Lim, M.Y., Louchart, S., Petta, P., Riedl, M. (eds.) ICIDS 2010. LNCS, vol. 6432, pp. 147–152. Springer, Heidelberg (2010)
12. O'Hara, K., Kindberg, T., Glancy, M., Baptista, L., Sukumaran, B., Kahana, G., Rowbotham, J.: Collecting and sharing location-based content on mobile phones in a zoo visitor experience. Comput. Supported Coop. Work 16(1-2), 11–44 (2007)

13. Ciolfi, L., McLoughlin, M.: Designing for meaningful visitor engagement at a living history museum. In: Proc. NordiCHI 2012, pp. 69–78. ACM, New York (2012)
14. Dionisio, M.: 7 Stories: Location Based Story-Delivery System. Master Thesis in Informatics and Engineering, CEEE, University of Madeira (UMA), Funchal, Portugal (2014)
15. Lochrie, M., Copic Pucihar, K., Gradinar, A., Coulton, P.: Time-wARpXplorer: creating a playful experience in an urban time warp. In: Proceedings of Physical and Digital in Games and Play Seminar, Tampere, Finland, May 29-30 (2013)
16. Čopic Pucihar, K., Coulton, P.: Exploring the Evolution of Mobile Augmented Reality for Future Entertainment Systems. Under review for the Journal of Computers in Entertainment
17. Olsson, T.: User expectations and experiences of mobile augmented reality services. Tampereen teknillinen yliopisto. Julkaisu-Tampere University of Technology. Publication 1085 (2012)
18. Pietroni, E.: An augmented experiences in cultural heritage through mobile devices: "Matera tales of a city" project. In: 2012 18th International Conference on Virtual Systems and Multimedia (VSMM), September 2-5, 2012, pp. 117–124 (2012)
19. Dourish, P., Anderson, K., Nafus, D.: Cultural Mobilities: Diversity and Agency in Urban Computing. In: Interact 2007 (2007)
20. Zheng, Y., Capra, L., Wolfson, O., Yang, H.: Urban computing: Concepts, methodologies and applications. ACM Trans. Intel. Sys. Tech. 5(3), Art 38 (September 2014)
21. Csikszentmihalyi, M.: Flow: The Psychology of Optimal Experience. NY Harper and Row (1990)
22. Chen, J.: Flow in games (and everything else). Commun. ACM 50(4), 31–34 (2007)
23. Magyaródi, T., Nagy, H., Soltész, P., Mózes, T., Oláh, A.: Psychometric properties of a newly established flow state questionnaire. The Journal of Happiness & Well-Being 1(2) (2013)
24. Tuters, M., Varnelis, K.: Beyond locative media: Giving shape to the internet of things. Leonardo 39(4), 357–363 (2006)
25. Nisi, V., Oakley, I., Haahr, M.: Location-Aware Multimedia Stories: Turning Spaces into Places. In: Barbosa, Á. (ed.) ARTECH 2008: Proceedings of the 4th International Conference on Digital Arts, Porto, pp. 72–82 (2008)
26. Galloway, A., Ward, M.: Locative Media As Socialising And Spatializing Practice: Learning From Archaeology. Leonardo Electronic Almanac 14(3) (July 2006)

Short Papers

Asterodrome: Force-of-Gravity Simulations in an Interactive Media Theater

Marcel Köster[1,2], Michael Schmitz[1], Soenke Zehle[1], and Burkhard Detzler[1]

[1] xm:lab, Academy of Fine Arts Saar, Saarbrücken Germany
[2] German Research Center for Artificial Intelligence (DFKI), Saarbrücken Germany
marcel.koester@dfki.de, {m.schmitz,s.zehle}@xmlab.org,
detzler@hbksaar.de

Abstract. This paper presents an interactive entertainment experience deployed in a configurable surround projection environment that we called the *media theater*. This immersive installation is based on a real-time space simulator displaying several asteroid belts with large amounts of objects orbiting a sun. The sun acts as a dynamic center of gravitation that can be controlled by users with the help of a tracking system. Furthermore, it allows users to experiment with gravity in order to see how their interaction manipulates all objects in space.

Keywords: Virtual reality, interactive environment, interactive installation, physics simulation, n-body simulation, motion tracking, projection mapping.

1 Introduction and Motivation

The project described in this paper exemplifies our cross-institutional and cross-domain approach to design games and interfaces for media architectures. We conduct these experiments as part of a broader inquiry into the future of immersion, with a particular emphasis on immersive storytelling and trans-medial scenarios that unfold across platforms. This kind of research not only requires a multidisciplinary methodology but also the use of complementary research infrastructures. For instance, some of the common experiments we conduct are performed on media facades, in so called green boxes using a markerless motion-capture system and some in the newly created interactive installation introduced in this paper.

We designed a configurable media environment called *the media theater* (see Figure 1) for various exhibition setups, realized in form of a flexible prototyping environment using projection mapping techniques. A first use case of our setup is an enhanced and extended version of a real-time gravity simulation framework by Köster et al. [7] for interactive installations like media facades and virtual-reality environments. In this scenario, we designed and integrated multi-user interaction with several asteroid belts orbiting an adjustable sun.

In the field of related space simulations, many different applications have been developed in the past. Some applications focus on the visualization and

© IFIP International Federation for Information Processing 2015
K. Chorianopoulos et al. (Eds.): ICEC 2015, LNCS 9353, pp. 359–366, 2015.
DOI: 10.1007/978-3-319-24589-8_27

Fig. 1. Sample setup of the media theater (configuration *deep-u*) with five projectors (two on the left, one in the front and two on the right)

exploration of gathered data sets. An example for such a system is *Cassie 3D* [8]. It was invented by the NASA and allows users to discover the details behind the Saturn Cassini mission, but without allowing further explorations of the outer space. Other applications focus on the simulation of fictional scenarios and experiments with gravity, like the *Universe Sandbox* [5], which is most similar to our framework. It offers a gravity engine based on Newton's laws of gravitation. Users can play with the stars and can watch the consequences of their influences. However, all available space simulations rely on desktop-interaction concepts and do not offer support for sophisticated interactive installations.

2   Simulation Framework

As stated by Köster et al. [7], each media facade requires a unique adaption of a specific interaction scenario. This is necessary to take advantage of the capabilities of the facade and to adapt to the requirements. This statement also holds true for other interactive installations like the presented *media theater*. Examples for such requirements are specific hardware and projection-display setups, as well as the available interaction features.

Our simulation framework is designed for media facades and interactive installations. The framework can adapt to arbitrary projection setups and supports different interaction methods. The core ingredients are a parallel force-of-gravity solver and an appropriate renderer that can handle the desired setups.

2.1   Rendering

In our space setting, several thousand objects are commonly visible in parallel and need to be rendered in an appealing way. Moreover, each object in space should appear as a unique object in the scene. These requirements are satisfied using a custom dynamic LOD renderer. It makes heavy use of procedurally generated geometry (for planets and asteroids) and adaptive LOD groups for triangular meshes. The actual rendering process of objects of a certain group is then performed with the help of geometry instancing [10]. This technique allows for rendering of many objects with the same base geometry in an efficient way. The dynamically adapted LOD for near objects is realized with the help of on-the-fly tessellation capabilities combined with geometry-displacement mapping [4]. Depending on the camera setup, the current performance and the current areas of interest from the observers' perspectives, we can automatically switch to image-based alternatives like parallax mapping [11] or bump mapping [2] that create the illusion of a displacement of the object geometry.

2.2   Physics

The physics part of the framework realizes a straight-forward force-of-gravity simulation. The gravitational-force between two objects is given by Newton's law of gravitation. The computation of the required forces between n different objects (or bodies) implies that every body can influence all other bodies. The force of gravity that is applied to the i-th object of such a simulation [9] is given by

$$\boldsymbol{F}_i := Gm_i \cdot \sum_{j \in \{1,\dots N\} \setminus \{i\}} \frac{m_j \hat{d}_{ij}}{|d_{ij}|^2}.$$

where

- G is the gravity constant $\approx 6.674 \cdot 10^{-11} \frac{m^3}{kg \cdot s^2}$,
- m_i is the mass of object i,
- d_{ij} is the distance vector that points from object i to object j and
- $\hat{d}_{ij}$ is the normalized distance vector.

Hence, we have to evaluate the forces F_i for all objects. An update of the acceleration vectors and the underlying object velocities and positions is performed once per step. However, in order to improve accuracy, multiple steps of the simulation per frame are performed. This avoids the occurrence of large force vectors, for instance.

In order to compute those vectors and performing the according position and velocity updates in real time, we can leverage the provided parallel computational power of the graphics-processing unit (GPU). The computation itself uses an hierarchical force-of-gravity algorithm related to the one of Barnes et al. [1]. If the number of objects falls below a certain threshold, we will adaptively switch to the direct $O(n^2)$ approach. However, we also perform several arithmetic and data-access pattern specific optimizations to improve the performance on a variety of different GPU accelerators.

For a proper realization of collisions, continuous collection detection based on spheres and ellipsoids is used. This kind of collision detection is perfectly suitable for the simulation: Nearly all objects in space can be roughly approximated by a sphere or an ellipsoid. Thus, collisions of two objects can be easily computed. It turned out that complex collision-detection functionality on the level of polygons or multiple spheres/ellipsoids cannot be distinguished from the approximated approach by an observer when using a large number of space objects. Furthermore, the collision logic can split or smash objects depending on their masses, velocity vectors and materials. If an object is smashed, it will be completely removed from the simulation. In the case of a subdivision operation, the object fragments will also be added to the internal simulation and will be treated as standalone objects.

3   Media Theater

The *media theater* was developed and installed as a configurable platform for various use cases: We aimed at supporting classic film screening situations as well as immersive interactive installations that employ a surround display plus ground projections. The theater is deployed in a large room under the roof with a pitched roof area and several roof beams that were used to frame the projection curtains and to fix projectors and cameras.

Six curtain elements shape a rectangular area with a 2:1 proportion (i.e. two curtain elements at the long sides and one curtain element for the short side). Each curtain element is the canvas of one projector and can be opened or hidden independently, such that a large number of configurations is supported.

Examples for possible setups are sketched in Figures 1 and 2. The first setup uses a so called *deep-u* format, in which visitors can enter a deep interactive installation. It is realized with two long projection curtains. Both sides use two projectors, whereas the rear uses a single projector. Additional bottom-projection from the top is also possible. In contrast to this configuration, the second setup focuses on the *long-u* format. It enables a more convenient and a more appealing setup for a larger number of observers and visitors (see Figure 3).

The general tracking capabilities feature arbitrary devices via a wireless network and motion tracking. In the case of external devices (like mobile phones), we rely on the support of the standard protocol for tangible user interfaces [6] (TUIO). This interaction support has been integrated to easily connect to the huge variety of available devices and applications. However, in order to provide a natural interaction concept and to animate a broad spectrum of observers and visitors to interact with a scenario, we also decided to integrate motion tracking. In our case, we make use of two depth cameras (two Asus Xtion Pro Live[1]).

We decided to use infrared-based cameras due to their robustness against external influences (like dramatic changes in term of lighting).

---

[1] |http://www.asus.com/Multimedia/Xtion_PRO_LIVE/

Fig. 2. Sample setup of the media theater (configuration *long-u*) with four projectors (one on the left, two in the front and one on the right)

Processing of raw-data information is performed by a so called interaction node that is an additional input-processing machine. It is connected via network to the actual simulation and rendering machines. This allows for high-performance and separate processing of large amounts of input information in form of CPU or GPU-based processing.

4 Use Case Deployment

The used configuration of the *media theater* is the *long-u* configuration (see Figure 2) with an additional bottom projection from the ceiling. This setup involves six projection surfaces: one on the left (plane 1), two in the front (plane 2), one on the right (plane 3) and two on the bottom (plane 4) (sketched in Figure 3).

The used scenario consists of three distinct (in the beginning) stable asteroid belts with different types of asteroids that are orbiting a central sun. We decided on different asteroid belts instead of a default solar system (like ours) since we want to ensure a continuously interesting simulation: A large number of objects in space appears overwhelming and fascinating. Furthermore, this variety of objects ensures continuous chain reactions and collision cascades. A common initial number of asteroids in the scope of the media theater is around $2^{17} = 131072$. This number can dramatically increase due to collisions and chain reactions. Only really small object fragments will be removed from the simulation upon collision, since they typically cannot be seen by an observer. After several interaction events and collisions in space, the average number of objects in the scene is around $280000 \approx 2^{18}$.

In contrast to previous work by Köster et al. [7], we also leverage temperature information combined with more detailed material specifications of space objects for rendering, mass computation and collision behavior. The previously used analogy for object sizes was: large objects in space imply a large mass, and

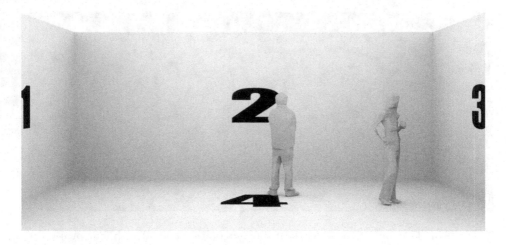

Fig. 3. Scenario setup with six projectors from a reference camera position

small objects imply a small mass. This slightly changes in the current setting. As soon as observers are able to definitely distinguish between light and heavy objects by their distinct appearance, we are able to slightly relax this constraint. For instance, the outer-most asteroid belt is the furthest one relative to the sun, and thus, could be hardly seen from an observer. Those asteroids can also become visible upon changing the material and temperature information to ice-like structures. The adapted sizes and the use of reflections and refractions from those asteroids will ensure a minimum visibility. A photo from the interactive installation can be seen in Figure 4.

4.1 Single- and Multi-User Interaction

As mentioned previously, the *media theater* features interaction via motion tracking from the ceiling. Two depth cameras capture every motion of visitors that are located inside of the interactive installation. Enabling user interaction for a single visitor is a non-problematic task. The user can be tracked according to the captured depth information from the interior of the installation. This location information can be used to manipulate and adjust the location of the central sun.

However, an interaction principle that allows for a natural and visitor-group-focused interaction is difficult to realize. In previous scenarios of media facades, we used multiple large-scale gravitational points in space (like multiple suns or larger planets) that could be controlled by users. This concept, however, makes a direct group-focused interaction hard, which would be a valuable choice for this setting.

Consequently, we decided to weight every visitor's influence according to the area he or she causes to appear in the depth image. People that are located close together will thus imply larger regions in the depth image. Furthermore, visitors can spread their arms to enlarge their captured regions, and therefore,

Fig. 4. Photo from the deployed scenario with the described virtual-camera configuration from Section 4.2. The photo was taken with the help of a wide-angle lens.

their weighting. The weighting factors, as well as the locations of the visitors are then used to control the sun. The target location of the sun can then be computed according to the mass center of all areas: The center of every detected visitor/group area is multiplied by its weighting factor, divided by the total weighting of all visitors and added to the target location.

In order to extract the required information from the depth images, we utilize the OpenCV library [3]. We subtract background information and try to find the largest connected regions, in which the depth differences are below a given threshold. By performing these processing steps we can determine the weights and locations of single and groups of visitors. Afterwards, we can compute the 2D location of the sun, interpolate the old location with the new location according to the elapsed time and can then send the target position to the simulation.

4.2   Projection Setup

The decision on a proper camera perspective that allows for an appealing and natural visualization for most observers is a sophisticated exercise. We decided on multiple virtual cameras oriented according to a visitor (height of the camera of about 1.7 meters above the ground) that is located in the center of the installation (around the location of the left human in Figure 3). This implies that we need four camera perspectives and have to render four images, one image with its corresponding camera perspective for each side. From a computer-graphics' perspective, we are rendering four images in a environment-mapping-based way.

This allows for a 3D-like immersive experience for visitors that are interacting with the simulation without the need for additional 3D equipment.

However, as shown in Figure 4, the perspective might not be optimal for observers that are not interacting with the installation. Experiments for adjusting and manipulating the camera positions and distortions to multiple observers on the fly would be an interesting extension in the future.

5   Conclusion

We presented an interactive installation called *media theater*. It supports many different configurations and interaction capabilities, like external devices based on TUIO or direct interaction via motion tracking. Due to its flexibility, it can be used as a rapid prototyping environment for a huge variety of interactive setups.

The installed real-time force-of-gravity simulation allows for experiments with gravity and appears fascinating due to the large number of presented space objects. Observers can directly interact with this scenario via the available motion-tracking features by manipulating a central sun. However, interaction is not limited to a specific amount of visitors, but also features interaction between multiple visitor groups. Furthermore, they are able to perceive a 3D-like experience in the center of the installation without the need for further 3D equipment.

In the future, we would like to experiment with dynamically adjusted camera perspectives to provide a multi-user 3D-like experience. Moreover, we plan to create further scenarios and to extend the interaction capabilities.

References

1. Barnes, J., Hut, P.: A hierarchical O(N log N) force-calculation algorithm. Nature 324 (1986)
2. Blinn, J.F.: Simulation of wrinkled surfaces. SIGGRAPH Comput. Graph (1978)
3. Bradski, G.: The OpenCV Library. Dr. Dobb's Journal of Software Tools (2000)
4. Cook, R.L.: Shade trees. In: Proceedings of the 11th Annual Conference on Computer Graphics and Interactive Techniques, pp. 223–231. ACM (1984)
5. Giant Army: Universe Sandbox (April 2015). http://universesandbox.com/
6. Kaltenbrunner, M., Bovermann, T., Bencina, R., Costanza, E.: TUIO: A Protocol for Table-Top Tangible User Interfaces. In: Proc. of the The 6th Int'l Workshop on Gesture in Human-Computer Interaction and Simulation (2005)
7. Köster, M., Schmitz, M., Gehring, S.: Gravity Games - A Framework for Interactive Space Physics on Media Facades. In: Proceedings of The International Symposium on Pervasive Displays, Perdis 2015 (2015)
8. NASA: Cassini (April 2015). http://saturn.jpl.nasa.gov/multimedia/CASSIE/
9. Nguyen, H.: GPU Gems 3. Addison-Wesley Professional (2007)
10. Pharr, M., Fernando, R.: GPU Gems 2: Programming Techniques for High-Performance Graphics and General-Purpose Computation. Addison-Wesley Professional (2005)
11. Policarpo, F., Oliveira, M.M., Comba, J.L.D.: Real-time relief mapping on arbitrary polygonal surfaces. In: Proceedings of the 2005 Symposium on Interactive 3D Graphics and Games. ACM (2005)

Exploring the Importance of "Making" in an Educational Game Design

Michail N. Giannakos[1], Varvara Garneli[2], and Konstantinos Chorianopoulos [1,2]

[1] Norwegian University of Science and Technology, Trondheim, Norway
michailg@idi.ntnu.no
[2] Ionian University, Corfu, Greece
bgarnelisch@gmail.com, choko@acm.org

Abstract. Educational games have been employed in many settings as a means to engage young students. Different genres and applications of games have been used to improve learning experience. The design or making of games in learning activities has been linked to teaching of new skills. Within this paper we explore and discuss the differences of involving young students into the game design and development process compared to just playing an educational game. In particular, we designed an educational math-game and an activity that involves children in playing or modifying the game, and we performed a between groups experiment with sixty students of the second grade of middle school (12 to 13 years old). Students formed three equivalent groups of twenty. The first group played the game, the second engaged with re-designing and modifying the game and the third (control) group solved the same exercises (with the educational game) on paper. The results showed that the making group exhibits certain attitudinal benefits. Hence, our findings suggest that learning through games should include more than just playing a well-designed game, it should also consider the involvement of students with various "making" affordances.

Keywords: Interaction design; empirical evaluation; serious games; learning; design principles.

1   Introduction

Contemporary research on interaction design for learning has focused mainly on the usability of the technology enhanced learning systems. Our thesis is that any learning environment (formal or informal) requires a consideration also for qualitative aspects, such as engagement and enjoyment. Ongoing research on game-based learning has focused on the evaluation of a teacher-led pedagogy. In this work, we suggest that a learning environment would benefit by considering educational games as a new medium for creative pedagogy and not only as a teacher-led tool or tool for just practicing. For example, teenagers have been reported to engage highly with malleable virtual environments, such as Minecraft, Little Big Planet 2, Roblox, Disney Infinity, and others; all supporting game making/modification as a core play mechanic.

© IFIP International Federation for Information Processing 2015
K. Chorianopoulos et al. (Eds.): ICEC 2015, LNCS 9353, pp. 367–374, 2015.
DOI: 10.1007/978-3-319-24589-8_28

In this work, we explore students experience with designing and developing an educational game. A fundamental principle of meaningful education is that all students can learn if the appropriate personalized conditions are given to them [12]. Research into multiple learning styles confirms that students learn in many different ways [14]. This perspective is crucial for all students and especially to those with fewer opportunities or lower performance to standard tests. Educational games have been proposed as a means to engage students. However, limited research has been conducted on the potential of students' involvement in the process of game making.

Our methodology is user-centered and considers the elaborate design and evaluation of an educational game. First, in collaboration with math and computer science teachers, we designed and developed a math game. Then, we investigated the impact of the making aspect on students' experience. The math-game is named "Gem-Game" and it is targeted to students that attend first and second class of middle school (12-13 years old).

After students' involvement with the respective process (playing, making, traditional learning), we used attitudinal surveys to measure their engagement. In addition, we performed some interviews in order to gather (qualitative) information on their motivation and their opinion regarding the respective instruction method and the content. We used quantitative method to analyze the results from the surveys and we triangulate our findings with the qualitative data extracted from the interviews.

2   Background and Research Questions

The use of educational games can be effective only if elements like goals, competition, challenges, fantasy and motivation are employed to facilitate learning. Young students are not always motivated to play an educational game. But certain design principles have been found to be extremely important on increasing students' motivation and interest to play an educational game [1].

A variety of environments have been developed by researchers to introduce game making concepts to children. Popular visual programming environments include Scratch [10] Alice and Storytelling Alice [8]. The idea of making games for learning instead of playing games to learn is one of the fundamentals of Constructionism. The design or making of games in learning activities has been linked to teaching of new STEM literacy skills [3, 4]. One common inspiration is the work of Papert and Harel [9] that stresses the importance of creating a 'felicitous' environment to facilitate learning. There are studies (e.g. [5]) supporting that learning by making is harder but it gives more substantial results.

As aforementioned, from a constructionist perspective, there are theoretical reasons for believing that making games can be educationally beneficial: Kafai, [6, 7] has argued that when making games, learners also construct knowledge and their relationship to it; "The learner is involved in all the design decisions and begins to develop technological fluency. Just as fluency in language means much more than knowing facts about the language, technological fluency involves not only knowing how to use new technological tools but also knowing how to make things of significance with those tools and most important, develop new ways of thinking based on use of those tools" ([6], p. 39). As technology has moved on opportunities have also arisen to develop new making pedagogies.

This work centers on investigating the impact of making pedagogy (e.g., modifying a serious game) on students engagement during the learning process.

3   Methodology

3.1   Gem-Game and Procedures

The main purpose of Gem-Game is to improve the mathematical skills of players/learners. The main character moves up or down dependent on the operation executed by the player (figure 1). So students also get a spatial idea of upwards movement when adding and downwards movement when subtracting. The final objective of the player is to retrieve his dog by collecting diamonds. To achieve this goal, the player must go through three different levels.

Fig. 1. Screenshot of the Gem-Game

In particular, the player must correctly add/subtract in order to reach each diamond that scrolls horizontally from right to left. For example, if the player is positioned on line 6, and the diamond is on line 1, the player must write -5 in order to reach the diamond. Notably, if the player makes a mistake, it is a constructive one, because the player can continue by typing a correction from the new position.

In addition to a group that played with Gem-Game serious game (experimental group 1), another group followed a more traditional paper-based pedagogy (control group). We also employed a third group (experimental group 2) in order to evaluate the effects of making pedagogy. Hence, students of the third group had the chance to get engaged with the game code by altering its scenario in the Scratch environment. In particular, students were involved with changing the fairy of the game, who helped the hero to achieve his goal. The participants changed the costume of the fairy and fit the dialogue properly and according their own preferences (e.g., see figure 2 next page).

Fig. 2. Example of how students altered the game scenario in the scratch environment

3.2   Sampling

The between groups experiment was consisted of sixty students, forty boys and twenty girls (12 to 13 years old). All the students who participated in the experiment attended the first grade of middle school. They formed three equivalent (age, gender, average grades) groups of twenty students; two of the groups were practiced with the math game (with a different way) and one (control) practiced traditionally by solving exercises on paper.

3.3   Measures

A wide range of data was collected to address our research question including surveys, short interviews and observations. During most of the sessions, one of the researchers/teachers was present to assist and observe the students. Regarding the quantitative data, we employed a questionnaire (5-point Likert scale from strongly disagree to strongly agree) that measures students' attitudes of immersion with the game and their intention to participate in the game. Table 1 lists the questionnaire items used to measure each factor and the source adapted from the literature.

We also conducted semi-structured interview with some students, these interviews focused on their motivations with the respective teaching practice and their opinion for mathematics and computing topics.

3.4   Statistical Analysis

First, we checked the validity of the questions used in the survey. Cronbach's α was found to be greater than 0.7 on both constructs. Next, we evaluated the reliability of the questions. The reliability of a question was assessed by measuring its factor loading onto the underlying construct. The factor analysis identified two distinct constructs: 1) Immersion (IMM); and 2) Intention to Participate (ItP); with factor loadings of the questions/items being greater than 0.7.

Table 1. Constructs and questions used, adopted from [1, 2].

Constructs	Questions Used
Intention to Participate* (ItP)	• Do you intend to repeat this activity? • Do you think that this activity must be part of the normal teaching procedure? • Do you wish that this practice will be continued in the future?
Immersion* (IMM)	• Do you forget the time as long as you are practicing? • Do you bother for what is happening around as long as you are practicing? • Do you forget the problems you have during your practice?

mean values of the questions were used for the analysis

To examine our research question regarding game making impact of students' experience, we conducted between groups t-test. We used three independent variables (playing, making, control) and two dependent variables (ItP, IMM). All statistical analyses reported were conducted with a significant level of 0.05.

4   Results

Based on the empirical results illustrated in Table 2, making pedagogy indicates a significant effect on students' intention to participate (ItP) in the learning activity. On the other hand, there is no significant effect on students' sense of immersion (IMM).

Table 2. Testing the effect of game play and game make on students' intention to participate and immersion with the process.

Con-structs	(I) Mean (S.D.)		(J) Control Group Mean (S.D.)	Mean Differ. (I-J)	Std. Error	Sig.
ItP	Playing Story Game Group	2.68 (1.22)	2.23 (1.10)	.450	.367	.615
	Making Game Group	3.35 (0.78)		**1.117**	**.301**	**.004***
IMM	Playing Story Game Group	2.58 (1.34)	2.32 (1.30)	.267	.417	.919
	Making Game Group	2.88 (1.26)		.567	.404	.507

*. The mean difference is significant at the 0.05 level.

Although our findings are preliminary, and there is a clear need for more in-depth investigations; by observing figure 3 (next page), we notice that making pedagogy exhibits certain benefits compared to game based learning and traditional learning.

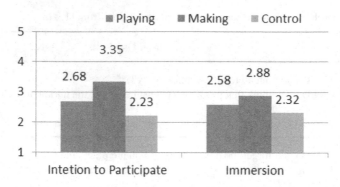

Fig. 3. Mean scores for intention to participate and immersion on each respective group

After the activity, students' participated in a semi-structured interview. Most of the students were familiar with playing an educational game; however students from the experimental groups were looking forward for the activity (since they were informed). At the end both experimental groups, found the activity amusing and easy.

During the semi-structured interviews with the students, the researcher guided the conversation in order to probe different aspects of students' motivation, attitudes and learning performance throughout the activity. In the conversations, students supported the idea of using video games at school. They were also positive on the possibility of introducing similar activities in other STEM courses (besides mathematics).

According to the informal data gathered from researcher's observations, students seemed enthusiastic with the game-play, particularly at the making group. Students' were experienced with many commercial games (e.g., Assassin's creed, league of legends) and they mentioned that although Gem-Game was simple, they found it very interesting with familiar game mechanics. As a result they did not get frustrated from the educational content, even at the very high and competitive levels (e.g., diamonds were moving faster). In particular, *the making group was more eager, with a very high intention to enroll on similar tasks in the future and plenty of ideas for further improvement of the game and the process.*

5   Conclusion and Discussion

In this work, we examined the importance of making affordances (e.g., modifying-extending a serious game) in students' engagement with an educational math-game. In addition to playing the math-game, students had the chance to get engaged with the game code by altering its scenario in the Scratch environment. Our findings suggest that students could benefit with the "making pedagogy" in gameplay. Thus, it is very important that we consider this issue and carefully examine how our educational game designs may address making affordances. From our early field studies we can support that the game making affordances could offer an enjoyable and engaging game-based learning process that requires further study.

Overall, it is important to use a variety of teaching tools and practices beyond the traditional (passive) teaching in order to facilitate the full spectrum of learning styles. Further research should perform similar studies over longer periods of time and for additional curriculum topics in order to be able to provide the overall picture of the effect of students' involvement in the process of making games and guide educators to use more teaching tools in a more effective way; this will assist students to achieve learning in a meaningful and creative way.

Based on our observations and interviews, when students were informed that they would practice in mathematics with an educational game, they became very eager. In contrast, the students that solved exercises on paper appeared to be less excited. All students were concentrated and completed their activity quite fast. Students who played the game liked the activity but some of them did not want to repeat it. They even asked if they could play another game. On the other hand the students that engaged with the game code wanted to keep refining the code and extending the game.

In summary our work in progress provides empirical evidence for the importance of the making aspect in an educational game design, however there are also certain limitations. First, the generalizability of the results must be carefully approached since the field study was conducted in a specific context (e.g., content, age). In addition, the introduction of other in-depth methods, such as video observations and log files analysis, will allow us to triangulate the results and have a complimentary picture of the findings. This will allow us to attain deeper understanding on how making affordances can be successfully employed in educational games design.

Further research should move across two paths: interaction design principles that transform curricula concepts into engaging serious games and pedagogy for interactive modification of serious games. The implications of this research concern the practice of both interaction designers and educators. Interaction design is needed in order to create engaging making mechanisms in games design and development, while educators need to consider pedagogies for employing serious games both as technological tool and a creative medium. Finally, in addition to interactions in learner-led pedagogy, further research should study the social interactions that happen between learners. Since education stands on a social science pillar, we suggest that the design of serious games should also consider their social embedding in everyday school and informal learning practices.

Acknowledgements. We would like to thank all the students and teachers for their participation during the game-design phase and the experiment.

References

1. Bopp, M.: Storytelling as a motivational tool in digital learning games. Didactics of Microlearning. Concepts, Discourses and Examples, pp. 250–266 (2007)
2. Bourgonjon, J., Valcke, M., Soetaert, R., Schellens, T.: Students' perceptions about the use of video games in the classroom. Computers & Education 54(4), 1145–1156 (2010)

3. Buechley, L., Eisenberg, M., Catchen, J., Crockett, A.: The LilyPad Arduino: Using Computational Textiles to Investigate Engagement, Aesthetics, and Diversity in Computer Science Education. In: Proc. CHI 2008, pp. 423–432. ACM Press (2008)
4. Chorianopoulos, K., Giannakos, M.N.: Design Principles for Serious Video Games in Mathematics Education: From Theory to Practice. The International Journal of Serious Games 1(3), 51–59 (2014)
5. Garneli, B., Giannakos, M.N., Chorianopoulos, K., Jaccheri, L.: Learning by Playing and Learning by Making. In: Ma, M., Oliveira, M.F., Petersen, S., Hauge, J.B. (eds.) SGDA 2013. LNCS, vol. 8101, pp. 76–85. Springer, Heidelberg (2013)
6. Kafai, Y.B.: Minds in play: Computer game design as a context for children's learning. Routledge (1995)
7. Kafai, Y.B.: Playing and making games for learning instructionist and constructionist perspectives for game studies. Games and Culture 1(1), 36–40 (2006)
8. Kelleher, C., Pausch, R., Kiesler, S.: Storytelling alice motivates middle school girls to learn computer programming. In: Proc. CHI 2007, pp. 1455–1464. ACM Press (2007)
9. Papert, S., Harel, I.: Situating constructionism. Constructionism, 1–11 (1991)
10. Resnick, M., et al.: Scratch: programming for all. Communications of the ACM 52(11), 60–67 (2009)
11. Robertson, J., Nicholson, K.: Adventure Author: a learning environment to support creative design. In: Proc. IDC 2007, pp. 37–44. ACM Press (2007)
12. Robinson, K.: Finding your element: How to discover your talents and passions and transform your life. Penguin Press, UK (2013)
13. Silver, J.: Awakening to maker methodology: the metamorphosis of a curious caterpillar. In: Proc. IDC 2009, pp. 242–245. ACM Press (2009)
14. Spalter, A.M., Simpson, R.M., Legrand, M., Taichi, S.: Considering a full range of teaching techniques for use in interactive educational software: a practical guide and brainstorming session. In: Proc. FIE, pp. 1–9. IEEE Press (2000)
15. Tan, L., Kim, B.: Learning by Doing in the Digital Media Age. In: New Media and Learning in the 21st Century, pp. 181–197. Springer, Singapore (2015)

Simple Games – Complex Emotions: Automated Affect Detection Using Physiological Signals

Thomas Friedrichs[1], Carolin Zschippig[2], Marc Herrlich[3],
Benjamin Walther-Franks[3], Rainer Malaka[3], and Kerstin Schill[2]

[1] OFFIS – Institute for Information Technology, Oldenburg, Germany
[2] Cognitive Neuroinformatics, University of Bremen, Germany
[3] Digital Media Lab, TZI, University of Bremen, Germany

Abstract. Understanding the impact of interaction mechanics on the user's emotional state can aid in shaping the user experience. For eliciting the emotional state of a user, designers and researchers typically employ subjective or expert assessment. Yet these methods are typically applied after the user has finished the interaction, causing a delay between stimulus and assessment. Physiological measures potentially offer more reliable indication of a user's affective state in real-time. We present an experiment to increase our understanding of the relation of certain stimuli and valence of induced emotions in games. For this we designed a simple game to induce negative and positive emotions in the player. The results show a high correspondence between our classification of participants' physiological signals and subjective assessment. However, creating a clear causality between game elements and emotions is a daunting task, and our designs offer room for improvement.

Keywords: Objective game evaluation, Psycho-physiology, Affective gaming, Valence detection.

1 Introduction

The role of emotions in human-computer interaction has received increased attention over the last years, and the user's emotions are nowadays recognized as an important part of the overall user experience. While the emotional impact has always been central to entertainment applications it is no longer limited to this area, but also considered important in areas such as business applications.

Measuring the user's emotional state and the impact of an interaction experience on it still relies mainly on subjective feedback from participants in user studies or observation and classification by experts. Questionnaires and similar tools are mostly suited for either pre- or post-experience assessment, but not for fine-grained real-time measurement or an online adaptation of the interaction. For example, when asking players after a game they might have difficulties remembering certain situations early in the game or certain events might overshadow the impact of others. Expert-based assessments are limited in the extent

© IFIP International Federation for Information Processing 2015
K. Chorianopoulos et al. (Eds.): ICEC 2015, LNCS 9353, pp. 375–382, 2015.
DOI: 10.1007/978-3-319-24589-8_29

and detail in which they can detect emotions, and require sophisticated alignment between assessors, as well as significant logistical overhead.

Psycho-physiological measurements of physical reactions can potentially allow objective, real-time assessment of the emotional state of users, thus enabling researchers and designers to make direct connections between design changes and the emotional impact. Once these connections are understood and formalized, the user experience can even be modified by automatically adapting to the user. With this goal in mind, the choice on which physiological parameters are to be measured becomes dependant on the ease of use of necessary sensors. It might not be practical to depend on the user wearing an electroencephalograph (EEG) cap or stick electrodes on facial muscles when playing a casual game on a mobile device, possibly in public.

We present further progress towards real-time, fine-grained measurement and classification of emotional valence in human-computer interaction without a prior calibration of the system to a specific player. In this we focus on video games, since emotions are particularly relevant to the gaming experience. We designed a game aimed at inducing positive and negative emotional states in the player at short but well defined intervals. Using this we observed and classified psycho-physiological data unobtrusively measured by electrocardiography (ECG) and electrodermal activity (EDA). We were able to successfully classify positive and negative emotional states according to the self-assessment of the participants across conditions by using psycho-physiological measures without prior knowledge on individual player reactions. We were less successful in inducing positive/negative emotional states in a controlled way with our game design.

2   Related Work

For a general overview of the recent work in Affective Computing, we point to the comprehensive review paper by Calvo [2] and the recently published *Oxford Handbook of Affective Computing* [3]. In addition to the studies mentioned in those publications, there has been a growing number of computer games that are either designed specifically as an affect manipulation tool or aim to utilize the affective state measured through physiological signals. Kivikangas et al. did an extensive literature review on psycho-physiological methods in game research in 2010 [8]. Since a comprehensive overview of the recent developments in the field is outside the scope of this paper, we limit ourselves to two highlights in order to illustrate the current state-of-the-art in affect-adaptive gaming research. Nogueira et al. have proposed the "Emotion Engine biofeedback loop system" to study and manipulate the affective player experience [11]. The Engine uses EDA, cardiovascular measures and EMG to infer the player's emotional state and can achieve 78% classification accuracy for valence if the player undergoes a personal calibration process. Chanel et al. studied the affective reaction of players to the game TETRIS via an EEG [4] aiming at implementing a dynamic adaptation of game difficulty. They succeeded in classifying valence with an accuracy of about 60%, leaving adapting the game as a future perspective.

3   Designing a Game for Measuring Valence

We specifically designed and implemented *Dino Run* as a tool for inducing positive or negative emotional valence. The tool should have clear influencing variables to allow us to manipulate the emotional impact dynamically. Measurement and classification of the emotional state is realized using psycho-physiological measures. Dino Run is a simple casual game, its core mechanics modelled after various successful games from the mobile game market. Great care was taken in game design to maximize the emotional impact and reduce noise in the measurements induced by complex and only intricately traceable cognitive processes. The main goal of Dino Run is to steer a little dinosaur through an obstacle course by jumping or ducking (cf. figure 1). The game is a typical side-scrolling game, with only jumping and ducking as vertical motion.

The goal of a tool for valence induction and measurement imposed two constraints that directed the design process. It had to be appealing to a broad audience, and the duration of gaming sessions should be kept to a minimum. Both constraints are satisfied by casual games, especially the so-called "one button" games popular on mobile devices. They are played by a large and diverse audience and the threshold to new players is very low. It can be assumed that many users are already familiar with such games, reducing the potential emotional impact of learning. Furthermore, the limited controls and the fixed set of game mechanics allow better control of game parameters in order to induce positive or negative emotional states.

In contrast to standard entertainment games, for our study design it was crucial to eliminate any redundant mechanics. In most games many different elements such as puzzles, collectables, power-ups, enemies, score systems are used in conjunction to make the game *fun*. Yet it is not apparent how these elements exactly affect players of different target groups. For our purposes we require the positive and negative conditions to be as symmetric and comparable as possible. We therefore pre-tested different mechanics before creating the final game design, including specific visual feedback, and special negative/positive items. The final game design included two mechanisms for inducing either positive or negative emotions based on the core locomotion mechanic of the game. They were designed to create a noticeable emotional change without the players consciously recognizing the change in the underlying game parameters. The first is an *adjustable collision detection and jumping force* of the character. Pretests confirmed that subtle changes regarding the hitbox sizes lead to increased collisions and negative performance of the players, which should impact their emotional state negatively, while not being noticed by the players. To reinforce the positive/negative affect, *positive and negative auditive feedback* was included in the game in the form of fanfares and buzzer sounds, respectively. Pre-tests confirmed this to work better than additional visual feedback, as this can easily be overlooked by players. The auditive channel is independent of the visual channel and has been successfully used to affect the emotional state of users [7].

We chose cardiac and electrodermal activity as psycho-physiological signals for valence detection, which can be unobtrusively measured by electrocardiography

Fig. 1. Experimental setup with ECG and EDA sensors

(ECG) and skin conductance measurement (SC). Heart rate variability (HRV) has been shown to be significant for valence detection [9] and in combination with EDA carries information about the respiration pattern, which has been shown to be influenced by valence [6].

4   User Study

For the study, students were recruited from the university campus. The participants (26 males and 21 females) were from different fields, backgrounds and had diverse gaming habits. Participants played the game while their electrodermal activity (EDA, i.e. skin conductance) and an electrocardiogram (ECG) were recorded. The ECG was done using an Olimex SHIELD-EKG-EMG on an Arduino Mega 2560, the Bluetooth-operated EDA sensor was a custom design [12]. After introducing the overall procedure, the EDA and ECG sensors were applied to fingers and lower arms, respectively. Participants were given instructions to avoid any obstacles in the game. Prior to beginning data acquisition, the participants had the opportunity to practice the controls in a basic test level that was free of any manipulations or feedback. Each game was internally divided into three phases: a neutral phase without any manipulation or feedback, the game phase E^1 where the players played either a positive (E_p^1) or negative game condition (E_n^1), and phase E^2, which could be positive or negative as well (E_p^2 or E_n^2). The phases lasted 60s, 150s and 150s. They were not explicitly communicated to the player, nor were there obvious indicators in game. From this set-up with full permutation, four participant groups result: people playing only the positive game condition ($E_p^1 \& E_p^2$), people playing the positive, then the negative condition ($E_p^1 \& E_n^2$), people playing negative, then positive ($E_n^1 \& E_p^2$) and people playing negative only ($E_n^1 \& E_n^2$). All participants were distributed randomly across the groups. Four groups were chosen to be able to compare

a) changing conditions within the game (positive to negative and vice versa) and b) changing reference conditions across trials (only positive or negative).

After finishing the task, the participants were asked to fill out an online questionnaire containing questions from the *Game Experience Questionnaire (GEQ)* [1] and a 9-point *Self Assessment Mannequin (SAM)* scale [10]. These questionnaires were chosen as they are based on two different models of emotion. There is currently no consensus in the affective systems research community on the most performant theoretical model of emotion in the human-machine interaction context, other than a strong tendency to use dimensional rather than discrete emotional models[2]. We support dimensional models, but view it as an open question to define the details of the dimensional space. Consequently we chose to attain the subjective ratings of our participants through a questionnaire based on a model with two axes for valence, labelled positive and negative affect (GEQ) and another questionnaire modelling valence on a single axis with the poles positive and negative (SAM).

5   Results

For the evaluation, data of 47 different participants was used. 38 data sets comprise of two conditions per person and 9 data sets comprise of one condition per person. Due to noise in the measurement, some data sets had to be removed from the analysis because the sensors failed randomly during the trials. However, the identification of the corrupted data was feasible because it was clearly distinguishable from the non-corrupted data (completely distorted signal).

The physiological data was preprocessed with digital filtering algorithms before a set of 13 features was extracted. The Biosig-toolbox [14] provided the algorithms to extract the RR-intervals in the ECG signal. The feature set comprised features derived by time domain methods as well as frequency domain methods, which have been shown to have psychophysiological significance in various publications [2]. The features chosen were: the standard deviation of the tonic and phasic component of the skin conductance, the slope of a linear approximation of the tonic component, the mean, standard deviation and root mean square of the RR-intervals, the root mean square and standard deviation of differences in interval lengths, as well as the power and normalized power in the high (0,15-0,4 Hz) and low (0,04-0,15 Hz) frequency range, plus the ratio of low to high frequency power. To improve the frequency resolution of the power density estimation, we used an autoregressive model with the model order of 16, as suggested in the literature [13]. A principal component analysis of the feature space reduced the number of features to 10, which explain 99% of the variance. This feature matrix was evaluated using a support vector machine (SVM), in order to infer the user's affective state from the physiological data during gameplay. The SVM was implemented using the libSVM library [5] in MATLAB.

First, we checked our working hypothesis that the game induces a positive affective state in the player during condition E_p and a negative affective state during condition E_n by training an SVM with the feature matrix and the conditions as labels. After a 10 fold cross validation with a training data/test data ratio of 9:1, the accuracy on training data was 60%. For the prediction the SVM did not reach chance level. This low prediction accuracy led us to the interpretation that the game might not have induced the expected valence during play, despite our careful design and pretesting.

We consequently tested our hypothesis by evaluating the subjective ratings reported by the players by means of the GEQ and by SAM. We specifically looked at GEQ items that rate the negative and positive affect induced by gameplay. Comparing the ratings for positive affect to those of negative affect revealed that for both game conditions the users rate positive affect higher then negative. Looking at the changes over time, we found the positive affect rating declining from first to second condition while the negative affect rating inclined. This was true for all games, when the condition was meant to induce a negative affect but also when it was meant to induce a positive affect. Figure 2 shows the mean and standard deviation of the GEQ ratings. We then performed a χ^2-test (hypothesis of independence and a normal distribution with $\mu = mean(GEQ)$) to see in more detail whether the valence of the condition has any significant influence on the GEQ votes, or if the votes are independent of the game condition. The χ^2 values of the votes for E^1 and E^2 are: $\chi^2_{E^1,p.a.r.} = 5,63$, $\chi^2_{E^1,n.a.r.} = 12,01$, $\chi^2_{E^2,p.a.r} = 6,70$ and $\chi^2_{E^2,n.a.r.} = 8,76$ (p.a.r. = GEQ positive affect rating, n.a.r. = GEQ negative affect rating). We interpreted these results as follows: in the first minutes of gameplay (E^1), playing the game induces positive affect in the players. If this condition is a negative one (E^1_n), the GEQ ratings on negative affect are significant (on a significance level of 5%). For the second game condition (E^2), both affect ratings depend upon the game condition on a significance level of 5%. While this indicates that the game's mechanisms

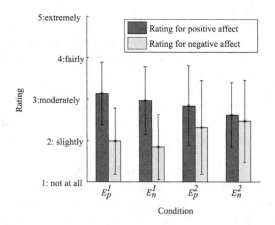

Fig. 2. Mean and standard deviation of the GEQ rating for positive and negative affect.

induce a discriminative player experience, the values also suggest that the game conditions are experienced significantly different depending on the time already played. Analysis of the SAM ratings showed these to be independent of the game condition label ($\chi^2_{E^1,SAM} = 4.94$, $\chi^2_{E^2,SAM} = 6.98$, both not significant on a 5% level). This led us to the hypothesis that a classifier trained with the subjective game experience obtained through SAM should produce better classification results, if the intended valence induction does indeed not match the objective overall experience of the player. The SVM trained with SAM labels grouped into $SAM \geq 5$: +1 and $SAM < 5$: -1 had a training accuracy of 75% and a test accuracy of 68.9%, supporting our hypothesis regarding the player experience.

6   Discussion and Future Work

The initial low performance of the classifier was substantially improved by using the SAM subjective rating of the game experience. Compared to literature values, a classification accuracy of almost 70% on data with very high subject variability is a promising result. Yet there is room for improvement. On the classification side, we will look into the temporal resolution of the features and take into account prior game events, in-game player actions and emotional stages. Also, we will look into alternative classification methods that allow for a more detailed resolution of the valence space, not just a binary positive/negative clustering. With these alternative methods, we are looking to classify on the basis of the two affect dimensions evaluated by the GEQ to see if this model will result in higher classification rates in our setting. A second point of discussion is the game design and its success in inducing the intended valence in a substantial intensity. The data obtained through the post-game questionnaires indicate that the reduction of game complexity may have been a key contributing factor to the increase in negative affect in condition E^2, since one dimension of the negative affect was attributed to increased boredom. Comparing our game to successful casual games, we identified the graphical design as one element to improve the game experience without introducing uncontrollable disturbance factors. Many side scrolling games change the visuals of the game, which contributes to the motivational aspect of curiosity without any impact on the game mechanics. As a next step, we will redesign the game in order to improve the affect induction and transfer our results towards the development of an adaptive game, manipulating the game parameters during gameplay to achieve a desired game experience.

7   Conclusion

We designed and implemented a simple video game as a controllable environment for the study of the player's emotional reaction during gameplay. In an empirical study with 47 participants, we mapped physiological data to the player's subjective game experience with an accuracy of approximately 70%. Our work demonstrates that automatic detection of affect valence using non-invasive physiological sensors is possible, and gives first insights into stimulating negative and positive emotional responses through game mechanics design. The results imply that the evaluation of a specific game design element or game mechanic can be facilitated. Thus, the choice of game mechanics and design elements for the evocation of an intended specific emotion (e.g. does this scene really scare the player?) can be grounded on data which, in contrast to post-game questionnaires, have a more direct temporal mapping between stimulus and response.

References

1. Brockmyer, J.H., Fox, C.M., Curtiss, K.A., McBroom, E., Burkhart, K.M., Pidruzny, J.N.: The development of the Game Engagement Questionnaire: A measure of engagement in video game-playing. J. of Experimental Social Psychology 45(4), 624–634 (2009)
2. Calvo, R.A., D'Mello, S.: Affect Detection: An Interdisciplinary Review of Models, Methods, and Their Applications. IEEE Trans. on Affective Computing 1(1), 18–37 (2010)
3. Calvo, R.A., D'Mello, S., Gratch, J., Kappas, A.: The Oxford Handbook of Affective Computing. Oxford University Press (2014)
4. Chanel, G., Rebetez, C., Pun, T.: Emotion Assessment From Physiological Signals for Adaptation of Game Difficulty. IEEE Trans. On Systems, Man, and Cybernetics 41(6), 1052–1063 (2011)
5. Chang, C.C., Lin, C.J.: LIBSVM: A library for support vector machines. ACM Trans. on Intelligent Systems and Technology 2, 27:1–27:27 (2011)
6. Ganglbauer, E., Schrammel, J., Deutsch, S.: Applying Psychophysiological Methods for Measuring User Experience: Possibilities, Challenges and Feasibility
7. Hébert, S., Béland, R., Dionne-Fournelle, O., Crête, M., Lupien, S.J.: Physiological stress response to video-game playing: the contribution of built-in music. Life Sciences 76(20), 2371–2380 (2005)
8. Kivikangas, J.M., Chanel, G., Cowley, B., Ekman, I., Salminen, M., Järvelä, S., Ravaja, N.: A review of the use of psychophysiological methods in game research. J. of Gaming & Virtual Worlds 3(3), 181–199 (2011)
9. McCraty, R., Atkinson, M., Tiller, W.A., Rein, G., Watkins, A.D.: The effects of emotions on short-term power spectrum analysis of heart rate variability. The American Journal of Cardiology 76(14), 1089–1093 (1995)
10. Morris, J.: Observations: SAM: the Self-Assessment Manikin; an efficient cross-cultural measurement of emotional response. J. of Advertising Research (December 1995)
11. Nogueira, P.A., Rodrigues, R., Nacke, L.E.: Guided Emotional State Regulation: Understanding and Shaping Players' Affective Experiences in Digital Games. In: AIIDE (2013)
12. Rachuy, C., Budde, S., Schill, K.: Unobtrusive data retrieval for providing individual assistance in aal environments. In: Int. Conf. on Health Informatics (2011)
13. Rajendra Acharya, U., Paul Joseph, K., Kannathal, N., Lim, C.M., Suri, J.S.: Heart rate variability: a review. Medical & Biological Engineering & Computing 44(12), 1031–1051 (2006)
14. Vidaurre, C., Sander, T.H., Schlögl, A.: Biosig: The free and open source software library for biomedical signal processing. Computational Intelligence and Neuroscience (2011)

Studying an Author-Oriented Approach to Procedural Content Generation through Participatory Design

Rui Craveirinha and Licinio Roque

Universidade de Coimbra
rui.craveirinha@gmail.com
lir@dei.uc.pt

Abstract. The paper describes the design research process of a procedural content generation tool aimed at supporting creative game design
processes. An author oriented approach to procedural content generation
tools is used where these tools can be manipulated so as to let authors
define the design space they want to explore and the design solution
they wish to find, therefore maintaining their creative agenda intact.
We present two Participatory Design exercises where game designers
were tasked with creating a complete Interface Design for an implementation of this approach. Content Analysis from participants' discourse
during these design exercises showed two important results. First, designers have trouble understanding how this procedural content generation
works, and how to express their design problem within its conceptual
framework. Second, subjects were averse to a pure optimization led approach to content generation and suggested the need for an exploratory
phase, where content is created only to grasp the design landscape, without having to specifically define the desired solution.

Keywords: Creativity Support Tools, Participatory Design, Prototyping, Human-Centered Design.

1 Introduction

Procedural Content Generation (PCG) tools promise enormous potential for
game design activities, as they may actively empower designers to create artifacts more effectively and efficiently, as well as expand their ability to explore
the creative space. However, PCG has been criticized for being confined to the
goal of efficient production of assets (scenery, levels, maps), and for producing
uninteresting, repetitive and/or unoriginal results [5]. And despite significant
investment into researching new methods and algorithms to improve the quality
of generated artifacts, there is little research done on how game designers can
meaningfully interface with PCG tools in a way that potentiates their creative
design process. This paper describes the two-stage design research process of a
PCG tool interface focused on realizing an authors' design agenda. At this stage,
the main objective was to clarify needs/requirements for an interface for creators

© IFIP International Federation for Information Processing 2015
K. Chorianopoulos et al. (Eds.): ICEC 2015, LNCS 9353, pp. 383–390, 2015.
DOI: 10.1007/978-3-319-24589-8_30

to interact with PCG algorithms. Towards that end, we involved game designers and researchers in a Participatory Design (PD) process, where they could design the user interface for the PCG approach. This design process served both for: a) designing an interface proposal from the perspective of its prospective users; b) providing a context to study how design practitioners would interact with this novel PCG approach. The outcome of this work was a series of findings related to how prospective users envision their interaction with a PCG-enabled game authoring system and, an interface model to build and user-study a prototype for such a system.

This paper goes on to describe the Participatory Design sessions, and the content analysis of the designers' discourse during these. Background section gives a brief overview of procedural content tools for games and the approach we are using, while the Methodology section outlines the PD exercises and how we analyzed results. Next we present the results from the PD sessions 1 and 2, with the content analysis of collected designers discourse. Finally, Discussion details our reections on these sessions.

2 Background

In the field of game design, the past years have seen the rise of research into Experience-Driven Procedural Content Generation (EDPCG)[15], a family of computational methods that allow for automatic or semi-automatic generation of videogame content aimed at improving player-experience. The aim is to strive for methods that can dynamically create content that is tailored to specific models of player experience. While results from these EDPCG methods are very promising, from our research positioning, they are limited in two regards: a) they are confined to experimental contexts, and are now only taking their first steps into becoming fully realized in actual game design processes (as an example of an early attempt, see [14]); b) most importantly, several of the reviewed methods ([7][13]) are focused on generating content that improves player-experience models, i.e., optimizing user reported aspects such as 'interest', or 'fun'. These models are built by correlating features of the game's content with player reported evaluations of the experience, so that features from levels that players find 'fun' are used when generating levels that are meant to optimize 'fun'. Hence, these models overlook authorial definition and intentional exploration of the player-experience spectrum (at best, an author can choose which user preference to optimize). While there is much value in this model-based approach, we have proposed an alternative, author-centric approach [2]. It works by transforming the design problem into a search-space mapping problem. The search-space is defined by designers choosing certain key elements of the game's design (henceforth called artifact features) to which they will forfeit control within set boundaries. These are the elements which a search algorithm then proceeds to vary until it finds the set of artifact elements that consistently elicit the target player experience. The target player experience is defined as a quantitative goal, established by setting optimal values or boundaries, for player experience indicators as defined by the game designers. Experience quality indicators are defined based on quantifiable aspects of logged user behavior, e.g. action rhythm, based on any count/frequency of specific actions within the game. General search algorithms can then try to solve the problem, iteratively generating artifacts, automatically measuring their mediated player experience with human players' participation, until a desirable solution is found. In this way, authors can use PCG to study/solve their design problems. In EDPCG terms, this is equivalent to letting authors design their own player-experience 'model'. For more on this approach, please refer to [2,3].

3 Methodology

To design the interface, our strategy was to do use Participatory Design. Participatory design is an approach to design where end-users are given a lead role in the process [8]; given that the goal was to provide game designers with a tool that they would find useful for their creative processes, providing them a key role in the design of this tool seemed an obvious fit, as their needs and wants should guide the design, and they are apt designers in the first place. Out of all strands in PD techniques [1], because we were considering how to develop an artifact for supporting PCG-based game design, we wanted designers themselves to engage in Prototype Sessions, to envision the interaction with this new technology. The purpose of these prototype sessions is to provide an environment where the end-users can create, interact with, and discuss low-res prototypes of the intended artifact. The advantages in employing a Participatory Design method are two-fold: one, to quickly adjust this approach's prototype interface to game designers mindset and practices so that, as a tool, it can actually benefit their design process; second, to start a preliminary study on the nature and impact that using such a tool could have in a game design context, namely as to adjusting game design activities. Because our research concerns the study of how design processes can use PCG tools, it is only natural that a design technique be used as a means to obtain data, given that one of the forefront subjects of design research concerns design praxeology[4].

Besides the participants designing of the interface by means of paper prototyping, audio recording from the exercises was used to support revisions and discourse analysis, allowing further insight into users' perceptions. While the main participant's focus was the creation of an interface prototype, hints on how designers would appropriate this technology should surface, as this would be intimately related with the mindset of participants and the way they describe and analyze interactions with the interface in respect to their design problem. Hence, so as to inspect these Participatory Design sessions, we used Content Analysis applied to participants' discourse during the design exercise, by means of open coding by a subjective coder [6]. An initial pass of all audio recordings was done in search of key concepts, after which a new pass was done for the coding proper. A third pass was then done to correct any coding errors. Naturally, forms of qualitative analysis are susceptible to biased interpretations and subjective manipulations [6]; in this case, given that only one author performed the analysis, one should temper the finality of any conclusions herein drawn. Since the purpose of this analysis was to complement users own design, by way of providing further insight into the rationale behind their expressed needs and specifications, seemed not to require further guarantees of objectivity. Furthermore, Relational Analysis was done by searching for occurrences of disparate concepts in time windows of one minute. Conclusions were drawn from the results of these analyses.

4   PD Session 1

The first PD session was to design an interface that would make the EDPCG approach usable to game designers. One designer and a computer engineer were developing a simple platform game, and their prototype was at the stage where this PCG approach could be used. They were told to draw the interface on paper whilst describing its workings orally. By grounding the exercise on their design process, we expected them to provide the best solutions for their work context. Coding for this session was divided into 3 major categories: a) data sources, b) UI elements and c) games design references. In terms of data, several gameplay experience measurements were mentioned, and so we subdivided counts in respect to the specific data type which they referred to. So, whenever a participant mentioned a gameplay metric, we counted one reference, the same for biometrics and subjectively determined qualities. Also, because the platform is focused on varying game features, every mention of these was counted. 'UI' related terms were divided into sub-categories: a) 'platform configuration', how data is inserted/edited/visualized in the application), b) 'application structure', how the program should be structured in terms of components and screen flow, c) how experience data should be processed visually when shown to users, and d) User Experience, references to usability and other user experience considerations). Game Design is the area we were most concerned with analyzing. We extracted 3 main categories in discourse, relating to the approach: a) 'optimization' of given experience goals, i.e. searching for the right set of features), b) 'experimentation' of different game variations, c) direct reference to 'player experience' qualities. We also registered problematic events: 'terminological misconception', registered whenever a participant used the wrong word for a given concept, the number of researcher directed 'queries' that were made, and expressions of doubt on either the working of the approach – 'Doubts (Approach)' – or its intended goals in terms of the creative design process –'Doubts (Goals)'.

Figure 1 shows the event count for each topic; we also accounted for a Proximity Analysis metric: the number of co-occurrence of concepts in one minute windows. A high number of 'App Config' (and App Config + App Structure pairs, 14 counts) counts means the session was dominated by a focus on screens for inserting/editing data into the PCG tools. This is further emphasized by high counts of two data concepts ('Metrics' and 'Features') and two very frequent co-occurrence pairs, 'App Config'+'Metrics' (11 counts) and 'App Config'+'Features' (9 counts) where subjects focused discourse on how to get data into the application. We find a significant number of co-occurrences with pairs 'App Config'+'Terminological

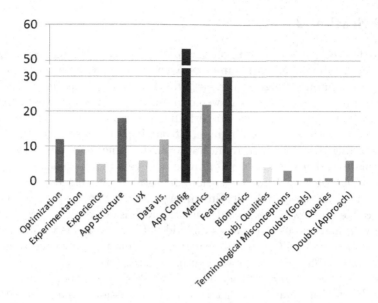

Fig. 1. Counting of references. Blue refers to Design topics, red to User Interface topics, green to Data topics and violet for problematic events.

Misconceptions'(6) and 'Features'+'Terminological Misconceptions' (7); as while describing the process of inserting/editing a specific type of data subjects mistook one type of data with another. Though the main focus of the approach is on finding the artifact that fulfils a certain experience (e.g. 'optimization'), the case for experimental testing of different cases was put forth, with no mention of target values. The number of events mentioning this approach was significant, and when queried if this experimentation should be a use case to be realized before optimization, one participant replied that *"yes, something along that line"*, an *"exploration"*. This means that this approach needed to be supplemented by a no target experimentation phase, where designers simply test out different variants of the same game. Also, participants struggled with finding appropriate values for target indicators. The pair 'App Config'+'Optimization' (13 occurrences), shows that there was a sequential order in the mindset of the process, starting with editing the data and following with the optimization of these values, *"For all these features, we can establish [here] their boundaries and values, and in that case, we then either optimize the rhythm or... "*. But optimization was not, as would be expected beforehand, a considerable focus of the session, and was only mentioned 12 times, and only in abstract, with no target values associated. This suggests that : designers struggle to find meaningful values for certain indicators *a priori* without data. Also, the focus on data visualization, even though not dominant, speaks of the importance of supporting visual data analysis, irrespective of whether or not optimization goals are met.

5 PD Session 2

The second session was to iterate on the first prototype. We realized a full PD workshop with 8 members of a game research laboratory, with backgrounds in game design, computer engineering, design (these include the members of the first session). In the second session, we counted both number of events and measured how much time was spent on certain discussion themes. The reason for this is that because of the large number of participants, discourse quickly lead to long winding discussions surrounding a single topic; counting these as singular events would result in a small number of events that could not represent the importance they took in the session. In terms of events we added coding for expressions implying difficulty in understanding some aspect of the platform, 'Trouble Understanding', and 'Functional misconceptions' regarding the platform working. Discussion themes include 'UI', which refers to all discussion of the interface design. 'Composed Features', a topic that revolved around the possibility of establishing complex game parameterizations, where each feature could vary in relation to a distinct one. 'Preset-Features', the proposal to add of a bundled set of default artifact features. Discussions that concerned how the game-artifact and the procedural platform should be integrated were coded with 'Code-Platform Integration'. Also, 'Data Mining', referring to a proposal for the use data mining techniques for harvesting of meaningful indicator data. Discussions arising from doubts on how the platform should operate were tagged with 'Platform operation'. Another discussion was referring to when to define Indicators, if before or after running a prototype test, 'Indicator Definition'. And also, strings of discussion focused on attempting to pinpoint 'Terminology' or come up with accurate conceptual definitions to integrate parts of platform.

As expected given the goal of designing the interface, 55.6% of discussion time concerned the 'UI' topic and it was also the main focal point of all co-ocurrences. More surprising is a non-negligible (9%) portion of time spent discussing how the platform operates, which is symptomatic of the approach's concepts and functioning being hard to comprehend. This is confirmed by the high number of problematic events: 10 'Terminological Misconceptions', 6 'Functional Misconceptions', 7 'UI doubts', 13 'Platform Doubts' and 22 'Researcher Queries'. The almost 15% of time spent on discussing terminology and underlying concepts seems of considerable importance in this respect as they imply a great deal of conceptual confusion. Highlighting this effect, terminology discussions lead to Terminological Misconceptions 8 times. In terms of which concepts subjects struggled more in pinning down, they were either the types of data (features), i.e., *"aren't these indicators [referring to features]?"*, or its procedural aspects . As one subject said: *"there is a conceptual base here that has yet to be defined, and it is very important"*, and *"the language is not completely defined"*. Nearly 10% was spent on determining how the approach should interoperate with games' prototype code; the preoccupation in this discussion was how to make the process seamless. Four major design proposals were forwarded during the sessions: 'Complex Features', 'Pre-set Features', 'Data Mining' and 'Indicator'. Apart from the latter, time spent on them was mostly negligible and none translated into new requirements. However, in all these cases, participants betray a desire to have an easy to set up application. Finally, the 'Indicator' discussion (determining when indicators should be defined, whether before starting a test or afterwards) did not take up as much time as other topics (5%), it actually lead to a new specification. In the end of the conversation, there was an agreement that new indicators should be able to be defined both a priori and a posteriori. This reinforces the need for an explorative content generation approach.

6   Discussion

Based on the results of content analysis from the PD sessions, and the resulting paper interface, a number of crucial requirements for the PCG application can be discerned.

Procedural Content Generation Needs a Metaphor. Before this PCG method can be operationalized in a game design scenario its functioning needs to be easier to understand and apprehend by its users. There was a consistent struggle from subjects to understand the nature of this tool: from the arise of queries and doubts, to outright terminological misunderstandings, there is ample evidence of difficulty in grasping the platform's goals, concepts and (non-technical) working process. The excess of concepts – features, indicators, etc. – without an intuitive semantic framework, as well as the approach's complex mode of operation, presented a high barrier of access to users. Furthermore, a new approach to design requires a new design language. Our approach to solve this is to propose a simple metaphor to encompass this approach, and then make sure both the application's terms and logic are coherent with it, so that users should have less difficulties to understand how this PCG method works. Currently, we are testing one possible solution for this problem.

Exploration Before Optimization. The other major difficulty that participants had was in how to define the game design problem and solution according to the metaphor of this procedural approach. It requires a reversal of the traditional game design flux – to decide on experiential qualities before game's material features – and it was never fully incorporated in subjects speech. In the first design session no values for experience indicators were ever discussed and in the second, little to no references were made on actual design cases and agendas that could be fulfilled with this approach. This puts forth the question of whether or not it is feasible for designers to reverse their mental processes in this way and use this tool as was foreseen. In both sessions a use-case was proposed for generating content without defining target experience indicators, so that users could better grasp the design landscape. Complementing this, the UI proposed by participants contains one window solely dedicated to presenting results from gameplay sessions, using plots and tables, and part of the discussion, in both session 1 and 2 was in reference to this topic. Thus, an integral part of this PCG application needs to be focused on how explore gameplay experience data that can inform the design process. In this way, designers can have exploratory phases to map out the design space, before committing to a design agenda that they want to optimize.

References

1. Crabtree, A.: Ethnography in participatory design. In: Proceedings of the 1998 Participatory Design Conference. Computer Professionals for Social Responsibility, pp. 93–105 (1998)
2. Craveirinha, R., Santos, L., Roque, L.: An author-centric approach to procedural content generation. In: Reidsma, D., Katayose, H., Nijholt, A. (eds.) ACE 2013. LNCS, vol. 8253, pp. 14–28. Springer, Heidelberg (2013)
3. Craveirinha, R., Roque, L.: Designing games with procedural content generation. In: Proceedings of the ACM SIGCHI Conference on Human Factors in Computing Systems (CHI 2015), Seoul, South Korea. ACM (2015)
4. Cross, N.: Design Research: A Disciplined Conversation. Design Issues 15(2), 5–10 (1999)
5. Hendrikx, M., Meijer, S., Van Der Velden, J., Iosup, A.: Procedural content generation for games: A survey. ACM Trans. Multimedia Comput. Commun. Appl. 9(1), 1:1–1:22 (2013)
6. Lazar, J., Feng, J., Hochheiser, H.: Research Methods in Human-Computer Interaction. Wiley (2010)
7. Pedersen, C., Togelius, J., Yannakakis, G.: Modeling player experience for content creation. IEEE Transactions on Computational Intelligence and AI in Games 2(1), 54–67 (2010)
8. Schuler, D., Namioka, A. (eds.): Participatory Design: Principles and Practices. L. Erlbaum Associates Inc. (1993)
9. Sears, A., Jacko, J.: Human-Computer Interaction Development Process. Human Factors and Ergonomics. Taylor & Francis (2009)
10. Shaker, N., Yannakakis, G.N., Togelius, J.: Towards Automatic Personalized Content Generation for Platform Games. In: Proceedings of the AAAI Conference on Artificial Intelligence and Interactive Digital Entertainment (AIIDE). AAAI Press (October 2010)
11. Smith, A.M., Mateas, M.: Variations forever: Flexibly generating rulesets from a sculptable design space of mini-games. In: IEEE Conference on Computational Intelligence and Games, CIG (2010)
12. Togelius, J., Nardi, R.D., Lucas, S.M.: Making racing fun through player modeling and track evolution. In: Proceedings of the SAB, Workshop on Adaptive Approaches for Optimizing Player Satisfaction in Computer and Physical Games, p. 70 (2006)
13. Togelius, J., Schmidhuber, J.: An experiment in automatic game design. In: IEEE Symposium on Computational Intelligence and Games (CIG 2008), pp. 111–118. IEEE (2009)
14. Yannakakis, G.N., Liapis, A., Alexopoulos, C.: Mixed-initiative co-creativity. In: Proceedings of the ACM Conference on Foundations of Digital Games (2014)
15. Yannakakis, G.N., Togelius, J.: Experience-driven procedural content generation. IEEE Transactions on Affective Computing 99 (2011) (PrePrints)

The Role of Embarrassment to Shape Public Interactions

Licia Calvi

Academy for Digital Entertainment, NHTV University of Applied Sciences,
Breda, The Netherlands
calvi.l@nhtv.nl

Abstract. Can audience embarrassment be used to shape interactions in public settings? Is this the threshold for an audience to step in and / or out of the interaction in performative interactions in public space?

The proliferation of mobile and ubiquitous devices has shifted the attention to the design of interactive systems for use in public settings. This design applies the notion of *performance* to attract and engage audiences. Because performance becomes such a core part of the interaction, the success of those interactive systems heavily depends upon the physical, social and emotional context in which they are to be used. Indeed, strangers around a potential user may hinder or encourage that individual's participation in the interaction. Similarly, the physical space in which the interaction takes place, public or semi-public space may as well facilitate audience participation or prevent it.

This paper investigates what characteristics of this setting (perceived / felt) can trigger audience participation in the interaction. A model based on the notion of performance and entailing some degree of felt embarrassment is applied to two cases to explain how the potential embarrassment implicit in any interaction in public space can be used to encourage users' participation in it.

Keywords: Performance, public space, embarrassment, social norms, design to limit embarrassment.

1 Introduction

Interacting with a system in a public setting is by far not straightforward for a potential audience, particularly if what is asked of them is to take part in a performative interaction that is one where performance lies at the core of the interaction itself. Because performing is in this case what users are expected to do, the success of those interactive systems heavily depends upon elements that have little to do with the system itself, but relate to the physical space and, particularly, to the social and emotional context in which the system is used. Indeed, strangers around a potential user may hinder as well as encourage that individual's participation in the interaction. Similarly, the physical space in which the interaction takes place, in the form of a public space like a train station or a semi-public space like a museum or a gallery, may as well facilitate audience participation or prevent it.

© IFIP International Federation for Information Processing 2015
K. Chorianopoulos et al. (Eds.): ICEC 2015, LNCS 9353, pp. 391–398, 2015.
DOI: 10.1007/978-3-319-24589-8_31

Several recent studies [1], [3], [10-11] have shown for example the influence that the mere presence of strangers has on the individual's intention to participate or not to participate in these interactions. VideoMob [10], for instance, is an interactive art installation based on Kinect technology that encourages strangers to connect across space and time. By presenting this art installation in various locations and contexts through the United States, the authors could collect hundreds of participants' responses to the interactive system and analyse their social behaviors when interacting with strangers in public space, in an attempt to identify what makes people trespass that invisible embarrassing threshold when expected to perform in public space.

Similarly, Hespanhol and his colleagues [11] have observed social encounters around large media façades. It is interesting to see in this study how people approach the interactive space, how they behave differently depending on the relative distance they are from this physical space and on the social situation they are in (i.e., alone, with friends or with children). Especially adults seem restrained to perform, mostly tend to look for other adults and to remain confined in this small clique when engaging in these interactions but appear less reluctant to step out of their comfort zone in the presence of kids.

From these few examples we can already see how the others, especially when strangers, can "invoke feelings of shyness and a desire to control the personal exposure associated with interactions" [3].

This is why we intend to investigate how public embarrassment can be transformed into an opportunity to play. In [4], we have referred to the notion of *experiential place* [6], as the way for people to break the social norms holding in a given context (cultural institutions in that case) and cross their emotional threshold to perform in public by for instance lying in a concert hall to intensify the music experience or dressing up as a cockroach when visiting a science museum. In this paper, we will embed this notion into a model to limit embarrassment when designing interactions in public space. This model is built by observing existing examples of such interactions and borrows elements from other accepted models of performance in HCI (see further).

In the next sections, we will first define what performative interactions are and present two different cases of performative interactions, "Schizophrenic Cyborg" [16-17] and "Presence" [7]. Further, we will describe the performance-based model we developed. We will then discuss the notion of felt embarrassment in the cases presented and analyse the way in which interaction can be shaped to limit embarrassment according to the model outlined.

2   Performative Interactions

Williamson et al. [21] define performative interactions as "any interaction or technology that is influenced by or affected by the spectacle resulting from its use, the public setting where it is used, or the presence of spectators as an audience" [21, p. 1546].

Based on this definition, they identify two types of performative interactions: those where technology is part of the artistic expression and rely on a *performer* actually performing on some kind of stage (we call them *performer-driven* interactions), and those with no official performer where it is the technology that triggers an audience to participate (we call them *technology-driven* interactions). Recent examples of performer-driven performative interactions are Joe Malia's "Scarf" [13], Philips "Skin Probe Bubble" [14], various performances by Stelarc [18], and "Schizophrenic Cyborg" by Sheridan and colleagues [16-17]. Examples of technology-driven performative interactions are "Presence" by Laura Dekker [7], "SMS Slingshot" by VR/URBAN [20] or "Text Rain" by Camille Utterback and Romy Achituv [19].

In "Schizophrenic Cyborg" [16-17], a performer is facing an audience with a screen hanging on his belly. The interface on his body displays an interaction that is in fact activated by another performer who is not visible to the public. So "Schizophrenic Cyborg" represents an example of a performative interaction where the performer puts on stage a situation using technology as part of the play in order to express something (therefore a performer-driven interaction). The role technology has is to create a confusion or misconception in the audience between the interaction enacted through the interface and the ways to achieve it. The audience has indeed no clue that what is displayed on the performer's body is not controlled by him but that he is himself part of the technology on stage (from here the name "cyborg") and that he himself, like the interface, is manipulated by the hidden performer. Just seeing the effects of this interaction but not the interaction itself, nor the cyborg undertaking any action, can of course cause various reactions in the public: these are all used by the hidden performer to shape the actual interaction. The cyborg is part of the technology and of the representation on stage and as such is not aware of the kind of interactions that the hidden performer is enacting, that is what will be shown on the screen and what reactions in the audience trigger it. In doing so the cyborg/device only provides a tangible and visible source for dialogue, despite the invisibility of the enacting power (the hidden performer).

In "Presence" [7], screens are displayed in a park and require an audience to move or dance in front of them provoking with their movements layers of video to reveal or hide (Fig. 1).

Fig. 1. Presence by Laura Dekker [7]

This is an example of a technology-driven performative interaction because the performance is determined by the audience movements that are triggered by the screen images. These screen images are related and engaged with the physical space, but they are not influenced by it, they are only affected by the social context, that is by the people present: who they are, what they do, if they play on their own or together. However, the audience willingness to perform or not is certainly affected by both.

In different ways both works (and the kind of performative interactions they enact) play with the notion of audience embarrassment although in one work this is more prominent and direct than in the other: in Dekker's work, as something the audience has to cope with and to overcome in order to participate in the interaction; in Sheridan's work, embarrassment is more about being able to understand who is in control of what in order to be able to react in an appropriate way. So, in a way, while in Dekker's work embarrassment can be felt more strongly because each individual needs to stand up for themselves to perform, in Sheridan's work, the audience seems to act more as a whole against the cyborg/hidden performer.

Both works and the way they use embarrassment can be better understood by looking at them through the lens of the performance-based model of interaction (see below). This model is intended to help design to limit embarrassment, so that more audience can trespass the threshold to interaction and become engaged in the performance.

Embarrassment has been described by Goffman [8-9] as that something people feel (being not at ease, or restrained) every time they violate the implicit social norms holding in the environment they are in. Technology may force people to violate these norms whenever they are pushed to move from the status of audience to that of performers (see in next section), that is, when the behavior they perform is front stage, which happens when people are in the centre of somebody's attention. Dekker's artwork is an example of this: people are encouraged to behave differently, possibly playfully, in a context (certainly physical, maybe even social and this depending on the nature of the audience around them) that would normally not allow this kind of behaviour. What makes it possible? What makes people not feel embarrassed to adopt an otherwise socially unacceptable behaviour? The feeling of being watched by others indeed mostly induce people to change behaviour, in general to behave socially, that is according to the accepted rules.

2.1 Models of Performative Interactions

Several models of performative interactions have already been developed [2], [15], [17]. They are based on the idea that for an interaction to occur, different audience roles are needed (performer / participant / observer) and that the interaction is confined within a given space (physical and / or psychological) for the audience to recognise and within which specific behavioral codes (or interactions rules) apply. In some cases [2] and [15], these roles are not static but may change as a result of the interaction evolving.

These models however do not seem to consider appropriately the space and the experience thereof of the people involved in the performance, regardless of the role they play in the initial interaction. We believe that it is precisely this experience that can help them cross that emotional threshold to perform in public without feeling embarrassed. This specific experience of the space lies at the heart of the model we have developed, that we called the performance-based model (Fig. 2).

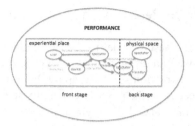

Fig. 2. The performance-based model

This model is very much in line with Benford's and Reeves's model [2] and [15] as it borrows from it audience differentiation and the notion of role transitions to account for the plasticity of the performative interaction. It also implies that these transitions must occur within a well-defined physical space. What we call performance in our model roughly corresponds to Reeves's performance frame [15] but our definition includes the physical and social context (the space) as well as its transformation into place. So it is in fact the context in which the performative interaction can ultimately take place. Here, the transition is from a physical space, i.e., the setting where the audience is and where the interaction can occur in practice, to an experiential place that is where the performance happens [4]. So the shift accounted for by this model is not physical rather it is cognitive. In a way, this experiential place is very similar to Huizinga's magic circle [12], in that the experience of it is not only memorable, but essentially meaningful. The recognition of this meaningfulness is what allows each individual participant to feel less unease in becoming a performer in front of an even unknown audience because they can add a personal meaning with each individual experience and in this way they can overcome their embarrassment to perform in public. Technology is part of this experience and in a way it is what makes the interaction possible especially in the technology-driven performative interactions discussed above.

The model in Figure 2 indeed displays the cognitive unfolding of the interaction rather than its ontological consistence. This unfolding is mainly visible in the transformation of the spectator moving from back to front stage [8-9], that is from being at the side of the interaction to being in the centre of it, and also from being part of an unfocused interaction, as a passer-by or a distracted observer, to a focused interaction, one the spectator is aware of and wittingly participating in. The performative interaction assumes the presence of a performer and a device (i.e., the technology in the definition by [21]) without specifying however the particular role this technology may take, or the function it may display. In this way, both forms of performative interactions mentioned above are accounted for. But their mere presence, of the performer and the device, is not enough: it is the spectator's transformation what sets the transition from physical space to experiential place in motion. This transformation implies the overcoming of some kind of felt embarrassment. In the next section, we will see how this model applies to the two cases presented earlier.

3   Embarrassment in Performative Interactions

If we apply the performance-based model to the two examples of performative interactions described above, we find different uses (or misuses) of it.

Dekker's performative interaction seems to apply the model in Fig. 2 almost literally: the audience has to recognise the possibility that, by stepping into the interaction, they will transform space into place by recognizing and attaching personal meanings to it. This recognition makes them forget about the physical and social setting they are in and their possible embarrassment with it. So, in this case (the possibly felt) embarrassment is part of the performative interaction, in fact it is essential for the interaction to take place, for people to recognize the magic circle [12] that allows them to step into the interaction and to play. Overcoming embarrassment is what makes the interaction possible. And passing this threshold is possible if users transform the physical space onto the experiential place.

In Sheridan's work on the contrary there is no physical space to be transformed, no experiential place to be filled with personal meanings, no magic circle to step into. There is a barrier between audience and performer / cyborg, and this is represented by the hidden performer, and by the interaction he is orchestrating behind the scene and without anybody being aware of: the audience that the messages are manipulated by others and not controlled by the performer / cyborg, the cyborg of what causes the audience's reactions. In this work therefore, the separation between physical space and experiential place remains and cannot be trespassed. The confusion and intended misconception generated by this set-up is what may cause embarrassment in the audience and in the cyborg but not one to be easily overcome by transforming space into place. Sheridan et al. [17] indeed report that the audience could recognize how the interaction was taking place (so that the cyborg was not in control of it) only if they had a high technical expertise: so nothing to do with the experience of stepping into the magic circle discussed above.

The question remains whether this effect is intrinsic in all performer-driven performative interactions that only use technology on stage or whether this is one of its possible uses. And whether from an HCI point of view one can appropriately speak of performative interactions only in the case where an audience is more actively engaged as in Dekker's example (so for technology-driven performative interactions).

4   Conclusion

In this paper, we have presented a model to explain performative interactions in public space, one that takes the possibility of participants' embarrassment into account and proposes a way to overcome it. A design for interactions in public space to limit embarrassment should account for a cognitive transformation of a physical space into an experiential place, one where the audience can feel emotions, have memorable experiences, attach meanings to it in a continuous and interactive way. This is when space becomes place.

The two cases discussed in this paper represent different yet specular instances of performative interactions. We have explained their different use of audience embarrassment under the light of a performance-based model of interaction. This model is in fact meant to limit embarrassment and to encourage audience engagement in the performative interaction. However, opposite uses (or misuses) are possible. Playing with the (im)possibility to shift from physical space to experiential place allows that.

The results of this analysis are very preliminary and do not allow for generalizations. However, they show that only in one type of performative interaction, the *technology-driven* one where technology is triggering the interaction as in Dekker's artwork, the concept of audience embarrassment can be appropriately applied as something that needs to be overcome in order to step into the interaction. As what shortens the distance among people (all actors) and makes people shift from a physical space to an experiential place and experience the interaction as pervaded with personal meanings. In the other type of performative interactions, the one where technology is part of the representation on stage (*performer-driven*), more uses seem to be possible and all depend on the performer's intentions. In the example discussed here, the (hidden) performer intended to create confusion and mislead the audience into believing that the cyborg was responsible for the interaction while he was also part of it in his dual role of performer and of technology (medium and message). Other performative interactions of this type (for instance Cillari's *Se mi sei vicino* [5]) still open up spaces for a dialogue with the audience and for this transformation (from space to place) to occur. Also here the performer is in fact in control of the interaction and the technology part of this stage representation. But the audience is 'pushed' to get closer (in Cillari's work literally and also physically).

These observations do not allow us to draw any final conclusion on the absolute validity of the model presented but advocate for more research on the types of performative interactions existing, their use of technology and the type of setting, both emotional, social and physical, they are embedded into.

Several questions still remain unanswered, in fact: what type of design can trigger users to cross the threshold? What elements should be present in the physical space to encourage this? Can we draw some guidelines on how to actually implement this design? Has the size of the audience an effect on the individual's intention to participate in the public interaction?

Acknowledgements. The author wishes to thank Laura Dekker for sharing her work with her.

References

1. Bekker, T., Johansen, S., van Kuijk, M., Schouten, B., Sturm, J., Vanden Abeele, V.: Playful Interactions Stimulating Physical Activity in Public Spaces. In: Proc. CHI 2013 Workshop, Experiencing Interactivity in Public Spaces (2013)
2. Benford, S., Crabtree, A., Reeves, S., Sheridan, J., Dix, A., Flintham, M., Drozd, A.: The frame of the game: Blurring the boundary between fiction and reality in mobile experiences. In: Proceedings SIGCHI 2006, pp. 427–436. ACM Press (2006)

3. Calcraft, P., Chalmers, D., Fisher, C., Rimmer, J., Wakeman, I., Whiting, L.: Mediating Exposure in Public Interactions. In: Proc. CHI 2013 Workshop, Experiencing Interactivity in Public Spaces (2013)
4. Calvi, L., Spence, J.: Engaging Audiences in Museums in a Performance Way. In: Proceedings of DRHA 2014 Conference. University of Greenwich's London eScholarship Repository (in press)
5. Cillari, S.: Se mi sei vicino (2006/2007), http://www.soniacillari.net/Se_Mi_Sei_Vicino_.htm
6. Ciolfi, L., Bannon, L.J.: Space, place and the design of technologically-enhanced physical environments. In: Proc. INTERACT 2015 Workshop, Workshop on Place and Experience in Human-Computer Interaction (2005)
7. Dekker, L.: Presence (2012), http://theretohere.co.uk/There_to_Here/Presence.htm
8. Goffman, E.: The presentation of self in everyday life. Doubleday, Garden City (1959)
9. Goffman, E.: Behavior in Public Places; Notes on the Social Organization of Gatherings. Free Press of Glencoe, NY (1966)
10. Grenader, E., Rodrigues, D.G., Nos, F., Weibel, N.: The VideoMob Interactive Art Installation Connecting Strangers through Inclusive Digital Crowds. In: Salah, A., Hung, H., Aran, O., Gunes, H., Turk, M. (eds) Behavior Understanding for Arts and Entertainment, Special issue, ACM Transactions on Interactive Intelligent Systems (TiiS) (in press)
11. Hespanhol, L., Tomitsch, M., Bown, O., Young, M.: Using Embodied Audio-Visual Interaction to Promote Social Encounters Around Large Media Façades. In: Proc. DIS 2014, pp. 945–954. ACM Press (2014)
12. Huizinga, J.: Homo Ludens: A Study of the Play-Element in Culture. Routledge & Kegan Paul, London (1949)
13. Malia, J.: Private Public, http://design-interactions2007-2014.rca.ac.uk/joe-malia/private-public (retrieved)
14. Philips Skin Probe Bubble, http://www.design.philips.com/philips/sites/philipsdesign/about/design/designportfolio/design_futures/dresses.page (retrieved)
15. Reeves, S.: Designing interfaces in public settings. Thesis submitted to The University of Nottingham for the degree of Doctor of Philosophy (2008)
16. Schizophrenic Cyborg, http://www.bigdoginteractive.com/cyborg.htm (retrieved)
17. Sheridan, J.G., Dix, A., Lock, S., Bayliss, A.: Understanding interaction in ubiquitous guerrilla performances in playful arenas. In: People and Computers XVIII—Design for Life, pp. 3–17 (2005)
18. Stelarc, http://stelarc.org/_.swf
19. Utterback, C., Achituv, R.: Text Rain, http://camilleutterback.com/projects/text-rain/
20. VR/URBAN, SMS, Slingshot, http://www.vrurban.org/smslingshot.html (retrieved)
21. Williamson, J.R., Koefoed Hansen, L., Jacucci, G., Light, A., Reeves, S. (eds.) Understanding performative interactions in public settings. Pers. Ubiquit. Comput., vol. 18 (2014)

Towards Smart City Learning: Contextualizing Geometry Learning with a Van Hiele Inspired Location-Aware Game

Matthias Rehm, Catalin Stan, Niels Peter Wøldike, and Dimitra Vasilarou

Aalborg University, Department of Architecture, Design, and Media Technology,
9000 Aalborg, Denmark
matthias@create.aau.dk

Abstract. We present an approach to geometry learning that is based on play. For a mobile and location-aware game, the concept of smart city learning is exploited to situate learning about geometric shapes in concrete buildings and thus make them more accessible for younger children. A game was developed in close collaboration with a local school and tested on a field trip and in class. A mixed measures evaluation is presented, where the quantitative results show a significant increase in correct answers in a standardized test and the qualitative analysis reveals increased motivation and curiosity for geometric concepts.

Keywords: Smart City Learning, Location-Aware Games.

1 Introduction

The notion of smart cities has been around for quite some time, but is often restricted to infrastructure or mobility aspects and does not focus on the actual users of a smart city. It is our conviction that the city itself can become the key element in creating smart learning environments that transcend traditional institutionalized learning by bringing learning back to where it originally belonged: everywhere. The work presented in this paper is related to our project on *Smart Cities for Smart Children*. The vision is to create a public space for learning experiences that transcend into all areas of the children's life by the use of modern mobile technology while at the same time establishing traditional institutions (like schools, libraries, museums, etc.) as hubs for information gathering and collaborative interactions. Learning is thus not confined to a traditional institutional setting but the children's living environment, i.e. the city itself, becomes an enchanted place allowing for discovering hidden knowledge in a playful manner. Smart cities, in our vision, become creative environments for realizing new ways of interacting with information (and with others), integrating real and virtual as well as social and emotional aspects.

In this paper we focus on STEM education, more precisely on primary school geometry learning. Based on Van Hiele's didactic approach (e.g. [4]) and in close collaboration with a local school, we developed a learning game that is on the

© IFIP International Federation for Information Processing 2015
K. Chorianopoulos et al. (Eds.): ICEC 2015, LNCS 9353, pp. 399–406, 2015.
DOI: 10.1007/978-3-319-24589-8_32

one hand integrated into the city scape surrounding the school and at the same time into the Math curriculum at the school.

2   Related Work

Smart City Learning The idea of smart city learning[1] is currently emerging as a research field and derives its motivation from the fact that esp. in Europe a rich cultural heritage can often only be experienced in a de-contextualized fashion (e.g. in museums) although it is deeply rooted in the corresponding urban scapes (e.g. [3]). Although primarily focused on cultural heritage and the museal field, the vision is very attractive for every type of location-, or more generally, context-aware system aiming at providing knowledge or skills to the user. The vision of smart city learning puts these approaches in a broader theoretical perspective, emphasizing the necessity of in-situ interactions with the learning content. In this respect, [2] present an analysis of the situated learning that happens on field trips and make suggestions at which points in the experience smart city technologies could become situated tools for initiating actions, triggering reflections, or relating learning episodes across contexts. In [5], a case study is presented that highlights the beneficial effects of situated learning experiences on a Biology field trip. The general idea behind such situated and experiential learning goes back to Kolb [6], who claims that learning has to take place in specific situations which provide rich contextual clues. In earlier work, it has been shown how this paradigm can be utilized in virtual learning environments, e.g. for increasing knowledge and skills about culture-specific gestures [9]. Transferred to a smart city learning scenario, it becomes crucial to integrate the city scape in the learning experience, making it an integral part of the learning.

(Mobile) Games for Learning Geometry. Several games have already been developed for teaching geometry. Lai and White [7] present a collaborative learning game that is loosely based on Van Hiele's didactic approach. Students work together to create and learn about quadrilaterals by each controlling a single corner point of the shape. The main benefit of this approach is that it forces students to communicate about the geometric concepts and thus develop geometric reasoning throughout the learning episodes. In line with van Hiele's approach of playful learning, Vitale and colleagues [12] present a computer-based geometry learning tool and show that grounded integration, which is closely related to Gestalt principles, yields better learning results than a numerical approach. Wallner and Kriglstein [13] report on a case study of a computer game for teaching geometry to elementary school children. In their concept they relate geometric shapes to real world objects found in nature in order to create a meaningful link between geometric concepts and the real world. As this is a desktop game this link is though only conceptual but not embodied and no results are presented.

A first embodied approach is presented in [14], describing a mobile mixed reality game for teaching about some geometric shapes (squares, rectangles, parallelograms). Players have to create the shapes by walking to the corner points in a

---

[1] Smart City Learning Observatory: http://bit.ly/1DxH8sp (visited 2 July 2015).

real environment. There is though no direct connection between the environment and the geometric concepts. All of these games were desktop based or aimed at classroom teaching. This is actually in line with van Hiele's earlier observations of the disembodied and de-contextualized way of the standard curriculum. Also, math field trips are rarely heard of, making it not the prime target for mobile and location-aware games. A rare exception of a math field trip is the work presented in [10] on a project for collaborative learning of geometry with in- and outdoor learning activities. The concept combines field trips for data collection as well as class room based collaborative 3D construction tasks and can be seen as one inspiration for the work presented in this paper.

3   From Van Hiele to Mobile Games

Van Hiele argues against the disembodied way in which geometry is taught in standard textbooks and instead argues for a playful approach situating geometric concepts in the everyday experience of the children [4]. He describes five levels of geometry understanding that a learner passes through (see e.g. [8] for a concise overview): (1) Visualization: holistic recognition of shapes; (2) Analysis: Knowledge about features of shapes; (3) Abstraction: Understanding relationships between features and shapes; (4) Deduction: Understanding of axioms, definitions, and proofs; (5) Rigor: Understanding of formal aspects of deduction.

Although not undisputed (see e.g. [11]; [1]), the different levels provide a useful descriptive tool of progress in geometry learning. Based on these ideas, the following guidelines for design of the mobile experience have been derived: (i) focus on the necessity of play during learning; (ii) connection between the real world and the abstract geometric concepts; (iii) difficulty relates to level of geometric understanding of the students.

With the vision of smart city learning as the driving motivational factor, a game was envisioned that should be based on geometric shapes found in buildings around the city and utilize these shapes on location for learning about geometric concepts. In close collaboration with a Math teacher from a local school it was soon decided to integrate the mobile experience into the third grade class curriculum. Thus, the concept was changed to allow for a field trip for testing the ideas on smart city learning. Additionally, the games would then also be available in class for further use during Math teaching. The teacher contributed to the game design process from the beginning, providing regular reality checks for game concepts as well as gamification elements.

During the field trip, children start at the school. On their mobile devices they see a map (Fig. 1 a), which shows their chosen avatar moving on the map in real-time. Approaching one of the locations triggers a reaction on the device, revealing a task for unlocking the game related to this location (Fig. 1 b). In our vision of smart city learning this would be a proactive behavior that could happen with any building in the city.

Calori and colleagues [2] analyzed learning trajectories on field trips and highlighted the ability of smart city technologies for triggering situated actions in-situ. The game design utilizes this advantage in the task of unlocking the location

Fig. 1. From left to right: (a) in-game map with the three locations; (b) unlocking game (first location); (c) shape shoot; (d) children engaged in shape shoot.

related games. This process is based on level 1 of van Hiele's approach (visualization). The vicinity to buildings with a rich repertoire of geometric shapes triggers situated interactions with these shapes. The children have to compare geometric shapes of the building to prototypes presented to them. Figure 1 (b) shows an example, where the rectangular windows are highlighted and the child has to select the geometric shape that is most similar to this (the rectangle).

For each location, a distinct mini game has been developed that is related to levels 1 (L1) and 2 (L2) of van Hiele according to the age of the children (3rd grade):

- Shape memory: Variant of the well-known memory game. Children are exposed to graphic representations of shapes that have to be matched to the names (L1) or properties (L2) of the shapes. Example: rhombus (L1), equilateral triangle (L2).
- Shape shoot: Two- and three-dimensional shapes move randomly around the screen. A shape becomes a target when the name of the shape or its properties is displayed at the bottom of the screen (Fig. reffig:fig1 c). Shooting is then realized by tapping on the shape. Example: cube (L1), equilateral triangle (L2).
- Shape recognition: Children are presented with a 3D object and asked to signify which (and how many) 2D shapes are used to build this object. This also supports the acquisition of level 3 skills (abstraction), where students are supposed to understand relations between shapes and their properties. Example: a cube consists of six squares.

4   Evaluation

In our vision of smart city learning, learning becomes an integrated part of living in the city, where learning experiences are pro-actively triggered by the surroundings of the learner and in relation to contextual factors. This is envisioned to increase the learner's curiosity about the material and stimulate his/her interest to examine the underlying concepts in more depth and beyond the specific intervention. The evaluation was thus set up as a mixed measures approach, where a quantitative part was a pre-/post-test with a standard measurement tool for knowledge on geometry. The qualitative part combines video observations from the field trip with a semi-structured interview with the teacher, in order to get

Fig. 2. Evaluation Process

insights into the actual practices that evolved around the use of the game. The whole process is shown in Figure 2.

The hypothesis for the quantitative part is

H1: The mean of correct answers in the standardized geometry test will be higher after the intervention.

4.1   Design

12 pupils (age 8-9) from a 3rd grade class at Skipper Clement International School in Aalborg (Denmark) participated in the study. Six Android phones with a screen resolution of 480x800 pixels have been used. The game was developed in Unity3D. The pre- and post-test questionnaire was adapted from a standard van Hiele level test [11] by taking only questions into account that related to levels 1 to 3 of geometry understanding. It consisted of 19 questions.

First, the children's level of geometric understanding was assessed using the standard questionnaire (see also Figure 2 for an overview). After a break of three days, the field trip took place, where the children spend 3 hours exploring the surroundings of the school and playing the games. A week later, the phones were handed to the teacher for in-class use for a period of two weeks. After a break of three days, the post-test questionnaire was administered, followed by the expert interview with the teacher.

4.2   Results and Discussion

A paired-samples t-test was conducted to compare the number of correct answers in the pre- and post-test conditions. There was a significant increase in correct answers for the post-test: pre-test (M=6.36, SD=1.80) vs. post-test (M=8.55, SD=1.81), t(10)= -3.52, p < 0.002. In order to get insights about the levels of geometric understanding, additional t-tests were run for all sets of level specific questions. Significant differences were found for level 1 questions: pre-test (M=3.27, SD=0.65) vs. post-test (M=4.55, SD=1.04), t(10)=-3.32, p<0.004. A tendency for better scores was found for level 2 questions: pre-test (M=2.00, SD=1.48) vs. post-test (M=2.64, SD=0.92), t(10)=-1.30, p=0.112. No significant result could be found for level 3 questions.

The hypothesis could not be rejected. Children performed significantly better after playing the game. The more detailed analysis revealed that this result is mainly depending on their performance on level 1 of geometry understanding. This could be expected for this age group. Additionally there is a tendency that children also got better with questions related to level 2.

4.3   Qualitative Findings

Observations are categorized according to three distinct phases: moving between locations, on location, and in class evaluation.

Moving. Six recurring categories of behavior were identified:
(1) Excitement due to novelty: Children were very excited by the map and the location tracking. Seeing their avatar move on the map prompted comments and discussions between the children.
(2) Discussions about the game: Children started talking about their performance and were comparing badges.
(3) Discussion about the location: Children showed great excitement when they figured out which building they were going to. When getting close, some of them wanted to start running to the location.
(4) Positive appraisal statements: Such statements mostly occurred directly after leaving a location.
(5) Discussions about the surrounding architecture: Children started investigating the buildings along the way and talked about their similarity to the target buildings.
(6) Navigation: While walking, most conversations were about navigation. The children were looking around relating the real world to the map on their screen, using the avatar position to get an idea of where they were and how far it was to the location. The children were very goal oriented and talked about what buildings could be at the locations they were going to.

On Location. The following recurring types of behavior were identified:
(1) Enthusiasm: The most prominent behavior was the enthusiasm shown when they unlocked a location or finished a level and got a badge.
(2) Immersion: Especially in the second location where children used headphones they became completely focused on the game. However, this also meant that they ignored their surroundings and did not spend much time with the actual building in this location.
(3) Frustration: For some children the geometric concepts in the game that relate to level 2 and 3 were hard to grasp.

In Class. Back in class, the children were prompted by their teacher to give feedback regarding the game. All of them gave positive comments and said that they enjoyed the game. They were very interested in the game development process. When asked whether the children wanted to play the game again they all said yes. After a break of one week, the teacher re-introduced the mini-games during Math classes. Children were very motivated to play the game. The log files show an average playing time of 150 minutes per child.

Interview. We summarize the findings that relate to the embodiment of learning and the resulting consequences.
(1) Field Trip and Location Awareness: The teacher points out the benefits of

integrating material from the field (i.e. geometric shapes from the actual buildings) because it allows showing the material in a different way. This makes it more likely that children internalize what they are supposed to learn. The way in which the material was introduced on location in the game was important because it showed how the shapes fit together and how they are used in the real world. The children enjoyed the field trip and talked a lot about it afterwards. Especially the concept of unlocking the different locations was frequently discussed.

(2) Educational Value: According to the teacher, the game got the children curious about the world around them and interested in geometric shapes. After the intervention, children started telling stories about shapes that they found and started asking questions about things they did not understand in relation to geometry. Additionally, they were able to figure out how to combine shapes to make more complex ones, for instance combining rectangle and semicircle for arches. The children also showed more confidence in class and were able to explain things to the teacher that they hadn't been able before.

(3) Motivation: The teacher experienced that the children were motivated to play the game in class and when interacting with it that they stayed focused on it. In fact, he states that they were much more focused than they usually are when given traditional classroom tasks. According to the teacher, the children have a lot of "junk" on their phones that entertains them without any educational value. From his perspective, the game accomplished making the children excited about the schoolwork.

5   Conclusion

In this paper, we present smart city learning as an emerging field for applications of location-aware games. By drawing on the children's natural environment for contextualizing learning experiences, we expect to see better learning results and higher engagement in the learning topics. To investigate this claim, a location-aware game for geometry learning has been developed. The game is based on a renowned didactic approach and was developed in close collaboration with stakeholders from a local school, where it was also evaluated.

Test scores for the participating class were significantly better after intervention. Moreover, the children were motivated playing the game, which is apparent from the average playing time. Qualitative data from observations and an interview with the teacher revealed that the game was successful in increasing the children's curiosity about geometric concepts. During the field trip, they started looking for geometric shapes in the buildings they encountered on the way, afterwards in class they started to tell stories about shapes and discuss other shapes they discovered at home. Thus, this case study confirms that embodying abstract learning goals in the real-life experience of the children has a beneficial effect, increasing their curiosity about the underlying concepts.

According to the teacher, these effects were persistent over the whole period of the study, which is a good indication that the game concepts were suitable. Moreover, contextualizing geometry learning by integrating it with the children's natural environment, in this case the surroundings of the school, has proven successful and warrants further explorations of the concept of smart city learning.

Acknowledgement. We would like to thank Skipper Clement International School, Aalborg, and especially Benjamin Gilbert, for their support and collaboration.

References

1. Burger, W.F., Shaughnessy, J.M.: Characterizing the van Hiele Levels of Development in Geometry. Journal for Research in Mathematics Education 17(1), 31–48 (1986)
2. Calori, I.C., Rossitto, C., Divitini, M.: Understanding Trajectories of Experiences in Situated Learning Field Trips. Interaction Design and Architecture(s) Journal - IxD&A 16, 17–26 (2013)
3. Giovannella, C., Iosue, A., Tancredi, A., Cicola, F., Camusi, A., Moggio, F., Baraniello, V., Carcone, S., Coco, S.: Scenarios for active learning in smart territories. Interaction Design and Architecture(s) Journal - IxD&A 16, 7–16 (2013)
4. van Hiele, P.M.: Developing Geometric Thinking Through Activities That Begin With Play. Teaching Children Mathematics 6, 310–316 (1999)
5. Kamarainen, A.M., Metcalf, S., Grotzer, T., Browne, A., Mazzuca, D., Tutwiler, M.S., Dede, C.: EcoMOBILE: Integrating augmented reality and probeware with environmental education field trips. Computers & Education 68, 545–556 (2013)
6. Kolb, D.A.: Experiential learning: experinece as the source of learning and development. Prentice Hall, Englewood Cliffs (1984)
7. Lai, K., White, T.: Exploring quadrilaterals in a small group computing environment. Computers & Education 59, 963–973 (2012)
8. Mason, M.: The van Hiele levels of geometric undestanding. In: Professional Handbook for Teachers – Geometry: Explorations and Applications. McDougal Inc., Boston (1998)
9. Rehm, M., Leichtenstern, K.: Gesture-Based Mobile Training of Intercultural Behavior. Multimedia Systems 18(1), 33–51 (2012)
10. Spikol, D., Eliasson, J.: Lessons from Designing Geometry Learning Activities that Combine Mobiel and 3D Tools. In: Proceedings of the 6th International Conference on Wireless, Mobile, and Ubiquitous Technologies in Education, pp. 137–141 (2010)
11. Usiskin, Z.: Van Hiele Levels and Achievement in Secondary School Geometry. The University of Chicago, Chicago (1982)
12. Vitale, J.M., Swart, M.I., Black, J.B.: Integrating intuitive and novel grounded concepts in a dynamic geometry learning environment. Computers & Education 72, 231–248 (2014)
13. Wallner, G., Kriglstein, S.: Design and Evaluation of the Educational Game DOGeometry – A case study. In: Proceedings of ACE (2011)
14. Wijers, M., Jonker, V., Kerstens, K.: MobileMath: the Phone, the Game and the Math. In: Proceedings of the 2nd European Game-Based Learning Conference (2008)

Posters

A Simultaneous, Multidisciplinary Development and Design Journey – Reflections on Prototyping

Achim Gerstenberg[1], Heikki Sjöman[1], Thov Reime[1],
Pekka Abrahamsson[2], and Martin Steinert[1]

[1]Department of Engineering Design and Mat.,
[2] Department of Comp. and Info. Sc.
NTNU, Høgskoleringen 1, 7491 Trondheim, Norway
{Achim.Gerstenberg,Heikki.Sjoman,Thovr,Pekkaa,
Martin.Steinert}@ntnu.no

Abstract. This paper proposes a wayfaring approach for the early concept creation stage of development projects that have a very high degree of intended innovation and thus uncertainty. The method is supported by a concrete game design example involving the development of a tangible programming interface for virtual car racing games. We focus onto projects that not only have high degrees of freedom, for example in terms of reframing the problem or iterating the final project vision, but are also complex in nature. For example, these can be projects that allow for the exploration and exploitation of **unknown unknowns** and serendipity findings. Process wise we are primarily focusing onto the early stage that precedes the requirement fixation, which we see as more dynamic and evolutionary in nature. The core conceptual elements that we have derived from the development experiences are: **simultaneous prototyping** in multiple disciplines (such as computer science, electronics and mechanics and engineering in general, **abductive learning** based on the outcome of rapid cycles of designing, building and testing prototypes (**probing**), and the importance of **including all the involved disciplines** (knowledge domains) from the beginning of the project on.

1 Introduction

To innovate incrementally is hard, to innovate "radically" harder still. Many an engineering project is fixating their requirements very early and then focus onto executing these predefined (and often unproven) specs as fast, as good, and as cost effective as possible. The usual outcome is a cost and/or time overrun if the innovative specs are to be met or a decrease in result quality. In a sense people perceive the innovation game often as a game under certainty with fixed variables and attribute values, fixed rules and thus predictable outcomes, hence it can be modeled, simulated and optimized. We argue that the innovation game is a game under uncertainty, with unknown unknowns that need to be discovered, evaluated and then discarded or embodied. The game is also played in a dynamic environment (opponents may counter and react) and even the rules are technically not fixed - take the Kobayashi Maru test situation as an example.

© IFIP International Federation for Information Processing 2015
K. Chorianopoulos et al. (Eds.): ICEC 2015, LNCS 9353, pp. 409 416, 2015.
DOI: 10.1007/978-3-319-24589-8_33

We argue that the development of highly innovative/uncertain and products is rather like an exploration journey. You have a vision where you want to end up and a general idea where your project is heading. However, neither can you know all the "moves" required to get there, nor can you accurately anticipate the effects and responses that one move will have in the future. Your expertise is your toolbox and it greatly helps in "playing your way through the project". Nevertheless the project is dependent on many unforeseeable events. In fact **unknown unknowns** (variables that are part of your problem/solution that you are neither aware off nor do you know their value) arise, serendipitous events present themselves, turning a complicated problem into a complex one - too complex to be planned out beforehand. We subsequently argue that sequential process models are not fitting for any innovative projects. [1,2].

The reference case [3] of designing a tangible game interface for racing games is used to extract reoccurring patterns during the design process and propose a method based on the experiences [4,5]

Our proposed method is based on abductive learning [6,7,8] and includes all involved disciplines from day one. This wayfaring model based on Steinert & Leifer [9] aims to allow the rapid requirement dynamics that become necessary during the development process.

2   Use of Wayfaring in the Example Case

Our example case is based on the **vision** of developing a physical car model as a tangible interface for manipulating/shape a digital car model in a virtual car racing game. A description of the project and the technical solution can be found in [3] This vision as an overarching goal was given to the developers instead of a precise list of requirements on how the technical solution is supposed to look like and the project architecture was allowed to emerge. This meant that the space of possible solutions is open, ambiguous and uncertain. In our example case, the problem became to identify car parts in the physical model that are attached to each other and to recognize the assembled structure. We explored the solution space by trying to come up with as many possible solutions to the problems as possible (divergent thinking). Possible ideas for solutions included measuring resistance, power dissipation of wireless communication devices or pulsed light communication for identifying connected pieces. For determining the structure we looked into a centralized structure with one central part that collects the data from all assembled parts and a decentralized structure that only required the detection and identification of neighboring parts. However, with no, or only little, experience it is unknown to us which of the suggested ideas was feasible to pursue. We call these unsolved uncertainties **unknown unknowns** because these open questions emerged during the development process and were in itself unknown to us before engaging the problem. We argued that resistors were the cheapest, simples and most reliable proposition and that just detecting neighboring car parts simplified the algorithm. Furthermore, having to use a specific center part restricted the liberty of freely using any car part separately in the virtual game. However, these are only arguments based on limited experience and in order to converge on the most promising proposal one has to build and test ideas to gain new knowledge. This repeating cycle of divergent and convergent thinking with designing, building and testing ideas is called **probing**. The probing cycles lead to **abductive learning** where the test result leads to design requirement changes and ideas for the next probing cycle. In our case, we realized that the measurement of the resistors fluctuates significantly. This lead to changes in the programming of the microcontroller that processes the measurement. The abductive learning from repeating cycles of probing leads to a **wayfaring** of opportunistically finding one's way through the project. This means that the test results of the last probing cycle shape the future development. Figure 1a) shows the first test of the resistor principle. There we discovered that the idea is feasible and that three electrical connections between car parts are needed. This lead to the development of the setup shown in figure 1b) that uses BitSnap connectors that serendipitously already had exactly three electrical connections and allow the user to easily manipulate the physical car model. Testing these BitSnap connectors revealed that these are mechanically not sufficiently robust and not genderless, thus limiting the combinations of mountable car parts. This learning resulted in the development of the customized connectors shown in figure 1 c) and d) where the first version in figure 1c) turned out to be also not genderless and subsequently lead to the development of the second version in figure 1d). This train of subsequent probing cycles showcases the wayfaring journey that can be successive or dead ended.

Progress is achieved by the emergence of new ideas as a result of previous probing cycles. Therefore, it is important to minimize the time spent and to maximize the learning outcome for each probing cycle. This accomplished by concentrating on just testing the **critical functions** by building a **low resolution prototype** that is reduced to the properties that are necessary to only test the critical function. An example for this is the testing of the resistor principle as it is shown in figure 1a). The critical function was to find out how resistors can be used to identify connected parts unambiguously. To save time we compromised robustness, automation of the measurement, looks and compactness of the system to focus only on the critical function and thus used prototyping boards, header wires and ohmmeters that were readily available in the lab.

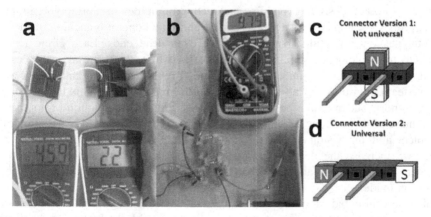

Fig. 1. a) first test of the resistor concept, b) testing with the BitSnap connectors, c) failed version of universal connector, d) successive version of a universal connector.

Imposing this train of thought to the entire project yields that prototypes that fulfill critical functions within different disciplines are merged as soon as they are available to test the system at large. The aim is to test and discover **interdependencies**. In our case, we combined the resistance measurement with a microcontroller, the information transmission to a PC and the virtual representation on the PC screen as soon as they were available in their most rudiment form. This means that all components from possibly different disciplines need to be **prototyped simultaneously**. Testing the entire system creates an **interlaced knowledge** between different disciplines. The structure recognition algorithm for example influenced the shape of the connectors and these changes had to be made in agreement with mechanical design of the car parts. This was possible because the developers of all disciplines were integrated from day one.

3   A Wayfaring Approach to Early Stage Concept Creation

In this part we describe a method that we derived from the project described above. The method has potential when finding and tackling previously unsolved engineering design problems that have no known existing solution. These problems are not necessarily complicated but rather complex according to Snowden and Boone [10]: they cannot be solved by asking experts to plan the final solution because they require the use of previously unproven and maybe even unknown concepts. In this context the development process becomes a wayfaring journey where the path towards fulfilling the vision emerges from making educated guesses and testing concepts, rather then a navigation journey along predefined waypoints. An optimum solution cannot be predicted when doing things that have never been done before. This method concerns only the early part of product development, the fuzzy front-end of concept creation, where the requirements of the product are not yet fixed. Figure 1 depicts such a wayfaring-inspired product development journey. This is a systematic and heuristic approach to developing something radically novel. The path to the end result will only be explored and discovered during the project. The journey consists of many probes. A probe is a circle of designing, building and testing of an idea or a prototype. In the figure 2, probes are depicted as multiple circles and may contain branching of ideas and prototypes on a multidisciplinary level or even dead ends. Each circle level corresponds to a role or a discipline in the project. At first, the team takes the best-guess direction based on the initial vision. Through multiple probing and prototype cycles the team then tries to find the big idea worth implementing. This journey can be long or short, but the main point is to learn fast with low-resolution prototypes. Through these prototypes one develops the requirements dynamically as perception of the problem and the vision of the solution will change during the journey. In a nutshell, we increase the degrees of freedom in the early design phase, develop requirements dynamically, and only then switch into classical engineering/project management mode.

While researching radical innovation projects, our chess analogy is lacking because in chess it is theoretically possible to calculate the move with the highest probability of winning the game. However, in the product design "game" the possible future moves, players, even the boundary conditions are often neither comparable nor foreseeable. There are **unknown unknowns** that create opportunities for extremely innovative solutions but also prevent us from predicting or simulating an optimum solution. In this analogy, the rules of the chess game can change without notice and we can only provide a journey overview in hindsight, roadmaps do not apply. The Hunter-Gatherer model by Steinert and Leifer [9] and Ingold [11] inspired this wayfaring concept.

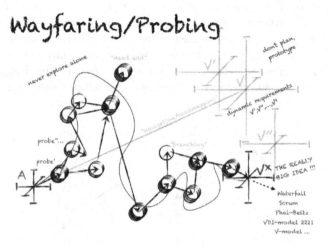

Fig. 2. Wayfaring journey in product development.

Many of our engineering problems are **multidisciplinary** and require interdependent knowledge between disciplines that cannot be covered by individuals or homogeneous teams. Two or more disciplines of the project are interdependent when design changes in one discipline lead to requirement adaptation in at least one other discipline. We argue that including team members or at least domain perspectives from all involved disciplines early in the project helps to reveal desirable and undesirable **interdependencies** already in early decision making phases. Even if actual deliverable input from every member is dispensable early on, the benefit of learning early overcomes the cost of participation. One of the greatest threats in new product development is the fear of failure [12]. According to Snowden [10] safe failing is identified as one of the cornerstones while innovating in the complex domain. The **interlaced knowledge,** developed through sense-making and justification of ideas to the other involved disciplines, is also beneficial when designing within one discipline while having the entire system in mind and thereby knowing when the other disciplines need to be taken into account and their input is needed [13]. This is a skill that can only be learned when combining all involved disciplines from the first day of the project.

The nature of trying out new concepts entails that outcomes cannot be guaranteed and some problems, opportunities and interdependencies are difficult, if not impossible, to foresee. When trying out something never attempted before we can no longer base our assumptions on past experiences and unexpected discoveries can arise. Snowden calls these discoveries **unknown unknowns** because we unknowingly discover something previously unknown [10]. In order to achieve these unexpected discoveries new experiences must be created from **probing ideas**. One of the ideas of probing is therefore to build and test prototypes that create completely new knowledge – knowledge that is impossible to accurately anticipate regardless of what our expectations may be. The concept of probing is depicted in Figure 2. Each probe is a prototype where new knowledge is deductively, inductively and/or abductively created and tested. The vision and requirements are then evolving dynamically until they are locked. The development cycle is executed through different roles of disciplines. Each probe is ideated through divergent thinking where open questions are asked in order to stimulate the creative process followed by convergent thinking, that evaluates and analytically benchmarks the ideas through proof-of-concept prototypes. The interesting interlaced knowledge lies in the boundaries of the different disciplines and presents the potential for serendipity discoveries.

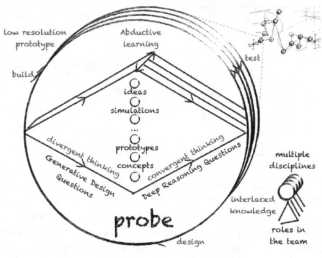

Fig. 3. Probing cycle

To continue with the chess analogy, we do not expect to win if we must plan all our moves (and anticipate the opponent's) in the beginning. However, if allowed to experiment and revert moves a thousand times during the game, it will quickly become a game of probing (or prototyping) multiple moves. Through not following an optimal game strategy, this will eventually lead to overall winning the game in case of a complex game scenario. Because the cost of probing is minimal, it allows us to explore opportunities that are not immediately perceived as profitable. It leads to moves that would normally not be taken, to discoveries that are normally not found, and may potentially lead to surprising and highly innovative ways of winning the game. Therefore, the aim must be to make the probing and the learning of ideas as low-risk (i.e. fast and cheap) as possible in order to create the experience needed to reflect, to understand the outcome, and then **abductively reason** and opportunistically choose the next step [14].

The notion is to put the focus on testing the **most critical functions**, thus leaving the development of the "nice to have" add-ons for later. It is preferable to utilize the resources for discovering the essentials and preferably fail there early. The probing removes uncertainty and an undiscovered problem is revealed before it forces undesired **requirement changes** at a later stage [15]. The testing usually involves building a **low resolution prototype** with the intention to either find the critical function or to build a prototype for user testing in order to avoid developing into an unnecessary direction. Low-resolution prototypes can be anything from cardboard models to Arduino hacks to proof-of-concept prototypes. Often developers have major problems in failing. Low-resolution prototypes in very fast iteration rounds do not resemble the finished object and are thus one way to allow and speed up experimentation. It seems to be inherent to human nature to fear failure, thinking it will cost too much. This can lead to a non-willingness to take risks and make cooperation hard with people from other disciplines. This skill of creative competence [16,12] does not come naturally. This is why changing the mindset into one that favors building prototypes with the option of failing safely before planning is critical while developing new concepts. Hence, despite the natural fear of failing, the mindset should be biased towards building low-resolution prototypes in order to gain experience instead of thinking the idea through and remaining with doubt.

Another finding is to **merge system components** as soon as possible in order to tackle potential integration issues very early on. This follows the same line of thought as aiming to discover unknown interdependencies as early as possible. Whenever a component individually fulfills its critical function, it ought to be integrated with other components to test its critical function in the context of the whole system. So, even when the system can and is divided into modules, integration should be tested while changes to the system are still easily possible. We believe that there is no point in fully developing one component and then risking requirement changes in other components that would endanger the previous development. This requires quasi-**simultaneous prototyping** to ensure that components can be merged. Thus in our context, simultaneous prototyping means understanding and probing ideas from multiple disciplines at the same time.

The **main purpose of probing** is to find solutions to the evolving problem by abductive reasoning and to continuously update the understanding of the problem. While probing different paths for the project one of the most important mindsets is to be opportunistic, to find, recognize and take chances that present themselves. Another benefit is the possibility to abandon disadvantageous concepts, "dead ends", in an early stage at the lowest cost and involvement possible. All in all, the wayfaring model calls for a bias towards action and learning in action.

4   Conclusions of Wayfaring

We propose a method suitable for developing new products with a high degree of uncertainty. It is largely based on including all disciplines related to the product from the beginning on and iterative cycles of probing ideas by designing, building and testing prototypes. The intent of this approach is to discover **unknown unknowns** and unexpected interdependencies early in order to minimizing losses due to failure and to spot opportunities and hitherto unknown potentials. Both, the initial problem statement and the targeted project vision remain in flux much longer than usually. The relatively early requirement fixation stage becomes a delayed dynamic requirement evolution process. The decisions to fix the dynamic requirements are made based on gained and tested information, based on learning cycles trough low-resolution prototyping and probing. We believe the headway and learnings, both in terms of breadth and depths have been superior to pre-planned or more traditional process models. We thus invite the community to deploy and test this approach in the early, pre-requirement definition phase and to share their insights.

Acknowledgments. We thank the project owner L. Nilsen, CEO of Metis Productions AS. This research is supported by the Research Council of Norway (RCN) through its user-driven research (BIA) funding scheme, project number 236739/O30.

References

1. Sanchez, R., Mahoney, J.T.: Modularity, flexibility, and knowledge management in product and organization design. Strategic Management Journal 17(S2), 63–76 (1996)
2. Baldwin, C., Clark, K.: Design Rules: The power of modularity. MIT Press (2000)
3. Reime, T., et al.: Proceedings of the 14th International Conference on Entertainment Computing, ICEC 2015, Trondheim, Norway, September 29-October 2, 2015. Springer (2015)
4. Eisenhardt, K.M.: Building Theories from Case Study Research. The Academy of Management Review 14(4), 532–550 (1989)
5. Yin, R.K.: Case Study Research: Designs and Methods. SAGE Publications (2013)
6. Burks, A.W.: Peirce's theory of abduction. Philosophy of Science 13(4), 301–306 (1946)
7. Eris, O.: Effective inquiry for innovative engineering design. Springer Netherlands (2004)
8. Leifer, L.J., Steinert, M.: Dancing with ambiguity: Causality behavior, design thinking, and triple-loop-learning. Information, Knowledge, Systems Management 10(1), 151–173 (2011)
9. Steinert, M., Leifer, L.J.: "Finding One"s Way': Re-Discovering a Hunter-Gatherer Model based on Wayfaring. International Journal of Engineering Education 28(2), 251 (2012)
10. Snowden, D.J., Boone, M.E.: A Leader's Framework for Decision Making. Harvard Business Review, 69–76 (2007)
11. Ingold, T.: Lines: a brief history. Routledge (2007)
12. Bandura, A.: Perceived self-efficacy in the exercise of control over AIDS infection. Evaluation and Program Planning 13(1), 9–17 (1990)
13. Türtscher, P., et al.: Justification and Interlaced Knowledge at ATLAS, CERN. Organization Science 25(6), 1579–1608 (2008)
14. Schön, D.A.: The reflective practitioner. Basic Books, New York (1983)
15. Kriesi, C., Steinert, M., Meboldt, M., Balters, S.: Physiological Data Acquisition for Deeper Insights into Prototyping. In: DS 81: Proceedings of NordDesign 2014, Espoo, Finland, August 27-29 (2014)
16. Kelley, T., Kelley, D.: Creative confidence: Unleashing the creative potential within us all. Crown Business (2013)

A Role-Switching Mechanic for Reflective Decision-Making Game

Thomas Constant[1], Axel Buendia[1], Catherine Rolland[2], and Stéphane Natkin[1]

[1] CNAM-Cédric, 292 Rue St Martin, FR-75141 Paris Cedex 03
[2] KTM-Advance, R&D et Innovation, 42 rue du Faubourg Poissonnière, 75010 Paris
{thomas.constant,axel.buendia,stephane.natkin}@cnam.fr,
catherine.rolland@ktm-advance.com

Abstract. This paper introduces issues about a methodology for the design of serious games that help players/learners understand their decision-making process. First, we discuss the development of a video game system based on a role-switching mechanic where the player becomes the game leader of the experience. Then, we introduce game mechanics designed to induce a specific behavior, overconfidence, that helps to understand the players' decision-making processes. Finally, we describe tools for measuring the players' self-reflection regarding their judgment process.

Keywords: serious game, game design, decision-making, overconfidence.

1 Introduction

Serious games for decision-making play an important role in management training [1]. But their use is too often limited to the training of a specific behavior, or to learn good habits. Video games offer the possibility of teaching a more reflexive experience [2]. They can be designed as decision-driven systems [3], tools created to help learners reflect on how they play [4], how they interact with the system [5]; thus, how they make a decision [6]. This paper presents issues about a game design methodology for serious games whose goal is to help learners gain a better understanding of their decision-making process, and to encourage players' reflexivity towards their own decision-making. The design is based on an asymmetrical gameplay: after the player has made a judgment task, and has taken a decision, s/he can become the "game leader" able to influence the other player. By switching roles, s/he may gain a better understanding of his/her own decision process. Our proposal to validate the mechanic's efficiency is to build a video game designed to develop and maintain an excessive confident behavior in the players' judgment, in order to promote the emergence of a reflexive stance of the player towards their decision processes. The first section of this paper introduces our model and its working conditions. The second section explains game mechanics useful for inducing overconfident behavior. These mechanics are, in effect, a translation of cognitive science principles regarding overconfidence into game variables. The third section proposes measurement tools for evaluating the game's efficiency.

© IFIP International Federation for Information Processing 2015
K. Chorianopoulos et al. (Eds.): ICEC 2015, LNCS 9353, pp. 417–423, 2015.
DOI: 10.1007/978-3-319-24589-8_34

2   Main Issue: Enlighten the Player's Decision-Making

2.1   Role-Switching Mechanic and Operating Conditions

Our main hypothesis is that a role-switching mechanic can help the players to develop a better understanding of their decision-making processes. However, we make the assumption that role-switching is not enough: the player can be good at playing but may not necessarily understand of how. To help players to be in a reflexive position about their abilities to make a decision, we introduce three conditions to support the role-switching mechanic:

- *A main condition:* when role-switching, the player must become the game leader of the game. In this role, s/he can use variables to impact the game experience. The game leader is the one who plays with the mechanics in order to alter the other player's judgment. S/he can achieve an optimal point of view of how the game works, and how it can alter the player's behavior.
- *A pre-condition:* before becoming the game leader, it is necessary that the player has been in the position of taking a decision for which s/he is confident about. The confidence must be assumed even if the decision was made in an uncertain situation, and may be biased by the context of the game. Players' judgment about their decision must be unequivocal if we want to help them to understand how it can be affected.
- *A post-condition:* after playing the game leader, it is necessary that the player is able to play his/her first role again, in order to measure the impact of the role-switching mechanic on his/her behavior.

For a serious purpose, we need to help the player to achieve this state of self-reflection. His/her way to make a decision has to be easier to understand and, as a consequence, the decision mechanisms have to be underlined by the system. Our proposal is to use cognitive fallacies in order to highlight judgment processes and explain why the player decision is biased.

2.2   Heuristic Judgment and Decision Making Processes

Heuristics and biases research allows to understand more precisely human judgment under uncertainty. Confronted with a complex question, decision-makers sometimes unwittingly substitute the question with an easier one. This process, called "attribute substitution", is an example of heuristic operating [7]. A heuristic represents a shortcut in the judgment process as compared with a rational approach to decision-making. Heuristics are "rules of thumbs" - simpler and faster ways to solve a problem, based on knowledge, former experiences, skills, and cognitive abilities (similar to memory or computational ability) [8,9]. If heuristic strategies are efficient most of the time, they can, however, occasionally lead to failure comparatively to a rational resolution of the full problem. These errors are called biases: markers of the use of a judgment heuristic. Identifying these markers allows researchers to better understand decision-making processes and reveal heuristic at work. Based on this approach, our methodology entails focusing on a single behavior in order to underline the player's decision-making process - chosen specifically because it frequently manifests itself in the comportment of game players: overconfidence.

2.3   Serious Game Concept and Context of Use

Before introducing specific game mechanics, we present the key elements of a gameplay chosen to illustrate the use of our methodology. The game is played by two players on two different computers. Players cannot see each other and cannot communicate directly, but they are aware of each other presence and role in the game. They play a narrative adventure game which apparent goal is to solve a sequence of criminal cases. Each player has a specific role. One of the players adopts the role of an investigator, gathering information to build a hypothesis for a given problem. S/he is confronted with various forms of influence, which are going to have an impact on his/her judgment. The other player personify the game leader, played by the other player, who is going to control the investigator access to information. S/he has access to multiple game variables useful to induce overconfidence in the other player's judgment (see below). After playing a sufficient number of levels in the same role (to be sure that the evaluation of the player's behavior is correct), the players exchange their roles: the game leader becomes the investigator, and reciprocally. By experimenting with these two gameplays, the player puts its own actions into perspective in order to understand how s/he made a decision.

3   Pre-Condition: Guiding the Player's Judgment

3.1   Variables to Orient the Player's Confidence

The overconfidence effect has been studied in economic and financial fields as a critical behavior of decision-makers [10]. It impacts our judgment of both our own knowledge and skills and those of others [11,12]. Overconfidence can be explained as a consequence of a person's use of heuristics such as availability and anchoring (defined in Section 3) [13,12]. Overconfidence is also commonly observed in player behaviors. In a card game, for example, beginners as well as experts can be overconfident with regard both to performance and play outcomes [14]. If we want to induce this behavior, the player's judgment has to be driven in a given direction. As a consequence, game mechanics must be related to expressions or sources of overconfidence in human behavior [15]. Then, based on game design methods for directing the behavior of the player [3,16], we derived game mechanics that can be used to produce the overconfidence effect. *Figure 1* presents some mechanics examples according to three major expressions of the overconfidence effect.

3.2   Core Gameplay

At the beginning of the level, the game leader introduces a case to the other player, the investigator. The investigator's mission is to find the culprit: s/he is driven through the level to a sequence of places where his/her is able to get new clues about the case, mainly by questioning non-playable characters.

	Difficulty	Anchoring	Confirmation
Definition	A decision-maker can be overconfident if s/he thinks that the task is too easy or too difficult [13,17].	Estimations are based on an anchor, a specific value they will easily memorize. The adjustments will be too far narrowed down towards this value to give an appropriate estimation. Anchor bias can induce overconfidence when evaluating an item or an hypothesis [18,12].	Confirmation bias reveals the fact that decision-makers often seek evidences that confirm their hypothesis, denying other evidences that may refute them [19,12].
Mechanic example 1	Setting up sensitive difficulty by restricting the player's exploration in time and space.	The game designer chooses a specific piece of information to use as an anchor. In order for it to be clear to the player that s/he has to use it the information must be important to the case.	The game designer classifies each piece of evidence according to how they support the investigation's solution and each of the red herrings.
Mechanic example 2	Setting up logical difficulty using puzzle game design, the intrinsic formal complexity of which can be controlled via given patterns and parameters.	In order to compare its impact on player judgment the game leader sets the anchor at different points and times in the game.	During the game, when giving evidence to the player, the game leader must give priority to evidence that favors a specific red herring.

Fig. 1. Variables and game mechanics to orient the player's behavior

But the investigator is allowed to perform a limited number of actions during a level, losing one each time s/he gets a new clue. Thus, the investigator is pushed to solve the case as fast as possible. The game leader is presented as the assistant of the investigator, but his/her real role is ambiguous: maybe s/he is trying to help the investigator, or maybe s/he has to push the investigator on the wrong track. This doubt is required to avoid biasing the investigator's judgment about the nature of the influence which target him/her. The investigator should not easily guess what the game leader is really doing, and should stay in a context of judgment in uncertainty. If this is not the case, the measure of the confidence of the player may be distorted. After several levels (several cases), the investigator becomes the new game leader, and vice versa. To win, the investigator must find the probable solution of a case depending on the clues s/he might have seen, associated with a realistic measure of his/her confidence. At the opposite, the game leader wins if s/he has induced overconfidence in the investigator's judgment, and if the latter didn't discover the game leader role.

4   Post-Condition: Measuring the Player's Behavior

4.1   Evaluation of the Player's Confidence

Two kinds of evaluations are used to assess the effectiveness of a serious game based on our role-switching model. The first ones focuses on the player's judgment through the evaluation of his/her confidence. Measurements of the investigator's overconfidence are based on credence calculation, which is used in overconfidence measurement studies [17]. This score assesses the players' ability to evaluate the quality of their decision rather than assessing the value of the decision itself. Variations of this score from one game session to an other can show the evolution of the players' confidence regarding their decision-making process. After playing, players must fill out a questionnaire survey in order to give a more precise evaluation of their progression and confidence [20].

4.2 Evaluation of the Player's Reflexivity

The second evaluations highlight the players' ability to assess their self-efficacy in terms of problem solving. Judgment calibration may engage the decision-maker in a reflexive posture on his/her ability to judge the quality of his/her decision that the overconfidence effect may bias [21]. But it is not enough for a long-lasting understanding of the behavior [22]. Therefore, in order to extend its effects, we design a re-playable game which can be experienced repeatedly within one or various training sessions. The role-switching mechanic allows the player to engage in a self-monitoring activity, by observing the behavior of other players and by experimenting on them. After several levels from this perspective, the player discerns how the investigator develops overconfidence, or tries to reduce it. Then the player resumes his/her first role and starts by giving new self-evaluations. This time, the player should give a more realistic assessment of his/her ability to solve the case. The variation of the players calibration score can give us a precise measure of the evolution of their behavior, and by extension, of their understanding on how they make a decision in the game. *Figure 2* presents the range of possible player behaviors that we can expect.

	Not confident	**Very confident**
The solution of the case given by the player is improbable	The player is aware of the weakness of his/her reasoning. <u>Well calibrated</u> *Score multiplied*	The player was too quick in his/her reasoning (and s/he has failed to seen the limits). S/he made a mistake in his/her reasoning. <u>Uncalibrated</u> *Player loses his points*
The solution of the case given by the player is probable	The player was too quick in his/her reasoning (and s/he realizes this). S/he is correct, but has no confidence in his/her reasoning. <u>Uncalibrated</u> *Player loses his points*	The player is correct as well as confident in his/her reasoning. <u>Well calibrated</u> *Score multiplied*

Fig. 2. Player behavior matrix

5   Conclusion and Future Works

This paper proposed a game design methodology for building serious games and the way of use to let the players gain a better appreciation of how they make a decision. This methodology is based on the heuristic approach to the analysis of human judgment as well as game design research that relates to decision-making and reflexivity. We then proposed rules and game mechanics designed to induce and control the overconfidence effect and to encourage the players' reflexivity regarding their decision-making. Finally, we introduced the idea of tools for measuring both the players' reflexivity and the effectiveness of the game itself. This methodology is currently being used to develop a prototype of the serious game, which will be evaluated in training courses at the Management & Society School of the National Conservatory of Arts and Crafts[1]. The prototype will be able to verify the proper functioning of the role-switching mechanic, its impact and its durability on the player's behavior.

References

1. Barth, I., Géniaux, I.: Former les futurs managers à des compétences qui n'existent pas: les jeux de simulation de gestion comme vecteur d'apprentissage. Management & Avenir 6(36), 316–339 (2010)
2. Constant, T., Buendia, A., Rolland, C., Natkin, S.: Enjeux et problématiques de conception d'un jeu sérieux pour la prise de décision. Revue ISI 20(1), 107–131 (2015)
3. Schell, J.: The Art of Game Design A Book of Lenses, 1st edn. Morgan Kaufmann Publishers, Burlington (2008)
4. Gee, J.P.: Surmise the Possibilities: Portal to a Game-Based Theory of Learning for the 21st Century. In: Clash of Realities 2008: Spielen in Digitalen Welten, 1st edn., Munchen, Deutschland (2008)
5. Papert, S.: Mindstorms: Children, Computers, and Powerful Ideas, 2nd edn. Basic Books, Inc., New York (1993)
6. Shaffer, D.W.: Epistemic Games. Innovate: Journal of Online Education 1(6) (2005)
7. Kahneman, D., Frederick, S.: A model of heuristic judgment. In: Holyoak, K.J., Morrison, R.G. (eds.) The Cambridge Handbook of Thinking and Reasoning, Cambridge, pp. 267–293 (2005)
8. Kahneman, D., Tversky, A.: Judgment under Uncertainty: Heuristics and Biases. Science 185(4157), 1124–1131 (1974)
9. Gigerenzer, G., Gaissmaier, W.: Heuristic decision making. Annual Review of Psychology 62, 451–482 (2011)
10. Bessière, V.: Excès de confiance des dirigeants et décisions financières: une synthèse. Finance Contrôle Stratégie 10, 39–66 (2007)
11. Johnson, D.D.P., Fowler, J.H.: The evolution of overconfidence. Nature 477(7364), 317–320 (2011)
12. Russo, J.E., Schoemaker, P.J.H.: Managing overconfidence. Sloan Management Review 33(2), 7–17 (1992)
13. Griffin, D., Tversky, A.: The weighing of evidence and the determinants of confidence. Cognitive Psychology, 411–435 (1992)
14. Keren, G.: Facing uncertainty in the game of bridge: A calibration study. OBHDP 39(1), 98–114 (1987)
15. Moore, D.A., Healy, P.J.: The Trouble with Overconfidence. Psychological Review 115(2), 502–517 (2008)

---

[1] For more informations about the School and the Conservatory: http://the.cnam.eu

16. Adams, E.: Fundamentals of Game Design, 2nd edn. New Riders, Berkeley (2007)
17. Lichtenstein, S., Fischhoff, B.: Do those who know more also know more about how much they know? Organizational Behavior and Human Performance 20, 159–183 (1977)
18. Kahneman, D., Tversky, A.: Intuitive prediction: Biases and corrective procedures. Eugene, Oregon (1977)
19. Koriat, A., Lichtenstein, S., Fischhoff, B.: Reasons for confidence. Journal of Experimental Psychology: Human Learning and Memory 6(2), 107–118 (1980)
20. Stankov, L., Lee, J.: Confidence and cognitive test performance. Journal of Educational Psychology 100(4), 961–976 (2008)
21. Stone, D.N.: Overconfidence in Initial Self-Efficacy Judgments: Effects on Decision Processes and Performance. OBHDP 59(3), 452–474 (1994)
22. Stankov, L., Lee, J., Paek, I.: Realism of confidence judgments. European Journal of Psychological Assessment 25(2), 123–130 (2009)

Adaptation to TV Delays Based on the User Behaviour towards a Cheating-Free Second Screen Entertainment

Rui Neves Madeira[1,2], Pedro Centieiro[2], and Nuno Correia[2]

[1] Escola Superior de Tecnologia de Setúbal, IPS, Setúbal, Portugal
rui.madeira@estsetubal.ips.pt
[2] NOVA-LINCS, DI, FCT, Universidade Nova de Lisboa, Monte da Caparica, Portugal
pcentieiro@gmail.com, nmc@fct.unl.pt

Abstract. Recent advances in technology created new opportunities to enhance TV personalization, providing viewers with individualized ways to watch TV and to interact with its content. Second screen applications are promising vehicles to enhance the viewers' experiences, but researchers need to take into account the effect that the TV delay has on viewers, in particular when watching broadcasted live events. In this paper, we propose a software-based solution to deal with TV delays. It is mainly directed for a gaming context in which the user has the means to control the synchronisation between the second screen application and the TV content. Taking this scenario into account, we implemented a cheating-detection mechanism to cope with the potential exploitation of the system by its users.

Keywords: Second screen, TV delays, broadcast live events, adaptation, ubiquitous personalization, user profile, game cheating.

1   Introduction

The quest for a personalized TV follows a path started with multichannel TV and has led us to Personal Video Recorder, Video-On-Demand and multiscreen TV [12]. Moreover, the proliferation of mobile devices, such as smartphones and tablets, allows TV viewers to become accustomed to "doing their own thing" [12]. So, if users have "individualized" ways for watching TV and for interacting with TV shows then this can be an opportunity to apply personalization to TV. Second screen applications (apps) are promising vehicles to accomplish personalization since they can provide show-related information and support "social viewing" through dedicated social networks, and even interactive experiences, through polls and quizzes, synchronised with the show content.

However, it is common for some viewers to get events on second screen apps that are not synchronised with the corresponding key moments in the TV broadcasts. The users' engagement can be ruined when a situation like this one occurs, since the app content may be presented too early (spoilers), or too late (obsolete content). Thus, second screen synchronisation is an important step towards TV personalization [12].

© IFIP International Federation for Information Processing 2015
K. Chorianopoulos et al. (Eds.): ICEC 2015, LNCS 9353, pp. 424–432, 2015.
DOI: 10.1007/978-3-319-24589-8_35

In order to address this issue, we use the Synchronisation Mechanism through User Feedback (SMUF), which relies on the feedback given by the users on how apps' key events are synchronised with the corresponding TV broadcasts' key moments [3]. SMUF provides a universal and simple interaction control to the users who become able to adjust their second screen experience according to how they are perceiving the TV delay. However, this mechanism presents a negative counterpart within gaming scenarios since users can easily find out how to exploit it. If users set up a delay higher than they actually have they will end up receiving the content on the second screen app after watching the corresponding content on TV. This can also happen in situations in which the synchronisation is made by automatic content recognition (ACR) methods, such as audio fingerprinting, where users can synchronise the app with the TV box at a past moment. On both cases, users will be able to win more points since they can, for instance, answer more questions correctly and within shorter time periods. In our context, these users are cheaters since they exploit the system to get an unfair advantage or achieve a target that they are not supposed to [13].

This paper presents a software-based solution that takes into account the users' interaction data, towards a cheating-free gaming experience while using SMUF. In order to achieve this goal, we need to counterbalance SMUF through the implementation of a Cheater-Detection Mechanism (CDM). We followed the generalized model for personalization provided by P^2MUCA [9] in order to build profiles for each user according to her/his gaming and syncing behaviours based on interactions data. If the user is detected with an "abnormal pattern" (e.g., several correct answers in a row in a very short time period) then s/he might be marked as cheater and the app delay can be automatically readjusted according to the app's game mechanics.

In order to understand how users interact with SMUF to find out the appropriate patterns that can tell us who might be a cheater, we collected users' interactions data while they were testing SMUF in WeSync, a mobile app that prompts users to interact on key events related to football TV broadcasts. Results from this study allowed us to gather important insights, which are very promising for future research on this area.

2   Background Research

Synchronisation can affect the user experience of the viewers, particularly when receiving key events on an app before watching them on the TV broadcast. A study by Centieiro et al. [2], in which users during a football match TV broadcast were prompted to bet if a goal would happen in a few seconds, showed that some users were frustrated or stressed for not being able to perform the action. This happened since the match on TV was delayed relatively to the real match and consequently to the match key events on the second screen app. It is in-line with the study of Kooij et al. [7], which states that a variation of the playout delay can go up to 6 seconds in TV broadcasts in the same country, and more than one minute in some web based TV broadcasts. Therefore, there are different solutions to synchronise a second screen app with TV content [3]. However, regardless of which type of synchronisation mechanism developers implement, whether based on ACR or SMUF, users can overcome and exploit it by setting up a false delay. The issue here is that users can manage to set a delay higher than they actually have in order to receive the content on the second screen app after watching the associated content on TV.

In our context, users that try to exploit the system are considered cheaters. Sometimes it is almost impossible to distinguish smart play, e.g., good use of tactics, from cheating, which is defined as "Any behaviour that a player may use to get an unfair advantage, or achieve a target that he is not supposed to be" [13]. Moreover, evolutionary psychology (EP) observes human nature as the result of a universal set of evolved psychological adaptations to recurring problems in the ancestral environment. EP considers the hypothesis that people have a cheater-detection module [4]. Cheating is a violation of a particular kind of conditional rule that goes along with a social contract. Social exchange is a collaboration system for mutual benefit and cheaters violate the social contract that governs social exchange [5]. The selection pressure for a dedicated cheat detection module is the presence of cheaters in the social world. Therefore, a CDM is needed as an adaptation complement arising in response to cheaters, ensuring the correct implementation of social exchange, which is essential for a game based social experience such as the one we are addressing here.

There are several approaches for cheating detection in games, but they are not directed to second screen gaming. Usually, those solutions are focused on online multiplayer environments, such as the one proposed by Laurens et al. [8], which monitors the player behaviour for indications of cheating play, and the one presented by Yeung et al. [14], which proposes a scalable method to detect whether a player is cheating, or not, based on dynamic Bayesian networks. Alayed et al. present another behavioural-based cheating detection in online first person shooters games using machine learning techniques [1], whilst Ferretti and Roccetti proposed an algorithm based on the monitoring of network latencies [6].

3   SMUF and the WeSync App

WeSync is a mobile app that prompts users to guess the outcome of corner kicks (Figure 1a), penalty kicks and free kicks during a football match. Users can also check their predictions' outcomes, as well as their friends' scores. Furthermore, WeSync also notifies users when a goal is scored (allowing them to quickly share their thoughts on social networks), or when a half starts or ends. However, when these events are not synchronised with the TV broadcast, users need to synchronise them by using SMUF, which can be done by adjusting a slider in a screen that appears right after each key event occurrence (Figures 1b-1c). Users rate their experience through SMUF, providing feedback on how the app is presenting the events. Each subsequent event is presented taking into account the previously provided feedback, in order to achieve the synchronisation between the app and the TV broadcast. Once users state that the app is synchronised, the screen with the slider stops from appearing right after each key event. A popup is shown explaining that from now on they still can adjust their experience whenever they wish by clicking on the top-right button that just appeared (Figure 1d).

We introduced four interaction cues to facilitate the user interaction: the temporal indication (e.g. "app is 3 seconds ahead"); the illustrative animation above the slider which behaves accordingly to the delay set, the overall colour of the slider and the animation, and the experience rating (e.g. "Great!", "Good!", "Fair.", and "Poor..."). The colour intervals and the experience rating values were based on the work done by Mekuria et al. [11]. Finally, we did not include any information regarding the live sports event, such as the match time - which could be used to compare the TV broadcast match time with the app match time to synchronise both feeds - since we wanted to have a universal synchronisation mechanism that could be deployed on any broadcast, regardless of the information presented on the TV screen.

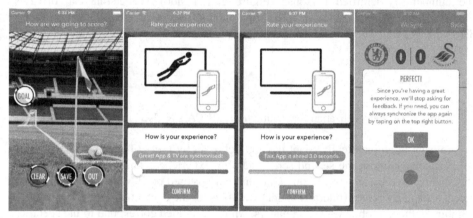

Fig. 1. (a) A key event that prompts users to predict a corner kick; (b) Initial screen of SMUF; (c) User setting a 3s delay; (d) Notification when the application is synchronised.

4 A Cheater-Detection Mechanism

We needed to implement a Cheater-Detection Mechanism (CDM) in order to cope with potential dishonest users (cheaters) as they can freely control the app delay with SMUF. Thus, app delays placed by a user should be personalized (automatically adapted) to benefit the users experience and its social exchange as a whole, persuading and preventing users from cheating. The implementation of CDM follows the generalized model for personalization provided by P^2MUCA and named X-Users [10], which can help us expressing what can be a cheater behaviour according to the users' gaming and syncing profiles. P^2MUCA is a personalization platform for multimodal ubiquitous computing applications that provides tools and services to help developers in the implementation of personalization solutions. The core of this platform is the personalization model that can be applied to different applications from different domains. The personalization model allows that user interactions with an application A may be used to personalize the experience of that same user when s/he starts interacting with a new application B. For instance, if a new app similar to WeSync is implemented and registered on P^{2}MUCA then a user with a cheater profile in WeSync can be already known by the new app, which allows from the beginning a fast adaptation to the delay set by the user, not requiring initial user interactions for the effect.

In order to use P^{2}MUCA and apply X-Users, we should decide a priori, at design time, what to personalize in WeSync. It is important that we know the app's potential end-users, mainly the specific ones that drive the personalization requirements. According to [10], the careful specification of personas can help to determine what to personalize (instances of personalization, i.e., the app delays in the case of WeSync) and the different options for each personalization. So, in X-Users, each personalization instance (Personalization) can have N different Personalization Options according to the number of identified Personas (Figure 2, left side). A Persona can drive N Personalization Options since an application can implement different Personalizations. The same Persona can even be the driver for Personalizations of different applications.

Fig. 2. The Personalization core entities of P^{2}MUCA's X-Users model (from [6]).

We want to automatically adapt the app delay set by users (TV viewers) according to their behaviours in the second screen gaming experience. This is a personalization that can be used by any app of this kind that is registered on P^{2}MUCA. So, we had to select a set of resources (interaction data variables) in the context of WeSync (Table 1), combining them to obtain two parameters, which combined correspond to the specified personas (Figure 2, right side).

Table 1. WeSync's Resources (interactions data used for personalization).

R	Resource	Description
1	keyEvents	(integer) Total of key events (questions) answered.
2	totalResponseTime	(double) Sum of the response time used for all answers.
3	totalCorrectResults	(integer) Total of correct answers.
4	currentUserDelay	(double) Current value of the app delay after last key event, placed by user.
5	totalDeltaUserDelay	(double) Sum differences between successive app delays at each key event.
6	totalUserDelay	(double) Sum of the app delays at each key event.

Each parameter is given by a mathematical expression that results in a numeric value representing a specific user behaviour in terms of the resources included. At each key event, the user will therefore have two values: the GamerProfile represented by equation (1), and the SyncerProfile represented by equation (2).

$$0.3 / (totalResponseTime/keyEvents) + 0.7 * (totalCorrectResults/keyEvents) \qquad (1)$$

$$0.5*currentUserDelay + 0.25*(totalDeltaUserDelay /keyEvents) + 0.25 * (totalUserDelay/keyEvents) \qquad (2)$$

These equations were determined after several iterations of simulations based on empirical data and domain knowledge. Furthermore, the weights were slightly refined with the user experiments study and the results confirmed the equations are appropriate for our goal (Table 4). We were mainly interested in discovering if at each key event (moment) a user should be marked as a cheater, or not. So, initially we decided to represent only two personas (cheater and non-cheater) and, for that, it was only needed a parameter (called TVViewerProfile). However, we found out that two parameters would make much more sense with the separation of resources into Gamer and Syncer profiles, giving us a greater granularity to work on. This way, we defined two options for each parameter (profile): High and Low (they revealed themselves as being appropriate as demonstrated by the results in Table 4). This way, P^{2}MUCA's clustering algorithm should divide users into two clusters for each parameter, receiving as input a parameter's vector composed of the parameter's values representing each user [10]. The permutations of these two options (clusters) of each parameter correspond to four personalization options (Table 2), the considered personas in our scenario: 1) Non-Cheater Tier-1; 2) Non-Cheater Tier-2; 3) Non-Cheater Tier-3; and 4) Cheater.

Table 2. Combinations of the two parameters options result in four personalization options.

GamerProfile / SyncerProfile	High Gamer Value	Low Gamer Value
High Syncer Value	Cheater	Non-Cheater Tier-3
Low Syncer Value	Non-Cheater Tier-2	Non-Cheater Tier-1

In our case study, we consider that a user should only be marked as a potential cheater (final profile) when both parameters (sub-profiles) result in high values. The three tiers of non-cheater should be treated equally by the app if it is not necessary to distinguish between the different sub-profiles of non-cheater users.

5   User Experiments and Data Collection

We carried out user experiments with the WeSync app in order to evaluate the SMUF's usefulness and viability in a gaming scenario and, more important, to collect important interactions data on gaming and syncing aspects. The user tests were conducted with 15 voluntary participants (11 male and 4 female) aged 23 to 45 ($\bar{x}$ = 31.5; σ = 7.4). The tests took place in a lab at our University campus and included two test sessions with participants being briefed before each one. In each session, participants watched an 8-minute highlight video from a football match, containing six key events to bet what the outcome would be. Since several TV providers have different delay values, it was set a random TV delay (values in range 0-6s) for each participant and video. Each participant had two initial moments to become familiar with SMUF, before the key events start appearing, allowing her/him to better understand how to set a delay.

After the first session, we asked participants to rate (with a 5-point Likert-type scale) six statements (Table 3) in a questionnaire regarding their SMUF experience and their cheating perception. Users were also free to write down any further comments and, at the end, we conducted a brief interview. Additionally, during each session, we also registered all the users' interactions data for the resources described in Table 1.

Table 3. Summary of the questionnaire results regarding: the SMUF experience (first 3 rows) and the cheating perception (last 3 rows).

Statements	Strongly Disagree	Disagree	Neutral	Agree	Strongly Agree
I had a good synchronisation experience.	6,67%	0,00%	13,33%	33,33%	46,67%
It is easy to use the synchronisation mechanism.	0,00%	13,33%	13,33%	33,33%	40,00%
This mechanism is useful to synchronise the application with the TV.	0,00%	6,67%	0,00%	20,00%	73,33%
This mechanism allows you to have an unfair competition.	6,67%	6,67%	33,33%	6,67%	46,67%
It is easy to cheat using the synchronisation mechanism.	0,00%	0,00%	20,00%	20,00%	60,00%
The mechanism motivates me to be honest when synchronising.	6,67%	6,67%	33,33%	26,67%	26,67%

The questionnaire's results were very positive regarding the users experience with SMUF. Table 3 shows that, in general, participants had a good synchronisation experience ($\bar{x} = 4.1$; $\sigma = 1.13$) and found it easy to use ($\bar{x} = 4.0$; $\sigma = 1.07$) and useful to synchronise the app with the TV ($\bar{x} = 4.6$; $\sigma = 0.83$). The remainder of the questionnaire also showed very interesting results. Although the majority of participants have agreed (6.67% agreed and 46.67% strongly agreed) that SMUF allows us to have an unfair competition ($\bar{x} = 3.8$; $\sigma = 1.32$), there are a considerable number of neutral opinions and two of them even stated that "the competition would not be unfair since everyone has the same conditions to cheat". Participants really found it easy to cheat using SMUF ($\bar{x} = 4.4$; $\sigma = 0.83$), generally after a few key events. Nonetheless, results showed participants felt motivated by SMUF to be honest ($\bar{x} = 3.6$; $\sigma = 1.18$). We believe this happens because of social and peer-pressure. It is interesting to refer that one participant told us s/he would be dishonest if s/he would perceive that others were cheating.

Furthermore, after the first session, we asked participants to indicate (using a 5-point Likert-type scale) how they behaved in terms of honesty when setting up the app delay for each key event. This was important to link gathered interactions data to users' perception on cheating. For example, no participants stated that they behaved like cheaters in this session and our results actually show no cheaters. Moreover, the results show that participants 1, 2 and 15 had a behaviour progression almost into cheater profile during session 1 and they confirmed that to us. Table 4 shows data of only six participants since these present the most interesting values to understand global results. Data are relative to the moment right after the conclusion of all 6 key events.

Table 4. Data results of 6 key-participants: final profiles, parameters and resources values.

P#-S#	TV Delay	Final Profile	GamerP. (Eq. 1)	SyncerP. (Eq. 2)	R2/ R1	R3/ R1	R5/ R1	R6/ R1	R4
1-S1	2,4	non-cheater tier-2	0,59	4,31	4,56	0,67	0,75	2,00	4,5
1-S2	0,2	non-cheater tier-1	0,21	3,17	3,84	0,17	0,17	1,75	2,0
2-S1	1,6	non-cheater tier-3	0,34	18,17	4,24	0,33	4,00	7,33	24,0
2-S2	4,5	non-cheater tier-1	0,52	5,92	5,95	0,33	0,67	2,67	6,0
11-S1	5,9	non-cheater tier-1	0,30	7,69	2,22	0,33	0,08	4,25	4,5
11-S2	3,3	cheater	0,53	16,88	2,54	0,67	1,67	8,92	12,0
12-S1	4,0	non-cheater tier-1	0,19	4,10	2,75	0,17	0,08	2,25	2,5
12-S2	4,4	cheater	0,67	14,50	3,42	0,83	2,00	7,33	12,0
14-S1	3,9	non-cheater tier-1	0,22	7,69	4,07	0,17	0,08	4,25	4,5
14-S2	5,7	cheater	0,71	26,13	4,60	0,83	1,58	12,83	21,5
15-S1	5,1	non-cheater tier-3	0,24	12,56	4,50	0,17	0,92	6,50	9,5
15-S2	0,8	cheater	0,56	12,73	3,79	0,67	0,92	6,83	8,5

In the second session, we asked each participant to set up an app delay for each key event according to a "behaviour guide" with indications (using a 5-point Likert-type scale: 1-"100% dishonest" and 5-"100% honest") on how we would like them to behave. This way, we would gather interactions data that would correspond to different profiles, having participants behaving according to our four options. As we have indicated, only four of them behaved like clear cheaters. It was easy for participant 15 as s/he almost did it in session 1. With the two sessions we got data corresponding to 30 users instead of only 15, which was better for testing purposes. The final profiles confirm the parameters equations previously presented. The final equations were obtained after several simulations with the collected data in which we were refining them in terms of the weight given to each resource.

6   Conclusions and Future Work

We described a new concept based on personalization to enhance cheating-free second screen experiences. This work provides a technology-independent and persuasive solution for competitive gaming contexts. We used a mobile app prototype called WeSync to test it. User tests were very positive and validated our ideas. The results showed that our approach is able to categorize the users based on profiles built from diverse resources combined to create parameters. We are already planning a thorough user study in a real environment to validate the resources and further refine the parameters. We will include a higher number of participants and mechanisms for cheating penalization and appealing (case of false positive cheaters) will be evaluated.

References

1. Alayed, H., Frangoudes, F., Neuman, C.: Behavioral-based cheating detection in online first person shooters using machine learning techniques. In: CIG 2013, pp. 1–8. IEEE Press (2013)
2. Centieiro, P., Romão, T., Dias, E.A.: From the Lab to the World: Studying Real-time Second Screen Interaction with Live Sports. In: ACE 2014, article 14. ACM (2014)
3. Centieiro, P., Romão, T., Dias, E.A., Madeira, R.N.: Synchronising Live Second Screen Applications with TV Broadcasts through User Feedback. In: 15th IFIP TC.13 INTERACT 2015. Springer (2015)
4. Cosmides, L.: The Logic of Social Exchange: Has natural selection shaped how humans reason? Studies with the Wason Selection Task. Cognition 31, 187–276 (1989)
5. Cosmides, L., Tooby, J.: Neurocognitive Adaptations Designed for Social Exchange. In: Buss, D. (ed.) The Handbook of Evolutionary Psychology, pp. 584–627. Wiley (2005)
6. Ferretti, S., Roccetti, M.: AC/DC: an algorithm for cheating detection by cheating. In: NOSSDAV 2006. ACM Press (2006)
7. Kooij, W., Stokking, H., Brandenburg, R., Boer, P.: Playout Delay of TV Signals: Measurement System Design, Validation and Results. In: TVX 2014, pp. 23–30. ACM (2014)
8. Laurens, P., Paige, R.F., Brooke, P.J., Chivers, H.: A Novel Approach to the Detection of Cheating in Multiplayer Online Games. In: ECCS 2007, pp. 97–106. IEEE Press (2007)
9. Madeira, R.N., Santos, P.A., Correia, N.: Building a platform for pervasive personalization in a ubiquitous computing world. In: MOBIQUITOUS 2014, pp. 345–346. ICST (2014)
10. Madeira, R.N., Santos, P.A., Vieira, A., Correia, N.: Model-based Solution for Personalization of the User Interaction in Ubiquitous Computing. In: 11th IEEE International Conference on Ubiquitous Intelligence and Computing (UIC 2014). IEEE (2014)
11. Mekuria, R., Cesar, P., Bulterman, D.: Digital TV: the effect of delay when watching football. In: EuroITV 2012, pp. 71–74. ACM (2012)
12. Videonet: Making TV more personal. Industry Report, http://www.v-net.tv/making-tv-more-personal (accessed May 11, 2015)
13. Yan, J.J., Choi, H.: Security Issues in Online Game. The Electronic Library 20(2), 125–133 (2002)
14. Yeung, S.F., Lui, J.C.S., Liu, J., Yan, J.: Detecting cheaters for multiplayer games: theory, design and implementation. In: CCNC 2006, vol. 2, pp. 1178–1182. IEEE Press (2006)

Exploring Deep Content in Physical Rehabilitation Games

Niels Quinten[1,2], Steven Malliet[2], and Karin Coninx[1]

[1] University of Hasselt, Martelarenlaan 42, 3500 Hasselt, Belgium
[2] LUCA School of Arts, C-Mine 5, 3600 Genk, Belgium
niels.quinten@uhasselt.be, steven.malliet@luca-arts.be,
karin.coninx@uhasselt.be

Abstract. This paper argues that game mechanics are important tools to combine rehabilitation therapy concerns with immersive game play. Through the practical design of a game we describe how properties of game mechanics (actions, attributes, dynamics, rules, space, and skill/chance) connect to elements of rehabilitation therapy (exercise motion, parameters, therapy context, goals, motion trajectory, and motion constraints). We aim to stimulate rehabilitation game researchers to consider applying the presented approach in their own designs.

Keywords: Game Design, Physical Rehabilitation, Deep Content, Design Research, Game Mechanics, Game Conventions.

1 Introduction

This study draws on theories developed in serious game design and applies these to the creation of a game for physical rehabilitation. Specifically we address the contstruct of deep content, defined by Isbister, et al., [3, p. 2043] as content that is tightly connected to a game's structure and is experienced as an integral part of the game.

2 Deep Content in Physical Rehabilitation Games

2.1 Physical Rehabilitation Exercises

Physical rehabilitation therapy is particularly effective when patients perform physical exercises repetitively and intensively [4]. Thus, an opportunity lies in matching these physical exercises with a virtual environment where the repetition of physical challenges results in winning [7]. Pery, et al. [7] note that rehabilitation games often fail to meet these expectations. Only a small amount of studies on games for rehabilitation are concerned with the close integration of rehabilitation and games, as most highlight only one of both topics [8].

© IFIP International Federation for Information Processing 2015
K. Chorianopoulos et al. (Eds.): ICEC 2015, LNCS 9353, pp. 433–438, 2015.
DOI: 10.1007/978-3-319-24589-8_36

2.2   Patient Disabilities

Designers of rehabilitation games have to consider patient disability resulting from cognitive [12], physical [1] and visual [9] impairments. In order for a customized game play to emerge, these impairments need to be incorporated as essential elements in design process rather than as external goals. This implies that designers of rehabilitation games cannot simply create adaptations of exisiting games, but should experiment with formats that are tailored to this specific context. For instance, Notelaers, et al. [5] note that the game interface should be adapted to accommodate patient disabilities by avoiding several elements that are common in commercial games. Vanden Abeele et al. [11] developed a design style that makes players understand the underlying game structure more easily and is simultaneously aesthetically pleasing.

3   Research Questions

While these are a few examples which cover the close integration of rehabilitation therapy and digital games, these often lack the situational knowledge needed to transfer research into practical design solutions [2]. In order to support the practical creation of physical rehabilitation games, we investigate how we can practically use the concept of deep content in the development of such a game. The following two research questions are formulated:

1. Which game design elements support the practical integration of rehabilitation exercises and game mechanics, for deep content to emerge?
2. How do patient impairments influence the design process when creating deep content in rehabilitation games?

4   Exploring Deep Content Through the Design of a Digital Rehabilitation Game Prototype

A digital game prototype was developed in which rehabilitation exercises and patient impairments have been integrated. A process of interaction or 'conversation' between the artist and the material of digital games took place, which is an essential requirement of design research [2].

4.1   Rehabilitation Components

In order to include rehabilitation exercises in the game mechanics, the approach of Octavia, et al. [6] was followed, with integration of several simple motions (e.g. horizontal, vertical and circular) that need to be performed with the most affected upper-limb. The following impairments were accounted for:

- Reduced dexterity (e.g. inability to use small buttons);
- Visual difficulties (e.g. inability to visually perceive a game world);

- Memory and cognitive processing problems (e.g. understanding the complexities of a game).

The Novint Falcon was selected as input device, allowing patients to move their hand in three dimensions (10 cm in each direction). The Unity3D game engine version 3.X was used to develop the prototype.

4.2   The Game Play of Flower Garden

In the resulting game, Flower Garden (see Fig. 1), patients grow and maintain flowers by performing simple rehabilitation exercises. All flowers created by singular players are placed in a virtual garden that is shown on a large screen in a public room of the rehabilitation centre. The goal of the game is to keep the flowers healthy, which depends on how well the predefined exercises are performed. Players design their own flowers by executing four main virtual actions: planting seeds, growing plants, healing plants, and coloring flowers. In real-life, these actions translate to the motions defined above. For instance, in order to plant a seed and color a flower, players complete the circular motions indicated by dashed lines. The average precision of the player while tracing a line is taken into account and has an impact on the health of the flower.

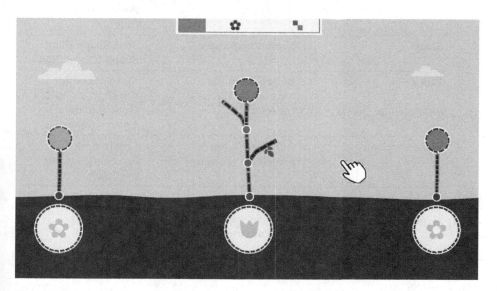

Fig. 1. In-game screenshot of 'Flower Garden' with three seeds and two types of flowers.

5   Results

5.1   Therapy Exercises and Game Mechanics

Flower Garden includes three main mechanics: planting seeds, growing/healing plants, and coloring flowers. As illustrated in Table 1, game mechanics possess six properties - actions, attributes, dynamics, rules, space, and skill/chance [10] - that structurally connect the rehabilitation world to formal game elements. First, the rehabilitation motions and their parameters are connected to the virtual world by using the properties 'actions' and 'attributes'. For instance, executing a horizontal motion in real-life represents growing a plant in the virtual environment. How well this motion is performed defines the value of the attributes.

Table 1. An overview of how game mechanics link the rehabilitation world and the game world

Game Mechanics	Rehabilitation World	Game World
Physical Components		
Actions	Horizontal motion	Planting a flower
	Vertical motion	Healing a flower
	Circular motion	Planting a seed
		Coloring a flower
Attributes	Quality of motion	Flowers' health flowers' type flowers' color
Space	Motion trajectory	Seed Shape Plant Shape Flower Shape
Rules	Be precise while completing the trajectory	Make a healthy flower Grow a plant Color a flower
Skills vs. chance	Adherence to a predefined trajectory	Create flowers according to your own taste
Contextual Components		
Dynamics	Multiple sessions 5 to 10 minutes of play time	Brief actions

5.2 Patient Impairments and the Virtual World

Flower Garden is a Construction and Management Game in which players progress by gradually earning and adding more virtual objects to a game world or model. As a result, the concept has a degree of cognitive and visual complexity that patients may not be able to deal with. We experienced a number of difficulties with regards to the patient impairments, including the use of an inventory system. Inventory systems can increase the visual complexity of the screen and the difficulty of the hand-eye coordination. In an attempt to resolve this, we integrated the inventory system into the action of planting a seed, both visually and functionally. Each time players plant a new seed, a new icon appears in the center of the seed's circle (see Fig. 1). Players can thus browse through the flowers automatically when planting a seed. This has the disadvantage that players are not able to see all available flowers at the same time, and the system would likely not be sustainable when more flowers were added.

6 Implications of Deep Content in Rehabilitation Games

The value of these results does not reside in the identification of game mechanics per se, but in the fact that these connect the game's content to its formal characteristics. In this manner, the mechanics become practical tools with which game designers and rehabilitation therapists can bridge the gap between their respective domains. Designers and therapists can, for instance, investigate which mechanics they want to include to facilitate rehabilitation exercises and how to do this.

In the prototype we designed, the virtual world and the interface were closely connected to the game's genre. Because we selected a specific genre in the beginning of the design process, undesirable entertainment game conventions were unconsciously included in the prototype. While the surface components (e.g. interface) could be adapted to patients relatively easily, the genre conventions underlying these components might be much harder to modify. Therefore, working with predefined concepts is not necessarily the most feasible solution for rehabilitation game design.

7 Conclusion

This paper raised two questions. The first question was how rehabilitation exercises and formal game qualities can be practically integrated in a rehabilitation game in order for deep content to emerge. The mechanics constituting our prototype contained a number of practical design components that were linked to essential parts of rehabilitation exercises. Game mechanics thus provided a conceptual tool to relate digital games to rehabilitation therapy. The second question was how patient disabilities can be taken into account during the design of a rehabilitation game in order for deep content to emerge. In our design, conventions of existing entertainment games unobtrusively slipped into the concept of a rehabilitation game. These conventions can potentially conflict with the disabilities of patients and should be treated with caution.

Acknowledgement. This work was supported by Hasselt University and LSM under Grant KOS 13 KM LS 225.

References

1. Ada, L., Canning, C.: Changing the way we view the contribution of motor impairments to physical disability after stroke. In: Refshauge, K., Ada, L., Ellis, E. (eds.) Science-Based Rehabilitation, pp. 87–106. Butterworth-Heinemann, Edinburgh (2005), http://www.sciencedirect.com/science/article/pii/B9780750655644500085
2. Cross, N.: Designerly ways of knowing. Springer, London (2006), http://public.eblib.com/choice/publicfullrecord.aspx?p=303690
3. Isbister, K., Flanagan, M., Hash, C.: Designing games for learning: insights from conversations with designers. In: Proceedings of the SIGCHI Conference on Human Factors in Computing Systems, pp. 2041–2044. ACM, Atlanta (2010), http://dl.acm.org/citation.cfm?id=1753637
4. Langhorne, P., Coupar, F., Pollock, A.: Motor recovery after stroke: a systematic review. The Lancet Neurology 8(8), 741–754 (2009), http://www.sciencedirect.com/science/article/pii/S1474442209701504
5. Notelaers, S., De Weyer, T., Robert, K., Raymaekers, C., Coninx, K.: Design Aspects for Rehabilitation Games for MS Patients. In: Proceedings of Design and Engineering of Game-like Virtual and Multimodal Environment, Berlin, Germany (2010), https://doclib.uhasselt.be/dspace/handle/1942/11089
6. Octavia, J.R., Coninx, K., Feys, P.: As I am not you: accommodating user diversity through adaptive rehabilitation training for multiple sclerosis patients. In: Farrell, V., Farrell, G., Chua, C., Huang, W., Vasa, R., Woodward, C. (eds.) Proceedings of the 24th Australian Computer-Human Interaction Conference, pp. 424–432. ACM, Melbourne (2012), http://dl.acm.org/citation.cfm?id=2414603
7. Perry, J.C., Andureu, J., Cavallaro, F.I., Veneman, J., Carmien, S., Keller, T.: Effective game use in neurorehabilitation: user-centered perspectives. In: Felicia, P. (ed.) Handbook of Research on Improving Learning and Motivation through Educational Games, pp. 683–725. IGI Global, Hershey (2011)
8. Quinten, N., Malliet, S.: Considering Design Concerns in Games for Physical Rehabilitation. In: Interactive Technologies and Games 2011 Conference Proceedings, Nothingham, GB, pp. 132–145 (2011)
9. Rowe, F., Brand, D., Jackson, C.A., Price, A., Walker, L., Harrison, S., Eccleston, C., Scott, C., Akerman, N., Dodridge, C., Howard, C., Shipman, T., Sperring, U., MacDiarmid, S., Freeman, C.: Visual impairment following stroke: do stroke patients require vision assessment? Age and Ageing 38(2), 188–193 (2008), http://www.ageing.oxfordjournals.org/cgi/doi/10.1093/ageing/afn230
10. Schell, J.: The Art of Game Design: A Book of Lenses. Morgan Kaufmann Publishers Inc., San Francisco (2008)
11. Vanden Abeele, V., Geurts, L., Husson, J., Windey, F., Annema, J.H., Verstraete, M., Desmet, S.: Designing Slow Fun! Physical Therapy Games to Remedy the Negative Consequences of Spasticity. In: Proceedings of the 3rd International Conference on Fun and Games, pp. 1–2. ACM, Leuven (2010), https://lirias.kuleuven.be/handle/123456789/297485
12. Zinn, S., Bosworth, H.B., Hoenig, H.M., Swartzwelder, H.S.: Executive function deficits in acute stroke. Archives of Physical Medicine and Rehabilitation 88(2), 173–180 (2007)

Games, from Engaging to Understanding: A Perspective from a Museum of Computing Machinery

Giovanni A. Cignoni, Leonora Cappellini, and Tommaso Mongelli

Fondazione Galileo Galilei, Museo degli Strumenti per il CalcoloLungarno
Pacinotti 43-44 c/o Università di Pisa – 56126 Pisa
giovanni@di.unipi.it, leonora.cappellini@gmail.com,
mog_tom@yahoo.it

Abstract. Science museums have a natural role in the building of *public under-standing* of science. For some time now, museums are particularly focused on *engaging* the public: it is a necessary condition to raise interest and cause active responses from the public. In this context, *gamification*, that is the usage of game dynamics to drive participation, is a way to engage the public.

The paper presents the experiences of the *Museum of Computing Machinery* of the University of Pisa in the adoption of gaming approaches for attracting and involving its public. Being a museum dedicated to computer science and its history, entertainment software has a noteworthy role. In particular, young people may be involved in projects aimed to the development of *toy games* and *mods*, two kinds of software artefacts that can still be faced as one-person projects – that is, simple, personal, and rewarding.

Keywords: Computing History, Museum, Gamification, Game modding.

1   Introduction

In 1985, the so-called *Bodmer Report* [1] set a pivotal point in relations among "science" and "public". There has never been a time when science and technology had been more related to progress and social wealth than in our age. Yet, people seem not to be really aware nor very interested in science. The Report pointed out such situation and set a new commitment in building the *public understanding* of science. Addressees of the Report were (and still are) schools, research communities, industries, political bodies, and, of course, museums dedicated to science and technology.

About thirty years after, the overall situation has not changed much. Still working to achieve the ultimate goal of public understanding, actors in the diffusion of scientific culture are today focused on strategic targets like *public engagement*. New ways have to be found to gain citizen interest and fascination, to involve them in the understanding and the development of science. *Gamification* is one strategy.

The paper presents the experiences of using gaming approaches carried out at the *Museo degli Strumenti per il Calcolo* (Museum of Computing Machinery, Museum in the following) [2] of the University of Pisa. As a Museum dedicated to computer science and its history, entertainment software plays a noteworthy role.

© IFIP International Federation for Information Processing 2015
K. Chorianopoulos et al. (Eds.): ICEC 2015, LNCS 9353, pp. 439–444, 2015.
DOI: 10.1007/978-3-319-24589-8_37

Smartphones, tablets, videogame consoles are very popular. Yet, paradoxically, the public is not really interested in understanding the science behind them: it is satisfied by their simple usage, sometimes by their bare possession as status symbols.

With the initiatives concerning games and video games the Museum tries to raise the general interest in information technologies and gadgets up to engage the public, the youngers in particular, in "true" computer science.

2   Games in the Museum Experience

Gamification is the usage of game dynamics to drive participation in non gaming contexts. While the term is recent, the idea is not. It is possible to find traces of planned gamification in the experiments of socialist competition like the *Stakhanovite movement* with all its surrounding mechanisms of records, awards and public praise [3]. The habit to gaming is however quite different today than in the days of Aleksei Stakhanov. For instance, thanks to video games there are much many gamers.

One of the recognized field of application for gamification is education [4] and Museums are committed in education. Moreover, they have to mark the difference with traditional teaching: museums are not schools and they have to attract and engage their public. No wonder that gamification is a sort of watchword.

In the following we will present three kinds of experiences carried out at the Museum. They can be seen as cases in gamification, but we prefer just to say that they concern games and computer games. For a rational and out-of-hype discussion about gamification in museums we suggest [5]. For a more comprehensive description of the Museum and of the underlying research project [6] we refer to [7].

2.1   Retro-gaming

Old video games have a characteristic vintage appeal for the large public: they played a large part in the childhood of many; even if they appear awkward and primitive to young people, they are still recognized as games. Many brands are still active. Temporary exhibits dedicated to video games are frequent events, organized by important institutions like the *Cité des Sciences* [8], or the *Smithsonian* [9]. There are also Museums dedicated to video games, one of the most known is in Berlin [10].

The *Night of Old Video Games* is a tournament that we organize as a yearly event, plus special editions. Qualifications and early phases are held in the afternoon and the final challenges in the evening. Due to the high appeal of old video games, the event is an easy success in terms of participation by players and spectators – a valuable mean of visibility for the Museum. But the initiative has also more noble goals.

As part of the schedule of the Night, brief speeches are held. They are used to talk about computer history topics. For instance, the last two editions were about *Super Mario Bros.* on the *Nintendo Entertainment System*, and *Ghosts'n Goblins* on the *Commodore 64*. The speeches covered topics with different perspectives:

1. *Technology*; like sound and graphics features of the NES and the C=64 ;
2. *Game art*; *Mario* is a long-running and successful franchise; the musical score of Ghosts 'n Goblins was a recognised masterpiece;

3. *Economy and culture*; Nintendo has celebrated 125 years of presence in the game
   industry, Commodore had a terrific success in the 80s, then is disappeared; both
   are good examples to discuss the ability to industrially exploit the opportunities offered by the available technologies.

During the tournament, the majority of the matches are played on software emulators
running on common modern PCs; only the finals take place on the original consoles
or computers. Playing on the originals has to be perceived as a special reward and a
rare occasion. It is a way to educate to respect and preserve the relics of the past.
Moreover, the emulators are a link to the present with a peculiar view on the evolution of computers: software can virtually make eternal the hardware.

2.2   Challenges on Old Machines

Some of the educational activities of the Museum challenge the visitors to operate old
machines. Using an old, strange device is a game of ability with a number of difficulties and the natural consequent satisfaction when the task succeeds.

It is easy to engage people by let them play with an old mechanical calculator like
a *Brunsviga*. The same happens for the hardware replica of the digital adder of the
first Italian computer. We can let people operate the replica under supervision. The
same is for pieces in the collection that are not very rare/antique and are sufficiently
sturdy. The feeling of having the special opportunity to operate an uncommon old
piece of computing machinery helps the visitor to enjoy the moment.

When the machines are very rare relics it is not possible to jeopardize them. Each
usage wears the mechanisms a little more: it has to be permitted only in very special
occasions and by expert hands only. In these cases we use software simulators.

Exploiting the success of "The Imitation Game" movie, in March the Museum organized an exhibition and a series of events played on the difference between the fiction and the real facts. We had an actual *Enigma* machine and we showed it working.
To let the public experience the Enigma, we used simulators to re-enact the true
World War II routines used to set-up the daily key and to encrypt messages. Being the
procedures (the actual ones, not the babble you see in the movie) quite complicated
and error prone, it was a real endeavour for visitors and students to successfully complete a whole cycle of set-up, encode and decode.

Fig. 1. A photo of the Macchina Ridotta and a screenshot of the simulator.

The simulator of the *Macchina Ridotta* (MR), is one of the most relevant results of the HMR project [11]. The MR was dismantled in late 1958 to reuse its electronic components in a second computer: no relics of the very first Italian computer survived. The simulator was developed starting from the retrieved blueprints and technical reports: today it makes possible to see the MR running again [12]. With such a background, the MR simulator is a set piece of the educational activities of the Museum. It is used to show the principles and the basic mechanisms that make the computers work. The main difference between the old computers and their modern descendants is that the former expose all their inner workings while the latter hide them behind friendly interfaces. Of course, operating the MR is awkward for today standards (see Fig. 1): its user interface is made of many switches and lights used to input and output binary data.

The simulators are software pieces, but they are not video games. It is the aura of old (even lost) machines, the hurdle of the complex procedures, the oddity of the interfaces and the way the challenge is thrown that build up the gaming feeling.

2.3   Ad hoc Edugames

The Museum is also experimenting the development of its own *edugames*. The occasion was given by the theme that the Tuscany Region proposed in the call for the events organized for the *Museum Night 2015*: sustainability.

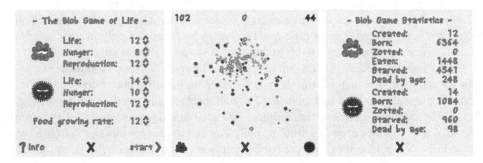

Fig. 2. Three screenshots of the prey-predator simulation game

We decided to use the Night to narrate the fragile equilibria of Nature, on which the sustainability of the Planet relies. Being a Museum devoted to computing, our interpretation of such idea is based on mathematical models and the ability to show them live using computer simulation technologies. For this purpose we developed a simple game to experiment with a small closed ecosystem where two species, prey and predators, interact. The game (see Fig. 2) lets the player modify the fundamental parameters of the species and observe the evolution of the ecosystem. Like a god, she/he may (or may not) intervene to create and kill individuals trying to recover a precarious equilibrium or to alter it to see what happens.

Besides ecosystems, the game is a good starting point to talk about historical mathematical models (like the Lotka-Volterra one) as well as modern simulation techniques (like the agent-based one) [13]. Moreover, the game is a case of software development taken on by the Museum itself, actually an one-man-project: a very small investment when compared to mainstream video game titles. We want to demonstrate to our public that programming may still be an activity on a human scale.

3   Further Engagement with Toy Games and Mods

Every museum can use video games to drive participation and engage its public. A Museum dedicated to computer science has a further motivation: video games are part of the history it has to preserve, study and disseminate. In this paper we presented the activities of our Museum which concern games and computer games.

Moreover, we believe that games can further help the building of public understanding of computer science. Games have a particular role in the history of computing. They were present since the beginning and were used in researches ranging from artificial intelligence up to human-machine interaction. When in the 80s information technology became a mass phenomenon, video games and *home computers* fired up curiosity about computer science and popularized programming up to the status of a hobby. Many people learned programming and enjoyed it as a new kind of *Meccano*.

We propose to renew those days by engaging people, the youngsters in particular, on simple software development projects. We identified *toy games* and *mods* as perfectly sized kinds of projects. Toy games are little video games, built using rapid development environments, relying on 2D graphics and based more on game dynamics than on elaborate plots and gorgeous sceneries. Mods [14] are modifications made to existing video games to change or add contents like equipment items, characters, sceneries, behaviours. Toy games and mods are software artefacts that can still be faced as one-man projects – that is, simple, personal, and rewarding.

An experiment about toy games is already in progress. The first cycle of the *Laboratorio di Videogiochi* (Video Game Lab in Italian) has been held from November 2014 to June 2015. Based on a weekly schedule, the Lab offers a crash course in gaming history, architecture, technologies and development processes, followed by a substantial set of programming lessons using Stencyl [15] to develop a game. The course was followed by a small class of 12 students of which only 6 were able to completely fulfill the final assignments.

While it is not possible to derive definitive conclusion, we can say that is difficult to recreate the happy moment of the 80s. The effort required to develop a toy game is low, but not insignificant and sufficient to discourage many. As a consequence, a modding lab is seen as an interesting alternative to engage the public in game development and has therefore been considered for future implementation among the activities held at the Museum.

Meanwhile, we want to stress the need of support from the industry of video games and electronic gadgets. The PC platform has to be supported as well as the moddability of the video games: this is the precondition to let people try, with reasonable effort, to be part of the amazing world of video game development.

The situation about mobile platform is more complex. The popularity of these devices is a great opportunity to engage people. However, it is hindered by the rise of the *walled garden* model of app distribution. This model dictates that apps have to be thoroughly scrutinized by platform owners before they can be made available. In some cases the store requires a fee even if the app is free. This is a large setback from the days of home computing.

Developing games for mobile platforms is possible, but the need of an external programming environment and the complicated distribution policies surely does not encourage people to try to program and to discover true computer science.

References

1. Bodmer, W.F. (ed.) The Public Understanding of Science. The Royal Society (1985)
2. Museo degli Strumenti per il Calcolo,
   http://www.facebook.com/MuseoStrumentiCalcolo
   (accessed July 3, 2015)
3. Nelson, M.J.: Soviet and American precursors to the gamification of work. In: Proc. of the 16th International Academic MindTrek Conference, pp. 23–26. ACM (2012)
4. de Sousa Borges, S., et al.: A systematic mapping on gamification applied to education. In: Proc. of the 29th Symposium on Applied Computing, pp. 216–222. ACM (2014)
5. Rodley E.: Gaming the museum – separating fad from function,
   http://exhibitdev.wordpress.com/2011/07/07/gaming-the-museum-separating-fad-from-function-part-four-of
   (accessed July 3, 2015)
6. Hackerando la Macchina Ridotta, http://hmr.di.unipi.it (accessed July 3, 2015)
7. Cignoni, G.A., Gadducci, F.: Using Old Computers for Teaching Computer Science. In: Tatnall, A., Blyth, T., Johnson, R. (eds.) HC 2013. IFIP AICT, vol. 416, pp. 121–131. Springer, Heidelberg (2013)
8. Vidéo, J.: Cité des Sciences, http://www.cite-sciences.fr/fr/au-programme/expos-temporaires/jeuvideo-lexpo/accueil-de-la-cite-du-jeu-video (accessed July 3, 2015)
9. The Art of Videogames. Smithsonian American Art Museum,
   http://americanart.si.edu/exhibitions/archive/2012/games
   (accessed July 3, 2015)
10. Computerspielemuseum, http://www.computerspielemuseum.de (accessed July 3, 2015)
11. Cignoni, G.A., Gadducci, F.: Rediscovering the Very First Italian Digital Computer. In: Proceedings of 3rd IEEE History of Electro-technology Conference. IEEE (2012)
12. Cignoni, G.A., Gadducci, F., Paci, S.: A Virtual Experience on the Very First Italian Computer. ACM Journal of Computing and Cultural Heritage 7(4), 21:1–21:23 (2015)
13. Kim, S., Hoffmann, C., Ramachandran, V.: Analyzing the Parameters of Prey-Predator Models for Simulation Games. In: Yang, H.S., Malaka, R., Hoshino, J., Han, J.H. (eds.) ICEC 2010. LNCS, vol. 6243, pp. 216–223. Springer, Heidelberg (2010)
14. Cignoni, G.A.: Reporting about the Mod Software Process. In: Ambriola, V. (ed.) EWSPT 2001. LNCS, vol. 2077, pp. 242–245. Springer, Heidelberg (2001)
15. Stencyl - Amazing Games without Code, http://www.stencyl.com (accessed July 3, 2015)

Interactive Painterly Rendering
for Mobile Devices

Dongwann Kang and Kyunghyun Yoon

School of Computer Science and Engineering,
Chung-Ang University, Seoul, Korea
{dongwann,khyoon}@cglab.cau.ac.kr

Abstract. Painterly rendering is among the most popular non-photorealistic rendering techniques and has been employed in many applications. Research on painterly rendering mainly focuses on automatically generating artistic results. In this study, we aim to develop an entertaining and interactive application for painterly rendering with touchscreen mobile devices. The proposed application provides user interaction for added enjoyment and ensures high-quality painterly results. We provide a method for finding the appropriate position of the brush stroke around the points touched by the user and for generating and rendering the brush stroke. With the proposed method, users can quickly generate high-quality painterly results.

Keywords: Non-photorealistic rendering, Painterly rendering, Stylization.

1 Introduction

Non-photorealistic rendering (NPR) [5,11,14] is an area of research in the field of computer graphics concerned with imitating the rules and practices of aesthetics and fine arts. In this field, research has attempted to simulate physical phenomena through the medium of the painting process and to mimic artwork styles. As a result of this research, a number of stylization methods are available that can plausibly imitate artistic styles. Moreover, with the increased use of mobile devices such as smartphones and tablet PCs, users can generate their own artwork using various mobile applications that employ these methods[2,1].

One common approach to NPR requires users manual control of the finished product in order to imitate artwork styles. Because this approach merely simulates physical phenomena[4,3], users must have a well-developed artistic sense or skill for drawing (or painting) akin to artists. However, it is difficult for most users to learn such artistic skills and develop an aesthetic sense.

Another NPR approach is to facilitate the style imitated by generating artistic results without the need for user expertise[7,6]. Most methods that adopt this approach automatically draw according to a particular painting style. Consequently, untrained users can obtain desirable results. However, users are almost completely uninvolved in the drawing process with this approach.

© IFIP International Federation for Information Processing 2015
K. Chorianopoulos et al. (Eds.): ICEC 2015, LNCS 9353, pp. 445–450, 2015.
DOI: 10.1007/978-3-319-24589-8_38

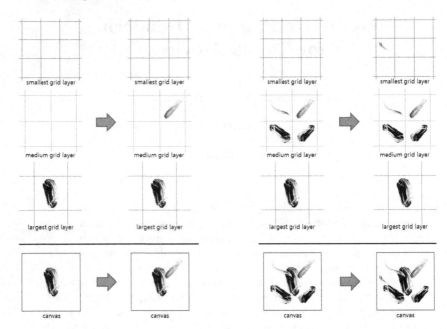

Fig. 1. The proposed interactive painting method. We select the largest grid layer among the grid candidates and paint a brush on it.

In order to design a popular NPR application, the latter approach is more suitable, insofar as a wider range of users will be able to utilize it. However, if users can only obtain results that are automatically generated, they will quickly lose interest in the application owing to limited user control. Therefore, an NPR approach in which users are involved in drawing process is needed, and this can be accomplished by providing the appropriate level of interaction without requiring pretrained skills.

In this paper, we propose an interactive algorithm for painterly rendering that runs on mobile devices. The proposed algorithm is based on previous methods[12], and it allows users to generate plausible painterly artwork easily. In Section 2, we describe our enhanced algorithm for painterly rendering. We present the results from evaluating our method in Section 3. Finally, we conclude with a summary of our method and discuss the directions for future development in Section 4.

2   Proposed Algorithm

Our study is based on [12]'s algorithm for painterly rendering. This algorithm automatically generates painterly images using a brush-stroke texture database and a photomosaic method[13,10,9]. However, users cannot participate in the painting process with [12]'s method, apart from choosing the input image and a limited number of rendering settings. To enhance user participation, we propose an interactive algorithm for painterly rendering in order to facilitate the direct involvement of the user during the painting process.

2.1   Basic Painterly Rendering Algorithm

This study follows the multiple-layered-grids approach proposed by [7]. First, we generate several grid layers. For each grid on each layer, a brush stroke is rendered. Smaller-sized grids correspond to layers at the upper levels. Consequently, only tiny grids are generated for the top layer.

According to the method in [7], a brush stroke is generated for each grid along the gradient of the input image. For our proposed algorithm, however, we employ [12]'s method to determine the most suitable brush stroke from a stroke-texture database and map it to the canvas. First, we sample the color of the input image at a point selected by the user through a touch interface in order to allow the user to choose the color of the brush stroke. Next, we select a brush-stroke texture from the database and map it to the canvas with the sampled color. Then, we resize the size of the texture to 1.5 times that of the grid in order to cover the area of the grid. Finally, we calculate the color distance between the grid area of the canvas and that of the input image. By repeating this process for all of the strokes in the database and selecting the one with the smallest distance, we can find the most suitable brush stroke. We then render this brush stroke to the canvas according to the texture-mapping process described above.

2.2   Interactive Painterly Rendering Algorithm

By using the method described in the previous section, we can obtain painterly rendering that is similar to the results from previous works[7,6,12]. Rather than performing the process automatically, we offer an interactive approach to the rendering. With our method, users can select the position of each brush stroke. If users are required to select all of the properties for the brush, such as the color, position, size, and shape, the process would be overly tedious for most untrained users. To alleviate such complexity, the size, texture, and color of the brush stroke are adaptively determined according to the position of the stroke selected by the user.

With our method, users input a point on the canvas by using a touch interface. The application then generates a circle with a predefined radius around that point and locates grids whose central points fall within this circle. Then, we eliminate the grids within the brush strokes that have already been generated. The remaining grids are candidates for the brush stroke that will be generated. By following the multilayered approach for rendering brush strokes according the size of the strokes, we select the largest grid among the candidates (Figure 1). If there are other grids that are equivalent in size to the largest grid, they are selected as well. In order to prevent the regularity of the brush location, we obtain the jittered point for the center of the selected grids and generate a brush stroke for that point using the method described in Section 2.1. When multiple grids are selected, we choose the most suitable brush stroke for rendering (i.e., the stroke with the minimum color distance).

If there are no more candidates within the circle generated at the point touched by the user, we then obtain the jittered point from the user-selected point and generate a grid with its center at the jittered point. Then, a brush stroke is generated using the method described above. Thus, the size of the grid is equivalent to the size of the grids at the top layer.

By iteratively performing the above process until the canvas is appropriately covered with a number of brush strokes, painterly results are generated interactively.

3 Results

Our experiments were conducted on an iPad 3. Figure 2 shows a comparison of the results from an automatic rendering approach, a manual approach, and our interactive approach. Table 1 summarizes the elapsed time for generating the results shown in Figure 2. For the automatic approach, we employed the basic method described in Section 2.1 and applied it in the order of each layer. With the manual approach, a user selected the size and orientation of the brush for each brush-stroke texture and rendered the brush stroke on a user-selected point using the iPads touch interface. For a given image, the user paints brush strokes by touching the screen

(a) input image (b) automatic approach (c) our interactive approach (d) manual approach

Fig. 2. A comparison of the results from several approaches. These results are generated by user1 in Table 1.

Table 1. The elapsed time for generating the results shown in Figure 2.

approach	elapsed time (s)		
	user1	user2	user3
automatic approach	51	50	55
our interactive approach	123	359	108
manual approach	549	786	451

Fig. 3. Various results from the proposed interactive method.

until he/she wants to finish painting. The experiments demonstrate that the automatic approach rendered the image more quickly to obtain a complete painterly result. The quality of the result appeared to be satisfactory. However, the user does not participate in the rendering process with the automatic approach, apart from selecting a few parameters such as the grid size and the number of layers. In contrast, the manual approach requires a considerable amount of time to complete the painting. Moreover, the quality of the result appeared to be the worst, probably because the user was unfamiliar with the interface and the painting method. Our interactive approach offered a balance between these approaches in terms of the elapsed time. Moreover, it is evident in Figure 2 that the user was able to focus on several interesting points. Because the proposed interactive approach allowed the user to be involved in the painting process, the users preferences and intent were appropriately reflected in the result. Figure 3 shows various results from the proposed interactive method by untrained users.

4   Conclusion and Future Work

In this paper, we proposed an interactive method for painterly rendering with an enhanced mobile application based on previous methods[12]. To facilitate user interaction, we developed a method that finds the appropriate position of the brush stroke around a point selected by the user, after which the brush stroke is generated, and the image is rendered. With our method, users can generate high-quality painterly results quickly and easily.

In future research, we plan to implement various styles of stroke-based rendering[8], such as watercolor, pen and ink, and pastel. To do so, we must reinforce the database to accommodate these various strokes and modify our rendering method to apply them appropriately.

Acknowledgment. This work was supported by a National Research Foundation of Korea (NRF) grant funded by the Korea government(MEST) (NRF-2013R1A2A2A01069032).

References

1. Mobilemonet, http://itunes.apple.com/us/app/mobilemonet/id395563116 (accessed September 21, 1998)
2. Toonpaint, http://toonpaint.toon-fx.com (accessed September 21, 1998)
3. Baxter, W., Wendt, J., Lin, M.C.: Impasto: A realistic, interactive model for paint. In: Proceedings of the 3rd International Symposium on Non-Photorealistic Animation and Rendering, NPAR 2004, pp. 45–148. ACM, New York (2004)
4. Curtis, C.J., Anderson, S.E., Seims, J.E., Fleischer, K.W., Salesin, D.H.: Computer-generated watercolor. In: Proceedings of the 24th Annual Conference on Computer Graphics and Interactive Techniques, SIGGRAPH 1997, pp. 421–430. ACM Press/Addison-Wesley Publishing Co., New York (1997)
5. Gooch, B., Gooch, A.: Non-Photorealistic Rendering. A. K. Peters, Ltd., Natick (2001)
6. Hays, J., Essa, I.: Image and video based painterly animation. In: Proceedings of the 3rd International Symposium on Non-Photorealistic Animation and Rendering, NPAR 2004, pp. 113–120. ACM, New York (2004)
7. Hertzmann, A.: Painterly rendering with curved brush strokes of multiple sizes. In: Proceedings of the 25th Annual Conference on Computer Graphics and Interactive Techniques, SIGGRAPH 1998, pp. 453–460. ACM, New York (1998)
8. Hertzmann, A.: Tutorial: A survey of stroke-based rendering. IEEE Comput. Graph. Appl. 23(4), 70–81 (2003)
9. Kang, D., Seo, S.H., Ryoo, S.T., Yoon, K.H.: A parallel framework for fast photomosaics. IEICE Transactions on Information and Systems 94-D(10), 2036–2042 (2011)
10. Kang, D., Seo, S., Ryoo, S., Yoon, K.: A study on stackable mosaic generation for mobile devices. Multimedia Tools and Applications 63(1), 145–159 (2013)
11. Kyprianidis, J.E., Collomosse, J., Wang, T., Isenberg, T.: State of the "art": A taxonomy of artistic stylization techniques for images and video. IEEE Transactions on Visualization and Computer Graphics 19(5), 866–885 (2013)
12. Seo, S., Ryoo, S., Park, J.: Interactive painterly rendering with artistic error correction. Multimedia Tools Appl. 65(2), 221–237 (2013)
13. Silvers, R.: Photomosaics. Henry Holt and Co., Inc., New York (1997)
14. Strothotte, T., Schlechtweg, S.: Non-photorealistic Computer Graphics: Modeling, Rendering, and Animation. Morgan Kaufmann Publishers Inc., San Francisco (2002)

Lessons from Practicing an Adapted Model Driven Approach in Game Development

Hong Guo, Hallvard Trætteberg, Alf Inge Wang, Shang Gao,
and Maria Letizia Jaccheri

Department of Computer and Information Science
Norwegian University of Science and Technology
Trondheim, Norway
{Guohong,hal,alfw,shanggao,letizia.jaccheri}@idi.ntnu.no

Abstract. Various authoring tools have been used to ease the game creation. However, these pre-defined tools may not be suitable for some emerging or special domains. We proposed an approach named Game Creation with Customized Tools (GCCT) to create tools for certain domains first, and then create games using these tools. GCCT is based on the widely applied Model Driven Development (MDD) approach. Despite the apparent appropriateness and benefits, MDD also has drawbacks. Among them, non-trivial cost for tools development is prominent. To address this, some enhancements were made in GCCT, and two case studies were performed to evaluate the cost and the productivity when involving GCCT. In this paper, we reported the results of the case studies as well as practical lessons we have learnt.

Keywords: Computer Game Development, Model Driven Development, Cost.

1 Introduction

Various authoring tools have been adopted to ease computer games creation by providing easy user interfaces and code automation. However, such tools usually do not address the complexity required by sophisticated games [1]. On the other hand, game engine tools are generally more powerful than authoring tools and they are the mainstream tools to create commercial games. But they are usually huge, complex, and sometimes lack usability, especially for beginners or amateurs. This makes the learning curve steep and using the tool cost expensive. What is more, both authoring tools and engine tools target pre-defined domains. Some emerging or innovative domains like pervasive games and education games may not be able to benefit from them. To ease the game creation especially for such specific domains, we propose an approach named Game Creation with Customized Tools (GCCT). By using GCCT, developers create tools according to specific domain requirements first, and then create games with these tools. GCCT is derived from the general Model Driven Development (MDD) approach [2] which has been proven effective in many domains [3, 4] to achieve higher productivity, shortened development cycle, and better software quality. The success of MDD was primarily achieved by providing high level and domain-specific abstractions (as the

© IFIP International Federation for Information Processing 2015
K. Chorianopoulos et al. (Eds.): ICEC 2015, LNCS 9353, pp. 451–456, 2015.
DOI: 10.1007/978-3-319-24589-8_39

base of easy user interfaces) as well as code automation. Despite the apparent fitness and strength, involving MDD may also bring risks. For instance, MDD is not easy and it imposes high development cost for (domain specific) tools development in addition to the game development [5]. Previous research about applying MDD for game development did not address this issue in depth. To alleviate this, some enhancements were made in GCCT, and two case studies were performed to evaluate the cost and the productivity when involving GCCT.

The remainder of this paper is organized as below. We illustrate the GCCT approach in Section 2. Section 3 introduces the settings and results of case studies. In Section 4 we talk about practical lessons we have learned from the case studies. Finally in Section 5, we introduce possible future works and conclude the paper.

2   GCCT Formalism

As mentioned earlier, the motivation behind GCCT is that we create tools according to the specific domain requirements first, and then create games with these tools. Compared with pre-defined and mostly fixed authoring tools or engine tools, tools in GCCT are highly customizable. The overall process of GCCT is shown in Fig. 1. As presented in the figure, the tools customization in GCCT consists of three parts: game feature customization, game editor customization, and game code generator customization. While game feature customization defines which game features should be supported in the tools (editor, code generator, etc.) and needs to be done according to the specific project/domain requirements firstly, game editor customization and game code customization can be done afterwards based on the game feature set that has been decided. For game editors, we select the style (textual, tree-based, table-based, diagrammatical, or graphical). And based on the style, we connect editor elements to the game feature elements. For game code generators, we define the rules regarding how code snippets should be generated according to the game features. The tools customization is formalized according to traditions of MDD approaches [6].

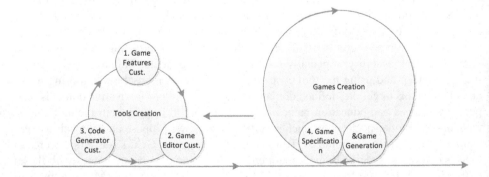

Fig. 1. GCCT Process View

In addition to the tools customization/creation, another part of GCCT is games creation. As shown in Fig.1, both parts are highly iterative. The necessity of intensive iterations in GCCT comes from the requirements of both the game domain and the MDD domain [2, 7, 8]. Although both parts are highly iterative, different parts are focused on when the projects progress. In the earlier stage of a project, usually more iterations of tools customization are performed, while several iterations of game creation may be used in order to validate the tools and provide feedback to improve the tools. In the latter stage of the projects, fewer iterations of tools creation may be performed because the tools have grown to be quite mature. And more games are developed in an iterative way. In order to fully play the strengths of MDD, more specialization and adaptation are done in GCCT in order to lower the technical barrier and the upfront and general cost. The main improvements are listed below, and the details were reported in [9].

- Instead of introducing a new Domain Analysis (DA) task [5], we propose to structure existing game design and level design tasks/documents in traditional game development to produce the DA outputs.
- Regulate and accelerate the DA task based on predefined domain vocabularies/ontologies (PerGO is proposed to be used for pervasive games domain [10]).
- Reuse existing working prototypes to construct the template of code generator.
- Utilize the state of the art and highly integrated language workbench tools [11].

3   Case Studies

Instead of addressing conventional computer games, we focused on the pervasive game domain in our research. This is mainly because pervasive games are innovative and there are no suitable authoring tools available for creating such games. Pervasive games have emerged during the last ten years. Such games involve more physical and social elements into the game, and blend game and everyday life by providing game experience all the time and everywhere [12]. The goals of performing the case studies include:

- To gain practical experiences of performing GCCT in general,
- To collect real project data regarding to the cost (for both tools and game software), and
- To gain lessons to reduce the cost.

We performed two case studies for this research. Prior to them, several pilot projects were carried out to get us familiar with model driven techniques as well as tools and libraries that would be used. We also gained some initial experience about how to perform MDD approaches in a more compact and efficient manner. Based on our experience, we consolidated and formalized the GCCT approach. Then we performed another two case studies with Realcoins and Realpacman to evaluate the GCCT approach. While Realpacman can be thought of a location-based variation of the traditional Pac-man game, Realcoins is a location-based treasure-hunting game which has been reported in detail in [9]. These two case studies were using similar settings. For Realcoins, we only recorded basic cost data, while for the latter Realpacman, we recorded detailed cost distribution for major tasks in addition to the basic cost data. This is because after performing the Realcoins case, we found that the actual productivity was decided by many factors, and identifying such critical factors was important in order to control cost and improve productivity.

Lines of Code (LoC) and Hours (Hrs) are used for evaluating cost and productivity [1, 13, 14]. Table 2 and Table 3 present the LoC and Hrs used for the two case studies. For models, we also recorded LoC to quantitatively estimate the workload. LoC of a model was got by counting the lines of code in the corresponding textual specification of the model (.ecore files in our case). The productivity increase is calculated based on the productivity of creating games in a manual way. We call the approach of manually creating games as Game Creation from Scratch (GCS). In Table 2 and Table 3, the gray cells indicate one-time costs of GCCT, while the dotted cells indicate repetitive costs of GCCT (for each game instance).

Table 1. Hours used by Realcoins and Realpacman

		RealCoins		RealPacman	
		Hrs	Percentage of Manual	Hrs	Percentage of Manual
GCS (Manual)		14	100%	8.267	100%
GCCT	Tools	11	78.6%	5.3	64.1%
	Game	0.75	5.4%	0.55	6.7%

Table 2. LoC used by Realcoins and Realpacman

		RealCoins		RealPacman	
		LoC	Percentage of Manual	LoC	Percentage of Manual
GCS (Manual)		1263	100%	363	100%
GCCT	Tools	255	20.1%	167	46.0%
	Game	59	4.67%	93	25.6%

From Table 2 and Table 3, we can see that by using GCCT, 5.4% and 6.7% of the manual development time was used for each new game instance. And the corresponding LoCs needed for GCCT were 4.67% and 25.6% of the manual ones. In another word, to develop every new game instance, using GCCT can be 4-20 times faster/cheaper than using GCS. The cost saving was very obvious. Although there was an upfront cost for the GCCT approach, it was relatively small. From the data in the two tables, this extra cost to develop GCCT tools required around 60%-80% time or 20%-50% LoC of manually developing one game instance. That is to say, this one-time cost might be paid back after two or three game instances were developed.

Despite the promising results in general, we also noticed that the data varied severely from case to case as a result of different domain complexity and practical factors. In the next section, we further introduce some practical lessons we have learned from the case studies in order to perform such a MDD approach in an efficient way.

4 Lessons Learnt

MDD is not a silver bullet [5]. The decision must be carefully made about whether or not to adopt MDD according to various aspects of the domains/projects. The actual productivity increase brought by involving MDD approaches may be influenced by many factors. From the case studies, we got some practical lessons about saving cost and therefore achieving a higher productivity increase.

1. *Start with stable but extensible meta-model.* This is important to make sure the tools are built up in an incremental way without frequent re-construction. During the pilot case studies, we did not have a common basic structure for the meta-models, which sometimes made it difficult to implement new features during the incremental process. And we had to re-create everything which made the overall development cycle much longer accordingly. But when we applied PerGO (in Realcoins and Realpacman) to build an extensible meta-model structure, such situation did not appear frequently.
2. *Make abstractions quickly with knowledge engineering.* Using PerGO in case studies helped us streamline domain analysis and define the meta-model quickly.
3. *Use easy-to-implement abstractions.* If it is difficult to find corresponding constructs to implement the meta-model concepts, building domain specific libraries will become much more difficult and time consuming. In addition, specifying the relationship among them in the code template gets even more difficult.
4. *Reuse codes of working prototypes to construct generators.* A working starting point made creating generator quicker and of less bugs.
5. *Generate complete codes.* If some codes (even several lines of code) need to be manually written after other parts have been automatically generated, it means this part of work will be repeated for all the iterations. Generating complete codes reduces the routine cost of iterations and makes the overall process much agile.
6. *Regulate structured process within one iteration.* The process should include both game design tasks and MDD related tasks. A reasonable and regulated process helps to reuse resources in an efficient way, smooth the task transition, and lower the routine cost for every iteration.
7. *Adopt highly automatic language workbench tools.* By doing so, many routine tasks like generating concept classes can be automated.
8. *Adopt highly integrated development environment.* Highly integrated development environment helps avoid some unnecessary tasks (like copying source codes from one tool to another, or changing formats of data due to different requirements from tools), and makes the overall process smoother.

5   Future Work and Conclusion

In this paper we have introduced GCCT, an enhanced MDD approach for computer game creation. We evaluated on the cost and the productivity when involving GCCT through case studies. In order to perform efficient MDD approaches in other projects, we presented some practical lessons we have gained from the cases. Consequently, we have identified some future work to address the cost issues: 1) we will explore major impact factors for the actual productivity increase of involving MDD approaches like GCCT; 2) we will observe how the cost of tools development and games development evolve as the project proceeds within iterations.

References

1. Furtado, A.W., Santos, A.L.: Using domain-specific modeling towards computer games development industrialization. In: 6th OOPSLA Workshop on Domain-Specific Modeling (DSM 2006). Citeseer (2006)
2. Kelly, S., Tolvanen, J.-P.: Domain-Specific Modeling Enabling Full Code Generation. John Wiley & Sons, Inc. (2008)
3. Hutchinson, J., Whittle, J., Rouncefield, M.: Model-driven engineering practices in industry: Social, organizational and managerial factors that lead to success or failure. Science of Computer Programming 89, 144–161 (2014)
4. Hussmann, H., Meixner, G., Zuehlke, D.: Model-Driven Development of Advanced User Interfaces. Springer Science & Business Media (2011)
5. Mernik, M., Heering, J., Sloane, A.M.: When and how to develop domain-specific languages. ACM Comput. Surv. 37(4), 316–344 (2005)
6. Guo, H., Gao, S., Krogstie, J., Trætteberg, H.: An Evaluation of an Enhanced Model Driven Approach for Computer Game Creation. In: Gaaloul, K., Schmidt, R., Nurcan, S., Guerreiro, S., Ma, Q. (eds.) BPMDS 2015 and EMMSAD 2015. LNBIP, vol. 214, pp. 499–508. Springer, Heidelberg (2015)
7. Adams, E.: Fundamentals of game design. New Riders (2010)
8. Gal, V., et al.: Writing for video games. In: Proceedings of the Laval Virtual, IVRC (2002)
9. Guo, H., et al.: RealCoins: A Case Study of Enhanced Model Driven Development for Pervasive Game. International Journal of Multimedia and Ubiquitous Engineering 10(5), 395–410 (2015)
10. Guo, H., Trætteberg, H., Wang, A.I., Gao, S.: PerGO: An Ontology towards Model Driven Pervasive Game Development. In: Meersman, R., et al. (eds.) Workshops at the OTM 2014. LNCS, vol. 8842, pp. 651–654. Springer, Heidelberg (2014)
11. Fowler, M.: Language workbenches: The killer-app for domain specific languages (2005)
12. Guo, H., et al.: TeMPS: A Conceptual Framework for Pervasive and Social Games. In: 2010 IEEE 3rd International Conference on Digital Game and Intelligent Toy Enhanced Learning, pp. 31–37. IEEE Press (2010)
13. Hernandez, F.E., Ortega, F.R.: Eberos GML2D: a graphical domain-specific language for modeling 2D video games. In: Proceedings of the 10th Workshop on Domain-Specific Modeling, Reno, Nevada, p. 1. ACM (2010)
14. Reyno, E.M., Carsí Cubel, J.Á.: Automatic prototyping in model-driven game development. Computers in Entertainment (CIE) 7(2), 29 (2009)

Measuring Latency in Virtual Reality Systems

Kjetil Raaen[1,2,3] and Ivar Kjellmo[1]

[1] Westerdals - Oslo School of Arts, Communication and Technology, Oslo, Norway
[2] Simula Research Laboratory, Bærum, Norway
[3] University of Oslo, Oslo, Norway

Abstract. Virtual Reality(VR) systems have the potential to revolutionise how we interact with computers. However motion sickness and discomfort are currently severely impeding the adoption. Traditionally the focus of optimising VR systems have been on frame-rate. Delay and frame-rate are however not equivalent. Latency may occur in several steps in image processing, and a frame-rate measure only picks up some of them. We have made an experimental setup to physically measure the actual delay from the user moves the head until the screen of the VR device is updated. Our results show that while dedicated VR-equipment had very low delay, smartphones are in general not ready for VR-applications.

Keywords: Latency, Virtual Reality, Framerate, Mixed Reality.

1 Introduction

The last years have seen a great increase in interest and popularity of Virtual Reality (VR) solutions. Some are dedicated hardware made specifically for VR, such as Oculus Rift. Others are Mobile VR solutions such as Samsung's Gear VR, HTC and Valves' new Steam VR and even the simplified solution Google Cardboard. Providing a stereoscopic view that moves with their head, these systems give users an unprecedented visual immersion in the computer generated world.

However, these systems all have in common the same potential problems when it comes to motion sickness and discomfort when using the VR solutions[2]. An important source of these problems is delay. This paper presents an apparatus for measuring delay as well as detailed measurements of delay in some popular VR systems.

Frame-rate is a measurement of how fast frames are sent through the rendering pipeline. Delay on the other hand defines the time it takes from a user triggers an action, such as turning the head, until results are visible on screen. Previous work by one of us[7] has, however indicate that there is no linear relationship between frame-rate and delay in traditional computer graphics setups. From this, we assume that frame-rate is not the best metric. If VR solutions work like other graphics output devices, there is a significant difference between frame-rate measured inside an application and actual update speed.

© IFIP International Federation for Information Processing 2015
K. Chorianopoulos et al. (Eds.): ICEC 2015, LNCS 9353, pp. 457–462, 2015.
DOI: 10.1007/978-3-319-24589-8_40

By using a light sensor and an oscilloscope we hope to measure the exact delays in VR applications. Finding out how much delay there is in virtual reality headsets would be helpful in when investigating the causes for motion sickness in virtual worlds, as well as providing guidance to people producing software for these systems.

2   Background

Previous research has suggested various methods for measuring delay in VR systems all the way back to the previous VR-hype in the early nineties. Earlier work has used cameras [6] or light sensors [8]. What they all have in common is that they rely on a continuous, smooth movement of the tested devices. DiLuca et al.[3] summarise a series of them, and suggest their own approach. Their approach is the most elegant we have found so far.

2.1   Sources of Delay

This section discusses the parts of the VR-pipeline that add most to the response delay. Components in the pipeline from the time the user moves until displays update are in general *black boxes*; documentation about how they work is often lacking. Thus, the only way to evaluate these delays is by measuring.

Screens used to display output add some delay, which can be divided into two parts: *screen refresh* and *response time*. LCD screens used in VR displays receive and display updated images at a fixed rate. This rate is termed *screen refresh* rate. Most modern screens update at 60 frames per second (FPS), or every 16.7 ms. *Response time* denotes the time the physical pixels take to change colour.

A *frame buffer* is memory used for holding a rendered frame about to be displayed on the monitor or VR-display. Modern renderers use at least two frame buffers. To avoid showing unfinished frames to the user, drawing happens in one buffer, while the other is being displayed. This practice is termed *double buffering*. Further, to avoid showing parts of two different buffers, it is common to wait for the next screen refresh before swapping. When double buffering is used, rendering follows the sequence: Assume frame 0 is the frame during which an event from an input device is registered. Frame 1 contains the result of the event, and at the time of frame 2 the result is sent to screen. This gives a minimum of 1 full frame time from input event to result on screen.

At 60 FPS this adds up to a minimum of one frame delay (17 ms) to a maximum of two frames (33 ms) delay. Further, not all hardware is capable of keeping up with the target frame-rate at all times. Slow hardware leads to significantly longer delays. An increased number of frame buffers in the pipeline increases this delay, because more steps are added between rendering and displaying data.

Dedicated VR equipment has tailor-made hardware and drivers that have been tweaked for low latency performance. The gyros of smartphones on the other hand are mainly intended for navigation or keeping the screen rotated the correct way, neither of which require fast response time or high accuracy.

2.2   Acceptable Delay

Empirical values for how long delay is acceptable is difficult to find. Davis et al. investigated a condition they term *cybersickness*[2] in analogy to motion sickness. They consider a range of options for the cause of these problems, delay among them. However they do not quantify delay that might lead to symptoms. Jarods [5] concludes that people reacts very differently to latency. Some people would hardly notice a 100 ms delay while other very sensitive people are able to perceive down to 3-4ms of latency.

Most design guidelines and measurements reports are from developers and of VR equipment and VR-software rather than scientists. John Carmack [1] states that a latency of 50 ms feels responsive but the lag when moving in the virtual world is noticeable. He recommends that latency should be under 20 ms. Neither methodology or background numbers and test results are presented.

3   Experiment Setup

To measure response time after abrupt movements, we need the virtual reality device to run a program that detects a small rotation and as fast as possible change the displayed picture. A simple program that detects rotation and changes the displayed picture would create solve this problem. However, we are interested in delays from actual 3D virtual reality software. Therefore we used a popular game engine, Unity 3D[1], and made a scene that creates abrupt changes based on headset movement. We tested multiple VR devices. Oculus Rift is a dedicated VR display solution, designed for this purpose. The other systems are smartphones, which developers have discovered have all the required hardware to run VR application and can also function as headsets.

The physical setup(fig 1) consists of the VR device (Oculus Rift, Smartphone etc.) mounted on a camera tripod. One light sensor is attached to the screen of the VR-device to register the virtual scene shifting from white to black. A laser pen is also attached to the virtual device pointing at another light sensor approx. one meter from the tripod setup. Both light sensors are connected to an oscilloscope. When we move the VR device by turning the tripod, the light sensor illuminated by the laser pen registers the disappearance of the light. When the movement is detected, light sensor connected to the virtual device screen measures the light shift from the white plane disappearing in the virtual scene.

This allows us to measure the time from when the physical movement starts until in movement is visible in the virtual scene. We measured 5-10 times on each device and we present an average of the measured values.

The virtual setup running on the VR-device is a simple completely black virtual 3D scene with a white self-illuminated plane and a virtual stereo camera. The virtual camera is set up with normal VR movement controllers. For the mobile phone setup the Durovis Dive SDK[2] was used while for the Oculus rift setup

---

[1] http://unity3d.com
[2] http://www.durovis.com/sdk.html

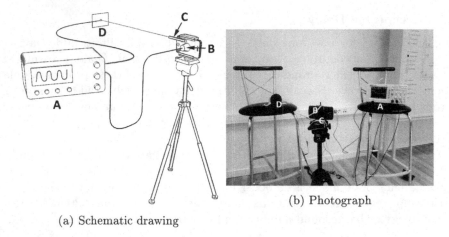

(b) Photograph

(a) Schematic drawing

Fig. 1. The Physical setup with the Oscilloscope (A), light sensor (B) attached to Virtual device, Laser pen (C) and light sensor (D) picking up the laser.

the Oculus Rift SDK[3] was used. This in order to set up a virtual reality scene with an absolute minimum of content optimised for a highest possible frame-rate, giving consistent values of multiple hundred frames per second and to use the build in VR movement controllers. The OculusRift devices were connected to a fast laptop[4].

The virtual scene consists of a white plane on a black background. The camera faces the white plane from a large distance and is set to a very narrow field of view. The scene is tweaked so that the display is completely white initially. Because of narrow field of view the camera is very sensitive to rotation. This means that even a small rotation in the headset leads to the screen changing colour from white to black, a change picked up by the light sensor.

4   Results and Discussion

Measured delay is simply the time from the light sensor illuminated by the laser changes from bright to dark until the light sensor attached to the screen reports the same change. Table 1 shows the results from the systems we tested. Unsurprisingly, the dedicated hardware has much faster response rate. Further, the smartphones do not give developers access to control the vertical synchronisation setting, and it seems from the numbers that it is always on.

For the dedicated VR displays, v-synch has a large effect on total delay. While the Virtual scenes with V-sync off the frame-rate in the application was as high as 3000 fps, the one with V-sync on would hold a steady frame-rate at 60 fps. Turning off this feature introduces introduce visual artefacts, but reduces the

---

[3] https://developer.oculus.com/
[4] Windows 7, Intel i7 - 3740 QM CPU @ 2,70 ghz, NVIDIA Quadro K2000M - 2048 mb DDR3

Table 1. Results from delay measurements.

VR Display	Avg.	Min.	Max.
Oculus Rift dev kit 1, v-sync ON	63 ms	58 ms	70 ms
Oculus Rift dev kit 1, v-sync OFF	14 ms	2 ms	22 ms
Oculus Rift dev kit 2, v-sync ON	41 ms	35 ms	45 ms
Oculus Rift dev kit 2, v-sync OFF	4 ms	2 ms	5 ms
Samsung Galaxy S4(GT-I9505)	96 ms	75 ms	111 ms
Samsung Galaxy S5	46 ms	37 ms	54 ms
iPhone 5s	78 ms	59 ms	96 ms
iPhone 6	78 ms	65 ms	91 ms

delay significantly. Without vertical synchronisation, these products can react very fast. Smartphones on the other hand are much slower, with delays close to 100 ms for most models. The exception is the Samsung S5 which has a delay less than 50ms. This result is similar to the Oculus Dev kit 2 with V-sync on. The screen in the Samsung S5 is actually the same as in the Oculus Dev kit 2 and the result confirms the similarity between the two devices.

These results come with some caveats. Despite our efforts, the rendered scene might not turn instantly from white to black between one frame and the next. Intermediate frames should show up as plateaus in the oscilloscope output, but we cannot be completely sure the animated movement did not show a frame or a few of parts of the white square. However, consistent results indicate that this is unlikely.

5   Conclusions and Future Work

We have presented a simple and precise solution for measuring delay in VR-systems. In contrast to DiLuca's [3] and other previous work, our system are able to detect delays in instantaneous, jerky movements. Earlier systems have generally relied on smooth, continuous movements, which are quite alien to a real user in a chaotic game. Jerald finds in 2012 [4] that users are most sensitive to delays when their movement changes direction. Current and future VR technology often employ prediction to reduce delay during continuous motion, which does work when motion changes. Thus, measuring delay for these sudden movements produces results more aligned with the sensitivity of users. Our setup does not require any modifications to the VR-systems to measure their delay, and can thus easily be applied to new hardware as soon as it becomes available.

Regarding how short delay is *good enough* both developer guidelines and than scientific papers mostly agree, placing ideal delay at less than 20 ms[4]. Even if the numbers comes from a simulated environment it gives a quality study of human perception when it comes to noticing latency.

With this in mind, it seems clear that the phones are too slow. Both of the latest models of iPhone, as well as the older Samsung have latencies around 100 ms, which all sources agree is far too slow. The older phones are not designed to run

VR systems, but these results give us a picture of the difference of yesterday's standards and the present specifications needed for pleasant VR experiences on mobil. In this picture the Samsung Galaxy S5 is closer to acceptable. Depending on which limits you use, an average value of 46 ms is either barely acceptable or somewhat too slow. However, Samsung markets some phones clearly as VR-devices, such as Samsung Note 4 and the upcoming Samsung Note 5. These are currently the only devices working with Gear VR, their new system for combining phones with VR. Our results from the Galaxy S5 indicates that some optimisations for VR are already included in this phone.

Oculus Rift in both versions respond extremely fast with v-synch off, fast enough to satisfy most guidelines. With synchronisation on, on the other hand, they are barely fast enough. The same guidelines that recommend 20 ms delay also claim v-synch is important for user experience. We found no way of satisfying both the delay requirement and the requirement to use vertical synchronisation at once. Oculus Rift is advertised to contain a built in latency tester. We did not find documentation on how to use the, nor did we find any description on how it works. Comparing our results with the output of this hardware would be interesting.

Development of new VR technologies, both dedicated and mobile, is progressing at a rapid pace these days, and not all the systems presented here will be current by the time this paper is published. The experiment setup on the other hand should be useable for any new system, and we hope to update our data with new systems when they become available. Other factors influencing user experience should also be studied in more detail, as well as their interaction with delay.

References

1. Carmack, J.: Latency Mitigation Strategies (2013),
   https://www.twentymilliseconds.com/post/latency-mitigation-strategies/
2. Davis, S., Nesbitt, K., Nalivaiko, E.: A Systematic Review of Cybersickness. In: IE 2014. ACM, New York (2014)
3. Di Luca, M.: New Method to Measure End-to-End Delay of Virtual Reality. Presence: Teleoperators and Virtual Environments 19(6), 569–584 (2010)
4. Jerald, J., Whitton, M., Brooks, F.P.: Scene-Motion Thresholds During Head Yaw for Immersive Virtual Environments
5. Jerald, J.J.: Scene-Motion- and Latency-Perception Thresholds for Head-Mounted Displays PhD thesis (2009)
6. Kijima, R., Ojika, T.: Reflex HMD to compensate lag and correction of derivative deformation. In: Proceedings IEEE Virtual Reality 2002 (2002)
7. Raaen, K., Petlund, A.: How Much Delay Is There Really in Current Games? In: ACM MMsys, pp. 2–5 (2015)
8. Swindells, C., Dill, J., Booth, K.: System lag tests for augmented and virtual environments. In: Proceedings of the 13th Annual ACM ..., vol. 2, pp. 161–170 (2000)

MindSpace: A Cognitive Behavioral Therapy Game for Treating Anxiety Disorders in Children

Barbara Göbl[1], Helmut Hlavacs[1], Jessica Hofer[2], Isabelle Müller[2],
Hélen Müllner[2], Claudia Schubert[2], Halina Helene Spallek[2],
Charlotte Rybka[2], and Manuel Sprung[2]

[1] University of Vienna, Research Group Entertainment Computing
[2] University of Vienna, Faculty of Psychology

Abstract. We describe the design process and implementation of the serious game MindSpace. MindSpace provides a playful setting for treating children with a variety of social and specific anxiety disorders. An age-appropriate approach is explained, taking a closer look on cognitive-behavioral techniques, how they are implemented within a game setting and what special needs to take into account when designing for children in a therapeutic context.

1 Introduction

Anxiety disorders are among the leading psychological conditions in children and adolescents. Research undertaken in western countries reports prevalence figures of 10% and higher. They can potentially lead to anxiety disorders and depression in adult age, substance abuse or even suicide attempts [8]. Cognitive Behavioural Therapy (CBT) is an established treatment form to tackle these psychological conditions. Research suggests that CBT is not only as effective as pharmacotherapy but might also be superior in maintaining long-term beneficial effects [7].

However, several issues remain. Low availability of trained CBT therapists, as well as financial or time related problems [10], hinder access to therapeutical treatment. Given the high prevalence of anxiety disorders, this led to exploration of different alternatives to face-to-face treatment, such as group treatment, self-help delivered via telephone or computer supported treatment [11,12]. Many approaches to computerized CBT (CCBT) have been taken in recent years. Video games are a popular approach amongst children and were already successfully applied in several medical and psychological fields such as chemotherapy, chronic disease management or post-traumatic stress disorder [3,13]. By developing the serious game *MindSpace*, we aim to address the above mentioned issues and support therapists and children during treatment.

2 Related Work

A variety of CCBT programs have been developed during recent years, with implementation being heavily dependant on resources, disorder and target group.

© IFIP International Federation for Information Processing 2015
K. Chorianopoulos et al. (Eds.): ICEC 2015, LNCS 9353, pp. 463–468, 2015.
DOI: 10.1007/978-3-319-24589-8_41

Regarding our young audience, projects such as *BRAVE-ONLINE* [14,15] and *Camp Cope-a-lot* [9] come into focus. *BRAVE-ONLINE* mimicks sessions as they take place in face-to-face therapy and is accompanied by a therapist who is introduced via telephone and keeps up contact via mail. It aims to attract children with cartoon images and appropriate multimedia content. The *Camp Cope-A-Lot* CD (CCCD) targets children aged 7-12. Various media are used to provide affective education, teach relaxation techniques, give homework and go through exposure situations. To motivate the child, computer games are introduced as rewards. Instructions are included to allow non-trained supervisors to support the child. *gNats* [5] provides a video game approach to CBT, targeting 10-15 year old adolescents. It is intended to be used alongside face-to-face therapy and showcases the positive responses of both clinicians and adolescents to CCBT. Another example is *Treasure Hunt*, also fully implemented within a game setting and designed to support face-to-face therapy. The player is taken upon a ship and sent on a treasure hunt. Several tasks and mini-games include the principles of CBT. It is important to mention, that evaluation of programs who are exclusive to face-to-face treatment showed improvement in anxiety and depression, even without the help of trained therapists [11].

3   Psychological Background

CBT combines cognitive and behavioral aspects and is based on the idea of emotion, thoughts and behavior deeply affecting our well-being [1]. One of the main goals is to identify, control and adjust irrational behaviour and damaging thoughts. Some of the main aspects included in child CBT treatments are: assessment, psycho-education, coping techniques, exposure procedures and contingency management [6]. *Assessment* refers to both a first diagnosis as well as monitoring of the changes over time. An important part of assessment is to identify anxiety-provoking situations and put them into order. *Psycho-Education* relays important and helpful information about anxiety and its workings. Inaccurate views on anxiety and treatment are addressed to positively influence cognition and expectations. Furthermore, *Coping Techniques* include methods to help the child relax such as breathing techniques and muscle relaxation. Also, an important task of CBT is to raise awareness about maladaptive thoughts or self-talk and help adapt. *Exposure Procedures* refer to a gradual confrontation with the client's fears. Counterconditioning combines exposure with incompatible reactions such as relaxation. Extinction, on the other hand, confronts a client with anxiety triggering stimuli while using cognitive and behavioral techniques to control the situation and lower anxiety to a lower, manageable level. Lastly, *Contingency Management* puts emphasis on the consequences of a client's behavior, setting behaviour modification as a major goal. A traditional approach within cognitive-behavioral therapy is to work with rewards.

4   MindSpace

To address the problem of child anxiety disorders, *MindSpace*[1] was developed by an interdisciplinary team of computer scientist and psychologists. Concepts and therapy modules provided within the MindSpace game are loosely based on the "Modular Approach to Therapy for Children with Anxiety, Depression, Trauma, or Conduct Problems" [4] (MATCH). It is an evidence-based, specialized CBT manual giving detailed instructions on how to proceed throughout child CBT.

4.1   Game Design

MindSpace is a 2D, Flash based, jump & run game, targeting children aged 7-12. Special focus was put on the skill level of our young target group as menus and buttons are mostly represented by graphics only, using simple, recognizable symbols and audio tutorials throughout the game. Game graphics and player characters are designed in a comic style, tailored to our young players.

There are a number of aspects that characterize MindSpace's unique approach to CBT. Firstly, while many programs are based on linked multimedia content, we provide an extensive game environment. Secondly, MindSpace is very flexible in adapting to the specific fears of children as it provides a large set of different anxieties and situations for exposure tasks. Lastly, MindSpace was designed to be self-explanatory, hence, while possible to use it as addition to face-to-face therapy, it is also intended to work with little to no assistance.

4.2   Let's Play MindSpace

Firstly, the player will go through an introductory phase, introducing the game and its context as well as gathering data about his or her anxieties. The **Fear Ladder** screen provides a list of pre-selected anxieties, represented with an icon and text, that can be sorted within the steps of the ladder. The game will henceforth focus on the top-most anxiety. In the next step, the **Fear Thermometer** is used to put situations into order according to how anxious the child is about them. Afterwards, the player will be taken to the **Cockpit** of his or her space craft, a fully graphical representation of the game's main menu. Five menu options are provided, each linking to another module of the game:

The **Education Button** starts the astronaut's training consisting of 3 different videos that teach the astronaut about anxiety and coping techniques. Clicking the window to **Open Space and the Solar System**, 10 planets are shown. Each planet represents a level which corresponds to a situation that has been sorted into the fear thermometer. Flags mark the planets he has successfully managed to play through, giving the player a sense of accomplishment. Levels lead through exposure situations but can also allow to collect up to 100 stars to trade in for playroom items. The **Playroom** represents a major part of the motivational system of the game. Here, players can use the collected stars

---

[1] http://barbarella.cs.univie.ac.at/mindspace/MindSpace.html

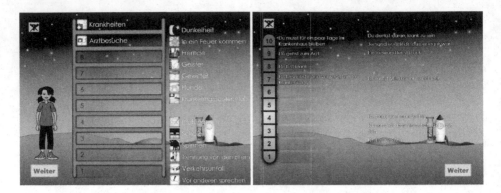

Fig. 1. Fear Ladder and Fear Thermometer

to exchange them for toys and items for their playroom. A further screen, the **Statistics Display** shows anxiety ratings for each individual level.

4.3   In-Game Exposure and Monitoring

The exposure situations are one of the core modules within the game. Each planet represents one of the situations sorted by the child using the fear thermometer. Exposure videos depict 15 different anxieties divided into 11 situations, each of them in different versions for both male and female players. This results in a total of 330 videos integrated in MindSpace, adding up to about 165 minutes of exposure material. Videos are composed using an age appropriate comic style[2]. They depict situations in third person perspective, starring the character chosen by the player. Common anxieties such as darkness, public speaking, school, strangers or traffic accidents are covered. Choice of anxieties was based on statistical data about pre-valence of specific anxieties in children [2].

Before and after exposure, measurements are taken on a scale from 1-10 indicating how much fear the child feels at this moment. This allows for monitoring progress and to provide optional rehearsals of coping and relaxation when measures are high.

4.4   In-Game Psycho-Education and Coping Techniques

Psycho-education and coping techniques, representing astronaut training, are included using instructional videos. In *Learning About Anxiety*, the goal is to introduce the workings of anxiety, explain how it occurs naturally and motivate the child for exposure practice and further treatment. The second video, *Cognitive STOP* introduces the STOP method. The children are taught to replace worried thoughts with better, helpful thoughts to handle anxious situations. Lastly, the *Quick Calming* video introduces relaxation techniques, helping the child to handle anxiety and relax when being fearful.

---

[2] http://www.pixton.com/

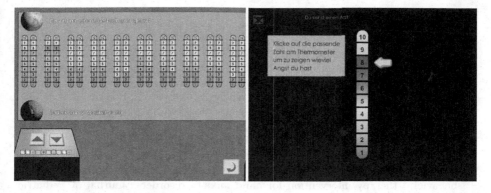

Fig. 2. The fear thermometer is a recurring motive used to display statistics and measure in-game anxiety

5   Conclusion

This paper provides a closer look on the CCBT game MindSpace and how psychological principles are implemented within a game setting. For one, we try to give insight into design considerations regarding our special target group. Both usability and game play need to be tailored to age and abilities. Also, therapy adherence is a important factor in psychological treatment that we tackle by including a reward system and additional motivational factors.

Experimental evaluation of MindSpace poses an important future task. While separate modules can be singled out for testing, such as efficacy of exposure tasks or the reward system, testing the overall effect of the game within clinical test groups is a long-term goal.

References

1. Kognitive Verhaltenstherapie, http://www.gesundheitsinformation.de/kognitive-verhaltenstherapie.2136.de.html
2. Beesdo, K., Knappe, S., Pine, D.S.: Anxiety and anxiety disorders in children and adolescents: Developmental issues and implications for DSM-V. The Psychiatric clinics of North America 32(3), 483–524 (2009)
3. Ceranoglu, T.A.: Video games in psychotherapy. Review of General Psychology 14(2), 141–146 (2010)
4. Chorpita, B.F., Weisz, J.R.: Modular Approach to Therapy for Children with Anxiety, Depression, Trauma, or Conduct Problems (MATCH-ADTC). Satellite Beach, FL: PracticeWise, LLC (2009)
5. Coyle, D., McGlade, N., Doherty, G., O'Reilly, G.: Exploratory evaluations of a computer game supporting cognitive behavioural therapy for adolescents. In: Proceedings of the SIGCHI Conference on Human Factors in Computing Systems, CHI 2011, pp. 2937–2946. ACM, New York (2011)
6. Gosch, E.A., Flannery-Schroeder, E., Mauro, C.F., Compton, S.N.: Principles of Cognitive-Behavioral therapy for anxiety disorders in children. Journal of Cognitive Psychotherapy: An International Quarterly 20(3), 247–262 (2006)

7. Gould, R.A., Otto, M.W., Pollack, M.H., Yap, L.: Cognitive behavioral and pharmacological treatment of generalized anxiety disorder: A preliminary meta-analysis. Behavior Therapy 28(2), 285–305 (1997)
8. Kendall, P.C., Compton, S.N., Walkup, J.T., Birmaher, B., Albano, A.M., Sherrill, J., Ginsburg, G., Rynn, M., McCracken, J., Gosch, E., Keeton, C., Bergman, L., Sakolsky, D., Suveg, C., Iyengar, S., March, J., Piacentini, J.: Clinical characteristics of anxiety disordered youth. Journal of Anxiety Disorders 24(3), 360–365 (2010)
9. Khanna, M.S., Kendall, P.C.: Computer-assisted CBT for child anxiety: The Coping Cat CD-Rom. Cognitive and Behavioral Practice 15(2), 159–165 (2008)
10. March, S., Spence, S.H., Donovan, C.L.: The efficacy of an internet-based cognitive-behavioral therapy intervention for child anxiety disorders. Journal of Pediatric Psychology 34(5), 474–487 (2009)
11. Proudfoot, J., Goldberg, D., Mann, A., Everitt, B., Marks, I., Gray, J.A.: Computerized, interactive, multimedia cognitive-behavioural program for anxiety and depression in general practice. Psychological Medicine, 217–227 (2003)
12. Proudfoot, J., Ryden, C., Everitt, B., Shapiro, D.A., Goldberg, D., Mann, A., Tylee, A., Marks, I., Gray, J.A.: Clinical efficacy of computerised cognitive-behavioural therapy for anxiety and depression in primary care: randomised controlled trial. The British Journal of Psychiatry 185(1), 46–54 (2004)
13. Radkowski, R., Huck, W., Domik, G., Holtmann, M.: Serious games for the therapy of the posttraumatic stress disorder of children and adolescents. In: Shumaker, R. (ed.) Virtual and Mixed Reality, Part II, HCII 2011. LNCS, vol. 6774, pp. 44–53. Springer, Heidelberg (2011)
14. Spence, S.H., Donovan, C.L., March, S., Gamble, A., Anderson, R., Prosser, S., Kercher, A., Kenardy, J.: Online CBT in the treatment of child and adolescent anxiety disorders: Issues in the development of BRAVE Online and two case illustrations. Behavioural and Cognitive Psychotherapy 36, 411–430 (2008)
15. Spence, S.H., Donovan, C.L., March, S., Gamble, A., Anderson, R.E., Prosser, S., Kenardy, J.: A randomized controlled trial of online versus clinic-based CBT for adolescent anxiety. Journal of Consulting and Clinical Psychology 79(5), 629–642 (2011)

Noise Modeler: An Interactive Editor and Library for Procedural Terrains via Continuous Generation and Compilation of GPU Shaders

Johan K. Helsing and Anne C. Elster

Norwegian University of Science and Technology (NTNU), Trondheim, Norway
johanhelsing@gmail.com, elster@ntnu.no

Abstract. In online procedural generation, content is generated as the game is running on the consumers computer. Our GPU-based Noise Modeler composites noise and other functions through a flow-graph editor similar to the ones used by procedural shader editors and offline terrain generators. Our framework enables non-programmers to edit models for procedural terrain while observing the effect of changes immediately in a real-time preview. Each time a change is made to the model, a corresponding GLSL shader function is automatically generated. The shader is then compiled, and used to render a real-time terrain preview.

Keywords: Online terrain generation, noise synthesis, real-time procedural content generation, stochastic implicit surface modeling.

1 Introduction and Background

In many recent games, an extremely vast and explorable world is one of the main features. Some recent games and their terrain models are shown below:

Ideally, the shipped game executable should be able to – without any involvement of humans – generate worlds that are virtually endless. Such terrains may be generated by combining and transforming noise functions [2, 4], and maybe running erosion algorithms on the generated terrain afterwards.

Issues with current approaches

Compositing noise is typically done by utilizing a noise generation library, such as libnoise or Accidental Noise Library. However, there are two problems with this approach: 1) these libraries are commonly written for the CPU and generating large amounts of terrain can be expensive and may limit the LOD. 2) tuning the terrain generation algorithm can be difficult. Whenever the terrain generation algorithm has changed, the game typically has to be rebuilt and relaunched in order to see if the change achieved the desired effect.

A game developer could improve the generation time by writing terrain generating code as a GPU shader [5, 7]. The issue with having a long feedback loop in the design process still remains. In the event of height-map-based terrain being

© IFIP International Federation for Information Processing 2015
K. Chorianopoulos et al. (Eds.): ICEC 2015, LNCS 9353, pp. 469–474, 2015.
DOI: 10.1007/978-3-319-24589-8_42

Table 1. Terrain models in some recent game engines. Static/dynamic indicates whether terrains are editable during run-time.

Engine	Released	Heightmaps	Displacement	Smooth voxel	Languages
Upvoid Engine	2014	No	No	Yes, dynamic	C#
Unity 4.3	2014	Dynamic	No	With plug-ins	JavaScript, C#, Boo
Unreal Engine 4	2014	Static	No	No	C++, UnrealScript
CryENGINE 3	2009	Dynamic	No	Prior to 3.5.3	C++
Torque Game Engine	2007	Static	No	No	C++, TorqueScript
Source Engine	2004	Static	Static	No	C++, Lua, Python, . . .
Panda 3D	2002	Dynamic	No	No	C++, Python

used, a solution could be to use a node-based procedural shader editor to assist in the development of the terrain shader. Such shader editors commonly let the terrain designer work with a graph-based editor to create a two-dimensional texture that can be previewed in real-time.

However, two issues arise from the fact that shader editors normally edit textures, not height maps, limiting previews are to diffuse maps, normal maps, bump maps and specular maps. Previews for height displacement maps are uncommon and diffuse and normal maps are a poor substitute. Also, these editors are commonly tied tightly to a specific rendering engine. This can be cumbersome when trying to integrate the terrain with other parts of the game engine, such as the AI and path finding.

Houdini, World Machine and Lithosphere, are three very useful graph-based noise synthesis tools that are commonly used to empower a traditional content creation process with procedural techniques. These tools, however, rely on creating terrain height map textures at, or before, build-time. They are hence not usable when creating an endless world, or a replayable game as discussed earlier.

This paper describes our Noise Modeler, a terrain generation framework designed to unify the flexibility and power of graph-based noise synthesis tools, such as Houdini, World Machine or Lithosphere, with in-game generation.

2 Our Approach

Current noise-synthesis tools offer real-time previews , but none of them are designed with in-game generation in mind. Due to their proprietary license and unavailable source code, there is little to be done with World Machine or Houdini. Lithosphere on the other hand, is AGPL3-licensed, so one way to remedy this would have been to extend or modify Lithosphere to also function as a library.

In ANL, libnoise, Lithosphere and many procedural shader editors, each node in the graph-model represents a 2D function. $f(x, y)$ which outputs a single value. Each node can have "sources", other nodes it depends on to calculate the result of $f(x, y)$. When terrain is generated, an output node is queried for its height at a given position. The graph is then traversed recursively to generate the output. Each node is responsible for querying its sources for the values needed to compute its output.

Our Noise Modeler, however, use nodes to represent function *calls*. I.e. the nodes are not using sources to answer a query, but model the the input position is inserted in one end of the graph and then the corresponding function calls are then executed, and the output is then read from the other end of the graph. This model is quite similar to the one used by Houdini.

The advantage of modeling the graph this way, is that the inputs and outputs of the graph are much more flexible with regard to supported terrain representations, i.e. it can easily be used to model voxel terrains, vector displacement terrains or layered terrains.

Our library has been carefully implemented without dependencies on the GUI application. The follwing are the main three modules:

model provides an object-oriented representation of function graphs and their relationships. The interface provides ways to modify and create new graphs.
serialization serializes and parses the model graphs to and from JSON.
code generation generates GLSL functions equivalent to the function graphs.

The generated code is stand-alone, i.e. it does not rely on any textures or other buffers to compute the function values. It is thus callable from a wide range of shader stages, including fragment, vertex, tessellation and compute shaders. Its limited set of GLSL functionality is also easily portable to most platforms.

2.1 Noise and Stochasticc Terrains

Stochastic interpolation may be used to generates terrains by evaluating a large batch of noise values at once. Mandelbrot [8] uses a two-dimensional **fractional Brownian motion (fBm)**, as an approximation of terrain altitudes. Fournier et al. [3] rendered terrains using **stochastic interpolation**, an approximation of **fBm** by recursively interpolating values with a pseudo-random offset proportional to the distance between the data points interpolated.

A **procedural noise function**, may be used to approximate fBm. Our Noise Modeler uses an unpredictable continuous function with range approximately $[-1, 1]$ and an approximate frequency of 1 Hz for this work. Ideally, the noise should also be isotropic, meaning that regardless of how you rotate the noise, it will look similar. A formal definition of procedural noise can be found in [7].

On its own, noise is not a very close approximation to fBm, but by combining the function with itself scaled to different frequencies and amplitudes, it is possible to get an approximation satisfactory for terrain generation. This implementation of fBm is a common choice among applications that need simple procedurally generated terrains. Babington [1] has for example used this implementation to generate terrains for the NTNU HPC-Lab snow simulator. Babington used the algorithm with Perlin noise as the noise function. Nordahl [10] enhanced this implementation by providing a GUI that could be used to adjust the inputs to the fBm function while the simulator was running. Musgrave [9] also contains a comprehensive guide on other ways noise can be used as a building block to create a wide range of natural structures.

2.2   Generating Shaders

Generating the shaders consists of the following four steps:

1. *Generate a function declaration for the graph based on the external inputs and outputs.* In the case of height map terrains, this is usually a function that takes a single two-dimensional vector as an input parameter and returns a single float as a value parameter.
2. *Generate unique variable declarations for all connected outputs.* For each node, look at which outputs have edges to other nodes. For each of those outputs, generate a unique id and use it to generate a declaration for a GLSL variable.
3. *Sort the nodes topologically* so that nodes come before the nodes their outputs are connected to.
4. *Generate code for each node.* For each node, generate declarations and assignments to default values for all of its inputs. For each of the connected inputs, generate an assignment to the unique variable of the corresponding output. Then generate code specific to the node type. i.e. for a multiplication node, perform a multiplication or for a noise node, generate a call to the noise generating function. At last, generate assignments to unique variables for any of the node's outputs that are connected.

2.3   Using the Shaders

The generated shaders functions may be used in the follwoing two ways:

1. *To generate a height map* If the world's position coordinates are specified as shader attributes, the shader function can be used to render a patch of height values onto a two-dimensional frame buffer which can be transferred back to the CPU. In this format the height map is typically usable by many game engines, and it may be used as if it was a regular height map loaded from disk.
2. *Directly offsetting a vertex in a vertex shader.* Given the length and width coordinates of a vertex on flat surface, the shader function can be used to move the vertex along the length axis to the appropriate height. This technique works well with a wide variety of level-of-detail and tessellation algorithms. The terrain preview in our Noise Modeler is implemented using this approach.

3   Results

The developed software achieved what it was designed to do: It is an implementation of a graph-based editor for implicit procedural terrain that does not require explicit geometry to be generated before build-time to be usable by game engines. Thus, it is a tool usable by games that are designed to have endless worlds and feature unique content every playthrough.

One such example usage of the library, is the terrain editor itself. i.e. it uses GLSL code generated by the library to show a terrain preview. Another example, is a simple command line application (nmcli) that simply generates a GLSL function given a file containing a serialized implicit terrain surface. At last a benchmark application was developed which demonstrates how explicit geometry (height maps) can be generated and transferred to CPU memory.

Our library demonstrates that our approach makes it possible to generate explicit geometry for implicit terrains at interactive rates. This has been demonstrated in two ways: Firstly, by running the editor itself, it can be observed that a terrain preview is rerendered at interactive rates as the model is edited.

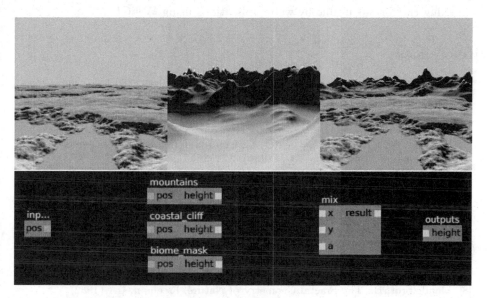

Fig. 1. Different biomes can be combined using a high-level mask, such as fractional-brownian motion (fbm) with a low frequency and few octaves.

Secondly, a more thorough benchmark was performed by Helsing [6]. In this benchmark, batch evaluation of large patches of a height map terrain was performed and compared with similar CPU-based noise libraries.

4   Conclusion

Most procedural terrain editors focus solely on generating height maps at the game developers computer, ignoring many powerful capabilities of procedural generation, the most important being replayability and vastness. Our framework shows that it is possible to model procedural terrains interactively in a user-friendly application, while at the same time retaining the ability to integrate with a game engine and generate explicit terrain geometry during run-time. The efficient computation of height values allowed an interactive, high-quality terrain preview to be updated with a vertex count comparable to state-of-the-art video games.

Our framework may be used to model height map terrains, and supports several popular algorithms for stochastic implicit terrains. Our framework may also model and generate GLSL code for — although not preview — other types of terrains, including voxel terrains and vector displacement terrains. It may thus integrate well with a variety of game engines with different approaches to terrain modeling.

Future work includes adding support for previewing additional types of terrain representations such as voxel terrain and vector displacement terrain. In addition an effort to port the library to JavaScript has been started[1] with the intention of making the format usable by web applications using WebGL.

References

[1] Babington, K.: Terrain Rendering Techniques for the HPC-Lab Snow Simulator. Master's Thesis. Norwegian University of Science and Technology (2012)

[2] Ebert, D.S., et al.: Texturing & Modeling: A Procedural Approach. Morgan Kaufmann (2003)

[3] Fournier, A., Fussell, D., Carpenter, L.: Computer Rendering of Stochastic Models. Communications of the ACM 25(6), 371–384 (1982)

[4] Gamito, M.: Techniques for Stochastic Implicit Surface Modelling and Rendering. PhD thesis. England: University of Sheffield (2009)

[5] Geiss, R.: Generating Complex Procedural Terrains Using the GPU. In: GPU Gems 3, pp. 7–37. Addison-Wesley Professional (2007)

[6] Helsing, J.K.: Framework for Real-Time Editing of Endless procedural Terrains. Master's Thesis. Norwegian University of Science and Technology (2014)

[7] Lagae, A., et al.: State of the Art in Procedural Noise Functions. In: Eurographics 2010-State of the Art Reports (2010)

[8] Mandelbrot, B.: The Fractal Geometry of Nature. Freeman, CA (1982)

[9] Kenton Musgrave, F.: Procedural Fractal Terrains. In: Texturing & Modeling: A Procedural Approach. Morgan Kaufmann (2003)

[10] Nordahl, A.: Enhancing the HPC-Lab Snow Simulator with More Realistic Terrains and Other Interactive Features. Master's Thesis. Norwegian University of Science and Technology (2013)

---

[1] https://github.com/johanhelsing/noisemodelerjs

Serious Games: Is Your User Playing or Hunting?

Sofya Baskin[1], Sharon Anavi-Goffer[1], and Anna Zamansky[2]

[1] Ariel University, Department of Behavioral Sciences, Ariel, Israel
[2] University of Haifa, Information Systems Department, Haifa, Israel

Abstract. There is an increasing demand for entertainment applications developed for pets, in particular for dogs and cats. However, play interaction between animals and technological devices still remains an uncharted territory both for animal behavior and entertainment computing scientific communities. While there is a lot of anecdotal evidence of pets playing digital games, the nature of animal-computer play interactions is still not understood. In this paper we report on empirical findings based on observing and analyzing dog-tablet game interactions. Using categories emerging from our data analysis, we construct an ethogram, a "catalogue" of behavioral patterns typical of dog-tablet interactions. Based on our data analysis, we hypothesize that the nature of the observed interactions is that of predatory behavior, in response to stimuli in the form of "prey-like" virtual objects displayed on the screen. Based on our hypothesis, we further propose some questions for future investigation, and raise some issues that need to be addressed by game developers when targeting dogs as their users.

1 Introduction

The emerging discipline of *animal-computer interaction* (ACI) [1] aims to understand the interaction between animals and computing technology within the contexts in which the animals habitually live. Interactions between dogs and technology have been studied mainly in the context of working and assistance dogs, trained to issue alerts (on upcoming seizures due to epilepsy or low blood sugar in diabetic patients), e.g., by pulling on a string 1 or pushing a button on a multi-touch screen [3]. But in these scenarios dogs interact with a device mainly because they are *trained* to do so. While digital game playing for the purpose of *entertainment* has been explored for other animals, such as apes [4], cats [5], and pigs [6], dog users remain underrepresented in this context. And yet dogs playing tablets is a wide-spreading phenomenon that seems to be here to stay. Hundreds of mobile applications have hit the market; over 10,000 YouTube videos can be found using the keywords "dog playing tablet". In the last years several dog training centers were reported to open classes teaching dogs to use mobile devices ([7,8]).

How should we design digital games for pets, in which they find some recreational or other positive value? So far these questions have mainly been addressed from ethical [9] and philosophical perspectives [5], in some sense in a top-down way, deriving game design principles from more general theoretical principles. In this paper we propose to take a bottom-up approach[1] by asking what can we learn about digital game design by observing what dogs actually do when playing digital games. To the best of our knowledge, behavioral characteristics of pet interactions with tablets have not been systematically investigated. These characteristics, however, are key to answering questions such as what constitutes an animal-computer play interaction, what it means for an animal to be engaged by a digital game, and how it perceives virtual objects. Exploring these questions calls for applying research methodologies from *ethology*.

Ethology is the comparative study of animal behavior, studying the biological roots and meanings of animal actions. One of the key steps in this process is constructing *ethograms*, which are quantitative descriptions of an animal's normal behavior. According to [11], "It is absolutely fundamental to any study of animal behavior to define what behavior types are being observed and recorded, and therefore production of an ethogram is always the first step in any animal behavior research". In this paper we take such a step by constructing an ethogram of typical behaviors dogs exhibit while playing digital games, based on analyzing video data of dog-tablet interactions.

2   The Empirical Study

Method. The first stage of the study included a careful selection of 32 videos of dogs playing digital games on tablet/iPad, according to the following selection criteria: (i) duration of each video: at least 25 seconds; (ii) minimal human intervention in the video fragment; (iii) dogs of small and medium breeds.

The main source for the video footage was YouTube. The benefits and limitations of using YouTube data for studying animal behavior have been extensively discussed in [12]. This methodology is based on the premise that the probability of capturing any given behavior is dramatically increased when the number of people obtaining the footage is not restricted to academics but is widened to the public. This is of course particularly true for the case of dog-tablet interaction: while a large variety of dogs is usually not easily available for academic studies, dog owners' videos of their pets are easily available. Nevertheless, there are limitations in terms of the use of such videos: they may not be chronologically or sequentially correct, they may be edited or even fake. For this reason we excluded from our analysis videos which included any type of editing, such as cutting scenes, speed modification, etc.

Results. An ethogram is a list of behaviors performed by particular individuals in a particular environment and for a particular purpose. Ethograms for the same species may differ depending on the individuals, environment and, most of all, the purpose of the research [11]. For constructing an ethogram, each video was tagged with behavioural patterns observed in it. The patterns were divided into the following three types:

---

[1] In a popular blog article [10] a similar approach was taken by looking at YouTube videos of dogs and cats playing iPad games. Their focus was however on the question whether dogs or cats are "better iPad players" (cats scored a higher proficiency). No description of the data collection and analysis methodologies was provided.

Attention to Tablet: Activities expressing an interest towards physical aspects of the tablet without getting into physical contact with it. This includes *eye-tracking the virtual object* and *head twisting*.

Actions Physically Directed at tablet: Activities based on a physical contact with tablet or moving around it, including scratching the tablet screen, catching the virtual object by teeth, pushing the tablet, licking the tablet, jumping around the tablet with attention to virtual object or performing fox jump. Fox jump (also known as a stiff legged jump) is a typically predatory movement, the dog rearing up on his hind legs and slamming both straightened and held rigid front legs down to the ground. The dog throws significant weight onto the front legs creating a great deal of downward force. Sometimes dogs do fox jumps in predatory games with small balls.

Actions not Directed at Tablet: Other activities not directly targeting the tablet, including heavy panting, nose licking, nervous yawn and catching the owner's hands.

The observed behavioral patterns together with their classification are summarized in Table 1 below. Their occurrence percentage (out of 32 videos) appears in brackets.

Table 1. Behavioral patterns classified according to basic types of behaviors

Category	Attention to tablet	Physically directed at tablet	Not directed at tablet
Behavior	Eye-tracking the object (87%) Head twisting (9%)	Scratching the screen (90%) Catching object by teeth (56%) Licking the tablet (25%) Fox jump (12,5%) Pushing tablet by nose (9%) Jumping around the tablet with attention to object (3%)	Heavy panting (16%) Trying to catch owner's hand (15%) Nose licking (9%) Nervous yawn (3%)

The distribution of game types was as follows (the number in brackets is the number of videos out of 32): fish catching (14), Fruit Ninja (10), running rat (4), running laser pointer (3), volleyball (1).

3   Discussion

Predatory Play or Serious Hunting?

All the observed behavioral patterns obtained in our ethogram directed at the tablet seem to be different types of either *predatory behavior or predatory play*. Predation is the act of an individual or group of individuals of one species (the predator) consuming an animal of another species (the prey). Predation (or hunting) consists series of stages: encounter, detection, recognition, attack, capture and consumption. Predatory play is a seemingly aimless manipulation of objects or rapid movements, but in fact may be similar to the first stages of predation without consumption.

The observed actions in the first two ethogram categories, attention to tablet and physically directed at tablet, may all be classified as different types of encounter, detection, recognition, attack, capture, all of which are components of both serious hunting and predatory play. Moreover, *none* of the dogs exhibit key social play postures such as play bow (the front-end-lowered rear-end-up position of play intention posture) and raised forepaw, reinforcing our belief that we are witnessing predatory behavior (either serious or playful). More concretely, the behavioral patterns we witnessed may be classified as fixed action patterns (FAPs) of predatory behavior, rather than social play behavior. FAPs are predictable, genetically predetermined and rigid sequences of behavior, triggered by simple stimuli called *sign stimuli* and resulting in simple responses [13]. Once triggered, these responses are unchangeable and must be carried to completion. In our context the sign stimuli are the virtual objects which have some characteristics of natural prey, such as size and mobility. Due to the fact that FAPs are genetically encoded reflex-like actions, the behavioral patterns in dog-tablet interactions with prey-like digital games are expected to be highly predictable, leaving almost no expressive freedom to the dog.

While all participants exhibited predatory behavior patterns, it is likely that their intensity varies depending to dog breed. In most breeds, the intensity of the predatory response has also been significantly reduced, while in others certain fragments of predatory patterns have been reinforced through selective breeding [14]. While in most breeds, the intensity of the predatory response has been significantly reduced, hunting breeds, save most of behavioral activities and, an opposite, some of predatory behaviors were increased [15].Terrier breeds have a strong predatory response that is directed toward small mammals, and are therefore expected to have the strongest reaction to prey-like digital game. It is interesting to explore the dependency of the behavioral patterns exhibited by participants on their breed.

We do not have enough data to make a clear distinction between predatory play and actual hunting. Moreover, the same dog may start out the interaction in predatory play, but end up hunting seriously (as we believe was the case in several videos). During this process, its frustration from not being able to perform the consummatory act may grow, as described next.

Digital Games - a Source of Frustration?
The third type of actions (not directed at tablet) deserves special attention. We believe that these actions may be signs of nervousness and frustration which take the following two forms:

Displacement Activity: Displacement (ambivalent) behavior occurs when an animal is in some kind of a motivational conflict between two or more tendencies. If such conflict remains unresolved, this is likely to result in a state of frustration and nervousness. Signs of such behavior are *nose licking* (generally considered a submissive behavior, showing ambivalence) and *yawning*, (if performed not during rest, it is also usually interpreted as displacement activity in ambivalent situations) [11].

Redirected Aggression: Aggressive behavior may be redirected towards other targets if the ones engaged in the confrontation are unreachable. The difference between this type of behavior and displacement activity is that in the former the target for the behavior is substituted, rather than the behavior itself. In our observations, redirected aggressions was expressed in situations where dogs playing tablet switched their attention to the hands of their owner during their interaction. Thus due to their inability to catch the virtual object, they redirected their aggression towards real objects. This also indicates that aggressive dogs playing with a tablet may be dangerous to their surroundings.

These types of behavior may be an indication of a significant motivational conflict caused by predatory motivation together with the inability to commit the final consummatory act (catching the virtual object), which leads to frustration and stress of the dog. This leads to the question which individual characteristics of participants, games or contexts are more likely to induce stress instead of enjoyment in game interactions.

Fruit Ninja, Running rat or Something Completely Different?

Predatory FAPs are triggered by sign stimuli, which is usually a subset of sensory information. Humans use a much richer set of sensory information than animals: e.g., observing that our virtual object has ears and nose of a particular form and has grey color, we classify it as a rat. However, dogs seem to have their own different subset of associations: e.g., they do not seem to make a clear distinction between a rat and a laser as the virtual moving object. Yet, they may distinguish between these objects and fish or Fruit Ninja objects: catching objects with their teeth mostly occurred in fruit ninja (7 out of 17) and fish catching (5 out of 17). Interestingly, while they exhibited a stronger predatory reaction to Fruit Ninja objects, fox jumps, strongly associated with predatory behavior, occurred *only* in animal-like objects (fish and rat). This leads to the question how behavioral characteristics of virtual objects are related to the different types of predatory behaviors.

4   Summary and Future Research

Videos of pets playing iPad games going viral on social networks, as well as an increasing number of applications with pets as their target audience call for a deeper understanding of animals' behaviors and perceptions in these interactions, as well as of the benefits and potential dangers of digital game playing for animals. While animal-tablet interactions have been explored for cats, apes and pigs, to the best of our knowledge, this is the first study which addresses dog behavior in this context.

In this paper we have presented a preliminary ethogram of dog behavior patterns during interactions with digital games. It unveils the complexity and ambiguity of dog-tablet interactions, showing a variety of predatory behavior patterns, ranging over exploration, physical acts directed at the tablet, signs of frustration and redirected aggression.

It is evident that dogs are easily attracted to digital games. In light of our results, one needs to take into account that some dogs may find digital games stressful. Nevertheless it seems that playing digital games has a potential of improving the dogs' welfare: by cognitive stimulation and enrichment, stress reduction, physical exercise via typical game movements, etc. We plan to further investigate this aspect, using non-invasive methods, such as cortisol level in saliva and heart rate measurements.

The limitations of our study need to be taken into account. An important issue is the use of YouTube videos, in light of the fact that we have no control over the conditions in which the video footage was taken. While this may be acceptable for producing a preliminary ethogram, further data needs to be collected in controlled experiments to validate the results.

References

1. Mancini, C.: Animal-computer interaction: a manifesto. Interactions 18(4), 69–73 (2011)
2. Robinson, C.L., Mancini, C., van der Linden, J., Guest, C., Harris, R.: Canine-centered interface design: supporting the work of diabetes alert dogs. In: The 32nd Annual ACM Conference on Human Factors in Computing Systems, pp. 3757–3766 (2014)
3. Zeagler, C., Gilliland, S., Freil, L., Starner, T., Jackson, M.: Going to the Dogs: Towards an Interactive Touchscreen Interface for Working Dogs. In: UIST ACM Symposium on User Interface Software and Technology Honolulu, HI, USA (2014)
4. Boostrom, H.: Problem-Solving with Orangutans (Pongo pygmaeus and Pongo abelii) and Chimpanzees (Pan troglodytes): Using the IPAD to Provide Novel Enrichment Opportunities. Diss. Texas A&M University (2013)
5. Westerlaken, M., Gualeni, S.: Digitally complemented zoomorphism: a theoretical foundation for human-animal interaction design. In: The 6th International Conference on Designing Pleasurable Products and Interfaces. ACM (2013)
6. Playing with pigs, http://www.wired.co.uk/news/archive/2013-03/11/human-animal-gaming
7. iPad classes for dogs, http://www.theregister.co.uk/2013/08/28/ipad_classes_for_dogs_offered_in_new_york/
8. iPad classes for dogs, http://www.padgadget.com/2014/03/21/idog-clinics-use-ipad-to-teach-dogs-to-read/
9. Väätäjä, H.K., Pesonen, E.K.: Ethical issues and guidelines when conducting HCI studies with animals. In: CHI 2013 Extended Abstracts on Human Factors in Computing Systems. ACM (2013)
10. Analyzing cat and dog tablet interactions, http://www.bigfishgames.com/blog/chew-on-this-analyzing-200-dogs-cats-playing-with-ipads/
11. Mills, D.S., Marchant-Forde, J.N.: eds. The encyclopedia of applied animal behaviour and welfare. In: CABI (2010)
12. Nelson, X.J., Fijn, N.: The use of visual media as a tool for investigating animal behaviour. Animal Behaviour 85(3), 525–536 (2013)

13. Gadbois, S., Sievert, O., Reeve, C., Harrington, F.H., Fentress, J.C.: Revisiting the concept of behavior patterns in animal behavior with an example from food-caching sequences in Wolves (Canis lupus), Coyotes (Canis latrans), and Red Foxes (Vulpes vulpes). Behavioural Processes 110, 3–14 (2015)
14. Fox, M.W.: The Dog: Its Domestication and Behavior. Garland Press, New York (1978)
15. Scott, J.P.: Genetics and the Social Behavior of the Dog. University of Chicago Press (1965)

Space for Seriousness?
Player Behavior and Motivation in Quiz Apps

Heinrich Söbke

Bauhaus-Universität Weimar, Bauhaus-Institute for Infrastructure Solutions (b.is), Germany
heinrich.soebke@uni-weimar.de

Abstract. Quiz apps as a genre have seen a huge leap in distribution over the past year. Their applicability to any subject matter of any subject area, along with their ubiquitous availability, means they could be considered as a potential learning tool. However, popular quiz apps are optimized for entertainment. Furthermore, multiple choice questions have so far been used predominantly for assessment but not for learning. We have examined popular quiz apps in a two-stage approach. First, test persons played quiz apps of their choice on a daily basis and took field notes. A questionnaire for an online survey was then developed from the results. Our research questions were: (1) What are the contexts in which quiz apps are played? (2) What game mechanics are perceived as motivating? The survey with 396 participants helped us identify usage characteristics and the main motivations for utilizing these apps. Among relevant findings are a distinct willingness to learn and the phenomenon of sociability, i.e. the motivation to play with and compete against friends.

Keywords: Quiz apps, Mobile gaming, Mobile learning, Game design, Educational app.

1 Introduction

The *QuizClash* app [1] came to the public's notice in Germany in the last months of 2013. This app is based on quizzes and employs simple game mechanics. Two players compete by answering multiple choice questions asynchronously in six rounds. The player with the most correct answers wins the match and is rewarded with a number of points. These points are accumulated and determine the rank within the overall community of players. The app has reached a huge audience: in January 2014 it had 8 million players in Germany [2], and by the end of 2014 almost 20 million players had created an account in the German version. Furthermore, a TV show in German public-service broadcasting has been built around this game [3, 4].

QuizClash is just one example of a popular quiz app. There are other apps which enjoy similar popularity, as *QuizUp* [5, 6]. So there seems to be a tremendous potential for quiz apps. From an educational point of view it is very significant that there is evidence for learning. Pawelka et al. [7] received first positive results employing a QuizClash-like prototype, although the sample size was small. During our own game play we too noticed learning effects. Furthermore, reports from players themselves

K. Chorianopoulos et al. (Eds.): ICEC 2015, LNCS 9353, pp. 482–489, 2015.
DOI: 10.1007/978-3-319-24589-8_44

often indicate that learning is both a result of and a requirement for playing such a game successfully [4, 8]. The question thus arises whether quiz apps can be used as an educational tool. They seem to employ an attractive and proven game principle. Furthermore, they manifest all the characteristics of mobile apps that lead to a huge number of players and are recognized as beneficial for learning, namely easy accessibility, ubiquitous availability and connectivity, to name but a few [9]. Additionally, they can be applied to a great range of subject areas and knowledge levels ([10, 11]).

In order to evaluate in how far these theoretical assumptions apply to the usage of quiz apps in the field, we conducted an online survey with two main research questions (RQs) in mind: *What usage contexts are prevalent?(RQ 1)* and *What are the main elements that motivate individuals to play these games?(RQ 2)*. Amongst other, RQ 1 aims at the hypothesis that apps are used in a more casual manner and support short sessions of play. RQ 2 should help to identify those game elements which lead to a high attraction of quiz apps.

Our article is structured as followed: First we describe the experiment design, the online survey and different aspects of its results: the context for playing quiz apps is delineated (RQ 1). Thereafter we discuss players' preferences (RQ 2). Finally, we present the most important findings, develop answers to the research questions and summarize them in a conclusion.

2   Survey

2.1   Method and Demography

We began our approach in an exploratory way. Eleven participants in a student project for educational media were each required to play a quiz app of their choice for at least five minutes a day. They were asked to write down their experiences as field notes. After one week, field notes were merged in order to exchange experiences. Field notes continued to be taken for another week. These experiences served as input for the online survey. For example, it was observed that *QuizClash* [1] had been used as a medium in a drinking game. From this we concluded that quiz apps may be played in company. We therefore asked about this characteristic in the survey.

The resulting online-survey consisted of 45 questions. A call for participation was distributed within the social environment of the student project. Both digital and non-digital channels were used. Pursuing the approach of snowball-sampling, we asked participants to forward the survey to their friends. Facebook as a social network service is one of the digital channels used. Friends and relatives were also addressed directly. The survey was open for participation for almost a month, from 15 December 2014 to 8 January 2015. There were 396 participants in all, aged from 14 to 65 years; the average age was 25.3, the median 23. 60% were female and 40% male. 33% indicated that they were working. Another 61% were students, either at university or an upper school.

238 (60%) of the participants confirmed their use of quiz apps. Reasons for not playing quiz apps are a lack of interest or time (79%), not being aware of quiz apps (20%), and not having an appropriate IT device (6%). Other reasons given as textual

responses include self-protection, quality of questions, data privacy concerns, no game partner and too many in-game-advertisements. A conclusion from this distribution is that the lack of suitable hardware is not a significant reason not to play quiz apps. Those participants who denied playing quiz apps, have been asked if they play other quiz-based games. 108 stated not to such games at all, but 50 acknowledged. They were asked in an open question to describe, why they are attracted by these games (see Fig. 4).

2.2   Contexts of Playing Quiz Apps

Device. Quiz apps are played predominantly on a smartphone. 89% of all participants named it as their device for using the app. Another 9% use it in combination with a tablet. Just 2% play a quiz app only on a tablet.

Usage Profile. Only 5% of all participants refer to themselves as regular app users. We used a 5-point Likert scale (1: sporadically – 5: regular) to get respondents to describe their regularity of use. More than 2/3 of users chose an irregular usage pattern (1 and 2 points). 17% could not decide. Results for the question "How often do you use your quiz app?" revealed a similar result (see Fig. 1). Again, 2/3 claimed to use the app a few times a month. A small group of 4% said they used such an app for more than 30 minutes a day. Thus, while quiz apps are generally used more sporadically, there seems to be a small faction of players who play these apps intensively. We also asked how long players had been using quiz apps. 39% have been playing for over a year, 59% for less than a year but longer than a month. Some players stated that they had stopped playing quiz apps because the novelty appeal was no longer given and they were unable to detect any new elements. Nevertheless, there seems to be a tendency towards the long-term use of such apps.

Frequency of usage

Fig. 1. How often do you use quiz apps? (n=238)

We wanted to know the situations in which quiz apps are used. There proved to be four main categories: apps are used mostly while travelling and commuting (68%), followed by use in one's spare time (63%), during breaks (48%), and during work or lectures (44%) (see Fig. 2). The last value may have been influenced by the high percentage of students in the survey. This value may also have been responsible for increasing the percentage of players who do not use sound because it is inappropriate for their environment. Among the answers in the "Other" category were hospital stay, before bedtime and on the toilet. This last answer is supported by Kientz et al. [12], who state that games are among gadget-based activities during a visit to the toilet.

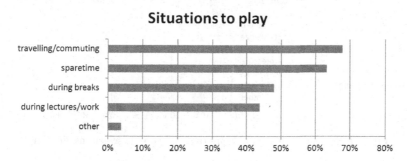

Fig. 2. In what situations do you use quiz apps? (n=238, multiple selections allowed)

2.3 Players' Preferences

Motivation. We asked players to choose their preferred reasons for playing quiz apps from a given set of possible motivations (see Fig. 3). Almost 70% of players indicated that they used these apps as a *pastime*. The next most important reasons are *sociability* and the prospect of acquiring new *general knowledge* (each scoring more than 50%). These reasons are followed by game-typical motivations such as *competition, fun, entertainment* and *challenge*. Importance is rarely attached to typical digital game features such as *achievements* and *avatar development*. Players are able to differentiate themselves from their friends and feel almost no *peer pressure*.

Reasons for Playing Quiz-Based Board Games. A third (50) of all respondents (158) who do not play quiz apps indicated that they played other quizzes, mostly board games such as *Trivial Pursuit* [13] and *Who Wants to Be a Millionaire?* (75%). They were asked to give reasons for playing those games in a non-digital form. It is striking to note that some reasons recur persistently – although no range of reasons was offered. These participants were not provided a closed question about their motivations as the app players, but an open question. Therefore we coded their answer using a coding scheme roughly based on the motivations indicated by the app placer faction. Fig. 4 shows the distribution of reasons named. *Learning* and *sociability* were mentioned by almost half the participants. These reasons were given more frequently than typical game attributes such as *challenge* and *fun and entertainment*. Motivations related to digital games, such as *avatar development* and *achievements* are not mentioned. Players differentiate between learning new facts and assessing their existing general knowledge.

Reasons to play quiz apps

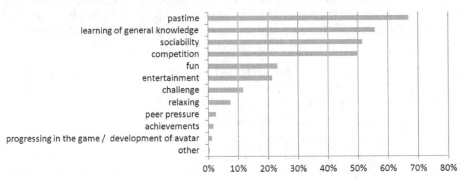

Fig. 3. Reasons for playing quiz apps (n=238, multiple selections allowed)

Reasons to play quiz-based games

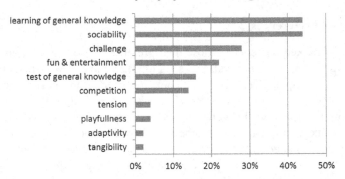

Fig. 4. Coded reasons ordered by frequency (n=50)

Opponents. Players prefer human opponents. We asked which type of opponent players usually faced: 92% compete with friends, 45% with random human opponents and 8% with bots. Another question looked at preferences for randomly assigned opponents or friends. 76% choose friends as their preferred opponents, while only 10% choose unknown opponents. For the remaining 15%, their preference depends on the situation.

Communities and Groups. Communities and groups are considered valuable for learning [14]. Thus we are interested in the extent to which quiz apps foster communities and groups. First, sociability is one of the most important reasons for playing quiz apps. Furthermore the technical support of groups is suggested as an improvement for the app.

We wanted to know if players use quiz apps in collaboration with other players. More than half of the players do this at least sometimes. The company of friends enables reflection: in another question we asked if questions and their answers were discussed.

55% mentioned direct conversations, and only 18% app chat and forums. Another 44% do not communicate about questions. Operating the app chat seems to be too cumbersome and using the forum means a change of medium. Therefore we assume that playing together with physically present friends is a prerequisite for reflection.

Games can foster friendship between players. Brüß et al. [15] found evidence in the social network game (SNG) Fliplife [16]: they asked players if they had developed friendships with other players originally unknown to them. 43% affirmed this assumption (n=267). As a measurement of the strength of the friendships that evolved, they asked if players had met in reality. 32% answered with yes, 52% had not met but did not exclude an encounter in future. We asked the same question: Has a player met a fellow player who s/he got to know in the quiz app? 8% of respondents confirmed. Although 8% is less than the equivalent percentage in the context of Fliplife, we consider it a remarkable figure. Fliplife is communication prone [17] whereas quiz apps rely more on previously formed groups.

Question Topics. Quiz apps often allow the player to select the topic for the questions. So what are the preferences when it comes to choosing a topic? Half the players prefer to choose from a given set of topics. This is implemented in *QuizClash* [1]. Another third wish to select from a larger catalogue of topics as in *QuizUp* [5]. The others voted for the option "Random topic". In another question we asked about the principles followed when players are able to influence the topic. The most influential principles are own strengths (84%) and personal interests (56%). However, assumed weaknesses of the opponent are also decisive elements (46%). Of negligible significance are "first topic that comes along" and "no strategy" (5%). Two respondents said they chose a topic according to their personal weaknesses in order to increase learning success.

3   Discussion

In the responses to RQ 1 (*What usage contexts are prevalent?*) we found evidence that quiz apps are mostly used in a casual way: they are played whenever people have some spare time and can become habitual. However, for educational use, it is important to examine if the urge to learn can lead to more regular play. Players are motivated to use such apps by the prospect of socializing with their friends. This has been observed in two ways. Firstly, most players prefer to play against their friends. Secondly, apps are used as a medium for playing a game in company with or against other people. These findings are also relevant for RQ 2 (*What are the main motivation elements to play these games?*). Quiz apps are mostly regarded as a leisure pastime. However, from an educational point of view participants indicated a strong motivation to improve their knowledge. One has to ask if this motivation can facilitate the educational process: how do players react to blatantly educational content in such an app? How can such content be integrated without endangering the high level of engagement? How do motivations change if there is an educational content? These are questions which have to be clarified in order to enable an educational application of quiz apps.

The survey participants mainly played *QuizClash* [1]. It may therefore not be feasible to draw general conclusions from the results. Equally, the participant sample is relatively young and may not be representative. However, we spread the call for participation broadly and managed to recruit a significant number of non app-players, which is why we are confident of representing a significant part of population. Nevertheless, we cannot estimate the percentage of app players and therefore the market potential of this app genre purely on the basis of this online survey.

A remarkable finding from an analysis of the field notes was the reluctance to pay for these apps. After all, the authors of the field notes were required to play such an app intensively, and more than half the field notes contained complaints about "disturbing advertisements". In the case of *QuizClash* it would have taken less than 3 € to switch off advertisements. Some of the students reported that they never install apps they have to pay for. Others mentioned that they had never set up a payment channel for app purchases before. One is therefore faced with the challenge of funding such an app in a manner that keeps it readily accessible.

4   Conclusions

The hype about quiz apps has declined. This was indicated by some survey participants who have since moved on to the next viral app. However, our findings suggest that there is a considerable core of players who are engaged in quiz apps continuously over a long period of time. As one main motivation of the players is learning (and players have reported that they do in fact learn from the apps), we consider quiz apps to be a promising educational tool. This estimation is additionally based on the high demand for sociability expressed by quiz app players in the survey. Despites of the genre's casual character, fellow players are seen as persons and not as mere resources, as can be observed in SNGs [18], and is even attributed to players in traditional multiplayer online games [19]. Therefore, the fact that quiz app players enjoy common play with friends is a valuable asset. One area of weakness to emerge from our survey is that individual players seem to have affinities to specific domains of content. These affinities have to be taken into account in designing a concept for educational use. A further issue is the disinclination to pay for an app, a challenge which has to be resolved.

References

1. FEO Media AB: QuizClash | Challenge your friends!, http://www.quizclash-game.com/
2. Trotier, K.: Fragen über Fragen - Die Wissens-App "Quizduell"erobert die Download-charts, http://www.zeit.de/2014/06/glosse-spiele-apps-quizduell
3. ARD: Quizduell - ARD | Das Erste, http://www.daserste.de/unterhaltung/quiz-show/quizduell/index.html

4. Sagatz, K.: ARD setzt "Quizduell" zunächst nicht fort,
   http://www.tagesspiegel.de/medien/game-over-ard-setzt-quizduell-zunaechst-nicht-fort/9975924.html
5. Plain Vanilla, QuizUp, https://www.quizup.com/
6. Russolillo, S.: QuizUp: The Next "It" Game App?,
   http://live.wsj.com/video/quizup-the-next-it-game-app/
7. Pawelka, F., Wollmann, T., Stöber, J., Lam, T.V.: Erfolgreiches Lernen durch gamifiziertes E-Learning. In: Plödereder, E., Grunske, L., Schneider, E., Ull, D. (eds.) 44. Jahrestagung der Gesellschaft für Informatik, Informatik 2014, Big Data - Komplexität meistern, 22-26, Stuttgart, Deutschland, pp. 2353–2364. GI (September 2014)
8. Hardinghaus, B.: Interview mit LeBernd: Bernd Schneider über Quizduell,
   http://www.spiegel.de/netzwelt/games/interview-mit-lebernd-bernd-schneider-ueber-quizduell-a-951529.html
9. Klopfer, E.: Augmented Learning: Research and Design of Mobile Educational Games. The MIT Press (2008)
10. Iz, H.B., Fok, H.S.: Use of Bloom's taxonomic complexity in online multiple choice tests in Geomatics education. Surv. Rev. 39, 226–237 (2007)
11. Collins, J.: Education techniques for lifelong learning: writing multiple-choice questions for continuing medical education activities and self-assessment modules. Radiogr. a Rev. Publ. Radiol. ..., 543–552 (2005)
12. Kientz, J.A., Choe, E.K., Truong, K.N.: Texting from the Toilet: Mobile Computing Use and Acceptance in Public and Private Restrooms. In: CHI 2013 (2013)
13. Bellis, M.: The History of Trivial Pursuit,
   http://inventors.about.com/library/inventors/bl_trivia_pursuit.htm
14. Lave, J., Wenger, E.: Situated learning: legitimate peripheral participation. Cambridge University Press (1991)
15. Brüß, F., Brunner, K., Hünemörder, J., Kühn, S., Meisgeier, K.: Fliplife als virtueller Third Place (2014)
16. Fliplife: Fliplife, http://fliplife.com/
17. Söbke, H., Londong, J.: A Social Network Game as virtual Third Place: Community Enabler in Virtual Learning Environments? In: Proceedings of World Conference on Educational Multimedia, Hypermedia and Telecommunications, pp. 518–531. Association for the Advancement of Computing in Education (AACE) (2015)
18. Söbke, H.: Gaming a Non-Game? A Long Term (Self-)Experiment about FarmVille. Well Play 4, 215–262 (2015)
19. Yee, N.: The Proteus Paradox: How Online Games and Virtual Worlds Change Us—And How They Don't. Yale University Press (2014)

Spheres of Play:
Designing Games and Interfaces
for Media Architectures

Michael Schmitz[2], Dominik Scholl[1], Julian Saraceni[1], Pascal Klein[2],
Carsten Blaser[1], Jorge Olmeda[1], Soenke Zehle[2], and André Miede[1]

[1] htw saar, Systemtechniklabor, Saarbrücken, Germany
http://www.htwsaar.de
[2] HBKsaar, xm:lab, Saarbrücken, Germany
http://www.xmlab.org

Abstract. The paper describes a game-based interaction scenario around an existing media architecture, developed to integrate aesthetic, social, and technological dynamics. On screen, the game unfolded as users moved across a globe, using a spherical input device to direct their avatars across a dynamic world of obstacles. Recalling the singularity and site-specificity of a performative intervention, the multidisciplinary project is part of a larger research effort that explores the use of media facades as an infrastructural core of complex interfaces for multiple forms of engagement and the co-creation of transmedial scenarios.

Keywords: Media facade, Urban HCI, User interfaces, Game design.

1 Introduction and Motivation

Part of the trend toward ambient media, the permanent integration of displays into buildings has facilitated the emergence of new aesthetic practices that combine visual media with a wide range of interaction technologies [3,6]. In these experiments, urban screens are no longer used simply as video walls, but as an infrastructural core of complex interfaces allowing for multiple forms of engagement and interaction [8]. The site of interaction is no longer the screen alone but the hybrid space created through the combination of a (permanent) media architecture and (temporary) forms of use, sometimes in combination with tangible interfaces to facilitate intuitive forms of interaction across a heterogenous audience. Such approaches create scenarios not usually associated with digital media: rather than lossless reproduction and infinite replay across an anonymous network of users, these collaborative scenarios recall the singularity and site-specificity of a performative intervention. As interface design strategies have to take this into account, they become increasingly multidisciplinary: the focus of design is not only the "content" to be displayed on a screen but the creation of a hybrid situation integrating aesthetic, social, and technological dynamics.

The fundamental principle of *tangible user interfaces* (TUIs), the tangibility of the interface and the material form of a digital resource [5], have been applied

© IFIP International Federation for Information Processing 2015
K. Chorianopoulos et al. (Eds.): ICEC 2015, LNCS 9353, pp. 490–495, 2015.
DOI: 10.1007/978-3-319-24589-8_45

to media facades in a few prototypes [2,4]. This approach maintains interaction with our everyday environment and situates the interface into real world context. This has the effect that users are enabled to utilise their experiences with the real world, the threshold for activity is lowered and the access bottleneck of common input devices bypassed (see e. g., [7]).

This paper presents an experimental game-based scenario that integrates a TUI to create such a hybrid scenario around an existing media architecture. On screen, the game unfolded as users move across a globe, using a spherical input device to direct their avatars across a dynamic world of obstacles. The input device (Sphero) was chosen because its design mimics the design of the game world, and its features and functionality allowed intuitive interaction.

The multidisciplinary design team included members from two research organizations: xm:lab (Experimental Media Lab) is an institute of the Academy of Fine Arts Saar (HBKsaar) – combining the autonomous aesthetic practices of art and design with research in information technologies, xm:lab develops and coordinates a wide spectrum of research projects at the intersections of art, design and technology. Saarland University of Applied Sciences (htw saar) is a research- and application-oriented university with strong regional ties, e. g., in the information and communication technology sector.

The following section of this paper describes the general technological and game design choices and outlines the implementation. The paper closes with a summary and general conclusions in Section 3.

2   Concept and Implementation

Technical Background: The HBKsaar media facade is a back projection screen, operated with five projectors inside the building. Accordingly, the whole canvas is subdivided into five smaller ones, where every small canvas covers a single window. In our setup, a single projector is used for every window, such that five projectors in total cover the whole media facade.

When looking at the enclosed edge (see Figure 1), a spectator gets the impression of volumetrically spreading 3D objects, which seem to be caught within the room confined by the projection canvases. The projectors have a resolution of 800×600 pixels each, summing up to a bit less than 4000×600 pixels, since some parts are covered at the shorter side (see Figure 1a). The projectors are connected to a single PC, which maps the computer desktop to a 3×2 grid (as seen in Figure 1b). The sixth part of the grid is fed to a monitor inside to facilitate the configuration of the system without interrupting the media facade output.

As a result of the back projection, the displayed content appears mirrored from outside of the building – thus, the render output must be mirrored by the active applications. There are different ways to communicate with the media facade. Its host is connected to the university's local network with access to the Internet. There is also a Wi-Fi hotspot with access to the university's network in front of the building. For this project, a Bluetooth dongle was installed at the roof of the building.

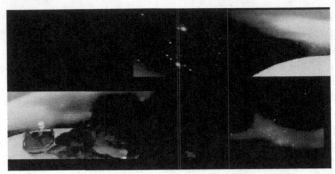

(a) The rendered image

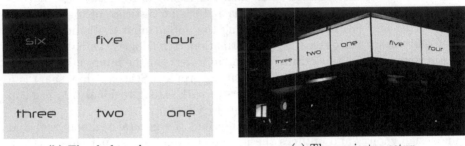

(b) The desktop layout   (c) The projector setup

Fig. 1. How the render output is put on the media facade

2.1   Game Concept

In this section we focus on game design decisions specific to the media facade
and do not discuss the general game design in detail. A major challenge when
designing a game for our media facade was to find a concept that fits to the
particular perspective, which is required for the 3D effect to work. The viewer
has to stand at a specific position across the street in order to see the projection
in an optimal way. Due to the fact, that the projection screen is located on
the first floor of the building, the viewer is looking upward to the stage, which
poses certain constraints to the 3D scene displayed at the facade, such that it is
e.g. impossible to see the ground floor of the virtual space. This makes it also
impossible to see the feet or the legs of a character walking inside this space.
Additionally, the front bottom corner of the building partly covers the back walls
of the virtual room. The only locations where a possible character would entirely
be visible, would be nearby the windows of the building or in the center of the
room some way above the floor. Another challenge is the placement of objects
or obstacles that appear in a game. However, these are the requirements for
creating a challenging game and the major source of interaction and fun.

A possible solution to the challenge of the limited view is to use the top
and the back walls of the room as mirrors. Obviously, this is rather complicated
for the player, since she would have to transfer/mirror the control commands.

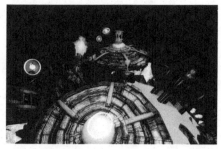

(a) The view when testing on PC   (b) The view on the facade

Fig. 2. The controllable character is placed at the center of the screen

We also considered to drop the 3D effect and to implement a 2D side-scrolling game including the edge or to use just the left, single screen for playing, while using the right and smaller part to display additional information. However, this would disregard the main characteristics of the media facade, which should be a central element of this installation.

The final solution we choose, was placing the character in a *fixed* position at the center of the screen as shown in Figure 2. For the game world, we chose the shape of a sphere, which resulted in two major benefits:

1. Due to the fixed camera position, it looks like the character is standing still and the world is moving. In combination with the sphere shaped world and the Sphero as an input device, we can transfer the way the player rotates the Sphero to the rotation of the game world, which yields a very simple and intuitive interaction metaphor.
2. All relevant parts of the sphere fit into the virtual space: The player sees only the part of the world, which is directly in front of the character, the rest of the world is hidden behind the horizon. This simplifies the scene and also simplifies the game by giving the player a better overview of the world.

2.2 Implementation

The implementation of the game was realized with Unity[1], a game development platform including a 3D game engine, scripting and animation environment. It allows to develop games for many common platforms, including Windows, Linux, Android, and game consoles. It is also often used for the development interactive art installations, such as virtual or augmented reality applications.

From a technical point of view, the game is structured in just a few main components. As shown in Figure 3, there is a central "GameMain" component, which initializes the game, handles the game progress using some utility classes and holds some general information such as the current score. During initialization,

---

[1] http://www.unity3d.com

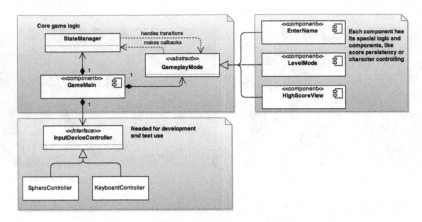

Fig. 3. Overview of the game architecture

there is also a switch to differentiate between the development mode on PC and the production mode for the media facade.

The game flow consists of several scenes. Each kind of scene is represented by a `GameplayMode`. Such a `GameplayMode` can be used in multiple scenes, i. e., the actual levels. There are the following modes:

1. "`Waiting`" mode, which starts a new game as soon as it recognizes user input.
2. "`NameInput`" mode, where the player can enter her name (with three digits).
3. "`Scoreboard`" mode, which shows the high scores after each level.
4. "`Level`" modes, which contain the actual game play.

The *Sphero*[2] ball contains both sensors and actors (motors), such that it can sense it's orientation and move independently on the ground. It can connect via Bluetooth to the host PC controlling the rendering on the media facade. There is a documented API for the Sphero with several SDKs including one for Unity3D. Unfortunately, these are designed to control the Sphero from mobile devices. The other way around, reading Sphero's sensor data for input purposes is poorly supported and documented, e. g., the APIs, including the Unity plugin, only work with mobile devices and are not usable on a Windows PC. Therefore, we had to develop new tools to read the Sphero's streamed sensor data and map the values to a set of keyboard commands. The game maps these input commands into one of seven possible horizontal rotation values (center and three steps for left and right each). For the user, this creates the illusion of analog control in order to achieve an important design goal: controlling a spherical world using a spherical input device. Due to the space constraints of this paper, further technical details are omitted.

3   Summary and Outlook

The scenario developed in this project exemplifies our cross-institutional approach to designing games and interfaces for media architectures. We conduct

---

[2] http://www.gosphero.com/sphero/

these experiments as part of a broader inquiry into the future of immersion, with a particular emphasis on immersive storytelling and transmedial scenarios that unfold across platforms. This kind of research not only requires a multidisciplinary methodology but the use of complementary research infrastructures – some of the experiments we conduct on the media facade, some in the media theater (immersion), and some in the green box using a markerless motion capture system. As we see it, the future of media experience design will have to take the becoming-ambient of display and interaction technologies into account; users will expect games and stories that are both situation-specific and unfold across devices. Our iterative research process links individual experiments conducted in different settings and allows us to compare and contrast the ways in which the use of different media architectures affects the aesthetic practices involved, from interface design to character development.

Future projects include collaborative research on game-based transmedial scenario development with xm:lab partners from the Connecting Cities Network, an international network of cultural organizations working with media architectures [1]. In this context, the academy's media facade serves both as a local infrastructure and as a node in an international network of arts-and-technology research.

References

1. Connecting Cities Network, http://www.connectingcities.net
2. Boring, S., Gehring, S., Wiethoff, A., Blöckner, A.M., Schöning, J., Butz, A.: Multiuser Interaction on Media Facades Through Live Video on Mobile Devices. In: Proceedings of the SIGCHI Conference on Human Factors in Computing Systems, CHI 2011, pp. 2721–2724. ACM, New York (2011)
3. Brynskov, M., Tscherteu, G.: Media Architecture Compendium, Vienna: Media Architecture Institute (2014), http://catalog.mediaarchitecture.org
4. Fischer, P.T., Zöllner, C., Hoffmann, T., Piatza, S.: VR/Urban: SMSlingshot. In: Proceedings of TEI 2010, pp. 381–382. ACM (2010)
5. Hornecker, E., Buur, J.: Getting a grip on tangible interaction: a framework on physical space and social interaction. In: CHI 2006: Proceedings of the SIGCHI Conference on Human Factors in Computing Systems, pp. 437–446. ACM, New York (2006)
6. Schoch, O.: My building is my display. In: Proc. eCAADe 2006 (2006)
7. Shaer, O., Hornecker, E.: Tangible user interfaces: past, present, and future directions. Foundations and Trends in Human-Computer Interaction 3(1-2), 1–137 (2010)
8. Struppek, M.: Urban Screens – The Urbane Potential of Public Screens for Interaction. In: "Screenarcadia" – Microwave – International New Media Arts Festival, festival book, Hong Kong (2010)

Supporting the Collaboration between Programmers and Designers Building Game AI*

Ismael Sagredo-Olivenza, Marco Antonio Gómez-Martín,
and Pedro A. González-Calero

Department Ingeniería del Software e Inteligencia Artificial
Universidad Complutense de Madrid, Spain
isagredo@ucm.es, {marcoa,pedro}@fdi.ucm.es

Abstract. The design of the behavior of non-player characters (NPCs) in a game is a collaborative task between programmers and designers. Nevertheless this collaboration is an open problem since the limits, responsibilities and competences are not well defined.

Behavior trees are the technology of choice nowadays for programming the behavior of NPCs, and they are first and foremost a programmers tool. In this paper we describe an experiment that shows that with the right division of labor and a reduced background in Programming, designers can also build behavior trees and thus find a principled way to collaborate with programmers in that task.

1 Introduction

Game development is a multidisciplinary task that involves professionals from different areas with different knowledge and sensibilities. The three main roles involved in the development of the artificial intelligence (AI) of non-player characters (NPCs) in a game are: artists (that are beyond the scope of the paper), which make the models and animations; programmers that implement behaviors; and designers, responsible for designing those behaviors.

Designers define how the characters must behave and programmers implement these behaviors, therefore, they should communicate between them and try to reach an agreement. This relation produces an iterative cycle of changes, because programmers can deliver an incomplete or inaccurate version of the behaviors to designers. Accordingly, designers need to validate these behaviors and then require the appropriate changes to programmers. This process ends when the behavior is accepted by designers.

To get a more fluid process, programmers usually develop authoring tools for designers. The goal is to get designers to become as autonomous as possible so they can modify certain parameters in order to configure behaviors to their needs. Different solutions have been explored (state machine, scripting, behavior trees...) but the most behaviors of the NPCs are stored in data files. These data file formats are seldom easy to understand or edit, hence, designers and

---

* Supported by the Spanish Ministry of Science and Education (TIN2014-55006-R).

K. Chorianopoulos et al. (Eds.): ICEC 2015, LNCS 9353, pp. 496–501, 2015.
DOI: 10.1007/978-3-319-24589-8_46

developers must have tools to edit or visualize them. If designers have a certain degree of autonomy, then they can test, modify or create parts of behaviors without the intervention of a programmer.

In this paper we present a methodology together with a tool (Behavior Bricks) for designing behavior trees that distinguish high-level behavior from low-level ones. We can think of these high-level behaviors as a simple description of the general behavior of an NPC, similar to the ones used in the early stages of design [1]. Our hypothesis is that, with the proper tools, designers can implement high-level behaviors while programmers implement the low-level ones in parallel.

The rest of this paper is structured as follows. Next Section describes behavior trees, Section 3 describes Behavior Bricks and our methodology for using it, and Section 4 describes the experiment. Finally Section 5 presents some conclusions and future work.

2   Behavior Trees

Behavior trees (BTs) are a modeling technique of behavior of an NPC. They were popularized for their utilization in Halo 2 [2] and Halo 3 [3], and they have similar representation capabilities of the traditional Finite State Machines (FSMs) [4,5]. The main problem of the FSMs and the Hierarchical FSM (HFSM) are the scalability of their transitions. When the problem grows, the number of relationships between states grows much faster than states and they become uncontrollable soon.

BTs improve scalability over FSMs thanks to remove these transitions, replacing them for internal nodes, which select the tasks that will run. By definition, BTs are hierarchical, therefore, it is very easy to have multiple abstraction-layers which improve their re-usability. Behavior trees have become popular thanks to the need to make increasingly complex behavior and the needs of the developers that were not comfortable with the existing techniques. Designers wish full control of the behavior but not all time. They need to delegate the most complex tasks to programmers [6]. In addition, designers want that the behaviors are driven by goals, but also that they are reactive to unexpected events and finally, they want that the chosen model is easy to use, easy to comprehend and, if possible, easy to draw.

3   Behavior Bricks and Its Methodology of Use

As we said before, designers must create behavior independently. For that reason designers need tools to simplify this task. In the market, there are some tools with this purpose like *NodeCanvas*[1], *Behavior Designer*[2] or *Behave*[3] among others.

---

[1] http://nodecanvas.com/

[2] http://www.opsive.com/assets/BehaviorDesigner/

[3] http://angryant.com/behave/

After analysing these editors, we have concluded that neither of them is adapted to our methodology because none of them has a correct abstraction system that allows to encapsulate the behaviors and the primitive tasks for reusing them. For those reasons, the authors have created a new BT framework named *Behavior Bricks*, a tool designed to be used by designers that are able to create, view and modify behavior trees and that, in addition, can be easily extended by programmers.

Behavior Bricks has two different modules: *Runtime module* and *visual editor*. Both runtime and editor are distributed as a extension of the game engine Unity3D[4].

3.1   Methodology

BTs can run sub-behaviors easily. These sub-behaviors can be used by designers within other behaviors like a simple primitive task. This mechanism may have different abstraction layers in a BT. We can define two different levels of details the *high-level* detail and the *low-level* detail. The low-level behavior can be defined as the behavior that can be reused in other behaviors. This behavior manages the concepts closer to scripting languages such as: target selection, follow a route, find a coverage, etc. The high-level behaviors can be defined as the behavior that describe the general behavior of the NPC. One of the purpose to create Behavior Bricks is to introduce this new methodology to develop the video games AI.

The responsibility of programmers in Behavior Bricks is two-fold. On the one hand, they must create the low-level primitives using the scripting language of the underlying engine and, on the other hand, we must implement with Behavior Bricks editor the low-level behavior.

A primitive task is defined establishing his name (that must be unique in the hierarchy) and optionally a collection of input and output parameters. The input parameters read their values from a blackboard stored in the behavior executor and the output parameters write its values in same blackboard.

The responsibility of designers in Behavior Bricks is make the high level behaviors using the visual editor. The designers using a subset of the internal nodes to simplify the BT complexity. This subset is formed by the following nodes: Sequences, selector, priority selector and the repeat decorator.

4   Experimentation

The experiment that we describe below demonstrates that it is possible and effective that non-technical designers implement high-level behavior with similar result to programmers, if they have been trained enough and they have a visual tool like Behavior Bricks. We have carried out this experiment with the students from the master program on Game Development at Complutense University of

---

[4] http://unity3d.com/

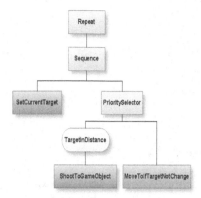

Fig. 1. The expected solution of the basic enemy behavior

Madrid, which includes two different itineraries: one for programmers and one for designers. These students have a diverse background, including: Computer Science, Mathematics, Journalism or Arts, and therefore is complex enough to validate our hypothesis. Before the experiment, the students had a class about BTs where they learned the concepts and how to use our tool.

4.1 The Experiment Environment

To carry out the experiment, we have used a prototype of a tower-defense video-game. In this prototype, the player's mission is to defend the base (or core) of a space mine. In this version, the player only can move his avatar and shoot against the enemies. Enemies appear in different spawning points and go to the base to destroy it.

Designers have described in a design document two types of enemies in the game: the basic enemy and the shield.

The *basic enemy* receives a target to its perception system, in this case only are available the core and the player. The selection of this target is random with different probabilities for each type of target. Perception is in charge of selecting the target that the NPC must consider. This perception is already done in the exercise and the students should not worry about it. To explain the behavior, we can see the expected solution in the figure 1.

The second exercise is divided in two parts: In the first part, the students must implement the low-level behavior *AttackTheCore*, when the initial target of the enemy is the core. The enemy should move next to the core and shoot it. This low-level behavior is very simple and it does not require the intervention of a programmer. The expected solution of this behavior can be seen in Figure 2a.

In the second part, the students must implement the high level behavior of the *Shield*. This NPC try to protect an enemy. While protecting the enemy, it should maximize the number of enemies protected by its shield. If the target dies, it try to find another enemy to protect. If not found an enemy to protect,

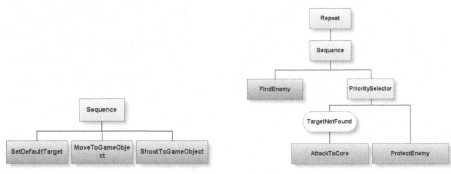

(a) The expected solution of the Attack-
TheCore behavior

(b) he expected solution of the Shield
behavior

Fig. 2. Second exercise formed by two parts

then it must attack the core. To explain the behavior, we can see the expected
solution in the figure 2b.

For both, the basic enemy and the shield, we provide the students a set of
primitive tasks and behaviors to be used. We can assume that this tasks would
be developed by programmer in a professional environment.

4.2   The Experiment

With this experiment, we want to evaluate if a correlation exists between the
knowledge of programming and their results using Behavior Bricks. To do this,
we have compared the marks obtained in a programming test and the marks
obtained in the practical exercises with Behavior Bricks.

In our hypotheses, we expected that the programming knowledge will help to
better solve the exercises, although it is not a barrier for designers that can also
create high-level behaviors with little training.

The sample of this experiment is of 25 students. They had 2 hours and 10
minutes to resolve the two exercises. Once completed the experiment, we have
evaluated these exercises. The score of each exercise has been as follow: 4 points
for the first, 2 points for exercise 2.1 since it is similar to the first one, and 4
points to exercise 2.2.

The plot that we can see in Figure 3a shows an evident correlation between
the result of the programming exam and the result of the exercise using Behavior Bricks. In addition, if we calculate the Pearson product-moment correlation
coefficient (PCC) we obtain a result of 0.525, which indicates that a correlation
exists (its value is greater than 0.5) but the correlation is not very pronounced.
Furthermore, the result agrees with the hypothesis that the technical knowledge is important to comprehend correctly BTs, but simplifying the model and
applying it in high-level behaviors, the designers can use it too.

If we carefully analyze the plot we find that given a basic programming knowledge, the differences between exercise results and exam do not follow any kind

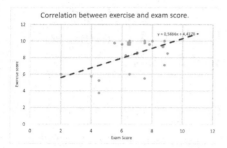

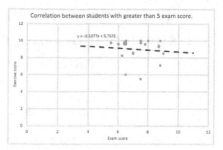

(a) Correlation between programming knowledge and exercise result

(b) Correlation with an exam score greater than 5

Fig. 3. Experiment results

of correlation. Figure 3b shows the distribution of the students who have passed the exam. In this figure we can observe this fact since there are no obvious correlation between both and the dispersion of the exercise result is very large. Even those students without technical skills have been able to complete at least the first exercise.

5   Conclusions and Future Work

Given the results from our experiments, we can conclude that, using a tool such as Behavior Bricks a designer with little training in the tool and little previous knowledge about Programming, can design high level behaviors of good quality within a reasonable time. In addition, we can conclude that given a minimum programming knowledge we have not found any differences in the results using Behavior Bricks, therefore, is not necessary to have high programming skills to create high-level behaviors using Behavior Bricks with our methodology.

In the future, we want to have more experiments with more subjects in order to validate other aspects of our methodology. We plan to compare our methodology with other in order to assess its comparative competitiveness, both in terms of developing effort, collaboration support and quality.

References

1. Hudson's, K.: The ai of bioshock 2: Methods for iteration and innovation. In: Game Developers Conference (2010)
2. Isla, D.: Handling complexity in the Halo 2 ai. In: Game Developers Conference (2005)
3. Isla, D.: Halo 3 - building a better battle. In: Game Developers Conference (2008)
4. Rabin, S.: 3.4. In: Implementing a State Machine Language. AI Game Programming Wisdom, vol. 1, pp. 314–320. Cengage Learning (2002)
5. Bourg, D.M., Seemann, G.: AI for Game Developers. O'Reilly Media, Inc. (2004)
6. Champandard, A.J.: Behavior trees for next-gen ai. In: Game Developers Conference (2005)

The Impact of Sensor Noise on Player Experience in Magic Window Augmented Reality Aiming Games

Farjana Z. Eishita and Kevin G. Stanley

Department of Computer Science, University of Saskatchewan, 110 Science Place, Saskatoon, SK S7N 5C9

Abstract. Augmented reality (AR) requires superimposing digital artifacts on real world scenes. Unfortunately, sensors used to render digital artifacts are subject to noise and imprecision, making the registration difficult in practice. Using a modified version of the Android operating system, we experimentally examined the impact of orientation sensor noise on player experience in three commercial AR aiming games employing different mechanics and input techniques.

1 Introduction

Game developers have always been early adopters of new technology, pushing the limits of what was technically feasible to craft new experiences for their audiences. With the mobile revolution, electronic play has moved away from the computer console or couch to permeate aspects of everyday life. However, the display area and processing power of handheld devices are limited, meaning players cannot inhabit virtual worlds that are as deep or richly textured as their desktop counterparts. A plausible workaround is to employ the real world as a game board, viewing the world through a smartphone camera, and rendering digital artifacts upon it. We call such games augmented reality (AR) games.

Augmented reality offloads much of the rendering load to the real world. Play environments not longer have to be drawn, they are viewed directly through a digital camera. While the rendering load is much lower, digital artifacts must be correctly placed within the scene, and viewed from the appropriate angle. To accomplish this, sensors initially developed to approximate a phone's position on Earth for navigation and determine phone orientation for screen rotation must now approximate the precision of a virtual camera in a video game. However, unlike the virtual camera used to render scenes in digital worlds, physical sensors are subject to noise, drift and error. In particular, determining the pose of the camera in space so that digital artifacts can be rendered from the appropriate angle, and aiming tasks within the game can be appropriately resolved, is of particular import. In this paper we present an experimental study of the impact of sensor noise on three different aiming games, and show that both noise and input type have an impact on the subjective play experience of participants.

© IFIP International Federation for Information Processing 2015
K. Chorianopoulos et al. (Eds.): ICEC 2015, LNCS 9353, pp. 502–507, 2015.
DOI: 10.1007/978-3-319-24589-8_47

2   Related Work

Location based games employ both orientation for aiming, and fixed real world coordinates. ARQuake [14] is a location-based AR shooting game. The digital artifact rendering occurs based on fiducial vision-based tracking. AR Battle commander [8] is a real-time strategy (RTS) AR game played in an outdoor environment. PasswARG [3] is a geo-tagged treasure hunt game where players find clues provided by the 3D characters located on POIs (Points of Interest) to find the password to unlock next level. Aiming AR games which soley employ accelerometers or gyroscopes are a significant game research area. Butterfly Effect [6] is an AR game dependent on orientation precision where player wears an HMD and wields a stick rendered as a tornado to collect virtual butterflies. Augmented Galaga [7] is an AR version of the famous arcade game Galaga. ARVe - Augmented Reality applied to Vegetal field [11] is a game for cognitive disable children. LittleProjectedPlanet [4] is an AR prototype of the famous PS3 game 'LittleBigPlanet'. Mind Wrap, Impera Visco, and Penalty kick are games implemented to demonstrate the user interfaces for handheld AR games [12].

3   Methodology and Experimental Setup

Many current commercially available MW smartphone games employ aiming with a handset as their primary mechanic. We chose three different games, each employing free aiming - aiming without the aid of visual marker tracking - to ensure that the comparisons reflected differences in aiming modality and not sensing technique. All three games require that players orient the phone to find targets, they differ in how players interact with those targets. All three of these games would be classified as casual arcade games, as they are meant to be played opportunistically and for short durations.

- Chase Wisply [1] is a ghost hunting game using a targeting crosshair.
- Skeeter Beater [9] makes players kill mosquitoes by tapping on the mosquito.
- Droid Shooting [5] requires players shoot robots with a trigger button.

There are several different methods for accessing phone orientation within the Android SDK. These games each use a different software interface. Zero mean Gaussian noise was inserted in a scaled manner in each of these interfaces. Droid Shooting uses accelerometer, Skeeter Beater uses the abstract Orientation sensor which fuses accelerometer, gyroscope and compass readings, and Chase Whisply uses the abstract Rotation Vector, derived from the abstract Orientation sensor.

Zero Mean Gaussian Noise (ZMGN) is a textbook noise model for physical sensors. As multiple small disturbances at various levels of the physical sensor and data acquisition are applied, Gaussian distributions tend to emerge. As the noise is zero mean, it can be added directly to the sensor signal without impacting the average performance. Sensor data error was injected at the operating system level as described below for each of the respective sensors. Through pilot testing we configured the standard deviation of sensor error to be at most 2.8% of the span of the input signal.

We used the Android Galaxy Nexus with AOSP 4.1 in all experiments. We recruited 24 participants (13 male, 9 female; aged from 20-35 years) After each experimental condition, participants completed the PANAS (Positive and Negative Affect Schedule) [2] survey, which measures positive and negative affect, and the IMI (Intrinsic Motivation Inventory) [13] survey, which measures perceived interest, competence, effort and tension.

4   Results

Both PANAS and IMI results were analyzed using a multivariate ANOVA. There was a significant difference among the games for players' positive in-game experience ($p = 0.033$, $F = 4.001$) and with noise level ($p = 0.001$, $F = 9.637$). While examining players' negative play experience, both game and noise level effects showed significant difference in variance (game: $p < 0.001$, $F = 11.645$; noise: $p < 0.001$, $F = 11.242$).

Interest and enjoyment of different gameplay was significant between games ($p = 0.025$, $F = 4.381$), and more so with noise ($p < 0.001$, $F = 12.407$). Competence displayed the highest significant difference among all effects (e.g. game, noise level, game-noise level) (game: $p < 0.001$, $F = 11.075$; noise: $p < 0.001$, $F = 33.591$, game-noise: $p < 0.001$, $F = 9.415$). Effort only differed by game ($p = 0.044$, $F = 3.611$). Players' tension had significant differences with noise level effect ($p = 0.001, F = 17.149$), but not with game.

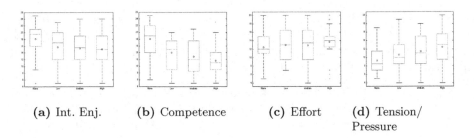

(a) Int. Enj.   (b) Competence   (c) Effort   (d) Tension/
                                                             Pressure

Fig. 1. IMI Responses from Chase Whisply

Although there was no significant difference between Low and Medium level in SK, competence showed significant difference in rest of the levels ($p < 0.001$ for relevant pairs). According to the pairwise comparison between subjects, other than Medium and High level of play, the tension/pressure variation was significant ($p = 0.006$). Subjective effort increased with each noise level ($p < 0.006$ for relevant pairs). As a result, there was a significant fall of interest and enjoyment of the gameplay with increased noise($p < 0.016$ for relevant pairs) [Figure 2].

For the game Skeeter Beater, almost all the parameters of IMI and PANAS showed significant interaction. In pairwise comparison of between parameters measured by PANAS and IMI, all of them showed significant difference, except for the difference between Medium and High noise. Noise impact appeared to saturate after a moderate amount of added noise. Although there was no significant difference between Low level and Medium level plays in SK, competence showed significant difference in rest of the levels ($p < 0.001$ for relevant pairs). According to the pairwise comparison between subjects, other than Medium and High level of play, the tension/pressure variation was significant ($p = 0.006$). Subjective effort increased with each noise level ($p < 0.006$ for relevant pairs). As a result, there was a significant fall of interest and enjoyment of the gameplay with increased noise($p < 0.016$ for relevant pairs). Figure 2 provides a box plots of players' experience with SK.

For the game Chase Whisply, the most significant difference among the different noise levels was observed in competence (pairwise always $p < 0.04$). Tension and pressure also increased pairwise with noise for No, Low and Medium ($p < 0.013$). For PANAS, only negative feelings were more pronounced with higher noise ($p < 0.0106$).

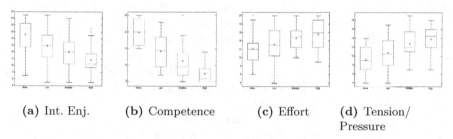

(a) Int. Enj.   (b) Competence   (c) Effort   (d) Tension/
                                                              Pressure

Fig. 2. IMI Responses from Skeeter Beater

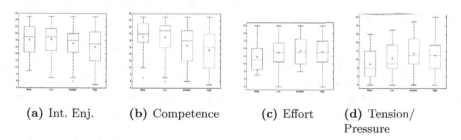

(a) Int. Enj.   (b) Competence   (c) Effort   (d) Tension/
                                                              Pressure

Fig. 3. IMI Responses from Droid Shooting

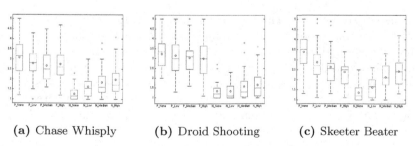

(a) Chase Whisply   (b) Droid Shooting   (c) Skeeter Beater

Fig. 4. PANAS Results of all three games

The least variance was observed in the game Droid Shooting. A noticeable variance was observed in competence ($p < 0.0144$) that went slightly lower with the increment of noise. Overall, a higher tension ($p = 0.0191, \chi^2 = 9.93$) was observed during DR gameplay with increasing noise [Figure 1].

5   Discussion and Future Work

Our primary findings indicate that noise can have a significant impact in MW AR aiming games, that this impact generally increases with increasing noise, and that the magnitude of this impact depends on the type of aiming mechanic and game mechanics. We suspect a combination of the more difficult aiming technique, which required aiming the phone like a camera while simultaneously tapping the screen, and the negative scoring mechanic caused greater levels of frustration and decreasing competence.

Players suffered more significant decreases in affect and competence in SK than in the other two games. We suspect a combination of the more difficult aiming technique, which required aiming the phone like a camera while simultaneously tapping the screen, and the negative scoring mechanic caused greater levels of frustration and decreasing competence. Because both DR and SK featured moving targets, but DR experienced a much smaller impact with respect to noise, we do not feel that moving targets in these cases were a dominant cause.

The uniformly decreasing competence observed in our experiments is particularly troubling for game designers, as it was noted in [10] that feelings of competency are one of the primary motivators for playing games. The sensitivity observed is particularly important because aiming is fundamental to almost all AR interactions.

While this work has made important contributions to the literature, there are several shortcomings that could be addressed in future work. First, we only focused on aiming games and magic window AR. Second, the games considered, while commercial, were limited in mechanic complexity, narrative scope and artistic design. Finally, while our sample size was large enough given to determine the primary effects, it was skewed towards the university community.

6   Conclusion

In this paper we have presented an experimental comparison between the impact of orientation sensor noise on commercial AR games on player experience. We have noted significant impacts of noise in all games tested, but more importantly differential sensitivity to noise.Game developers should consider the interaction mode carefully when designing new interactive experiences to either avoid or masks the noise sensitivity observed, employ more sophisticated filtering techniques and integrate the potential for noise into the overall game design.

Acknowledgments. We acknowledge Natural Sciences and Engineering Council of Canada (NSERC), Graphics, Animation and New Media (GRAND) for funding and Ansgar Depping for his cooperation and guidance in the statistical analysis.

References

[1] Chase whisply, author = Google Play, https://play.google.com/store/apps/details?id=fr.tvbarthel.games.chasewhisply&hl=en (accessed February 17, 2015)

[2] Crawford, J.R., Henry, J.D.: The Positive and Negative Affect Schedule (PANAS): Construct validity, measurement properties and normative data in a large non-clinical sample. British Journal of Clinical Psychology 3(43), 245–265 (2004)

[3] Eishita, F.Z., Stanley, K.G., Mandryk, R.: Iterative Design of an Augmented Reality Game and Level-Editing Tool for Use in the Classroom. In: 6th IEEE Consumer Electronics Society Games, Entertainment, Media Conference (2014) (to appear)

[4] Löchtefeld, M., Str, W., Rohs, M., Krüger, A.: LittleProjectedPlanet: An Augmented Reality Game for Camera Projector Phones. In: Artificial Intelligence:Proc. of MRIW (2009)

[5] Google Play: Droid shooting, https://market.android.com/details?id=jp.co.questcom.droidshooting (accessed February 14, 2012)

[6] Norton, M., Macintyre, B.: Butterfly Effect: An Augmented Reality Puzzle Game Marleigh Norton and Blair MacIntyre 2. Design for Real World Constraints. In: Proceedings of the Fourth IEEE and ACM International Symposium Mixed and Augmented Reality, pp. 5–6. IEEE Comput. Soc. (2005)

[7] Park, A., Jung, K.: Augmented Galaga on Mobile Devices. Flying, pp. 888–897 (2007)

[8] Phillips, K., Piekarski, W.: Possession techniques for interaction in real-time strategy augmented reality games. In: Proceedings of the 2005 ACM SIGCHI International Conference on Advances in Computer Entertainment Technology, ACE 2005, p. 2. ACM Press, New York (2005)

[9] Google Play: skeeter, https://play.google.com/store/apps/details?id=com.cogtactics.skeeterbeater&hl=en (accessed December 17, 2014)

[10] Przybylski, A.K., Rigby, C.S., Ryan, R.M.: A motivational model of video game engagement. Review of General Psychology 14(2), 154–166 (2010)

[11] Richard, E., Billaudeau, V., Richard, P., Gaudin, G.: Augmented Reality for Rehabilitation of Cognitive Disabled Children: A Preliminary Study. 2007 Virtual Rehabilitation (2), 102–108 (2007)

[12] Rohs, M.: Marker-Based Embodied Interaction for Handheld Augmented Reality Games Marker-Based Embodied Interac-. Virtual Reality 4(5) (2007)

[13] Ryan, R.: Control and information in the intrapersonal sphere:An extension of cognitive evaluation theory. Journal of Personality and Social Psychology (43), 450–461 (1982)

[14] Thomas, B., Close, B., Donoghue, J., Squires, J., Bondi, P.D., Piekarski, W.: First Person Indoor/Outdoor Augmented Reality Application: ARQuake. Personal and Ubiquitous Computing 6(1), 75–86 (2002)

Towards a Framework for Gamification-Based Intervention Mapping in mHealth

Helf Christopher, Patrick Zwickl, Helmut Hlavacs, and Peter Reichl

University of Vienna,
Währingerstraße 29, 1090 Vienna, Austria
http://cs.univie.ac.at/

Abstract. Given increasing obesity rates, reduced physical activity and other unhealthy practices, mobile gamification-based health applications have gained momentum in motivating individuals towards behavioral change. The lack of corresponding frameworks enabling the efficient cooperation between health professionals and independent game developers has resulted in a clutter of mHealth apps, which uncoordinately make use of large numbers of motivational techniques, gamification metrics and health data. In this paper, a unified user-centered framework is proposed, running health applications crafted by external developers within a sandbox, and thus mitigating the most concerning privacy and safety issues. It is capable of differentiating between apps on intervention-level granularity and tailoring suggested treatments based on users and their current environment, and aims at maximizing motivational impact in order to sustain and facilitate healthy lifestyles in the long run.

Keywords: mHealth, eHealth, Gamification, Individualisation, Health Intervention, Framework.

1 Introduction

Overweight, obesity and lack of physical activity are considered a major public health concern worldwide. Studies indicate that by 2030, up to almost 58% of the world's adult population could be either overweight or obese [9]. A sedentary lifestyle on the other hand can be directly linked to serious health consequences in forms of chronic diseases, such as diabetes, hypertension or heart problems [8,9]. This alarming development has encouraged developers to utilize new technologies to create mobile health (mHealth) applications [15] and has also given rise to novel gamification approaches that aim at increasing the individual's engagement with systems by providing elements such as play, fun, reward, challenge, social context, visually appearing aesthetics or creative interaction types. Nevertheless, applications in the health domain targeting behavior change are often developed without or little involvement of health professionals [4] and thus subsequently have been found to be only weakly backed by scientific evidence or validation [1,3]. Furthermore, most gamified applications nowadays individually collect, process and analyze health data and thus try to motivate users in form

© IFIP International Federation for Information Processing 2015
K. Chorianopoulos et al. (Eds.): ICEC 2015, LNCS 9353, pp. 508–513, 2015.
DOI: 10.1007/978-3-319-24589-8_48

of island solutions. The high fragmentation of these applications leads to the conclusion that users need a large number of apps in order to achieve the often desired lifestyle change [5]. Gamification metrics among these apps are additionally often not comparable and designed incoherently due to the high competition among developers in this field. Consequently, it is imperative to create a holistic framework in which both serious game and gamification developers as well as health professionals can operate independently for the benefit and motivation of the user. In this context, the main contribution of this paper is the definition of a holistic mHealth framework of a highly-modularized system for gamified applications. The framework and subsequent implementations are developed within the EU project PRECIOUS[1].

2 Related Work

Few approaches have been made hitherto with respect to combining mHealth interventions with motivational aspects, such as gamification elements. A recent and promising eHealth framework named the Behavioural Intervention Technology Model (BIT) [10] depicts a high-level model following three existing and comparable design models and includes design intentions from different stakeholders. Another model being complementary to the BIT approach [7] is Intervention Mapping (IMA) [2]. Instead of describing a technical framework, it is a protocol on how to create health-related interventions. Both models address limitations of existing models [7] and thus underline the lack of frameworks in this field in addition to highlighting the importance of key stakeholder inclusion in app-development, such as health professionals [6]. Another important point with regards to motivational aspects are a framework's capability to adapt to user needs and circumstances. A study by Orji, Mandryk et al. showed for instance that different gamer types based on the BrainHex classification [11] responded differently to game mechanics in the context of health behavior change, thus emphasizing the need to tailor health determinants to various gamer types for example. Implemented Behaviour Change Techniques (BCT) for instance are often not considered along with the individual's personality and characteristics [10], which generally leads to the conclusion that people may need multiple apps to initiate and maintain behavior change [5].Even though gamification has been suggested as a design pattern [13], dynamic interventions based on gamification elements represent an entirely new concept to the field of health applications, which are often of rather static nature with regards to user characteristics and environments. They often lack understanding of behavioral interventions, where feedback loops and responsive or reactive systems are crucial for the success of health interventions [12]. In general it can be said that there exists a large gap between current clinical interventions based on scientific methods and iterative gaming and app technology design [14]. Most designers and human-computer-interaction professionals place an emphasis on usability, aesthetics and engagement, whereas health researchers focus on efficacy and often personal treatment.

---

[1] http://www.thepreciousproject.eu

Current suggestions for eHealth models have already tried to bridge this gap, but have placed an emphasis on specific intervention problems rather than creating a framework where apps can deliver arbitrary interventions within a single framework.

3   Towards a Framework for Gamification-Based Intervention Mapping

While today isolated applications are hardly aligned to each other, future health frameworks have to provide the required umbrella for synchronizing individual efforts to optimally target common goals, i.e., the improvement of the user's health. As a consequence, the goal of the presented framework is threefold: Firstly, it needs to provide a structured and consistent translation of interventions, medical treatments or other user-specified aims into an actual implementation delivered through apps developed by externals. Secondly, it needs to facilitate the actual development of serious games or gamification-based health apps by providing both straightforward but privacy-aware access to relevant data as well as a standardized motivational system, i.e., system-wide rewarding schemes. Thirdly, the framework needs to initiate interventions based on psychological user characteristics such as gamer types or preferred BCTs, as well as availability of requirements of a desired intervention, such as time, location or weather conditions for instance. Similar to [10], the term "intervention" (IV) will be referred to as a single interaction with a single element of the system, whereas we refer to a set of of IVs delivered by apps as treatments (TMs). In the context, an app is considered to be potentially developed by externals with limited control by the platform, and is run within the framework itself. Figure 1 shows the big picture of the framework's components.

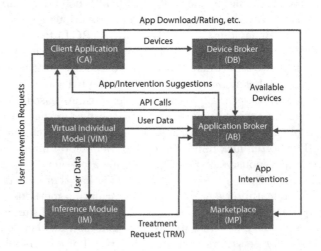

Fig. 1. Overview of the presented framework.

The overall architecture of the framework consists of several components which are described in brief in the following.

The **Client Application (CA)** serves as the main application for the user with execution of potential apps developed by externals. It is the single trusted point of interaction of the user with the system and moderates access to the back-end functionalities. Mainly, it implements a sandbox for running externally developed apps, e.g., a food intake diary realized with HTML5 and JavaScript (JS), as well as central, sandbox-independent functionality for personalization of the system. With this design, we can guarantee data protection as well as straightforward developer access to commonly used functionalities. Furthermore, developers have easy access to all the health data, analysis and gamification metrics offered by the platform e.g. through a JS API, which is bundled with the CA, and which also offers native resources and functionalities like available sensors (geolocation, heartrate, camera, etc.) or algorithms (step counters, etc.). Users can overview, like, filter, browse, hide and launch applications according to their needs, while suggestions are made by the framework itself dynamically according to preferences and set goals. The **Virtual Individual Model (VIM)** is a collection of historic user states which are collected and aggregated over time. Each state then contains several parameters and variables capturing both the user and their environments, as well as health-related micro and macro goals of the user following continuous needs assessment. The **Inference Module (IM)** represents the "clinical" part of the framework and is designed to create treatments based on user-specific parameters and different sets of rules. Starting from parameters from the VIM such as health indicators or treatment preferences, recipes represented as "if-this-then-that"-like rules trigger so-called "Treatment Requests" (TMR) based on health parameter thresholds and user contexts (e.g., location) and are targeted at improving health conditions or to implement change objectives. Main recipes could be based on general health guidelines issued for instance by public institutions, whereas both developers and users can adjust and create their own rules, i.e. users may specify to be notified when sitting for more than two hours. The **Application & Device Brokers (AB, DB)** are generally responsible for selecting potential ways to operationalize the suggested treatment by the IM. First, the DB module is contacted to gather available actuators and devices for the TMR. Once one of the CAs has been opened by the user, the best fitting app (i.e. matching TRM requirements, whether the user has enough time for necessary tasks, etc.) is triggered. The selection algorithm should also consider the popularity and ranking of apps within the marketplace, not only on a global level, but also with respect to users and user type specifics, i.e. which apps have worked best for which gamer type in which context. A **Gamification Interface** is provided additionally to facilitate and standardize the gamification aspects of the framework, such as specifically designed metrics forming a global inter-app reward system which are required to reflect healthy activities. In general, the aim is to achieve a systemic integration of gamification aspects, such that the relative achievement, progress and motivational status of the users are *a)* (quantitatively) comparable within a social group; both users and apps can access the user's current status measured in system-wide understandable metrics, e.g., coins, levels, leaderboard positions, and *b*) can be attributed to apps, i.e., reflecting the status within the app and the contribution to the health goals. A Gamification API, e.g., available via the JS API in the CA, will be the central entrance point for applications to access features with regard to gamification and associated health metrics, individualization and motivation. Besides the aim of a homogeneous interface, comparable metrics and the collaborative support for the user, the multifacetedness and creativity of individual apps are an asset, which need to be supported by limiting restrictions. Thus, the framework will provide means to access and set gamification metrics on the one hand, but also to create own metrics, badges or leaderboards on app-level on the other hand.

4   Discussion and Conclusion

The presented framework defines an approach of translating isolated app-based interventions into a holistic user-centered treatment implementation that not only tailors to the users themselves, their context and environment, but also eliminates common barriers between apps, which is to our knowledge a novelty in the eHealth domain. With this approach, we can aggregate efforts and creativity of individual apps to jointly address the goals of individual beings with their personality, needs, desires and background, while at the same time creating a platform that is able tackle privacy issues and reduce the cost of change for the entire spectrum of eHealth. Whereas the framework can help developers to formalize game ideas in terms of health-related IVs by adhering to it's structure and conventions, a multitude of different stakeholders can interact with the framework through our recipe-based intervention selection approach, hence providing transparent means for integrating the expertise of health professionals with limited technical backgrounds. The increasing smartphone adoption rates we see today on a global scale paired health interventions delivered through mobile technologies point to the conclusion that health apps will be deeply integrated into medical practices of the future. Holistic frameworks are thus promising for facilitating the cooperation of different stakeholders in the area of eHealth. The approach of fully utilizing the strength of modular apps in a coordinated way seems to be a promising balancing act towards targeting a very heterogeneous and unhealthy society. Our model is intended to be at a sufficiently high level to be generalizable for different eHealth problems, however, details such as the actual structure or categories of IVs or IVRs need to be specified upon implementation of the framework. Furthermore, the efficacy of dynamic app-selection for certain users needs to be evaluated and tested in long-term studies. Future work has to shed light on algorithms that align the current context and status of the user, required and available interventions, as well as health goals. Moreover, we will focus on the operationalization and implementation of the proposed framework.

Acknowledgements. This project has received funding from the European Union's Seventh Framework Programme for research, technological development and demonstration under grant agreement no 611366.

References

1. Azar, K.M., Lesser, L.I., Laing, B.Y., Stephens, J., Aurora, M.S., Burke, L.E., Palaniappan, L.P.: Mobile applications for weight management: theory-based content analysis. American Journal of Preventive Medicine 45(5), 583–589 (2013)
2. Bartholomew, L.K., Parcel, G.S., Kok, G., Gottlieb, N.H., Fernandez, M.E.: Planning health promotion programs: an intervention mapping approach. John Wiley & Sons (2011)
3. Boulos, M.N.K., Brewer, A.C., Karimkhani, C., Buller, D.B., Dellavalle, R.P.: Mobile medical and health apps: state of the art, concerns, regulatory control and certification. Online Journal of Public Health Informatics 5(3), 229 (2014)
4. Buijink, A.W.G., Visser, B.J., Marshall, L.: Medical apps for smartphones: lack of evidence undermines quality and safety. Evidence Based Medicine, ebmed–2012 (2012)
5. Conroy, D.E., Yang, C.H., Maher, J.P.: Behavior change techniques in top-ranked mobile apps for physical activity. American Journal of Preventive Medicine 46(6), 649–652 (2014)
6. Craven, M.P., Lang, A.R., Martin, J.L.: Developing mhealth apps with researchers: multi-stakeholder design considerations. In: Marcus, A. (ed.) DUXU 2014, Part III. LNCS, vol. 8519, pp. 15–24. Springer, Heidelberg (2014)
7. Crutzen, R.: The behavioral intervention technology model and intervention mapping: The best of both worlds. Journal of Medical Internet Research 16(8) (2014)
8. Haslam, D., Sattar, N., Lean, M.: Obesitytime to wake up. Bmj 333(7569), 640–642 (2006)
9. Kelly, T., Yang, W., Chen, C., Reynolds, K., He, J.: Global burden of obesity in 2005 and projections to 2030. International Journal of Obesity 32(9), 1431–1437 (2008)
10. Mohr, D.C., Schueller, S.M., Montague, E., Burns, M.N., Rashidi, P.: The behavioral intervention technology model: An integrated conceptual and technological framework for ehealth and mhealth interventions. Journal of Medical Internet Research 16(6), e146 (2014)
11. Nacke, L.E., Bateman, C., Mandryk, R.L.: Brainhex: preliminary results from a neurobiological gamer typology survey. In: Anacleto, J.C., Fels, S., Graham, N., Kapralos, B., Saif El-Nasr, M., Stanley, K. (eds.) ICEC 2011. LNCS, vol. 6972, pp. 288–293. Springer, Heidelberg (2011)
12. Navarro-Barrientos, J.E., Rivera, D.E., Collins, L.M.: A dynamical model for describing behavioural interventions for weight loss and body composition change. Mathematical and Computer Modelling of Dynamical Systems 17(2), 183–203 (2011)
13. Oduor, M., Alahäivälä, T., Oinas-Kukkonen, H.: Persuasive software design patterns for social influence. Personal and Ubiquitous Computing 18(7), 1689–1704 (2014)
14. Paredes, P.: Design principles for the conceptualization of games for health behaviour change. In: CHI 2013 (2013)
15. Riley, W.T., Rivera, D.E., Atienza, A.A., Nilsen, W., Allison, S.M., Mermelstein, R.: Health behavior models in the age of mobile interventions: are our theories up to the task? Translational Behavioral Medicine 1(1), 53–71 (2011)

Demonstrations

[self.]: Realization/Art Installation/Artificial Intelligence: A Demonstration

Axel Tidemann[1] and Øyvind Brandtsegg[2]

[1] Department of Computer Science, Norwegian University of Science and Technology
Trondheim, Norway
`tidemann@idi.ntnu.no`
[2] Department of Music
Norwegian University of Science and Technology, Trondheim, Norway
`oyvind.brandtsegg@ntnu.no`

Abstract. This interactive installation paper describes [self.], an open source art installation where the people interacting with it determine its auditory and visual vocabulary. When the system starts, it knows nothing since the authors have decided that it should be without any kind of bias. However, the robot is equipped with the ability to learn and be creative with what it has internalized. In order to achieve this behaviour, biologically inspired models are implemented. The robot itself is made up of a moving head, mounted with a camera, projector, microphone and speaker. As an art installation, it has a clear robotic visual appearance, although it is designed to demonstrate life-like behaviour. This is done by making the system start in a "tabula rasa" state, forming categories and concepts as it learns through interaction. This is achieved by linking sounds, faces, video and their corresponding temporal information to form novel sentences. The robot also projects an association between sound and image; this is achieved using neural networks. This provides a visual and immediate way of seeing how the internal representations actually learn a certain concept.

Keywords: artificial intelligence, robot, interaction, art.

1 Background

The original goal was to draw attention to how AI will effect human society, and subsequently what the man-machine-interaction can be like. To achieve this goal, various AI techniques were employed. A design goal was to reach for some sort of primitive consciousness, no matter how simple or fraught with errors it might be. This is of course in itself an enormously ambitious goal, but given the constraints (i.e. it being an art installation), we were not confined to rigorous standards or metrics, such as the Turing test or running up a staircase. Instead, we could focus on the *perceived* intelligence, knowing that the AI techniques implemented on the robot were devised in order to achieve such a goal. The art installation context gives a certain freedom from this kind of scientific measurement, rather

© IFIP International Federation for Information Processing 2015
K. Chorianopoulos et al. (Eds.): ICEC 2015, LNCS 9353, pp. 517–522, 2015.
DOI: 10.1007/978-3-319-24589-8_49

putting the emphasis on how the different aspects of the intelligence can inspire reflection in the participants.

The art installation wanted to examine the relationship between technology and humans, and relates to language, philosophy and the contemporary (over-)focus on self realization. In order to highlight this, the robot had a raw design, with no attempt at anthropomorphization at all. The user interface was therefore rather crude, with exposed motors and wires, in order to illustrate what comprises an artificial intelligence. The user experience depends squarely on the behaviour of the robot.

2   Materials and Methods

Instructions on how to build the robot as well as source code to run it has been published online[1]. The architecture of the robot can be seen in Figure 1. The robot employs well-known methods from the sound processing and AI literature. The robot was built with an off-the-shelf moving head for stage lightning which was gutted except for the motors. On top of the moving head, a projector, USB camera, microphones and a speaker was mounted. The final build of the robot is seen in Figure 2.

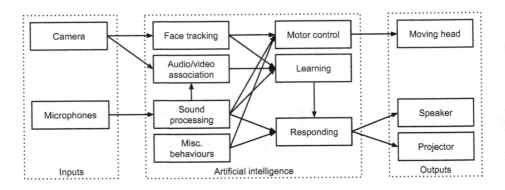

Fig. 1. The overall design of [self.] See the text for details pertaining to each module, the arrows indicate signal paths.

To enable the robot to sense the horizontal position of the sound source, two microphones were mounted on the moving head. These were mounted in a X-Y stereo configuration, allowing an amplitude comparison between the two to give information about the sound source's position. Using this information, the robot can turn towards the person talking to it. Figure 1 describes the overall architecture of [self.].

---

[1] www.github.com/axeltidemann/self_dot

The robot is equipped with a Kalman filter [8] to do face tracking. Csound[2] is used for both audio input and output. Csound is an open source programming language for sound with a rich API. Transient detection is used to segment the audio, this is done based on the amplitude slope and is therefore independent of the absolute amplitude. Upon detection of a transient, audio recording starts. It is stopped when the signal drops below a certain threshold, this is typically 6 dB below the initial transient. Before passing on the audio segment to other parts of the system, silent/noisy parts are deleted.

The raw WAVE files created by Csound are then processed by a biologically inspired model of the inner ear [9], an analysis based on a bio-mimetic "cascade of asymmetric resonators with fast-acting compression". The output is referred to as a neural activation pattern (NAP). This is different from a Fourier spectrum since the NAP has features that correspond to auditory physiology. The NAP is used for learning audio concepts, as well as building a transformation from audio to video.

We wanted to enhance the expressive capabilities of the robot by projecting an association between sound and image. [self.] records video at the same time as it records audio, and this video along with the NAP can then be used to train a neural network that represents a visual memory of the interaction. Echo State Networks (ESNs) [7] are used to form this audio/video transformation. The ESN is trained as follows: when a certain segment is to be learned, the NAP is used as input to the ESN and the corresponding images are used as the output of the ESN. The ESN then learns a mapping from the auditory domain to the video domain, and provides the visual output.

Both face tracking and sound localization influence motor control. Face tracking uses the estimation of the position of the face to rotate the moving head directly in front of the face. Similarly, the localization of sound in the horizontal plane guides the moving head to position it towards the sound source. The face tracking can be thought of as a higher level cognitive function than the sound localization. The organization of these two levels are inspired from Brooks' subsumption architecture [2], a sound can inhibit the motor signals determined by the face tracking. When someone is standing right in front of [self.] but not talking to it, the robot will then turn towards someone else who starts talking.

A crucial part of [self.] is its ability to learn and form categories by clustering similar sounds together. The robot builds an episodic audio-visual memory from each interaction. Similar sounds are clustered together, based on the Hamming distance [5] between sounds of roughly the same length. In this module, face recognition is also implemented. The "Face tracking" module also outputs the face it extracts from each image. Facial recognition is done by Support Vector Machines [4], and the different learning techniques are chosen based on empirical testing.

Context analysis is performed on the recorded audio segments, and this is used to create a set of quality dimensions. They forms a multi-dimensional web of associations, where dynamic weights are applied to each quality dimension.

---

[2] www.csounds.com

This is balanced and weighed similarly to fuzzy logic, where a variable can have partial membership in several relevant contexts. The response is based around the loudest sound perceived in a sentence, and this initiates the association that [self.] uses to generate a response, by comparing the Hamming distance of the new sound (i.e. NAP) to the ones already in memory. [self.] then looks for associations to this sound by looking up the various contexts, as described above. For instance, it can look for similar sounds, sounds uttered by the same face, and sounds in the same sentence or a specific time span. This creates a chain of associations, which yields a repository of sounds that are used to build a response sentence.

The visual output comes from the corresponding audio-visual ESN that was trained earlier. This network is then fed the NAP of the new sound, and the output is sent to the projector. This distributed representation of the audio/video-transformation gives a visual output that varies in accordance with how well the network recognizes the sound. If the sound is very similar to what it has been trained on, the visual output will typically consist of clear images. However, if the sound is very different from the original training sound, the resulting sequence of images will show this difference, e.g. as grey blurs or flashing images. This provides a more "life-like" visual presence of the robot, and provides some intuition into the learning process of [self.]. The memories are not retained forever - if a memory is not recalled, it will fade away as time passes.

Although [self.] is not pre-programmed with any kind of knowledge, it is programmed to perform certain behaviours over time since it is an installation. These are mostly implemented to avoid being caught in a "catatonic" state, and exhibit more life-like behaviour. There are three such behaviours: 1) *Idling:* the robot will search for a face in a pseudo-random pattern if it does not see anyone or hear anything for a certain period of time. Upon finding a face, [self.] finds the sounds it knows this person has said earlier, and uses these to initiate an interaction. If [self.] has not said anything for a certain period of time, it will start talking to itself, i.e. say something on its own. 2) *Dream state:* each night [self.] goes through all the memories experienced throughout the day. The learning process clusters similar sounds together, forming categories. Sometimes this clustering contains errors. The similarity between sounds in the same cluster can be estimated by calculating a sparse representation of the sounds [9], and those that are too different from the others are removed from the category. This resembles what the brain does during sleep [10], and can be thought of as some sort of "mental hygiene" process. 3) *Optimization of parameters for the response mechanism:* as described above, the various associations between sounds, faces and their sequences make it possible to form a multi-dimensional web that can be used to create a response. A large number of interdependent parameters needs to be adjusted in order to achieve the desired behaviour. The parameters themselves are sensitive to the state of the memory, i.e. how many memories are stored and their inherent sequences. [self.] is able to optimize these parameters on its own by using a genetic algorithm [6]. As a consequence, [self.] writes a part of its own behavioural program by the use of evolution.

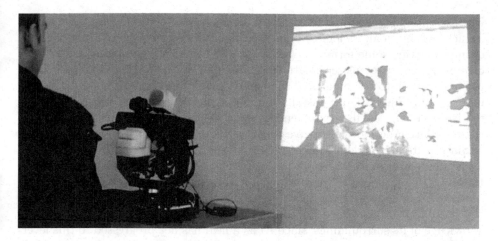

Fig. 2. A person interacting with [self.]

Sound output comes from the speaker mounted on top of the projector, using Csound as the audio engine. In order to make the sound output more life-like and with a character corresponding to the person who taught the given word, the sound is transformed using granular [1] and spectral[3] transformation techniques. These transformations are subtle, with the goal of providing a gentle coloring and personalization of the sound, similar to what the ESN does in the video domain.

The primary moving head constitutes the motor output of [self.], which it uses to locate people. This is seen in figure 2. A secondary moving head (not pictured) is placed a few metres from the main moving head. This is similar to the main head, except it only contains an ultrasonic speaker. The purpose of an ultrasonic speaker is to create a tight sound beam[4], and we use the motorized head to direct this beam around the room. This speaker is used to play back the secondary associations of [self.] to the sounds it perceives, somewhat akin to "what you think about while speaking". These sounds are time stretched using granular techniques and the sound beam reflects on the wall of the room. This is intended to create an impression of "being inside the mind" of [self.] since its secondary associations are projected as sound all around the room, and the time stretching creates a dreamy slow moving representation of the secondary sounds.

3   Performance

When creating the art installation, the focus has been to avoid pre-programming the robot with knowledge, and letting the robot build up its own knowledge base from scratch through interaction. When seeing the system in action, the authors observe how this design choice encourages interactivity, since people interacting

---

[3] www.csounds.com/manual/html/SpectralRealTime.html
[4] www.holosonics.com/technology.html

with [self.] find it rewarding to recognize themselves or someone else they know. To achieve this goal, biologically inspired models are implemented, as a means of implementing some form of cognition in the robot. By employing the web of contexts, it can also answer creatively, something that is further enabled by the use of evolution to write parts of the behavioural programme. This is discussed more in [11]. Since the art installation is completely open in terms of what it receives as input, the user experience is dependent on what it learns throughout the installation period, which gives it an organic feel.

Since [self.] is completely open source, we envision that it can be used also as a research platform for the interplay between people and artificial intelligence. However, the authors are very aware that the system is far from being a truly sentient AI. Even though the robot learns like a child, it currently does not have the possibility to grow into an adult in terms of reasoning power and deeper knowledge of its surroundings, since AI as a field has not progressed to this level yet. On the other hand, this serves as a motivation to continue implementing models of human cognition to get closer to this goal. This kind of *cognitive incrementalism* has been regarded as a way of achieving full-blown human cognition by gradually adding cognitive bells and whistles to an entity [3].

References

1. Brandtsegg, Ø., Saue, S., Johansen, T.: Particle synthesis – a unified model for granular synthesis. In: Linux Audio Conference (2011)
2. Brooks, R.: A robust layered control system for a mobile robot. IEEE Journal of Robotics and Automation 2(1), 14–23 (1986)
3. Clark, A.: Mindware. Mindware (2001)
4. Cortes, C., Vapnik, V.: Support-vector networks. Machine Learning 20(3), 273–297 (1995)
5. Hamming, R.: Error detecting and error correcting codes. The Bell System Technical Journal 29(2), 147–160 (1950)
6. Holland, J.H.: Adaptation in Neural and Artificial Systems. University of Michigan Press, Ann Arbor (1975)
7. Jaeger, H., Haas, H.: Harnessing Nonlinearity: Predicting Chaotic Systems and Saving Energy in Wireless Communication. Science 304(5667), 78–80 (2004)
8. Kalman, R.E.: A new approach to linear filtering and prediction problems. Journal of Fluids Engineering 82(1), 35–45 (1960)
9. Lyon, R.F., Rehn, M., Bengio, S., Walters, T.C., Chechik, G.: Sound retrieval and ranking using sparse auditory representations. Neural Computation 22(9), 2390–2416 (2010)
10. Stickgold, R., Hobson, J.A., Fosse, R., Fosse, M.: Sleep, learning, and dreams: Off-line memory reprocessing. Science 294(5544), 1052–1057 (2001)
11. Tidemann, A., Brandtsegg, Ø.: [self.]: an Interactive Art Installation that Embodies Artificial Intelligence and Creativity. ACM Cognition + Creativity (to appear)

Bridging Tangible and Virtual Interaction: Rapid Prototyping of a Gaming Idea

Thov Reime[1], Heikki Sjöman[1], Achim Gerstenberg[1],
Pekka Abrahamsson[2], and Martin Steinert[1]

[1] Department of Engineering Design and Materials, NTNU,
Richard Birkelands vei 2B, 7492 Trondheim, Norway
{Heikki.Sjoman,Achim.Gerstenberg,
Martin.Steinert}@ntnu.no, Thov@stud.ntnu.no
[2] Department of Computer and Information Science, NTNU, Sem Sælands vei 9,
7491 Trondheim, Norway
pekkaa@ntnu.no

Abstract. The Fibo Car is an example for a game interface that allows a user to modify a virtual car in a racing game through assembling tangible car parts. This paper describes the 6 week development journey towards a fully functional proof of concept prototype, reflections on the process as well as the technical details of the prototype.

1 Introduction

The basic idea of the Fibo Car game project is that the player can construct a real world car model out of tangible building blocks. The structure of the model is digitally recognized and it influences the properties of the virtual model in the car racing game.

In this paper we focus solely on the development of the tangible objects, the structure recognition, and a virtual representation without any gameplay. The game idea is related to games like Kerbal Space Program [1] or Besiege [2] except that the constructing takes place tangibly like in LEGO Mindstorms [3].

The solution presented here has one central part that can detect the attached neighboring parts. The identification is realized by measuring and identifying part-specific resistances with an Arduino Uno microcontroller board [4] wired to a PC. A virtual representation of the identified tangible model is then shown on a screen. The latest version of the prototype is shown in figure 1.

The upcoming section describes the development journey of the first 6 weeks. It includes failures, dead ends, and gives reasons for the actions taken. We concentrated on development speed using a process with rapid iteration cycles in favour of fast learning and quick improvement without project control by predefining requirements and a priori budgeting.

K. Chorianopoulos et al. (Eds.): ICEC 2015, LNCS 9353, pp. 523–528, 2015.
DOI: 10.1007/978-3-319-24589-8_50

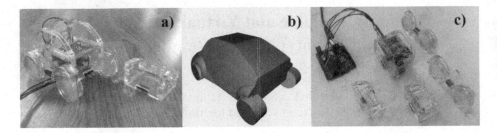

Fig. 1. Latest proof of concept prototype showing the tangible model in a) and the corresponding virtual representation in b). All available tangible car parts of the latest prototype are shown in c).

2   Development Journey

The project started with a presentation of the basic game idea by the problem owner to the developers. The aim was to reach a common ground on the project vision and the reasons behind the idea. This initiated a brainstorming about possible solutions. The main challenge was perceived to be the structure recognition. Therefore, we started by exploring possible technical solutions on paper. When considering radio communication and information through light signals, measuring resistances turned out to be the easiest to develop and cheapest alternative. Concerning the algorithm for structure recognition, we realized that it is simpler if each car part is only detecting its nearest neighbor instead of all parts detecting the entire structure. Therefore, resistance identification and neighbor detection were chosen to be pursued. The resistor solution was tested with resistors on a solderless prototyping board measured with ohmmeters. The principle was confirmed as functional. The idea here was to make sure as early, simple and fast as possible that principles worked with components already available in the lab in order to minimize the amount of time wasted in case it did not work. In the beginning of the **second week** of the development journey, we determined that we require three electrical connection points for connecting two car parts. This fit with the already existing BitSnap connectors [5] that had three electric connection points. They used magnets and their own shape to ensure a consistent and non-ambiguous electrical connection. Those BitSnap connectors were designed to be soldered onto a circuit board, and solderless prototyping boards were too large to fit into the car parts. Knowing that the principle worked, we decided that spending time for manufacturing a soldered circuit board version was a safe investment. The result is shown in figure 2 on the left. From this prototype we learned that the BitSnap connectors were mechanically not rigid enough to support the weight of the car parts. Furthermore, the connectors were not symmetrical, meaning that only matching pairs were combinable. This was in conflict to the fundamental idea of allowing any given car piece to connect. Anyhow, the structure recognition technically worked. Therefore, we continued developing the remaining critical functions such as measuring the resistors with a microcontroller, sending this data to a PC and displaying the measurement on a screen. We decided to not bother with improving the connectors at this point in time to save time towards achieving the critical functions of our envisioned game idea. The microcontroller measurement was prototyped using an Arduino Uno because it is easy to develop, immediately accessible in the lab, and already offers the software to display the results of the measurement on a computer screen. After merging the existing development stages and fulfilling the critical functions as early as possible (digitally recognizing a structure of mechanically attached objects, transferring this data to a PC, and displaying it) we could now focus on improving the existing solution. During **week three**, we intended to focus on shrinking the Arduino microcontroller solution to a size that is suitable for embedding in a car part. Light Blue Beans [6] appeared to be a suitable solution that is already available in the lab. They also had the advantage of replacing the wire connection between the Arduino and the PC by wireless Bluetooth communication. One upcoming problem with Light Blue Beans was that they only have two analogue inputs. This lead to the use of shift registers to channel many measurements through few input pins on the microcontroller. The shift register also work in combination with the Arduino Uno and the Arduino was kept because it is more convenient to program.

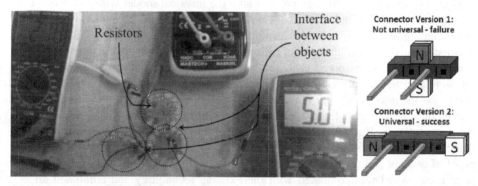

Fig. 2. Left: the resistances on the connected circuit boards in the middle are unique for each connection and measured by ohmmeters. Right: two sequent designs of a mechanically more stable connector.

Week four started with developing mechanically stronger and symmetrical connectors. This was implemented by using larger and stronger magnets and using pin connectors to further stabilize mechanically. The first design is shown in figure 2 in the top right. However, this design turned out to be impossible to connect to an identical connector because the magnet orientation would not match. It required a matching counter piece and was thus no improvement to the previous solution with the BitSnaps. The bottom right design solved this problem. This design flaw was discovered by building and testing the design in a very rough way instead of technically drawing and machine producing the parts. This decreases the risk of design errors and thereby saves more costly resources at a later development stage when such errors have more profound implications.

All electrical components were now on two large breadboards that required a lot of space. The components had to be merged on one platform so that they would all fit safely inside a physical shell. This was accomplished by soldering all components (transistors to control a shift register, reference resistors and header connectors) compactly onto a custom circuit board.

The next issue to be tackled was to advance the virtual representation from a line of text to a car look-a-like representation. We took two approaches into account: The first was a photograph based version where the PC would display a corresponding picture for every possible combination of parts. The second was using 3D models for representation of the car structure. We decided to develop the second option because the number of pictures needed for the first was inconveniently large when scaling up the number of car parts. We used Processing [7] to process the data coming from the Arduino, determining the structure and displaying the models on the PC screen. The system was first tested by displaying a rocket and a chair as substitutes for the virtual car model. Only after verifying the concept, we continued to make virtual representations of the car parts using a CAD software and importing those models to Processing. After confirming that Processing was a reasonable option for displaying a digital representation, **week five** began by drawing the car model parts and implementing them within Processing. At the same time, we also pursued the implementation of Light Blue Beans to make the physical model wireless. However, we experienced that Windows 8.1 did not allow importing serial data via Bluetooth. We could not instantly resolve this problem with the resources at hand and therefore decided to move back to the proven technology to not lose more time with this issue. During **week six** we explored switches, buttons and potentiometers as extra tangible inputs to alter the car parts. Since the gameplay did not yet exist, the visual representation was the only possibility to make adjustments to. We showed that this extension was technically functional and could also be used to change non-visual properties in the game later on. But there was no meaningful reason to develop something further that had no use at the current development stage. Therefore, we stopped after the proof of concept and continued to make a laser cut physical car model in acrylic. The acrylic car model was combined with the existing technology and combined all aspects from physical model to structure recognition and virtual representation. Figure 1 shows the prototype after these six weeks of development.

3   Reflections on the Development Process

It turned out that our process was very similar to the wayfaring process described by Steinert and Leifer [8]. Both processes are largely based on rapid iteration cycles of design, build and testing ideas as early and quickly as possible. We tested the most critical functions with the resources that are readily available in the lab to fail early and mitigate the risk of losing advances that become unusable due to a later design changes. The early testing lead to learnings that shaped the development journey; the design emerged over time.

4   Detailed Description of the Latest Prototype

The final prototype consists of one central part connected to a PC, and four external objects that can be attached to the central part. The central part has four connectors, one on each vertical side, on which external parts can be attached; each external part has only one connector. When no external parts are attached to the central part, a 3D model resembling the central part is displayed on the connected PC screen. Upon attaching an external part to the central part, a virtual 3D model resembling the attached part is automatically updated.

The identification of the neighboring car parts is achieved by the measurement of resistors through the connectors on the sides of the car parts. All connectors are made from 4 pin headers where two alternating pins are pulled out (see figure 2, bottom right). In the external parts' headers, a resistor is placed with one pin hole between its two legs. In the central part headers, two wires are connected to the female pins that the external connectors will fit into. Thus, when an external part connector is connected to a central part connector, we get a closed loop that runs through one wire into one of the central part header pins, through the male pin on the external part header, through the resistor, and back across to the other wire. This design is made with the intention of having multiple 'central parts' in the future that can measure each other's resistors. So far in this prototype, the central part pins that connect to the external header serve only for structural integrity.

The connector wires are connected to an analogue gate and ground on an Arduino Uno. The Arduino is able to calculate the resistance between ground and the analogue gate by comparing it to a reference resistor between its 5 volt supply and ground. Because there are four connectors and we use only one analogue gate, a shift register is used to control which connector has current at any time. The shift register is placed on a custom made circuit board along with the reference resistor, four transistors, two rows of headers for the connector wires, and a series of headers for easy connection of wires from the Arduino. Three wires connect three digital pins on the Arduino to the shift register. The shift register is connected to the gate pins on the transistors which open the current through the various connectors. Thus, the loop through ground, resistor, and analog gate is controlled. The circuit board is placed inside the central part and connected to the Arduino through a total of six wires (three digital, 5V, ground, and analogue).

When measuring the resistors, the Arduino uses as sequence of North, West, South, and East when the central part is seen from above. For each measurement, the value is serial printed, and a semicolon is added between the values. Processing 2.2.1 imports the string through the COM port on a PC. Before Processing can use the data for anything, it must convert the string into integers and store them in an array. The semicolons act as delimiters for the values. Processing then takes each value in the array and compares it to a set of thresholds.

Processing displays a rotating 3D model resembling the central part in a window. Depending on which interval between thresholds a certain measured value is, Processing displays a corresponding 3D model next to the central part. The correct position is acquired by the position of the value in the array, thus the reason for the compass sequence in the Arduino.

All 3D models are made in Autodesk Inventor [9] and converted into an .obj format. Processing loads the models in the setup of the script, and only displays them when receiving not NULL values from the Arduino.

The physical objects are made from laser cut pieces of 5mm thick acrylic plastic sheets. All pieces are modeled and assembled in Inventor before converting to a 2D format fit for cutting. The pieces are then assembled together with circuit board, central part connectors, and external connector. The pieces are held together with hot glue and clear tape so that broken pieces can be removed and retrofitting is easier.

5   Future Plans

In the near future, we will focus on improving the existing prototype by including wireless communication, universally orientable connectors, alternate modes of inter-object communication, more than one 'smart part', and how to merge our tangible programming prototype with actual gameplay. We will continue to use a wayfaring mind set as we are satisfied with the results it has yielded so far. Looking further ahead, developing and testing of real gameplay is needed before we can undergo user testing and subsequent reiterations.

Acknowledgments. We extend our most sincere gratitude to project owner Leonore Alexandra Nilsen, CEO of Metis Productions AS, for giving us this challenge and introducing us to the Fibo Car Project. This research is supported by the Research Council of Norway (RCN) through its user-driven research (BIA) funding scheme, project number 236739/O30.

References

1. Web page about "Kerbal Space Program", https://kerbalspaceprogram.com/en/?page_id=7 (retrieved April 28, 2015)
2. "Besiege" sandbox game, http://www.besiege.spiderlinggames.co.uk/ (retrieved April 28, 2015)
3. lEGO Mind Storms EV3, http://www.lego.com/en-/mindstorms/?domainredir=mindstorms.lego.com (retrieved April 28, 2015)
4. Arduino Uno microcontroller board, http://www.arduino.cc/en/Main/HomePage (retrieved April 28, 2015)
5. Little Bits Electronics, BitSnaps, http://littlebits.cc/accessories/bitsnaps (retrieved April 28, 2015)
6. Lightblue Beans, https://punchthrough.com/bean/ (retrieved April 28, 2015)
7. Processing programming language, https://processing.org/ (retrieved April 28, 2015)
8. Steinert, M., Leifer, L.: 'Finding One's Way': Re-Discovering a Hunter-Gatherer Model based on Wayfaring. Int. J. Eng. Educ. 28(1), 251–252 (2012)
9. Autodesk Inventor, http://www.autodesk.com/products/inventor/overview (retrieved April 28, 2015)

Can Interactive Art Installations Attract 15 Years Old Students to Coding?

Michail N. Giannakos, Finn Inderhaug Holme, Letizia Jaccheri,
Irene Dominguez Marquez, Sofia Papavlasopoulou, and Ilse Gerda Visser

Norwegian University of Science and Technology (NTNU), Trondheim, Norway
{michailg,letizia}@idi.ntnu.no, {finninde,ilsegv}@stud.ntnu.no,
contact@namtarucreations.com
sofia.papavlasopoulou@gmail.com

Abstract. In this art demonstration we will present the art installations which are at the center of a creative development program for young students with the name KODELØYPA. KODELØYPA is based on the philosophy of creative reuse of recycled materials and the open-source software Scratch and Arduino. KODELØYPA is based on an empirically validated framework, designed and implemented by researchers and artists.

Keywords: Creative activities, software and hardware development, physical–digital creativity, art and technology.

1 Introduction

The Norwegian University of Science and Technology (NTNU) offers six science frameworks for Norwegian primary and secondary schools with the objective of raising interest in various science disciplines from physics, chemistry, mathematics, biology, energy, to coding. The framework, dedicated to raise interest in coding is based on the hypothesis that the interactions between the children and the artifacts in a creative activity are vital [5]. In this framework children learn coding by playfully interacting with digital artifacts that also exhibit physical and aesthetical characteristics. Such artifacts allow children to learn by iteratively testing and rebuilding their designs [2]. The interactive installations presented by this paper are the concrete results of our efforts to develop an authentic environment for creative learning that helps school children, to build their own digital game based on the interplay of digital and physical objects. KODELØYPA represents a good example of novel directions in the creative learning. In particular, in this paper we focus on the artifacts specifically designed and created for the workshop program where children collaboratively engaged in modifying interactive artworks that react to events in the physical world [6].

2 KODELØYPA: An Approach to Enhance Creative Learning

KODELØYPA is based on open source software and hardware and consisted of tutorials on open source tools, artifacts, creative sessions and students' demonstrations/

© IFIP International Federation for Information Processing 2015
K. Chorianopoulos et al. (Eds.): ICEC 2015, LNCS 9353, pp. 529–532, 2015.
DOI: 10.1007/978-3-319-24589-8_51

presentations. Up to date, KODELØYPA has organized four workshops, allowing 63 students to be introduced to coding (about 15 children per workshop). Our thesis is that coding skills improve children understanding of the design and functionalities that underlie all aspects of interfaces, technologies, and systems we encounter daily. It is important that everyone should use code in some ways for expressive purposes to better communicate, interact with others, and build relationships.

Fig. 1. Left: The artist organizes old computer pieces and other garbage to prepare the components to be used for the physical phase. Right: One of the assistant animates the spider installation by help of motors.

KODELØYPA is based on a well-documented and validated framework [4, 5]. It enables children to engage in programming languages (i.e., Scratch) and programmable hardware platforms (i.e., Arduino), to enable them to become the creators and programmers of their own playful experiences. KODELØYPA takes place at NTNU's premises. Children attending the workshops are instructed and assisted by one artist, and 6 assistants; who have organized the process in advance (Fig. 1). The art demonstration will present the artifacts developed during KODELØYPA (Fig. 2 shows one art installation).

3   Requirements for the Exhibitions

In the demonstration we will illustrate the process (Fig. 3), as well as the tangible results from the KODELØYPA program. These are interactive installations made by a team of artists, designers, and programmers for the purpose of enabling young students to become creators of interactive experience with both artistic and technical qualities.

We can exhibit up to five interactive installations. They vary in size but they are all smaller than 1 cubic meter. Each one can be connected to a PC and is programmable. A screen with a video about the program will be provided.

Fig. 2. One concrete installation: the swan.

Fig. 3. Picture from one workshop: children play, program, interact with the assistants.

References

1. Buechley, L., Eisenberg, M., Catchen, J., Crockett, A.: The LilyPad Arduino: Using Computational Textiles to Investigate Engagement, Aesthetics, and Diversity in Computer Science Education. In: Proc. CHI 2008, pp. 423–432. ACM Press (2008)
2. Cassell, J.: Towards a Model of Technology and Literacy Development: Story Listening Systems. Journal of Applied Developmental Psychology 25(1), 75–105 (2004)
3. Edwards, C., Gandini, L., Forman, G.: The hundred languages of children: the Reggio Emilia approach to early childhood education, 2nd edn. Ablex Publishing, NJ (1998)
4. Giannakos, M.N., Jaccheri, L.: What motivates children to become creators of digital enriched artifacts? In: Proceedings of the 9th ACM Conference on Creativity & Cognition, pp. 104–113. ACM Press (2013)
5. Jaccheri, L., Giannakos, M.N.: Open source software for entertainment. In: Herrlich, M., Malaka, R., Masuch, M. (eds.) ICEC 2012. LNCS, vol. 7522, pp. 604–607. Springer, Heidelberg (2012)
6. Papert, S.: Mindstorms: Children, Computers, and Powerful Ideas. Basic Books, New York (1980)
7. Price, S., Rogers, Y.: Let's get physical: the learning benefits of interacting in digitally-augmented physical spaces. Computers & Education 43(1-2), 137–151 (2004)

Digital Art Application Development: A Project to Increase Motivation in Systems Development Courses for Bachelor Students in Computer Engineering

Anniken Karlsen and Robin T. Bye

Aalesund University College, Aalesund, Norway
{ak,roby}@hials.no

Abstract. In this demonstration, we present some in-progress results of using digital art application development as an example of entertainment computing for increasing motivation and participation in a computer engineering undergraduate systems development course, with the purpose of improving the chances of reaching the intended learning outcomes. By stimulating motivation and participation via an openly defined project description of making an interactive art application in a competitive context, a variety of interesting project outcomes were produced, despite the fact that the project did not count towards the final grading of the course. The students made their applications by combining existing programming skills with the programming language Processing, lessons in Human-Computer-Interaction and software development methodologies.

Keywords: Art and motivation, Creative activities, Digital creativity, Teaching, Software engineering.

1 Introduction

Aalesund University College (AAUC) offers a variety of bachelor education programs. As part of becoming a computer engineer, software development is vital. Programming is introduced in the first study year. In the second year, this competence is further developed. Specifically, in the fourth semester course Systems Development and Modeling, the teachers have been trying for years to increase the motivation for projects where the outcome does not directly count as a grading criterion, only the final exam does. Last year a competition project was initiated based on requirements and specifications from a private company [1]. This year another competition was initiated. This time the project mission was provided by the teachers and deliberately made more open, with the goal of developing a digital art application as an example of entertainment computing to stimulate creativity and fun as part of the development process.

The use of digital technology in contemporary art is often referred to as new media art [2]. Software engineering, including systems development and modelling, are key elements in succeeding bridging the gap between the worlds of the computer programmer and the artist. In higher education, the combination of art and computing can be used for the benefit of attracting students to computer science and providing a stimulating framework for studying software engineering issues (e.g., see [3]).

© IFIP International Federation for Information Processing 2015
K. Chorianopoulos et al. (Eds.): ICEC 2015, LNCS 9353, pp. 533–538, 2015.
DOI: 10.1007/978-3-319-24589-8_52

The idea of using entertainment computing such as new media technology for teaching computer engineering courses is not new. Whilst the domain of entertainment technology can be divided into the four fields of games; sports; novels and movies; and art [4], there seems to be a focus in computing education on programming computer games (e.g., simple versions of classic games like Pac-Man or Space Invaders) or toy robots such as Lego Mindstorms (mindstorms.lego.com) [5]. Indeed, at AAUC, we are using the highly advanced, yet easy to use 3D game engine Unity (www.unity3d.com) for a variety of courses as well as for research. In this paper, on the other hand, our approach of using digital art as the vehicle for teaching a computer engineering course appears to be a less trodden path.

Central to the course and its use of the above mentioned student project is the adoption of an active learning paradigm, which is dominant in many of the engineering courses taught at AAUC and have recently also been the focus of education research in a joint computer and automation engineering course on microcontrollers offered at AAUC [6]. A key factor for achieving intended learning outcomes is the students' approach to learning [7, 8]. Many studies have tried to identify factors that promote deeper learning [e.g., 9,10], that is, learning associated with understanding in contrast with surface learning, where focus is on memorizing facts and procedures, and with little or no understanding as a result [8]. According to one definition by Prince [11], active learning is any learning activity or teaching method that actively involves the students in the learning process, usually associated with cooperative learning, problem-based learning, and practical exercises. Of these learning activities, particularly cooperative learning strategies have shown the best learning effects [e.g. 12, 13, 14, and 15].

Common characteristics of new media include new types of entertainment experiences; interactive as opposed to passive experiences; and integration of spatial, social, mental, and physical presence [16]. The creation of a digital art application as presented here encompasses much of these in an "integrated presence" [16], combining physical presence (team work, programming, discussions, etc.) with mental presence (study literature, watch and judge the art created by the application, etc.). Indeed, computer programming is a creative form of art itself, which combined with the excitement of creating an interactive art application triggers a number of enjoyable entertainment experiences such as curiosity, pleasingness, pride, perception of being in control, etc. [17].

2   About the Project

The class of 24 students was divided into 6 groups, each with 4 students. All groups were given the same task of designing an interactive application for generating digital art but were free to approach the problem as they desired. When first introducing the project to the students, they seemed surprised. One student stated that he was not into art and did not feel particularly creative. Another stated that he had no insight into visualization and animation. A third stated that programming was not among his favorites. He therefore worried that the project would be too demanding. As a response to these worries, the students were shown a variety of visual art applications found on the Internet. They were also introduced to Processing, a programming language created to make programming interactive graphics easier [18]. The language was made by Reas and Fry who were frustrated with how difficult it was to write this type of software with the programming languages they usually used [19]. By combining Processing with previous insights into the Java programming language, soon after the students made colorful lines and figures on the screen. Many of these became blue-prints and ideas for brushes, a basic painting tool, to be found in the future art applications. Some of the students seemed amazed of what they were able to make and words like fun and interesting started to fill the room.

Stimulating creativity is one of the aspects highlighted by the Norwegian Ministry of Knowledge in the national curriculum for 3-year bachelor degrees in engineering (Universities and Colleges Act, 2005) [20], based on the vision of an engineer as socially committed, creative and dynamic, with the ability to actively contribute to future challenges. Adding to this, The National Council for Technological Education [21] in their guidelines for engineering education also emphasizes the ability to be skilled at working independently as well as in engineering teams. Obviously, letting the students collaborate in groups with much freedom in choosing their own design decisions stimulated both creativity and dynamic teamwork. The students eagerly investigated how they could use their previous programming knowledge together with the capabilities of Processing to make an application for generating artistic pictures. They got new ideas, and some of them seemed to burst into excitement.

3   Competition and Creativity as a Driving Force for Learning

To develop the art applications the students started by investigating the capabilities of Processing [19] as a programming tool. By challenging them to first make some simple forms and figures and then systematically making the tasks more complicated they all showed great progress in making visualizations and animations on the screen. Between lectures the students continued the work at school or at home. They all used an agile development method with several meetings and incremental deliveries.

The teachers' main experience was that the climate of positive competition mixed with creative thinking and doings improved motivation and thereby increased student participation even though the project did not per se count on the grading. One of the students stated that he now saw programming as fun and engaging. Another highlighted that he had never experienced such a progression in obtaining knowledge in other courses he had attended.

4   Awards Ceremony for Worthy Winners

On the final day of the course, each student group demonstrated their application to the other student groups and a jury panel of externals (see Fig. 1 for a screenshot).

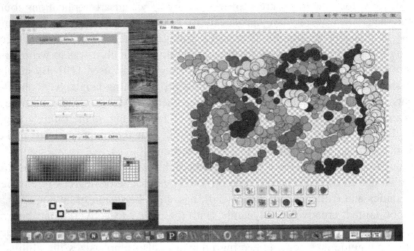

Fig. 1. Screenshot from one of the applications

The panel was invited to choose the winner app and constituted one academic, one architect, one professional artist and one person from a private computer company. The teachers themselves did not take part in the formal evaluation to pick a winner. The jury did an overall evaluation based on the technical quality and complexity of the app, its usability, the artistic quality of the generated art, and the presentation skills of the group. An artistic lithograph was given to each member of the winning group and the second best group.

5   Results and Conclusions

The main project outcomes reported by the students were joy, engagement and increased capability and trust in their personal software development skills by having developed creative applications. The need to make decisions on their own mixed with an informal creative competition made this a continuous learning process motivating further engagement in programming and graphics.

As teachers, we observed that the students were able to write large and complex software, integrating and synthesizing computer code and libraries readily available with their own code tailored for their own art application. Thus, the student project served as a suitable practical test-bed for the various theoretical aspects of the course. It is also worth mentioning that the class results from the final examination were overall very good although we have no rigorous evidence linking the project to these results at this time. Finally, a number of in-depth tape-recorded interviews with students in focus groups will be analyzed with the prospect of further improving the course design and informing future research. We will report on the findings from the interviews in a subsequent paper.

According to [6], there are at least three important factors for succeeding with an active learning paradigm as presented in this paper. The first factor is the effect of instant feedback, which is well known as a basis in behavioral learning. Programming graphical art applications gave the students immediate feedback about their code and if something was working or not, thus the positive effect of instant feedback was achieved. The second factor is the bi-directional interaction between lectures and practical work, where both affect each other positively. The project served as a suitable domain for applying theory, thus making lectures more worthwhile and easy to absorb. The third factor is related to critique against problem-based learning in the literature. According to a survey of 800 meta-studies, Hattie [22] found that problem-based learning has no effect on achieving intended learning outcomes. Instead, there is a positive effect from problem-solving learning [6]. The reason for this is likely provided by Sotto [23], who claims that students spend too much time searching and sorting information in problem-based learning compared to problem-solving learning. Presumably, it appears that the readiness of available tools, an easy-to-use programming language like Processing, and the immediate visual feedback turned our project into a problem-solving one, where students quickly were able to focus on solving the actual problem.

In this demonstration, we illustrate tangible results from the art application competition, remembering that these are applications made by teams of students that in advance did not feel particularly creative and/or capable of making art on the computer screen. The end-results obviously proved them wrong.

Acknowledgements. The authors wish to thank our enthusiastic students and in particular the winning group consisting of Stein Sæter, Terje Eik, Erik Espenakk, and Tony André Haugen. In addition, we are grateful for the valuable insight provided by Professor Letizia Jaccheri during the preparation of this paper.

References

1. Karlsen, A., Kristiansen, H.: Undervisningsrefleksjoner fra et konkurranseprosjekt i samarbeid med næringslivsaktør. Norsk konferanse for organisasjoners bruk av informasjonsteknologi (NOKOBIT 2014), Open Access at:
   http://obj.bibsys.no/index.php/NOKOBIT/index
2. Trifonova, A., Jaccheri, L., Bergaust, K.: Software engineering issues in interactive installation art. Int. J. Arts and Technology 1(1), 43–65 (2008)
3. Giannakos, M.N., Jaccheri, L.: Designing creative activities for children: the importance of collaboration and the threat of losing control. In: Proceedings of the 12th International Conference on Interaction Design and Children. ACM (2013)
4. Altman, E., Nakatsu, R.: Interactive Movies: Techniques, Technology and Content. Course Notes. In: SIGGRAPH 1997, vol. (16), ACM (1997)
5. Overmars, M.: Teaching computer science through game design. Computer 37(4), 81–83 (2004)
6. Schaathun, W., Schaathun, H.G., Bye, R.T.: Aktiv læring i mikrokontrollarar. Artikkel presentert på MNT- konferansen 2015 og under vurdering for publisering i Uniped (2015)

7. Gynnild, V.: Læringsorientert eller eksamensfokusert? Nærstudier av pedagogisk utviklingsarbeid i sivilingeniørstudiet. PhD, NTNU, Trondheim (2001)
8. Marton, F.: Phenomenography – describing conceptions of the world around us. Instructional Science 10, 177–200 (1981)
9. Marton, F., Booth, S.: Learning and awareness. Lawrence Erlbaum, Mahwaw (1997)
10. Prosser, M., Trigwell, K.: Understanding learning and teaching: The experience on higher education. Society for Research in Higher Education / Open Univeristy Press, Buckingham (1999)
11. Prince, M.J.: Does active learning work? A review of the research. Journal of Engineering Education 93(3), 223–231 (2004)
12. Bowen, C.W.: A Quantitative Literature Review of Cooperative Learning Effects on High School and College Chemistry Achievement. Journal of Chemical Education 77(1), 116 (2000)
13. Foldnes, N.: Cooperative Learning in the Flipped Classroom: A Randomized Experiment. Unpublished manuscript (2014)
14. Johnson, D., Johnson, R., Smith, K.: Active Learning: Cooperation in the College Classroom (2 utg). Interaction Book Co, Edina (1998)
15. Springer, L., Stanne, M., Donovan, S.: Effects of small-group learning on undergraduates in science, mathematics, engineering and technology: A meta-analysis. Review of Educational Research 69(1), 21–52 (1999)
16. Nakatsu, R., Rauterberg, M., Vorderer, P.: A new framework for entertainment computing: from passive to active experience. In: Kishino, F., Kitamura, Y., Kato, H., Nagata, N. (eds.) ICEC 2005. LNCS, vol. 3711, pp. 1–12. Springer, Heidelberg (2005)
17. Vorderer, P., Klimmt, C., Ritterfeld, U.: Enjoyment: At the heart of media entertainment. Communication Theory 14(4), 388–408 (2004)
18. Greenberg, I., Xu, D., Kumar, D.: Processing – Creative coding and Generative Art in Processing 2. Friendsof – an Apress company (2013)
19. Reas, C., Fry, B.: Getting Started with Processing. O'Reilly (2010)
20. Kunnskapsdepartementet. Ny forskrift om rammeplan for ingeniørutdanning, Kunnskapsdepartementets internettside med lenke til lovdata (2011), http://lovdata.no/dokument/SF/forskrift/2011-02-03-107
21. Nasjonalt råd for teknologisk utdanning. Nasjonale retningslinjer for ingeniørutdanning: På vei mot fremtiden! (2011) (Downloaded May 11, 2015) http://www.uhr.no/documents/Nasjonale_retningslinjer_for_ing eni_rutdanning_ENGELSK.pdf
22. Hattie, J.: Visible learning: A synthesis of over 800 meta-analyses relating to achievement. Routledge (2013)
23. Sotto, E.: When teaching becomes learning: A theory and practice of teaching, vol. 2. Continuum, London (2007)

Pedal Tanks

A Multiplayer Exergame Based on Teamwork and Competition

Kristoffer Hagen, Stian Weie, Konstantinos Chorianopoulos,
Alf Inge Wang, and Letizia Jaccheri

Norwegian University of Science and Technology,
Trondheim, Norway
{kiffihagen,stianwe}@gmail.com
{choko, alfw, letizia}@idi.ntnu.no

Abstract. This installation presents a multiplayer stationary bicycle exergame for four players. The game is played in teams of two, where the players compete to outmaneuver the opposition. Pedal Tanks is being developed to increase the physical activity levels of people struggling to find motivation to exercise. Inspiration for the gameplay has been found in the computer game industry, using elements from contemporary popular computer games and combining them in a cohesive way yields an exergame that is both familiar and engaging. Both the software and hardware used has been custom-made to create an immersive experience where the user forgets that he/she is exercising while playing.

Keywords: Exergame, exertion game, active video game, computer game, sedentary lifestyle, competitive multiplayer, physical activity.

1 Introduction and Motivation

Computer games have become one of the most popular activities of everyday life for youths and adults alike. More time is being spent on television, computer and other gaming devices than any other activity apart from sleeping [8]. We are also living increasingly sedentary lifestyles, replacing physical activity with sedentary activity. In the last five years alone, average computer use by youths has increased by 40 minutes per day, or the equivalent of 240 hours a year [7]. This lifestyle, characterized by increased time spent in front of a screen and decreased physical activity, has been shown to increase the risk of both physical as well as psychological illness [4, 5]. These trends motivated us to investigate the potential of promoting physical exercise in tandem with providing gaming-type entertainment. We wanted to create an ordinary computer entertainment game where exercise equipment is used as a game controller – an exergame. Exergames make it possible for many to combine their favorite hobby with physical activity. This can therefore provide a significant contribution to deter the impending sedentary lifestyle epidemic.

© IFIP International Federation for Information Processing 2015
K. Chorianopoulos et al. (Eds.): ICEC 2015, LNCS 9353, pp. 539–544, 2015.
DOI: 10.1007/978-3-319-24589-8_53

This installation will demonstrate our current prototype of Pedal Tanks. Our objective is to develop a video game that can provide continued motivation to exercise. While our proposal is aimed primarily at people already familiar with computer games, it may also be of interest for those who have yet to venture into this domain. Distinct from many existing efforts in the field of exergames, Pedal Tanks aims combat the retention issue often found in exergames [6] by utilizing tried-and-true features found in some of the most popular computer games [2, 9].

Game	Teambased multiplayer	Competitive multiplayer	Different playable classes	Persistent progression
LoL	Yes	Yes	Yes	Yes
WoW	Yes	Yes	Yes	Yes
Dota 2	Yes	Yes	Yes	Yes
CS:GO	Yes	Yes	No	No
Diablo 3	Yes	No	Yes	Yes
Minecraft	No	Yes	No	No
Hearthstone	Yes	Yes	Yes	Yes
Battlefield	Yes	Yes	Yes	Yes
Archeage	Yes	Yes	Yes	Yes
Smite	Yes	Yes	Yes	Yes
Sum	9 of 10	9 of 10	8 of 10	8 of 10

Fig. 1. Features found in the most popular computer games

Pedal Tanks has applications for people who normally have difficulty motivating themselves to go to the gym, exercise, move regularly, and stay in shape. It presents the opportunity to achieve an appropriate level of physical fitness while doing something that is enjoyable.

2   Prototype Hardware

The prototype is based on a stationary bicycle enhanced with hardware components. On the wheel, a pattern of black and white sectors has been attached, and above the pattern, two optical sensors are mounted. A small offset in the placement of the optical sensors generates a 2 bit gray-code [3] when the wheel, and thereby sectors, beneath revolves. This method creates a resolution of two orders of magnitude (dependent upon the number of black and white sectors) greater than the magnetic sensor normally used, effectively removing any sense of input delay and mapping movement into the game with very high accuracy. Six buttons are positioned on the handlebars, two in the front and four behind, in positions naturally accessible in a bicycling pose.

Both the controller and the sensors are connected to a microcontroller (in our case an Arduino[1]) that converts the analog input into a digital signal and prepares it for transmission to the game via a virtual COM port over USB. Figure 2 shows the prototype bike with sensors and buttons.

Fig. 2. Bicycle prototype

3   The Game of Pedal Tanks

Pedal Tanks is an online multiplayer capture the flag arena game. Each player drives a tank in a 3rd person view for the duration of the game, as seen in Fig. 3. The tanks are controlled by the pedals on the bike and the six buttons on the handlebar, two for turning and four for firing the cannon and performing other actions in the game. The tanks are selected from a pool of vehicles at the start of the game. Certain tanks are slow, powerful, and defensive; others are fast, fragile and superior at capturing the flag. Each tank comes equipped with a predetermined set of two actions, or abilities, that the players can activate during the game. These two abilities, together with the tank's innate characteristics, define that tank's role in the team. Deft use of the tank's abilities drastically improves the chance to succeed in the game. The players must effectively utilize all the strengths of their tanks in order to gain the advantage. Each game consists of a preselected number of rounds that end once one team manages to capture the flag, or the two minute timer runs out.

---

[1] http://www.arduino.cc/

Fig. 3. Screenshot from the game during play

After every game, the players are rewarded with experience points based on their performance, and new types of tanks will become available as the players advance in level. This aspect of persistence not only heightens the players' investment in the game, but also affords control over the learning curve and complexity of the game, allowing new players to start out with simple classes of tanks and unlock more complex ones as they grow accustomed to the game. Having many different varieties of tanks for both player and opponent dramatically increases the replay value of the game, a feature that can be found in many of the most popular video-games [1]. With two games very seldom having the same combination of tanks, the players can continuously discover new interactions and strategies, causing the game to feel "fresh" even after many hours of play.

Movement in the game is encouraged through the objectives; guarding your flag from opponents and getting their flag back to your base, and through gameplay mechanics such as the ability to regenerate ammunition based on the distance moved within the game. The best strategy is not always to go as fast as possible, sometimes it is better to sneak into the opponents' base, or simply wait for them to make a tactical mistake and exploit it. On the other hand, when a player acquires the opponents' flag, it is usually best to return to home-base to capture the flag as fast as possible. After a player has been eliminated, and in between rounds, there is a short break in which the player(s) can catch their breath before they reinitiate play. This gameplay generates a beneficial high-intensity interval training for the users, providing good physical benefits per time played, ensuring the efficacy of the game.

The theme of the game was selected based on common denominators in contemporary popular computer games. While some might find the theme foreign, the target audience will feel very familiar with the concept. Other themes can be explored and applied to the game, without significant change in the gameplay, in order to make it more appealing for other audiences.

Pedal Tanks has been designed for an immersive and natural-feeling experience. The players are in full control of their avatar. Being fit is an advantage but not a requirement. A tactical mind is equally important and so is the hand-eye coordination required to make precise and accurate moves with the tanks. This lets players of different fitness levels and with different levels of computer game experience both feel a sense of mastery and enjoy the game.

Fig. 4. A game of Pedal Tanks

References

1. Ferrari, S.: From Generative to Conventional Play: MOBA and League of Legends. In: DiGRA 2013 (2013)
2. Forbes, "Riot games league of legends officially becomes most played pc game in the world",
   http://www.forbes.com/sites/johngaudiosi/2012/07/11/riot-games-league-of-legends-officially-becomes-most-played-pc-game-in-the-world/ (accessed November 29, 2014)
3. Gray, F.: Pulse code communication,
   http://www.google.com/patents/US2632058 (accessed November 1, 2014)

4. Hu, F.B.: Sedentary lifestyle and risk of obesity and type 2 diabetes (2013)
5. Lakka, T.A., Laaksonen, D.E., Lakka, H.M., Männikö, N., Niskanen, L.K., Rauramaa, R., Salonen, J.T.: Sedentary Lifestyle, Poor Cardiorespiratory Fitness, and the Metabolic Syndrome (2003)
6. Macvean, A., Robertson, J.: Unserstanding exergame users' physical activity, motivation and behavior over time. In: SIGCHI Conference on human Factors in Computing Systems, pp. 1251–1260 (2013)
7. Norwegian Health Informatics, http://nhi.no/forside/urovekkende-lavt-niva-av-fysisk-aktivitet-41842.html (in Norwegian) (accessed January 11, 2015)
8. Rideout, V.J., Foehr, U.G., Roberts, D.F., Generation, M.: Media in the Lives of 8-to 18-Year-Olds. Henry J. Kaiser Family Foundation
9. Statista, "Most played pc games on gaming platform raptr in april 2015, by share of playing time", http://www.statista.com/statistics/251222/most-played-pc-games/ (accessed March 5, 2015)

The Vocal Range of Movies - Sonifying Gender Representation in Film

Marcello A. Gómez Maureira and Lisa E. Rombout

LIACS Media Technology, Leiden University,
Niels Bohrweg 1, Leiden, Netherlands
http://mediatechnology.leiden.edu

Abstract. Research has shown that in contemporary movies, male characters consistently outnumber female characters. In recent years, the number of speaking roles identified as female has declined or remained stable. Guidelines like the Bechdel and Mako Mori test have emerged as a method of evaluating gender representation in film. In this study, a more abstract and experiential form of evaluation is proposed. The per-segment sonification of the assigned gender of a character and the amount of lines they have in that segment of the script creates an audio file, showcasing the gender-representation in the movie dynamically. Two focus groups, one specifically consisting of young filmmakers, have expressed their interest in this form of movie-sonification. Expressed wishes for additional features and other suggested improvements are taken into consideration for the creation of the next prototype.

Keywords: Gender, Sonification, Representation, Data Perceptualization, Movie, Film, Audio.

1 Introduction

In a changing landscape of cultural norms, popular media such as movies can reflect as well as influence the current values of society. Trend-analysis of popular movies can therefore offer insightful information about these norms and values. In 2012, Bleakley et al. [1] presented an analysis of the 855 top-grossing films from 1950 to 2006. They concluded that for the main roles, male characters consistently outnumbered female characters by two to one. Female characters where further increasingly likely to be involved in explicit sexual content, and both genders saw a rise in involvement with violent content. A year later, Smith et al. [2] concluded that in the 100 most successful films in 2012, just 28.4 percent of the 4475 speaking characters were female. In 2009, this was 32.8 percent. The amount of speaking lines is, for most films, a representative measure for the importance of a character. Behind the camera, a similar gender-representation pattern emerges, with only one in five directors, producers or writers being women - a figure that has remained stable over time. This suggests that there is a link between gender-representation behind and in front of the camera.

© IFIP International Federation for Information Processing 2015
K. Chorianopoulos et al. (Eds.): ICEC 2015, LNCS 9353, pp. 545–550, 2015.
DOI: 10.1007/978-3-319-24589-8_54

1.1   Existing Evaluation Methods

The Bechdel test (see Fig. 1a) famously checks whether 1) there are at least two female characters in the movie, who 2) have a conversation with each other, about 3) something other than a man. One estimation is that at least 40% of popular movies do not pass it [3]. From a self-described "little joke" it has become a sort of industry standard to bring the representation of women in cinema to attention. However, it also has several drawbacks. It is hard to give an objective measure: what counts as a character and a conversation is not defined. It does not work for movies with very few characters or dialogue, as these often fail the test automatically. This last problem led to the creation of the similar Mako Mori test [4], which a movie passes if it has 1) at least one female character, 2) who has her own narrative arc, 3) that is not about supporting a man's story.

As both the Bechdel and similar tests works in terms of 'passing' them and rules that need to be adhered to, they are often misunderstood as a verdict on whether a movie is sexist or not. However, while passing the Bechdel test is certainly an indication of a certain gender representation, is does not necessarily say anything about gender depiction.

1.2   Sonification of Gender

In this study we are interested in devising a method to intuitively grasp the gender balance in a movie, without a rule system that the movie needs to 'pass' or an otherwise seemingly objective measure of sexism. The goal is to induce thought and discussion about gender representation in movies by separating it from the rest of the movie to be viewed on its own. We decided to focus on the amount of speaking lines as a good benchmark for a characters importance in the movie.

2   Methods

2.1   The Sonification Process

The very first prototype sonifications were made by analyzing the scripts by hand. A list of five main characters was determined by amount of speaking lines. Each was assigned a different pitch. The scripts were divided into segments, and in each section the number of words spoken by each character was measured. This data was then used to create a sonification, using the Sonification Sandbox [5] - an application that allows the mapping of data to sound.

The resulting sonification goes through the segments in order, with tones signifying that a character speaks and volume being dependent on the amount of words they have in that section. Scene descriptions are also represented and result in silent parts whenever the selected five characters do not have lines. Thus, action-heavy movies tend to have more stretches of silence than movies that feature a lot of dialogue. The results were three audio-files of radically different movies ('American Beauty', 'Thelma and Louise', 'Indiana Jones').

(a) 'Dykes to Watch Out For' by Alison   **(b)** Prototype GUI
Bechdel, 1985

Fig. 1. Bechdel test (left) and our gender sonification prototype (right)

An informal presentation of the results provided some interesting insights and the movies were paired to their sonifications with relative ease by the participants. The next step was to make the sonification an automated process. Scripts of various popular movies were collected in the 'Fountain' format - an open-source format for script-writing. We then created a prototype program (see Fig. 1b) that could load the script file, analyze it, present sonification options to a user and then create the audio output in wave format. In the analyzation step of the program, the source script is broken down in dialogue and action segments based on the formatting provided by the 'Fountain' file format. The program creates a list of all movie characters by looking at which names precede a dialogue segment, establishes a total word count per character and presents the six characters with the most lines to the user.

After the analysis, the user chooses whether or not to include each of the six characters, assigns their gender, and adjusts the sonification settings in terms of tone length, beats per minute, and dialogue length per tone. Tone length and beats per minute determine the overall speed of the sonification and can be considered as simply two ways of letting a user set the speed. Dialogue length per tone represents the amount of letters that each tone-segment contains. The default setting of 3000 means that the source script uses 3000 letters per tone-segment and creates tones for each character included within that count. If three characters have a dialogue of 1000 letters within a tone-segment, three notes will sound at the same time, each of them at $1/3$ of the full volume.

In the sonification, female characters are represented by a higher pitched sound, and male characters by a lower pitch, as this is the option most likely to be intuitive to the listener [6]. In addition, we differentiated between characters with smaller changes in pitch. In the first prototype, this was done by age, as adult female voices get lower with age while male voices get higher, so this is again a realistic option [7]. In the current prototype, age is not factored in and the pitch within a gender's pitch range is fixed in order of amount of dialogue.

2.2   Focus Groups

Two small focus groups (N=3 and N=4) were organized to test the current prototype and discuss the resulting sonifications. Participants were between 18 and
29 years of age, 6 female, 1 male. The first group was a mix of different people,
the second group consisted of Dutch film-students. The groups listened to two
audio-files, knowing which movies they were based on but initially not how the
sonification worked. After first impressions, they were explained more about the
mechanism and the reasons behind the project, and made their own sonifications
with the program. They were asked for their first impressions, thought and ideas
on the sonifications, opinions on gender representation in movies in general, and
wishes as a movie-audience and/or as movie-creators.

3   Results

Most of the participants thought the sonification had something to do with
the storyline or who the main characters were before they were told what kind
of information (gender representation based on amount of dialogue) was sonified. After the sonification parameters were explained, some participants found
it difficult to clearly distinguish between individual characters based on their
pitch. Several participants noted that some movies sounded more different than
expected. The first group remembered 'V for Vendetta' as a mostly male dominated movie, and were surprised to hear many high tones.

One group noted that the pitch-differences made female-centered movies seem
very happy, but male-centered movies sounded like "funeral music". Movies like
'Frozen' and 'Sister Act' sounded more musical, with many tones at once - an
effect of many characters having dialogue lines in a given scene.

We found that only some participants described themselves as conscious of
gender representation in movies. One participant noted that they might unconsciously notice it. They agreed that there was usually a huge overlap between gender representation and film genre. One participant noted that situations where
expectations were not met would be most interesting for sonification, such as
"when you know it's an action movie but you hear only high notes".

Most participants noted that, just as with the Bechdel test, the way each
gender was depicted in the movie was not translated into the audio-file. Although some regarded this as a loss, most agreed that it would be difficult to
introduce this information in an objective manner. Participants were divided
on whether the sonification was too abstract to gain meaningful information
about the movie. Some thought it was too vague, but one participant noted
that it "gave me an understanding that is perhaps more accurate than just data,
because representation is not always factual".

Participants noted that the separation of the visual element worked well to
experience the movie in a more unbiased manner, also noting that with some
additional information brought in, a sonification could act as a spoiler-free trailer.

The first focus group largely agreed on a distinction between the perceived quality of the movie itself in whether gender-representation was important to them.

One of them noted they "would only care about more ambitious movies, not about the ones that you already know will be stupid". Others agreed that gender-representation was interesting from a research-perspective, but did not much factor into their own private choice of movies. The second group wondered how significant speaking lines really are for judging the importance of a character. They thought the combination of the "associative qualities of sound" and the "hard facts of word-counting" was interesting, but could also be confusing.

3.1   Recommendations

Most participants would have liked the sonification to offer more information, particularly on the quality or topic of the conversation, the story-line or the movie genre. Mentioned ways to translate this were in speed, volume, sound-origin and different instruments. Some mentioned that this would also increase the chance that a person less interested in gender issues might want to hear the sonification. Multiple participants were interested in whether movies of the same genre would sound the same, or whether their own favorite movies would. Participants noted that it could be interesting to see how different people sonify different movies, as so many elements are subjective. The second group was interested in sonifying the (short) movie scripts they were currently working on for their studies - these sounded about as they had expected.

4   Conclusion and Discussion

From our focus groups we learned that the sonification of gender is not self-explanatory even if an audience is aware that an aspect of a movie is sonified. As such, it is necessary to make the purpose as well as the mapping clear from the beginning on if the goal is to promote a focused discussion. While gender sonification is essentially a qualitative representation of gender balance in a movie, it has been identified as very data-driven. We think that, due to the subjective nature of what constitutes as balanced representation, an intuitive approach can be useful, but many participants expressed their desire to see more tangible data on this subject. Clearly, gender sonification cannot be a replacement for an in-depth analysis using more traditional forms of reporting data. As such we anticipated that it could be considered unpractical and vague. However, it can also be understood as a playful method to add a experiential component to the representation of data. In our small focus groups we were indeed pleased with the amount of discussion the sonifications evoked. Acting as a starting point for such conversation is, as we consider it, the main function of this form of data representation.

Arguably, this effect is harder to achieve outside of a dedicated focus-group environment - meaning that the system must promote and facilitate such discussions. One possible way to do this is through letting users compare their expectations with the reality, another to promote a social experience were multiple users share their thoughts about a sonification. A movie/sonification pairing game, as was done with our first prototype, could also bring unexpected results to light and facilitate discussion.

A downside of our mapping scheme is that we largely lose the rhythm of the movie, since we mainly focus on text (scripts have some descriptions of actions but this does not translate well to screen-time). Since we focus specifically on gender representation, however, we consider this an acceptable loss.

Adding more information to the audio can be useful for pointing out unanticipated combinations of elements - like a genre associated with a certain gender that turns out to feature mostly characters from another gender. This has the additional benefit of being able to inform on representation of different sexualities, for instance by pointing out there is a love scene featuring only male characters. Additionally, it might get people interested for whom just gender representation is not an interesting enough factor when choosing or evaluating a movie. This can mean focusing on the story-line or genre, but also to incorporate the representation of other minority groups. One obvious example would be characters of a non-binary gender, who are currently largely ignored not only in the film industry, but also in our prototypes so far.

We think the strength of this representation is to be found in the balance between simplicity and narrative power. There is no important other information present to distract from the main point of the audio, thus drawing attention to an issue that might have escaped attention when watching the actual movie. At the same time, it is still interesting and organic, as it changes over time, different characters can be heard and a little bit of the flow of the movie is discernible. It does not give clear-cut answers on what the gender-representation is or how it should be, leaving room for different opinions and their exchange.

References

1. Bleakley, A., Jamieson, P.E., Romer, D.: Trends of sexual and violent content by gender in top-grossing us films, 1950–2006. Journal of Adolescent Health 51(1), 73–79 (2012)
2. Smith, S.L., Choueiti, M., Scofield, E., Pieper, K.: Gender inequality in 500 popular films: Examining on-screen portrayals and behind-the-scenes employment patterns in motion pictures released between 2007-2012. Study by the University of Southern California Annenberg School for Communication & Journalism (2013)
3. Website, B.: Bechdel test movie list (2015) (Online; accessed April 28, 2015)
4. Peterson, P.: Beyond the bechdel test: Two (new) ways of looking at movies (Online; accessed April 28, 2014)
5. Walker, B.N., Cothran, J.T.: Sonification sandbox: A graphical toolkit for auditory graphs (2003)
6. Titze, I.R.: Physiologic and acoustic differences between male and female voices. The Journal of the Acoustical Society of America 85(4), 1699–1707 (1989)
7. Honjo, I., Isshiki, N.: Laryngoscopic and voice characteristics of aged persons. Archives of Otolaryngology 106(3), 149–150 (1980)

Workshops and Tutorials

Workshop: AI and Creativity in Entertainment

Axel Tidemann and Agnar Aamodt

Department of Computer and Information Science
Norwegian University of Science and Technology
{tidemann,agnar}@idi.ntnu.no

1 Workshop Objective

Many different artificial intelligence/machine learning concepts are driving mechanisms behind entertainment systems. Further, computational creativity (CC) is an area with increased focus within entertainment computing as well as AI. This workshop provides a forum where AI and creativity can be discussed within the context of entertainment computing and related areas, as described in the main conference call.

Entertainment and creativity are intrinsically linked, and different approaches address this combination. This include systems with predefined strategies for creative behaviours as well as systems that are able to be creative on-the-fly. CC focuses on the formalisms of how known concepts can be combined or tweaked in order to form novel solutions; a core research question then becomes how to perform these combinations/mutations in an intelligent manner. Both CC methods targeting creativity within and for the computer, as well as methods for helping humans to be more creative, are relevant here.

Of main interest for the workshop is the cross-pollination between artificial intelligence and computational creativity, in the context of entertainment systems. However, work focusing on either AI or CC is also of interest as long as the ties between the two method areas in some way are addressed and discussed.

So, the overarching themes of the workshop are the same as that of the main ICEC conference (e.g. health, education, media, sport, core areas of entertainment computing, including games) but with a focus on the AI&CC methodologies running at the core of such systems. Within this scope, more specific methods of relevance include (but are not limited to):

- Modeling, design, system architectures, and development methodologies
- Cognitive architectures and systems, bio-inspired architectures
- Machine learning, data mining including text mining, intelligent data analysis
- Situation interpretation, event detection, decision support
- Case-based, rule-based, and model-based reasoning
- Neural networks, evolutionary algorithms, swarm intelligence
- Natural language processing, language and speech generation
- Image understanding, image composition, video streaming
- Intelligent user interfaces, dialogue systems, interactivity

© IFIP International Federation for Information Processing 2015
K. Chorianopoulos et al. (Eds.): ICEC 2015, LNCS 9353, pp. 553–555, 2015.
DOI: 10.1007/978-3-319-24589-8_55

Within the scope of the workshop are also papers addressing Art and Entertainment, given that they have a methodology related to AI and/or CC. Art is of course creativity per se, and this line should foster discussions across various fields and disciplines, with a common theme of exploring the methodologies that govern the various manifestations (e.g. physical, visual, auditive) of such systems.

2   Background/Relevance of Workshop Topic

The field of entertainment computing presents a plethora of possibilities when it comes to making use of the above-mentioned topics. This workshop will have a stronger focus on the underlying mechanisms that enable entertainment computing, and is therefore very relevant to the conference. Special focus is on the computational creativity part of entertainment computing, which is not part of the main conference.

3   Expected Workshop Outcomes

The workshop will encourage collaboration between the participants, which will hopefully lead to publications. Some focus will also be on skill development.

4   Expected Number of Participants

20-30.

5   Length of the Workshop

Full day.

6   Workshop Due Dates

1st of August 2015: Deadline for workshop paper submission
21st of August 2015: Notification
1st of September 2015: Camera ready due
29th of September 2015: Workshop helt at ICEC 2015, Trondheim, Norway

7   Workshop Chairs

Axel Tidemann, NTNU axel.tidemann@gmail.com
Agnar Aamodt, NTNU agnar@idi.ntnu.no
Odd Erik Gundersen, NTNU odderik@idi.ntnu.no

Note: Program Committee is being organized at the time of submission.

8   Organizer CV

Axel Tidemann received the M.S. and Ph.D. degrees in Computer Science from The Norwegian University of Science and Technology (NTNU), Norway, in 2006 and 2009, respectively. Since 2011, he is a Post-Doctoral Researcher with NTNU, supported by the "Next Generation Control Centres for Smart Grids" project. He researches the use of data driven and machine learning methods to do time series prediction. In addition, he has a focus on using machine learning to model human cognition.

Agnar Aamodt received the Ph.D. degree in Computer Science from The University of Trondheim, Norway, in 1991. He is a professor of Computer Science and Artificial Intelligence in the Department of Computer and Information Science, Norwegian University of Science and Technology. His main research area is artificial intelligence methods for decision-support systems, with a focus on interactive problem solving and experiential learning in knowledge-based systems.

Creating Video Content for Oculus Rift

Scriptwriting for 360°-Interactive Video Productions

Mirjam Vosmeer and Ben Schouten

Interaction and Games Lab,
Amsterdam University of Applied Sciences
Postbus 1025, 1000 BA Amsterdam, The Netherlands
{m.s.vosmeer,b.a.m.schouten}@hva.nl

Abstract. In this workshop, we will first discuss previous experiences with producing and/or watching video content for Oculus Rift, or other 360° video devices. After determining the challenges and possibilities, we will works towards developing concepts for settings and stories for this particular medium.

Keywords: interactive narrative, digital storytelling, scriptwriting, content development, Oculus Rift.

1 Introduction/Workshop Background

Oculus is awesome for games, but it's the future of movies, was the headline of an article that was published in January 2014 in technology and lifestyle magazine *Wired* (Watercutter, 2014). After Facebook paid 2 billion dollar to take over the company Oculus VR in March 2014 (Solomon, 2014), the headset Oculus Rift became world famous practically overnight. In the past year, researchers and developers who had gotten hold of the first series of developer kits have been presenting their latest findings on technology festivals and conferences all over the world, and discussing the challenges they encountered when producing 360 degrees content for this device (for instance, Vosmeer and Schouten, 2014). Especially developers who explore the possibilities of creating real life video content (instead of VR content), find themselves probing a new field of media production that offers characteristics of video games on one hand, but on the other hand feels like a movie in which the viewer is watching a scene that is displayed all around him or her.

While using Oculus Rift, the viewer has the sense of literally being in the center of the scene. Because the footage has been recorded in 360 degrees, the viewer has the strange sense of being present in the movie, almost as if he or she is playing a part in it, instead of watching from the outside. This relates directly to the theoretical concept of 'presence', which is defined as 'being in the story world' (Roth et al, 2012). The perspective is actually more related to the position of a video game player than that of a movie watcher. After all, gamers are used to being able to look all around in the game world, in order to explore the surroundings and detect enemies or other game elements. When watching a movie, viewers are presented with the one frame that has been

© IFIP International Federation for Information Processing 2015
K. Chorianopoulos et al. (Eds.): ICEC 2015, LNCS 9353, pp. 556–559, 2015.
DOI: 10.1007/978-3-319-24589-8_56

chosen by the director to present the story through. One of the challenges that producers face is that they need to find ways to tell stories for surround video content that suit the sense of presence that users experience. One solution to this problem is adding voice-over narration: the voice of someone talking who is not visible on the screen (Kozloff, 1988).

In our first study, we have experimented with different voice over perspectives that would best suit the immersive qualities that 360° video content offers its users. It turned out that a second person perspective gave the audience the best sense of *presence*: of actually being a part of the narrative that was presented.

Our second study focused on creating an interactive story that could be produced for Oculus Rift. We developed a concept, explored different ways of interactive storytelling, and eventually produced a short interactive drama for Oculus Rift that was presented in Amsterdam in January 2015.

The 360° point of view implies several other difficulties for the producer. Firstly, it is not possible to work with a traditional film set in which a scene may be recorded. As the camera records the world in 360°, everything around the system will be seen. This problem also applies for the floor of the set, and the ceiling. As these angles will also be available for the future viewer, both the floor and the ceiling of the set need to be fully presentable, which means for instance that it is not possible to make use of elaborate lighting systems (Vosmeer and Schouten, 2014). Another issue involves camera movement: while the viewer takes the point of view of the camera, and is able to look around in the scene, he or she is not able to move through the space in which the scene was filmed. The only possible movement is the one that was recorded when shooting the scene.

The camera position within a setup like this also has profound impact on the way that stories may be told. A scene that is written with the intention to be watched from 360°, may take different viewer perspectives into account. For instance, the story could be told in such a way that the camera is not part of the narrative, but just registers the scene like a fly on the wall. Another option however, would be to include the viewer position within the story, and have characters react towards the camera as if it is another character participating in the scene. Experiments like these, in which actors react to a camera, are of course known within traditional cinema as well. With this new technology, however, experiments with new ways of storytelling are imaginable in which the option of the viewer to look around within the scene - and for instance discover pieces of information and new interpretations - could be essential to the way a plot unfolds.

Another interesting possibility that this kind of media production offers, is the use of so called *hot-spots*: it is possible to insert interactive points in the video that can be activated by the user by focusing his or her gaze on it for several moments (this can be compared to clicking a link or touching a screen). These interactive points can be used to activate the next part of the story. For instance: in our Oculus Rift video 'A Perfect Party', the user was told by the voice over that he was hosting a party, but that it would be nice to have some music. If the user than fixed his gaze on the DJ for a few seconds, the DJ would step forward and start playing music, which would result in the guests starting to dance.

2   Workshop

In this half-day workshop, we will first present a short overview of our previous studies into content creation for Oculus Rift, and explain the challenges and possibilities that we came across. Secondly, we will discuss the attendants' own earlier experiences with 360° video content, and invite them to reflect on the narrative aspects that they have encountered there. In the third part of the workshop, attendants will be asked to think of possible settings in which an Oculus Rift narrative could be placed, taking into account the production boundaries that were discussed earlier. During the fourth and last part of the workshop, we will discuss the settings, think of story concepts that might be written for these particular settings, and consider whether using a voice over could add useful extra information to the scene. Note that the focus will be on developing concepts and narratives, rather than on dealing with technical issues.

3   Workshop Outcomes

During this workshop, we hope to develop new concepts for settings and stories that can be produced for Oculus Rift. After attending the workshop, the participants will have gained new insights into the production challenges and narrative possibilities of producing 360° interactive stories.

4   Participants

I think that a maximum of 12 participants would be a good number for this workshop, but I have no specific names yet.

5   CV Information

Mirjam Vosmeer is coordinator of the Interaction & Games Lab at the Amsterdam University of Applied Sciences. She has a PhD in communication science and an academic background in game studies, psychology and media entertainment. Her further professional background includes television production, scriptwriting and game concept development. She is project manager of Interactive Cinema, a collaboration between the Netherlands Film Academy and the Amsterdam University of Applied Sciences. For this project, she has conducted several experiments into interactive storytelling for 360° video content. Ben Schouten is professor Playful Interaction at Eindhoven University and lector Play and Civic Media at the Amsterdam University of Applied Sciences

Acknowledgement. This workshop proposal is part of the Interactive Cinema project, within the Amsterdam Creative Industries Network. The Interactive Cinema project is a collaboration between the Netherlands Film Academy and the Amsterdam

University of Applied Sciences. The pilot for this workshop has been presented on March 27 (2015), for a group of screenwriting students who have graduated from the Dutch Film Academy.

References

1. Kozloff, S.: Invisible Storytellers. University of California Press, Berkeley (1988)
2. Roth, C., Klimmt, C., Vermeulen, I.E., Vorderer, P.: The experience of interactive storytelling: Comparing "Fahrenheit" with "Façade". In: Anacleto, J.C., Fels, S., Graham, N., Kapralos, B., Saif El-Nasr, M., Stanley, K. (eds.) ICEC 2011. LNCS, vol. 6972, pp. 13–21. Springer, Heidelberg (2011)
3. Solomon, B.: Facebook buys Oculus virtual reality gaming startup for 2 billion. In: Forbes 2014 (2015),
4. http://www.forbes.com/sites/briansolomon/2014/03/25/facebook-buys-oculus-virtual-reality-gaming-startup-for-2-billion/
5. (retrieved March, 2015)
6. Vosmeer, M., Schouten, B.: Interactive Cinema: Engagement and interaction. In: Mitchell, A., Fernández-Vara, C., Thue, D. (eds.) ICIDS 2014. LNCS, vol. 8832, pp. 140–147. Springer, Heidelberg (2014)
7. Watercutter, A.: Oculus Is Awesome for Games, But It's the Future of Movies (2014), http://www.wired.com/2014/01/oculus-movies/ (retrieved March, 2015)

Game Mechanics Supporting Pervasive Learning and Experience in Games, Serious Games, and Interactive & Social Media

J.M. Baalsrud Hauge[1,2], T. Lim[3], S. Louchart[4], I.A. Stanescu[5], M. Ma[6], and T. Marsh[7]

[1] Bremer Institut für Produktion und Logistik (BIBA) University of Bremen, Germany
[2] Royal institute of Technology, Stockholm, Sweden
[3] Heriot-Watt University, Scotland, UK
[4] The Glasgow School of Art (DDS), Scotland, UK
[5] Advanced Technology Systems, Targoviste, Romania
[6] University of Huddersfield, UK
[7] Griffith University, Griffith Film School, Brisbane, Australia
t.lim@hw.ac.uk, s.louchart@gsa.ac.uk, baa@biba.uni-bremen.de,
ioana.stanescu@ats.com.ro M.Ma@hud.ac.uk, dr.tim.marsh@gmail.com

Abstract. This workshop investigates the mechanisms for behaviour change and influence, focusing on the definition of requirements for pervasive gameplay and interaction mechanics, procedures, actions, mechanisms, systems, story, etc.) with the purpose of informing, educating, reflecting and raising awareness. By connecting various experts such as designers, educators, developers, evaluators and researchers from both industry and academia, this workshop aims to enable participants share, discuss and learn about existing relevant mechanisms for pervasive learning in a Serious Game (SG) context.

Research in SG, as a whole, faces two main challenges in understanding: the transition between the instructional design and actual game design implementation [1] and documenting an evidence-based mapping of game design patterns onto relevant pedagogical patterns [2]. From a practical perspective, this transition lacks methodology and requires a leap of faith from a prospective customer to the ability of a SG developer to deliver a game that will achieve the desired learning outcomes. This workshop aims to present and apply a preliminary exposition though a purpose-processing methodology to probe, from various SG design aspects, how SG design patterns map with pedagogical practices

1 Introduction

Government, commerce, marketing, health, energy efficiency and sustainability identify and use a wide range of non-digital information-based devices including policies and legislation when attempting to persuade, influence or change behaviour of the citizen or group of citizen, but are information, education or awareness sufficient, or are other techniques and devices needed?

© IFIP International Federation for Information Processing 2015
K. Chorianopoulos et al. (Eds.): ICEC 2015, LNCS 9353, pp. 560–565, 2015.
DOI: 10.1007/978-3-319-24589-8_57

Due to their immersive nature and engaging qualities, games, SGs, and interactive and social media have an important role to play in the way information is provided and change facilitated. Towards this, we have identified the following three main synergistic areas of focus for this workshop:

1. To learn, educate, inform and make aware.
2. To encourage reflection, contemplation and deliberation.
3. To determine pervasive mechanisms that influence behaviour change.

There are a number of existing games and game communities that address research aspects of these areas. Amongst them are Games for Change [1], Persuasive Games [2] and Alternate Reality Games [3].

Experiences that resonate or linger following an encounter (gameplay, interaction) have been shown to encourage reflection and potentially act as trigger for behaviour change [4]. Other examples that aim to address aspects of these areas come from Ian Bogost's game development company Persuasive Games who design games to represent arguments that aim to influence players to take action through gameplay [2]. However, there are still several gaps in order to understand exactly how Serious Game Mechanics (SGM) interacts with Learning Mechanics. An improved understanding of the relation would help in the design of better pervasive game mechanics.

2   The SGM Approach

SGs represent a complex system of intertwined experiences influencing and motivating not only to play and engage with a proposed experience, but also to express and reflect on a gaming activity during and after experiencing it. In this context, game activities, various levels of SGM, motivational elements, competition, challenge etc. are all inter-related elements through which a gaming experience can be defined. Purposeful learning is in itself an aspect specific to SGs. The methodological approach towards identifying SGMs is a simple approach, which focuses on the nature of game mechanics associated with the specific aspect of purposeful learning [5].

All of these elements can be described in terms of Purpose, Process and Structure, in the sense that SGMs elements are designed for a reason and have a purpose connected to a gaming and learning experience [6, 7]. This purpose is generally achieved through a process in which activities, information or events represent the structural tangible elements of the overall element described (Figure 1).

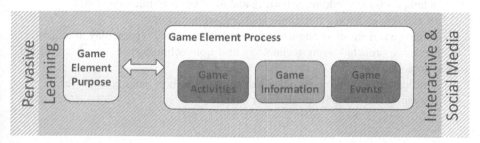

Fig. 1. Pervasive & Social SG element methodological approach.

Pervasive technologies open up new opportunities for game-enhanced learning experiences. However, providing adapted game experiences based on the learner location remains an open challenge. Context/ location identification represents a first stage in generating customized sequences of learning. Defining context/ location-sensitive, user-centred customization sequences are still subject to debate.

At the same time, socially intense virtual experiments are powerful tools to engage learners. It is equally important to consider not only their potential to stimulate learners, but also to annoy them. Maintaining a balanced stimulus based on Social Media is a key ingredient in achieving success. Social networks should play a critical role in stimulating learning, it is important to achieve an in-depth understanding on how to balance the amount of information posted on social networks and how revealing the information is.

3   Objective

This workshop focuses on identifying and analyzing the criteria of design, development and assessment of pervasive, socially textured gaming methods and technologies (mechanics, procedures, actions, mechanisms, systems, story, etc.) [8, 9] that interactively inform and educate, develop skills, encourage reflection, raise awareness, and influence behaviour change.

Specific objectives include:

1) Identify opportunities and challenges associated with SG implemented in context-aware, socially intensive environments.

2) Analyse the transformation processes of SGM and of pedagogical constructs in pervasive and social contexts.

3) Validate the extension of the Purpose-Processing Methodology (PPSM) based on pervasive and social experiences.

4) Discuss the pedagogical implications of adaptive learning experiments.

In particular, we intend to discuss how the different aspects influence the SGM-LM interaction in pervasive and social contexts:

a) Mechanics/experience to inform or provide a message or argument.

b) Character and role-play to enact/become complicit in historical, social and perhaps difficult events/scenarios;

c) Techniques for embedding messages and arguments in interactive story;

d) Entertaining and non-entertaining gameplay/interaction;

e) Encourage reflection during and following an encounter (gameplay, interaction);

f) Blended approaches using technology and non-technology, & in-game and off-game approaches

g) Gamification – applying gaming characteristics to non-gaming activities;

h) Motivating and sustaining behaviour change.

4 Target Participants

The workshop targets designers, developers, evaluators and researchers from both academia and industry involved in the topics above. In addition, we are interested in educators and participants with an interest in games, SGs, social media and on-line design, to share and discuss the issues presented above.

5 Workshop Program

The proposed workshop will last half a day and will run as follow:

1. Presentation of emerging blends of technologies that impact learning experiences: Serious Games Mechanics, Pervasive Learning & Social Media — 30 min

SGMs are seen as the relationship between pedagogical patterns and game design patterns [5]. The process of investigating the links between the two lies between the instructional design requirements and the actual game/game-play design. This 30 minutes session will provide a definition of SGM and suggest a purpose-processing methodology (PPSM) to identify the link. The extension of the methodology to incorporate Pervasive Learning and Social Media features is discussed and stimuli for reflection are provided.

2. Game play session — 1 hour, 30 min

The participants will experiment the presented methodological approach and framework. Participants will be divided into groups working with two different aims:

1) To analyze existing games from a pervasive and social perspective; and
2) To design new gameplays that take advantage of the benefits of pervasive and social contexts.

The organizers will provide a set of state of the art SGs to be played and analyzed.

3. SGM card game — 1 hour, 45 min

This activity is based on the board game "cards against humanity". The groups of participants will use the cards to sketch a pervasive, socially-driven SG integrating mechanisms that influence behaviour change. To stimulate creativity, participants will be handed blank cards, enabling them to integrate other mechanics than those provided by the organizers, such as those identified in the previous session and mechanics participants consider relevant.

Each SG that has been designed during this session will be presented and workshop participants will be able to rate the SGMs that they find most useful in a pervasive and social SG approach. The mechanics used will be analyzed and feedback will be collected in a matrix format that will specifically identify mechanics relevant in pervasive and social contexts.

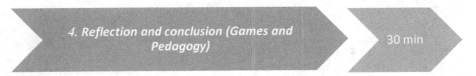

Based upon the result of game play session, we will analyze, discuss and show how different aspects of the proposed methodological approach and framework can effectively support the design process, increasing the quality of the outcomes and decreasing the time to market. We will also discuss typical issues encountered during the design process, as well as challenges in finding the right SGMs for specific purposes.

6   Main Outcomes

Participant will be invited to contribute to specific conference and journal papers based on the Pervasive & Social SG element methodological approach, reflecting findings and value-adding contributions to the field.

Acknowledgments. This workshop is based upon previous experience and similar workshop held at ICEC 2013 in Sao Paolo, Brazil, GameDays 2014 in Darmstadt, Germany and Gala Conference 2014 in Bucharest, Romania. Part of the work has been partially funded under the EC 7FRP GALA, Psymbiosys (EC H2020) and by the Unitatea Executiva pentru Finantarea Invatamantului Superior, a Cercetarii, Dezvoltarii si Inovarii (UEFISCDI) in Romania, Contract no. 19/ 2014 (DESiG).

References

1. Games for Change, http://www.gamesforchange.org
2. Alternate Reality Games, http://www.argn.com
3. McGonigal, J.: Reality Is Broken: Why Games Make Us Better and How They Can Change the World. Penguin Press, New York (2011)
4. Bogost, I.: Persuasive Games: The expressive power of videogames. The MIT Press (2007)

5. Arnab, S., Lim, T., Carvalho, M.B., Bellotti, F., de Freitas, S., Louchart, S., Suttie, N., Berta, R., De Gloria, A.: Mapping learning and game mechanics for serious games analysis. British Journal of Educational Technology (2014), doi:10.1111/bjet.12113
6. Suttie, N., Louchart, S., Lim, T., Macvean, A., Westera, W., Brown, D., Djaouti, D.: Introducing the "Serious Games Mechanics" A Theoretical Framework to Analyse Relationships Between "Game" and"Pedagogical Aspects" of Serious Games. Procedia Computer Science 15, 314–315 (2012)
7. Carvalho, M.B., Bellotti, F., Berta, R., De Gloria, A., Islas Sedano, C., Baalsrud Hauge, J., Hu, J., Rauterberg, M.: An activity theory-based model for serious games analysis and conceptual design. Computers & Education 87, 166–181 (2015) ISSN 0360-1315, http://dx.doi.org/10.1016/j.compedu.2015.03.023..
8. Bellotti, F., Kapralos, B., Lee, K., Moreno-Ger, P., Berta, R.: Assessment in and of Serious Games: An Overview. Advances in Human-Computer Interaction, Article ID 136864 (2013), doi:10.1155/2013/136864
9. Bellotti, F., Berta, R., De Gloria, A.: "Designing Effective Serious Games: Opportunities and Challenges for Research", Special Issue: Creative Learning with Serious Games. Int.l Journal of Emerging Technologies in Learning (IJET) 5, 22–35 (2010)

Making as a Pathway to Foster Joyful Engagement and Creativity in Learning

Michail N. Giannakos[1], Monica Divitini[1],
Ole Sejer Iversen[2], and Pavlos Koulouris[3]

[1] Norwegian University of Science and Technology (NTNU), Trondheim, Norway
{michailg,divitini}@idi.ntnu.no
[2] Participatory IT Center, Aarhus University, Aarhus, Denmark
oiversen@cs.au.dk
[3] Ellinogermaniki Agogi, Athens, Greece
pkoulouris@ea.gr

Abstract. The International Workshop of Making as a Pathway to Foster Joyful Engagement and Creativity in Learning (Make2Learn) aims to discuss the introduction of creative and joyful production of artifacts in the learning processes. A variety of environments have been developed by researchers to introduce making principles to young students. Making principles enable them foster co-creativity and joy in learning processes and construct knowledge. By involving students in the design decisions they begin to develop technological fluency and the needed competences, in a joyful way. Make2Learn aims to bring together international researchers, educators, designers, and makers for the exploration of making principles towards the acquisition of 21st Century learning competences, by employing the state of the art aspects of entertainment technologies, new media, gaming, robotics, toys and applications. The main objective is to build a research community around this topical area. In particular, Make2Learn aims to develop a critical discussion about the well-established practices and entertainment technologies of the maker movement, and expected outcomes of putting them into practice under different spaces such as Hackerspaces, Makerspaces, TechShops, FabLabs etc. This will allow us to better understand and improve the value of Maker philosophy and the role of entertainment technologies to support teaching and learning.

Keywords: Maker movement, entertainment technologies, creativity, knowledge construction, technological fluency, constructionist.

1 Background

Digital artifacts that enable people to exchange, create, and distribute information have, in the past couple of decades, profoundly reshaped the way we work and live [8]. The creative production of digital artifacts and use of entertainment technologies in learning activities has been linked to teaching new computer and design literacy skills [2]. Common inspiration is the work of Papert [7] that stresses the importance of creating a 'felicitous' environment to facilitate learning. The idea here is that the

© IFIP International Federation for Information Processing 2015
K. Chorianopoulos et al. (Eds.): ICEC 2015, LNCS 9353, pp. 566–570, 2015.
DOI: 10.1007/978-3-319-24589-8_58

students benefit from being happy and in a carefree and creative environment. In accordance with Papert, Csikszentmihalyi's [4] research has exhibited that students' motivation is highly predictive of achievement; however, educational systems neglect creative and joyful aspects on learning activities. Educational programmes focus on recall and reproduction abilities instead of emphasizing the development of problem solving, creative thinking and decision-making abilities.

Digital artifacts have the potential to make the symbolic and abstract manipulations involved in creative procedures more concrete and manageable for young students [3]. For example, artifacts allow students to learn by iteratively testing, rebuilding their designs and working collaboratively. The interactions between the young students and the artifacts in creative and joyful activities are vital [5]. During the past decade, we have seen an increased appearance of environments and community spaces offering diverse opportunities for young students to facilitate learning through construction. Environments like Scratch, Alice and Storytelling Alice and spaces like Hackerspaces, Makerspaces, TechShops, and FabLabs have allowed researchers to empirically investigate the potential benefits of the maker movement towards the acquisition of 21st Century learning competences. Collecting and discussing around those advances will allow us to formulate better understanding of several technical and practical aspects that could be valuable in designing effective making activities to foster joyful engagement and creativity in learning.

2   Objectives

The advances of digital environments, entertainment technologies, manufacturing equipment and community spaces offer diverse opportunities for making practices to facilitate learning, especially when supported by engaging and joyful entertainment technologies and designed in an appropriate pedagogical manner. From current research, it is difficult to tell what aspects of environments, engaging-entertainment technologies, applications, equipment and practices can have a positive impact.

The current drive in many countries to teach design and technology competences to all has potential to empower and support making as a creative, joyful and problem-solving tasks. However, there are a number of challenges in ensuring that procedures, tools and environments, embody appropriate progression and engender motivation and joyful. This workshop will attempt to address these key research challenges.

One of our main objectives is to bring together researchers, educators, designers who are interested for the exploration of making principles and supportive entertainment technologies towards the acquisition of 21st Century learning competences. Make2Learn aims to provide an environment where participants will get opportunities to: develop their research skills; increase their knowledge base; collaborate with others in their own and complementary research areas; and discuss their own work.

3   Making Instruments: Tools, Kits and Spaces to Support Creativity

Cultures of making—like, social practices of hacking, DIY, and craft—rise in prominence, and design researchers have taken note, because of their implications for sustainability, democratization, and alternative models of innovation, design, participation, and education [1]. Designing tools, kits and spaces to support constructionism and creativity via new modalities, not only leverages more authentic connections to engagement but also extends learning opportunities as youth align computing, engineering and interaction design.

Tools to support creativity can be described as tools that enable people to express themselves creatively and to develop as creative and critical thinkers [8]. Tools, like computational systems and environments that people can use to generate, modify, interact and play with, and/or share artifacts such as programs, diagrams, artifacts, installations, designs, images, and music; these tools can help us to enhance people's creativity if designed and applied properly. Drawn from a large pool of diverse studies, Shneiderman et al. [10] have defined twelve "design guidelines" (called also patterns) to guide the development of creativity support tools:

1. Support exploration,
2. Low threshold, high ceiling, and wide walls
3. Support many paths and many styles,
4. Support collaboration,
5. Support open interchange,
6. Make it as simple as possible—and maybe even simpler,
7. Choose black boxes carefully,
8. Invent things that you would want to use yourself,
9. Balance user suggestions with observation and participatory processes,
10. Iterate, iterate—then iterate again,
11. Design for designers,
12. Evaluate your tools.

These principles are distinguished from other user interface principles because they emphasize on easy exploration, rapid experimentation, and fortuitous combinations that lead to innovations [10]. These twelve principles allow designers not only to develop successful tools to support creativity but also to improve different commercial products like programming environments, design, brainstorming, composite music etc.

Many types of physical and digital products as well as toys can offer learning experiences that foster students' creativity and 21st century skills. Related tool categories include diverse new media, smart environments, physical and digital games, robotics, toys and so forth. Various types of construction kits are also often reinforce joyfulness, creativity, engagement and learning. However, most of the available construction kits are focusing on a very specific set of skills and competences, and support a non-systematic ad-hoc learning model.

Creativity is often supported by physical products as well as tangible technologies. For instance in OurToys [6], students build their own digital game/story with physical objects; this raised their awareness for technology, explored their design and development boundaries as well as increase their collaboration while learning and playing through the making process. Another interesting mean to enhance creativity is designing and developing wearable products. For instance, designing wearable controllers, interfaces and boards where young programmers can manipulate objects not only on the screen but also in the physical world provide a compelling application of creative learning [2].

In addition to available toolkits, technologies and environments for creative learning, there are some dedicated spaces to introduce students to the making movement principles, such as Hackerspaces, Makerspaces, TechShops, FabLabs etc. On the top of these spaces there are also events like, Lego League Junior and Maker Faires. But again, most of the available events and spaces are focusing on a very specific set of skills and competences with an ad-hoc organization/participation.

4 Conclusions and the Way Ahead

The advances of digital environments, technologies, manufacturing equipment and community spaces offer diverse opportunities for making practices to facilitate learning, especially when supported by engaging and joyful entertainment technologies and designed in an appropriate pedagogical manner. From current research, it is difficult to tell what aspects of environments, technologies, applications, equipment and practices can have a positive impact.

The current drive in many countries to teach 21st century skills to all has potential to empower and support making as a creative, joyful, problem-solving and critical thinking tasks. However, there are a number of challenges in ensuring that procedures, tools and environments, embody appropriate progression and engender motivation and joyful.

To explore the future of technologies, tools, and various spaces to foster engagement and creativity in learning, we seek to promote interest in well-established tools and practices of the maker movement, and expected outcomes of putting them into practice under different spaces such as Hackerspaces, Makerspaces, TechShops, FabLabs etc. This will allow us to better understand and improve the value of Maker philosophy as well as to accelerate the process of disciplinary convergence. We aspire to bridge computer science, design, HCI and related disciplines to encourage ambitious research projects that could yield potent tools for many students to use. This workshop is implemented with an aim to collect high quality studies around this topical area, to envision what the next generation of technologies, environments, spaces and practices might look like. In particular, future work need to:

1. Accelerate research on Maker Movement by proposing ways to create greater interest and synergies among researchers, educators, students, policymakers, and industrial developers,

2. Promote rigorous multidimensional and multidisciplinary methods and implement rigorous experimentation strategies and metrics for in-depth longitudinal case studies,

3. Design tools, kits and spaces for individuals to promote "low floor" (easy to get started) and a "high ceiling" (opportunities to create increasingly complex projects over time) opportunities for young students.

Acknowledgments. We would like to thank the workshop Program Committee members for contributing to the success of Make2Learn as well as the workshop and conference chairs for their constructive comments and their helpful assistance during the preparation and throughout the workshop.

References

1. Bardzell, J., Bardzell, S., Toombs, A.: Now that's definitely a proper hack: self-made tools in hackerspaces. In: Proc. CHI 2014, pp. 473–476. ACM Press (2014)
2. Buechley, L., Eisenberg, M., Catchen, J., Crockett, A.: The LilyPad Arduino: Using Computational Textiles to Investigate Engagement, Aesthetics, and Diversity in Computer Science Education. In: Proc. CHI 2008, pp. 423–432. ACM Press (2008)
3. Cassell, J.: Towards a Model of Technology and Literacy Development: Story Listening Systems. Journal of Applied Developmental Psychology 25(1), 75–105 (2004)
4. Csikszentmihalyi, M.: Creativity: Flow and the Psychology of Discovery and Invention. Harper Collins (1996)
5. Giannakos, M.N., Jaccheri, L.: What motivates children to become creators of digital enriched artifacts? In: Proc. C&C 2013, pp. 104–113. ACM Press (2013)
6. Giannakos, M.N., Jaccheri, L.: Code Your Own Game: The Case of Children with Hearing Impairments. In: Pisan, Y., Sgouros, N.M., Marsh, T. (eds.) ICEC 2014. LNCS, vol. 8770, pp. 108–116. Springer, Heidelberg (2014)
7. Papert, S.: Mindstorms: Children, Computers, and Powerful Ideas. Basic Books, New York (1980)
8. Resnick, M., et al.: Design Principles for Tools to Support Creative Thinking. Technical Report: NSF Workshop Report on Creativity Support Tools. Washington, DC (2005)
9. Ryokai, K., Lee, M.J., Breitbart, J.M.: Children's storytelling and programming with robotic characters. In: Proc. C&C 2009, pp. 19–28. ACM Press (2009)
10. Shneiderman, B., et al.: Creativity support tools: Report from a US National Science Foundation sponsored workshop. International Journal of Human-Computer Interaction 20(2), 61–77 (2006)

Playful Experiences and Game Concepts for Multi-screen Environments

Jeroen Vanattenhoven and David Geerts

Centre for User Experience Research, KU Leuven – iMinds
Parkstraat 45 bus 3605, 3000 Leuven – Belgium
{jeroen.vanattenhoven,david.geerts}soc.kuleuven.be

Abstract. In this workshop we will focus on how to design for playful experiences in multi-screen environments (smartphone, tablet, PC and TV), how existing gaming concepts can or cannot be transferred to the design of novel multi-screen formats, and how current insights in sociability, genres and attention can inspire new game concepts. These insights should ultimately lead to novel concepts for multi-screen formats utilising the opportunities offered by the recently increased functionality and interactivity. We will invite experts from industry and academia to discuss the latest research efforts and applications, analyse the current "gamified" media landscape, and formulate essential directions for future research.

Keywords: Gaming, playful experiences, multi-screen, sociability, media.

1   Introduction

In the past decade many living rooms, and by extension homes, have been turned into multi-screen environments. It is not uncommon to see households with multiple smartphones, tablets, laptops and televisions, often being used at the same time. Research on how people's consuming behaviours are changing is growing, but research on how to design good multi-screen experiences that use this multitude of screen-based devices is however scarce. An area where the synchronised use of multiple screens is being increasingly studied is that of second-screen applications for television. The uses of second-screen applications include among others Social TV [1], companion apps (e.g. Beamly), and additional content about a drama series such as Game of Thrones[1]. The increased interactivity also allows for playful experiences and gaming. A popular example is the app for the quiz show 'Blokken' in Flanders[2]: the quiz involves two people competing by answering questions for points – a traditional quiz – and by playing a version of Tetris on the show. For this show a second screen app was created so viewers could play along. The potential of playful experiences within a multi-screen environment are plentiful but still under explored. Our work-

---

[1] http://mashable.com/2014/02/03/second-screen-tv-apps
[2] http://deredactie.be/cm/vrtnieuws/
  cultuur%2Ben%2Bmedia/media/1.2251025

© IFIP International Federation for Information Processing 2015
K. Chorianopoulos et al. (Eds.): ICEC 2015, LNCS 9353, pp. 571–574, 2015.
DOI: 10.1007/978-3-319-24589-8_59

shop aims to fill this gap by studying how new multi-screen formats can be created that allow for playful experiences with smartphones, tablets, pc's and television.

2   Aim

The aim of our workshop is to gather the latest insights, experiences and results on novel formats for multi-screen environments that involve some form of gamification or insights from gaming. We will delve into issues such as (but not limited to):

- **Evaluating game experiences in gamified multi-screen formats**. Current literature on the evaluation of gaming experiences might be reused for gamified multi-screen formats. However, since the latter is not just a game, some of the gaming insights might not (entirely) applicable in the new domain.
- **Social dynamics influencing existing gaming insights**. In the living room different kinds of social interaction occur [6]. Even without multiple screens the complexities of the social dynamics are vast [5]. What is the role of the social mechanics during a gamified show? What are the differences in experience between members of a household playing against each other, and all households watching the show playing against each other in a more widespread competition?
- **The role of the genre**. The genre of a program has an important influence on the social interaction [3] and second-screen interaction it allows [4]. As gaming mechanisms are very likely to augment the experience of novel formats, it is essential to understand with which kinds of programs this would work.
- **Distracting vs. complementing the gaming experience**. Certain game elements might be engaging; the might be more fun than the actual program, but ultimately distract[3] the viewer from the main content on the TV. In what ways can we ensure that the added gamification is really complementary to the entire viewing experience?
- **Engagement with the audience**. How does the addition of game like elements into a program influence the engagement with the audience? What kind of engagement with the audience do broadcasters currently try out? What are the uses, effects of such engagement? What does this demand from the program makers? How can such engagement be strengthened, steered, and measured?
- **The TV as a second screen for games**. Should we make the TV the second screen (or third or fourth) in some cases? How can our TV screen form an excellent addition to games played on tablet or smartphone?

3   Workshop Format

Our workshop is aimed at academics and practitioners who are working on gaming and playful formats for multi-screen environments (including smartphones, tablets,

---

[3] https://gigaom.com/2013/09/11/abc-executive-second-screen-apps-can-be-a-distraction

pc's and television). We have good relations with several broadcasters (VRT, NPO, RBB, TVC), with development companies delivering innovative second-screen formats (Small Town Heroes, Peoples Playground, Angry Bites), game development companies (Larian, GRIN, Studio 100) and will certainly invite them to participate in our workshop. In addition, we will spread our call for papers in the ACM TVX and Fun & Games communities among others. In total we aim for 20 to 25 participants, possible invitees: Joost Negenman (NPO), Hendrik Dacquin (Small Town Heroes), Ammar Tijani (Peoples Playground).

We foresee the submission deadline on 10/07/2015 and the notification on 14/08/2015. The outcome of our full day workshop will be a mapping of the different aspects of multi-screen entertainment; an indication of which aspects that have been covered by academia and/or by industry; and the gaps which have to be explored in the future. We will a toolkit created to support participatory mapping exercises [5].

Schedule:

1. 09.00h-09.15h: Welcome & Introduction
2. 09.15h-10.45h: Pecha Kucha style presentations: Our participants will be asked to prepare a compelling and feisty presentation about their contribution to the workshop, in order to avoid becoming a passive mini-conference, and at the same time offer them the opportunity to tell their story. In addition, we will strongly encourage participants to read each other's contributions before coming to the workshop.
3. 11.00h-12.30h: Mapping the workshop contributions: To get the mapping started and keep the participants awake and active, we will start mapping the relevant aspects in the participants' contributions. They would write down the key concepts on post-its and past them on large sheets of paper or white-boards – one for research contributions, one for industry contributions. After this first phase we will review the current mapping, and review and structure the content properly.
4. 13.30h-15.15h: Mapping related work: In this exercise, making use of the structure of the workshop contributions, we will now map important related efforts in academia en industry, and write down the aspects related to formats for multi-screen environments.
5. 15.30h-16.40h: Bombs away, mortal locks and the big question marks: Participants now receive 1 bomb, 1 lock and 1 question mark to place on the mapped post-its [5]. The bomb indicates where the participants expect or experience great difficulties - these are then written down. The opposite of the bomb is the lock: these mapping items describe a guaranteed winner in our area. Finally, the areas we still know too little about will be indicated by a question mark. These areas will form important directions for future research.
6. 16.40h-17.00h: Closing: At the end of the workshop we will do a wrap-up of the main conclusions and insights gained during the day. Consequently, we will plan follow-up activities such as a suitable venue for a next workshop, the organisation of a special issue for the Entertainment Computing Journal, and the launch of a community website on this topic.

4   Organizers' Background

Jeroen Vanattenhoven is senior researcher at the Centre for User Experience Research of the iMinds research institute and the KU Leuven. He has been involved in Flemish and EU research and innovation projects on social media, Social TV, and second-screen for more than eight years. Earlier research efforts focused on gaming experience and evaluating different controls in games. Currently, he is working in the TV-RING project focusing on social and contextual recommendations, and second-screen applications for TV. He is also Work-in-Progress chair of ACM TVX2015.

Dr. David Geerts has a PhD in Social Sciences at the KU Leuven and is Research Manager of the Centre for User Experience Research (CUO) of KU Leuven and iMinds at the faculty of Social Sciences. David is specialized in human-centered design and evaluation of (social) interactive television. He organized many workshops, special interest groups, and tutorials at international conferences. David Geerts is member of the IFIP TC14 WG6 on Entertainment Computing, is co-founder of the Belgian ACM SIGCHI chapter (CHI Belgium), is part of the TVX steering committee and is general chair of the ACM international conference on interactive experience for television and online video (ACM TVX2015).

References

1. Basapur, S., Mandalia, H., Chaysinh, S., Lee, Y., Venkitaraman, N., Metcalf, C.: FANFEEDS: Evaluation of Socially Generated Information Feed on Second Screen As a TV Show Companion. In: Proceedings of the 10th European Conference on Interactive Tv and Video, pp. 87–96. ACM, New York (2012)
2. Dreessen, K., Huybrechts, L., Laureyssens, T., Schepers, S.: MAP-it. A participatory mapping toolkit. Cahiers FAK 3 (2011)
3. Geerts, D., Cesar, P., Bulterman, D.: The implications of program genres for the design of social television systems. In: Proceedings of the 1st International Conference on Designing Interactive User Experiences for TV and Video, pp. 71–80. ACM, New York (2008)
4. Geerts, D., Leenheer, R., De Grooff, D., Negenman, J., Heijstraten, S.: In Front of and Behind the Second Screen: Viewer and Producer Perspectives on a Companion App. In: Proceedings of the 2014 ACM International Conference on Interactive Experiences for TV and Online Video, pp. 95–102. ACM, New York (2014)
5. Lull, J.: The Social Uses of Television. Human Communication Research 6, 197–209 (1980)
6. Vanattenhoven, J., Geerts, D.: Second-Screen Use in the Home: An Ethnographic Study. In: Proceedings 3rd International Workshop on Future Television, EuroITV 2012, p. 12. Springer, Berlin (2012)

Quantum and Entertainment Computing

Nikitas M. Sgouros

Department of Digital Systems, University of Piraeus
18534, Piraeus, Greece
sgouros@unipi.gr

Abstract. Quantum computing offers a radically different paradigm for dealing with information and its processing. This tutorial seeks to serve as a springboard that can inform and motivate entertainment computing researchers to delve into this new and exciting field and investigate novel ways for utilizing quantum-computational concepts in their work both from a theoretical and a practical point of view.

Keywords: Quantum Computing, Quantum Mechanics, Computational Methodologies for Entertainment, Theory and Practice of Entertainment.

1   Introduction

Quantum Computing seeks to develop a radically different paradigm for dealing with the character of information and its processing. This is because it is based on a set of rules governing the behavior of subatomic particles that is fundamentally different from the set of rules governing our everyday experience of the physical world. Contrary to the classical view, in the quantum world particles can be in multiple states at the same time, obey non-local constraints in their behavior, exhibit probabilistic behavior during observation and pose inherent limitations on the amount of knowledge we can have about them. What is more interesting in this case is that there exists a well-defined quantum theory able to accurately capture all the quirkiness of the quantum world. It is only recently that the implications of this theory for computation have become an active area of study and this has led to the development of abstract models for quantum computation with impressive potential. Another promising research area investigates the implications of this theory for the processing of knowledge and the roles it can play in addressing problems in the social sciences.

Entertainment Computing, on the other hand, seeks to develop computational models of entertainment, a task that is significantly complex due, among other reasons, to the difficulty in defining something as 'entertaining'. The problem stems from the fact that entertainment is primarily a phenomenological concept and as such it can be substantiated on an individual basis. Consequently, entertainment lacks the generality of objective properties and relies on subjectivity and context. It is for this reason that Quantum Computing provides an interesting alternative in capturing entertainment since it can deal with notions such as state, uncertainty, contextuality,

K. Chorianopoulos et al. (Eds.): ICEC 2015, LNCS 9353, pp. 575–577, 2015.
DOI: 10.1007/978-3-319-24589-8_60

subjectivity and transformation in completely new and unexplored ways. This tutorial seeks to provide an introduction to this new and exciting computing paradigm and explore the ways by which its models can provide possible building blocks for the theory and practice of entertainment computing.

2   Objective and Intended Audience

The tutorial will seek to familiarize entertainment computing researchers with recent developments in quantum computing and investigate possible synergies between these two fields. The tutorial is oriented towards entertainment computing researchers with minimal exposure to quantum computing who wish to obtain an overview of the quantum field and try out prototype applications on the intersection between the quantum and the entertainment worlds.

3   Content

Although it might seem idiosyncratic to suggest that quantum theory that deals with the behavior of subatomic particles can be useful in thinking about computational forms of entertainment, we believe that there are very interesting insights to be gained from synergistic interactions between these two research areas. This tutorial will seek to describe in a simplified manner (by keeping the mathematical details to a minimum) the major features of quantum theory that can be relevant to this endeavor and provide references for further study. We will describe basic notions in quantum computing such as quantum state, superposition, entanglement, measurement, dynamics and algorithms. We will then turn our attention to specific examples of how these concepts can be used in the development of entertainment applications. We will present prototypes for games and narrative applications that incorporate elements of quantum behavior in their development and operation. The tutorial will conclude with a discussion of possible ways by which further synergies between quantum and entertainment computing can be pursued.

4   Structure

The tutorial will run for 4 hours. During the first half the participants will get familiarized with essential features of Quantum Mechanics and Quantum Computing. The second half will focus on outlining possible synergies between Quantum and Entertainment Computing and getting a hands-on experience with related applications in these fields. All the material for the tutorial will be available online after the event. The following table summarizes the tutorial structure.

Time	Activity
8:30-9:15	Quantum Mechanics and its postulates
9:30-10:15	Quantum Computing Essentials
10:30-11:15	Drawing Synergies between Entertainment and Quantum Computing
11:30-12:15	Experimentation with Quantum Computing Applications in Entertainment
12:15 -	Discussion & Conclusions

5   Organizer Details

Nikitas M. Sgouros is a Professor in the Department of Digital Systems at the University of Piraeus, Greece working on Entertainment Computing, Multimedia Systems, Artificial Intelligence and Robotics. He has also been a Director of the M.Sc. in Digital Systems and a Deputy Director of this Department. Prof. Sgouros is the author of more than 60 publications in scientific journals and conferences. He holds a PhD in Computer Science from Northwestern University, USA (1994) a M.Sc. with distinction in Artificial Intelligence from the University of Edinburgh, UK (1990) and a Diploma in EECS from the National Technical University of Athens, Greece (1988).

Acknowledgements. Presentation of this tutorial was partially supported by the University of Piraeus Research Center.

References

1. Nielsen, M.A., Chuang, I.L.: Quantum Computation and Quantum Information. Cambridge University Press (2010)
2. Mermin, N.D.: Quantum Computer Science: An Introduction. Cambridge University Press (2007)
3. Yanofsky, N.S., Manucci, M.A.: Quantum Computing for Computer Scientists. Cambridge University Press (2008)
4. Merzbacher, E.: Quantum Mechanics. Wiley (1997)
5. Susskind, L., Friedman, A.: Quantum Mechanics – The Theoretical Minimum. Basic Books (2014)

Tutorial: Service-Oriented Architecture (SOA) Development for Serious Games

Maira B. Carvalho[1,2], Jun Hu[1], Francesco Bellotti[2], Alessandro De Gloria[2], and Matthias Rauterberg[1]

[1] Eindhoven University of Technology, Netherlands
{m.brandao.carvalho,J.Hu,G.W.M.Rauterberg}@tue.nl
[2] University of Genoa, Italy
{franz,adg}@elios.unige.it

Abstract. This tutorial aims to introduce the benefits of applying a service-oriented architecture (SOA) approach to serious games developers. For that end, we propose a hands-on session in which we will provide information on state-of-the-art services for serious games and guide developers in rethinking one of their existing games or game ideas using our SOA framework for serious games.

Introduction

Serious games are typically conceived as one-of-a-kind products fully customized to meet specific learning requirements. This leads to high costs, long production processes and low reusability of the final product and its components, which are all factors that hinder large scale deployment of serious games [4]. The SOA approach has been described as a desirable and beneficial solution for the field, enabling serious games developers to reduce costs and time to market, while enabling flexibility in the development and reuse of software parts [2].

In a previous work [3], we proposed the first steps of a SOA framework to support reusability of serious game components, using elements from the Activity Theory-based Model for Serious Games (ATMSG) [1]. The framework aims to facilitate the serious game development process and to increase the overall quality of the process and of the final product. This is achieved by encouraging the use of interoperability standards and proposing a consistent structure across game components.

However, migrating to a SOA approach for serious games development can have a relatively high learning curve. It involves time and costs to refactor the code, and it can result in increased complexity in testing. For this reason, it is important that developers get acquainted with ways to minimize costs and perform quality assurance. It is also desirable that they are encouraged to identify opportunities to reuse existing components and to share knowledge and best practices.

Given the benefits, but also the added complexity of applying SOA for serious games, we propose this tutorial as a forum for serious games developers to better

© IFIP International Federation for Information Processing 2015
K. Chorianopoulos et al. (Eds.): ICEC 2015, LNCS 9353, pp. 578–580, 2015.
DOI: 10.1007/978-3-319-24589-8_61

understand what such a migration represents and which opportunities for reuse there are, so that they are able to make informed decisions on the suitability of SOA for their practice.

Intended Audience and Schedule

The tutorial targets serious game developers and designers, and particularly participants who have ongoing projects or ideas that could be converted into a service-oriented architecture.

This is a half-day tutorial. The schedule is detailed below.

Welcome (15min)

Content (60min) We will briefly discuss the benefits of using a service-oriented architecture in the development of serious games, drawing on previous successful experiences [2]. We will then present our SOA framework for serious games. The framework is focused on providing a toolbox of reusable components that are relevant for the development of educational serious games within different genres and domains, with particular emphasis in assessment and adaptivity. It also offers recommendations on which development standards can be employed by developers to maximize compatibility with other existing components. Finally, we will introduce a list of existing services, free and otherwise, that currently can be used by developers in their own projects.

Break (15min)

Hands-on session (120min) The second part of the tutorial will be a practical one: we will guide the participants in applying the structure of the framework to one of their own games or game ideas. We will help them identify which changes would be needed to convert their games to a SOA architecture. We will provide suggestions of requirements and evaluation metrics to help developers determine if these services are suitable to the scale and scope of their projects. This session will also allow them to identify if there are any components in common between their projects which are not yet available as services, and which could benefit from shared development efforts.

Evaluation (30min) The last part of the tutorial will be a short evaluation of the framework and of the tutorial. We will collect the participants impressions on the framework and discuss their views on the applicability of the framework in different projects.

Expected Outcomes

At the end of the tutorial, participants will have a clear roadmap of what is needed to convert their serious game or game idea to a SOA architecture. This will include an indication of which components of the game could be reused from readily available services, and which ones would have to be developed from scratch. Participants will be able to identify shared needs and possibly establish collaborations to develop these common components, to the benefit of all involved.

We also expect to improve the SOA framework itself, by collecting the participants' evaluation of the framework quality, relevance and applicability in their own practice. Furthermore, we will be able to gauge which components would be most useful for a larger number of serious games developers, which in turn will be an indication to the serious games community of relevant topics for future research and development.

Acknowledgment. This work was supported in part by the Erasmus Mundus Joint Doctorate in Interactive and Cognitive Environments, which is funded by the EACEA Agency of the European Commission under EMJD ICE FPA n 2010-0012.

References

[1] Carvalho, M.B., Bellotti, F., Berta, R., De Gloria, A., Islas Sedano, C., Baalsrud Hauge, J., Hu, J., Rauterberg, M.: An activity theory-based model for serious games analysis and conceptual design. Computers & Education 87, 166–181 (2015)

[2] Carvalho, M.B., Bellotti, F., Berta, R., Gloria, A.D., Gazzarata, G., Hu, J., Kickmeier-Rust, M.: A case study on service-oriented architecture for serious games. Entertainment Computing 6, 1–10 (2015)

[3] Carvalho, M.B., Bellotti, F., Hu, J., Baalsrud Hauge, J., Berta, R., De Gloria, A., Rauterberg, M.: Towards a service oriented architecture framework for educational serious games. In: Proceedings of the 15th IEEE International Conference on Advanced Learning Technologies (ICALT 2015), Hualien, Taiwan, July 6–9 (2015)

[4] Hauge, J.B., Stanescu, I., Carvalho, M.B., Lim, T., Arnab, S.: Serious games mechanics and opportunities for reuse. In: 11th eLearning and Software for Education Conference (eLSE 2015), Bucharest, Romania (2015)

Author Index

Printed in the United States
By Bookmasters